varcut

Fodor's

THE AMALFI COAST, CAPRI & NAPLES

5th Edition

New York, Toronto, London, Sydney, Auckland

varcaturo

Be a Fodor's Correspondent

Your opinion matters. It matters to us. It matters to your fellow Fodor's travelers, too. And we'd like to hear it. In fact, we need to hear it.

When you share your experiences and opinions, you become an active member of the Fodor's community. That means we'll not only use your feedback to make our books better, but we'll publish your names and comments whenever possible. Throughout our guides, look for "Word of Mouth," excerpts of your unvarnished feedback.

Here's how you can help improve Fodor's for all of us.

Tell us when we're right. We rely on local writers to give you an insider's perspective. But our writers and staff editors—who are the best in the business—depend on you. Your positive feedback is a vote to renew our recommendations for the next edition.

Tell us when we're wrong. We're proud that we update most of our guides every year. But we're not perfect. Things change. Hotels cut services. Museums change hours. Charming cafés lose charm. If our writer didn't quite capture the essence of a place, tell us how you'd do it differently. If any of our descriptions are inaccurate or inadequate, we'll incorporate your changes in the next edition and will correct factual errors at fodors.com immediately.

Tell us what to include. You probably have had fantastic travel experiences that aren't yet in Fodor's. Why not share them with a community of like-minded travelers? Maybe you chanced upon a beach or bistro or B&B that you don't want to keep to yourself. Tell us why we should include it. And share your discoveries and experiences with everyone directly at fodors.com. Your input may lead us to add a new listing or highlight a place we cover with a "Highly Recommended" star or with our highest rating, "Fodor's Choice."

Give us your opinion instantly at our feedback center at www.fodors.com/feedback. You may also e-mail editors@fodors.com with the subject line "Italy Editor." Or send your nominations, comments, and complaints by mail to Italy Editor, Fodor's, 1745 Broadway, New York NY 10019.

You and travelers like you are the heart of the Fodor's community. Make our community richer by sharing your experiences. Be a Fodor's correspondent.

Buon Viaggio! (Or simply: Happy traveling!)

Tim Jarrell, Publisher

FODOR'S THE AMALFI COAST, CAPRI & NAPLES

Editor: Matthew Lombardi

Editorial Contributors: Linda Cabasin, Erica Duecy, Robert I. C. Fisher, Carolyn Galgano, Rachel Klein

Writers: Martin Wilmot Bennett, Fergal Kavanagh, Katie Parla, Chris Rose, Mark Walters, Jonathan Willcocks

Production Editor: Carrie Parker

Maps & Illustrations: Mark Stroud, Moon Street Cartography; David Lindroth, Inc.; Mapping Specialists, *cartographers*; Bob Blake, Rebecca Baer, *map editors*; William Wu, *information graphics*

Design: Fabrizio La Rocca, *creative director*; Guido Caroti, Siobhan O'Hare, *art directors*; Nora Rosansky, Tina Malaney, Ann McBride, *designers*; Melanie Marin, *senior picture editor*

Cover Photo: (Villa Rufolo, Ravello, Amalfi Coast) P. Narayan/age fotostock

Production Manager: Amanda Bullock

5th Edition

ISBN 978-1-4000-0735-6

SPECIAL SALES

This book is available at special discounts for bulk purchases for sales promotions or premiums. Special editions, including personalized covers, excerpts of existing books, and corporate imprints, can be created in large quantities for special needs. For more information, write to Special Markets/Premium Sales, 1745 Broadway, MD 6-2, New York, New York 10019, or e-mail specialmarkets@randomhouse.com.

AN IMPORTANT TIP & AN INVITATION

Although all prices, opening times, and other details in this book are based on information supplied to us at press time, changes occur all the time in the travel world, and Fodor's cannot accept responsibility for facts that become outdated or for inadvertent errors or omissions. So **always confirm information when it matters,** especially if you're making a detour to visit a specific place. Your experiences—positive and negative— matter to us. If we have missed or misstated something, **please write to us.** We follow up on all suggestions. Contact the The Amalfi Coast, Capri & Naples editor at editors@ fodors.com or c/o Fodor's at 1745 Broadway, New York, NY 10019.

PRINTED IN SINGAPORE

10 9 8 7 6 5 4 3 2 1

CONTENTS

MAPS

ABOUT THIS BOOK

Our Ratings

Sometimes you find terrific travel experiences and sometimes they just find you. But usually the burden is on you to select the right combination of experiences. That's where our ratings come in.

As travelers we've all discovered a place so wonderful that its worthiness is obvious. And sometimes that place is so experiential that superlatives don't do it justice: you just have to be there to know. These sights, properties, and experiences get our highest rating, **Fodor's Choice,** indicated by orange stars throughout this book.

Black stars highlight sights and properties we deem **Highly Recommended,** places that our writers, editors, and readers praise again and again for consistency and excellence.

By default, there's another category: any place we include in this book is by definition worth your time, unless we say otherwise. And we will.

Disagree with any of our choices? Care to nominate a place or suggest that we rate one more highly? Visit our feedback center at www.fodors.com/feedback.

Budget Well

Hotel and restaurant price categories from ¢ to $$$$ are defined in the opening pages of each chapter. For attractions, we always give standard adult admission fees; reductions are usually available for children, students, and senior citizens. Want to pay with plastic? **AE, DC, MC, V** following restaurant and hotel listings indicate if American Express, Diners Club, MasterCard, and Visa are accepted.

Restaurants

Unless we state otherwise, restaurants are open for lunch and dinner daily. We mention dress only when there's a specific requirement and reservations only when they're essential or not accepted—it's always best to book ahead.

Hotels

Hotels have private bath, phone, TV, and air-conditioning. We indicate whether they operate on the European Plan (a.k.a. EP, meaning without meals), Breakfast Plan (BP, with a full breakfast), Modified American Plan (MAP, with breakfast and dinner) or American Plan (AP, including all meals). We always list facilities but not whether you'll be charged an extra fee to use them, so when pricing accommodations, find out what's included.

Listings	
★	Fodor's Choice
★	Highly recommended
✉	Physical address
✛	Directions or Map Coordinates
⌂	Mailing address
☎	Telephone
🖷	Fax
⊕	On the Web
✍	E-mail
💷	Admission fee
☉	Open/closed times
Ⓜ	Metro stations
▭	Credit cards
Hotels & Restaurants	
🏠	Hotel
⌆	Number of rooms
⚬	Facilities
¶◎¶	Meal plans
✕	Restaurant
⚮	Reservations
⚲	Smoking
⚑♀	BYOB
✕🏠	Hotel with restaurant that warrants a visit
Outdoors	
🏌	Golf
⚶	Camping
Other	
☾	Family-friendly
⇨	See also
✉	Branch address
☞	Take note

Experience the Amalfi Coast, Capri & Naples

WHAT'S WHERE

The following numbers refer to chapters.

2 Naples. Italy's third-largest city is wonderfully situated, with the gorgeous Bay of Naples spread out before it and mighty Mount Vesuvius as a backdrop. Its streets are packed with people, cafés, pizzerias, and an amazing number of Norman and baroque churches. Perhaps the most operatic city in world, Napoli can seduce you one moment and exasperate you the next: it's lush, chaotic, friendly, scary, amusing, confounding, and very beautiful.

3 Around the Bay. East of Naples lie **Pompeii** and **Herculaneum**, the most completely preserved cities of classical antiquity, along with **Vesuvius,** which buried them in ash and mud in AD 79. West of Naples are the **Campi Flegrei**—Fields of Fire. The area sits on a mass of molten lava (two major seismic faults intersect here) and is studded with ancient sites, from the Greek city of **Cumae** to the **Lago d'Averno**, once thought to be the gateway to hell.

4 Capri, Ischia, and Procida. History's hedonists have long luxuriated on Campania's islands. The most famous, rocky **Capri**, mixes natural beauty and *dolce vita* glamour. In summer, the day-trippers are legion, but even crowds don't

spoil the charm. Twice the size of Capri, **Ischia** has Campania's most beautiful white-sand beaches and is known for its spas, thermal baths, and mineral springs. Nearby **Procida** is a rugged island of fishing villages, domed houses, and sweeping views.

5 Sorrento and the Sorrentine Peninsula. Directly across the water from Naples, **Sorrento** was until the mid-20th century a small, genteel resort. Now the town has expanded along its famous cliffs, but the historic center remains a belle epoque treasure, with picturesque alleyways and palm-shaded cafés.

6 The Amalfi Coast. Heading from Sorrento to the south side of the peninsula, you enter the spectacularly scenic Amalfi Coast, traversed by a road that must have a thousand turns, each with a beautiful view. Amid the crystal lagoons and vertiginous cliffs, sunbaked towns compete for the title Most Beautiful. **Positano** is probably the world's most photographed fishing village; **Amalfi** is adorned with medieval monasteries, Arab-Sicilian cloisters, and the coast's grandest cathedral; **Ravello,** perched 1,500 feet over the famously blue Bay of Salerno, is blessed with some of Italy's most beautiful gardens and villas.

Villa Literno

Marina di Lago di Patria

Marina di Varcature

Cumae

Lago d'Averno

Pozzuoli

Baia

Procida Miseno
Porto

Ischia
Porto

Forio

Barano
D'Ischia

Sant'
Angelo

Ischia

Isola
d'Ischia

Procida

Isola di
Procida

Tyrrhenian Sea

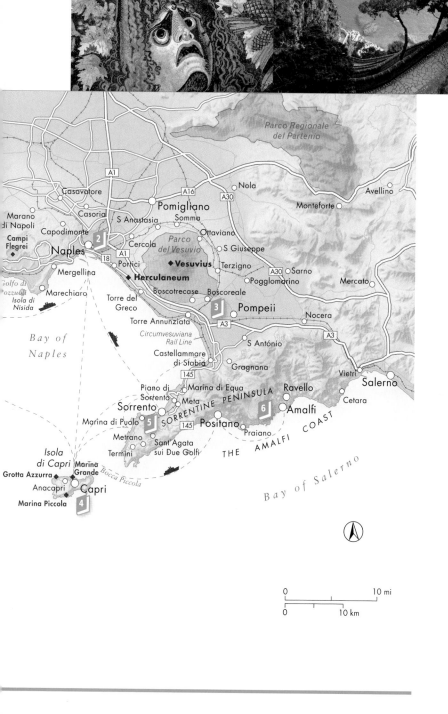

CAMPANIA PLANNER

When to Go

In April, May, and early June, southern Italy is at its best—the weather is generally pleasant and flowers are in bloom. Easter is a busy time for most tourist destinations; if you're traveling then, have lodging reserved in advance. In May the ocean water is warm enough for swimming, and beaches are uncrowded.

Temperatures can be torrid in summer, making it a less-than-ideal time to visit. The archaeological sites swarm with visitors, and the islands and Amalfi Coast resorts are crowded. If you seek a beach, keep in mind that during August all of Italy flocks to the shores.

From late September through early November you'll find gentle, warm weather, and acres of beach space; swimming temperatures last through October. Watch the clock, however, as the days get shorter. At most archaeological sites you're rounded up two hours before sunset—but by then most crowds have departed, so afternoon is still a good time to see Pompeii and Herculaneum.

Early winter is relatively mild, but later in the season cold fronts can arrive and stay for days. In resort destinations, many hotels, restaurants, and other facilities close from November until around Easter.

Getting Here

Major gateways to Italy are Rome's Aeroporto Leonardo da Vinci, better known as **Fiumicino** (FCO), and Milan's **Aeroporto Malpensa** (MIL). To fly into most other Italian cities you need to make connections at Fiumicino and Malpensa or another European airport.

Located just 8 km (5 mi) outside Naples, **Aeroporto Capodichino** (NAP) serves the Campania region. It handles domestic and international flights, including several flights daily between Naples and Rome (flight time 45 minutes). In Rome you can also take the airport train to Termini station and catch a train to Naples. It typically takes about an hour to get from the airport to the station, and the trip from Rome to Naples is around 90 minutes.

Italy's airports are not known for being new, fun, or efficient. Security measures, including random baggage inspection and bomb-sniffing dogs, may seem daunting, but they don't pose any problems for the average traveler. For further information about getting into the region, see the Travel Smart chapter at the end of this book.

What to Pack

In summer stick with light clothing, but toss in a sweater in case of cool evenings, especially if you're headed for the islands. Sunglasses, a hat, and sunblock are essential. In winter, bring a coat, gloves, hat, and scarf. Winter weather is milder than in the northern and central United States, but central heating isn't always reliable. Bring comfortable walking shoes in any season.

As a rule, Italians dress well. They do not usually wear shorts. Men aren't required to wear ties or jackets anywhere except in the most formal restaurants, but are expected to look reasonably sharp—and they do. A certain modesty (no bare shoulders or knees) is expected in churches, and strictly enforced in many.

If you stay in budget hotels, **take your own soap.** Many such hotels do not provide it or give guests only one tiny bar per room. Washcloths, also, are rarely provided even in three- and four-star hotels.

Restaurants: The Basics

A meal in Italy has traditionally consisted of five courses, and every menu you encounter will still be organized along this five-course plan:

First up is the *antipasto* (appetizer), often consisting of cured meats or marinated vegetables. Next to appear is the *primo*, usually pasta or soup, and after that the *secondo*, a meat or fish course with, perhaps, a *contorno* (vegetable dish) on the side. A simple *dolce* (dessert) rounds out the meal.

This, you've probably noticed, is a lot of food. Italians have noticed as well—a full, five-course meal is an indulgence usually reserved for special occasions. Instead, restaurant meals are a mix-and-match affair: you might order a primo and a secondo, or an antipasto and a primo, or a secondo and a contorno.

The crucial rule of restaurant dining is that you should order at least two courses. It's a common mistake for tourists to order only a secondo, thinking they're getting a "main course" complete with side dishes. What they wind up with is one lonely piece of meat.

Hotels: The Basics

Hotels in Italy are usually well maintained (especially if they've earned our recommendation in this book), but in some respects they won't match what you find at comparably priced U.S. lodgings. Keep the following points in mind as you set your expectations, and you're likely to have a good experience:

■ First and foremost, rooms are usually smaller, particularly in cities. If you're truly cramped, ask for another room, but don't expect things to be spacious.

■ A "double bed" is commonly two singles pushed together.

■ In the bathroom, tubs are not a given—request one if it's essential. In budget places, showers sometimes use a drain in the middle of the bathroom floor. Washcloths are a rarity.

■ Most hotels have satellite TV, but there are fewer channels than in the United States, and only one or two will be in English.

■ Don't expect wall-to-wall carpeting. Particularly outside the cities, tile floors are the norm.

Speaking the Language

Because Naples and the surrounding resort areas see many English-speaking tourists, in restaurants and hotels you're bound to find someone with a rudimentary understanding of English. On the other hand, if you're fluent in Italian you still may not be able to follow conversations heard on the street; locals often use dialect that even fellow Italians have a hard time deciphering. But locals speak standard Italian as well, so you can still benefit from knowledge of the language.

Italy from Behind the Wheel

Having a car in Italian cities is almost always a liability—nowhere more so than in Naples. In the towns of the Amalfi Coast parking is hard to come by, and on the islands of the bay car access is very limited. In short, you're usually better off not renting a car in this part of the country. If you do get one, be aware that Italians tend to be aggressive drivers—expect tailgating and high-risk passing. Your best response is to stick to a safety-first approach; the *autostrada* is one place where you don't want to "go native." On the upside, Italy's roads are well maintained. Note that wearing a seat belt and having your lights on at all times are required by law.

CAMPANIA TODAY

. . . remains distinctly different from the North

Southern Italy is slap bang in the middle of the Mediterranean, so it's no wonder that it has experienced invasions and migrations for millennia, many of which have left their mark culturally, linguistically, and architecturally.

The southerners, despite the homogenizing influences of television and education, really *are* different from Italians farther north. Under an ostensibly sociable and more expressive exterior, they are more guarded when dealing with strangers, less at home with foreign languages, and more oriented toward the family than the community. The trappings of affluence, like cars and scooters, become essential status symbols here, which in part explains why Naples is congested and noisy.

. . . has issues when it comes to local politics

Politics tends to be clientelistic in large swaths of the south. In this climate of mutual back-scratching and with unemployment rates (13.6%) twice the national average, the main preoccupation for many voters is *il posto fisso* (a steady job).

Votes are all too often cast for the politician who promises opportunities for career advancement—or lucrative contracts—preferably in the public sector. Over the years, this approach has insured inefficiencies, if not outright corruption.

. . . endures national political upheaval

The political landscape in Italy as a whole is less stable than in any other industrialized nation. The country has had a new government an average of about once a year since the end of World War II, and hopes are slim that the situation will change much in the near future.

This virtual turnstile outside the prime minister's office takes a toll on Italy in any number of ways: economic growth is slow in part because businesses are continually adapting to new sets of government policies, and polls show that rank-and-file Italians are increasingly cynical about their political institutions. As a result, they're much less likely to trust in or depend upon the government than neighbors elsewhere in Europe do.

. . . has its economic ups and downs

While the north has developed relatively rapidly in the past 50 years, the Italian entrepreneurial spirit in the south struggles to make good. Despite a pool of relatively cheap, willing labor, foreign investment across the entire south is merely one-tenth of that going to the northern region of Lombardy alone.

The discrepancy can be attributed in large part to the stifling presence of organized crime. Each major region has its own criminal association: in Naples, it's the *Camorra*. The system creates add-on costs at many levels, especially in retail.

It is not all bad news though. Southern Italy has woken up to its major asset, its remarkable cultural and natural heritage. UNESCO lists 14 World Heritage Sites in southern Italy alone, while the last decade has seen the creation of several national parks, marine parks, and regional nature preserves. Environmental and cultural associations have mushroomed as locals increasingly perceive the importance of preserving across the generations.

In general, the small average farm size in the south (5.8 hectares, under 15 acres) has helped preserve a pleasing mosaic of habitats in the interior. Landscape and product diversity has been aided by the promotion

of traditionally grown products by the European Union and its PDO (Protected Designation of Origin) project.

. . . lives with the black market

Nobody knows how big Italy's black-market economy is, though experts all agree it's massive. Estimates place it at anywhere from a fourth to a half of the official, legal economy.

Put another way, if the highest estimates are correct, Italy's black-market economy is about as large as the entire economy of Mexico or India. If the black-market figures were added to Italy's official GDP, the country would leapfrog France, the U.K., and China to become the world's fourth-largest economy.

The presence of the black market isn't obvious to the casual observer, but whenever a customer is not given a printed receipt in a store or restaurant, tobacco without a tax seal is bought from a street seller, or a product or service is exchanged for another product or service, that means the transaction goes unrecorded, unreported, and untaxed.

. . . is getting older

Italy is the oldest country in Europe (worldwide, only Japan is older)—the result of its low birth rate, relatively strict immigration standards, and one of the highest life expectancy rates in the world. As of 2009, the average Italian was 42.5 years old, and the number keeps rising.

The result is a remarkably stable population: the total number of Italian residents rises just 0.1% per year.

But the situation is putting a strain on the country's pension system and on families, since elderly family members are likely to live with their children or grandchildren in a country where nursing homes are rare.

The trend also has an impact on other areas, including politics (where older politicians are eager to promote policies aimed at older voters) and the popular culture (where everything from fashion to television programming takes older consumers into consideration).

. . . misses the lira

Italy was among a dozen European Union countries that switched to the euro currency at the start of 2002. For many Italians, the change was not a welcome one.

In day-to-day conversations, the euro is blamed for higher prices and for the handing over of more control of the Italian economy to bureaucrats in Brussels, the seat of the European government.

The most common complaint is that many vendors simply took the old prices in *lire* and erased three zeros, meaning something that used to cost 1,000 lire (around 0.52 euro) now costs one euro.

Many Italians still value purchases in their beloved lira. Years after the switch, it is still common to hear someone in the midst of a negotiation argue the price in the now-dead currency, "Eight euros? But that's 16,000 lire!"

CAMPANIA
TOP ATTRACTIONS

Spaccanapoli, Naples

(A) To learn why people fall in love with Naples, stroll down this arrow-straight road through the heart of the city. It's all here: gorgeous churches, café-lined piazzas, colorful shops, and, most of all, the exuberant Neapolitans, engaged in the drama of their daily lives. (⇨ *Chapter 2*)

Museo Archeologico Nazionale, Naples

The National Archaeological Museum has arguably the world's finest collection of classical artifacts. The most impressive finds from Pompeii and Herculaneum—everything from sculpture to carbonized fruit—are on display; a visit before heading to the ruins makes the experience significantly richer. (⇨ *Chapter 2*)

Pio Monte Misercordia, Naples

(B) Among the many impressive churches in Naples, this one bears special mention for its altar painting, Caravaggio's *Seven*

Acts of Mercy, the city's most heralded artwork. (⇨ *Chapter 2*)

Underground Naples

(C) In Naples the locals point to the ground and say there's another city underneath. This is *Napoli Sotterranea,* a netherworld of ancient Greek quarries, Roman streets, medieval aqueducts, and World War II bomb shelters. Parts have been cleaned up and made accessible to the public. (⇨ *Chapter 2*)

The Ruins around Vesuvius

(D) This may be the closest you'll ever get to time travel. Thanks to Vesuvius blowing its top in AD 79, the towns at its base were carpeted in fallout and preserved for posterity. Allow a good half day to look round bustling Pompeii or the more compact, less busy Herculaneum. For the best Roman frescoes, head to the Villa of Oplontis between the two ancient cities. (⇨ *Chapter 3*)

La Piazzetta, Capri

(E) Sitting in one of the cafés on this main square, watching the world go by, is a classic Capri experience. It's at its best in the evening, when day-trippers have departed and locals make an appearance. (⇨ *Chapter 4*)

Villa San Michele, Capri

Emperor Tiberius himself would have been impressed by this antique-rich 19th-century villa. Make a wish while standing on the Sphinx Parapet; here, high atop Anacapri, it feels like anything is possible. (⇨ *Chapter 4*)

The Amalfi Drive

(G) The road along the Amalfi Coast combines the thrills of a roller-coaster ride with some of the most spectacular views anywhere. If you're taking a car, you'll need a confident driver who can keep his eyes on the road. Go by bus if you want a seasoned pro behind the wheel. (⇨ *Chapter 6*)

Belvedere of Infinity, Villa Cimbrone, Ravello

(F) This sky-kissing terrace, set amid gorgeous gardens and overlooking the bluest bay in the world, is the high point, in more ways than one, of any trip to the Amalfi Coast. (⇨ *Chapter 6*)

Positano

(H) Whitewashed houses cascade down to the azure sea in this remarkable village, described by the artist Paul Klee as "The only place in the world conceived on a vertical rather than a horizontal axis." (⇨ *Chapter 6*)

The Temples of Paestum

(I) These are some of the best-preserved ancient Greek monuments found anywhere (including Greece). Paestum's remoteness from the main tourist routes means its seldom overrun by crowds. The best times to absorb the grandeur of the three temples are daybreak and dusk. (⇨ *Chapter 6*)

TOP EXPERIENCES

Stepping Back in Time

The regions to the west and east of Naples are two of the world's greatest treasure troves of Greek and Roman antiquity. Quick to appreciate the sybaritic possibilities of Campania Felix—"happy land"—the ancient Romans built palatial country residences and luxurious resorts. Although the finest art relics have been moved to the Museo Archeologico in Naples, there's still plenty to see at the original ancient sites.

The most famous, rightly, is Pompeii, but it's well worthwhile to check out some of the many other notable locations, including Baia, pleasure spot of the Roman emperors; Lake Averno, legendary entrance to Hades; Oplontis, perhaps once home to Mr. and Mrs. Nero; and Cumae, where from her cave the famous Sibyl announced to kings and emperors her portents of the future.

Simply Fabulous Food

It's no wonder *la cucina Napolitano* has won the hearts (and stomachs) of millions: the rich volcanic soil and fertile waters surrounding the city provide abundant and varied seafood, Vesuvian wines, vine-ripe tomatoes, and luscious fruits.

This food is simple and earthy, at once wholesome and sensual, as sophisticated in its purity as the most complex cuisine, as inspired as the great art and architecture born out of the same culture. Like Michelangelo freeing the prisoners that dwelt within the stone, chefs in Campania seem intuitively to seek out the essence of what they are preparing—exhibit 1 being that Neapolitan delight, pizza.

It's worth noting that in Campania, as in much of Italy, the most revered (and most expensive) restaurants are often found in the countryside or in small, remote towns.

These are places for food pilgrimages, where you can escape the city and indulge in a long, opulent meal free from distractions. A notable example is Don Alfonso 1890, the region's most famous temple of fine dining, located in the mountainside village of Sant'Agata on the Sorrentine Peninsula.

Neapolitan Baroque

Of the numerous artistic styles on display in Naples, none suits the city's temperament better than the baroque—the style that came to the fore in the 17th century and continued in the 18th century under the Bourbon kings.

In a city of volcanic passions, the flagrantly emotional, floridly luxurious baroque—a style that seems perpetually on the point of bursting its bonds—found immediate favor. With untrammeled individualism given full play, the results, visible throughout the city center today, are dramatic, dynamic, and sometimes wonderfully showy. Like the city itself, the decorative scheme is diffuse and disjunctive, with little effort to organize everything into an easily understood scheme.

Taking to the Water

Despite its miles of beautiful coast, Campania's beaches can be disappointing—most are small stretches of coarse sand. That doesn't mean you shouldn't pack your swimsuit, but leave any Caribbean-inspired expectations behind.

The area around Positano has good beach-going options: Spiaggia Grande (the main beach) is pleasant; a little farther west, Spiaggia di Fornillo gets better; and you can go by boat to the remote Spiaggia di Laurito for a leisurely day of swimming and lunching on seafood. On Ischia, the best sandy beach is at Citara, south of Forio, and on Capri you can take a dip in

the waters around the famous Faraglioni rock formation.

Your may not be won over by the sand, but the water itself is spectacular, with infinite varieties of blue shimmering in the sun, turning transparent in the coves. And you may have as much fun on the water as in it. In particular, boating around Capri is a classic experience, allowing you to see sights that are either remote or entirely inaccessible by land.

Edenic Gardens

"What nature gives you makes you rich," they say in Campania. One look at Capri's perfectly tonsured palm trees, Sorrento's frangipani, and Amalfi's lemon trees laden with golden fruit, and you know what they mean.

So it's not surprising to learn that one of the major joys of this region is the abundance of spectacular gardens. Many of the most celebrated gardens were created by English green-thumbs, such as the 18th-century "romantic" garden planted by Sir William Hamilton (and his Lady Emma) at the royal palace of Caserta, the 19th-century medieval-style garden designed by Sir Francis Reid at Ravello's Villa Rufolo, and Lord Grimthorpe's relentlessly picturesque paradise created in the early 20th century at Ravello's Villa Cimbrone. When it comes to gardens, Campania is *incomparabilo*.

The Glories of Spring

In April and May, *all* of Campania seems like a garden. Wherever you look—roadsides, archaeological sites, public gardens, even along railroad tracks— you're likely to see a dazzling array of natural colors.

From seemingly untended fields of scarlet poppies, to overflowing flowerboxes on the streets of Naples, to the yellow umbels of giant fennel on Capri, this is the Mediterranean at its most explosive. Come back in June and much of the tapestry will have faded, with plants dispersing their seeds for next year's show.

Il Dolce Far Niente

"The sweetness of doing nothing" has long been an art form in Italy—particularly in southern Italy. This is a place where life's pleasures are warmly celebrated, not guiltily indulged.

Of course, doing "nothing" doesn't really mean nothing. It means doing things differently: lingering over a glass of wine for the better part of an evening as you watch the sun slowly set; savoring a slow and flirtatious evening *passeggiata* along the main street of a little town; and making a commitment—however temporary—to thinking that there is nowhere that you have to be next, and no other time than the magical present.

Along the Amalfi Coast, it's easy to achieve such a state of mind. No matter where you choose to situate yourself, you can hardly go wrong: there's quiet little Ravello, stunningly positioned on a hilltop lookout; the vertical fishing village of Positano, where a tranquil sunset is a balm to the soul; and Amalfi with its Moorish passageways and other hints of a long, multicultural history.

On Capri the pace picks up a little, and in Naples a lot, but there's still a sense of taking life's pleasures where you find them. The sense of enjoyment is, fortunately, infectious.

QUINTESSENTIAL CAMPANIA

Il Caffè (Coffee)

The Italian day begins and ends with coffee, and more cups of coffee punctuate the time in between. To live like the Italians do, drink as they drink, standing at the counter or sitting at an outdoor table of the corner bar. (In Italy, a "bar" is a coffee bar.) A primer: *caffè* means coffee, and Italian standard issue is what Americans call espresso—short, strong, and usually taken very sweet. *Cappuccino* is a foamy half-and-half of espresso and steamed milk; cocoa powder *(cacao)* on top is acceptable, cinnamon is not. If you're thinking of having a cappuccino for dessert, think again—Italians drink only caffè or caffè *macchiato* (with a spot of steamed milk) after lunchtime. Confused? Homesick? Order caffè *americano* for a reasonable facsimile of good-old filtered joe.

Il Calcio (Soccer)

Imagine the most rabid American football fans—the ones who paint their faces on game day and sleep in pajamas emblazoned with the logo of their favorite team. Throw in a dose of melodrama along the lines of a tear-jerking soap opera. Ratchet up the intensity by a factor of 10, and you'll start to get a sense of how Italians feel about their national game, soccer—known in the mother tongue as *calcio*. On Sunday afternoons throughout the long September-to-May season, stadiums are packed throughout Italy. Those who don't get to games in person tend to congregate around television sets in restaurants and bars, rooting for the home team with a passion that feels like a last vestige of the days when the country was a series of warring medieval city-states. How calcio mania affects your stay in Italy depends on how eager you are to get involved. At the very least, you may notice an eerie

If you want to get a sense of contemporary Italian culture and indulge in some of its pleasures, start by familiarizing yourself with the rituals of daily life. These are a few highlights—things you can take part in with relative ease.

Sunday-afternoon quiet on the city streets, or erratic restaurant service around the same time, accompanied by cheers and groans from a neighboring room. If you want a memorable, truly Italian experience, attend a game yourself. Availability of tickets may depend on the current fortunes of the local team, but they often can be acquired with help from your hotel concierge.

Il Gelato (Ice Cream)

During warmer months, *gelato*—the Italian equivalent of ice cream—is a national obsession. It's considered a snack rather than a dessert, bought at stands and shops in piazzas and on street corners, and consumed on foot, usually at a leisurely stroll (⇨ *see La Passeggiata, below)*. Gelato is softer, less creamy, and more intensely flavored than its American counterpart. It comes in simple flavors that capture the essence of the main ingredient. (You won't find Chunky Monkey or Cookies

'n' Cream.) Standard choices include pistachio, *nocciola* (hazelnut), caffè, and numerous fresh-fruit varieties. Quality varies; the surest sign that you've hit on a good spot is a line at the counter.

La Passeggiata (Strolling)

A favorite Italian pastime is the *passeggiata* (literally, the promenade). In the late afternoon and early evening, especially on weekends, couples, families, and packs of teenagers stroll the main streets and piazzas of Italy's towns. It's a ritual of exchanged news and gossip, window-shopping, flirting, and gelato-eating that adds up to a uniquely Italian experience. To join in, simply hit the streets for a bit of wandering. You may feel more like an observer than a participant, until you realize that observing is what la passeggiata is all about.

MAKING THE MOST OF YOUR EUROS

Below are suggestions for ways to save money on your trip, courtesy of the Travel Talk Forums at Fodors.com.

Transportation

"Don't hire a tour, take the train to Pompeii, or stay on it to Sorrento and take the bus down the coast." —JoanneH

Food and Drink

"Book a hotel room with a mini fridge—you can keep tap water cold to save on buying bottled water constantly. You can also buy great food from the markets or small shops to have picnics in your room. If you aren't a foodie and don't care about having all your meals in a sit down restaurant you can really save a lot this way. Many people mention picnics as a way to save on food cost, but having the flexibility that a small fridge in the room allows can make a big difference." —isabel

"Bars always have two different prices: If you have your coffee at the counter it's cheaper than when a waiter serves it at a table (*servizio al tavolo*)." —quokka

"Visit wine fill-up shops in Italy; get table wine from the cask for 2–3 euros a liter. In Rome we would get them filled at the Testaccio market . . . I will usually ask at the local bar where I go for my coffee." —susanna

"If you aren't hungry, skip to *secondo*—the 'second course.' Rarely do Italians eat a *primo e secondo* when they go out." —glittergirl

Sights

"You really don't realize how much money you spend on museums, places of interest, tours, etc., since it's 'six euros here,' 'ten euros there,' until you add them all up or worse yet, see the total on the credit card bill when you return home. When people ask me what I want for Christmas/

my birthday, I ask them to purchase my tickets for specific sights/tours online, print them out and give those to me for presents. I just inform them the days that I will be there and give them the websites. It's easy for them and saves me money." —goferfan512

"Always visit the tourist offices and get the free guides for what is going on." —gotkids

Shopping

"So many travellers especially during the first couple of trips to Europe feel the need to buy souvenirs for so many people back home. I quit doing that ages ago. Even if you buy inexpensive items if you feel you have too many people to buy for (example, if I buy this for Trisha I must buy something for Joyce) etc., it can be surprising how all the items can add up. And often although people think it is nice to be remembered it was not their trip so the souvenirs really do not mean that much to them and often just adds to the 'stuff' they already have in their homes." —LoveItaly

Lodging

"When looking up lodging, I mostly check the official websites of the cities I want to visit or italian websites aimed for italians tourists. I've been able to find very good deals on inexpensive and wonderful B&B's or hotels that I've haven't been able to find on regular foreign-tourist-oriented websites or bookguides." —Castellanese

"Go off-season—March or November have better air prices and also accommodations, particularly if you stay in apartments, which you can rent for much less off-season (and plan some meals in-house—make the noon meal your biggest of the day, then have a small dinner in the apartment)." —bobthenavigator

Naples

WORD OF MOUTH

"We liked Naples very much from our first moments in the city. If there is a city whose people appear more filled with the sheer joy of life, I have not yet been there!"

—ekscrunchy

WELCOME TO NAPLES

Certosa di San Martino

TOP REASONS TO GO

★ **Vistas of Vesuvius:** Ride the funicular to the Vomero and from San Martino and Castel Sant'Elmo feast on the views across the city to the slumbering volcano.

★ **Museums and Churches:** Engross yourself in cultural heritage, from the remarkable finds of Pompeii at the Museo Archeologico to the masterpieces on display in the city's *palazzos, churches, and castles.*

★ **The Underworld:** Naples is honeycombed with subterranean quarries, aqueducts, and catacombs. You can walk a kilometer or more in them, stopping beneath the stage where Nero once performed and continuing deeper into the Greek and Roman quarries from which the city above was born.

★ **Walking Spaccanapoli:** This part of town is where you experience most intensely the energy, chaos, and bursts of beauty that make Naples the most operatic of cities.

1 Toledo and Quartieri Spagnoli. The central Toledo district has a concentration of monuments, including the sumptuous apartments of the Palazzo Reale and the broad open space of Piazza Plebiscito. Built by Viceroy Pedro di Toledo to bring some order to the city, the pedestrianized Via Toledo leads into the grid of Quartieri Spagnoli, a sort of NATO base of its time, where Spanish soldiers were deployed between campaigns to guard the palazzos of the ruling class.

2 The Lungomare. The area along the harbor west of Toledo consists of two quarters, Santa Lucia and Chiaia. Both areas are thin on culture and geared to *la dolce vita*: in Santa Lucia you can expect serenades from street musicians over dinner, while most locals head for their favorite trattoria up a side street in Chiaia.

Frescoed cloister
of the Santa Chiara
complex

Funicular
M Metro stop

GETTING ORIENTED

In Naples "up and down"
is often as accurate a form
of direction as "to and fro."
From the bay, the city rises
up steep hillsides, which
you can ascend with the
help of three funiculars, as
well as strategically placed
ascensori (elevators). Via
Toledo, one of the major
thoroughfares, serves as a
north–south axis. Farther
north, the long Corso
Vittorio Emmanuele, a panoramic strip of road, runs
up along the Vomero link-
ing the sea-level southwest
with the elevated northeast.

Charles III of Bourbon statue on
facade of the Palazzo Reale

3 **Vomero.** Connected
to the city below by three
funiculars, the Vomero hill
offers a peaceful contrast to
the hustle downtown. The
Certosa at San Martino, a
monastery turned museum
complex is a highlight,
with magnificent works
of art, wraparound views
of Naples, and gardens
fit for contemplation.

4 **Spaccanapoli.** For
art and archaeology,
this must be one of the
most exquisitely packed
neighborhoods on earth,
and at the same time it
teems with vibrant street
life. The United Nations
has dubbed the district an
open-air museum—which
in this case feels like
an understatement.

NAPLES PLANNER

Beyond First Impressions

If you're arriving in Naples by train, don't expect to be instantly charmed. Piazza Garibaldi, which is home to the Stazione Centrale, the main railroad terminal, is a battered place—crowded, messy, and inhospitable, with the local bus station perched in the middle of a tangle of intersections. Long-time home to street sharks and souvenir-hawkers, the piazza is now also a meeting point for eastern European guest workers, who have become a growing presence in the city.

When you make your way beyond Piazza Garibaldi, first impressions begin to mellow: delightfully and unforgettably, Naples reveals itself as a cornucopia of elegant boulevards, treasure-stocked palaces, the world's greatest museum of classical antiquities, the stage-set neighborhood of Spaccanapoli, and scores of historic churches. Naples becomes *Napoli la bella*, a city that centuries of romantics have deemed one of the most beautiful in the world.

Making the Most of Your Time

Three to four days will be enough to give you a taste of the city and see you through the main monuments, as well as factor in a breather to one of the islands in the bay. Always make a contingency plan for each day. Naples can be fraying on the nerves and tiring in terms of legwork, so head for one of the city parks (Villa Comunale, Floridiana, or Capodimonte) for well-earned *riposo* in between doses of *cultura*.

Sightseeing days should begin no later than 9, as most churches are usually open only from 7:30 until noon or 12:30, reopening only after the afternoon siesta, from 4 or 4:30 until about 7. Most museums have extended hours, with a few even open in evenings; however, this usually means that rooms may be open on a rotating basis, and if you're making a special journey to see a particular exhibit, it's worth phoning to check if it's viewable. If you come to Naples by car, park it in a garage as fast as you can, agree on the cost in advance, and then forget it for the duration of your stay (otherwise, city driving is not for the fainthearted, theft is a constant risk, and parking a nightmare).

Finding a Place to Stay

If you want seafront accommodation in Naples, remember that rooms with a view come at a sizable premium, and there are likely to be three busy lanes of traffic between you and the shoreline.

Taking advantage of pedestrianization schemes, several competitively priced hotels close to Piazza Plebiscito and in the Chiaia area, offering similar services, better public transport connections, and more touring options within walking distance.

Resist the temptation to stay near Piazza Garibaldi by the Stazione Centrale just because it's a transport hub: the area has high pollution levels during the day and is unsafe (and unpleasant) for evening strolls after 8:30 PM.

To avoid sleep-disturbed nights, ask for a *camera tranquilla* (quiet room) regardless of where you stay.

The Campania Artecard

The Campania Artecard is a big boon for museum lovers. This pass offers free or discounted admission to almost 50 museums and monuments over a three- or seven-consecutive-day period for the city or the whole region, as well as discounted services ranging from audio guides to theater tickets and car parks.

The benefits depend on the pass: a three-day pass gets you free admission to the first two sites you visit, then half price for the others, plus free transport—including the Alibus from the airport and the Metro del Mare around the bay (Naples and Campi Flegrei: €13; anywhere in the region, including Pompeii, Herculaneum, Caserta, and Paestum: €25; there are generous youth discounts).

The seven-day card (€28) gives free entrance to two sites, a 50% discount to others, but no free transport.

As sites and discounts are frequently updated, check ⊕ www.campaniartecard.it for the latest information.

Cards are available at all the major participating museums and archaeological sites, at main city hotels, as well as at the airport and the station.

A Tipping Tip

Neapolitans are easily recognized in coffee bars elsewhere in Italy by the tip they leave on the counter when ordering. This habit does not necessarily ensure better service in bars in Naples, notorious for their fairly offhand staff, but you do blend in better with the locals.

In restaurants, service is usually included unless stated otherwise (in which case 5%–10% is reasonable). In pizzerias, tips are rarely given unless you have splurged on side dishes or sweets, or have had particularly good service.

Visitor Information

The numerous tourist offices in Naples aren't always open when they claim to be, but most are generally open from Monday to Saturday 8:30–8 and Sunday 8:30–2 except where noted.

There's an **EPT** (Ente Provinciale per il Turismo) office in Stazione Centrale (⊠ *Stazione Centrale, Piazza Garibaldi* ☎ *081/268779*), where the people are quite friendly and helpful; the main administrative center (with an atmosphere of baroque mothballs) is in Piazza dei Martiri (⊠ *Piazza dei Martiri 58, Chiaia* ☎ *081/4107211*), and is open weekdays 8:30–2. There's also a branch at Stazione Mergellina (☎ *081/7612102*). The **AACST** (⊠ *Piazza Gesù Nuovo, Spaccanapoli* ☎ *01/5523328*) specializes in information on old Naples but generally just gives out brochures. A second office, which is closed Sunday, is handily inside the Palazzo Reale.

"Built like a great amphitheater around her beautiful bay, Naples is an eternally unfolding play acted by a million of the best actors in the world," Herbert Kubly observed in his *American in Italy.* "The comedy is broad, the tragedy violent. The curtain never rings down." Is it a sense of doom from living in the shadow of Vesuvius that makes some Neapolitans so volatile, so blind to everything but the pain or pleasure of the moment?

A huge zest for living, and crowded conditions, are the more probable causes. But whatever the reason, Naples remains the most vibrant city in Italy—a steaming, bubbling, reverberating minestrone in which each block is a small village, every street the setting for a Punch-and-Judy show, and everything seems to be a backdrop for an opera not yet composed.

It's said that northern Italians vacation here to remind themselves of the time when Italy was *molto Italiana—really* Italian. In this respect, Naples—Napoli in Italian—doesn't disappoint: Neapolitan rainbows of laundry wave in the wind over alleyways open-windowed with friendliness, mothers caress children, men break out into impromptu arias at sidewalk cafés, and street scenes offer Fellini-esque slices of life. Everywhere contrasting elements of faded gilt and romance, rust and calamity, grandeur and squalor form a pageant of pure *Italianità*—Italy at its most Italian.

As the historic capital of Campania, Naples has been perpetually and tumultuously in a state of flux. Neapolitans are instinctively the most hospitable of people, and they've often paid a price for being so, having unwittingly extended a warm welcome to wave after wave of invaders. Lombards, Goths, Normans, Swabians, Spanish viceroys and kings, and Napoleonic generals arrived in turn; most of them proved to be greedy and self-serving. Still, if these foreign rulers bled the populace dry with taxes, they left the impoverished city with a rich architectural inheritance.

Much of that inheritance is on display in the Spaccanapoli district, where the Piazza Gesù Nuovo and the surrounding blocks are a show-place for the city's most beloved churches and a showcase for the city's greatest attraction, the Neapolitan people. On the piazza, watch and rub elbows with them. Let their charm, gaiety, effervescence, and undiluted spontaneity pull you into their unique and glorious concept of life and living. You'll soon begin to sense that Neapolitans are possibly the happiest people in the world. In an hour or two you'll feel like part of the *famiglia* yourself.

Compared to most other great metropolises of the world, Naples has little tourist infrastructure, forcing you to become a native very quickly, as you'll find out if you spend some time wandering through the gridlike narrow streets of the old center. Lost? You'll be taken in hand (probably by way of mamma's house). Hungry? Can't think of the right word? A translation is shouted out over the din, and a single word is never sufficient when 10 will do—as you could have seen one September afternoon when an English couple asked for directions to the Church of Pio Monte della Misericordia. One passerby started explaining, but another man suddenly thought of a still shorter way and butted in. In no time 8 or 10 people were volubly offering their own directions. The arguing that ensued was not unfriendly; a torn racing form was the only casualty. The inquiring couple never learned the shortest—or, for that matter, any other—way to Pio Monte. But the sun was warm, the sky was blue, and there are plenty of other beautiful churches in Naples.

EXPLORING NAPLES

Updated by
Martin Wilmot
Bennett

Naples, a bustling city of some 1.2 million people, can be a challenge for visitors because of its hilly terrain and its twisty, often congested streets. Though spread out, Naples invites walking; the bus system, funiculars, and subways are also options for dealing with weary legs.

The city of Naples stretches along the Bay of Naples from Piazza Garibaldi in the east to Mergellina in the west, with its back to the Vomero Hill. From Stazione Centrale, on Piazza Garibaldi, Corso Umberto I (known as the "Rettifilo") heads southwest to the monumental city center—commonly known as "Toledo"—around the piazzas Bovio, Municipio, and Trieste e Trento; here is the major urban set piece composed of the Palazzo Reale, Teatro San Carlo, and Galleria Umberto Primo.

To the north are the historic districts of old Naples, most notably Spaccanapoli, I Vergini, and La Sanità; to the south, the port. Farther west along the bay are the more fashionable neighborhoods of Santa Lucia and Chiaia, and finally the waterfront district of Mergellina. The residential area of Vomero sits on the steep hills rising above Chiaia and downtown.

At the center of it all is picturesque Spaccanapoli—the heart of the *centro storico* (historic center), called the Decumanus Inferior in Roman times. The entire quarter takes its name from its main street, a partly pedestrianized promenade referred to as Spaccanapoli. Rather confusingly, this street changes its name—Via Benedetto Croce and Via San

Massive Castel Nuovo overlooks the bay in the heart of Naples.

Biagio dei Librai, among others—as it runs its way through the heart of old Naples. The area is particularly suited to strolling. The slopes are manageable, and a gridlike street layout makes navigation extraordinarily simple. The *vicoli* (side streets) are seldom more than 100 meters long, and the high number of intersections means there is always a square on hand where you can take a coffee and watch life go by, a favorite Neapolitan activity.

Tying much of this geographic layout together is the "spine" of the city, Via Toledo—Naples' major north–south axis, which begins at Piazza Trieste e Trento and heads up all the way up to Capodimonte. It's basically one straight road with four different names (five if you count the official name of Via Roma, which is how the locals refer to it). Via Toledo links Piazza Trieste e Trento with Piazza Dante. Going farther north you get into Via Pessina for about 100 yards, which takes you up to the mega-junction with the Museo Archeologico Nazionale. North of that, you head up to the peak of Capodimonte by traveling along Via Santa Teresa degli Scalzi and then Corso Amedeo di Savoia. To make things a bit more confusing, parts of Via Toledo are pedestrianized—that means no buses or scooters, thankfully—from just south of Piazza Carità (where Via Toledo/Roma intersects with Via Diaz) all the way to Piazza Trieste e Trento.

GETTING AROUND NAPLES

PUBLIC TRANSIT

Naples's rather old Metropolitana (subway system), also called Linea 2, provides fairly frequent service and can be the fastest way to get across the traffic-clogged city.

The other urban subway system, Metropolitana Collinare (or Linea 1), links the hill area of the Vomero and beyond with the National Archaeological Museum and Piazza Dante. Trains on both lines run from 5 AM until 10:30 PM.

For standard public transportation, including the subways, buses, and funiculars, a Giranapoli pass costs €1.10 and is valid for 90 minutes as far as Pozzuoli to the west and Portici to the east; €3 buys a *biglietto giornaliero*, good for the whole day.

Bus service has become viable over the last few years, especially with the introduction of larger buses on the regular R1, R2, and R3 routes. Electronic signs display wait times at many stops.

PARKING

If you come to Naples by car, find a garage, agree on the cost, and leave it there for the duration of your stay. (If you park on the street, you run the risk of theft.) **Garage Cava** (⊠ *Via Mergellina 6* ☎ *081/660023*), **Grilli** (⊠ *Via Ferraris 40, near Stazione Centrale* ☎ *081/264344*), and **Turistico** (⊠ *Via de Gasperi 14, near port* ☎ *081/5525442*) are all centrally located, safe, and open 24 hours a day.

TAXIS

When taking a taxi in Naples, make sure that the meter is switched on at the start of your trip. Trips around the city are unlikely to cost less than €10 or more than €20. Set fares for various destinations within the city should be displayed in the taxi, as should extra charges for things like baggage and night service. For trips outside the city, negotiate your fare before getting in. Watch out for overcharging at three locations: the airport, the railway station, and the hydrofoil marina. And in peak summer weeks, don't forget that most cabs in Naples have no air-conditioning—which the city's buses and metro do have—and you can practically bake if caught in one during a half-hour traffic jam.

TOURS

Handily close to the port is the terminal for double-decker buses belonging to **City Sightseeing** (⊠ *Piazza Municipio* ☎ *081/5517279* ⊕ *www.napoli.city-sightseeing.it*). For €22 you can take two or three different excursions, giving you reasonable coverage of the downtown sights and outlying attractions like the Museo di Capodimonte.

For in-depth tours of Naples, the **Comune di Napoli** (⊠ *Piazza Municipio* ☎ *081/5422090* ⊕ *www.comune.napoli.it*) occasionally offers English-language guided tours. These tours are a great way to see monuments that are otherwise off-limits.

A welcome center in the old town, the **Centro di Accoglienza Turistica Museo Aperto Napoli** (⊠ *Via Pietro Colletta 89* ☎ *081/5636062* ⊕ *www.museoapertonapoli.it*), offers €6 audio guides you can listen to as you wander around.

TOLEDO: THE MONUMENTAL CITY CENTER

Naples' setting on what is possibly the most beautiful bay in the world has long been a boon for its inhabitants—the expansive harbor has always brought great mercantile wealth to the city—and, intermittently, a curse. Throughout history, a who's who of Greek, Roman, Norman, Spanish, and French despots has quarreled over this gateway to Campania. Each set of conquerors recognized that the area around the city harbor—today occupied by the Molo Beverello hydrofoil terminal and the 1928 Stazione Marittima—functioned as a veritable welcome mat to the metropolis and consequently should be a fitting showcase of regal and royal authority. This had become imperative because of explosive population growth, which, by the mid-16th century, had made Naples the second-largest city in Europe, after Paris. With the mass migration of the rural population to the city, Naples had grown into a capricious, unplanned, disorderly, and untrammeled capital. Thus, the central aim of the ruling dynasties became the creation of a *Napoli nobilissima*— a "most noble" Naples.

The monuments they created remain prominent features of the city center: one of the most magnificent opera houses in Europe, a palace that rivals Versailles, an impregnable *castello* (castle), a majestic church modeled on Rome's Pantheon, and a 19th-century shopping galleria are landmarks that characterized the shifts among the ruling powers, from the French Angevins to the Spanish Habsburgs and Bourbons and, later, the postunification rise of the bourgeoisie and the regime of Mussolini. In contrast to the intense intimacy of the Spacca, the official center of Naples unrolls its majesty with great pomp along its spacious avenues and monumental piazzas.

TOP ATTRACTIONS

❼ ★ Castel Nuovo *(New Castle)*. Known to locals as Maschio Angioino in reference to its Angevin builders, this imposing building is now used more for marital than military purposes, its being partly a government registry office. Looming Angevin stonework is upstaged by the white four-tiered triumphal entrance arch, ordered by Alfonso of Aragon after his entry into the city in 1443 to seize the throne from the increasingly unpopular and beleaguered Angevin Giovanna II. (She had promised Alfonso the throne on her death in return for some much needed protection, only to switch allegiances to a fellow Angevin prince.) Completed by Francesco Laurana and others, the arch on its first level shows the king riding a triumphal cart accompanied, Roman fashion, by a procession of followers. At the top, as if justifying Alfonso's claim to the throne, stands the Archangel Gabriel in the act of slaying a demon. Add four orders of Corinthian columns, rose reliefs, and putti, and you have self-promotion that was built to last. As you enter, admire on the arch's side walls Renaissance soldiers sporting the latest military fashion.

Across the courtyard within is Sala Grande, also known as the Sala dei Baroni. Alfonso's triumphal arch notwithstanding, his son King Ferrante soon found himself waging a war at the Pope's bidding against Florence. In 1486 the local barons hatched a plot against him. King Ferrante reacted by inviting them here for a wedding banquet, which

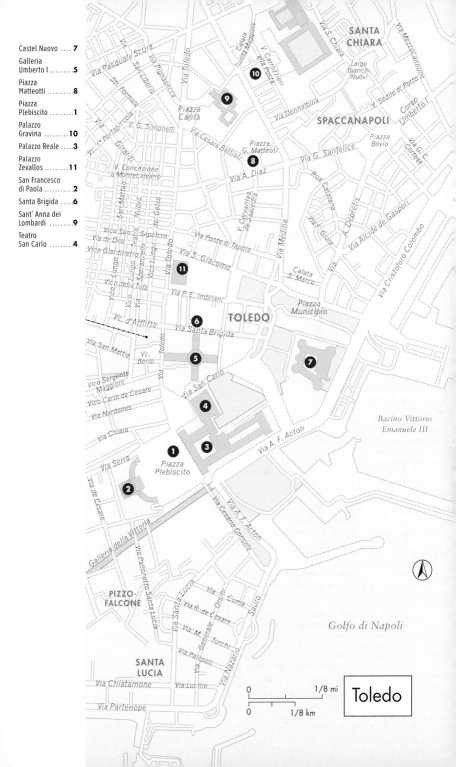

Toledo

A GOOD WALK: NAPOLI NOBILISSIMA

In a day filled with monarchist grandeur, it's fitting to start out at **Caffè Gambrinus,** in the very center of Naples on Piazza Trieste e Trento, between Piazza del Plebiscito and Piazza Municipio. This ornate café was once the rendezvous for Italian dukes, prime ministers, and literati. Treat yourself to a cappuccino and a pastry as rich and velvety as the surroundings, then step outside into the grand **Piazza del Plebiscito ❶**, which makes an imposing setting for **San Francesco di Paola ❷**, the domed 19th-century church built by Ferdinand I.

From here head directly across the piazza to take in the facade of the **Palazzo Reale ❸** then enter the palace from Piazza Trieste e Trento, walk up the grand staircase of its Scalone d'Onore, and tour the spectacular 18th- and 19th-century salons of the Museo dell'Appartamento Reale. To visit the adjacent **Teatro San Carlo ❹**, head back down to the piazza and make a right turn in the Piazza Trieste e Trento. Opera lovers will want to take a guided tour of the famous red-and-gold theater.

Across the way is the vast, elegant **Galleria Umberto I ❺**, an ancestor of the shopping mall. Walk through it to Via Santa Brigida and tour the Church of **Santa Brigida ❻**. Head back through the Galleria and then gently downhill on the Via San Carlo and the Via Vittorio Emanuele III; you'll come to the usually light-drenched Piazza Municipio, for years a sprawling building site for the Municipio metro station. To appreciate some of the technical difficulties faced by the subway engineers, peer down into the various layers

of civilization from Roman times on. Above the piazza rises the imposing fortress of the **Castel Nuovo ❼**. From the outside, study its great sculpted triumphal arch of Alfonso of Aragon; inside, explore the museum and Hall of the Barons.

Head across Piazza Municipio to Via Medina until you reach the 20th-century complex at **Piazza Matteotti ❽**. Then trip across the centuries by continuing up Via Monteoliveto to its pedestrianized piazza, where you can find both the quiet church of **Sant'Anna dei Lombardi ❾** and the Tuscan-influenced rusticated facade of **Palazzo Gravina ❿**.

Make a left leaving Sant'Anna dei Lombardi and head over to Piazza Carità for ice cream at La Scimmia, then take the 10 or so blocks down Via Toledo (the main thoroughfare of the area, often referred to as Via Roma) back to the Piazza Trieste e Trento; along the way, take in the 17th-century opulence of the **Palazzo Zevallos ⓫**, do some window-shopping, and pick up a hot, flaky *sfogliatella* pastry at Mary's by the entrance to Galleria Umberto. You'll arrive back at Piazza Trieste e Trento in time to seek out a leisurely lunch. (See "Where to Eat" for a number of good options.)

TIMING

Not including stops at the Palazzo Reale and Castel Nuovo museums, this walk will take about three hours. There's no escaping the crowds, but if you start early you may catch the spectacular Piazza del Plebiscito *senza gente* (without people).

turned promptly into a mass arrest. (Ferrante is also said to have kept a crocodile in the castle as his special executioner.) In the stupendous 28 meter high vault is a luminous hole toward which spider 16 massive rather sinister arms of reinforcing piperno stone quarried from nearby Pozzuoli. You can also visit the Sala dell'Armeria, where a glass floor reveals recent excavations of a Roman baths from the Augustan period, and a collection of skeletons of 20 to 40 year olds dating back to the Angevin period.

The next room, on the left is the Cappella Palatina. Among the wall frescoes particularly noteworthy is Nicolo di Tomaso's painting of Robert Anjou, one of the first realistic portraits ever. Others, or bits of them anyway, are by various Giotteschi, as the followers of Giotto are known. Giotto's own work in the same chapel was destroyed in a 1456 earthquake and now only remains in Petrarch's poems.

Meanwhile, making up the loss somewhat, the castle's first floor hosts a small gallery with works by Luca Giordano (again), Caracciolo, Solimena, and Maria Preti, as well as a beautiful early Renaissance Adoration of the Magi that once adorned the altar of the Palatine chapel. The painting is by Marco Cardisco and the three Magi are none less than the three Aragonese kings Ferrante I, Ferrante II, and Charles V. ✉*Piazza Municipio, Toledo* ☎*081/7952003* 💶*€5* 🕐*Mon.–Sat. 9–6* Ⓜ*Montesanto (in construction: Piazza Municipio).*

3 **Palazzo Reale.** One of the showplaces of Naples, the Palazzo Reale, or Royal Palace, was meant to be the apotheosis of Bourbon power in the city. Renovated and redecorated by successive rulers, once lorded over by a dim-witted king who liked to shoot his hunting guns at the birds in his tapestries, and filled with salons designed in the most deliciously lavish 18th-century Neapolitan taste, it remains a palatial pile. The Spanish viceroys commissioned it in 1600, ordering Swiss architect Domenico Fontana to build a suitable new residence for Philip III, should he chance to visit Naples (which he didn't); the immense complex was not completed until 1843 (by Gaetano Genovese). The palace saw its greatest moment of splendor in the 18th century, when Charles III of Bourbon became the first permanent resident; during that century Luigi Vanvitelli filled in half the arcades in the lower register of the facade to strengthen it, and Ferdinando Fuga created the State Wing after the accession of Ferdinand IV in 1759. Today this wing comprises the Museo dell'Appartamento Storico, or **Royal Apartments,** where visitors can get a taste of Bourbon glory.

To view these 30 rooms on the second floor, enter from Piazza Trieste e Trento and head toward the *Biglietteria* (ticket booth). You'll be channeled through the bookshop and past medieval archaeological remains toward the monumental Scalone d'Onore. Montesquieu, the French 18th-century writer, considered this to be the finest staircase in Europe, and it does set a tone for the glitter and grandeur to come. The first doors on the right open into the **Court Theater,** built by Ferdinando Fuga for Charles III, who in 1763 had created an opera company for private performances of comic opera. Damaged by World War II bombing, it was restored in the 1950s; note the resplendent royal box, which

abandons the lure of monumentality for intimate luxury. Following are the suite of rooms around the courtyard that constitute the royal apartments. Through a series of antechambers, you eventually reach Room VI, the **Throne Room,** with wine-red striped-silk walls and gilded stuccos representing the 12 provinces of the Kingdom of the Two Sicilies; the ponderous Empire-style throne in fact dates from after 1850.

The decoration picks up in the **Room of the Ambassadors** (Room VIII), where a pair of choice 18th-century Gobelin tapestries grace the light-green walls while the ceiling painting honoring Spanish military victories is by local artist Belisario Corenzio and his school (1610–20). Room IX, with pale gold walls and a simple white vault, was the bedroom of Charles's queen, Maria Amalia of Saxony, and hides a small, brilliantly gold private oratory in the corner, with beautiful paintings by Francesco Liani of Parma (1760).

The **Great Captain's Room** (Room XI), small and square, has wonderful ceiling frescoes by Battistello Caracciolo (1610–16)—all velvet, fire, and smoke, they reveal the influence of the visit by Caravaggio to Naples— a jolly series by Federico Zuccari depicting 12 proverbs on small wood panels, along with, last but not least, a Titian portrait (circa 1543) of Pier Luigi Farnese. Room XII, the **Flemish Hall,** has a rather brash 19th-century gilded ceiling with 12 paintings representing the coats-of-arms of the kingdom's provinces and a large neo-Gothic centerpiece depicting the 12th-century Tancred and Constance.

Room XIII was **Joachim Murat's writing room** when he was king of Naples; he brought with him from France some regal furniture by the great French *ébeniste* (cabinetmaker) Weisweiller, originally commissioned by Marie Antoinette and completed through commissions of his own (including the desk and two dignified clocks) in 1812. The next few rooms combine ponderous 19th-century furnishings and rather better baroque paintings: Room XVII, in particular, has a good selection of paintings by followers of Caravaggio; Room XVIII has an intensely colored Guercino depiction of the biblical Joseph dreaming; and Room XIX is full of still lifes from the important Neapolitan school. The huge Room XXII, painted in green and gold with kitschy faux tapestries, is known as the **Hercules Hall,** for in a moment of glory it once housed the *Hercules Farnese.* The authentic tapestries are from the Royal Factory of Naples (1783–89), but the things to look at here are the porcelain creations from Sèvres, including the Atlas with his starry globe and the huge green chrome vase (1812) opposite, painted by Louis Béranger.

The **Palatine Chapel,** redone by Gaetano Genovese in the 1830s, is, as chapels go, a disappointing affair, having been gussied up with an excess of gold, but it has a stunning Technicolor intarsia altar from the previous chapel (Dionisio Lazzari, 1678). Note the false-perspective panels, which almost propel the altar into the stratosphere of bad taste. Also here on a long-term loan is the famous *Presepio* (Nativity) scene of the Banco di Napoli—it may lack the spectacular setting of the *Presepio Cuciniello* in the Museo di San Martino but has even better sculpture, with pieces by important sculptors such as Giuseppe Sammartino, Francesco and Antonio Viva, Francesco Celebrano, and others. There are

Continued on page 42

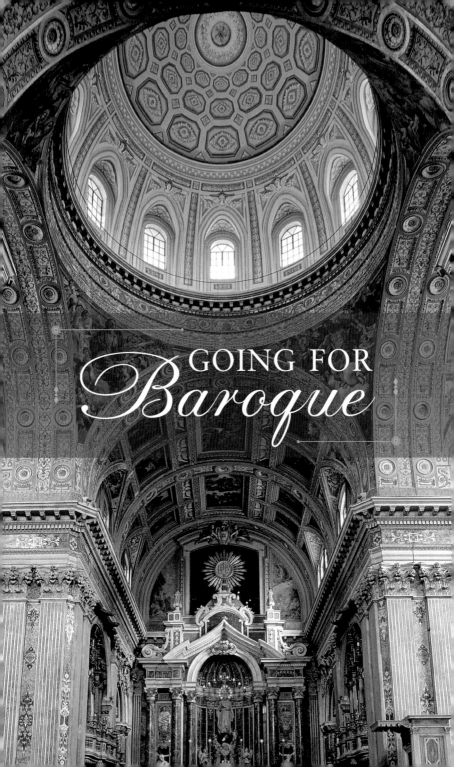

GOING FOR *Baroque*

Even charitable observers would say that excess, fake opulence, and exaggeration are typical Neapolitan qualities. It's not surprising, then, that the baroque, an artistic style that revels in details added to swirls added to flourishes added to twists—a style that is playful, theatrical, dynamic, and seems permanently about to burst its bonds—should find one of its most spectacular showcases in Naples.

The very word "baroque" derives from a Portuguese word describing an impressive-looking but worthless type of pearl, and was originally used as an insult to describe the flagrantly emotional, floridly luxurious style that surfaced in Europe around 1600. Critics now use baroque to describe a style more than a period.

It's a style that found immediate favor in a city of volcanic passions. Like the city itself, the decorative scheme is diffuse and disjunctive, with little effort to organize everything into an easily understood scheme.

Contradictions still abound in Naples: plenty with want; grandeur with muddle; beauty with decay; the wide bay, lush countryside, and peaceful sky harboring the dense, chaotic city, sheltered by the ever-present threat of the slumbering Mount Vesuvius. In this context, the vivid, dramatic baroque style feels right at home.

NAPLES AND BAROQUE: A MATCH MADE FOR HEAVEN

At the beginning of the 17th century, thanks to the Counter-Reformation, the Catholic Church was busy making an overt appeal to its congregants, using emotion and motion to get its message across—and nowhere was this more blatant than in Naples, which, as the most populous city in Italy at the time, had more clerics (some 20,000) than even Rome. Baroque artists and architects, given an open invitation to indulge their illusionistic whims on church cupolas and the like, began arriving in Naples to strut their aesthetic stuff.

The most representative practitioner of Neapolitan baroque was **Cosimo Fanzago (1591–1678)**. A Lombard by birth, he traveled to Naples to study sculpture; even when decorating a church, he usually covered it head to toe with colored and inlaid marbles, as in

his work at the Certosa di San Martino atop the Vomero hill.

Preceding Fanzago by two decades was **Caravaggio (1571–1610)**, who moved to Naples from Rome. This great painter took the city by storm, with an unflinching truthfulness and extroverted sensuality in his work. Experts will continue to argue to what degree Caravaggio was or wasn't a baroque painter, but certainly his use of chiaroscuro, a quality common in baroque art, can be seen dramatically in his Neapolitan paintings *The Flagellation of Christ* and *The Seven Acts of Mercy*.

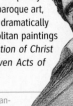

(preceding page) The dome of Gesú Nuovo; (top) *St Bruno* by Cosimo Fanzago; (bottom) Caravaggio

BAROQUE TECHNIQUES: TRICKS OF THE TRADE

MEMENTO MORI. Lest all the sumptuous decoration should appeal too directly to the senses, the Church (as the major sponsor of the baroque) felt it was necessary to remind people of their ultimate message: *memento mori*—"remember that you will die." Don't be surprised if, in the midst of the most delicate and beautiful inlaid marble floor, you find leering skulls. In the tiny church of **Purgatorio ad Arco** ❶ in Spaccanapoli, a winged skull by Fanzago awaits salvation.

DOMES: LOOK UP! If there was one thing baroque architects loved, it was a dome—Exhibit One being the **Duomo di San Gennaro** ❷. Domes offered space and height and

lots of opportunities to trompe your oeil. Even in the tightly packed old center of Naples, domes manage to make you feel as if you are in an enormous, heavenly space. This is in part due to their acoustic qualities, which reduce the city and its noisy inhabitants to swirling whispers and echoes.

MARVELOUS MARBLE. Making the most of the large quantities of marble quarries in Italy, baroque architects outdid their Renaissance predecessors. They used softer kinds of stone and developed intricate, interlaced patterns of

different colored marble, such as seen in the **Certosa di San Martino** ❸.

KEEPING IT (HYPER)REAL. Getting solid marble or stone to "move" was one of the skills of any baroque sculptor worth his chisel. Giuseppe Sammartino, who sculpted the **Veiled Christ** ❹ in the Capella Sansevero, was so good at his craft that it was rumored (falsely) his boss had him blinded so he couldn't repeat his genius anywhere else. In Gesù Nuovo a dead Christ lies near the entrance in a glass case, often giving visitors cause

to stop momentarily as they think they've stumbled across a real person. It is common to find saints' marble effigies still dressed in real period clothes.

OUT OF THE SHADOWS. Chiaroscuro ("light-dark") is the word most often used to describe baroque painting, with its mixture of bright shafts of light and thick shadows. Figures loom out of the dark while the main action is highlighted by dazzling beams of light—as in Rubino's *Apollo and Marsyas* ❺ at the Museo di Capodimonte.

TROMPE L'OEIL. Literally "tricking the eye," trompe l'oeil is an illusionist method of painting that consists, quite simply, of making things look like something they're not. Angels lean over balconies and

out of paintings, walls become windows, and skylights bestow views into heaven itself, as grandly displayed in Luca Giordano's *Triumph of Judith* ❻ at the Certosa di San Martino. There is something very baroque in trompe l'oeil's sense of trickery, of something being built upon nothing.

STAIRWAYS TO HEAVEN. The principles of movement and ascension naturally conveyed by a staircase made baroque architects drool with possibilities. Staircases can often be seen with winged banisters, as if those simply climbing the steps were on a journey into a higher realm. The staircase in the entrance of the Royal Palace in Naples splits and divides and splits again, its movement magnified

and reflected dizzyingly by the windows and mirrors surrounding it. At the Palazzo della Spagnola in the Sanità neighborhood, the M.C. Escher–esque staircase boasts steps wide enough to ride a horse up them—which is precisely what they were used for in the 17th century.

ON STAGE. If some of the more extravagant interiors of Neapolitan churches remind you of theater sets, you're not far off. Many designers crossed over into ecclesiastical work, usually having first been noticed in the theater. Many arches over altars are made from a reinforced form of papier-mâché, originally used in theatrical productions.

The church of San Francesco di Paolo was designed to emulate Rome's Pantheon.

some pleasant 19th-century landscapes in the next few rooms, as well as Queen Maria Carolina's Ferris wheel–like reading lectern (which enabled her to do a 19th-century reader's version of channel surfing). Speaking of reading, another wing of the complex holds the **Biblioteca Nazionale Vittorio Emanuele III**, the largest library in southern Italy and one of the most important in the country. Begun, as with so many other Bourbon collections, with Farnese bits and pieces, it was enriched with the priceless papyri from Herculaneum found in 1752 and opened to the public in 1804. You can view these and a splendid selection of manuscripts and rare editions in the elegant rooms open to visitors. To use the library for scholarly research, you need to apply for a card. The library also has a lovely garden, which looks out on the Castel Nuovo. ⊠*Piazza del Plebiscito, Toledo* ⊕*www.palazzorealenapoli.it* ☎*081/400547, 848/800288 schools and guided tours* ⊠*€4* ☉*Thurs.–Tues. 9–7* Ⓜ*Dante (in construction: Piazza Municipio).*

NEED A BREAK? Across from the Palazzo Reale is the most famous coffeehouse in town, the **Caffè Gambrinus** (⊠*Piazza Trieste e Trento, near Piazza del Plebiscito* ☎*081/417582*). Founded in 1850, this 19th-century jewel once functioned as a brilliant intellectual salon. The glory days are over, but the inside rooms, with amazing mirrored walls and gilded ceilings, make this an essential stop for any visitor to the city. To its credit, the café doesn't inflate prices to cash in on its fame.

⓫ **Palazzo Zevallos.** Tucked inside this beautifully restored palazzo, which
★ houses the Banca Intesa San Paolo (one of Italy's major banks), is a small museum that's worth seeking out. Enter the bank through Cosimo

CLOSE UP

How to Cross the Street in Naples

Long considered a threatened species, the Naples pedestrian is gradually being provided with a more friendly environment. Once Piazza Garabaldi has been negotiated, traffic in much of Naples is no more off-putting than in other Italian cities. (Accident rates involving pedestrians are higher in Rome.) In fact, large tracts of Naples are open to pedestrians only. That's the case for most of Via Toledo—called by Stendhal "the most beautiful street in the world" and by Sartre, less romantically, "a long hygienic clearing in this pox-ridden city." Leading off it is the fashionable Via Chiaia, a destination for posh shopping and the birthplace of the pizza Margherita. Piazza del Plebiscito, once reduced to a parking lot, is also now an ideal space to stroll through, touched by a pleasant sea breeze.

That being said, crossing major thoroughfares in Naples still takes some savvy. In a city where red traffic lights may be blithely ignored, especially by two-wheelers, walking across a busy avenue can be like a game of chess—if you hesitate, you capitulate. Some residents just forge out into the unceasing flow of traffic, knowing cars invariably slow down to let them cross. (A trick for the fainthearted: look for an elderly couple—when they cross, you *know* it will be safe.) Look both ways even on one-way streets, as there may be motorcyclists riding against the flow. Areas where you have to be particularly vigilant—and cross at the lights—are around the Archaeological Museum and on Via Marina outside the port, as well as the ever-challenging Piazza Garibaldi.

Fanzago's gargoyled doorway and take the handsome elevator to the upper floor. The first room to the left holds the star attraction, Caravaggio's last work, *The Martyrdom of Saint Ursula*. The saint here is, for dramatic effect, deprived of her usual retinue of a thousand followers. On the left, a face of pure spite, is the king of the Huns, who has just shot Ursula with an arrow after his proposal of marriage has been rejected. Opposite the painting is an elaborate map of the city of Caravaggio's day, not so different from now. ✉ *Via Toledo 185, Piazza Plebiscito* ☏ *081/400547* ⊕ *www.palazzozevallos.com* 💳 *€3* 🕐 *Mon.–Sat. 10–6.*

❶ Piazza Plebiscito. After spending time as a carpark, this square was restored in 1994 to one of Napoli Nobilissima's most majestic spaces, with a Doric semicircle of columns resembling Saint Peter's Square in Rome. It was originally built under the Napoleonic rule. When the Napoleonic regime fell, Ferdinand, new king of the Two Sicilies, ordered the addition of the Church of San Francesco di Paola. On the left as you approach the church is a statue of Ferdinand and on the right his father, Charles III, both clad in Roman togas. Around dusk the floodlights come on, to magical effect. The square is aired by a delightful sea breeze and on Sunday one corner becomes an improvised soccer stadium where local youth emulate their heroes.

❷ San Francesco di Paola. Modeled after Rome's Pantheon, this circular ★ basilica is the centerpiece of the Piazza del Plebiscito and remains one of the most frigidly voluptuous examples of the Stil Empire, or neoclassic style, in Italy. Commissioned by Ferdinand I in 1817 to fulfill a vow he had made in order to enlist divine aid in being reinstated to the throne of the Kingdom of the Two Sicilies, it rose at one end of the vast parade ground built several years earlier by Joachim Murat. It managed to transform Murat's inconveniently grandiose colonnade—whose architect was clearly inspired by the colonnades of St. Peter's in Rome—into a setting for restored Bourbon glory. The church also usefully fulfilled a prophecy by the 15th-century saint Ferrante d'Aragona, for whom it is named, that one day a large church and square would occupy the crowded site. Pietro Bianchi from Lugano in Switzerland won a competition and built a slightly smaller version of the Pantheon, with a beautiful coffered dome and a splendid set of 34 Corinthian columns in gray marble; but the overall lack of color (so different from the warm interior of the Pantheon) combined with the severe geometrical forms produces an almost defiantly cold space. To some, this only proves the ancients did sometimes know their own architecture better. Art historians find the spectacle of the church to be the ultimate in neoclassic *grandezza*; others think this Roman temple is only fitting to honor Jupiter, not Christ. In any event, the main altar, done in gold, lapis lazuli, and other precious stones by Anselmo Caggiano (1641), was taken from the destroyed Church of the Santi Apostoli and provides some relief from the oppressive perfection of the setting. ⊠ *Piazza del Plebiscito, Toledo* ☎ *081/7645133* 🕘 *Mon.–Sat. 6:45–noon and 4:30–5:30, Sun. 8–noon* Ⓜ *Dante (in construction: Piazza Municipio).*

❾ **Sant'Anna dei Lombardi.** Long favored by the Aragonese kings, this church, simple and rather anonymous from the outside, houses some of the most important ensembles of Renaissance sculpture in southern Italy. Begun with the adjacent convent of the Olivetani and its four cloisters in 1411, it was given a baroque makeover in the mid-17th century by Gennaro Sacco, although this is no longer so visible, as the bombs of 1943 rather radically altered the decoration and led to a modern restoration favoring the original *quattrocento* (15th-century) lines. The wonderful coffered wooden ceiling adds a bit of pomp. Inside the porch is the tomb of Domenico Fontana, one of the major architects of the late 16th century, who died in Naples after beginning the Palazzo Reale.

On either side of the original entrance door are two fine Renaissance tombs. The one on the left as you face the door belongs to the Ligorio family (whose descendant Pirro designed the Villa d'Este in Tivoli) and is a work by Giovanni da Nola (1524); the tomb on the right is a masterpiece by Giuseppe Santacroce (1532) done for the del Pozzo family. To the left of the Ligorio Altar (the corner chapel on the immediate right as you face the altar) is the Mastrogiudice Chapel, whose altar contains precious reliefs of the *Annunciation* and *Scenes from the Life of Jesus* (1489) by Benedetto da Maiano, a great name in Tuscan sculpture. On the other side of the entrance is the Piccolomini Chapel, with a *Crucifixion* by Giulio Mazzoni (circa 1550), a refined marble altar (circa 1475), a funerary monument to Maria d'Aragona by another prominent Florentine sculptor, Antonello Rossellino (circa 1475), and on the right,

Teatro San Carlo, Naples' grand opera house, was rebuilt in only nine months after burning to the ground in 1816.

a rather sweet fresco of the Annunciation by an anonymous follower of Piero della Francesca.

The true surprises of the church, however, are to the right of the altar, in the presbytery and adjoining rooms. The chapel just to the right of the main altar, belonging to the Orefice family, is richly decorated in pre-baroque (1596–98) polychrome marbles and frescoes by Luis Rodriguez; from here you continue on through the Oratory of the Holy Sepulchre, with the tomb of Antonio D'Alessandro and his wife, to reach the church's showpiece: a potently realistic life-size group of eight terra-cotta figures by Guido Mazzoni (1492), which make up a Pietà; the faces are said to be modeled from people at the Aragonese court. Toward the rear of the church is Cappella dell'Assunta, with a fun painting in its corner of a monk by Michelangelo's student Giorgio Vasari, and the lovely Sacrestia Vecchia (Old Sacristy), adorned with one of the most successful decorative ensembles Vasari ever painted (1544) and breathtaking wood-inlay stalls by Fra' Giovanni da Verona and assistants (1506–10) with views of famous buildings. ⊠ *Piazza Monteoliveto 15, Toledo* ☎*081/5513333* ⊙ *Tues.–Sat. 9–noon* Ⓜ *Dante (in construction: Toledo).*

❹ **Teatro San Carlo.** La Scala in Milan is the famous one, but San Carlo is more beautiful, and Naples is, after all, the most operatic of cities. Built in eight months and 10 days in 1737 by Angelo Carasale for Charles III of Bourbon—and opened on the king's saint's name day—it burned down in 1816 and was rebuilt, with its facade of five rustic gray arches surmounted by an elegant loggia, in a mere nine months. This time the architect was Antonio Niccolini, working under the impetus of

Fodor'sChoice

★

Domenico Barbaja, the Milanese director appointed by Joachim Murat in 1810. Barbaja, San Carlo's most legendary director, started out as a waiter in a tavern and enriched himself through a talent for gambling. Obviously wanting to remain part of the new regime, he bet the king that he could have the theater open within nine months. More important, he also managed in the same year to convince Gioacchino Rossini to come to Naples as conductor and house composer; Stendhal hailed Ferdinand's wise retaining of Barbaja and his prompt sponsorship of the theater as a "coup d'état" for the deep and immediate bond it created between the ruler and his opera-loving populace. This was further cemented by the many operas composed for the house, including Donizetti's *Lucia di Lammermoor* and Rossini's *La Donna del Lago.*

In the theater, nearly 200 boxes are arranged on six levels, and the huge stage (12,000 square feet) permits productions with horses, camels, and elephants and even boasts a removable backdrop that can lift to reveal the Palazzo Reale Gardens. Above the rich red-and-gold auditorium is a breathy ceiling fresco, by Giuseppe Cammarano, suitably representing Apollo presenting poets to Athena. At many performances, however, all eyes strayed to the sumptuous royal box, which seats 15 and is topped by a gigantic gilded crown. Check the San Carlo Web site, the local press (*Il Mattino, La Repubblica, Corriere della Sera*), or the *Qui Napoli* for information on performances, or pick up the annual program at the ticket office and get ready for a great evening of opera. Performance standards are among the highest in Europe at the San Carlo—even the great Enrico Caruso was hissed here—although some locals really come to study the fashion show in the auditorium, not the Verdi on stage. If you can't catch a performance, try to take the 30-minute guided tour (€5) to see the splendid theater—as Stendhal wrote: "The first impression one gets is of being suddenly transported to the palace of an oriental emperor. There is nothing in Europe to compare with it, or even give the faintest idea of what it is like." ⊠ *Via San Carlo 101–103, Toledo* ☏*081/7972331 box office, 081/7972412* 🖷*081/400902* ⊕*www.teatrosancarlo.it* ⊙*Guided tours daily 9–6, but not during rehearsals* Ⓜ*Dante (in construction: Piazza Municipio).*

WORTH NOTING

❺ **Galleria Umberto I.** The centerpiece of a clean-up of Naples following the 1885 cholera epidemic, when swaths of buildings between Spaccanapoli and Palazzo Reale were knocked down, this shopping complex was designed by Emanuele Rocca as a sort of smaller glass and cast-iron relative to the Galleria Vittorio Emmanuele in Milan. Now a large section of it is scaffolded off, but this does not prevent young Neapolitans using the other part on Sunday as an improvised football field while their less energetic elders window-shop. ⊠*Entrances on Via San Carlo, Via Toledo, Via Santa Brigida, Via Verdi, Toledo* Ⓜ*Montesanto (in construction: Piazza Municipio).*

❿ **Palazzo Gravina.** A dignified Renaissance palace in the Tuscan style, the palazzo was begun in 1513 for Ferdinando Orsini, duke of Gravina, by Gabriele d'Angelo, a student of Alberti and Brunelleschi. The monumental doorway was added by Mario Giuffredo in a restoration of 1762–72, and an extra story was added in 1839, which is clearly visible from the beautiful courtyard. Largely burned down in 1848 by Swiss Guards trying to flush out a group of armed patriots, it now houses the modern School of Architecture. Visitors are allowed access to the courtyard. ⊠ *Via Monteoliveto 3, Monteoliveto* ☎*081/7955877* Ⓜ *Montesanto (in construction: Toledo).*

8 Piazza Matteotti. Renamed after the opposition politician whom Mussolini had murdered, this Piazza is an example of Fascist architecture, with "Anno 1936 XIV E. Fascista" on the side of the massive post office a reminder of an era ending in Nazi occupation and a ferocious four-day battle in which the German army was expelled and Allied forces retook the city. Opposite the post office, from the same Fascist epoch, is the ominously named Casa del Mutilato.

6 Santa Brigida. The Lucchesi fathers built this church around 1640 in honor of the Swedish queen and saint who visited her fellow queen, Naples' unsaintly Giovanna I, in 1372 and became one of the first persons to go on record as denouncing the loose morals and irrepressible sensuality of the Neapolitans. The height of the church's dome was limited to prevent its interfering with cannon fire from nearby Castel Nuovo, but Luca Giordano, the pioneer painter of the trompe l'oeil Baroque dome, effectively opened it up with a spacious sky serving as the setting for an *Apotheosis of Saint Bridget* (1678), painted (and now in need of considerable restoration) in exchange for his tomb space, marked by a pavement inscription in the left transept. ⊠ *Via Santa Brigida 72, Toledo* ☎*081/5523793* ⊙ *Daily 6:45–12:45 and 4:30–7:30* Ⓜ *Dante (in construction: Piazza Municipio).*

THE VOMERO TO THE LUNGOMARE

Neapolitans often say their town's glories are vertical—the white *guglia* (religious obelisk) of the historic quarter, the eight-story tenements of Spaccanapoli, and Vomero, the towering hill that overlooks the city center. Even longtime residents love to head up here to gaze in wonder at the entire city from the balcony belvedere of the Museo di San Martino. Before them, a rich spread of southern Italian amplitude fills the eye: hillsides dripping with luxuriant greenery interspersed with villainously ugly apartment houses, streets short and narrow—leading to an unspeakable as well as unsolvable traffic problem—countless church spires and domes, and far below, the reason it all works, the intensely blue Bay of Naples. To tie together the lower parts and upper reaches of the city, everyone uses the *funicolare*—the funicular system that runs on three separate routes up and down the Vomero.

Thanks to the funiculars, you can readily take in many of Naples' aristocratic pleasures and treasures on the same day: the chic Piazza dei Martiri sector; the gilded 19th-century Villa Pignatelli; three major landmarks that crown the Vomero hill—the Villa Floridiana, the Certosa di San Martino, and the Castel Sant'Elmo; down to the Lungomare, the grandest stretch of waterfront in Naples. In the 19th century Naples' waterfront harbored the picturesque quarter that was called Santa Lucia, a district dear to artists and musicians and known for its

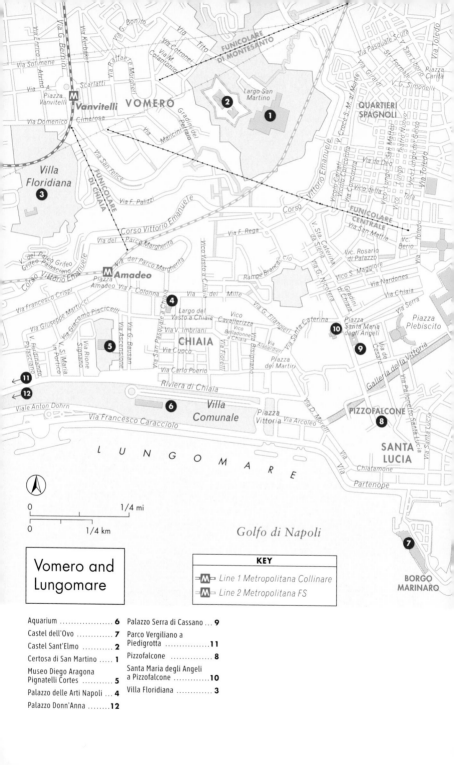

Vomero and Lungomare

A GOOD WALK: VOMERO/LUNGOMARE

Begin at the main station of the Funicolare Centrale, on the tiny Piazza Duca d'Aosta, opposite the Via Toledo entrance to the Galleria Umberto I. After two hillside stops, get off at the end of the line, Stazione Fuga, near the top of the Vomero Hill. To get to the Castel Sant'Elmo/Certosa di San Martino complex, head out from the station, turning right across the pedestrianized Piazza Fuga toward the escalator, then left on Via Morghen. At the next junction, Via Scarlatti—the main thoroughfare of the neighborhood—turn right uphill and take the escalator (or steps), cutting twice across the snakelike Via Morghen, then follow the path around the left side of the Montesanto funicular until you run into the Via Tito Angelini. This street, lined with some of Naples' best belle epoque mansions, leads to the **Certosa di San Martino** ❶ past the adjoining **Castel Sant'Elmo** ❷, which commands magnificent 360-degree vistas over city and sea to Vesuvius.

After viewing this enormous complex, backtrack to Via Scarlatti until you make a left on Via Bernini at Piazza Vanvitelli. This piazza, with no shortage of smart bars and trattorias, remains the center for the Vomero district, and is a gathering point for talented street performers.

Walk right onto Via Cimarosa for two blocks until you reach the entrance to the **Villa Floridiana** ❸, today a museum filled with aristocratic knickknacks and surrounded by a once-regal park. After viewing the villa, make a right from the park entrance on Via Cimarosa for two blocks until you reach the Stazione Cimarosa of the Chiaia funicular,

which will take you back down to the Lungomare area.

From the Amedeo funicular station walk down Via del Parco Margherita, past Piazza Amedeo, making a left onto Via Colonna. Stop at the rambling **Palazzo delle Arti Napoli** ❹ if there's an exhibit that catches your eye; otherwise take the first right turn down off Via Colonna onto the steps at the top of Via Bausan. The steps will take you down toward the Riviera di Chiaia (*chiaia* means "beach" in the Neapolitan dialect), where a final right turn brings you to the **Museo Diego Aragona Pignatelli Cortes** ❺. From here cross the Riviera to the waterfront park of the Villa Comunale and its world-famous **Aquarium** ❻.

Follow the Riviera past the Piazza della Vittoria onto Via Partenope to reach the spectacular **Castel dell'Ovo** ❼. From here, a walk north on Via Chiatamone takes you to the Piazza dei Martiri, where you can join chic Neapolitans shopping the boutiques, bookstores, and antiques shops lining the streets that radiate off the piazza (particularly the designer-dense stretch between Via Carlo Poerio and Via dei Mille).

The area around Piazza dei Martiri is excellent for both snacking and more substantial meals. From here it's a relatively short walk back to one of the funiculars (the Centrale and Chiaia are roughly equidistant from the piazza), or you can catch any number of buses westward along the areas main artery, the Riviera di Chiaia.

fishermen's cottages. The fishermen were swept away when an enormous landfill project extended the land out to what is now Via Nazario Sauro and Via Partenope, the address for some of Naples' finest hotels. Today, the waterfront promenade has lost much of its former color, but it still retains a uniquely Neapolitan charm.

TIMING

As always in Naples, it's best to start out early in the morning to fit most of your sightseeing in before the lunch break—and the midday heat. Aim to get to the San Martino complex atop the Vomero hill at opening time and allow at least three hours to take it in along with the Castel Sant'Elmo and an additional half-hour for the Villa Floridiana. If you prefer a leisurely wander or wish to visit an exhibition at Castel Sant'Elmo, go straight to the Borgo from the Riviera di Chiaia following the seafront, and then swing back to Villa Pignatelli and the Aquarium.

TOP ATTRACTIONS

❻ Aquarium. Originally named by the Greeks after the mermaid Parthenope (who slew herself after being rejected by Odysseus, at least in the poet Virgil's version), it's only fitting that Naples should have established one of Europe's first public aquariums in 1874. At the time—when, not so incidentally, the public imagination was being stirred by Jules Verne's Captain Nemo and Hans Christian Andersen's Little Mermaid—technological innovations came into place to funnel seawater directly from the bay into the aquarium tanks, which showcase some 200 species of fish and marine plants (undoubtedly better off here than in the somewhat polluted Bay of Naples, their natural habitat). Officially named the Stazione Zoologica, founded by the German scientist Anton Dohrn, and housed in a Stil Liberty building designed by Adolf von Hildebrandt, the aquarium quickly became the wonder of Naples for children and art-exhausted adults. Today the ground floors contain the aquarium tanks—fishy "living rooms" decorated with rocks and plants of the region and illuminated by skylights. ⊠ *Stazione Zoologica, Viale A. Dohrn, Chiaia* ☎ *081/5833263 for information and library visits* ⊕ *www.szn.it* ⊠ *€1.50* ⊗ *Mar.–Oct., Tues.–Sat. 9–6, Sun. 9:30–7:30; Nov.–Feb., Tues.–Sat. 9–5, Sun. 9–2* Ⓜ *Piazza Amedeo.*

❼ Castel dell'Ovo. The oldest castle in Naples, the Castel dell'Ovo sits on
Fodor's Choice the most picturesque point of the bay, standing guard over the city it
★ protects. Occupying the isle of Megaris, it was originally the site of the Roman villa of Lucullus—proof, if you need it, that the ancient Romans knew a premium location when they saw one (for the same reason, some of the city's top hotels share the same site today). By the 12th century, it had become a fortress under the Normans; it was once the prison of Conradin and of Beatrice, daughter of Manfred, last of the Hohenstaufen rulers. The castle's gigantic rooms, rock tunnels, and belvederes over the bay are among Naples' most striking sights as well as a magical setting for the temporary contemporary-art exhibitions sponsored by the city council.

You enter the castle not through its main entrance with its forbidding trio of cannons, but by descending the steps on the left into the sleepy Borgo Marinaio. Continue alongside the forbidding castle walls and,

Castel dell'Ovo provides impressive views of the bay, the city, and looming Vesuvius.

opposite Oste Pazzo, enter the Spartan hall. An elevator takes you up to the battlement level. Walk up to the roof's Sala della Terrazze for a postcard-come-true view of Ischia. Then, as the odd car honk drifts across from inland, use the tiled map to identify the sights of the city and maybe plot an itinerary for the rest of the day.

As for the egg of the castle's name, the poet Virgil, rather anachronistically, is supposed have hidden an egg in the walls. The egg, like the blood of San Gennaro, was believed to have protective powers, but only as long as it remained intact. If it broke, disaster would strike. The belief was taken so seriously that when in the 15th century under there was an earthquake, followed by a Hungarian invasion, followed by a plague, Queen Giovanna I brought forth an intact egg, solemnly declaring it to be the Virgilian original, in order to quell the people's panic. ✉ *Santa Lucia waterfront, Via Partenope* ☎ *081/2400055* ✉ *Free* ⊙ *Weekdays 8–2.*

❷ **Castel Sant'Elmo.** Perched on the Vomero, this massive castle is almost the size of a small town. It was built by the Angevins in the 14th century to dominate the port and the old city and remodeled by the Spanish in 1537. The parapets, configured in the form of a six-pointed star, provide fabulous views: the whole bay on one side; on another, the city spread out like a map, its every dome and turret clearly visible; and to the east, slumbering Vesuvius.

> **WORD OF MOUTH**
>
> "Although there is not much to see at the castle itself, the views of Naples from the walls make the Castel Sant'Elmo one of my favorite places." —willit

Once a major military outpost, the castle these days hosts occasional cultural events. You get in free if you have a ticket to the adjoining Certosa di San Martino. ✉ *Largo San Martino, Vomero* ☎ *081/5784030* 💶 *€3* 🕐 *Wed.–Mon. 8:30–7:30* Ⓜ *Vanvitelli.*

❶ **Certosa di San Martino.** Atop a rocky promontory with a fabulous view of

the entire city, and with majestic salons that would please any monarch, the Certosa di San Martino is a monastery that seems more like a palace. In fact, by the 18th century Ferdinand IV was threatening to halt the order's government subsidy, so sumptuous was this *certosa*, or charter house, which had been started in 1325 under the royal patronage of Charles of Anjou. With the Carthusians' vast wealth and love of art, it was only a matter of time before dour Angevin Gothic was traded in for varicolored Neapolitan Baroque, thanks to the contributions of many 17th- and 18th-century sculptors and painters. Although the Angevin heritage can be seen in the pointed arches and cross-vaulted ceiling of the Certosa Church across the courtyard just opposite the ticket barrier, the church was overhauled from 1631 onward, partly as a response to Naples' deliverance from Vesuvius the same year.

The sacristy leads into the later Cappella del Tesoro, with Luca Giordano's ceiling fresco of Judith holding aloft Holofernes's head and the painting by Il Ribera (the *Pietà* over the altar is one of his masterpieces). The main baroque style note was set by Cosimo Fanzago (1591–1678), an architect, sculptor, and decorator who was as devout as he was mad. His polychrome marble work is at its finest here in the church, while he displays a gamut of sculptural skills in the **Chiostro Grande** (Great Cloister), also adding the curious small monks' graveyard, bounded by a marble balustrade topped with marble skulls. Fanzago's ceremonial portals at each corner of the cloister are among the most spectacular of all baroque creations—aswirl with Mannerist volutes and Michelangelo-esque ornament, they serve as mere frames for six life-size statues of Carthusian saints, who sit atop the doorways, judging all with deathless composure.

Just by the entrance to the monastery's terraced gardens is the **Quarto del Priore,** which was the residence of the only monk who had any contact with the outside world. It's an extravaganza filled with frescoes, 18th-century majolica-tile floors, and paintings, with extensive gardens where scenic *pergolati* (roofed balconies) overlook the bay—a domicile that might be called the very vestibule of heaven.

Most of the monastery, which was suppressed in 1831, now serves as a museum. For a sound introduction to monastic life and a well-signposted history of the Carthusians and San Martino, see the panoramic renovated galleries of the **Museo dell'Opera** around the Chiostro Grande. Room 24 has a helpful 18th-century scale model of the monastic complex; Room 26 has 19th-century paintings of monastic life. Dalbono's 13 gouaches of Vesuvius in various angry poses are attractively displayed in Room 28. If you're beginning to think that the 17th century in Naples was all grand masters and opulence, Room 37 and the various paintings depicting the plague might change that impression.

Nearby, the **Sezione Presepiale,** open only during the winter holiday season, holds the greatest collection of Nativity crèches in the world. Ranging in size from a nutshell to an entire room, they offer supreme evocations of 18th-century life. Many figures are garbed in exquisite costumes and have portraitlike faces. The most noted is the *Presepe Cuciniello,* with more than 160 shepherds, eight dogs, countless angels, Moors, chickens, cheese wheels, beggars, and dwarfs, all worshiping the Holy Family against a brilliant blue sky. ⊠ *Largo San Martino 5, Vomero* ☎ *081/2294589* 🎟 *€6 includes admission to Castel Sant'Elmo* ⊗ *Thurs.–Tues. 8:30–7:30. Some rooms are often closed (Quarto del Priore) depending on staffing* Ⓜ *Vanvitelli.*

❾ **Palazzo Serra di Cassano.** By the late 18th century, Via Monte di Dio
★ had become one of Naples' poshest addresses. Lined with palazzi and villas, it was chosen by Prince Aloisio Serra di Cassano for his family palace, designed by Ferdinando Sanfelice, the most important architect of domestic architecture in Naples. In this city where spectacle and love of show have always been important, the appropriately gigantic double-flight staircase that Sanfelice built in the palace courtyard wouldn't have been out of place in a lavish 1950s MGM musical. When his son Gennaro was executed as one of the participants in the 1799 revolution, the prince closed the building down in protest, and it remained closed for 200 years. Today the Istituto Italiano per gli Studi Filosofici, an institute devoted to philosophy studies, occupies much of the palazzo; it offers a full calendar of courses and lectures throughout the year. ■ TIP➡To view the staircase, ask the *portiere* (concierge) for permission (*"Posso vedere lo Scalone?"* should do the trick). ⊠ *Via Monte di Dio 14, Pizzofalcone* ☎ *081/7642652* ⊕ *www.iisf.it* ⊗ *Weekdays 8–1 and 3–7, Sat. 8–noon.*

WORTH NOTING

❺ **Museo Diego Aragona Pignatelli Cortes.** Set behind what, except for the palm trees, would be a very English expanse of lawn, this salmon-pink building with its Athenian style porch was built in 1826 for Ferdinand Acton, the son of English aristocrat Sir John Acton. In 1841 it was bought up by the Rothschild family, who brought in Gaetano Genovese—he of the Palazzo Reale's sumptuous staircase—to design the Salotto Rosso and the ballroom. The villa then passed to a distant ancestor of Spanish conquistador Hernando Cortes, and eventually to the Italian State in 1955.

The villa contains a sumptuous collection of porcelain and a *biblioteca-discoteca*—a collection of classical and operatic records. It also hosts part of Banco di Napoli's collection of paintings, including works by masters of Neapolitan Baroque; another room containing 18th and 19th century landscapes. ⊠ *Riviera di Chiaia 200* ☎ *081/76112356* 🎟 *€2* ⊗ *Wed.–Mon. 8:30–1:30* Ⓜ *Piazza Amedeo.*

❹ **Palazzo delle Arti Napoli.** Occupying the enormous Palazzo Rocella, the Palazzo delle Arti di Napoli—or PAN as it's conveniently called—acts as a temporary exhibition center for contemporary arts and as a permanent center for art research and documentation. Given the size of the building (6,000 square meters—roughly 60,000 square feet—on three floors), expect several exhibitions at any one time, featuring artists of international stature. There is also a fine bookshop with works on contemporary artists, both international or Italian, as well as other books on Naples. ⊠ *Via dei Mille 60, Chiaia* ☎*081/7958605* ⊕*www. palazzoartinapoli.net* ⊠*€5* ⊗*Mon.–Sat. 9:30–7:30, Sun. 9:30–2:30* Ⓜ*Piazza Amedeo.*

⑫ **Palazzo Donn'Anna.** One of the great icons of romantic Naples and immortalized many times over the centuries in paintings, this bay-side palace (now with privately owned apartments) adorns the shoreline of Posillipo, the superb suburb that sits just to the west of the Mergellina harbor, the westernmost sector of the city center proper. The palace we see was designed by Cosimo Fanzago in 1642 for Princess Donn'Anna Carafa, the beautiful local-born wife of the Duke of Medina, the Spanish Viceroy of Naples, who proceeded to abandon her when he was recalled to Spain. Although the interior is closed, the porticoed terrace—with fantastic views over the Bay of Naples—may be open (ask at the gate for access to the courtyard). Fanzago's palazzo arose on a site that once housed 14th-century Queen Joan's private palace, where, according to legend, she lured young fishermen to a night of passion before throwing them into the sea. The best way to get to the palazzo is to take Bus 140 from Piazza Vittoria. Nearby is Bagni Elena, one of the most convenient city beaches, if you want a quick dip in rather murky waters or a laze in the sun. ⊠*Piazza Donn'Anna 9, Posillipo.*

⑪ **Parco Vergiliano a Piedigrotta.** At the western end of the city in Mergellina district lies one of Naples' most undervisited spots, the Parco Vergiliano, named after the great ancient Roman poet Virgil (and not to be confused with the Parco Virgiliano, at the western end of the Naples suburb, Posillipo). The park is most famed for its legendary Bay of Naples vista. Immortalized in countless postcards and pizza-parlor paintings—you know, it's that one showing a lone umbrella pine tree sitting on a bluff overlooking all of the Bay of Naples and the city, with Vesuvius in the background—the vista is situated not far from "Virgil's Tomb." Unfortunately, the legendary pine tree is no longer standing. The small park is still beautiful and is, according to legend, the site of the poet's tomb, now judged to be an anonymous Roman *columbarium* (funerary monument). It's set not far from both the Crypta Neapolitana, an ancient Roman tunnel, which is now being extensively restored in eager anticipation of opening (perhaps in 2008), and the tomb-memorial of Giacomo Leopardi, the noted 19th-century poet. Gain access to the park from behind the church of Santa Maria di Piedigrotta, close to Piazza Piedigrotta, just outside the Stazione di Mergellina station. The park rises to the left immediately after the railway bridge crossing Via Piedigrotta, just before the road tunnel entrance. ⊠*Parco Vergiliano a Piedigrotta, Salita della Grotta 20, Mergellina* ☎*081/669390* ⊠*Free* ⊗*9–1 hr before sunset.*

⑧ **Pizzofalcone** *(Falcon's Beak).* In the 7th century BC, Pizzofalcone *was* Naples. The ancient Greeks had settled here because, legend says, the body of the siren Parthenope had been found washed ashore on the beach at the foot of the Pizzofalcone Hill, then known as Monte Echia. More than two millennia later, in the 18th century, the hill, mere feet from the bay and the Castel dell'Ovo, became a fashionable address as

Naples' rich and titled sought to escape the congestion and heat of the city center. The rocky promontory soon became studded with baroque palaces and Rococo churches.

You can walk up to Pizzofalcone by taking Via G. Serra just to the right-hand colonnade of the Church of San Francesco di Paola, on Piazza del Plebiscito, to Pizzofalcone's main piazza, Santa Maria degli Angeli; or take the elevator during daylight hours (never the dark staircase) by the bridge on Via Chiaia. The leading sights are the palazzi along Via Monte di Dio—including Palazzo Serra di Cassano—and the churches of La Nunziatella and Santa Maria degli Angeli. Like other parts of Naples, Pizzofalcone harbors both palaces and slums; unlike other parts, it's off the beaten path, so don't stop to answer questions from seemingly innocuous strollers. ⊠*Piazza Santa Maria degli Angeli, accessed via elevator at Ponte di Chiaia on Via Chiaia, Pizzofalcone.*

⑩ Santa Maria degli Angeli a Pizzofalcone. In 1590 the princess of Sulmona, Costanza Doria del Carretto, commissioned this church not far from her palace on Pizzofalcone. In the 17th century the church was given to the Theatine order and enlarged by an architect belonging to the order. The lively vault and dome frescoes are by Giovanni Beinaschi from Turin, better known as a painter of genre scenes, and there are some good paintings by Luca Giordano and Massimo Stanzione tucked away in the smaller side chapels and oratory. ⊠*Piazza Santa Maria degli Angeli, Pizzofalcone* ☎*081/7644974* ☉*Daily 7:30–11:30 and 5:30–7.*

❸ Villa Floridiana. Now a chiefly residential neighborhood, the Vomero Hill was once the patrician address of many of Naples' most extravagant estates. La Floridiana is the sole surviving 19th-century example, built in 1817 on order of Ferdinand I for Lucia Migliaccio, duchess of Floridia—their portraits are by the main entrance. Only nine shocking months after his first wife, the Habsburg Maria Carolina, died, when the court was still in mourning, Ferdinand secretly married Lucia, his longtime mistress. Scandal ensued, but the king and his new wife were too happy to worry, escaping high above the city and court gossip to this elegant little estate. Designed by architect Antonio Niccolini in neoclassic style, the house is now occupied by the **Museo Nazionale della Ceramica Duca di Martina,** a museum devoted to the decorative arts of the 18th and 19th centuries. Countless display cases on the upper floor are filled with what Edith Wharton described as "all those fragile and elaborate trifles the irony of fate preserves when brick and marble crumble": Sèvres, Limoges, and Meissen porcelains, gold watches, ivory fans, glassware, enamels, majolica vases. Sadly, there are no period rooms left to see. Outside is a park designed in the English style by Degenhardt, who also designed the park at Capodimonte. Too bad—graffiti defaces the Grecian Tempietto and the lawns are worn bare by aspiring soccer players. ⊠*Via Cimarosa 77, Vomero* ☎*081/5788418* ☜*€2.50* ☉*Museum Wed.–Mon. 8:30–1:15; park daily 8:30–1 hr before sunset* Ⓜ*Vanvitelli.*

NEED A BREAK? Walking down the fashionable Via Scarlatti in the Vomero, a bustling pedestrian precinct, you'll come upon Caffè Scarlatti (⊠ *Via Scarlatti 106/108, Vomero* ☎ *081/3723027)*, which produces a wide range of cakes and waist-threatening delicacies. If you need something more substantial, look at the *rosticceria* selection on the left.

SPACCANAPOLI: THE HEART OF NAPLES

If your plan for Naples is just to do the sights, you'll see the city, but you'll miss its essence. To get that, you need to discover Spaccanapoli, the unforgettable neighborhood that is the heart of old Naples. A buzzing hive of daily chaos in a constantly re-created grid of ancient patterns, this densely populated neighborhood presents the city's most familiar face. This is the Naples of peeling facades and enough waving laundry to suggest a parade; of arguments in the streets (or are they gossiping? It's sometimes hard to tell) swelling to operatic proportions, often with onlookers adding their comments to supplement the lyrical principals; of small alleyways fragrant with freshly laid flowers at the many shrines to the Blessed Virgin. Here, where the cheapest pizzerias in town feed the locals like kings, the full raucous street carnival of Neapolitan popular culture is punctuated with improbable oases of spiritual calm. All the contradictions of Naples—splendor and squalor, palace and slum, triumph and tragedy—meet here and sing a full-throated chorale. The amazing thing is that it seems, somehow, more real in its conscious theatricality. And, paradoxically, it also seems impossible to remain stressed out in the midst of all this ricocheting vitality.

But the Spacca is not simply picturesque. It also contains some of Naples' most important sights, including a striking conglomeration of churches—Lombard, Gothic, Renaissance, baroque, rococo, and neoclassical. Here are the majolica-adorned cloister of Santa Chiara; the sumptuous Church of the Gesù Nuovo; two opera-set piazzas; the city duomo (where the Festa di San Gennaro is celebrated every September); the Cappella Sansevero; the greatest painting in Naples—Caravaggio's *Seven Acts of Mercy* altarpiece—on view at the Church of Pio Monte; and Via Gregorio Armeno, where shops devoted to *Presepe* Nativity scene (crèche) wares make every day a rehearsal for Christmas. And even though this was the medieval center of the city, night owls will find that many of Naples' most cutting-edge clubs and bars are hidden among its nooks and alleys.

This area is best explored by starting out at its heart, the Piazza Gesù Nuovo (approachable from all directions but easily reachable from Via Toledo by heading eastward from Piazza Carità through the pedestrianized Piazza Monteoliveto and then up Calata Trinità Maggiore), then heading east along the Spacca street to the Duomo, then back along Via dei Tribunali. The Via dei Tribunali is often referred to as part of the city's Decumano Maggiore, but as it's only one block over from the Spacca, the entire region is also commonly grouped under the name Spaccanapoli. Wherever you head, you'll find half of Naples's populace crowded at your elbow, all pursuing life *con gusto*.

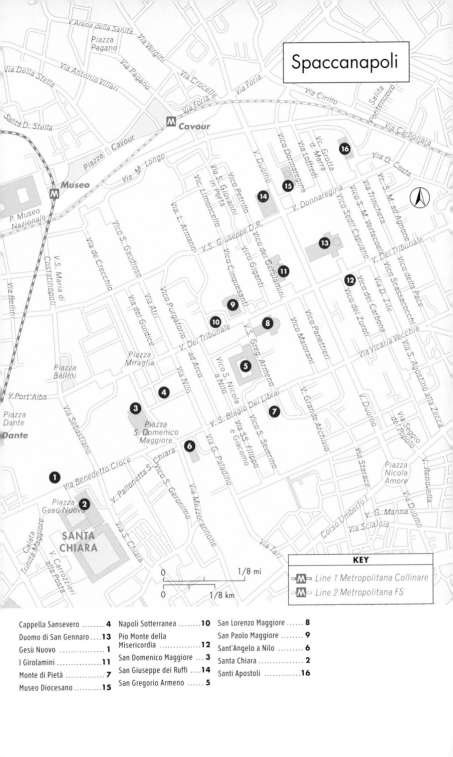

Spaccanapoli

TIMING

Because many churches open at 7:30 and close for the afternoon around 1, it's imperative to get an early start to fit in as many sights as possible before the midday break. Scaturchio in Piazza San Domenico is the perfect place for a post-lunch espresso. Then fit in a bit of shopping by browsing around Piazza Dante, Port'Alba, and the Via Santa

WORD OF MOUTH

"Cappella Sansevero will be a quick stop, as it's a small museum, but the Shrouded Christ is truly beautiful. If I ever get back to Naples, it would be the first thing I would go back to—I was awed."
—cynstalker

Maria di Costantinopoli for used books and antiques, or head over to the Via San Gregorio Armeno to pick out a manger figure to take back home—but remember that many shops close for three hours, from 1:30 to 4:30. By 4 many of the churches reopen. Plan on a good two hours to walk this route, plus a quarter to a half hour for each of the principal churches you decide to visit. However, Spaccanapoli is the most memorable part of Naples so take a full day, if you can, to explore its varied pleasures.

TOP ATTRACTIONS

4 Fodor'sChoice ★

Cappella Sansevero. Rightly one of the emblematic monuments of Naples in the popular imagination, this dazzling masterpiece, the funerary chapel of the Sangro di Sansevero princes, combines noble swagger, overwhelming color, and a touch of the macabre—which is to say, it expresses Naples perfectly. The di Sangros were renowned military leaders as far back as the Dark Ages, and they boast no fewer than six saints in their family (who are portrayed in the chapel's painted roundels between the windows). The chapel was begun in 1590 by Giovan Francesco di Sangro, the result of a vow to be fulfilled if he were cured of a dire illness. He lived for another 14 years, which was good for the building campaign, but the present aspect of the chapel is due to his descendant Raimondo di Sangro, prince of Sansevero, who had it completely redone between 1749 and 1770. (His tomb and portrait are halfway down on the right.)

Youthful portraits show this fascinating character with a pronounced pointy chin. Confident and sophisticated in his tastes, legendarily brilliant, and an important mover in Naples' Enlightenment, this princely intellectual, mad scientist, and inventor was accused of just about everything then considered base: atheism, alchemy, and Freemasonry. The last two are likely: he seems to have been a Grand Master of the Freemasons, and his claim to be able to reproduce the miracle of San Gennaro's blood got him kicked out of the Fraternity of the Treasure of San Gennaro. He left a personal touch in the basement, down the stairs to the right, where two glass cases house a pair of "anatomical machines," which are astonishing even if fake. Purporting to be an encyclopedic reconstruction of the blood vessels of an adult male and a pregnant female, they are supposedly based on two of the prince's servants, who fell victim to his curiosity when he injected them while still alive with what is conjectured to be a mercury solution that hardened their arteries.

Continued on page 62

WALKING SPACCANAPOLI

Spaccanapoli is the informal designation given to the long, straight street running down the middle of Naples's *centro storico* (historic center). The name has also come to stand for the neighborhood surrounding the street, an area that's chaotic, vibrant, edgy, colorful, noisy, mysterious, and very beautiful. In other words, it's the essence of Naples. A walk along Spaccanapoli takes you past peeling palaces, artisans' workshops, many churches and street shrines, stores of all sorts, bars, and people young and old.

left, Via San Gregorio Armeno; top right, church of Gesú Nuovo; bottom right, a *presepe* shop window

A STROLL THROUGH THE HEART OF NAPLES

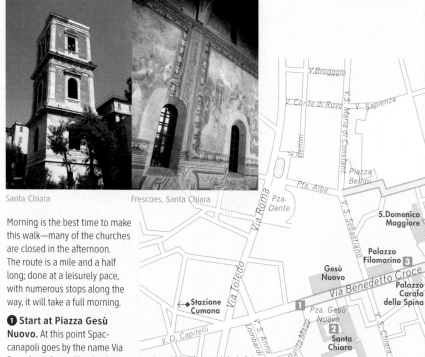

Santa Chiara

Frescoes, Santa Chiara

Morning is the best time to make this walk—many of the churches are closed in the afternoon. The route is a mile and a half long; done at a leisurely pace, with numerous stops along the way, it will take a full morning.

❶ **Start at Piazza Gesù Nuovo.** At this point Spaccanapoli goes by the name Via Benedetto Croce. The Guglia dell'Immacolata, an extravagant carved-stone spire honoring the Virgin Mary, stands in the middle of the district's largest square. The forbidding 15th-century facade of the church of **Gesù Nuovo** suits the building's original function as a fort; it was converted into the city's most extravagant baroque church by the Jesuits in the 18th century.

❷ **Cross the road and enter the church of Santa Chiara.** Originally built by Robert of Anjou in the early 1300s and reconstructed after a direct hit from a bomb in 1943, the church is light, airy, and spacious. Look for the traces of the Giotto frescoes behind the altar. A side

entrance leads to a delightful vine-laden cloister decorated with hundreds of majolica tiles, an unexpected outbreak of peace in noisy Naples.

❸ **Head east on Spaccanapoli.** You'll cross Via San Sebastiano, a street filled with music shops frequented by students from the nearby

Piazza Gesú Nuovo

conservatory; it can be a veritable symphony in the morning. **Palazzo Filomarino**, former home of philosopher Benedetto Croce and now the site of his library, is on the left as you continue. Next on your right is architect Cosimo Fanzago's **Palazzo Carafa della Spina**; coachmen once used the mouths of the gargoyles at the entrance to tamp out their torches.

❹ **Continue east to Piazza San Domenico Maggiore.** The rear of the church of San Domenico Maggiore, the Palazzo Corigliano (today part of the university), and

Piazza San Domenico Maggiore

Chapel of San Gennaro

Capella Sansevero

Duomo di San Gennaro

Via Tribunali

Pio Monte della Misericordia

Via Vicaria Vecchia

Purgatorio ad Arco

S.Lorenzo Maggiore

Cappella Sansevero

San Gregorio Armeno

SPACCANAPOLI
Via S.Biagio dei Librai

Monte di Pietà

0   1/8 mi
0   1/8 km

Marionettes in a shop window.

another spire contribute to one of Naples's most charming squares. Outdoor cafés (including Scaturchio, one of Naples's most celebrated pastry shops) give the piazza the feel of an open-air living room. Heading up the right-hand side of the piazza, swing right onto Via Francesco de Sanctis, where you find the fascinating **Cappella Sansevero**, the tomb-chapel of the Sangro di San Severo family.

5 Return to Spaccanapoli on Via Nilo. Where the two streets intersect you pass a statue of the Egyptian river god Nile reclining on a pedestal. (A few steps beyond, Spaccanapoli's street name changes to Via San Biagio dei Librai.) Several blocks down on the right is the ornate palazzo **Monte di Pietà**, and beyond it the storefront Ospedale delle Bambole (Doll Hospital).

6 Turn left (north) when you reach Via Duomo. The next main intersection is Via Tribunali, the other great thoroughfare of the district. Take a right to reach the **Pio Monte della Misericordia**, which contains one of the greatest 17th-century altarpieces in Europe, Caravaggio's *Seven Acts of Mercy*. Return to the Via Duomo to visit the **Duomo di San Gennaro** and its spectacular chapel.

7 Head west on Via dei Tribunali. After a short block you'll reach one of the street's many imposing churches, the gigantic **San Lorenzo Maggiore.** Its 18th-century facade hides a Gothic-era nave and—surprise—one of the most interesting archaeological sites in the city.

8 Turn left onto Via San Gregorio Armeno. This may be the most charming street in Naples. The towering campanile of the Rococo church of **San Gregorio Armeno** arches over the street, which is lined with *presepe* (crèche) stores.

9 Continue west along Via Tribunali. Stop to note the curious brass skulls outside the church of **Purgatorio ad Arco** on your right—touch them to bring good luck. At the end of Via Tribunali, turn right into Piazza Bellini and stop for a drink at one of the leafy square's many cafés.

Murder in the Cathedral?

Most of the frescoes of the San Gennaro chapel are by the Bolognese artist Domenichino, but his compatriot Guido Reni was originally engaged to paint the cycle, and thereby hangs a tale.

When he arrived in Naples, Reni found himself so harassed and threatened by jealous local artists, who were indignant that the commission had been given to an outsider, that he gave up the job and fled town. Ultimately he was replaced by the great Domenichino, who came to Naples only after the viceroy himself guaranteed his protection.

Domenichino started painting under armed guard beginning in 1630 and had almost completed the work in 1641 when he died suddenly; poisoning was suspected. The committee charged with finding his replacement pointedly refused to consider a Neapolitan painter, instead selecting the Roman Giovanni Lanfranco, who bravely (and quickly) finish the dome. It was Lanfranco who painted the dome's frescoed vision of Paradise.

Prince Raimondo is generally credited with the design of the splendid marble-inlay floor; he hired Francesco Maria Russo to paint the ceiling with a *Glory of Paradise* (1749) and also hired a team of up-and-coming sculptors, whose contributions remain the focal point for most visits here: the showpiece is smack in the middle of the chapel, Giuseppe Sammartino's *Veiled Christ* (1753). The artist was only 33 years old when he sculpted this famous work, which was originally meant to be placed in the crypt. It was too good to leave down below; the audacious virtuosity of the clinging drapery showing the wounds underneath is one of the marvels of Neapolitan sculpture. A taste for the outré and extravagant had already been demonstrated by other statues in the chapel, especially Francesco Quierolo's *Disillusion*, to the right of the altar, with its chisel-defying net making a spectacular transition to empty space. This Genovese sculptor also did the female statue representing *Sincerity* on the right and the commemorative *Altar to St. Odorisio* between the two Allegories. Antonio Corradini, who came to Naples from the Veneto region via Rome, is responsible for the allegorical statue to the left of the altar, *Veiled Modesty* (1751), widely considered his masterpiece; he also sculpted the funerary monument and allegorical figure of *Decorum*, on the inside of the front wall to the right of the exit. Francesco Celebrano contributed the stunning funerary monument above the front door, depicting Cecco di Sangro in of one of his most famous moments: believed dead in battle, he was set in a coffin, only to climb out again wielding a sword and ready to fight. ⊠ *Via de Sanctis 19, Spaccanapoli* ☎ *081/5518470* ⊕ *www.museosansevero.it* 🎫 *€6* ⊙ *Mon. and Wed.–Fri. 10–5:10, weekends 10–1:10.*

 Duomo di San Gennaro. The shrine to the paterfamilias of Naples, San
★ Gennaro, the city's cathedral is home to the saint's devotional chapel, among the most spectacular—in the show-biz sense of the word—in the city. With a colonnade leading to an apse bursting with light and Baroque splendor, the Duomo's nave makes a fitting setting for the

The chapel of the Duomo di San Gennaro in Spaccanapoli.

famous **Miracle of the Blood,** when the blood of the martyred San Gennaro liquefies (hopefully) in its silver ampule every September 19 before an audience of thousands massed in front of the Duomo's altar. *San Genna, fa'o miracolo! Fa ampresso! Nun ce fa suffrì!* yell the congregants during the ritual— "Saint Genna, do the miracle! Hurry up! You'll pay for it if you don't do it!" If St. Januarius (to use his ancient Latin name) doesn't cooperate, however, it's usually the city that winds up paying, or so the locals believe: eruptions of Vesuvius, cholera outbreaks, and defeats of the Naples soccer team have all been blamed on the saint when the *miracolo* has failed to occur.

The Duomo was first established by Charles II of Anjou, using imported French architects, on the site of a previous structure, the Cattedrale Stefania (AD 570), and next to an even earlier structure, the still-extant Basilica di Santa Restituta (4th century AD). Already restored in 1456 and 1484, it was largely redesigned in 1787 and 1837. The original facade collapsed in the earthquake of 1349, and the present pseudo-Gothic concoction is a modern (1877–1905) fake by Enrico Alvino and Giuseppe Pisanti, which, however, reemploys the doors—still majestic in spite of extensive damage—from the 1407 facade. The central door, by Antonio Baboccio, features a *Madonna and Child* by Tino da Camaino under its arch. Inside, the splendid nave welcomes all, with a gilt wooden ceiling (1621) and golden roundels painted above the pillars by Luca Giordano and his school depicting various saints. From the nave head to the right side of the church to see the chapel devoted to the city's patron saint.

The **Cappella del Tesoro di San Gennaro,** or Chapel of the Treasure of Saint Januarius, was built in 1608–37 by the Theatin architect Francesco Grimaldi to fulfill a desperate vow pronounced by city fathers during an outbreak of the plague (January 13, 1527), some 80 years earlier. The chapel honors San Gennaro (250–305), one of the earliest Christian martyrs; as bishop of Benevento, he was executed at Pozzuoli during the rule of Emperor Diocletian. The entrance to the chapel is marked by a heavy gilt-bronze baldachin gate (1668–86) by noted architect Cosimo Fanzago, who also designed the chapel's superb floor, and is flanked by statues of Sts. Peter and Paul by Giuliano Finelli. Inside, the elegant Greek-cross plan is decorated everywhere possible with gold, colored marble, bronze, and paint, but nothing could be too overdone for the home of San Gennaro's most famous DNA sample and the fabulous treasure of jeweled offerings bestowed by numerous sovereigns. The 40-odd *brocatello* columns, with their musty tones of dried roses, were sent from the quarries of Tortosa in Valencia, Spain. The high altar on the back wall (1689–90), designed by the painter Francesco Solimena, seems to swell as it tries to contain the opulence of the central relief, created in silver (circa 1692) by Giovan Domenico Vinaccia (who inserted into it a portrait of himself holding eyeglasses). Above the altar, against the wall, is a large bronze of St. Gennaro on his bishop's throne by onetime Bernini assistant Giuliano Finelli. Also behind the altar are two silvered niches donated by Charles II of Spain to house the reliquaries containing the blood of the saint (the right-hand one) and his skull. This latter reliquary consists of the famous gilded medieval bust done by three French artists (1305) set on a silver base from 1609, the actual repository of the precious vials of the saint's blood.

Note Il Ribera's *San Gennaro in the Furnace* (1647), on the right-hand wall—perhaps the most beautiful church painting in Naples. Dating from his early Neapolitan period, it clearly shows the influence of Velasquez in the figures on the left, and it's imbued with a Mediterranean luminosity that is rare in his work. The chapel, a veritable church-within-a-church, also has its own sacristy (sometimes closed), which contains a luxurious washbasin by Cosimo Fanzago. This room leads into a suite of rooms with frescoes by Giacomo Farelli and a splendid altarpiece by Massimo Stanzione; at the back are kept the 51 statues of the "co-patron" saints, displayed in the chapel proper in May and September and which accompany the reliquary of the blood on its annual procession to Santa Chiara.

The main altar sits in the resplendent apse redesigned in 1744 by Paolo Tosi and framed by two magnificent jasper columns found in a dig in 1705. A staircase on either side of the entrance to the presbytery (high altar area) descends to the Caraffa Chapel, better known as the **Succorpo di San Gennaro,** or, more simply, the crypt (1497–1506), a Renaissance masterpiece by Tommaso Malvito in the form of a rectangular room divided into three naves by rows of columns. Malvito also carved the imposing statue of Cardinal Oliviero Caraffa, who commissioned the chapel.

Coming back up into the nave and continuing in a counterclockwise direction, you find the Chapel of San Lorenzo, with highly restored frescoes by Lello da Orvieto (circa 1314–20). This chapel hides an elevator that ascends through one of the corner towers to the roof, which offers an intimate yet panoramic view of the historic quarter. Nearby is the tomb of Pope Innocent, sculpted in 1315 and redone in the 16th century by Tommaso Malvito. The sarcophagus to the left belongs to Andrea of Hungary, the unfortunate consort of Queen Joan I, who allegedly had him strangled in Aversa (at least the dogs at the foot of the deceased show a little sadness). Beyond the tombs of Pope Innocent XII and the late-Renaissance chapel of the Brancaccio family, a door leads to the Chapel of Santa Restituta. The **Cappella di Santa Restituta** is in fact the oldest church in Naples, dating from the 4th century AD and, according to tradition, built by order of the first Christian emperor, Constantine, on the site of a temple to Apollo. It was dedicated to Santa Restituta in the 8th century when the martyr's relics were transferred to the church. Outside the Duomo (on the south side) is the ticket booth for the various showpieces in the cathedral (entrance: €7). This includes entrance to the flashy but somewhat dry **Museo del Tesoro di San Gennaro** housing religious works by silversmiths over the centuries, the Baptistery of San Giovanni in Fonte—a square room with an octagonal dome, built by Bishop Soterus in the middle of the 5th century, which still dazzles with its rare, gorgeous, and important early Christian mosaics, the Royal Chapel, and the underground archaeological site. ✉ *Via Duomo 147, Spaccanapoli* ☎*081/449097 Duomo, 081/294764 museum* ⊕*www.museosangennaro.com* ✆*€7* ⊙*Daily 8:30–12:30 and 4:30–7.*

❶ **Gesù Nuovo.** *Opulenza* and *magnificenza* are the words that come to
★ mind when describing this floridly baroque church, the centerpiece of the Piazza del Gesù Nuovo. Its formidable diamond-point facade is actually a remnant of the Renaissance palace of the Sanseverino princes (1470), destroyed to make way, in 1584–1601, for a generically stupendous exercise in the full-throated Jesuit style, albeit one with an unusual Greek-cross plan. The dome has been rebuilt twice (this is an earthquake zone); the present version dates from the early 19th century. The bulk of the interior decoration took more than 40 years and was completed only in the 18th century. You can find the familiar baroque sculptors (Naccherino, Finelli) and painters. The gracious *Visitation* above the altar in the second chapel on the right is by Massimo Stanzione, who also contributed the fine frescoes in the main nave: they're in the presbytery (behind and around the main altar). In the chapel to the left of the main altar is a frescoed vault by the young Francesco Solimena, who became a leading baroque painter, and on either side is a wonderful gallery of reliquary portraits, each placed in its own opera box. Like many churches in Naples, much of the interior was undergoing restoration at this writing. ✉*Piazza Gesù Nuovo, Spaccanapoli* ☎*081/5578111* ⊙*Daily 7–12:30 and 4–7:30.*

❼ **Monte di Pietà.** Lush and lavish, this baroque-era landmark is a must-
★ see for anyone interested in Neapolitan decorative arts. As Spaccanapoli was home to both Naples' poorest and richest residents, the latter formed several charitable institutions, of which the Monte di Pietà was one of the most prominent. At the beginning of the 16th century,

Beneath the city you can tour Napoli Sotterranea (Naples Underground), an extensive network of tunnels, caverns, and aqueducts.

it constructed this palazzo (F. Cavagna, 1605), with a grand courtyard leading to the Cappella della Pietà, with gilt stuccoes and beautiful frescoes by Belisario Corenzio. Leading off the chapel are a number of salons, including the Sala delle Cantoniere, with inlaid marbles and precious intarsia woodwork. Since most Neapolitan residential palace interiors are private or have disappeared, this 17th-century enfilade of salons offers a rare glimpse of Naples at its most sumptuous. Concerts and theatrical performances are often held in the courtyard in summer. Today the palazzo is an office for the SanPaolo Banco di Napoli. ⊠ *Via Biagio dei Librai 114, Spaccanapoli* ☎*081/5517074* ◷*Sat. 9–7, Sun. 9–1* Ⓜ*Piazza Cavour (in construction: Duomo).*

⓯ Museo Diocesano. Situated opposite the Archbishop's palace, this museum
★ incorporates the baroque church of Santa Maria Donnaregina Nuova. Started in 1617 and consecrated 50 years later for the Francescan nuns (les Clarisses) in the attached cloister, the church replaced the Gothic Donnaregina Vecchia, which was damaged by earthquake. In more modern times the building was used as legal offices before being closed completely, becoming prey to the occasional theft, not to mention bomb damage during the World War II. In September 2008, it was reborn as a museum. Instantly recognizable by the fresco of the Virgin above the entrance, the building houses the work, brilliantly restored, of late Gothic and Renaissance masters, and many of the main practitioners of the Neapolitan baroque.

On the ground floor, as suits the church's name, the artwork centers on the life of the Virgin Mary, beginning with the first chapel on the left and French painter Charles Mellin's beautiful depiction of the Immaculate

Conception (1646), while on the other side of what was once the nave is an equally fine Madonna and Child by Massimo Stanzione. Also on the left is a space rich in Gothic and Renaissance statuary from the former church. You then take the elevator upstairs to where the nuns once attended Mass, concealed from the congregation by a special screen. The hundred works on show follow a theme of life as an Imitation of Christ. There is also the rare chance see roof paintings close up, with state of the art floodlights displaying the restoration to maximum effect.

In the antisacristy, in the middle of a 1735 fresco, is a very large hole caused by the 1980 earthquake. It's minor disaster in one sense, but also a revelation: beyond the visible wooden trellis used to support the plasterwork, you can see another painting from a few centuries before—an explicit example of the city's layers artistic heritage.

In the vault of the nave are the frescoes by Francesco de Benedictis, including the Ascension of the Virgin (1654). In what the former Presbytery at the end are the last two works of Luca Giordano (1705). the Miracle at Cana and a mystically lit Sermon on the Mount. On the wall in front is an even larger fresco, "Miracolo delle rose," by Giordano's one-time pupil Francesco Solimena. Story goes that jealous rivals objected to Cardinal Caracciolo that giving the commission to the young, handsome artist would pose a danger to nuns. ⊠ *Largo Donnregina, Spaccanapoli* ☎ *081/5571365* ⊕ *www.museodiocesanonapoli. it* ⊙ *Mon. and Wed.–Sat. 9:30–4:30, Sun. 9:30–2* Ⓜ *Piazza Cavour (in construction: Duomo).*

➓ **Napoli Sotterranea.** Outside San Paolo Maggiore (on your right as you're coming out) on Piazza San Gaetano along Via dei Tribunali is one of

the entrances to *Napoli Sotterranea*—Underground Naples. This is a fascinating tour through a portion of Naples' fabled underground city and a good initiation into the complex layering of history in the city center. ∎ TIP➔ Be prepared to go up and down a lot of steps, and handle a few narrow corridors—remember that temperatures in summertime will be much lower undergound than at street level, so bring a wrap. In all, allow 1½ hours to complete the whole tour. Efforts to dramatize the experience—amphoras lowered on ropes to draw water from cisterns, candles distributed to negotiate narrow passages like in pre-electric days, objects shifted to reveal secret passages—combined with excellent guiding in English make this particularly exciting for children.

After a descent into "Naples' stomach," the first stop is an amphitheater that until 1999 was part of a parking garage. On this spot Nero performed three times. During one of his performances an earthquake struck and—so Suetonius relates—the emperor forbade the 6,000 spectators to leave. The rumbling, he insisted, was only the gods applauding his performance.

Across a small street above, a second descent takes you down 30 meters to what was originally part of a 400-km system of quarries and aqueducts. The aqueducts were used from Greek times right up to the 1845 cholera epidemic. In 1942 a section was reopened to provide air-raid shelter big enough to sleep 3,000 people. A further descent takes you to the Greco-Roman quarry and what might be called the Genesis of the city: soft tufa stones were cut from here and then raised to the surface.

Finally, prepare for a highly claustrophobic 1-km walk with only a candle to light your way. Eventually at the end of the aqueduct you come to first a Greek then a much larger Roman cistern. You then ascend to near the entrance where there is a small display of Second World War uniforms. ⊠*Piazza San Gaetano 68, Spaccanapoli* ☎*081/296944* ⊕*www.napolisotterranea.org* ☉*Daily; tours weekdays at noon, 2, and 4, weekends at 10, noon, 2, 4, and 6; evening tour on Thurs. at 9* ☜*€9.50* Ⓜ*Piazza Cavour.*

⑫ **Pio Monte della Misericordia.** One of the defining landmarks of Spac-
FodorśChoice canapoli, this octagonal church was built around the corner from the
★ Duomo (practically in front of its constantly used side door) for a charitable institution founded in 1601 by seven noblemen. The institution's aim was to carry out acts of Christian charity: feeding the hungry, clothing the poor, nursing the sick, sheltering pilgrims, visiting prisoners, ransoming Christian slaves, and burying the indigent dead—acts immortalized in the history of art by the famous altarpiece painted by Caravaggio (1571–1610) depicting the *Sette Opere della Misericordia* (or *Seven Acts of Mercy*) and now the celebrated focus of the church. In this haunting work the artist has brought the Virgin in palpable glory, unforgettably borne atop the shoulders of two angels, right down into the street—and not a rhetorical place, but a real street of Spaccanapoli (scholars have in fact suggested a couple of plausible identifications) populated by figures in whose spontaneous and passionate movements the people could see themselves given great dignity. Along with other paintings in the church, the sculptures by Andrea Falcone on its porch refer to this commitment. The original church was considered too small and destroyed in 1655 to make way for the new church, designed by Antonio Picchiatti in 1658–78.

The extraordinary expressiveness and efficiency of the Caravaggio altarpiece can be judged by comparison with the church's other paintings, commissioned from Neapolitan painters after Caravaggio hit the road again (to Malta) to stay one step ahead of the law. In particular, in the painting to the left of the altar, *St. Peter Rescuing Tabitha* (1612), Fabrizio Santafede is clearly struggling to modify his Technicolor formalist style to suggest the dramatic impact of the altarpiece—but the figures here merely occupy the space of the painting, rather than animate it. Upon seeing Caravaggio's altarpiece, a number of artists changed their styles radically, although often giving a personal interpretation to one aspect of Caravaggio's style. The painting to the right of the exit door is a beautiful work by one of the best of the Neapolitan Caravaggesques, Giovan Battista Carraciolo, who was 29 years old when the slightly older artist came to town. Depicting the *Liberation of St. Peter* (1615), the composition is almost shockingly spartan, nearly all dark brown with contained blocks of white, red, and flesh tones. For more paintings of the Neapolitan Seicento, head up the staircase to the church's small **Pinacoteca,** a museum of 17th- and 18th-century paintings. ⊠*Via dei Tribunali 253, Spaccanapoli* ☎*081/446973* ⊕*www.*

2

piomontedellamisericordia.it ⊘ *Thurs.–Tues. 9–2:30* 🖂 *€5, including audioguide* Ⓜ*Piazza Cavour (in construction: Duomo).*

❺ **San Gregorio Armeno.** Set on Via San Gregorio Armeno, the street that
★ is lined with Naples' most adorable Presepe—or Nativity crèche scene–
emporiums—and landmarked by a picturesque campanile, this convent
is one of the oldest and most important in Naples. The nuns (often the
daughters of Naples' richest families) who lived here must have been
disappointed with heaven when they arrived—banquets here outrivaled
those of the royal court, hallways were lined with paintings, and the
church was filled with gilt stucco and semiprecious stones. Described
as "a room of Paradise on Earth" by Carlo Celano and designed by
Niccolò Taglicozzi Canle, the church has a highly detailed wooden
ceiling, unique papier-mâché choir lofts, a shimmering organ, candlelit
shrines, and important Luca Giordano frescoes of scenes of the life of
St. Gregory, whose relics were brought to Naples in the 8th century
from Byzantium. From the convent's cloister (entrance off the small
square up the road—buzz on the entry phone) you can gain access to
the nuns' gallery shielded by 18th-century jalousies and see the church
from a different perspective. Other areas off the cloister, such as the
Salottino della Badessa—generally not on view, as this is still a working
convent—are preserved as magnificent 18th-century interiors. ✉*Piazzetta San Gregorio Armeno 1, Spaccanapoli* ☎*081/5520186* ⊘*Mon.–
Sat. 9–noon, Sun. 9–1* Ⓜ*Dante.*

❽ **San Lorenzo Maggiore.** One of the grandest medieval churches of the
Decumano Maggiore, San Lorenzo features a very unmedieval facade
of 18th-century splendor. Due to the effects and threats of earthquakes,
the church was reinforced and reshaped along baroque lines in the
17th and 18th centuries, and remaining from this phase is the facade
by Ferdinando Sanfelice (1742) based on the sweeping curves of Borromini's Filomarino altar in the Church of Santi Apostoli. Begun by
Robert d'Anjou in 1265 on the site of a previous 6th-century church,
the church's single, barnlike nave reflects the desire of the Franciscans
for simple spaces with enough room to preach to large crowds. Numerous statues and paintings from the 14th century are indicative of San
Lorenzo's importance during this period. In 1334, in fact, Boccaccio
met and fell in love with his fabled Lady Fiammetta here, and in 1343
another great Italian poet, Petrarch, resided in the monastery next door.
The transept is announced by a grandiose triumphal arch, while the
main altar (1530) is the sculptor Giovanni da Nola's masterpiece; notice
the fascinating historical views of Naples in the reliefs.

The apse was built by an unknown imported French architect of great
caliber, who gives here a brilliant essay in the pure French Angevin style,
complete with an ambulatory of nine side chapels that is covered by a
magnificent web of cross arches. The most important monument in the
church is found here: the tomb of Catherine of Austria (circa 1323),
by Tino da Camaino, one of the first sculptors to introduce the Gothic
style into Italy. The left transept contains the 14th-century funerary
monument of Carlo di Durazzo and yet another Cosimo Fanzago masterpiece, the **Cappellone di Sant'Antonio**—*cappella* (or small chapel)
being too diminutive a word, especially in this behemoth of a church.

Caravaggio's Seven Acts of Mercy

The most unforgettable painting in Naples, Michelangelo Merisi da Caravaggio's *Seven Acts of Mercy*—in Italian, the *Sette Opere della Misericordia*—takes pride of place in the Church of Pio Monte della Misericordia, as well as in nearly all of southern Italy, for emotional spectacle and unflinching truthfulness.

Painted in 1607, it combines the traditional seven acts of Christian charity in sometimes abbreviated form in a tight, dynamic composition under the close, compassionate gaze of the Virgin (the original title was *Our Lady of Mercy*).

Borne by two of the most memorable angels ever painted, she flutters down with the Christ child into a torch-lighted street scene.

Illuminated in the artist's landmark chiaroscuro style (featuring pronounced contrasts of light, *chiaro*, and deep shadow, *scuro*), a man is being buried, a nude beggar is being clothed, and—this artist never pulled any punches—a starving prisoner is being suckled by a woman.

Caravaggio, as with most geniuses, was a difficult artist and personality. His romantic bad-boy reputation as the original bohemian, complete with angry, nihilistic, rebel-with-a-cause sneer and roistering and hippielike lifestyle, has dominated interpretations of his revolutionary oeuvre and tend to present him as an antireligious painter.

This is perhaps understandable—most of the documents pertaining to his life relate to his problems with the law and make for a good story indeed (he came to Naples after killing a man in a bar brawl in Rome, where

his cardinal patrons could no longer protect him).

But in spite of (or perhaps because of) his personal life, Caravaggio painted some of the most moving religious art ever produced in the West, whittling away all the rhetoric to reveal the emotional core of the subject.

His genuine love of the popular classes and for the "real" life of the street found expression in his use of ordinary street folk as models.

If his art seems to surge directly from the gut, his famous "objectivity" of observation and reduced palette have clear antecedents in paintings from his home region in northern Italy.

The simplicity and warts-and-all depictions of his characters show a deeply original response to the Counter-Reformation writings on religious art by Carlo Borromeo, a future saint, also from Lombardy.

The *Seven Acts of Mercy*, the first altarpiece commissioned for the new church of the charitable institution, has been called "the most important religious painting of the 17th century" by the great 20th-century Italian art critics Roberto Longhi and Giuliano Argan, and if that may not be immediately obvious, it's nevertheless easy to imagine the impact this astonishing painting had on artists and connoisseurs in Naples.

Naples affected his style, too: he began to express visual relations purely in terms of dramatic light and shadow, which further exalted the contrasts of human experience.

Outside the 17th-century cloister is the entrance to the **Greek and Roman** *scavi*, or excavations, under San Lorenzo, which are a good initiation to the ancient cities beneath the modern one. Near the area of the forum, these digs have revealed streets, markets, and workshops of another age.

> **WORD OF MOUTH**
>
> "I really enjoyed the Basilica di Santa Chiara—it has a big garden in the interior with lovely tile details. Very peaceful in the middle of a busy city!" —orangetravel

Next door to the church is the **Museo dell'Opera di San Lorenzo,** installed in the 16th-century palazzo around the *torre campanaria* (belltower). In Room 1 ancient remains from the Greek Agora beneath combine with modern maps to provide a fascinating picture of import and export trends in the fourth century BC. The museum also contains ceramics dug up from the Svevian period, many pieces from the early middle ages, large tracts of mosaics from the 6th century basilica, and helpful models of how the ancient Roman forum and nearby buildings must have looked. ⊠ *Via dei Tribunali 316, Spaccanapoli* ☎ *081/2110860* ⊕ *www.sanlorenzomaggiore.na.it* ⌨ *Excavations and museum €5* ⊙ *Mon.–Sat. 8–6:30 and Sun. noon–6; excavations and museum Mon.–Sat. 9–5:30 and Sun. 9:30–1:30* Ⓜ *Dante.*

② Santa Chiara. Across from the Gesù Nuovo and offering a stark and telling contrast to the opulence of that church, Santa Chiara is the leading monument of Angevin Gothic in Naples. The fashionable church for the nobility in the 14th century, and a favorite Angevin church from the start, Santa Chiara was intended to be a great dynastic monument by Robert d'Anjou. His second wife, Sancia di Majorca, added the adjoining convent for the Poor Clares to a monastery of the Franciscan Minors so she could vicariously satisfy a lifelong desire for the cloistered seclusion of a convent; this was the first time the two sexes were combined in a single complex. Built in a Provençal Gothic style between 1310 and 1328 (probably by Guglielmo Primario) and dedicated in 1340, the church had its aspect radically altered, as did so many others, in the baroque period, when the original wooden roof was replaced with a vault dripping in stuccos. A six-day fire started by Allied bombs on August 4, 1943, put an end to all that, as well as to what might have been left of the important cycle of frescoes by Giotto and his Neapolitan workshop: Giorgio Vasari, writing in the mid-16th century, tells us that the paintings covered the entire church. The most important tomb in the church towers behind the altar. Sculpted by Giovanni and Pacio Bertini of Florence (1343–45), it is, fittingly, the tomb of the founding king: the great Robert d'Anjou, known as the Wise. To the right of the altar is the tomb of Carlo, duke of Calabria, a majestic composition by Tino da Camaino and assistants (1326–33), and answering it on the side wall is Tino's last work, the tomb of Carlo's wife, Marie de Valois.

Around the left side of the church at Via Santa Chiara 49/c is a gate leading to the **Chiostro delle Clarisse,** the most famous cloister in Naples. It's clear here that we are not dealing with any normal convent; the benches and octagonal columns upholding the trellis of vine shading this privileged garden comprise a light-handed masterpiece of painted

Fodor's Choice
★

The cloister at Santa Chiara is a tranquil oasis in the midst of hectic Spaccanapoli.

majolica designed by Domenico Antonio Vaccaro, with a delightful profusion of landscapes and light yellow and green floral motifs realized by Donato and Giuseppe Massa and their studio (1742). Where the real vines leave off and the painted ones take over was once hard to say, but much of the cloister is now being replanted, so the complete effect is missing. The elegant 14th-century porch around the garden is enlivened by fading frescoes. In the back corner you can enter the Museo dell'Opera, built on the visible remains of an old Roman bath establishment and containing some interesting sculptural fragments from the damaged church (look for Giovanni da Nola's moving wooden *Ecce Homo* of 1519 on the upper floor) and objects illustrating life in the cloister. ✉ *Piazza Gesù Nuovo, Spaccanapoli* ☎ *081/7971231* ⊕ *www.santachiara.info* ✉ *Museum and cloister €5* ◷ *Church: daily 7–12:30 and 4:30–6:30. Museum and cloister: Mon.–Sat. 9:30–5:30, Sun. 9:30–2* Ⓜ *Dante (in construction: Piazza Borsa-Università).*

WORTH NOTING

⓫ **I Girolamini/Quadreria dei Girolamini.** The Girolamini is another name for the Oratorians, followers of St. Philip Neri, to whom the splendid church I Girolamini is dedicated. Built in 1592–1619 by the Florentine architect Giovanni Antonio Dosio, the dome and gray-and-white facade were rebuilt after a design by Ferdinando Fuga (circa 1780) in the most elegant neoclassic style. Hit by Allied bombs in 1943, the intricate carved-wood ceiling is still being restored, and the church has been closed for decades. Yet you can still get a good look at the grandiose fresco (1684) by Luca Giordano on the inside of the entrance wall.

The Oratorians also built the Casa dei Padri dell'Oratorio, down the block at Via Duomo 142. Step through its gate to see the two improbably calm and disciplined cloisters, designed by the Florentine architects Giovanni Antonio Dosio, Dionisio di Bartolomeo, and Dionisio Lazzari sometime around 1600. Just off the larger cloister enclosing a prolific forest of citrus, fig, and loquat trees is the Quadreria dei Girolamini. With its high-quality, intimate collection of 16th- and 17th-century paintings, the gallery more than compensates for the adjacent church being closed. Here, too, is one of the most gloriously decorated 18th-century libraries in Europe, the 60,000-volume Biblioteca dei Girolamini, now used by scholars. In fact, this area was an important nucleus of intellectual life in the Renaissance and baroque periods, thanks to the presence of the Girolamini Library. Directly across the street as you exit the Girolamini, note an inscription by Naples' profusely subtle philosopher, historian, and politician Benedetto Croce (1866–1952) that marks the house in which his illustrious predecessor, Giambattista Vico, lived for nearly 20 years. On the left is the Palazzo Manso, where the Marchese di Villa hosted the noted 16th-century poet Torquato Tasso. ⊠ *Via Duomo 142, Spaccanapoli* ☎ *142/08129444* 🎟 *Free* 🕑 *Mon.– Sat. 9–12:50* Ⓜ *Piazza Cavour.*

❸ San Domenico Maggiore. One of the largest churches of Spaccanapoli, this Dominican house of worship was originally constructed by Charles I of Anjou in 1238. Legend has it that a painting of the crucifixion spoke to St. Thomas Aquinas when he was at prayer here. This early structure, however, was nearly gutted by a fire three centuries later and, in 1850, a neo-Gothic edifice rose in its place, complete with a nave of awe-inspiring dimensions. In the second chapel on the right (if you enter through the north door) are remnants of the earlier church—14th-century frescoes by Pietro Cavallini, a Roman predecessor of Giotto. Along the side chapels are also some noted funerary monuments, including those of the Carafa family, whose chapel, to the left of Cosimo Fanzago's 17th-century altar, is one of the most beautiful Renaissance-era set-pieces in Naples. ⊠ *Piazza San Domenico Maggiore 8/a, Spaccanapoli* ☎ *081/459188* 🕑 *Mon.–Sat. 8:30–noon and 4–7, Sun. 9–1 and 4:30–7* Ⓜ *Dante.*

⓮ San Giuseppe dei Ruffi. Half a block up from the Duomo, this late-17th-century church, built by Dionisio Lazzari, features a dramatically baroque facade. Inside, look for the armored wooden figure of a winged Michael slaying a rather docile dragon on the nave's right end. Behind a gate rises the altar, layer after baroque layer, Lazzari's sumptuous gold and marble (1686) topped by the putti and the figures of Hope and Charity by Matteo Bottigliero (1733). If you arrive around 7:30, most mornings you'll hear the nuns beautifully singing early mass. ⊠ *Piazza San Giuseppe dei Ruffi 2, Spaccanapoli* 🕑 *Mon.–Sat. 7:30–1 and 4–6, Sun. 7:30–10:30* Ⓜ *Piazza Cavour.*

❾ San Paolo Maggiore. Like Santi Apostoli, this church was erected for the Theatin fathers in the late 16th century (1583–1603), the period of their order's rapid expansion. This was another instance where Francesco Grimaldi, the (ordained) house architect, erected a church on the ruins of an ancient Roman temple, then transformed it into a Christian basilica. Spoils from the temple survive in the present incarnation, especially the two monumental Corinthian columns on the facade holding up a piece of their architrave to form a portal over the entrance door. The cloaked torsos of the ancient gods, which used to lie under the statues of Peter and Paul, have been moved. An earthquake knocked down the original facade in 1688, and World War II, coupled with decades of neglect, did further damage to the marble facing along the aisle and to the ceiling, both of which have now been restored. ⊠ *Piazza San Gaetano, Spaccanapoli* ☎ *081/454048* ☉ *Weekdays 9–1 and 3–6, Sat. 9–1* Ⓜ *Dante.*

❻ Sant'Angelo a Nilo. Originally built by Cardinal Brancaccio in the late 1300s, this church was redesigned in the 16th century by Arcangelo Guglielminelli. Inside the graciously beautiful interior is the earliest evidence of the Renaissance in Naples: the cardinal's funerary monument, sculpted by the famous Donatello and the almost-as-famous Michelozzo in 1426–27. The front of the sarcophagus bears Donatello's contribution, a beautiful bas-relief *Assumption of the Virgin;* upheld by angels, the Virgin seeming to float in air. ⊠ *Piazzetta Nilo, along Via San Biagio dei Librai, Spaccanapoli* ☎ *081/5516227* ☉ *Mon.–Sat. 9–1 and 4–6, Sun. 8:30–noon* Ⓜ *Dante.*

⓰ Santi Apostoli. This baroque church in a basic Latin-cross style with a single nave shares the piazza with a contemporary art school in a typically anarchic Neapolitan mix. Built (1610–49) by the ordained architect Francesco Grimaldi for the Theatin fathers above a previous church, itself built on the remains of a temple probably dedicated to Mercury, it's worth a quick peek inside for its coherent, intact baroque decorative scheme. There are excellent paintings on the inside of the entrance wall and on the ceiling by Giovanni Lanfranco (circa 1644), with a good number painted by his successors Francesco Solimena and Luca Giordano. For lovers of baroque architecture, there's an altar in the left transept by the great architect Francesco Borromini. Commissioned by Cardinal Ascanio Filomarino, this is the only work in Naples by this architect, whose freedom from formality so inspired the exuberance of the baroque in southern Italy, although its massive virile flourish of monochrome gray stone comes as a bit of a shock in the midst of this polychromed city. ⊠ *Largo Santi Apostoli 9, Spaccanapoli* ☎ *081/299375* ☉ *Mon.–Sat. 9–noon, Sun. 9–1* Ⓜ *Piazza Cavour.*

MUSEO ARCHEOLOGICO NAZIONALE TO PORTA CAPUANO

It's only fitting that the Museo Archeologico Nazionale—the single most important and remarkable museum of Greco-Roman antiquities in the world (in spite of itself, some observers say)—sits in the upper *decumanus,* or neighborhood, of ancient Neapolis, the district colonized by the ancient Greeks and Romans. Repository of many of the greatest surviving art treasures of antiquity—including most of the celebrated finds from Pompeii and Herculaneum—the museum has so many rooms it almost constitutes its own walking tour. As Naples' preeminent

The Salone della Meridiana, on the top floor of the Museo Archeologico, is one of the largest rooms in Europe.

treasure trove, it deserves your undivided attention. Happily, it's open all day (its core collection, that is). But if two hours are your limit for gazing at ancient art, nearby you'll discover some of the lesser-known delights of medieval and Renaissance Naples, along with the city's lush botanical gardens (which are set in the neighborhood quarter known as Carlo III). Along the way you'll visit churches that are repositories for magnificent 15th- and 16th-century art and sculpture the Museo Madre, the city's flagship museum of modern art; and the famed Porta Capuana, one of the historic gates to the city walls.

TOP ATTRACTIONS

❶ **Museo Archeologico Nazionale** (*National Museum of Archaeology*). Those who know and love this legendary museum have the tendency upon hearing it mentioned to heave a sigh: it's famous not only for its unrivaled collections but also for its off-limit rooms, missing identification labels, poor lighting, billows of dust, suffocating heat in summer, and indifferent personnel—a state of affairs seen by some critics as an encapsulation of everything that's wrong with southern Italy in general.

Fodor's Choice ★

Precisely because of this emblematic value, the National Ministry of Culture has decided to lavish attention and funds on the museum in a complete reorganization. This process has been ongoing for some time and looks as if it will continue for a while longer. Ticketing has been privatized and opening hours extended (for the center-core "masterpiece" collection, that is; other rooms are subject to staffing shortages and can be closed on a rotating basis). Some of the "newer" rooms, covering archaeological discoveries in the Greco-Roman settlements and necropolises in and around Naples, have helpful informational panels in

A History of the Museo Archeologico

First built in 1585 as a cavalry barracks, then used as a law court, then a university, the building housing the Museo Archeologico Nazionale became a museum, in part, only in 1777. With Italian unification in 1860 it became exclusively so, housing the fabulous Farnese collection, which is now accompanied by finds from Herculaneum, Pompeii, Capua, and other parts of Magna Grecia (as Southern Italy was once known).

The origins of the collection can be traced in part to some dynastic luck. The Farnese family's last surviving member, Elizabetta, was married to Philip V of Spain. On her death in 1766, her son, the Bourbon Charles III, King of Naples and Sicily, was left with one of the biggest cultural heirlooms of all time. The Farnese family had from Renaissance times used its papal offices to gain something of a monopoly on antiquities, not to mention works by the Renaissance masters. When one of the family married a Medici princess, they acquired the Medici collection as well. A further windfall came in their taking over the collection of another papal family, the Orsinis.

The 1587 will of Cardinal Alexander Farnese—later Pope Paolo III—stipulated that the collection remain in Rome. Risking the disapproval of then Pope Pius VI, Charles's son Ferdinand ignored the dictate and arranged for the transfer of probably the world's most valuable batch of statues to Naples. Hercules, Zeus, Athena, and Venere Callipige headed south, along with satyrs, gladiators, and fauns, eventually to be put on display in 1801. (Most can now be seen on the ground floor.) Unlike many other works in Italy, they escaped further kidnapping to France under the Napoleonic occupation, thanks to the efforts of Naples governor Joachim Murat.

With the restoration of Ferdinand, the museum acquired a new name, the Royal Bourbon Museum, and a considerable expansion to house stunning finds from Pompeii and Herculaneum—most of which are now on the first floor. With works like these being unearthed, it's no surprise that *la febbre da rovine* (ruin fever) set in and Naples became a top venue on the Grand Tour circuit.

It didn't hurt the museum's popularity when Francesco II (1825–30) opened the Gabinetto Secreto (Secret Cabinet) to display X-rated finds from Pompeii. After a visit to the museum with his wife and daughter, the same Francesco decided the exhibit should have limited access. Garibaldi on Italian Unification declared the restrictions on the Cabinet to be a symbol of Bourbon backwardness and pledged to reopen it. During the 20th century it was closed again, only becoming totally accessible in 2000.

During World War II, the museum's collection was moved to Montecassino to escape the Allied bombing of Naples. (Fortunately, unlike many churches, the museum was not hit.) When things turned dangerous at Montecassino, the collection ended up for a while in the Vatican Museums in Rome—their original home—only returning to Naples after the war.

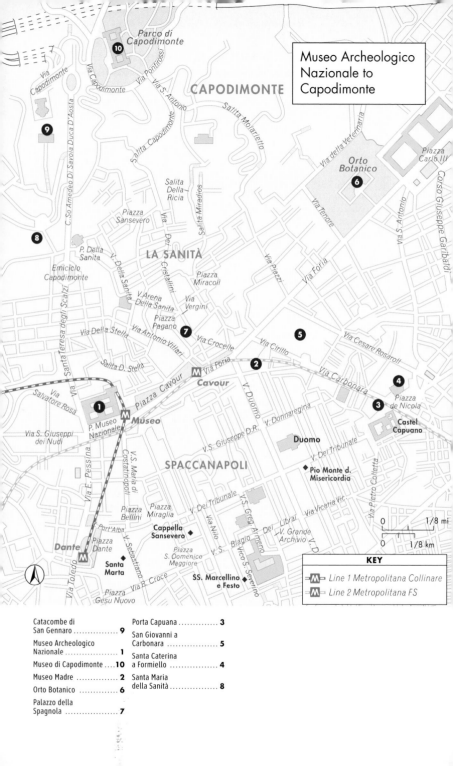

Museo Archeologico
Nazionale to
Capodimonte

English. A fascinating display (free) of the finds unearthed during digs for the Naples metro has been set up in the Museo station close to the museum entrance.

Even if some rooms may be closed, this still leaves available the core of the museum, a nucleus of world-renowned archaeological finds that puts most other museums to shame.

> **WORD OF MOUTH**
>
> "The artifacts from Pompeii at the Museum of Archaeology were incredible, especially the mosaics! Some of them were done in pieces no bigger than an 1/8"! Absolutely amazing." —Dayle

It includes the legendary Farnese collection of ancient sculpture, together with local sculptural finds, and almost all the good stuff—the best mosaics and paintings—from Pompeii and Herculaneum. The quality of these collections is unexcelled and, as far as the mosaic, painting, and bronze sections are concerned, unique in the world.

As you enter the building, the ticket booth is on your right opposite the bookshop. To view the remarkable Farnese collection of ancient marble sculpture, take the right-hand corridor at the end of the entrance atrium and follow the signs. If you're going to devote some time to the museum, though, it makes more sense to start your visit on the top floor, which contains some of the more demanding works on the eye, and work your way down. It's worthwhile to invest in an up-to-date printed museum guide, as exhibits are generally poorly labeled, and have a habit of changing location. Alternatively, you might try the audioguide (€6; ID required), though for a collection of this magnitude it is woefully incomplete. ⊠ *Piazza Museo 19, Spaccanapoli* ☎ *081/440166* ⊕ *www.archeona.arti.beniculturali.it* ☞ *€6.50, €10 for special exhibits* ☉ *Wed.–Mon. 9–7.*

❷ **Museo Madre.** Don't be misled by the scaffolding across the street: Museo
★ d'Arte Contemporanea Donnaregina or Madre for short, with 8,000 square meters of exhibition space and a host of young helpful attendants, is very much up and going—in fact it's the third most visited museum in Naples. The artworks on the first floor were mostly installed in situ by their creators, while on the second floor a "historic" gallery features works by such 20th-century luminaries as Rauschenberg, Oldenburg, and Warhol. For a complete contrast, the museum includes in the Gothic church of Donnaregina across a courtyard. It also hosts temporary shows by major international artists and is the only museum in Europe to stay open until midnight (Friday and Saturday). ⊠ *Via Settembrini 79, San Lorenzo* ☎ *081/19313016* ⊕ *www.museomadre. it* ☞ *€7, free Mon.* ☉ *Mon., Wed., Thurs., Sun. 10–9, Fri. and Sat. 10 AM–midnight* Ⓜ *Piazza Cavour.*

❻ **Orto Botanico.** Founded in 1807 by Joseph Bonaparte and Prince Joachim
★ Murat as an oasis from hectic Naples, this is one of the largest of all Italian botanical gardens, comprising some 30 acres. Nineteenth-century greenhouses and picturesque paths hold an important collection of tree, shrub, cactus, and floral specimens from all over the world. Next to the Orto Botanico, with a 1,200-foot facade dwarfing Piazza Carlo III, is one of the largest public buildings in Europe, the Albergo dei Poveri, built

in the 18th and 19th centuries to house the city's destitute and homeless; it's now a UNESCO World Heritage Site awaiting an ambitious restoration scheme. ☒ *Via Foria 223, Carlo III* ☏*081/449759* ⊕*www. ortobotanico.unina.it* ☒*Free* ⊙*By appointment weekdays 9–2.*

❺ **San Giovanni a Carbonara.** This often overlooked church is an engaging
★ complex of Renaissance architecture and sculpture. Its curious name is the result of its location during medieval times near the city trash dump, where refuse was burned (carbonized); this location is just outside the Capuana Gate of the old city walls. Its history starts in 1339, when the Neapolitan nobleman Gualtiero Galeota gave a few houses and a vegetable garden to a small convent of Augustinian monks who ministered to the poor neighborhood nearby.

To enter the church, go up the dramatic staircase in piperno stone with a double run of elliptical stairs—modeled after a 1707 design by Ferdinando Sanfelice (similar to other organ-curved stairways in Rome, such as the Spanish Steps). Upon entering the rectangular nave, the first thing you see is the Monument of the Miroballo family, which is actually a chapel on the opposite wall, finished by Tommaso Malvito and his workshop in 1519 for the Marchese Bracigliano; the magnificent statues in the semicircular arch immediately set the tone for this surprising repository of first-class Renaissance sculpture.

To the right—beyond the skeletal main altar, which has been stripped of its 18th-century baroque additions—is the suitably royal (59-foot-tall), if not megalomaniacal, funerary monument of King Ladislas (who funded the original church) and Joan II, finished by Marco and Andrea da Firenze in 1428. Four monumental female statues of Virtues hold up the sarcophagi of Ladislas and his sister, as well as statues of the two monarchs seated on thrones, and, finally, an energetic armed Ladislas on horseback being blessed by a bishop (the king died excommunicate, but you can buy anything in Naples). A door underneath this monument leads to the **Ser Caracciolo del Sole** chapel, with its rare and beautiful original majolica pavement—the oldest (1427) produced in Italy, from a workshop in Campania, it shows the influence of Arab motifs and glazing technique.

Coming back out into the nave and immediately turning right at the altar, you enter another circular chapel, the **Caracciolo di Vico** chapel. This cohesive, sophisticated ensemble shows how Italian art history, first written by Tuscans with a regional agenda, tends to simplify the evolution of Renaissance art and architecture at the expense of other centers. The dating for the chapel is the object of debate; usually given as 1517, with the sculptural decor complete by 1557, the design (usually attributed to Tommaso Malvito) may go back to 1499 and thus precede the much more famous Tempietto in Rome, by Bramante, which it so resembles. In fact, the chapel's superlative quality has led some scholars to reject the traditional attribution and give it to Bramante himself or one of the Sangallos under the assumption that such a fine work should naturally be by someone quite famous.

Coming once again into the nave, see if the next door on the right is open (or ask the custodian): this leads to the small rectangular room of the **Old Sacristy,** commissioned by the Caracciolo di Sant'Erasmo. The walls are decorated with 18 richly colored fresco panels depicting scenes from the Old and New testaments as well as saints and doctors of the Church, painted by Giorgio Vasari, disciple of Michelangelo and godfather of Renaissance art history. You can be thankful this great church is off the path of tour groups so you can absorb the ordered beauty of the decoration in peace. ✉ *Via San Giovanni a Carbonara 5, Decumano Maggiore* ☏*081/295873* ⊙ *Mon.–Sat. 9:30–1* Ⓜ *Piazza Cavour.*

WORTH NOTING

❸ **Porta Capuana.** Its elegance heightened by the spruced-up pedestrianized piazza on which it stands, this great ceremonial gateway is one of Naples's finest landmarks of the Renaissance era. Ferdinand II of Aragon commissioned the Florentine sculptor and architect Giuliano da Maiano to build this white triumphal arch—perhaps in competition with the Arco di Trionfo found on the facade of the city's Castel Nuovo—in the late 15th century. As at Castel Nuovo, this arch is framed by two peperino stone towers, here nicknamed Honor and Virtue. Across Via Carbonara stands the medieval bulk of the **Castel Capuano,** once home to Angevin and Aragonese rulers until it was transformed in 1540 by the Spanish Viceroy into law courts, a function it still fulfills today. On Sunday this is a meetingplace for Naples' *extracommunitari* (immigrants), who chat in their native tongues—from Ukrainian and Polish to Twi and Igbo. ✉ *Piazza San Francesco, Carlo III.*

❹ **Santa Caterina a Formiello.** After a complete makeover completed in July 2008, this church is eminently visitable, the full explanations of its paintings and sculptures on display worthy of a good museum. The Formiello in the name refers to the *formali,* the nearby underground aquaduct, which, history relates, the Aragonese also used to capture the town from beneath. The church facade in dark piperno stone was designed for the Dominicans by Tuscan architect Romolo Balsimelli, a student of Brunelleschi.

The side chapels are as interesting for their relics as for their art. In the Orsini Chapel on the left are the elaborately framed remains of St. Helodorus and other Dominican saints, while the fourth chapel displays some 20 skulls of the martyrs of Otranto, brought to Naples by King Alfonso in 1490. The event referred to is the Ottoman sack of Otranto in 1480, when 813 Christians were executed for refusing to renounce their faith. (More martyrs' skulls occupy a much larger cabinet in Otranto's cathedral.) Depicted in the rather surrealistic altar painting is the headless Antonio Primaldo, whose body, through the strength of faith, stands upright to confound his Ottoman executioner.

In the fifth chapel a cycle of paintings by Giacomo del Po depicts the life and afterlife of Saint Catherine, while in the vault Luigi Garzi depicts the same saint in glory. Up in the rather faded dome painted by Paolo di Mattei, Catherine, together with the Madonna, implores the Trinity to watch over the city. Below are the tombs of the Spinelli family, feudal loyalty to the Aragonese cause being rewarded by something of a family Pantheon. The sumptuous altar is by Lorenzo Fontana. ✉ *Via Carbonara, Decumano Maggiore* ☏*081292316* ⊙ *Mon.–Sat. 9–1* Ⓜ *Piazza Garibaldi.*

TOWN AND COUNTRY:
LA SANITÀ TO CAPODIMONTE

The Parco di Capodimonte is the crowning point of the vast mountainous plain that slopes down through the city to the waterfront area. Nearly 5 km (3 mi) removed from the madding crowds in the *centro storico,* the sylvan and verdant mount of Capodimonte is enjoyed by locals and visitors alike as a favored escape from the overheated city center. With its picture-perfect views over the entire city and bay, the park was first founded in the 18th century as a hunting preserve by Charles of Bourbon. Before long, partly to house the famous Farnese collection which he had inherited from his mother, he commissioned a spectacular Palazzo Reale for the park. Today this palace is the Museo di Capodimonte, which contains among its treasures the city's greatest collection of old-master paintings. Here, rooms virtually wallpapered with Titians, Caravaggios, and Parmagianinos will be your reward for making the effort to reach this area of the city, accessible only by vehicles on wheels rather than rails.

If you're feeling intrepid—and not carrying anything of value—you might like to deviate into La Sanità, one of Naples' most densely populated and uncomfortably lawless neighborhoods, still studded with legendary palaces and gilded churches. In the district known as I Vergini (so-called after an inscription found on a ancient Greek tomb in the area relating to the women who had dedicated their virginity to the Greek goddess Eunostos), you can catch your breath at the haunted Catacombs of San Gaudioso. Alternatively, avoid the hassle at street level by taking a fascinating tour with Napoli Sotterranea (⊕*www. napolisotterranea.org*) to the Cimitero delle Fontanelle.

TOP ATTRACTIONS

⑩ Museo di Capodimonte. The grandiose 18th-century neoclassic Bourbon
★ royal palace, in the vast Bosco di Capodimonte (Capodimonte Wood), which served as the royal hunting preserve and later as the site of the Capodimonte porcelain works, is a spectacular setting for Naples' finest collection of old-master paintings and decorative arts. Perched on top of a hill overlooking all of Naples and the bay, the palace was built in 1738 by Charles III of Bourbon as a hunting retreat, then expanded by Antonio Medrano—architect of the Teatro San Carlo—to become the repository of the fabled Farnese art collection Charles inherited from his mother, Elizabeth Farnese. For this art-loving king, however, collecting was not enough; to compete with his father-in-law, Frederick Augustus, the Elector of Saxony, who had founded the celebrated Meissen porcelain factory, Charles decided to set up his own royal factory, opposite the Capodimonte Palace, and before long, the "soft-paste" porcelain figurines of Pulcinello, biscuit vendors, and pretty nymphs were the choicest collectibles for Europe's rich. Fittingly, the most unique room in the palace is entirely crafted from porcelain (3,000 pieces of it)—**Queen Maria Amalia's Porcelain Parlor** (1757–59), built for the royal palace at Portici but relocated here.

But Capodimonte's greatest treasure is the excellent collection of
paintings, well displayed in the
Galleria Nazionale on the palace's
first and second stories. Before you
arrive at this remarkable collection,
a magnificent staircase leads to the
royal apartments, where you'll find
beautiful antique furniture, most of
it on the splashy scale so dear to the

Bourbons, and a staggering collection of porcelain and majolica from
the various royal residences. The walls of the apartments are hung with
numerous portraits, providing a close-up of the unmistakable Bourbon
features, a challenge to any court painter. The main galleries on the first
floor are devoted to work from the 13th to the 18th century, including
many familiar masterpieces by Dutch and Spanish masters, as well as
by the great Italians: Simone Martini's *St. Louis Crowning King Robert*
(1317), Masaccio's *Crucifixion* (1426), Giovanni Bellini's *Transfigura-
tion* (1480), Annibale Carracci's *Pietà* (1600), Parmigianino's *Antea*
(1531), Gentileschi's *Judith and Holofernes* (1630), Caravaggio's *Flagellation* (1607–10), and a bevy of famous Titians, including the *Danaë*
(1545).

On the top floor, a set of galleries features international contemporary
art—including Andy Warhol's *Mount Vesuvius,* painted when the artist
visited Naples in 1985—while the second floor holds extensive collections of 14th- to 19th-century Neapolitan painting and decorative arts,
including plenty of dramatic renditions of Vesuvius in all its raging glory.
When you've had your fill of these, take time to admire the genuine
article from the shady parkland outside, designed by Ferdinando Sanfelice and then adapted into the "natural" English style, which affords
a sweeping view of the bay. On weekends, you can rent bicycles (€3
per hour; ID required) by the Porta Piccola entrance to explore several
circuits inside this large city park. You can get to the museum via Bus
24 from Piazza Municipio or Piazza Carità, or by Bus C57, R4, or C63
from outside the Archaeological Museum. ⊠ *Via Miano 2, Porta Piccola, Via Capodimonte, Capodimonte* ☎848/800288 *for information
and tickets for special exhibitions* ⬚€7.50, *after* 2 PM €6.50 ⊗ *Daily
8:30–7:30; ticket office closes at 6:30.*

WORTH NOTING

❾ **Catacombe di San Gennaro.** These catacombs—designed for Christian
burial rather than as refuges—go at least as far back as the 2nd century
AD. This was where St. Gennaro's body was brought from Pozzuoli in
the 4th century, after which the catacombs became a key pilgrimage
center. The 45-minute guided tour of the two-level site takes you down
a series of vestibules with fine frescoed niche tombs. The imposing bulk
of the early-20th-century church looms over the site (Madre del Buon
Consiglio), apparently inspired by St. Peter's in Rome. ⊠ *Via Capodimonte 13, next to Madonna del Buon Consiglio church, Capodimonte*
☎081744371 ⬚€5 ⊗ *Guided tours Tues.–Sat. 9, 10, 11, noon, 2, 3,
Sun. 9, 10, 11, noon.*

❼ Palazzo della Spagnola. Built in 1738 for the Neapolitan aristocrat Marchese Moscati, this palazzo is famed for its external "hawk-winged staircase," believed to follow the design of star architect Ferdinando Sanfelice and decorated with sumptuous stucco and a bust and panel at the top of each flight. The palace was at one point owned by a Spanish nobleman, Don Tommas Atienza, thus the name "della Spagnola." In the left corner of the courtyard in the back, a nondescript metal door leads to a tunnel running all the way to Piazza Carlo III—another example of the Neapolitan underground. The top floor of the palazzo houses Museo di Totò (not yet open at this writing), named for and honoring one of Naples's great film actors, who lived nearby. ⊠ *Via Vergini 19, Sanità* ⊙ *Daily 7–7*

❽ Santa Maria della Sanità. This baroque, Greek cross–shaped basilica, replete with majolica-tile dome, was commissioned by Dominican friars in the early 17th century. The church contains a small museum of 17th-century Counter-Reformation art—the most flagrantly devotional school of Catholic art—and includes no less than five Luca Giordano altarpieces. Elsewhere, the richly decorated elevated presbytery, complete with double staircase, provides the only note of color in the gray-and-white decoration. This also provides access to the noted Catacombe di San Gaudioso. ⊠ *Via della Sanità 124, Sanità* ☎ *081/5441305* ⊙ *Mon.–Sat. 9:30–12:30 and 5–7:30, Sun. 9:30–12:30*

NEED A BREAK?	In teeming Via dei Vergini, give in to temptation with a pastry from Pasticceria dei Vergini (⊠ *Via dei Vergini 66, Vergini* ☎ *081/455989*) to enjoy a truly calorie-bursting Neapolitan specialty. If you don't have a sweet tooth, pick up a sandwich from da Salvatore, a tiny snack bar next door.

WHERE TO EAT

Let's be honest: you really want a traditional Neapolitan dinner against the backdrop of Vesuvius with a great show of Neapolitan love songs to get you crying into your limoncello. There's no reason to feel guilty, because even the natives love to get into the spirit. But listening to someone warble "Santa Lucia" while feasting on a pizza *Margherita* (with basil, mozzarella, and tomatoes) from a table overlooking the bay is just one example of the pleasures awaiting diners in Naples. From *vitello alla Principe di Napoli* (veal garnished with truffles) to sea bass in *acqua pazza*—that is to say, poached in water "maddened" with anchovy, bay leaves, *peperoncino*, and olive oil—to Neapolitan pastries like the light, fluffy, exotic *babà al Rhum,* the city expresses its gastronomic self in many ways. The *haute*-hungry should look elsewhere (particularly Ristorante Don Alfonso 1890 and the Torre Saraceno, both just across the bay near Sorrento) and so should those in search of newer-than-now nouvelle flights of fantasy served on designer plates. While these can be found, the cuisine in Naples is by and large earthy, pungent, and *buonissima,* as attested to by those signature dishes: *mozzarella in carrozza* (mozzarella cheese fried in a "carriage" of two slices of bread); *polpo alla luciana* (octopus stewed with garlic, peppers, and tomatoes); *risotto ai frutti di mare* (seafood risotto); and *spaghetti*

Neapolitan Folk Songs at Your Table

If you want to hear *canzoni napoletane*—the fabled Neapolitan folk songs—performed live, you can try to catch the city's top troupes, such as the Cantori di Posillipo and I Virtuosi di San Martino, in performances at venues like the Teatro Trianon. But an easier alternative is to head for one of the city's more traditional restaurants, such as La Bersagliera or Mimì alla Ferrovia, where most every night you can expect your meal to be interrupted by a *posteggiatore*. These singers aren't employed by the restaurants, but they're encouraged to come in, swan around the tables with a battered old guitar, and belt out classics such as "Santa Lucia," "O' Surdato Innamurate," "Torna a Surriento," and, inevitably, "Funiculi Funiculà."

These songs are the most famous of a vast repertoire that found international fame with the mass exodus of southern Italians to the United States in the early 20th century. "Funiculi Funiculà" was written by Peppino Turco and Luigi Denza in 1880 to herald the new funicular railway up Vesuvius. "O Sole Mio," by Giovanni Capurro and Eduardo di Capua, has often been mistakenly taken for the Italian national anthem. "Torna a Surriento" was composed by Ernesto di Curtis in 1903 to help remind the current Italian prime minister how wonderful he thought Sorrento was (and how many government subsidies he had promised the township).

The singers are more than happy to do requests, even inserting the name of your *innamorato* or *innamorata* into the song. When they've finished they'll stand discreetly by your table. Give them a few euros and you'll have friends for life (or at least for the night).

---

puttanesca (streetwalker's spaghetti with black olives and bitter capers). In Naples it is still the old reliables that apply, the recipes time-tested by centuries of mammas that still manage to put meat on your bones and smiles on your faces.

This means pizzerias aplenty. As the birthplace of pizza, Naples prides itself on its vast selection of pizzerias, the most famous of which—Da Michele or Sorbillo—deserve the encomium "incomparable." Many Neapolitans make lunch their big meal of the day, and then have a pizza for supper, with a late-night treat—*ogni tanto* (every now and then)—perhaps enjoying the light seabreezes out at Marechiaro accompanied by some of the Mediterranean's best produce, like at Da Cicciotto. Note that "pizzerias" in Naples does not simply mean the linoleum-floored, neon-lighted ones you'll find back in New York City—they range here from holes-in-the-wall to full-scale restaurants.

When it comes to *i secondi* (main dishes), you won't be disappointed by the *salsicce* (pork sausages), but the reason visitors to Naples want to eat seafood is a good one: geography. Naples' position, hugging a rich bay, has guaranteed that marine creatures feature prominently on local menus. Marinated seafood salad (*insalata di frutti di mare*) is a classic antipasto, as well as marinated white anchovies (*alici*). Spaghetti *con le vongole veraci* (with clams, garlic, and a baby's fistful of chopped Italian parsley) is of course a popular and dependable standard, as are myriad variations on linguine or fresh pasta with mixed seafood (mussels, shrimp, clams, and so forth), usually "stained" with fresh cherry tomatoes. As for seafood Neapolitan style, the best—*spigola* (sea bass), *pesce spada* (swordfish), and, if you can find it, *San Pietro* (sort of a sole for grown-ups)—is grilled simply and ennobled with a splash of olive oil and a squeeze of lemon. When it's not on the menu—and many top delicacies are only available if you ask the waiter—go for the *pezzogna* (blue-spotted bream), as you can be almost sure it hasn't been fish-farmed. Fresh calamari, kissed lightly by a grill, can be exquisitely delicate, but the fried version, which can be uniquely satisfying, is, alas, too often done these days with frozen squid. Another good way to have fish is *all'acqua pazza* (literally, in crazy water), poached with anchovy, bay leaves, red pepper, and olive oil, a brew said to have been invented by returning fishermen using seawater to cook up a meal on the beach.

There isn't a surfeit of expensive, luxury restaurants in Naples: most Neapolitans will go out of town for a high-end restaurant meal, heading to gastronomic enclaves on the Sorrento peninsula or up country close to Puglia. That said, if you stay in town you're likely to be pleasantly surprised. Palazzo Petrucci in the old town opened to much fanfare in 2007 and offers palatal treats at excellent prices—surrounded by late Renaissance elegance. Other new entries, Coco Loco and Radici, fill a quality niche in the more up-market area of Chiaia, close to the waterfront and the Villa Comunale. Wherever you go, be prepared to deviate from the menu (locals rarely ask for one) and ask the waiter for the chef's special *piatto* (dish). At the lower end, service may be rough and ready, but then again, this is Naples, and you don't expect to be served by liveried wait staff when your restaurant sits at the end of an alley. Note that many restaurants in Naples close for at least a week around August 15th to celebrate the Ferragosto holidays.

WHAT IT COSTS IN EUROS					
	¢	$	$$	$$$	$$$$
AT DINNER	under €20	€20–€30	€30–€45	€45–€65	over €65

Prices are for a three-course meal (*primo*, *secondo*, and *dolce*), excluding wine.

CITY CENTER

Appropriately, the monumental city center environs feature Naples' most iconic restaurants.

$$
SOUTHERN
ITALIAN
★

✕**Amici Miei.** A place favored by meat eaters who can't take another bite of sea bass, this small, dark, and cozy den is well loved for specials such as tender carpaccio with fresh artichoke hearts, and a rice-and-arugula dish featuring duck breast. There are also excellent pasta dishes, such as *orecchiette* with chickpeas or *alla barese* (with chewy green turnips), or that extravaganza, the *carnevale lasagne,* an especially rich concoction relied on to sustain revelers in the build up before Lent. Everyone finishes with a slice of chocolate and hazelnut *torta caprese.* ✉ *Via Monte di Dio 78, Chiaia* ☎ *081/7646063* ✍ *Reservations essential* ⊟ *AE, DC, MC, V* ⊘ *Closed Mon. and July and Aug. No dinner Sun.* ✛ *D5.*

Continued on page 92

THE SIMPLE GOODNESS OF NEAPOLITAN FOOD

"But there's nothing to it!" cry food snobs when Neapolitan cuisine is mentioned among the higher rungs of the world's culinary ladder. And they might be right—after all, there are no secret spices or special skills needed in its preparation.

The best fresh ingredients are all you need when the local produce is this good

But indeed, simplicity is the key, and the best fresh ingredients are what Napoli has in spades. Long, fleshy, deep-red San Marzano tomatoes grow on the fertile slopes of Vesuvius. The olive groves of the Cilento provide fragrant oil. Buffalo chew the grass on the plains toward Caserta, north of Naples, producing milk that makes the best mozzarella cheese in the world. And Neapolitans have long used the fish-filled waters of the bay to their gastronomic advantage. Tiny fish are marinated, fried, and eaten whole, or used to flavor sauces. Swordfish are sliced up to make steaks. Clams, mussels, and octopus are ubiquitous, and usually enhanced with oil, lemon juice, garlic, and parsley, rather than masked with sauces.

With it all being so simple, you'd think you could replicate it at home. But it's never quite the same: perhaps it's that the water is different, or that you can never quite get the right variety of tomato. Or maybe it doesn't taste the same simply because you're not in Napoli anymore.

Classic Neapolitan dishes featuring the best of the sea and the field.

PIZZA: THE CLASSIC MARGHERITA

Locally grown San Marzano tomatoes are a must.

The best pizza should come out with cheese bubbling and be ever-so-slightly charred around its edges.

Only buffalo-milk mozzarella or *fior di latte* cheese should be used.

The dough has to use the right kind of durum wheat flour and be left to rise for at least six hours.

Be prepared: ranging from the size of a plate to that of a Hummer wheel, Neapolitan pizza is pretty different from anything you might find elsewhere in Italy—not to mention what's served up at American pizza chains. The "purest" form is the *marinara*, topped with only tomatoes, garlic, oregano, and olive oil.

OTHER FAVORITES ARE . . .

- **CAPRICCIOSA** (the "capricious"), made with whatever the chef has on hand.

- **SICILIANA** with mozzarella and eggplant.

- **DIAVOLA** with spicy salami.

- **QUATTRO STAGIONE** ("four seasons"), made with produce from each one.

- **SALSICCIA E FRIARIELLI** with sausage and a broccoli-like vegetable.

A PIZZA FIT FOR A QUEEN

Legend has it that during the patriotic fervor following Italian unification in the late 19th century, a Neapolitan chef decided to celebrate the arrival in the city of the new Italian queen Margherita by designing a pizza in her—and the country's—honor. He took red tomatoes, white mozzarella cheese, and a few leaves of fresh green basil—reflecting the three colors of the Italian flag—and gave birth to the modern pizza industry.

Margherita of Savoy

ONLY THE BEST

An association of Neapolitan pizza chefs has standardized the ingredients and methods that have to be used to make pizza certified DOC (*denominazione d'origine controllata*) or STG (*specialità tradizionale garantita*). See the illustration on the opposite page for the basic requirements.

Buffalo-milk mozzarella

FIRED UP!

The Neapolitan pizza must be made in a traditional wood-burning oven. Chunks of beech or maple are stacked up against the sides of the huge, tiled ovens, then shoved onto the slate base of the oven where they burn quickly at high temperatures. If you visit Pompeii, you will see how similar the old Roman bread-baking ovens are to the modern pizza oven. The *pizzaiolo* (pizza chef) then uses a long wooden paddle to put the pizza into the oven, where it cooks quickly.

A pizzaiolo at work

PIZZERIE

There are hundreds of restaurants that specialize in pizza in Naples, and the best of these make pizza and nothing else. As befits the original fast food, *pizzerie* tend to be simple, fairly basic places, with limited menu choices, and quick, occasionally brusque service: the less complicated your order, the happier the waiters.

Typical pizzeria in Naples

THE REAL THING

Naples takes its contribution to world cuisine seriously. The Associazione Verace Pizza Napoletana (www.pizzanapoletana.org) was founded in 1984 in order to share expertise, maintain quality levels, and provide courses for aspirant pizza chefs and pizza lovers. They also organize the annual Pizzafest—three days in September, dedicated to the consumption of pizza, when *maestri* from all over the region get together and cook off.

Simple, fresh toppings

IT AIN'T JUST PIZZA . . .

Spaghetti con le vongole

While the most famous of Neapolitan foods can be eaten standing up, there is more to local cuisine than pizza. Don't even think about leaving without having tried these Napoli classics.

HOW SIMPLE IS NEAPOLITAN CUISINE?

Take a handful of tomatoes and squeeze them into a pan along with a drizzle of olive oil, a pinch of salt, and some fresh basil leaves. Leave them in just long enough to warm through. Boil some pasta for just as long as it needs. Put it all together, and you have *pasta al pomodoro fresco*, one of the most delicious dishes Italy has to offer. There really is nothing to it!

■ **SPAGHETTI CON LE VONGOLE:** spaghetti topped with different kinds of clams, from the tiny *lupini* to the big red *fasullari*, still in their shells.

■ **IMPEPATA DI COZZE:** mussels, thrown in a pot, heated up, and served with lots of fresh black pepper.

■ **BACCALÀ:** dried salt cod, fried and served with some fresh herbs. Once you try it, you'll understand why many Neapolitans regard it as the authentic taste of home.

■ **POLPETTINE AL RAGÙ:** meatballs in tomato sauce. Italian food's biggest export has never tasted as good as in Napoli.

■ **PESCE ALL'ACQUA PAZZA:** fish in "crazy water," with garlic, a few small tomatoes, then some of the water from the fish added to the hot oil. The bubbles are what make it "crazy."

■ **PARMIGIANA DI MELANZANE:** layers of eggplant, mozzarella, and tomato sauce baked in the oven.

■ **PASTA ALLA GENOVESE:** not from Genoa, as its name may suggest, but invented by a Neapolitan chef named Genovese. Onions are added to a ham bone and cooked for hours, then added to the pasta.

"POOR FOOD"

During the winter when the best fresh produce isn't so abundant, Neapolitans head for the store cupboard and soak large quantities of dried cannellini beans, chickpeas, and lentils. These are then made into hearty soups, to which any kind of pasta can be added. They're great as filling and warm dishes, but because *pasta fagioli*, *pasta ceci*, and *pasta lenticchie* are regarded as "poor food" (the kind of thing you make at home), they aren't often found on restaurant menus.

Baccalà alla vicentina, a traditional Italian codfish stew

LA FRITTURA

Forget all that stuff about the Mediterranean diet being so healthy. Lots of pizzerie and roadside stalls will offer you a selection of *frittura*—deep-fried balls of dough and seaweed, fried sliced eggplant, fried potato croquettes, fried zucchini flowers. Eat them with your fingers, and don't feel guilty.

Fried zucchini flowers

CAKE SEASON

Like everything else, cakes are seasonal. If you're visiting over Christmas, check out the teeth-challenging *rococò*, made of hazelnuts, or the softer *struffoli*, tiny balls of fried pastry doused in honey. Carnival time (mid-February to mid-March) is for *chiacchiere*—large, flat slices of light pastry sprinkled with icing sugar—while Easter sees rivalries for the best *pastiera*, a rich cake filled with ricotta, sifted grain, and orange or rose water. Around All Souls' Day (late October), cake shops fill up with *torrone* (soft or hard nougat). Two Napoli classics are, thankfully, available year-round: the large soft sponge *babà*, soaked in rum, and the *sfogliatella*, sweet and spicy ricotta cheese wrapped in short crust or puff pastry.

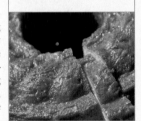
Rum-soaked *babà* cake

LIMONCELLO

No serious meal is complete without a final *liquore*, and the local limoncello is the best of the lot. Made from the zest of lemons, lots of sugar, and pure alcohol, limoncello is very sweet, very strong, and must be served very cold.

Limoncello

U CAFFÈ

Whether to help you digest a big meal, give you a morning pickup, or accompany a cake, *u caffè* (to give coffee its name in the local dialect) is a Neapolitan rite. You can have it in its pure state, small and black with a teaspoonful of sugar, or order *nocciola* (with hazelnut syrup), *macchiato* (with a dash of frothy milk), or *corretto* (with a shot of liqueur) varieties. If you want to keep to local customs, never ask for a cappuccino after a meal. It's considered bad for digestion.

U caffè

$$
PIZZA

✕**Brandi.** Forget that this historic place gave the world *pizza Margherita*—the classic combo of tomato sauce, mozzarella, and basil, named after King Umberto's queen. This is, hands down, one of the most picturesque restaurants in Italy. Set on a cobblestone alleyway just off chic Via Chiaia, it welcomes you with an enchanting wood-beam salon festooned with 19th-century memorabilia, saint shrines, gilded mirrors, and bouquets of flowers, beyond which you can see the kitchen and the *pizzaioli* (pizza makers) at work. That's the good news. Unfortunately, most of Naples stays away, considering the pizzas are far, far better elsewhere, and finding the service somewhat off hand. But there's no denying the decor is *delizioso* and if tourists like Chelsea Clinton, Bill Murray, and Gerard Depardieu have dined here, why not you? ✉*Salita Sant'Anna di Palazzo 1, Toledo* ☎*081/416928* ▭*AE, DC, MC, V* ✆*Closed Tues.* ✛*D4.*

¢–$
NEAPOLITAN
★

✕**Cantina della Tofa.** Located two blocks up one of the narrow alleys that lead off Via Toledo into the Quartieri Spagnoli, this small, welcoming restaurant serves traditional Neapolitan fare that goes beyond standard pasta with seafood or tomatoes. Try the *vellutata di cicerchie,* a creamy soup made from beans that are a cross between chickpeas and fava beans. The orange-walled dining room has large wooden tables that seem more Tuscan than Campanian. Service is friendly and unhurried. ✉*Vico Tofa 71, Piazza Municipio* ☎*081/406840* ▭*No credit cards* ✆*Closed Sun. and 3 wks in Aug.* ✛*D3.*

$$
NEAPOLITAN

✕**Ciro a Santa Brigida.** Just off Via Toledo, Ciro has been an obligatory entry on any list of Neapolitan cooking (as opposed to cuisine) since 1932, when Toscanini and Pirandello used to eat here. Popular with business travelers, artists, and journalists, Ciro is famous for a wide variety of favorites, with an emphasis on rustic food, from very fine pizzas and justly famed versions of pasta *e fagioli* to the classic *sartù*—rice loaf first concocted by baroque-era nuns—and the splendid *pignatiello e vavella,* shellfish soup. The menu looks too large for all its items to be good, but the owners must be doing something right, as the place is often packed with Neapolitan regulars. The old waiters are darling wherever you sit, but try to get a table upstairs, which has a more pleasant atmosphere. ✉*Via Santa Brigida 71, Toledo* ☎*081/5524072* ⊕*www.ciroasantabrigida.it* ▭*AE, DC, V* ✆*Closed Sun. and last 2 wks in Aug.* ✛*D4.*

$$
NEAPOLITAN
★

✕**Trattoria San Ferdinando.** Almost the first doorway on the right as you go up Via Nardones from Piazza Trieste e Trento—ring the bell outside to get let in—this cheerful trattoria is open in the evening only from Wednesday to Friday, with the fine intention of running a restaurant for the sheer pleasure of it. Try the traditional (but cooked with a lighter modern touch) pasta dishes (especially those with *verdura,* fresh leaf vegetables) and excellent fish. Close to the San Carlo Theater and aptly decorated with playbills and theatrical memorabilia both ancient and modern, this is an excellent place to stop after a visit to the opera. ✉*Via Nardones 117, Toledo* ☎*081/421964* ▭*AE, DC, MC, V* ✆*Closed Sun. No dinner Sat.–Tues.* ✛*D4.*

SPACCANAPOLI

Spaccanapoli is now one of *the* evening locations where *buona cucina* meets both low- and high-brow culture (what a change from 15 or 20 years ago, when it was a dark and dangerous part of town). The teeming alleyways and 17th-century palazzi house many inexpensive places to eat, which begin to fill up after 9 PM. For a classier restaurant, try Palazzo Petrucci on the main square of San Domenico Maggiore, at the very cultural heart of Spaccanapoli.

¢ ✕**Gino Sorbillo.** There are three restaurants called Sorbillo along Via
PIZZA dei Tribunali; this is the one with the crowds waiting outside. Order
★ the same thing the locals are here for: a basic Neapolitan pizza (try the unique pizza al pesto or the stunningly simple marinara—just tomatoes and oregano). They're cooked to perfection by the third generation of pizza makers who run the place. The pizzas are enormous, flopping over the edge of the plate onto the white marble tabletops. ✉ *Via dei Tribunali 32, Spaccanapoli* ☎ *081/446643* ⊟ *AE, DC, MC, V* ⊗ *Closed Sun. (except Dec.) and 2 wks in Aug.* ⊕ *E2.*

¢–$ ✕**La Cantina di Via Sapienza.** With a balanced array of mainly land-based
NEAPOLITAN cuisine, owner-manager Gaetano attracts students and young professionals to this unpretentious eatery—mainly regulars from the school of medicine round the corner. It's busy and not big enough (expect to share a table—and if your fellow diners are not shy, why should you be?), but the prices can't be beat, and the daily selection of a good dozen vegetable side plates merits a detour of its own, even if you're not a vegetarian. ✉ *Via Sapienza 40, Spaccanapoli* ☎ *081/459078* ⊟ *No credit cards* ⊗ *Closed Sun. and Aug. No dinner* ⊕ *E2.*

$ ✕**La Vecchia Cantina.** On a rather dark side street in the tattier section
NEAPOLITAN of Spaccanapoli, this place is well worth seeking out for its combination of old-style Neapolitan hospitality and attention to the quality of its food and wine. The place is run as a family affair, with Gianni out front while his mother Nunzia and wife Maria are busy in the kitchen, much like a typical Neapolitan household. An accumulation of kitsch decorations completes the feeling, and everyone who comes here seems to know each other. The pasta with chickpeas is a must, and *baccalà fritto* (fried salt cod) is a specialty. Backed up with a selection of wines from all over Italy, this place is a great value. ✉ *Via S. Nicola alla Carità 13–14, Spaccanapoli* ☎ *081/5520226* ⊟ *AE, MC, V* ⊗ *Closed Tues.; Sun. June–Aug.; and 2 wks Aug. No dinner Sun.* ⊕ *D3.*

¢–$ ✕**Lombardi à Santa Chiara.** Right on Spaccanapoli opposite the Palazzo
PIZZA Croce, home to the philosopher and historian Benedetto Croce, this is one of the city's most famous pizzerias, packed night after night. The young crowd heads down into the more boisterous basement, while the atmosphere upstairs is calmer and more congenial to conversation at standard decibel levels. On the ground floor you can watch the

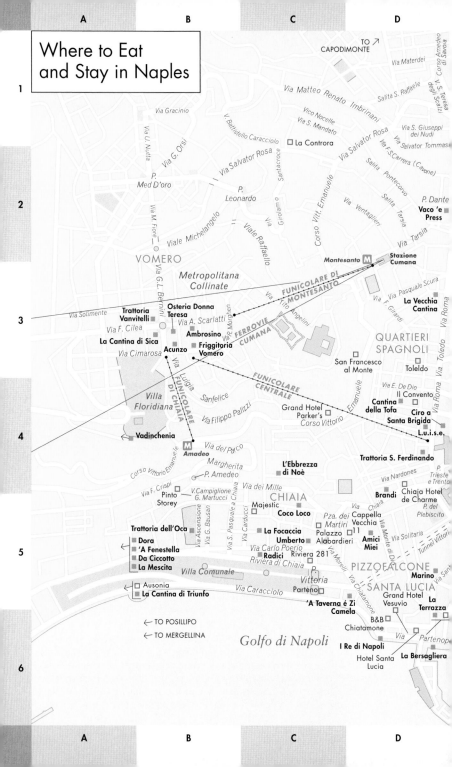

Where to Eat and Stay in Naples

A   B   C   D

TO CAPODIMONTE

Via Materdei

Corso Amedeo di Savoia

V. S. Scarlatti

Via Gracinio

Via Matteo Renato Imbriani

Salita S. Raffaele

Vico Nocelle
Via S. Mandato

Via S. Giuseppe dei Nudi

Via U. Nutta

Via G. Orsi

V. Battistello Caracciolo

Santacroce

Via Salvator Rosa

Via F-S. Carrera (Cavone)

Via S. Salvator Tommas

□ La Controra

P. Med D'oro

P. Leonardo

Girolamo

Santacroce

Corso Vitt. Emanuele

Salita Pontecorvo

Salita Tarsia

P. Dante

Vaco 'e Press

Via M. Fiore

Viale Michelangelo

Viale Raffaello

Via Ventaglieri

Via Tarsia

VOMERO

Metropolitana Collinate

Montesanto Ⓜ Stazione Cumana

Via G.L. Bernini

FUNICOLARE DI MONTESANTO

Via S. Pasquale Scura

Via Solimente

Trattoria Vanvitelli

Osteria Donna Teresa

Via A. Scarlatti

Via R. Morghen

Via F. Girardi

Via F. Cilea

Ambrosino

FERROVIE CUMANA

La Vecchia Cantina

Via Toledo

La Cantina di Sica

Acunzo

Friggitoria Vomero

QUARTIERI SPAGNOLI

Via Cimarosa

Via Luigia Sanfelice

FUNICOLARE CENTRALE

San Francesco al Monte

□ Toleldo

Via Roma

Villa Floridiana

Via Filippo Palizzi

Grand Hotel Parker's

Corso Vittorio

Via E. De Dio

Il Convento

Cantina della Tofa

Ciro a Santa Brigida

Vadinchenia

Ⓜ Amadeo

Via del Parco

Margherita

Emanuele

L.u.i.s.e.

Trattoria S. Ferdinando

Corso Vittorio Emanuele

P. Amedeo

L'Ebbrezza di Noè

Via Nardones

P. Trieste e Trento

Via F. Crispi

Pinto Storey

V. Campiglione
G. Martucci

Via dei Mille

CHIAIA

Via Chiaia

Brandi

Chiaja Hotel de Charme

P. del Plebiscito

Majestic

Coco Loco

Pza. dei Martiri

Cappella Vecchia

Via Solitaria

Via Ascensione

Via S. Pasquale a Chiaia

Via Carducci

La Focaccia

Palazzo Alabardieri

11

Amici Miei

Tunnel Vittori

Trattoria dell'Oca

Via G. Bausan

Umberto

Via Carlo Poerio

Radici

Riviera 281

Via Morelli

PIZZOFALCONE

□ Dora

■ 'A Fenestella

■ Da Ciccotto

■ La Mescita

Riviera di Chiaia

P. Vittoria

SANTA LUCIA

Marino

Villa Comunale

Parteno

Grand Hotel Vesuvio

La Terrazza

□ Ausonia

■ La Cantina di Triunfo

Via Caracciolo

'A Taverna é Zi Camela

Via Monte di Di

Via Chiatamone

B&B
Chiatamone

Via Partenop

← TO POSILLIPO

← TO MERGELLINA

Golfo di Napoli

I Re di Napoli

Hotel Santa Lucia

La Bersagliera

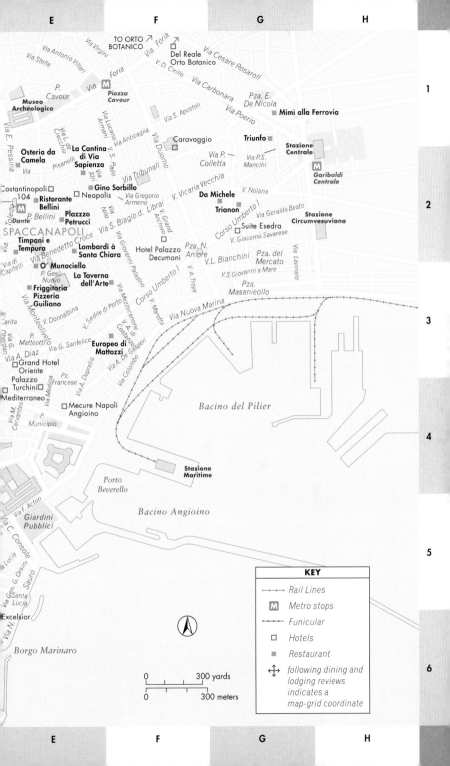

pizzaioli working the pizza dough, manipulating each pie as if it were a live creation. ⊠ *Via Benedetto Croce 59, Spaccanapoli* ☏*081/5520780* ⊟*AE, MC, V* ⊙*Closed last 3 wks in Aug.* ✛*E2.*

$ **⨯O' Munaciello.** Right on Piazza Gesù, this restaurant is a good place to
NEAPOLITAN sit outside, relax, and people-watch after a tour around Spaccanapoli. It caters to diverse palates and budgets: pizzas are served here at lunchtime and there is a menu of small plates for €8. Alternatively, opt for the single dish *linguine al coccio*, combining pasta with locally caught fish. ⊠*Piazza del Gesù Nuovo 26–27, Spaccanapoli* ☏*081/5521144* ⊟*AE, DC, MC, V* ✛*E2.*

$–$$ **⨯Osteria da Carmela.** Conveniently close to the archaeological museum,
ITALIAN yet surprisingly off the tourist beat, this small eatery is patronized by *professori* from the nearby Academy of Fine Arts and theatergoers from the Teatro Bellini next door. A specialty here is the blend of seafood with vegetables—try the *tubettoni con cozze e zucchini* (tube-shaped pasta with mussels and zucchini) or a *risotto mare e monti* (garnished with prawns and mushrooms). The service is both swift and obliging. ⊠ *Via Conte di Ruvo 11–12, Spaccanapoli* ☏*081/5499738* ⊟*AE, DC, MC, V* ⊙*Closed Sun.* ✛*E2.*

$$$ **⨯Palazzo Petrucci.** Nestled in a 17th-century mansion facing *Piazza San*
NEAPOLITAN *Domenico Maggiore*, Palazzo Petrucci doesn't lack for dramatic din-
Fodor'sChoice ing options. Choose between tables under the vaulted ceiling of the
★ former stables, in the gallery where a glass partition lets you keep an eye on the kitchen, or in the cozy room overlooking the piazza. Fortify yourself with a complimentary glass of prosecco before making the agonizing choice between the à la carte offerings and the *menu degustazione* (€40). A popular starter is *lasagnette baccalà con scarole e pinoli tostati* (layered cod with escarole and roasted pine nuts). The *paccheri all'impiedi* (tube-shaped pasta served standing up) in a rich ricotta and meat sauce is an interesting twist on an old regional favorite. ⊠*Piazza San Domenico Maggiore 4, Spaccanapoli* ☏*081/5524068* ✍*Reservations essential* ⊟*AE, DC, MC, V* ⊙*Closed most of Aug. No dinner Sun., no lunch Mon.* ✛*E2.*

$ **⨯Ristorante Bellini.** Worth visiting just to observe the waiters, who all
NEAPOLITAN seem to have just stepped off the stage of a Neapolitan comedy at the nearby Teatro Bellini, this spot claims a proud perch on the corner of the chicly bohemian Piazza Bellini. But if the neighborhood remains suave, this staple Neapolitan restaurant proudly retains its old-world feel. Good bets here include a fine (if rather small) pizza, and classic fish dishes such as linguine *al cartoccio* (baked in paper) or *all'astice* (a type of small lobster). Go up the narrow stairs to get to the spacious upper rooms, or squeeze in at one of the pavement tables in summer. ⊠ *Via Santa Maria di Costantinopoli 79, Spaccanapoli* ☏*081/459774* ⊟*DC, MC, V* ⊙*Closed Sun. June–Sept. and 1 wk in Aug.* ✛*E2.*

¢–$ **⨯Timpani e Tempura.** A tiny shrine to local culinary culture with no
NEAPOLITAN tables, but where you're invited to perch yourself at the bar-style coun-
★ ter, this place isn't comfortable but is worth the squeeze for its *timballi di maccheroni* (baked pasta cakes) and its unique *mangiamaccheroni*, spaghetti in broth with caciocavallo cheese, butter, basil, and pepper. High-quality wines by the glass make this a spot for a swift but excellent

lunch. You can also buy cheese and salami to take home with you. ✉ *Vico della Quercia 17, Spaccanapoli* ☎*081/5512280* ▭*No credit cards* ⊘*No dinner* ✛*E2.*

THE PORT AND PIAZZA GARIBALDI

Forget waterfront restaurants and outdoor candlelighted terraces. This is an area noted for fine no-nonsense eating, with some of the city's most traditional restaurants offering excellent value for money. If returning to base after dark, stick to well-lighted main roads or ask one of the restaurant staff to order a taxi.

¢ | PIZZA | Fodor's Choice | ★

✕**Da Michele.** You have to love a place that has, for more than 130 years, offered only two types of pizza—marinara (with tomato, garlic, and oregano) and *margherita* (with tomato, mozzarella, and basil)—and a small selection of drinks, and still manages to attract long lines. The prices have something to do with it, but the pizza itself suffers no rivals, and even those waiting in line are good-humored; the boisterous, joyous atmosphere wafts out with the smell of yeast and wood smoke onto the street. At almost all times there is a wait for a table; get a number at the door and hang out outside until it's called. Note: the restaurant is off Corso Umberto, between Piazza Garibaldi and Piazza Amore. ✉ *Via Sersale 1/3, Piazza Garibaldi* ☎*081/5539204* ▭*No credit cards* ⊘*Closed Sun. and last 2 wks in Aug.* ✛*G2.*

$$ | NEAPOLITAN

✕**Europeo di Mattozzi.** Within walking distance of the port, master of ceremonies Alfonso runs his restaurant like a tight ship, maintaining a banter with staff and customers alike. The choices are extensive, though you'll probably be steered towards fixed-price meals (€30 or €40, depending on the number of courses). If on the menu, opt for the delicately served *pesce bandiera* (long-fin banner fish), a welcome change from the standard seafood pasta dish. ✉ *Via M. Campidisola 4–8, Port* ☎*081/5521323* ▭*AE, DC, MC, V* ⊘*Closed Sun. and last 2 wks in Aug. No dinner Mon. and Tues.* ✛*F3.*

$–$$ | NEAPOLITAN

✕**La Taverna dell'Arte.** As its name suggests, this gracious trattoria on a small side street near Naples' main university is popular with actors, but it manages to remain welcomingly low-key. Warmed with touches of wood, it prides itself on its fresh interpretations of Neapolitan classics: excellent salami, mozzarella, and *frittura* (fried vegetables) among the appetizers, cabbage soup fragrant with good beef stock, and meat and fish grilled over wood. Typical Neapolitan desserts, such as babas and the familiar crunchy almond cookies called *quaresimali*, are served with homemade liqueurs. ✉ *Rampe San Giovanni Maggiore 1/a, Port* ☎*081/5527558* ⌖*Reservations essential* ▭*MC, V* ⊘*Closed Sun. and last 2 wks in Aug. No lunch* ✛*F3.*

$$ | NEAPOLITAN | ★

✕**Mimì alla Ferrovia.** Clients of this Neapolitan institution have included Fellini and that magnificent true-Neapolitan comic genius and aristocrat of dubious lineage, Totò. Mimì manages to live up cheerfully to its history, proudly serving fine versions of everything from pasta *e fagioli* (with beans) to the sea bass *al presidente*, baked in a pastry crust and enjoyed by any number of Italian presidents on their visits to Naples. Not so much a place to see and be seen as a common ground where both the famous and the unknown can mingle, feast, and be of good cheer, Mimì's sober beige-and-green hues, accented with updated art deco features, pale-yellow tablecloths, and retro bentwood chairs, pleasantly tone down the bustle. Given the fairly seedy neighborhood, splurge on a taxi there and back especially at night. ⊠ *Via A. D'Aragona 19/21, Piazza Garibaldi* ☎ *081/289004* ⊕ *www.mimiallaferrovia.com* ⊟ *AE, DC, MC, V* ⊙ *Closed Sun. and last 2 wks in Aug.* ✛ *G1.*

¢ ✕ **Trianon.** Across the street from its archrival Da Michele—and without
PIZZA the lines outside—this is a classic pizzeria with a simple yet upscale art nouveau ambience expressed in soothing tile and marble. More relaxed and upmarket than its rival, Trianon does the classics (Margherita, marinara) in an exemplary manner, but you can also feast on pizza with sausage and broccoli greens, while the signature pizza Trianon comes with eight different toppings. ⊠ *Via P. Coletta 46, Piazza Garibaldi* ☎ *081/5539426* ⊟ *No credit cards* ✛ *G2.*

¢ ✕ **Triunfo.** A strikingly clean place near the Stazione Centrale (take a
PIZZA left turn about halfway along Via A. Poerio as you walk away from Piazza Garibaldi), in a neighborhood that has seen better times, this restaurant sticks out for the quality of its pizza and draws a devoted clientele. The selection of cold antipasti, with lots of simply prepared vegetables, is a welcome change from the usual fried offerings, and the house pizza, with prosciutto and artichokes, makes a wonderful summer dinner. ⊠ *Vicolo II Duchesca 10, Piazza Garibaldi* ☎ *081/268948* ⊟ *DC, MC, V* ⊙ *Closed Mon.* ✛ *G1.*

SANTA LUCIA AND CHIAIA

While Santa Lucia is a classic choice for both chic and touristy fish restaurants with that just-how-you-imagined-Naples sea view, the upscale area of Chiaia is a favorite with both locals and discerning expatriates and is likely to offer better value.

$$ ✕ **'A Taverna 'e Zi Carmela.** Not far from the Villa Comunale gardens, this
NEAPOLITAN is a reasonable, family-run alternative in the pricey Santa Lucia area. Don't pay attention to the haphazard decor; the pizza is excellent, from the ubiquitous basics to such original specialties as the brashly named *incazzata*, a calzone stuffed with spicy pasta *all'arrabbiata* (for those who can't decide if they want pizza or pasta). If you do want pasta, try the hearty gnocchi with beans, or the superb house spaghetti with fresh tomato and a perfectly cooked medley of fresh seafood. ⊠ *Via Niccolò Tommaseo 11/12, Chiaia* ☎ *081/7643581* ⊟ *AE, DC, MC, V* ⊙ *Closed Wed. Sept.–June and 1 wk in Sept.* ✛ *D5.*

$$$ ✕ **Coco Loco.** This place has taken the Naples dining scene by storm,
NEAPOLITAN thanks to the innovative cuisine of master chef Diego Nuzzo, a stylish
★ ambience, and a quiet location off Via Filangieri, a 10-minute walk from the Palazzo Reale. If possible, take a table in the more-spacious outdoor section in the square, and then be pampered with subtle dishes like *insalata di aragosta e gamberi alla catalana* (lobster and prawn salad garnished with citrus). ⊠ *Piazzetta Rodinò 31, Chiaia* ☎ *081/415482* ⊟ *AE, DC, MC, V* ⊙ *Closed Sun. and 3 wks in Aug. No lunch July–Sept.* ✛ *C5.*

$$$ ✕ **Dora.** Despite its location up an unpromising-looking *vicolo* (alley)
NEAPOLITAN off the Riviera di Chiaia, this small restaurant has achieved cult status for its seafood platters. It's remarkable what owner-chef Giovanni can produce in his tiny kitchen. Start with the pasta dish linguine *alla Dora,*

Caffè Gambrinus, across from the Palazzo Reale, is the most famous coffeehouse in town.

laden with local seafood and fresh tomatoes, and perhaps follow up with grilled *pezzogna* (blue-spotted bream). Like many restaurants on the seafront, Dora has its own guitarist, who is often robustly accompanied by the kitchen staff. ✉ *Via Fernando Palasciano 30, Chiaia* ☎ *081/680519* ⏚ *Reservations essential* ▭ *AE, DC, MC, V* ⊘ *Closed Sun., 2 wks in Dec., and 2 wks in mid-Aug.* ✛ *B5.*

$$ ╳ **I Re di Napoli.** With its inviting blue-and-green custom-tile interior
PIZZA and tables set along the seafront drive, this chic pizzeria is an essential hangout for Naples' gilded youth—so if you want better service and are not interested in fashion statements, go early evening and avoid peak times like weekends when Via Partenope is positively heaving. Thirty kinds of pizza plus a fine selection of salads and an ample buffet make the place a refreshing change from the more minimal *pizzerie*. The various stuffed pizzas named after kings are classics with a modern twist: try the *Boccone di Re Ferdinando*, filled with *speck* (lean cured pork), *provola* cheese, and artichokes. ✉ *Via Partenope 29/30, Santa Lucia* ☎ *081/7647775* ▭ *AE, MC, V* ✛ *D6.*

$$ ╳ **La Bersagliera.** On the picturesque Borgo Marinaro—the port at Santa
ITALIAN Lucia—in the shadow of the looming medieval Castel dell'Ovo, this spot is touristy but fun, with an irresistible combination of spaghetti and mandolins. Dalí and De Chirico, Sophia and Marcello all came here in the grand old days to enjoy uncomplicated time-tested classics, such as spaghetti with mixed seafood and eggplant *alla parmigiana*. Recent additions to the menu include octopus and swordfish carpaccio. But as any Neapolitan will tell you, simple grilled fish always tastes better when seasoned with sea air and a waterfront view. ✉ *Borgo Marinaro*

10, Santa Lucia ☎081/7646016 ⊕*www.labersagliera.it* ▤*AE, DC, MC, V* ⊗*Closed Tues. in July, Aug., and Nov.–Apr.* ⊕*D6.*

$$$ ✕**La Terrazza.** The Hotel Excelsior's Terrazza attracts A-list stars visiting
ITALIAN the area with its Pompeian-red marble floorings and brown leather fur-
nishings (all aimed at highlighting the gold cutlery, *capisce?*). A breath-
taking buffet counts as an appetizer (but would be a banquet in itself
for mere mortals), while the à la carte menu creates a fusion of Italian
regional culinary styles. Dress up, and expect to be impressed. ⊠*Hotel
Excelsior, Via Partenope 48, Santa Lucia* ☎081/7640111 ▤*AE, DC,
MC, V* ⊕*D6.*

$ ✕**L'Ebbrezza di Noè.** A small bar leads into a larger dining area decorated
ITALIAN in the style of a very elegant farmhouse. Owner Luca has an enthusiasm
★ for what he does that is quite moving—as you sip a recommended wine
you can sense that he hopes you like it as much as he does. The atten-
tion paid to the quality of the wine carries over to the food—here you
can taste delicate *carpaccio di chianina* (thinly sliced Tuscan steak), rare
cheeses such as the Sicilian *ragusano di razza modicana* and the local
caciocavallo podolico, and a daily selection of hot dishes. ⊠*Vico Vetri-
era a Chiaia 8b/9, Chiaia* ☎081/400104 ▤*AE, DC, MC, V* ⊗*Closed
Mon. No lunch* ⊕*C4.*

¢–$ ✕**Marino.** Just around the corner from the Borgo Marinaro and the
PIZZA Hotel Vesuvio, this famous pizzeria offers up its delights in a cool white-
and-blue room. Try the house specialty, the Anastasia, with cherry
tomatoes and lots of premium mozzarella. A wide sidewalk and partial
pedestrianization of Via Santa Lucia make this a pleasant outdoor venue
in summer. ⊠*Via Santa Lucia 118/120, Santa Lucia* ☎081/7640280
▤*AE, MC, V* ⊗*Closed Mon. and Aug.* ⊕*D5.*

$$$ ✕**Radici.** Combining low-key elegance with well-tried combinations
NEAPOLITAN of Mediterranean cuisine, Radici is one of a cluster of restaurants on
★ Naples' busy Riviera di Chiaia opposite the leafy gardens of the Villa
Comunale. Master of ceremonies, Agostino, steers you through the
elaborate choices on offer, where dishes invariably taste as good as they
sound. Faced with a pasta favorite, *ravioli di ricotta di bufala profumata
al limone e vongole veraci* (ravioli filled with lemon-scented buffalo
ricotta, served with clams) and the delicate *riso giallo sauté ai frutti di
mare e crostacei, verdurine di stagione* (rice garnished with sea food
and fresh greens), you could be forgiven for indecision. ⊠*Riviera di
Chiaia 268, Chiaia* ☎081/2481100 ▤*AE, DC, MC, V* ⊗*Closed Sun.
No lunch except Fri. and Sat.* ⊕*C5.*

$–$$ ✕**Trattoria dell'Oca.** The bright, clean, simple decor reflects this place's
NEAPOLITAN lighter take on occasionally heavy Neapolitan food, also echoed in the
younger crowds who pack this place on weekends. The soupy pasta *e
piselli* (with peas) is a wonderful surprise for anyone who has bad memories of pea soup, while the penne *alla scarpariello* (pasta quills with
fresh tomato, basil, and pecorino cheese) is a specialty to set the taste
buds quivering. ⊠*Via S. Teresa a Chiaia 11, Chiaia* ☎081/414865
▤*AE, DC, MC, V* ⊗*Closed 3 wks in Aug. and Sun. June–Sept. No
dinner Sun. Oct.–May* ⊕*B5.*

$–$$ ✕**Umberto.** Run by the Di Porzio family since 1916, Umberto is one of
NEAPOLITAN the city's classic restaurants. It combines the classiness of the Chiaia

neighborhood and the friendliness of other parts of the city. Try the *tubettini 'do tre dita* ("three-finger" pasta with a mixture of seafood), which bears the nickname of the original Umberto. Owner Massimo and sister Lorella (Umberto's grandchildren) are both wine experts and oversee a fantastic cellar. Umberto is also one of the few restaurants in the city that caters to those who have a gluten allergy. ⊠ *Via Alabardieri 30–31, Chiaia* ☎*081/418555* ⊕*www.umberto.it* ▤*AE, DC, MC, V* ⊘*Closed Mon. and 3 wks in Aug.* ✛*C5.*

$$
ITALIAN
✕**Vadinchenia.** Though it identifies itself as a cultural and gastronomic association, Vadinchenia has all the trimmings of a high-class restaurant. You will be steered through an innovative menu against a backdrop of refreshingly minimalist decor. Adventurous palates will enjoy such bold combinations as *paccheri alle alici e pecorino* (pasta with sardines and sheep's milk cheese), and meat eaters will delight in the *filletto al vino e sale grosso* (steak cooked in wine and rock salt). In winter, round off the meal with the *purée di castagna* made from local chestnuts. ⊠ *Via Pontano 21, Chiaia* ☎*081/660265* ⚖*Reservations essential* ▤*AE, DC, MC, V* ⊘*Closed Sun. and Aug. No lunch* ✛*B4.*

MERGELLINA AND POSILLIPO

These ritzy bay-side suburbs feature some of the most popular restaurants in Naples. Several of these spots are found at the end of waterfront cul-de-sacs, so unless you have your own wheels, taxis will be the most convenient option.

$$–$$$
NEAPOLITAN
✕**'A Fenestella.** This restaurant is picturesquely perched over a beach in Posillipo near the end of a long winding side road, and has long capitalized on its location. The landmark comes with its own legend: the story goes that in the 19th century any Juliet would promise herself simply by appearing at the window ("fenestella" in the local dialect) to the Romeo sailing in the boat below, thus inspiring the famous Neapolitan folk song. Today, the restaurant is blatantly traditional, with a comfortable decor and the usual suspects on the menu. (For more stylish food and people, and better value for money, head across the road to Da Cicciotto.) ⊠*Calata del Ponticello a Marechiaro 23, Posillipo* ☎*081/7690020* ⊕*www.afenestella.it* ▤*AE, MC, V* ⊘*Closed Wed. lunch, Sun. dinner* ✛*A5.*

$$$
NEAPOLITAN
★
✕**Da Cicciotto.** One of Naples' best-kept secrets, this chic and charming spot corrals more than a few members of the city's fashionable set— there's a fair chance you'll find a Neapolitan count or off-duty film star enjoying this jewel. A tiny stone terrace overlooks a pleasant anchorage, centered around an antique column, with seats and canopy exquisitely upholstered in blue-and-white matching-but-mixing fabrics. You can appreciate the outdoor setting at either lunch or dinner, and don't even bother with a menu—just start digging into the sublime antipasti and go with the waiter's suggestions. ■TIP➜ Cicciotto is at the end of the same long winding road that leads to the famed 'A Fenestella restaurant and shoreline, so phone for the restaurant's free shuttle service if starting out from the city-center. ⊠*Calata del Ponticello a Marechiaro 32, Posillipo* ☎*081/5751165* ⚖*Reservations essential* ▤*AE, DC, MC, V* ✛*A5.*

$$
NEAPOLITAN
✕**La Cantina di Triunfo.** Founded by Carmine Triunfo in 1890 and now run by great-grandson Antonio (who looks after the wines) and his mother

Tina (who looks after the kitchen), this place has recently made a successful bid to move upmarket. Well-prepared *cucina povera* ("poor people's food") still dominates, from the antipasto of hot peppers, salami, and cheese to the famous *vermicelli alle vongole fujute* (pasta with "escaped" clams, flavored with a dose of seawater). Dinners here are fixed price (€30), there's no written menu, and choice is limited to two dishes of the day. ✉*Riviera di Chiaia 64, Mergellina* ☎*081/668101* ✍*Reservations essential* ▭*DC, V* ☉*Closed Sun. and Aug. No lunch* ⊹*A5.*

$$ ✕**La Mescita.** Close to Cape Posillipo and a short walk from the Parco
NEAPOLITAN Virgiliano, this trattoria-cum-pizzeria is a good place for a wintertime
★ plate of fresh seafood like *spaghetti ai ricci* (spaghetti with sea urchins) or a land-based *paccheri alla Genovese* (pasta garnished with an onion and meat sauce). Rather noisy outside tables—it's near the end of the C21, C31, 140 bus routes—make this more of a winter and evening venue, with pleasing alcoves inside for greater privacy. ✉*Discesa Coroglio 88, Posillipo* ☎*081/5983375* ✍*Reservations essential* ▭*AE, DC, MC, V* ☉*Closed Mon.* ⊹*A5.*

VOMERO

Sitting on top of the hill, the wealthy residential Vomero doesn't look like the first place you'd pick to eat out in. However, if you've been on a shopping spree on Via Scarlatti or taking in the Castel Sant'Elmo, you could do worse than stick around for a bite. Absence of tourists means that there are still a few stalwart places frequented by locals.

¢–$ ✕**Acunzo.** If you see a line of hungry-looking patrons near the top
PIZZA station of the Chiaia Funicular, you'll know you are close to Pizzeria Acunzo. To avoid anxious waits, many like to get here as soon as it opens for the busier evening session at 7:30. When ordering, note that few variations on the pizzas are permitted; but then owner Michele and his wife Caterina have been running the establishment since 1964 and have a tried-and-tested product. The house specialty, pizza Acunzo, comes replete with a daunting list of ingredients, but ends up being *fenomenale.* ✉*Via Cimarosa 60–62, Vomero* ☎*081/5785362* ▭*AE, MC, V* ☉*Closed Sun.* ⊹*B3.*

$$ ✕**La Cantina di Sica.** This rustically elegant trattoria serves variants on
NEAPOLITAN traditional faves: the *tubettoni al pesce spada* (small pasta tubes with succulent pieces of swordfish), *peperoni imbottiti* (peppers stuffed with bread crumbs, olives, and capers), and the *parmigiana di melanzane* (layers of tomato, eggplant, and mozzarella baked in the oven) are all excellent. The kitchen's take on the traditional Neapolitan *pastiera* is as good as, if not better than, anybody's mamma ever made it. ✉*Via Bernini 17, Vomero* ☎*081/5567520* ▭*DC, MC, V* ☉*Closed Mon. and Aug.* ⊹*B3.*

¢ ✕**Osteria Donna Teresa.** Donna Teresa has managed to keep a piece of
NEAPOLITAN old-style Napoli alive on the otherwise modern and unspectacular Via Kerbaker. A tiny place, this restaurant is always full of clients who are treated like children (and that means being encouraged, if not actually forced, to eat everything on their plates). Patrons flock here at lunchtime, in particular for a fill of classic *pasta e fagioli* (with beans), *pasta e ceci* (with chickpeas), or solid helpings of fried anchovies or baccalà

(salt cod). ⊠*Via Kerbaker 58, Vomero* ☎*081/5567070* ⊟*No credit cards* ⊘*Closed Sun. and Aug.* ✛*B3.*

$ ✕**Trattoria Vanvitelli.** A small low-key entrance on Piazza Vanvitelli opens
ITALIAN into a labyrinth of underground cellars and a large covered courtyard surrounded by palazzos. This bustling eatery suits both a wide range of palates and budgets: pizzas and several variants of *filletto* (fillet steak) are highly recommended, while the three-course special at lunchtime for €9 is a great bargain. Portions are large, so be conservative when ordering. ⊠*Piazza Vanvitelli 9c, Vomero* ☎*081/5563015* ⊟*AE, DC, MC, V* ✛*B3.*

FOOD ON THE GO

If you get caught up in the chaotic head-spinning atmosphere of downtown Napoli, you might not even be able to sit still for an hour to eat. If so, follow the locals and indulge in some of the delicious quick snacks that Neapolitans have dreamed up to assuage hunger in a short time and at a low price. Many of Naples' specialties can be consumed while standing up—a fantastic advantage if you've got little time or money.

¢ ✕**Ambrosino.** Once they opened for business, the owners of this grocery
NEAPOLITAN store quickly realized that people were eating the produce as soon as it was handed to them so they added a counter. Now you can take your pick from the pizzas and pasta dishes, or ask the owners to make up a *panino* (sandwich) by choosing the ingredients from the huge range of excellent cheeses, vegetables, and meats on display. A uniformly excellent quality of ingredients makes up for the rather spartan surroundings. ⊠*Via Scarlatti 49, Vomero* ☎*081/3721170* ⊟*AE, DC, MC, V* ⊘*Closed Sun. in July and Aug., and 3 wks in Aug.* ✛*B3.*

¢ ✕**Friggitoria Pizzeria Giuliano.** A favorite place of students from the adja-
PIZZA cent school of architecture, Giuliano has an old-style glass cabinet in which are kept *arancini* (balls of fried rice) the size of tennis balls, and deep-fried pizzas filled with mozzarella, tomato, prosciutto, or ricotta, that can fill that yawning void in your stomach—even if you have to sit down on the steps in the square afterward to recover. ⊠*Calata Trinità Maggiore 31–33, Spaccanapoli* ☎*081/5510906* ⊟*No credit cards* ✛*E3.*

¢ ✕**Friggitoria Vomero.** Popular with kids heading home from school, this
NEAPOLITAN spot also often draws guilty-looking adults attracted by its greasy brown
★ paper bags filled with deep-fried eggplant, zucchini, zucchini flowers, *zeppole* dough balls, or potato croquets—the Neapolitan versions of Proust's madeleines. Forget all that stuff about the Mediterranean diet being so healthy and indulge in some oil-drenched bliss. ⊠*Via Cimarosa 44, Vomero* ☎*081/5783130* ⊟*No credit cards* ⊘*Closed Sun. and Aug.* ✛*B3.*

¢ ✕**La Focaccia.** While the flat, pan-cooked focaccia is enough to make
ITALIAN pizza fundamentalists wince (coming as it does from Rome), this place makes mouthwatering slices of crunchy-bottomed snacks with a variety of toppings. Skip the predictable tomato variations and go for the delicious potato-and-rosemary focaccia with melted provola (smoked mozzarella). Washed down with a beer, this makes for a great speedy

lunch or late-night snack. ⊠ *Vico Belledonne a Chaia 31, Chiaia* ☎*081/412277* ⊟*No credit cards* ✛*C5.*

¢ ✕**L.u.i.s.e.** Elbow your way through the crowds at lunchtime, point NEAPOLITAN to what you want in the tempting glass counter, and pay for it at the cash desk. If you're lucky you'll get a seat, but if not you can still enjoy the usual *frittura* (fried dough balls and potato croquets stuffed with mozzarella), the tangy cheese pies (*sfoglino al formaggio*), the pizza *scarola* (an escarole pie with black olives), or slices of omelets stuffed with spinach, peppers, or onions. The immaculately liveried waiters aren't polite, but they are quick. ⊠ *Via Toledo 266–269, Toledo* ☎*081/415367* ⊟*No credit cards* ✛*D4.*

¢ ✕**Vaco 'e Press.** Stoke up here before or after your visit to the Museo NEAPOLITAN Archeologico, a five-minute walk away. This busy eatery close to the metro station in Piazza Dante has a bewildering variety of hot meals, pizzas, vegetable pies and rolls, and even has seating at the back. As usual in this type of establishment, pay at the *cassa* before you eat. ⊠*Piazza Dante 87, Spaccanapoli* ☎*081/5499424* ⊟*No credit cards* ✛*D2.*

CAFÉS AND COFFEE

Naples is ground zero for coffee lovers. Espresso was invented here and is still considered by the Neapolitans to be an essential and priceless part of their cultural patrimony (the word *espresso*, by the way, should probably be understood here in its meaning "pressed out," rather than the more common interpretation of "quick"). For many cognoscenti, Naples has the best coffee in the world. Almost any bar you walk into, no matter how dingy or how close to the train station, is likely to serve up an espresso that would make any Malibu hot spot wilt in envy.

Even Italian bars (meaning coffee bars) are generally tied to, as English pubs once were with brewers, a coffee roaster–distributor. The sponsoring brand is indicated with a sign on the outside, so you can choose your bar by looking for the sign of your favorite brand. Brands tend to be highly regional; the most widely advertised Neapolitan brand is Kimbo, but Moreno, Salimbene, and Tico are considered far superior by the cognoscenti. Some small, family-run cafés still roast their own.

You won't find any double low-fat mochas with extra vanilla here, though there are certain permitted variations: *corretto*, with a shot of grappa or the local moonshine thrown in; *al vetro*, in a glass; *macchiato*, "stained" with a burst of steamed milk; and, of course, cappuccino. On the whole, coffee is a Neapolitan sacred ritual with precise rules. Cappuccino, for instance, is essentially a breakfast beverage, accepted in the afternoon with a pastry but looked strangely at after a meal (they claim it's bad for the liver). Many Italians like to order a glass of water (*bicchiere d'acqua*) with their coffee as a chaser. As for flavored coffees, Neapolitans, like all Italians, stubbornly believe that you only add flavorings to coffee to hide imperfections in the original grind. Coffee is perhaps the one feature of life in which Neapolitans don't gild the lily. Why fix what works?

Gran Caffè Aragonese (⊠*Piazza San Domenico Maggiore 5, Spaccanapoli* ☎*081/5528740*) offers a fine coffee in the heart of historic

Spaccanapoli: sit out on the Piazza San Domenico or inside in the elegant tearoom with its marble-top tables. In the heart of the congested city center, the small **Caffè del Professore** (✉ *Piazza Trieste e Trento 46, Piazza Municipio* ☎ *081/403041*) offers a superb espresso, as well as a house specialty, the *caffè nocciolato*, which is sweetened with a coffee-and-walnut syrup.

The most famous coffeehouse in town is the **Caffè Gambrinus** (✉ *Via Chiaia 1/2, Chiaia* ☎ *081/417582*), catercorner to the Palazzo Reale across the Piazza Trieste e Trento. Founded in 1850, this 19th-century jewel functioned as a brilliant intellectual salon in its heyday but has unfortunately fallen into a Sunset Boulevard–type existence, relying on past glamour, at the mercy of tourists and their pitiless cameras, and with often indifferent service. However, the opening and renovation of some of its long-closed inside rooms, replete with amazing mirrored walls and gilded ceilings, still makes it an essential stop for any visitor to the city. You may find it more worthwhile to continue along the Via Chiaia shopping street with its fashionable clothes shops as far as **La Torteria** (✉ *Via Filangieri 75, Chiaia* ☎ *081/405221*) not only for its excellent coffee but also for its selection of beautiful-looking cakes—concoctions of cream, chocolate, and fruit that look like Abstract Expressionist paintings with their swirls of color. A fave with Via Chiaia shoppers is **Bar Guida** (✉ *Via Dei Mille 46, Chiaia* ☎ *081/426570*), which offers you not only the luxury of being able to sit down, but also has a decent range of savory light meals. **La Caffetteria** (✉ *Piazza dei Martiri 30, Chiaia* ☎ *081/7644243*) is a classic address in the chic Chiaia district, and it has a second space in Vomero. Both addresses sell their famous coffee-flavored chocolates in the shape of tiny coffeepots. The **Gran Bar Riviera** (✉ *Riviera di Chiaia 183, Chiaia* ☎ *081/665026*) has good profiteroles and fresh tiramisu, and is an excellent late-night stopover for clubbers—a cappuccino and cornetto in the small hours are classic post-dancing pick-me-ups. If you're near the Borgo Marinaro waterfront, **Megaride** (✉ *Via Borgo Marinaro 1, Santa Lucia* ☎ *081/7645300*), on the port under the shadow of the Castel dell'Ovo, provides a romantic outdoor setting for a coffee or aperitif.

Piazza Bellini, in the Spaccanapoli area, also contains a gaggle of good and hip cafés, and almost any of the pastry shops listed below will have excellent coffee.

PASTRY AND GELATO SHOPS

On the whole, Neapolitan pastry tends to suffer from the excesses that mark most southern Italian desserts: Falstaffian enthusiasm rather than precision in technique, ricotta clogging up everything, sentimental glops of glaze, and effusive dousings of perfumed syrups (one local specialty, babà al rhum, often succumbs to this last vice). But the Neapolitan tradition of pastry is an old and venerable one, and the most classic local invention in matters of *pasticceria* (pastry making), the *sfogliatella*, is a true baroque masterpiece, with puff pastry cut on a bias and wrapped around a nugget of cinnamon-sugar ricotta to form a simple but intricate shell. These are best eaten hot, and they are easy to find in Naples this

Sfogliatelle are a classic Neapolitan pastry.

way. The classic address for sfogliatelle is **Pintauro** (✉ *Via Toledo 275, Toledo* ☎*081/417339*). The excellent **La Sfogliatella Mary** (✉*Galleria Umberto 66, Toledo* ☎*081/402218*), just at the Via Toledo entrance to the Galleria Umberto, offers a broader array of pastries than the name suggests. For a hot-out-of-the-oven morsel as soon as you get off the train, **Attanasio** (✉*Vico Ferrovia 2, Piazza Garibaldi* ☎*081/285675*), hidden away off Piazza Garibaldi, is justifiably famous.

Scaturchio (✉*Piazza San Domenico Maggiore 19, Spaccanapoli* ☎*081/5516944*) is the essential Neapolitan pastry shop. Although the coffee is top-of-the-line and the ice cream and pastries quite good—including the specialty, the *ministeriale,* a pert chocolate cake whipped with rum-cream filling—it's the atmosphere that counts here (though not the luxe, it's a rather unprepossessing sort of place). In the heart of Spaccanapoli, it's where nuns, punks, businesspeople, and housewives commune on the good things they all have in common. If you're look-ing for an alternative to coffee, try the city's only hot chocolate bar: **Chocolat** (✉*Via San Pietro a Maiella 8, Spaccanapoli* ☎*081/299840*) offers 35 different types of hot chocolate as well as milk shakes and ice cream in the summer months.

The largest number of good pastry shops are in the upscale Chi-aia neighborhood. **Moccia** (✉*Via San Pasquale a Chiaia 21, Chiaia* ☎*081/411348*) is often said to be the finest pasticceria in the city, and it has great babas (decorated, should you wish, with whipped cream and wild strawberries) and an out-of-this-world pound cake injected with just the right dose of intense lemon curd. Connoisseurs will say the most refined pastry in town can be found at **Gran Caffè Cimmino**

(✉ *Via G. Filangieri 12/13, Chiaia* ☎*081/418303*). Most of the city's many lawyers congregate here, to celebrate or commiserate with crisp, light cannoli; airy lemon eclairs; *choux* paste in the form of a mushroom laced with chocolate whipped cream; and delightful wild-strawberry tartlets.

All these addresses will have exemplary ice cream as well, but you may prefer a more informal setting. **Scimmia** (✉*Piazza Carità 4, Toledo*), in the center of town, scoops out a luscious variety of ice-cream flavors. Just off Via Gramsci, a five-minute walk west of the Villa Comunale and the American Consulate, is the highly rated gelateria **Remy** (✉*Via F. Galiani 29/A, Mergellina* ☎*081/667304*).

> ## WORD OF MOUTH
>
> "A *must* is sfogliatelle. I was overcome with joy at Sfogliatella Mary. The other classic option is Scaturchio, the most famous cafe in Naples and a reputed master when it comes to sfogliatelle. The trick in eating this multilayered pastry is to get it when it's hot. You will noticed signs touting 'caldo' at bakeries throughout the area…this is when you want to strike. Just prepare yourself! And do not forget the amazing little fried treats sold street-side—for about 1 euro you can get a paper cone of friend vegetables, seafood, etc etc." —ekscrunchy

If you're going to abandon your low-cholesterol diet, this is definitely the place to do it, preferably with a selection of their *semi-freddi* (a cross between ice cream and mousse).

Chocolate lovers will be relieved to know that **Gay Odin** (✉ *Via Toledo 214, Toledo* ☎*081/400063* ⊕*www.gay-odin.it*), Naples' most famous *cioccolateria,* has seven stores around town, all recognizable by their inviting dark-wood art nouveau decor; try the signature chocolate forest cake (*foresta*) or their unusual "naked" chocolates (*nudi*), a suave mixture of chestnuts and walnuts, some with a whole coffee bean wrapped in the center. **Cioccolateria Perzechella** (✉ *Vico Pallonetto a S. Chiara 36, Spaccanapoli* ☎*081/5510025*) looks set to challenge Gay Odin's supremacy in the chocolate world. How can it not, since owners Pina and Giulia have rather shamelessly devised the *Tre Re* ("three kings")—three hazelnuts stuck together with chocolate in honor of King Ferdinand II, revolutionary Masaniello, and Naples' unofficial saint, the soccer player Diego Maradona. They just may tip the scales with their *Torna a Surriento*—Sorrento orange peel dipped in dark chocolate.

A small alleyway leading off the side of the Gesù Nuovo toward Via Toledo hides a little-known jewel that is worth the detour! **Gallucci** (✉ *Via Cisterna dell'Olio 6, Spaccanapoli* ☎*081/5513148*), founded in 1890, specializes in fruit-filled chocolates (the cherry and grape are memorable) and also produces a delightfully original local cult item, chestnuts filled with marsala. It also produces the most fantastically packaged Easter eggs, all with huge silver or gold bows, that you are ever likely to see.

WHERE TO STAY

Updated by
Chris Rose

For a long time, staying in Naples meant gritting your teeth and praying your credit card could stand the cost of one of the impressive seafront landmarks—or risking one of the gloomy little hostels crowded around the Piazza Garibaldi railway station. Fortunately, the options have improved over recent years, with the addition of many new places to stay, from top-end hideaways to simple, family-run B&Bs and *pensioni*. Usually small and intimate, and often set in historic *palazzi*, these sometimes have a quaint appeal that fortunately does not preclude modern plumbing. But whether you're in a five-star hotel or a more modest establishment, you may enjoy one of the greatest pleasures of all: a room with a view. In this case it's not *any* view, but the lay-down-and-die panorama of the Bay of Naples and Vesuvius, so be sure to ask for a bay-side room if your hotel can provide one—though be warned that *"camere panoramiche"* often cost more than regular rooms.

Since Naples is not known for peace and quiet, it's good news that it features a bevy of hotels that deliver exactly that—most accommodations are cool and tranquil sanctums, with the emphasis on cool. As one of Europe's hottest and busiest cities, its hotels feature some of the strongest air-conditioning around (when making reservations, be sure to inquire if there is a supplement for air-conditioning). Bear in mind that high seasons in Naples are really the "shoulder seasons" elsewhere—April to June and September to October—so be sure to book well in advance if visiting then. Assume all hotels reviewed here have air-conditioning, telephones, TV, and private bath, unless otherwise noted.

WHAT IT COSTS IN EUROS				
¢	$	$$	$$$	$$$$
FOR TWO PEOPLE	under €75	€75–€125	€125–€200	€200–€300	over €300

Prices are for two people in a standard double room in high season including tax and service.

LUNGOMARE AND SANTA LUCIA

This prominent stretch of seacoast, with an unsurpassed view of the Bay of Naples, naturally has the greatest concentration of luxury hotels in the city, although more reasonable lodging is available on the side streets.

$ ★   **B&B Chiatamone.** The Chiatamone is a budget alternative to its showy big brothers, nestled in on the first floor of an elegant 19th-century palazzo on the long, narrow street that runs immediately behind the seafront. Still, befitting the elegant neighborhood, it stands above a regular B&B with its refined rooms, each one named after a classic Neapolitan song. Several are minisuites, with spacious living areas and beds tucked up away on a mezzanine floor. Most of the Chiatamone's guests are Italians—which could be a pro or con, depending on what you're looking for. **Pros:** well-located both for the seafront and the city center. **Cons:** rooms are dark, with no sea view. ⊠ *Via Chiatamone 6, Chiaia* ☎ *081/0608129* ⊕ *www.hotelchiatamone.it* ⇱ *6 rooms* ⚙ *In-*

room: *Kitchen (some). In-hotel: Bar, public Internet* $\equiv$*AE, DC, MC, V* ⧖*BP* ⊹*D6.*

$$ ⚑ **Chiaia Hotel de Charme.** No views, but there's plenty of atmosphere
★ in these converted first-floor apartments that occupy a spruce 18th-century palazzo, part of which includes a converted historic brothel. Above the fireplace in the cozy entrance hall, the distinguished-looking chap with the moustache in the painting is the Marchese Nicola Le Caldano Sasso III, original owner of the building, whose granddaughter Mimi now runs the place. Antiques, many of them original to the Marquis's home, give a personal touch to the elegant guest rooms (most have whirlpool baths). The location is tops, a two-minute walk from Piazza Plebiscito and the Royal Palace and a stagger from the liveliest nightlife in town in the backstreets around Piazza dei Martiri. **Pros:** central location on bustling; pedestrians-only street. **Cons:** small rooms get hot in summer (a/c notwithstanding); on second floor of historic palazzo—elevator is small and the stairs are steep. ⊠*Via Chiaia 216* ☎*081/415555* ⊕*www.hotelchiaia.it* ⟿*27 rooms* ⚙*In-room: Safe, Internet. In-hotel: Bar* $\equiv$*AE, DC, MC, V* ⧖*BP* ⊹*D4.*

$$$$ ⚑ **Excelsior.** A swarm of maharajahs, emperors, and Hollywood legends has stayed at this hotel, a grand-tradition outpost since 1909. The exterior, with the hotel's name magnificently picked out in Pompeian red, is awash in elegant detail, while the interior is a symphony of soaring columns, gilded French doors, and Venetian chandeliers. Today the hotel caters to corporate chiefs, its ballrooms host company meetings, and the breakfast is delicious. Discreet but attentive service gives the hotel a personal touch—if you even want to hire a yacht, the concierge can oblige. After a day of sightseeing, repair to the peaceful piano bar, where the barman mixes the driest martini in town—ask for a Hemingway. The restaurant La Terrazza, dressed up with antique red accents and vermeil tableware, serves first-rate food, and the terrace with sweeping views of the bay makes summer dining out a memorable event. **Pros:** great views from the breakfast room and the rooftop terrace; spacious rooms. **Cons:** the busy road outside is a challenge to cross, and the traffic noise may keep you up; decor feels a little dated. ⊠*Via Partenope 48, Santa Lucia* ☎*081/7640111* ⊕*www.excelsior.it* ⟿*109 rooms, 12 suites* ⚙*In-hotel: 2 restaurants, bar, gym, public Internet, parking (fee)* $\equiv$*AE, DC, MC, V* ⧖*BP* ⊹*D6.*

$$$–$$$$ ⚑ **Grand Hotel Vesuvio.** You'd never guess from the modern exterior that
Fodor'sChoice this is the oldest of Naples' great seafront hotels—the place where Enrico
★ Caruso died, Oscar Wilde escaped with lover Lord Alfred Douglas, and Bill Clinton charmed the waitresses. Fortunately, the spacious, soothing interior compensates for what's lacking on the outside. Guest rooms are done in luxurious, traditional style with antique accents, vibrantly colored walls, and gleaming bathrooms. The best ones overlook the bay. You can pamper yourself at the spa, where there are myriad special services (though they come at a price). The famous Caruso restaurant sits atop the hotel, affording wonderful views. **Pros:** luxurious atmosphere; historic setting; location directly opposite Borgo Marinaro. **Cons:** extra charge for health club and Internet use; reception staff can be snooty; not all rooms have great views. ⊠*Via Partenope 45, Santa Lucia*

Fodor'sChoice ★

Hotel Palazzo Decumani

Grand Hotel Vesuvio   Costantinopoli 104

☏*081/7640044* ⊕*www.vesuvio.it* ⇌*146 rooms, 17 suites* ⌂*In-room:
Safe, refrigerator, Internet. In-hotel: Restaurant, bar, gym, spa, Internet
terminal, parking (paid)* ▭*AE, DC, MC, V* ⍣*BP* ✛*D6.*

$$$$
★ 🏨**Hotel Santa Lucia.** Neopolitan enchantment can be yours if you stay
here, for right outside your window will be the port immortalized in the
song "Santa Lucia," bobbing with hundreds of boats, lined with seafood restaurants, and backed by the medieval Castel dell'Ovo. Even if
your room doesn't have this bay-side view, you're likely to be impressed
by the hotel's luxurious, quietly understated polish. The lobby is aglow
with antiques, chandeliers, and full-length portraits of Neapolitan aristocrats. The comfortable guest rooms are traditional, if somewhat bland
(and some are small for the price), but bathrooms are paved in terra-
cotta, and some are equipped with whirlpool bath. Just off the lobby,
the restaurant Megaris is a good spot for luxe hotel dining. **Pros:** great
views; close to the main port, so convenient for trips to the islands
and along the coast. **Cons:** rooms disappointingly modern and boxy;
the entrance is on the busy Via Partenope. ⊠*Via Partenope 46, Santa
Lucia* ☏*081/7640666* ⊕*www.santalucia.it* ⇌*107 rooms* ⌂*In-hotel:
Restaurant, bar, public Internet* ▭*AE, DC, MC, V* ⍣*BP* ✛*D6.*

$$–$$$
★ 🏨**Parteno.** Undoubtedly proud of their premier address—"No. 1" on
Naples's main waterfront street—welcoming owners Alex Ponzi and
mother Adele have installed an exclusive and elegant bed-and-breakfast
near the Villa Comunale, five minutes from Castel dell'Ovo and 15
from the hydrofoils to the bay islands. The surprisingly quiet rooms
are tastefully decorated with period etchings and gouache views of
Naples. One looks onto the bay; the others face a side street, fortunately
removed from the swirling traffic on the bay-side avenue. Breakfast
(served in your bedroom if you wish) is the real treat here—one of a
tempting range of specialty Neapolitan pastries will accompany your
caffè. **Pros:** located in the five-star neighborhood, without the five-star
price; friendly, helpful staff. **Cons:** though helpful, the staff's English
is a bit shaky; except for the "Azalea" room, rooms are neither large
nor light. ⊠*Via Partenope 1, Santa Lucia* ☏*081/2452095* ⊕*www.
parteno.it* ⇌*6 rooms* ⌂*In-hotel: Room service, Wi-Fi* ▭*AE, DC,
MC, V* ⍣*BP* ✛*C5.*

$$–$$$
Fodor'sChoice
★ 🏨**Riviera 281.** An apartment in the 18th-century Palazzo San Teodoro,
perfectly located on the elegant Riviere di Chiaia immediately across
the road from the Villa Comunale park, Riviera 281 is the probably
the most refined of the B&B places that have sprung up across the city.
It feels like a home away from home, with even a small kitchen should
you want to try your hand at Neapolitan cooking. Furnishings resemble
what you see in the neighborhood's swish interior-design shops—the
feeling is cool and modern, but owner Elena makes sure there's an old-
fashioned Neapolitan welcome. **Pros:** a sea view for a comparatively
low price. **Cons:** only three rooms, so you need to book well in advance.
⊠*Riviera di Chiaia 281, Chiaia* ☏*081/7641427* ⊕*www.riviera281.it*
⇌*3 rooms* ⌂*In-hotel: Internet* ▭*DC, MC, V* ⍣*BP* ✛*C5.*

PIAZZA GARIBALDI TO LA SANITÀ

Hardly the nicest or most interesting part of town to stay in, the Piazza Garibaldi area is noisy and edgy. It's handy if you have to get an early train in the morning, but otherwise you're better off putting some distance between you and the central station.

$–$$ ☂ **Del Real Orto Botanico.** Located near Naples' noted botanical gardens, this 18th-century building has been turned into a spacious hotel, an eight-minute taxi ride from the airport and a short bus ride from the bustling center of town. Owner Michele Catuogno's attention to detail is what makes the hotel stand out. Antiques—for sale, no less—adorn the public rooms; 200 guidebooks and art catalogs are available to help aclimate you to this less-frequented historic area of Naples; and service is excellent. A courtesy car will take you to the airport or train station during the day. Front rooms are noisy if you leave the balcony window open, but they face the gorgeous tropical gardens of the Orto Botanico; a better bet may be the back, particularly on summer nights. All rooms are spacious, decorated in stylish, soothing greens and beiges, but the real stunner is the fabulous roof-terrace bar–restaurant—fresh grilled fish a specialty—with views over the gardens and the Sanità right up to Capodimonte. **Pros:** near the Archaeological Museum; some rooms overlook the botanical gardens. **Cons:** pretty far from other attractions; noisy location. ⊠ *Via Foria 192, Carlo III* ☎ *081/4421528* ⊕ *www.hotelrealortobotanico.it* ⚲ *36 rooms* ⚠ *In-hotel: Restaurant, bar* ⊟ *AE, DC, MC, V* ⦿*BP* ⊕*F1.*

$$ ☂ **Suite Esedra.** Squashed into a tiny piazza off frantic Corso Umberto—one of the main roads leading away from Piazza Garibaldi—this is a hotel that's convenient to transportation as well as just a few blocks from the heart of the historic neighborhood of Spaccanapoli. The decor, based on an astrological theme, takes itself lightly enough to work. Each guest room expresses a different planet or sign of the zodiac, all in the coolest faux-Memphis style, with plenty of sleek woods and Philippe Starck–esque touches. The hotel is in a densely packed district (reach out your window and you can practically touch the building across the way), and guest rooms on the small side, except for two suites that have their own private terrace with whirlpool. Still, the lobby, library, and dining room are all suavely decorated, and in a nice touch, at breakfast guests sit round one large table, rather like a house party. **Pros:** well priced for what it offers. **Cons:** small rooms; Corso Umberto is chaotic and not particularly attractive. ⊠ *Via A. Cantani 12, Piazza Garibaldi* ☎*081/5537087* ⊕*www.esedra.hotelsinnapoli.com* ⚲*17 rooms* ⚠*In-hotel: Restaurant, bar, gym* ⊟ *AE, MC, V* ⦿*BP* ⊕*G2.*

SPACCANAPOLI AND PIAZZA MUNICIPIO

Spaccanapoli is Naples' most picturesque quarter, so if you're looking for classic Neapolitan atmosphere, this is the place to roost. The flip side of the coin is the nearby area around Piazza Municipio; it's the bustling heart of the modern city, and it has a collection of upscale, large-capacity business hotels, along with some delightful finds housed in historic buildings.

$$ ☂ **Caravaggio.** In a 17th-century palazzo on a tiny square behind the Duomo, this place takes its name from the painter of the amazing *Sette*

2

Opere della Misericordia altarpiece, which can be seen in the chapel opposite. Spaccanapoli's first "modernist" hotel, it's atmospherically furnished with blocks of volcanic stone in the entrance hall, while the guest rooms (some of which include a Jacuzzi) are all refreshingly light and airy. **Pros:** great location for sight-seeing. **Cons:** in an old building with small rooms and unreliable climate control; Piazza Sforza is as dark and creepy now as it was in Caravaggio's day. ⊠*Piazza Riario Sforza 157, Spaccanapoli* ☎*081/2110066* ⊕*www.caravaggiohotel. it* ⟲*11 rooms* ⌂*In-hotel: Bar, public Internet* ▤*AE, DC, MC, V* ¹⊙¹*BP* ⊕*F2.*

$$$ ⊞**Constantinopoli 104.** An oasis of what Italians call *stile liberty* (art
Fodor'sChoice deco style), with impressive colored glass fittings, this calm and elegant
★ hotel sits in the bustling *centro storico* near the Museo Archeologico Nazionale. Each room is individually decorated. Ask for a room with a balcony in the warmer months and enjoy your breakfast alfresco, or opt for one of the garden rooms that open onto the small swimming pool. **Pros:** perfectly situated for the centro storico; swimming pool (a rarity in Neapolitan hotels). **Cons:** difficult to find from street; located on second floor with access by steep steps or small elevator. ⊠*Via Costantinopoli 104, Spaccanapoli* ☎*081/5571035* ⊕*www. costantinopoli104.com* ⟲*19 rooms* ⌂*In-room: Safe, refrigerator, Internet. In-hotel: Bar, pool, laundry service, parking (paid)* ▤*AE, DC, MC, V* ¹⊙¹*BP* ⊕*E2.*

$$$ ⊞**Grand Hotel Oriente.** This is an excellent businessperson's hotel with
★ all the conveniences and a great location. A three-minute walk away is the Via Toledo, leading down to Piazza Plebiscito and the Royal Palace. Despite the severe marble facade, the interior is welcoming: after a long day it's a boon to return here and find comfortable, soundproof guest rooms and friendly, professional staff. **Pros:** well located for Via Toledo shops and city center; refreshingly modern. **Cons:** large building site for multiyear metro project right outside the front door; parking expensive. ⊠*Via Diaz 44, Toledo* ☎*081/5512133* ⊕*www.grandhoteloriente.it* ⟲*131 rooms* ⌂*In-room: Safe (some). In-hotel: Restaurant, bar, Internet terminal, parking (paid)* ▤*AE, DC, MC, V* ¹⊙¹*BP* ⊕*E3.*

$$–$$$ ⊞**Hotel Palazzo Decumani.** Opened in 2008, the Decumani is a welcome
Fodor'sChoice addition to the small list of higher-end hotels in Spaccanapoli. The
★ design here is pleasingly contemporary—no heavy, ornate furnishings, but instead an emphasis on light and space (both in short supply in old Naples). The services and professional approach are on a par with the grander hotels on the seafront or the Corso Vittorio Emanuele. The Decumani is a great choice for comfortable lodgings in the heart of classic Napoli. **Pros:** well-located for both transportation links and sightseeing; large rooms and bathrooms; soundproofed windows. **Cons:** the location on a side street can be hard to find—you'll need a map to come and go on foot. ⊠*Piazzetta Fortunato Giustizio 8, Spaccanapoli* ☎*081/4201379* ⊕*www.palazzodecumani.com* ⟲*28 rooms* ⌂*In-room: Wi-fi. In-hotel: Restaurant, bar* ▤*DC, MC, V* ¹⊙¹*BP* ⊕*F2.*

$$ ⊞**Il Convento.** In a 17th-century palazzo tucked away in the Quartieri
★ Spagnoli, Il Convento is conveniently close to Via Toledo. Rooms are small but elegant, with original architectural features such as arched or

beamed ceilings. They are decorated in simple, modern Mediterranean style. Two junior suites have private roof gardens. **Pros:** close to cafés and shops; free Internet access. **Cons:** church bells may wake you in the morning; on a busy street; tiny lobby. ⊠ *Via Speranzella 137/A, Toledo* ☎*081/403977* ⊕*www.hotelilconvento.com* ⚲*12 rooms, 2 suites* △*In-room: Refrigerator. In-hotel: Bar, Internet terminal* ⊟*AE, MC, V* ⊺⊙⎮*BP* ✛*D4.*

$$–$$$ ⬚**Mediterraneo.** This large, modern, efficient business hotel that manages to be comfortable and pleasant, and is within walking distance of both the Teatro San Carlo and Spaccanapoli. The entire lobby area has an elegant feel, dressed in nouveau Mediterranean colors, and the rooms are similarly attractive. A nice plus here is the beautiful roof garden. **Pros:** convient to the port; attractive rooftop breakfast terrace. **Cons:** restaurant food is mediocre. ⊠ *Via Nuova Ponte di Tappia 25, Toledo* ☎*081/7970001* ⊕*www.mediterraneonapoli.com* ⚲*256 rooms* △*In-room: Internet. In-hotel: Restaurant, bar* ⊟*DC, MC, V* ⊺⊙⎮*BP* ✛*E4.*

$$ ⬚**Mercure Napoli Angioino.** In the heart of town, right off Piazza Municipio in the shadows of the famed Castel Nuovo, and close to the Teatro San Carlo, this popular hotel with a sober yet luminous lobby and quiet, tastefully appointed guest rooms. It's a good choice if you're taking a boat from the nearby Molo Beverello. **Pros:** good location near the port and sights. **Cons:** on a busy road; less character and charm than many Naples hotels. ⊠ *Via De Pretis 123, Toledo* ☎*081/5529500* ⊕*www. mercure.com* ⚲*85 rooms* △*In-hotel: Restaurant* ⊟*AE, DC, MC, V* ⊺⊙⎮*BP* ✛*E4.*

$–$$ ⬚**Neapolis.** On a narrow alley off the humming Via Tribunali close to Piazza Bellini, this relatively new hotel looks out over the 13th-century Pietrasanta bell tower. A mix of modern and traditional style furnishings, with a lovely warm terra-cotta floor and data ports in every room, make this a good bet if you want to stay in the Spacca, Naples' fascinating medieval center. **Pros:** great location in the heart of the *centro storico*. **Cons:** difficult to find; a closed window won't always keep out the roar of passing scooters. ⊠ *Via Francesco Del Giudice 13, Spaccanapoli* ☎*081/4420815* ⬚*081/4420819* ⊕*www.hotelneapolis.com* ⚲*18 rooms* △*In-room: Internet. In-hotel: Bar* ⊟*AE, DC, MC, V* ⊺⊙⎮*BP* ✛*E2.*

$$ ⬚**Palazzo Turchini.** Directly behind the impressive *fontana di Nettuno,*
★ just a few minutes' walk from the Castel Nuovo, Palazzo Turchini is one of the more-attractive smaller hotels in the city center. Its location is an 18th-century building with older roots, and the elegant design mixes historical styles, as seen in the combination of marble floors and wooden fittings throughout the hotel. Rooms are small but surprisingly quiet despite being on a busy street, and many offer views over the roofs and domes of the old town. **Pros:** good location for centro storico and the port, more intimate than neighboring business hotels. **Cons:** buffet breakfast not impressive, Via Medina can get very busy. ⊠ *Via Medina 21, Toledo* ☎*081/5510606* ⊕*www.palazzoturchini.it* ⚲*27 rooms* △*In-room: Safe, Internet. In-hotel: Bar, public Internet terminal* ⊟*AE, DC, MC, V* ⊺⊙⎮*BP* ✛*E4.*

2

$$ ⊞**Toledo.** A centuries-old palazzo has been tastefully transformed into this boutique hotel, a two-minute walk up from Via Toledo, near Spaccanapoli and the Royal Palace. Rooms are furnished in a pleasing rustic style, while the leafy rooftop terrace provides a quintessentially Neapolitan backdrop for your breakfast. **Pros:** convenient location for Via Toledo shopping. Great views from the roof garden. **Cons:** rooms are small; by foot, it's a steep walk up Via Montecalvario. ✉ *Via Montecalvario 15, Toledo,* 📠081/406800 ⊕*www.hoteltoledo.com* ↗18 rooms ⌂*In-hotel: Bar, public Internet* ☰*AE, DC, MC, V* ⦿*BP* ⊹*D3.*

CHIAIA, VOMERO, AND POSILLIPO

Chiaia is the ritziest residential neighborhood of Naples, studded with 19th-century mansions and an elegant shopping district bordering the Villa Comunale gardens by the water. Above Chiaia rises the Vomero hill, offering great vistas of the bay. The bay-side atmosphere continues at Mergellina, a transportation hub set at the far western end of the Riviera di Chiaia, and beyond at the suburban coastal district of Posillipo.

$ ⊞**Ausonia.** The spic-and-span rooms of this hotel are decorated in a nautical motif, giving it a homey feel. In the courtyard of a building on the waterfront at Mergellina, this is quite handy if you're taking a boat from the Mergellina pier. On the other hand, perhaps this is why some guests have said they suffer from cabin fever after staying here a few nights—the constant presence of boats and windows like portholes may have you thinking you're on board a ship **Pros:** one of the few hotels in the Mergellina area; away from the hubbub of the center and convenient to the port. **Cons:** located inside a larger palazzo—make sure you have the address written down. ✉*Via Caracciolo 11, Mergellina,* ☎081/682278 ⊕*www.hotelausonianapoli.com* ↗20 rooms ⌂*In-hotel: public Internet* ☰*AE, MC, V* ⦿*BP* ⊹*A5.*

$ ⊞ **Cappella Vecchia 11.** Glamorously located, one of the city's outstanding budget options lies just a stone's throw from the Platinum Card ★ square of Naples, Piazza dei Martiri, now colonized by the likes of Cartier, Ferragamo, and Versace. Protected from the city hubbub by being set on a quiet, cobblestoned street (and in a building with an even quieter courtyard), this small B & B has six amply-sized guest rooms decorated in a breezily modern way: Ikea colors, contemporary furnishings, and paintings by local mod artists. Warming it all up are the smiles and impeccably attentive charms of owner Stefano Raja, who likes to joke "I don't speak Italian" and loves to make foreigners feel at home in Naples. **Pros:** fabulous location; friendly staff. **Cons:** lack of room phones; prefers cash payment. ✉*Vicolo Santa Maria a Capella Vecchia 11, Chiaia,* ☎081/2405117 ⊕*www.cappellavecchia11.it* ↗6 rooms ⌂ *In-room: no telephone. In-hotel: public Wi-Fi* ☰*AE, MC, V* ⦿*BP* ⊹*C5.*

$$$–$$$$ ⊞**Grand Hotel Parker's.** This landmark hotel, which first opened its doors in 1870, continues to serve up a supremely elegant dose of old-style atmosphere and surprisingly personal service. It welcomes visiting VIPs, ranging from rock stars to Russian leaders, who probably enjoy the hotel decor, an homage to the neoclassical style, brought to Naples by Napoléon and his general Joachim Murat. Gilt-trimmed Empire bureaus, shimmering chandeliers, fluted pilasters, and ornate ceilings

all glitter. Set midway up the Vomero hill, and a bit of a walk from its funicular stops, the hotel's perch offers fine views of the bay and distant Capri. Drink it all in from the superb rooftop-garden restaurant, which proffers regional specialties. **Pros:** excellent restaurant; fabulous views. **Cons:** a good walk or taxi ride from city center and seafront; not quite as grand as it once was. ⊠ *Corso Vittorio Emanuele 135, Vomero* ☎*081/7612474* ⊕*www.grandhotelparkers.com* ⤢*83 rooms* △*In-room: Safe. In-hotel: Restaurant, bar, parking (paid)* ▭*AE, DC, MC, V* |○|*BP* ⊹*C4.*

¢   🏨 **La Controra.** You get a unique experience here, at what is probably the cheapest place to stay in the city. Originally a monastery, but recently turned into what the owners modestly describe as a "backpackers' hostel," the Controra provides its own entertainment: it hosts film showings, art exhibitions, alternative conferences, and themed parties. There are only a few private rooms, but if you have a spirit of adventure and like meeting others, the kitsch retro-designed dorms here offer the perfect place to do so. **Pros:** the energetic, arty, funky vibe; international clientele. **Cons:** don't expect the facilities of a luxury hotel; location is slightly odd, higher up than the old town but lower than the Vomero; hidden behind a crumbling church. ⊠ *Piazzetta Trinità alla Cesarea 231, Vomero* ☎*081/5494014* ⊕*www.lacontrora.com* ⤢*3 rooms with shared bath, 4 dorms* △*In-room: Wi-fi, no TV, no a/c* ▭*DC, MC, V* |○|*BP* ⊹*C2.*

$$ 🏨 **Palazzo Alabardieri.** Just off the chic Piazza dei Martiri, Palazzo Ala-
★   bardieri is a top choice among the city's growing number of smaller, modern luxury hotels. A spacious marble-floored lobby makes the place seem bigger than it actually is, yet maintains a feeling of discretion and intimacy. The hotel prides itself on its comfortable accommodations, especially its marble bathrooms. **Pros:** impressive common areas; central yet quiet location (a rare combination). **Cons:** no sea view; difficult to reach by car. ⊠ *Via Alabardieri 38, Chiaia* ☎*081/415278* ⊕*www. palazzoalabardieri.it* ⤢*29 rooms* △*In-room: Safe, Internet. In-hotel: Bar, Internet terminal, parking (paid), some pets allowed* ▭*AE, DC, MC, V* |○|*BP* ⊹*C3.*

$$$ 🏨 **Paradiso.** This impressive hotel on the hillside of Posillipo is famous for the views of the Bay of Naples from its rooms, its roof-garden restaurant, and its garden terrace. From your own flower-bedecked balcony you can also take in the immediate neighborhood, less enchantingly filled with apartment buildings. Although the hotel is at the western edge of the city, the nearby funicular takes you efficiently to the harbor port and transportation hub of Mergellina, at the end of the Riviera di Chiaia. **Pros:** sweeping view of the bay; posh Posillipo neighborhood is quieter and safer than city center. **Cons:** some rooms face inland, so ask for a *camera con vista*; funicular service is infrequent, and the alternative is a long walk up a steep hill or a taxi ride into the city center. ⊠ *Via Catullo 11, Posillipo* ☎*081/2475111* ⊕*www.bestwestern. it* ⤢*74 rooms* △*In-hotel: Restaurant, bar, parking (paid)* ▭*AE, DC, MC, V* |○|*BP* ⊹*A5.*

$$ 🏨 **Pinto Storey.** This fascinating hotel overflows with warmth and
★   charm—its late-19th-century (but fully renovated) style makes you feel

2

like a character in a period movie. The simple and airy guest rooms are on the fourth and fifth floors of an elegant building off the chic Piazza Amedeo. Rooms here are always in demand, so book far in advance. **Pros:** safe neighborhood; near public transportation. **Cons:** not close to major sights; rickety elevator; only a few rooms have views. ⌧ *Via G. Martucci 72, Chiaia* ☎*081/681260* ⊕*www.pintostorey.it* ☎*16 rooms* ♿*In-room: Safe, refrigerator, Internet. In-hotel: Internet terminal* ⊟*AE, MC, V* †○†*EP* ✛*B4.*

$$–$$$ 🏠 **San Francesco al Monte.** This high-end hotel retains hints of its former life as a Franciscan monastery: the small lobby leads to narrow corridors lined with doors that look dauntingly cell-like, until you enter and find surprisingly spacious, simply decorated rooms, many with their own hot tubs, antique furnishings, majolica-tile floors, and stunning views of the city below and the bay beyond. The hotel's restaurant serves regional specialties, and the wine bar has a selection of smaller dishes. **Pros:** rooftop pool; several dining options. **Cons:** isolated location; need a taxi if you're going out at night. ⌧*Corso Vittorio Emanuele 328, Vomero* ☎*081/4239111* ⊕*www.hotelsanfrancesco.it* ☎*44 rooms* ♿*In-room: Safe, refrigerator, Internet. In-hotel: 2 restaurants, bar, pool, parking (paid)* ⊟*AE, DC, MC, V* †○†*BP* ✛*D3.*

NIGHTLIFE AND THE ARTS

THE ARTS

Lively and energetic yet also chaotic and often difficult to follow, the cultural scene in Naples reflects the city's charming yet frustrating character. Schedules of events are published in daily newspapers, particularly *Il Mattino, La Repubblica,* and *Corriere della Sera, and the freesheet City* and listings magazine *Zero 81,* though they can't be relied on to cover everything that is happening, or frequent last-minute changes of program or venue. The best source of information is word of mouth (ask the receptionists in your hotel what's going on this evening) or by keeping your eyes peeled for the theater and concert posters that wallpaper much of the city center. Information and ticket sales are provided by the following ticket agencies:

Box Office (⌧*Galleria Umberto I 17, Piazza Municipio* ☎*081/5519188* ⊕*www.boxol.it*). **Concerteria** (⌧*Via Schipa 23, Chiaia* ☎*081/7611221*). **FNAC** (⌧*Via Luca Giordano 59, Vomero* ☎*081/2201000*).

CONCERT HALLS AND THEATERS

In addition to the world-famous Teatro San Carlo, Naples has several other leading concert halls and theaters. Each theater generally plans its entire season—which usually runs October through May—in advance with a printed schedule. The **Augusteo** (⌧*Piazza Augusteo, Piazza Municipio* ☎*081/414243* ⊕*www.teatroaugusteo.it*) is a large, centrally located theater off Via Toledo that usually presents commercial Italian theater and concerts.

Galleria Toledo (⌧*Via Montecalvario 36, Spaccanapoli* ☎*081/425824*) attracts the hip set with high-quality fringe and avant-garde theater presentations. **Teatro Nuovo** (⊠ *Via Montecalvario 16, Spaccanapoli* ☎*081/425958* ⊕*www.nuovoteatronuovo.it*) is another venue for the avant-garde. **Teatro Bellini** (⊠ *Via Conte di Ruvo 14, Spaccanapoli* ☎*081/5491266*) is a gilded belle epoque theater that presents plays and concerts of a more traditional flavor. **Teatro delle Palme** (⊠ *Via Vetriera 12, Chiaia* ☎*081/418134*) is a rather ugly postwar-plywood, auditorium-cum-movie theater, which regularly hosts chamber music concerts presented by the Associazione Alessandro Scarlatti. **Teatro Mercadante** (⊠*Piazza Municipio, Piazza Municipio* ☎*081/5513396*), a belle epoque theater with an ultramodern foyer, hosts touring productions of invariably high quality. The **Teatro Politeama** (⊠ *Via Monte di Dio 80, Chiaia* ☎*081/7645001*) could almost be considered an off-Broadway playhouse, considering its challenging bill of fare, which includes much contemporary dance. The Teatro San Carlo company uses it for contemporary works, which they don't dare perform in their hallowed temple. For a satisfying Neapolitan "soul" experience, catch a local singer like Lina Sastri or Lara Sansone warbling at the **Teatro Sannazzaro** (⊠*Via Chiaia 157, Chiaia* ☎*081/418824*); traditional Neapolitan plays by Edoardo di Filippo are also often presented here, and they also program shows by younger Italian bands and singers. **Teatro Trianon** (⊠*Piazza Calenda 9, Spaccanapoli* ☎*081/2258285*) is a refurbished cinema opened in 2003 to provide a "home for Neapolitan song," mixing showings of classic Neapolitan movies with local comedies and frequent concerts by traditional Neapolitan musicians (not to be missed if you want to feel tearful while singing along to "Turna a Surriento"). For those with a knowledge of Italian, the **TAM Tunnel** (⊠*Gradini Nobili 1, Chiaia* ☎*081/682814*) has a solid program of cabaret and stand-up.

FILM

Neapolitans take their cinema seriously: the city has many cinema and video stores and rental outlets, and several cinemas even run their own "cineforums" one day a week to cater to more discerning cinemagoers. From the end of June to mid-September, open-air cinemas come into their own, and provide film aficionados with a chance to catch up on movies they missed during the year. Remember, however, that your favorite movie star will be speaking fluent Italian on the big screen—the dubbers still have a stranglehold on the industry.

The city's love fest with the movies reaches its high point every year with the Napoli Film Festival, usually presented every June at different locations across the city—the 2008 festival found a home in the impressive surroundings of the Castel Sant'Elmo and the nearby **America Hall** (⊠*Via Tito Angelini 21, Vomero* ☎*081/5788982*). Moviegoers should also look out for the **Warner Village Metropolitan** (⊠ *Via Chiaia 149, Chiaia* ☎*081/5511247*) a city-center multiplex in the American style, with as much popcorn as you can eat.

OPERA AND CLASSICAL MUSIC

Opera is a serious business in Naples. Not the music, that is, but the costumes, the stage design, the players, the politics. Anyone who aspires to anything absolutely has to be present at the season's major openings, where what's happening on the stage and in the pit are secondary to the news of who is there, who they're with, and what they're wearing. Given this, it's hardly surprising that the city's famous San Carlo company does not offer a particularly challenging repertoire but spends time endlessly redressing the classics. All this takes place in the historic **Teatro San Carlo** (⊠ *Via San Carlo 101–103, Piazza Municipio* ☎ *081/7972412 box office, 081/7972331* ⊕ *www.teatrosancarlo.it*), the luxury liner of opera houses in southern Italy. In 2008 the concert hall underwent a massive renovation, with everything from the seats to the gold inlay on the ceiling fescoes being replaced, and the statue of the mermaid Parthenope (missing since 1969) being restored to its position on the building's facade. The program, however, remains traditional, although the choice of Benjamin Britten's comparatively obscure opera *Peter Grimes* (directed by English conductor Jeffrey Tate, who follows in the illustrious footsteps of former conductors Riccardo Muti and Claudio Abbado) to open the new house in January 2009 hints at a newfound adventurousness. The company is usually of very high quality—and if they're not on form, the audience lets them know. Although rotten vegetables are terribly passé, catcalls and boos are perfectly acceptable.

For the opera and ballet season (generally December through June), many seats are presold by subscription but there are usually some seats available if you go to the box office several days before the performance (unless a superstar is performing). If you are under 30, you can buy an unsold ticket one hour before the curtain rises for €15. Otherwise, for some opera performances, tickets can only be bought five days before the performance, but at other times you can buy tickets weeks in advance. You can book ahead using a credit card on the theater's Web site. Unlike many leading opera companies in the United States, the San Carlo does not operate on a revolving repertory schedule: each opera or ballet is usually scheduled for a minirun, generally over a 10-day period.

Prices vary due to both seat location and date. The front rows of the stalls, known as *poltronissime,* might cost as much as €200 for a performance on the first night of an opera, while up in the sixth tier, the Balconata VI, you would pay a fifth of that price, or much less if you go on a later night. Prices are always highest at first nights with the best opera divas, then fall off as top performers are sometimes substituted after a few nights. If you get a box seat, keep in mind that there are as many as six people sharing a box, so it's worth getting there early to get a front seat. Some people tip the *maschere* (ushers), and this is especially appreciated if they have fixed you up with a better seat than the one you were allocated originally (maybe a season ticket holder didn't show up). Ballet and concert performances are up to 50% less expensive than operas. One way of getting into the San Carlo for much less is to go on a guided tour (weekends only, 2 to 3:30). At €6.50, you soak up some of its magnificence, which might be preferable to paying 50 times as much and sitting through five hours of the Ring cycle. For complete information, contact the **box office,** which is open Tuesday to Sunday 10 to 7, and one hour before performances.

Mamma Mia, Sophia!

Given Naples' size and rich cultural life, it is strange that it has produced so few internationally famous people. The exception of exceptions, of course, is Sophia Loren.

Like many things in Naples, Sophia Loren's life story is a tangled mixture of truth and myth. Strictly speaking, Loren is not Neapolitan but instead comes from the town of Pozzuoli, just outside Naples. It is in Pozzuoli that the first of her myths lies—that she was raised in "slums," or that she pulled herself out of the grinding poverty of postwar Napoli.

Born on September 20, 1934, to mother Romilda Villani and a fly-by-night father, Sofia Villani Scicolone (bearing both her mother's and father's names) certainly didn't find a silver spoon in her mouth at birth, but there is nothing to suggest that she was any worse off than anyone else who lived through the crippling hardships of that period. However, Sophia herself played her part in creating and perpetuating the rags-to-riches tale:

"The two big advantages I had at birth were to have been born wise and to have been born in poverty," she famously said.

She managed to survive being born dangerously underweight, only to find herself a refugee from bomb-hit Pozzuoli during World War II. Following the war, Sofia was so thin that she was nicknamed *la stuzzicadente*— "the toothpick." Her mother, whose own dreams of acting had been constrained by her far-from-wealthy family, encouraged the young Sofia toward the stage, turning their house into a bar to entertain GIs stationed in town. At the same time, Sofia found herself rapidly developing the curvaceous figure, feline eyes, and voluptuous lips that became her defining characteristics. In 1951 both mother and daughter managed to land bit parts in biblical epic *Quo Vadis?* and Sofia filled out her earnings by posing regularly for magazine photo stories.

It was during this time that she came to the attention of film director and producer Carlo Ponti, a meeting that would change her life and also give rise to myriad myths concerning Sophia's personal life.

Ponti was 22 years her senior and had launched the career of Gina Lollobrigida; now he set about trying to launch Sofia's. After briefly changing her surname to "Lazzaro" (the Italian for "Lazarus"—so beautiful she could wake the dead), Ponti selected the more northern-sounding "Loren" (out of deference for the vogue for Scandinavian actresses) and altered the "f" in her first name to a more international "ph."

He allegedly also suggested that she do something about her wide hips and long nose, but Sophia refused, being proud of her figure—later quipping, "Everything I have, I owe to spaghetti."

She soon had her first major breakthrough playing a feisty pizza-seller in Vittorio de Sica's *L'Oro di Napoli* ("The Gold of Naples," 1954), which was soon followed with bigger roles alongside Marcello Mastroianni in *La Fortuna essere donna* ("Lucky to be a Woman!" 1956) and Cary Grant in *The Pride and the Passion* (1957). Starring with the leading men of the day inevitably set tongues wagging, but not without reason: Grant had proposed to her, apparently forcing Ponti to do the same—despite the fact that he was already married. Ponti managed to obtain a divorce in Mexico, and he and Sophia married.

Immediately he was labeled a bigamist back home in Italy, and questions were raised about the validity of their marriage, but married they stayed: "I needed a father. I needed a husband. I was adopted by Carlo, and I married my father," said Sophia.

Sophia's most successful decade followed, with one great film after another, including the Napoli-set *It Started in Naples*; *Ieri, Oggi, Domani* ("Yesterday, Today, and Tomorrow"); *Matrimonio all'italiano* ("Marriage, Italian Style"); and *La Ciociara* ("Two Women"), for which she deservedly won an Oscar for her harrowing portrayal of a mother trying to protect her daughter in war-torn Rome.

Following the birth of two children, Sophia spent most of the '70s promoting her lines of eyewear and perfume, popping up only in a few substandard films.

Today, Sophia has a fairly complex relationship with her hometown, not aided by the fact that she had to enter in secret following her scandalous marriage, and later was forced to spend two weeks in prison in 1982 for tax evasion charges—she was eventually cleared of wrongdoing.

Despite having been made a *Cavaliere della Repubblica* (an honorary citizen of Pozzuoli) and having a cinema named after her just down the road from where she was born, her public appearances in town are rare.

Nevertheless, local gossip has it that *La Loren* still makes frequent incognito visits to the city, arriving by private boat and mooring in Posillipo. So if you happen to see a tall, impossibly glamorous seventysomething hidden behind a pair of large sunglasses while you're walking around Naples, check carefully.

Naples features a reasonable calendar of classical and chamber music concerts; check the newspaper listings and street posters for information about concerts frequently held in the historic churches of the city.

The **Associazione Alessandro Scarlatti** (⊠ *Piazza dei Martiri 58, Chiaia* ☎*081/406011*) organizes a series of chamber music concerts at various venues across the city, including the auditorium of the Castel Sant'Elmo and the Villa Pignatelli—check their Web site for details. The **Centro di Musica Antica Pietà de' Turchini** (⊠ *Via Santa Caterina da Siena 38, Spaccanapoli* ☎*081/402395* ⊕*www.turchini.it*), based in the early-baroque church of Santa Caterina da Siena, offers an excellent season of early music that runs from October to early May. Even if madrigals aren't your thing, it's worth visiting just for the location.

A NEOPOLITAN NIGHT ON THE TOWN

Long queues are common at the more popular spots as people endlessly haggle about being on the guest list or try to avoid paying in some other way. Be patient and enjoy the experience—many long-standing friendships have been formed in queues outside nightclubs in Naples. But remember that planning a night out in Napoli is rather like planning a military campaign, with many phone calls made, appointments fixed, changed, not met, and plans B, C, and D coming into action.

NIGHTLIFE

Nightlife in Naples begins well after the sun has gone down. If you're going to a club, don't even think about turning up before 11, as more than likely it'll still be empty, and don't plan on going to bed much before 3. Yet if you're willing to stay up late enough, and prepared to hang around outside places where there's sometimes more going on in the street than in the clubs themselves, Naples offers distractions for night owls of all persuasions. The designer-clad young and not-so young hang out in the area around Chiaia and Mergellina; a more artsy post-student crowd congregates around Piazza Bellini; the rawer, punkier edge prefers to hang around on Piazza del Gesù or Piazza San Domenico. Clubs tend to open and close or change name, style, or ownership with bewildering rapidity, so be sure to check locally before planning a night out. The best way to find out what's going on is to keep your eyes on the flyers that cover Spaccanapoli or check the monthly publication *Zero 81*.

Many dance clubs issue a drink card (prices vary, €15 is average) at the door that must be returned when you leave, stamped to show you've consumed at least one drink. After the first or second drink, other drinks usually run less (about €5). Via Cisterna dell'Olio hosts the tiny but agreeably funky **Superfly** (⊠ *Via Cisterna Dell'Olio 12, Spaccanapoli* ☎*347/1272178*), where a DJ spinning classic jazz stands next to the bartender and regularly changed photographic exhibitions line the walls. Just around the corner from the Superfly bar, **Kinky Klub** (⊠ *Vicolo della Quercia 26, Spaccanapoli* ☎*081/5521571* ⊕*www. kinkyjam.com*) is actually a reggae bar. The place fills up quickly that in summer the whole scene spills out onto the street. Nearby Piazza Bellini is somewhat more relaxed than the club-studded alleyways of Spacca, and you might even be able to sit down at a proper table. **Caffè Intramoenia** (✉ *Piazza Bellini 70, Spaccanapoli* ☎*081/290988* ⊕*www. intramoenia.it*) is the granddaddy of the bars here—set up as a bookshop in the late 1980s, it still has its own small publishing house and a variety of the attractive titles are on sale. Seats in the heated veranda are at a premium in winter, though many patrons sit outside year-round. If Piazza Bellini is too packed, head around the corner to **Perditempo** (✉ *Via San Pietro a Maiella 8, Spaccanapoli* ☎*081/444958* ⊕*www. perditempo.org*), which advertises *libri, vini e vinili* ("books, wine, and vinyl"). Set up as a used book and record store, it is now a relaxed place to enjoy a glass or two and peruse their stock. **Kestè** (✉*Largo S. Giovanni Maggiore 26, Spaccanapoli* ☎*081/5513984* ⊕*www.keste. it*) nestles in the small square in front of the Orientale University. Cool chrome furnishings contrast with the old arched ceiling inside but try to bag one of the few tables out in the beautiful square. A DJ spins tunes, and there's live jazz on the tiny stage on weekends. The nearby **Aret 'a Palm** (✉*Piazza S. Maria La Nova 14, Spaccanapoli* ☎*339/8486949*) shares the same vibe, though its dark-wood interior, marble-top bar, and red plush seats suggest Paris far more than the Mediterranean. There's often impromptu live music as owner and guitarist Alan Wuzburger picks out some of his tunes. One stalwart of the Spaccanapoli scene is **Velvet** (✉*Via Cisterna dell'Olio 11, Spaccanapoli* ☎*347/8107328* ⊕*www.velvetzone.it*). It's in a dark and somewhat labyrinthine basement with arched doorways leading into ever smaller rooms, and has a mixture of live bands and DJs of every stripe, from Italy and abroad. **Risingsouth** (✉*Via San Sebastiano 19, Spaccanapoli* ☎*081/447001* ⊕*www.risingrepublic.com*) has become a fixture of the center's club scene. More upscale than its rival Velvet, the long narrow room with eclectic furnishings (fake Louis XIV chairs alongside '80s-style chrome-and-matte black divans) hosts a mixture of hip European DJs, occasional live acts, and film screenings. It now has a sister club **Rising Mutiny** (✉*Via Bellini 15, Spaccanapoli* ☎*3358790428*), designed in a similar style but concentrating more on live acts, from Italian singer-songwriters to U.S. indie-rockers.

A dressier crowd hangs out in the Chiaia zone. **S'move** (✉*Vico dei Sospiri 10, Chiaia* ☎*081/7645813* ⊕*www.smove-lab.net*) is somewhere between a bar and a club, with its high-tech bar leading into an oriental-style room complete with scatter cushions if you want to arrange yourself artfully on the floor to the chill-out sound track. It fills around midnight with a young crowd that wears its clothes so that the designer labels show.

Miles (✉*Via S. Pasquale 47, Chiaia* ☎*081/405000*) is named after "Davis," though its music policy has shifted from cool jazz to hard techno, which nevertheless manages to get the slightly older crowd here moving. It's sumptuously furnished, with long leather divans and zebra-stripe bar stools where you can sit and watch the acrobatic barman shake and stir cocktails under the moody blue lights. The bar entitled simply **66** (✉*Via Bisignano 58, Chiaia* ☎*081/415024*) describes itself as a "fusion bar." Some prefer it as a chic place to have an aperitif (help yourself to the snacks beautifully laid out on the bar). Other patrons, who look like they've just popped out of one of the area's designer clothes shops, come here to dine and listen to the chilled-out DJ in one of the ethnic-themed rooms upstairs.

Chandelier (⊠ *Vico Belledonne a Chiaia 34–35, Chiaia*) is even more chic than its neighbors, a minimalist long white space dominated by, appropriately enough, a large chandelier. It shakes off its somewhat haughty cool as the night wears on; however, don't think about stopping here if you're still wearing beach shorts. Dress up, and fit in.

Jazz fans should seek out the **Otto Jazz Club** (⊠ *Salita Cariati 23, Chiaia* ☎ *081/5524373*), a staple of the city's trad jazz scene. **Around Midnight** (⊠ *Via Bonito 32/a, Vomero* ☎ *081/7423278* ⊕ *www.aroundmidnight. it*) regularly features live contemporary jazz from Europe and the U.S.

If you can't face any chaotic nightlife after the all-too-chaotic daylife of Naples, there's the civilized option of the *enoteca,* not exactly a wine bar, but a place where you can stop for a drink or meet up with friends without having to shout over the music or hang around on the street outside for hours, and have something more substantial to eat than peanuts and pretzels. The **Enoteca Belledonne** (⊠ *Vico Belledonne a Chiaia 18, Chiaia* ☎ *081/403162* ⊕ *www.enotecabelledonne.com*) is something of an institution among inhabitants of Chiaia. Between 8 and 9 in the evening it seems like the whole neighborhood has descended into the tiny space for an *aperitivo.* The small tables and low stools are notably uncomfortable, but the cozy atmosphere and the pleasure of being surrounded by glass-fronted cabinets full of wine bottles with beautiful labels more than makes up for it. A particularly quiet and refined option in Chiaia is **L'ebbrezza di Noè** (⊠ *Vico Vetriera a Chiaia 9, Chiaia* ☎ *081/400104* ⊕ *www.lebbrezzadinoe.com*). A small bar leads into a larger dining area decorated in the style of what seems to be a very elegant farmhouse. The attention paid to the quality of the wine is backed up by that of the food—more than just a "prop," here you can taste delicate slices of Tuscan steak *carpaccio di chianina* or rare cheeses such as the Sicilian *ragusano di razza modicani.*

SPORTS AND THE OUTDOORS

Updated by
Mark Walters

For complete news and information about sporting events, check the newspapers *Il Mattino, La Repubblica,* and *Corriere della Sera,* and the free English-language monthly guide *Qui Napoli.* Many sporting facilities in Naples, such as those for golf and horseback riding, are run as private clubs, so they are not listed here. The major sports area of Naples is the Fuorigrotta area, to the west of the city center, site of the Stadio San Paolo (soccer stadium).

BEACHES, SPAS, AND WATER SPORTS

Beaches are few and far between in Naples proper, although out of desperation Neapolitans like to take to the Lungomare rocks that line the waterfront from the Castel dell'Ovo to the little port of Mergellina.

The water here was recently declared officially safe to swim in, though it's still only the very young and very reckless who dive in. For true swimming pleasure, head to the Posillipo coast that lies just west of the Mergellina harbor. Here are three ancient fishing ports: **Giuseppone a Mare**, at the end of Via Ferdinando Russo; **Marechiaro**, at the end of Discesa Marechiaro; and **La Gajola** (local dialect for "The Cage"), at the end of Discesa Gajola. These are quite picturesque spots immortalized in Neapolitan songs, landscape paintings, and poetry.

The more policed and costly facilities in the Posillipo zone are **Bagno Elena** (⊠ *Via Posillipo 14, Posillipo* ☎*081/5755058* ⊕*www.bagnoelena.it*), alongside the splendid Palazzo Donn'Anna from where you can now rent canoes or motorboats; **Gabbiano** (⊠ *Via Marechiaro 115, Posillipo* ☎*081/5755650*); **Le Rocce Verdi** (⊠ *Via Posillipo 68, Posillipo* ☎*081/5756716*); **Marechiaro** (⊠*Calata Ponticello a Marechiaro 33, Posillipo* ☎*081/7691215*); and **Villa Imperiale** (⊠ *Via Marechiaro 90, Posillipo* ☎*081/5754344*). Of course, for the best paradisiacal beaches head to Ischia and the Amalfi Coast.

SOCCER

Matches by the Napoli team are played at the **Stadio San Paolo** (☎*081/2395623* ⊕*www.calcionapoli1926.it*), in a suburb to the west of Mergellina (beware: *very* raucous crowds on their way to a game can clog up public transportation throughout the city). The team has sadly fallen on hard times since the mid-'90s, although promotion from the Series C third division in 2006 has got the team's loyal fans dreaming once again. Tickets are fairly easy to come by and range from about €6.60 for the *curva* (at the highest tier of the giant stadium) to €20 for the more comfortable *tribuna* stand. Even though the great Maradona's days are long gone, it's still worth a visit for a heady experience in which the fans are more interesting to watch than whatever's happening on the pitch. The stadium is across the piazza from the Ferrovia Cumana train station at Mostra and can also be reached via the Metro Line 2 stop at Piazzale Tecchio, and via the new Metro Line 6 stop at Mostra. Tickets are available through **Azzurro Service** (⊠ *Via F. Galeota 17, Fuorigrotta* ☎*081/5934001*) near the stadium, **Box Office** (⊠*Galleria Umberto I 17, Toledo* ☎*081/5519188* ⊕*www.boxofficenapoli.it*), and **Concerteria** (⊠ *Via Schipa 23, Chiaia* ☎*081/7611221*).

SHOPPING

Updated by
Chris Rose

Naples is a fascinating and largely underrated city for shopping. From the delightful *Presepe* (Nativity scene) shops that transform Via San Gregorio Armeno into a perpetual Christmas morning to its noted leather-goods emporia, the city's rich history of skilled workmanship means it abounds in unique souvenirs and gifts, including some of the world's best ties (**Marinella**), crèche figures (**Ferrigno**), masks (**Nel Regno di Pulcinella**), shoes (**Mario Valentino**), and intarsia tabletops (**Domenico Russo**). At the other end of the price scale are world-famous, dirt-cheap bootleg CDs of Italian and Neapolitan music for you to check out. A sense of adventure is once again the key, especially in the open markets, which are worth a visit just as a social experience—bargaining here is an art and a necessity (watch your wallet and leave the expensive extra camera lenses at the hotel).

Shops are generally open from around 9:30 in the morning to 1:30, when they close for lunch, reopening around 4:30 and staying open until 7:30 or 8. Most stores are closed Sunday, but certain higher-volume addresses have procured a license allowing them to open on Sunday morning. Sales run twice a year, from mid-January to mid-March for the fall–winter collections and from mid-July to early September for the spring–summer collections, with half-price discounts common.

MARKETS

Shopping in an outdoor market is an essential Neapolitan experience; do prepare yourself against pickpockets (relax—just don't wear your tiara). Food markets are all over town, offering a Technicolor feast for the eyes as well as free street theater. The **Mercato di Porta Nolana** (*Via Carmignano, Piazza Garibaldi*), open Monday–Saturday 8–6 and Sunday 8–2, is just south of Piazza Garibaldi, with a great display of seafood. The **Mercatino della Pignasecca** (⊠*Spaccanapoli*), several blocks west of Piazza Carità off Via Toledo, is open Monday–Saturday 8–2 and is the best place in the city for fruit and vegetables. For low price and surprisingly high-quality clothing and linen, go to the **Mercatino di Antignano** (⊠*Piazza degli Artisti, Vomero*), open daily 8–1. The **Mercatino di Posillipo** (⊠*Viale Virgilio, Posillipo*) takes place once a week, on Thursday mornings. Get there early to get the best bargains. In Chiaia, the **Bancarelle di San Pasquale** (⊠*Via San Pasquale, Chiaia*) takes place every morning, with a smaller but higher quality selection of shoes, bags, and clothing.

Clothes merit a special mention. Neapolitans are the world masters of the used-clothing trade and also specialize in, well, let's call them unofficial brand-name knockoffs, sometimes of excellent quality. If you trust your eye, you can have a field day: you might find excellent shoes made by the same factories that turn out top brands, quality leather purses, or secondhand cashmere at the price of discount-store cotton. Of course, quite often you have to wade through a lot of dismal stock of no interest in order to get to the good stuff, but that's part of the fun. Over the last few years, a large number of Chinese merchants have moved in, lowering prices, but also some of the quality of the clothes on offer. The best stomping ground is the **Mercato di Ponte Casanova** (⊠*Porta Capuana, Piazza Garibaldi*), which is open Monday–Saturday 8–sunset and which must have the world's greatest collection of jeans and a surprising number of untagged name-brand items at half price. The **Mercatino di Poggioreale** (⊠*Via Nuova Poggioreale, Piazza Garibaldi*) is a little farther out, but provides a vast selection of shoes of all styles and sizes at uniformly low prices. The above-mentioned markets of **Antignano** in Vomero and **San Pasquale** in Chiaia also have a good selection of clothing.

The Galleria Umberto I isn't as grand as it once was, but it's still a popular meeting place in the city center.

SHOPPING DISTRICTS

Most of the luxury shops in Naples are along a crescent that descends the Via Toledo to Piazza Trieste e Trento and then continues along Via Chiaia to Via Filangieri and on to Piazza Amedeo, as well as continuing south toward Piazza dei Martiri and the Riviera di Chiaia. Within this area, the Via Chiaia probably has the greatest concentration and variety of shops (and caffè–pastry shop Cimmino, on the corner of Via Filangieri and Via Chiaia, makes for an excellent rest stop along this route). The area around Piazza Vanvitelli, and Via Scarlatti in particular, in the Vomero also has a nice selection of shops outside the tourist zone. This area can be conveniently reached by funicular from Piazza Amedeo or the Cumana station. Used-book dealers tend to collect in the area between Piazza Dante, Via Port'Alba, and Via Santa Maria Constantinopoli toward Piazza Bellini. The shops specializing in Presepi (Nativity scenes) are in Spaccanapoli, on the Via San Gregorio Armeno.

SPECIALTY STORES

ART GALLERIES
With the opening of two new museums dedicated to contemporary art, the gallery scene in Naples has been kick-started back into life, following a slump after the death of Lucio Amelio, the gallery owner who brought international superstars like Andy Warhol and Joseph Beuys to the city, and who was instrumental in creating the Arte Povera and Transavanguardia movements. Along with established galleries, a number of more modish spaces have opened, often showing local artistic talent.

Raucci Santamaria (✉ *Corso Amedeo di Savoia 190, Spaccanapoli* ☎ *081 /7443645* ⊕ *www.raucciesantamaria.com*) specializes in international artists including Mat Colishaw, Ugo Rondinone, and Tim Rollins. **T293** (⊠*Piazza G. Amendola 4, Chiaia* ☎*081/19728116* ⊕*www.t293.it*) has a space in the heart of the Chiaia shopping district, often puzzling passersby with some of its more challenging displays of contemporary art. **Galleria Lia Rumma** (⊠ *Via Vannella Gaetani 14, Chiaia* ☎*081/7643619* ⊕*www.gallerialiarumma.it*) has a status-heavy array of artists, including Cindy Sherman, Anselm Kiefer, and Vanessa Beecroft, along with Neapolitan photographer Mimmo Jodice. **Galleria Scognamiglio** (⊠ *Via M. D'ayala, Chiaia* ☎*081/400871* ⊕*www. mimmoscognamiglio.com*) has built a fine reputation and shows work by international artists including Antony Gormley and local mainstay Mimmo Paladino. **Galleria Trisorio** (⊠*Riviera di Chiaia 215, Chiaia* ☎*081/414306* ⊕*www.studiotrisorio.com*) shows international artists of the caliber of Rebecca Horn and William Eggleston. **Changing Role** (⊠*Via Chiatamone 26, Santa Lucia* ☎*081/19575958* ⊕*www. changingrole.com*) works frequently with photographers and designers to produce distinctly modish, energetic work. At the **Fondazione Morra Greco** (⊠*Largo Avellino 17, Spaccanapoli* ☎*081/210690* ⊕*www. fondazionemorragreco.com*) influential collector Maurizio Morra Greco has put his private collection on display, and also holds frequent shows by emerging artists.

BOOKS AND PRINTS
Naples is a paradise for bibliophiles. It helps if you read Italian, of course, but you can find a reasonable selection of delightful surprises in French- or English-language publications as well. The best area to hunt is between Piazza Bellini and Piazza Dante, along the streets of Via Santa Maria di Constantinopoli, Via San Sebastiano, and Via Port'Alba. The largest bookstore in town is **La Feltrinelli** (⊠*Piazza dei Martiri, Chiaia* ☎*081/2405411* ⊕*www.lafeltrinelli.it*), with its extensive range of books, CDs, and DVDs, and an inviting coffee bar on the lower ground floor and a space for daily meetings and book launches. Another branch of **Feltrinelli** (⊠*Via Tommaso D'aquino 70, Piazza Municipio* ☎*081/5521436*) has a much larger selection of English-language books. **Libreria Guida** (⊠*Via Port'Alba 20/23, Spaccanapoli* ☎*081/446377* ⊕*www.guida.it*) has a wide selection of local interest books in English and Italian and an expert staff. **FNAC** (⊠*Via Luca Giordano 59, Vomero* ☎*081/2201000* ⊕*www.fnac.it*) is the Neapolitan branch of the French chain, and has a huge basement brimming with books and CDs, as well as a coffee bar and meeting space.

Rare-book enthusiasts will want to check out **Casella** (⊠*Via Carlo Poerio 92, Chiaia* ☎*081/7642627* ⊕*www.librantichi.com/casella*), just above the Riviera di Chiaia, a famous source that also specializes in authors' autographs. **Colonnese** (⊠*Via San Pietro a Maiella 32/33, Spaccanapoli* ☎*081/459858* ⊕*www.colonnese.it*), near Via Port'Alba, has a wide assortment of antique postcards and magical objets d'art. If you're an art history student and pictures are what matter, browse the booksellers near Piazza Bellini and take Via Port'Alba to Piazza Dante, where **Alpha** (⊠*Via Sant'Anna dei Lombardi 10, Spaccanapoli* ☎*081/5525013* ⊕*www.alphalibri.com*) has a great selection of cut-rate art books. For antique prints and engravings, the most famous shop in town is **Bowinkel** (⊠*Piazza dei Martiri 24, Chiaia* ☎*081/7644344*), in the Chiaia area; it also has antique postcards, watercolors, photographs, and fans. **Arethusa** (⊠ *Riviera di Chiaia 202/b, Chiaia* ☎ *081/411551* ⊕ *www.arethusanapoli.it*) specializes in collectible posters and has an excellent selection of both rare and inexpensive editions.

CLOTHING AND
ACCESSORIES

Neapolitans are famous for their attention to style, and Naples abounds in clothing stores for every pocketbook. **Melinoi** (⊠ *Via Benedetto Croce 34, Spaccanapoli* ☎ *081/5521204*) is particularly known for its originality—as well as Romeo Gigli. It also stocks clothes and accessories by a number of French designers, with an eye for uniqueness of style. **Livio de Simone** (⊠ *Via Domenico Morelli 15, Chiaia* ☎ *081/7643827* ⊕ *www. liviodesimone.it*) is a Neapolitan designer famous for his bright, printed-textile designs, and who has a range of less traditional clothing.

International chains are present, of course. A good selection of affordable clothes can be found at **Benetton** (⊠ *Via Chiaia 203/204, Chiaia* ☎ *081/405385*), which continues to represent easy Italian chic to most of the world. Up the price scale, **Emporio Armani** (⊠ *Piazza dei Martiri 64, Chiaia* ☎ *081/425816*) is in the highly chic Piazza dei Martiri. Just down the road its even more upscale brother **Giorgio Armani** (⊠ *Via Calabritto 1, Chiaia* ☎ *081/2451303*). The French **Hermès** (⊠ *Via Filangieri 53/57, Chiaia* ☎ *081/4207054*) is on the increasingly chic Via Filangieri. A landmark of the Chiaia area is the luxe outfitter **Versace** (⊠ *Via Calabritto 7, Chiaia* ☎ *081/7644210*). Beloved by stylemeisters, **Prada** (⊠ *Via Calabritto 9, Chiaia* ☎ *081/7641323*) is yet another Chiaia area emporium.

A number of smaller, local, or more exclusive shops are also worthy of notice. **Amina Rubinacci** (⊠ *Via dei Mille 16, Chiaia* ☎ *081/415486* ⊕ *www.aminarubinacci.it*) is the queen of knitwear, featuring her famous "ostrich" pullover and a wide range of colors in sweaters. **Maxi Ho** (⊠ *Via N. Nisco 23/27, Chiaia* ☎ *081/427530*) has the latest in men's and women's fashion trends. Italy wouldn't be Italy without shoes, and **De Liberti** (⊠ *Via Chaia 1470, Chiaia* ☎ *081/416064* ⊕ *www. deliberti.it*) offers a wide range of cutting-edge fashion footwear (often at the edge of the wearable).

Furla (⊠ *Via Filangieri 58, Chiaia* ☎ *081/412190*) offers a range of accessories from scarves to bags to shoes at surprisingly accessible prices. **Barbaro** (⊠ *Galleria Umberto I 3/7, Piazza Municipio* ☎ *081/414940*) has a stylish choice of name designers.

If your credit card is crying in pain, head for **Lo Stock** (⊠ *Via Fiorelli 7, Chiaia* ☎ *081/2405253*), a large basement in which designer-label end-of-lines can be found at hugely reduced prices. You have to be prepared to rummage and hope they've got your size, as all items are one-offs only. A branch with clothes for babies and children is directly across the street.

Naples is a surprisingly good city for male fashion and tends to spoil its male clotheshorses (many would use the word *peacocks*). Gents can outfit themselves head-to-toe Italian-style by stopping at **Fay** (⊠ *Via Filangieri 29* ☎ *081/403816* ⊕ *www.fay.it*), where the classic jackets and overcoats are on sale alongside Hogan shoes (entirely Italian, despite the name). Leading Italian and international designer

The Doll Hospital in Spaccanapoli is a Neapolitan institution.

brands at reasonable prices are at **Jossa** (✉ *Via Carlo Poerio 43, Chiaia* ☎ *081/7649835*), off the Piazza dei Martiri above Riviera di Chiaia. Finely tailored shirts with hand-sewn buttonholes can be found at **Luigi Borelli** (✉ *Via Filangieri, Chiaia* ☎ *081/4238273* ⊕ *www.luigiborelli. com*). If you feel like indulging in a custom-made suit, try **Blasi** (✉ *Via dei Mille 29/31/35, Chiaia* ☎ *081/415283*), which also has some soigné ready-to-wear items. You'll find high-class souvenirs that are more immediate and more accessible at **Marinella** (✉ *Riviera di Chiaia 287, Chiaia* ☎ *081/2451182* ⊕ *www.marinellanapoli.it*), where Maurizio Marinella, grandson of the founder, Eugenio, cuts made-to-measure ties for the world's royalty and other sensitive necks—these are widely considered by globe-trotting VIPs to be the finest ties in the world. The selection of fabrics is so vast it's impossible *not* to find the perfect tie. **Argenio** (✉ *Via Filangieri 15, Chiaia* ☎ *081/418035*) is another famous and exclusive address for men's accessories, and former supplier of scarves, cuff links, buttons, tiepins, and so forth to the royal Bourbons of the House of the Two Sicilies.

Mario Valentino (✉ *Via Calabritto 10, Chiaia* ☎ *081/7644262*) offers fine handmade footwear in his fashionable shoe store. **Spatarella** (✉ *Via Toledo 284, Spaccanapoli* ☎ *081/401376*) is a top source for shoes by local craftsmen, as well as for high-quality belts, purses, and luggage.

CRAFTS
AND GIFTS

The classic handicraft of Naples is the Presepe—or Nativity crèche scene—with elaborate sets and terra-cotta figurines and elements of still life. The tradition goes back to the medieval period, but its acknowledged golden age arrived in the 18th century. The tradition is alive and flourishing; although the sets and figurines retain their 18th-century

2

aspect, the craftsmen keep their creativity up-to-date with famous renditions of current political figures and other celebrities. The scenes are appropriately completed with a profusion of domestic animals and food of all sorts, meticulously rendered. A number of the smaller articles make great Christmas tree ornaments, if you don't feel up to adopting an entire Bethlehem-on-the-bay Nativity scene. Shops cluster along the Via San Gregorio Armeno in Spaccanapoli, and they're all worth a glance, but the most famous is **Ferrigno** (⊠ *Via San Gregorio Armeno 10, Spaccanapoli* ☎*081/5523148*). *Maestro* Giuseppe Ferrigno himself died in 2008 but the family business continues, still faithfully using 18th-century techniques. If you're seriously bitten by the Presepe-collecting bug, you can find rare antique Nativity figures at **Marisa Catello** (⊠ *Via Santa Maria Costantinopoli 124, Spaccanapoli* ☎*081/444169*). **Gramendola** (⊠ *Via San Gregorio Armeno 51, Spaccanapoli* ☎*081/5514899*) offers the noted creations of Matteo Principe.

The **Ospedale delle Bambole** (⊠ *Via San Biagio dei Librai 81, Spaccanapoli* ☎*081/203067*)—a tiny storefront operation—is a world-famous "hospital" for dolls, a wonderful photo-op, and a great place to take kids. **Nel Regno di Pulcinella** (⊠ *Vico San Domenico Maggiore 9, Spaccanapoli* ☎*081/5514171*) is the workshop of famous Pulcinello maker Lello Esposito. This shop, a converted 16th-century stable, also offers some wonderful model volcanoes and the traditional good-luck symbol of the city, a red horn.

Music lovers can get a prestigious mandolin at **Liuteria Calace** (⊠ *Vico San Domenico Maggiore 9, Spaccanapoli* ☎*081/5515983* ⊕*www.calace.it*) or a greater range of instruments along Via Costantinopoli, close to the Naples Conservatorio.

Elegant office supplies—notebooks, pens, and stationery—can be had at **P & C** (⊠*Largo Vasto a Chiaia 86, Chiaia* ☎*081/418724*), a treasure trove for writing enthusiasts. **Egraphe** (⊠*Piazza L. Miraglia 391, Spaccanapoli* ☎*081/446266* ⊕*www.egraphe.it*) is a tiny hole in the wall crammed with notebooks of every style and size, different kinds of handmade papers, and unusual pens and pencils.

HOUSEHOLD DECORATION AND ANTIQUES

For household linens, **La Cage** (⊠*Largo Duca della Ferrantina 10, Chiaia* ☎*081/403811*) has the most exclusive selection in Naples. The national chain **Frette** (⊠ *Via dei Mille 2, Chiaia* ☎*081/418728*) is justifiably famous throughout Italy for the quality of its sheets, towels, and bedspreads.

A good address for hand-painted ceramic tiles is **Capri Due** (⊠*Via Scarlatti 61–65, Vomero* ☎*081/5789400*), in the Vomero. **Domenico Russo e Figli** (⊠*Via Bisignano 51, Chiaia* ☎*081/7648387*) continues the centuries-old Neapolitan tradition of marble-inlay work, creating precious tables and console tops. Mario Muscariello produces museum-quality replica furniture (they copied the ancient furniture from Herculaneum for the Getty Museum) at **Il Cirmolo** (⊠ *Via Santa Maria di Costantinopoli 32, Spaccanapoli* ☎*081/451140*). **Salvatore Molino** (⊠ *Via Alabardieri 21/22, Chiaia* ☎*081/426505*) painstakingly handcrafts furniture, using time-tested techniques.

If you're interested in original antiques, several prestigious dealers are clustered along Via Domenico Morelli south of Piazza dei Martiri. **Arte Antica** (⊠ *Via Domenico Morelli 45, Chiaia* ☎*081/7646897*) has a fine display of porcelain objects. **Maurizio Brandi** (⊠ *Via Domenico Morelli 11, Chiaia* ☎*081/7643906*) is known for its 17th- and 18th-century Neapolitan antiques. **D'Amodio** (⊠ *Via Domenico Morelli 6/bis, Chiaia* ☎*081/7643872*) is the place for historic majolica. **Florida** (⊠ *Via Domenico Morelli 13, Chiaia* ☎*081/7643440*) is famous for its painting on glass and silver rococo and neoclassic style candelabra. Fine collectible 20th-century furniture and objects (basically art nouveau and art deco) can be seen in Chiaia at **Nabis** (⊠ *Via Cavallerizza a Chiaia 52, Chiaia* ☎*081/422493* ⊕*www.nabis.it*).

JEWELRY   The densest selection of goldsmiths' and jewelers' shops is located around the old jewelry-makers' quarter, Via degli Orefici (Street of the Goldsmiths), between Corso Umberto and Via Marina. The area is noisy and frenetic, and many of the shops here are aimed at the wholesale market, but this means that bargains abound. The nearest you get to a gold supermarket in Naples is **Presta** (⊠ *Via Scialoia 2–10, Piazza Garibaldi* ☎*081/5545282*), which has unbelievably competitive prices. In the center of Spaccanapoli is the upscale **Gioielleria Caso** (⊠*Piazza San Domenico Maggiore 16, Spaccanapoli* ☎*081/5516733*), which has antique jewelry and silver and great coral works. **Brinkmann** (⊠*Piazza Municipio 21, Piazza Municipio* ☎*081/5520555*) is noted for its exquisite collection of watches that incorporate rare coins. **Ventrella** (⊠ *Via Carlo Poerio 11, Chiaia* ☎*081/7643173*) is a posh salon showing original designs by the most exclusive contemporary workshop. **Bulgari** (⊠ *Via Filangieri 40, Chiaia* ☎*081/400856*) showcases internationally famous jewelry on posh Via Filangieri. Almost directly opposite Bulgari is its rival for high-end jewelry, **Damiani** (⊠ *Via Filangieri 15, Chiaia* ☎*081/405043*). More unusual jewelry (in the form of silver charms) can be found at **Dodò** (⊠ *Via Filangieri 58, Chiaia* ☎*081/418245* ⊕*www.dodo.it*).

Naples has also long been famous for its coral and cameos, and although the raw material now comes most often from the Far East, it's Neapolitan technique and inspiration that transform the shells and coral into works of art. A number of touristy shops along the Sorrento coast sell cameos of varying quality and price, but if you want to see how beautiful they can get, go to Torre del Greco and visit **Mattia Mazza** (⊠ *Via Marconi 70, Torre del Greco* ☎*081/8814866*). **Giovanni Apa** (⊠ *Via E. de Nicola 1, Torre del Greco* ☎*081/8811155* ⊕*www.giovanniapa.it*) is a longstanding source for coral. When in Naples, however, visit **Ascione** (⊠*Piazzetta Matilde Serao 19, Piazza Municipio* ☎*081/4211111* ⊕*www.ascione.it*), a century-old family firm which has a showroom-cum-gallery hidden away in a wing of the Galleria Umberto, including pictures of traditional methods of working coral.

Around the Bay: From Pompeii to the Phlegrean Fields

WORD OF MOUTH

"The view from the top of Vesuvius is incredible, because you see the whole Gulf of Naples laid out below. . . . You really get the sense of being in a volcanic region."

—Emma_L

AROUND THE BAY

TOP REASONS TO GO

★ **Archaeological Treats:** Thanks to the destructive yet preserving powers of Vesuvius, you can see what ancient Roman life was like when visiting Pompeii and Herculaneum.

★ **Walking on Volcanoes:** Along with the more hackneyed trip up Vesuvius, experience the otherworldly Solfatara, an active crater just outside Pozzuoli that belches sulfur fumes.

★ **Sweeping Views:** Look seaward from the Acropolis at ancient Cumae and imagine you're a Greek colonist just arrived on the Italian mainland in the 8th century BC.

★ **A Gastronomic Splurge:** See how the Romans have revived their reputation as *bons viveurs* in restaurants at modern Pompeii, or enjoy the day's catch on the waterfront at Pozzuoli.

★ **For Contemplation:** As an alternative to the tourist bustle at other sites, head for Oplontis, a Roman villa oozing charm and tranquility with astoundingly well-preserved frescoes.

Ancient sculpture at Herculaneum

Roman fresco from Villa Poppaea in Oplontis

1 **Vesuvius and environs.** If you head southeast from Naples you immediately run into the *Comuni Vesuviani*, towns with wondrous archaeological sites often sandwiched between once-opulent Bourbon era villas and ugly 20th-century housing developments, all set against the fertile but threatening backdrop of Vesuvius. This is the place to immerse yourself in Roman society, art, and architecture.

2 **Campi Flegrei.** Starting from the western suburbs of Naples, the Phlegrean Fields stretch in a coastal belt all the way to the coast at Cumae. Pockmarked with volcanic craters, this was where Rome's senators and emperors came to spend the summer months, tapping the geothermal energy to enhance their downtime with steam baths and swims. It is no coincidence that this remains a favorite excursion for Neapolitans in the 21st century.

GETTING ORIENTED

3

Around the Bay includes two main areas, the area dominated by Vesuvius to the southeast and the Campi Flegrei along the coast west of Naples. The Vesuvian area is served by the Circumvesuviana railway from both Naples and Sorrento, which are the major bases for day trips. Although Naples is the obvious base for the Campi Flegrei, public transportation from Naples to the main sites beyond Pozzuoli becomes more sporadic, so if you have a few days to spare, opt to stay in one of the country-style hotels in situ.

Pozzuoli

AROUND THE BAY PLANNER

When to Go

This part of the Mediterranean is at its best in spring and fall.

Winter months occasionally reserve chilly surprises for visitors, with roads on the upper slopes of Vesuvius becoming dangerously icy at times.

In April, May, September, and October watch out for the hordes of (nonpaying) schoolchildren at archaeological sites.

Pozzuoli rewards its overheated summer visitors with evening performances in the amphitheater, and other sites such as the baths at Baia and the theaters at Pompeii also have summertime events.

Nature lovers will be pleased to know that this part of the Mediterranean, especially the verdant Campi Flegrei, becomes a floral feast at springtime, while the north-facing slopes of Vesuvius are still awash with color as late as June and July.

Making the Most of Your Time

Allow two full days for visiting the major sites of Herculaneum, best combined with Vesuvius, and Pompeii, which can be neatly bracketed with more rarefied Oplontis.

All these sites will need to be backed up by a visit to the Museo Archeologico Nazionale in Naples, which houses all the major finds from the various sites.

For several buildings in Pompeii you need to make Internet reservations at least 24 hours ahead of time (⊕ www. arethusa.net), so a little advance planning is necessary.

In the Campi Flegrei, prioritize the sites in Pozzuoli, especially the amphitheater, Rione Terra, and the Solfatara.

With more time to spare, head for the outlying site of Cuma or tour the monumental archaeological park in Baia and the spectacular museum in Baia castle.

Finding a Place to Stay

Though much of the Vesuvian area is embraced by the Vesuvius National Park, don't expect well-appointed *agriturismi* or rustic lodgings—or, for that matter, hotels that have you sighing with pleasure when you throw open the shutters. Your best bet is to use either the Sorrentine Peninsula or Naples as a base (though not the less than salubrious Piazza Garibaldi area around the train station).

In the Campi Flegrei, given the limited transportation options, staying in situ becomes more desirable, though access to a car may be essential for some transfers. If on a tight budget, consider the youth hostel in Pompeii—quiet yet very central—or a cabin on the well-equipped campsite of the Solfatara near Pozzuoli.

WHAT IT COSTS (IN EUROS)					
	¢	$	$$	$$$	$$$$
Restaurants	under €20	€20–€30	€30–€45	€45–€65	over €65
Hotels	under €75	€75–€125	€125–€200	€200–€300	over €300

Restaurant prices are for a first course (*primo*), second course (*secondo*), and dessert (*dolce*). Hotel prices are for two people in a standard double room in high season, including tax and service.

Getting Around by Train

The main station in Naples (Stazione Centrale, at Piazza Garibaldi) is the main hub for public transport both east and west of Naples. A branch of the aptly named **Circumvesuviana railway** (☎ 800/053939 ⊕ www.vesuviana.it) serves the main archaeological sites at the foot of Vesuvius. Trains leave from the Porta Nolana–Corso Garibaldi station in Naples, stop at the main terminal at Piazza Garibaldi 10 blocks away, and then head southeast for Sorrento (about two trains per hour; €1.80 to Ercolano and Torre Annunziata, €2.40 to Pompei Scavi–Villa Dei Misteri).

For the Phlegrean Fields to the west of Naples, take the Cumana line run by **SEPSA** (☎ 800/001616 ⊕ www.sepsa.it), with trains every 15–20 minutes, from the terminus at Piazza Montesanto near Montesanto Metropolitana station. Alternatively, take the **FS Metropolitana Linea 2** (☎ 800/568866 ⊕ www.trenitalia.com) to Pozzuoli from either the main Piazza Garibaldi station or the more welcoming station of Mergellina, with departures every 10–15 minutes. This will drop you near the amphitheater and the Solfatara crater.

Getting Around by Bus

Train travel is generally preferable to bus; local roads can be frustratingly slow. The cultural association **Retour** (⊕ www.retourcampiflegrei.com) organizes seasonal departures of the Campi Flegrei on a hop-on-hop-off sightseeing bus from Piazza Municipio-Largo Castello in Naples. Tickets cost €10 a day or €15 for two consecutive days. The bus makes various stops in Naples before heading on to Pozzuoli, Cuma, Baia, Lucrino, and Monte Nuovo.

Getting Around by Boat

The **Metro del Mare** (☎ 199/600700 ⊕ www.metrodelmare.com) is a scenic seasonal option for getting around the bay. Commuter ferries serve all the main ports; they're more expensive and slower than ground transport, but provide spectacular views. Line 1 is particularly useful, with stops in Bacoli (Baia), Pozzuoli, Naples, Portici, Ercolano, Torre del Greco, Torre Annunziata, Castellmmare di Stabia, and Sorrento. Line 2 connects Pozzuoli and Sorrento (€9). Consult the Web site for departure times, which vary with the season.

Getting Around by Car

Pompeii is a short distance off the A3 Naples–Salerno Autostrada (toll from Naples or Nocera: €1.60), but this major highway with only two lanes in each direction can get congested with ill-disciplined drivers and seemingly never-ending roadwork. A car could be useful for exploring the Campi Flegrei region on the west side of Naples, especially for sites like Cumae and Lake Avernus where public transport is either infrequent or nonexistent. From Naples, travel toward Pozzuoli on the Tangenziale—the Naples bypass (toll: €0.65)—exiting at the appropriate junction.

Most archaeological sites are fairly accessible by car. Use a *parcheggio custodito* (attended parking lot), particularly at Pompeii and Herculaneum, and avoid on-street unattended parking. Metered parking (look for the blue lines on the street) is scarce in most places.

Off the main highways, signposting is sometimes poor, with road signs suffering intense competition from advertising placards, so navigating becomes an invaluable skill. The westbound Tangenziale (Napoli–Pozzuoli) should be avoided Saturday evenings and Sunday in summer (crowds heading out of Naples for nightlife or beaches). Road conditions are usually good, though surfaces near the top of Vesuvius can become icy in winter.

CAMPANIA'S WINE RENAISSANCE

Two thousand years ago, wine from Campania was considered some of the best in the Roman Empire. But in recent centuries, the region's wine production—and quality—declined precipitously, only to be raised from mediocrity in the past 20 years. Now Campanian wine is once again arousing the passions and palates of wine connoisseurs.

A vinous renaissance is underway: traditional grape varieties like Aglianico and Piedirosso (reds), and Fiano and Falanghina (whites) have halted the southward expansion of "foreign" (i.e., Northern Italian) intruders like Sangiovese and Trebbiano. There is a new spirit of pride and achievement in the region, evidenced by the rapid increase in production of DOC—Controlled Denomination of Origin—wines, meaning they are recognized by Italy's system for ensuring quality wines. Like those in Tuscany to the north, wineries are increasingly opening their doors to the public.

LABEL TERMS

Italian wine laws are complex. Fortunately wine labels feature some indications of quality and style. The most rigorous classification—with restrictions on geographic zone, grape variety, and production methods—is DOCG (Denominazione di Origine Controllata e Garantita), followed by DOC (Denominazione di Origine Controllata); and IGT (Indicazione Geografica Tipica), which has the fewest restrictions. Other wine label terms to look out for: "vino di tavola" means basic table wine; "riserva" indicates the wine was aged longer than usual; "classico" signifies a well-respected, traditional style; "secco" means dry; and "dolce" indicates sweet.

Aglianico (Taurasi)

The most renowned regional red variety is Aglianico, which makes Taurasi near Avellino, the first-ever Southern Italian wine to receive a DOCG label in 1993. The varietal has been called "the Barolo of the south" for its structure and ability to age. Aglianico produces full-bodied red wines with crisp acidity, robust tannins, and complex flavors of plum and spice. These wines are excellent with grilled steak, pizza, and pasta with meat ragù.

Fiano (Fiano di Avellino)

This classical white grape shows best in the volcanic soils of Avellino, where it has garnered DOCG status. The wine expresses strong flavors of honey, spices, and nuts. It is excellent as an aperitivo, and pairs well with tough-to-match artichokes, as well as seafood fettucine and most fish dishes.

Coda di Volpe

An ancient full-bodied white grape grown near Naples. Until recently, it was used as a blending grape with Falanghina and Greco (in the white Vesuvio DOC) or Fiano. Now it is possible to find the crisp, medium-bodied Coda di Volpe bottled by itself. The varietal is excellent with gently prepared (not grilled) shellfish dishes or panfried fish as it is fairly neutral and can be overwhelmed by strongly flavored foods.

Falanghina

An ancient white grape that may have been a base for the fabled Falernum, the most highly prized wine of the Roman period. This varietal has experienced a revival in recent years. It is a full-bodied, fresh tasting white wine with fruity notes. Falanghina can be found in many DOC wines by itself, and famously is blended with Greco and Biancolella to make Capri Bianco, the DOC white wine from the island of Capri. Falanghina is acidic enough to pair well with grilled and fried seafood dishes.

Greco (Greco di Tufo)

Greco is a Campanian variety that does best around the village of Tufo, where it has DOCG status. The soil there is a sulphurous soft rock called *tufo* (*tuffeau* in French). Greco is a light white wine that expresses ripe stone fruits, like peaches, with notes of almond and citrus. It is great served as an aperitivo and matched with cold antipasto.

Piedirosso (aka Per'e Palummo)

This late-ripening red grape variety produces a fruity wine with notes of cherries and herbs. It is the main grape in the red wines of Vesuvio DOC and Capri DOC. Piedirosso pairs well with pizza, cured meats, and grilled vegetables.

Opposite page: A wine cellar in Campania.
top right: A Campania vineyard.
bottom left: Black grapes grow in Naples.

Updated by
Katie Parla

You can get to Naples by train, bus, or car, or you can "arrive" aboard a boat. If you're lucky enough to travel by water, a peacock's tail of splendor unfolds before you as you enter the vast Golfo di Napoli, the Bay of Naples. Enshrined in 1,001 travel posters, this pulse-tingling vista offers a turquoise-rimmed crescent of isles, hills, azure sea, ancient cities, and modern villas, all arrayed around the bay to the east and west of Naples.

But on each side of the city the earth fumes and grumbles, reminding us that all this beauty was born of cataclysm. Along the coast to the west are the Campi Flegrei, the Phlegrean Fields of the ancients, where the crater of the Solfatara spews satisfyingly Dante-esque gases and where hills like Monte Nuovo have a habit of emerging overnight. Nearby are the dark, deep waters of Lago d'Averno, the lake that was allegedly the ancient doorway to the Underworld, realm of the pagan afterlife ruled over by the god Hades. To the southeast of Naples slumbers Vesuvius, the mother of all mounts, looking down from its 4,000-foot height at the coastal strip stretching from modern and ancient Pompeii all the way to Naples. With potential destruction ever at hand, it is small wonder that southern Italians—and in particular Neapolitans—obey to the letter Horace's precept, *carpe diem*, "seize the day."

Even with the world's most famous volcano looming over the scene like a perpetual standby tombstone, visitors should feel relatively safe. The observatory on Vesuvius's slopes keeps its scientific finger on the subterranean pulse and will warn when signs of misbehavior become evident, so you need not worry about becoming an unwilling exhibit in some encore of Pompeii. You can simply concentrate on the memorable sights that fringe the spectacularly blue bay. The entire region is rife with legend and immortal names. Sixteen kilometers (10 mi) to the west of Naples lies an area where the emperors Claudius and Nero schemed and plotted in their villas, Virgil composed his poetry, and the Apostle Paul landed to spread the Gospel. Here, in and around what was called the Phlegrean (burning) Fields, are ancient sites, such as the Greeks' first colony in mainland Italy, the city of Cumae, home of the famed Cumaean Sybil; the luxury-loving Baia, whose hot springs and dissolute living made it ancient Rome's most fashionable pleasure dome; and the Amphitheater of Pozzuoli, whose subterranean galleries are better preserved than even those at Rome's Colosseum. Here are the Campi Flegrei—inspiration for Dante's *Inferno*—and the sulfur-bound Solfatara, the "Little Vesuvius." Leapfrogging over Naples and spread out east along the bay are the glittering Bourbon palace of Portici, the ancient noble villa at Oplontis, and, in the shadow of Vesuvius, Herculaneum and Pompeii—among the largest archaeological sites in Europe. Nowhere else in Italy is there a comparable mingling of natural vigor with the remains of antiquity.

EXPLORING AROUND THE BAY

When it comes to Campania's overflowing basket of treasures of the ancient world, everyone starts with Pompeii, and rightly so. After touring this massive ghost town, work your way clockwise around Mt. Vesuvius to nearby Oplontis and Herculaneum, two other spectacular excavations, and then shoot off at a tangent to the Museo Archeologico Nazionale in Naples to study the many artistic masterworks excavated from these towns. The lower slopes of Vesuvius—the most densely inhabited volcanic region in the world—are crisscrossed by major roads and several railway lines, providing easy access to most of the archaeological sites. To make a chronological departure from classical times, while in Ercolano make a short detour to take in the sumptuous Royal Palace of Portici and a Vesuvian villa, such as the attractively restored Villa Campolieto, both built during Bourbon rule in the 18th century. The best form of transportation is the Circumvesuviana light railway, its stations never more than a 10-minute walk from the major sites.

But this is just the beginning of the ancient wonders the Bay of Naples has in store for travelers. Pompeii and the towns mentioned above are set to the southeast of Naples, but you'll really get awash in mythical folklore if you also head to the *west* of Naples. Pompeii and Herculaneum were favored by middle- and upper-middle-class Romans but when the emperors and patricians wanted to party they headed to this area, from Puteoli (Pozzuoli—where Petronius set much of his famous *Satyricon*, the unique novel that looks though some keyholes during Nero's time) to Baia, where the Emperors built their pleasure palaces, to Cumae, home of the famed Cumaean Sibyl. Every tour group since Cicero has marched through Pompeii and environs, but you'll really win the classical sweepstakes if you also tour the sites west of Naples.

VESUVIUS AND ENVIRONS

Though barely more than a third as tall as the perennially active Mt. Etna, its Sicilian counterpart, Vesuvius, with its relatively modest 4,189-foot height, has achieved unparalleled status in the collective consciousness of the Italians and the world. For centuries this intermittently active volcano had offered a spectacle to visitors who flocked to the Bay of Naples to marvel at its small-scale eruptions, ever-present plumes of smoke, and thundering fumaroles. In the mid-18th century, in fact, the entire court of Naples set up shop in Portici, at the foot of the mountain, building summer villas that served as ringside seats to the volcano's hypnotic pyrotechnics.

Vesuvius's eruptions—from the ancient era through the 18th century—had long been legendary, but the volcano's lethal handiwork only became apparent to modern minds when the Roman towns of Pompeii and Herculaneum were discovered by accident and then excavated in the late 18th century. As it turned out, having been buried since the famous AD 79 eruption, these towns promptly became the most celebrated archaeological sites in Europe, offering up untold artistic treasures (the finest of which are on display at Naples's incredible Museo Archeologico Nazionale).

Today, thousands of visitors arrive every day to sites around the bay, most with one eye monitoring 'O Vesuvio, just a few miles away. There have been around 30 eruptions of various magnitudes in the past 2,000 years, the most recent of which took place in 1944. This might be construed as good news, but many vulcanologists think it's ominous when a living volcano is so silent—only two eruptions have occurred in the 20th century—and they now maintain a constant watch.

PORTICI

7 km (5½ mi) southeast from Naples, 1 km (½ mi) northwest from Ercolano.

GETTING HERE

To get to Portici by car, take the A3 Naples–Salerno highway and exit at "Portici." Portici is well connected to Naples by train and in fact has two stations. The FS (state train line) station, located near the port, links Portici to Naples and Salerno) while the Circumvesuviana, on Via Liberta' connects Portici to Naples, Ercolano, Torre del Greco, Torre Annunziata, Pompeii, and Sorrento. City buses No. 157 and 255 depart Naples' Piazza Municipio for Herculaneum, via Portici, regularly. No. 255 continues on to Torre del Greco as well.

EXPLORING

Portici, whose Reggia, or Royal Palace, offers a peek into the gilded lives of the 18th-century rich and famous, is set rather incongruously within the urban sprawl of the *Comuni Vesuviani*. In the 1730s, the area was chosen by the first Bourbon king of the Two Sicilies, Charles III, as the site for a royal palace that would be sufficiently close to Naples for him to be able to return to the capital at a moment's notice, yet far enough away for the king and his entourage to indulge in hunting, one of the main Bourbon pursuits. No matter that courtiers were worried by the proximity of Vesuvius; Charles refused to show concern at any imminent danger, proclaiming, "God, the immaculate Virgin, and San Gennaro will protect us." The royal presence in the area triggered a boom in real estate, with more than 120 ducal villas being built in the subsequent half century on a stretch of land that came to be known

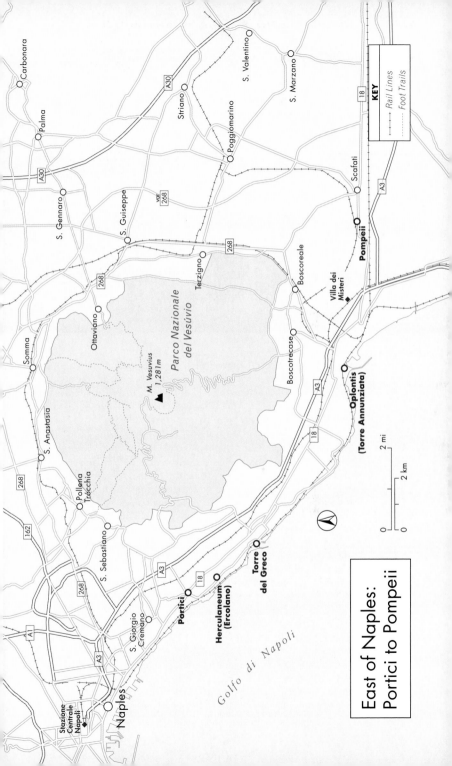

East of Naples: Portici to Pompeii

KEY

Rail Lines
Foot Trails

Carbonara

Palma

S. Gennaro

A30

A30

Striano

S. Valentino

S. Marzano

Poggiomarino

S. Guiseppe

VdT
268

Scafati

268

18

A3

Pompeii

Terzigno

Boscoreale

Villa dei
Misteri

Ottaviano

268

Parco Nazionale
del Vesúvio

Boscotrecase

Somma

M. Vesuvius
1,281 m

Oplontis
(Torre Annunziata)

S. Anastasia

A3

18

S. Pollena
Trócchia

268

S. Sebastiano

162

268

A3

S. Giorgio
Cremano

18

Portici

A1

Herculaneum
(Ercolano)

A3

Torre
del Greco

Golfo di Napoli

Naples

Stazione
Centrale
Napoli

2 mi

2 km

0

0

Portici's Palazzo Reale is one of the main landmarks of the Bourbon presence in Italy.

as the *Miglio d'Oro* (Golden Mile). Here life became one long gala, with costume balls, picnics, concerts, and entertainment, some of which enchanted the likes of Goethe and Lord Byron. Today, progress is being made by the *Ente per le Ville Vesuviane* (Vesuvian Villa Association) to purchase and restore the villas to their former glory.

Fodor'sChoice ★ The showpiece is Portici's Reggia (palace), or **Palazzo Reale.** Straddling the Via Nazionale delle Calabrie (Statale 18), the main road that led south of Naples in past centuries, now renamed Via Università, this royal palace was designed by the architect Canevari, who added a layout of 75 acres of woodland, but its actual construction was overseen and executed by another architect, Ferdinando Fuga, 1738–42. It stands impressively at the foothills of Vesuvius and enjoys sweeping views across the Bay of Naples from both its south-facing inner courtyard and its upper floors. Although the agricultural faculty of Naples University still occupies most of the palace, the cultural heritage ministry has taken over a few of the rooms on the *piano nobile* (main floor) and currently uses them for temporary exhibitions, thereby restoring to the public one of the main landmarks of Bourbon history and architecture.

The palace is on a trolley-bus route (No. 255) between Ercolano and Portici, a 10-minute walk northwest up Corso Resina from the Herculaneum archaeological site. Purchase tickets at a tobacco shop or newsstand along the Corso and ask for the *"fermata del tram-bus"* (tram-bus top). The Reggia's bus stop is unmistakable, in the middle of the courtyard right between the northern and southern wings. Head for the university porters' lodge on the seaward side (in parking lot just beyond) and mount the monumental staircase leading up to the piano nobile. At the risk of developing a crick in your neck, admire the well-preserved 18th-century trompe l'oeil frescoes decorating the walls and the ceiling and generally enjoy these now-hallowed halls of academe. Horatio Nelson would have walked up the same staircase on his way to a royal banquet held in his honor by King Ferdinand IV and Queen Carolina in 1798, where he sat opposite and first met Sir William Hamilton and his wife, Emma. At the time the palace was used as a repository for many of the early finds from Herculaneum, now in the Museo Archeologico in Naples, and it was noted particularly for the decorative 18th-century panels from the finest salon—called the porcelain, or china, room—which were subsequently moved to the Royal Palace of Capodimonte, where they can still be admired today. ✉ *Via Università 100, Portici* ☏ *081/7754850* 🎫 *Reggia is free, exhibits have variable admission charge* ✆ *Sept.–July, weekdays 9–6.*

Opposite the entrance to the Royal Palace of Portici lies the **Orto Botanico** *(Botanical Garden),* founded in 1872. It's housed within the palace grounds and abuts the magnificent Holmoak Wood, the hunting preserve of the Bourbon kings. The garden's original specimens were severely damaged in World War II, when the botanical institute was requisitioned and the garden used as a vehicle parking area by Allied forces. Since then the collection has recovered and expanded, with a delightfully shady palmery, an impressive variety of cycads, and some unusually large specimens of the exotic Asian tree *Ginkgo biloba.* Since there are virtually no signposts in the garden, ask to see the rare southern African desert plant *Welwitschia mirabilis,* and the native but endangered primrose *Primula palinuri.* ✉ *Via Università 100, Portici* ☏ *081/7755136* ⊕ *www.museiagraria.unina.it* 🎫 *€4* ✆ *Daily, but by reservation only.*

There are other signature villas of the famed Miglio d'Oro, but many—including the Villa d'Elboeuf, and Villa Signorini—are either being renovated or are open only for group visits. However, to the west of Portici (in the rather dreary suburban town of San Giorgio a Cremano) is the **Villa Bruno,** now restored to its original late 18th-century grandeur. Past its gentle yellow-and-gray outer walls and remodeled neoclassical facade you'll find a small museum devoted to locally born actor and film director Massimo Troisi. The rest of the building is office space and closed to the public. At the back of the villa is a pergola walkway, a small auditorium used for concerts, and extensive lawns offering a welcome respite from San Giorgio's incessant traffic. The villa is best reached from the Cavalli di Bronzo stop of the Circumvesuviana railway between Naples and Portici. Outside the station, turn right down Via Cavalli di Bronzo for about five minutes until you come to the villa on your left. ✉ *Via Cavalli di Bronzo 20, San Giorgio a Cremano* ☏ *081/5654395* 🎫 *Free* ✆ *Weekdays 9–7, Sat. 8–1 and 5–9, Sun., 9–9.*

WHERE TO EAT

× **A' Cantinella do Cunvento.** A short walk down Via Università from the Royal Palace of Portici brings you to this unpretentious ristorante–pizzeria, known to the locals as Da Peppino after its owner-manager Giuseppe. Although crowded at lunchtime with staff from the nearby college, this spot has down-to-earth service and prices that are hardly

SOUTHERN ITALIAN

donnish. The competitive all-in-one price—an incredibly good value—includes first course (pasta or rice), main (octopus salad is a specialty), and fruit for €7.50. ⊠ *Via Università 64, Portici* ☎*081/7755301* ⊟*No credit cards* ⊗*Closed Sun.*

HERCULANEUM (ERCOLANO)

Fodor'sChoice
★ *12 km (8 mi) southeast of Naples, 40 km (25 mi) northwest of Salerno.*

GETTING HERE

To get to Herculaneum by car, take the A3 Naples–Salerno highway and exit at "Ercolano." Follow signs for the "Scavi" (excavations). The Circumvesuviana connects Herculaneum to Naples, Portici, Torre del Greco, Torre Annunziata, Pompeii, and Sorrento with frequent departures and arrivals. City buses No. 157 and 255 depart Naples' Piazza Municipio for Herculaneum, via Portici, regularly. No. 255 continues on to Torre del Greco as well.

VISITOR INFORMATION

The **Ufficio Turistico** (⊠ *Via IV Novembre 82, Ercolano* ☎*081/7881243*) is open 9–2, closed Sunday.

EXPLORING

A visit to the archaeological site of Herculaneum neatly counterbalances the hustle of its larger neighbor, Pompeii. And although close to the heart of the busy town of Ercolano—indeed, in places right under it—the ancient site seems worlds apart, and you have the sensation of being catapulted back into the past, for here there is ample supply of ancient allure and splendor (unlike Pompeii, whose site is much more ruined). Like Pompeii, Herculaneum was buried by Vesuvius's eruption in AD 79. Unlike Pompeii, it was submerged in a mass of volcanic mud that sealed and preserved wood and other materials including food (whereas at Pompeii, most organic matter rotted away over time). Much smaller than its famous neighbor, the settlement of Herculaneum was a wealthy resort town, and a greater portion of what was found has been left in place. Several villas have inlaid marble floors that evoke the same admiration as the mosaics in Naples' Museo Archeologico. Elsewhere it's possible to gauge how the less privileged lived: more remains of the upper stories than in Pompeii, so you can view the original stairs to the cramped, poorly lighted rooms that gave onto the central courtyard. Here there's more of a sense of a living community than Pompeii is able to convey. Like all the other sites in the Vesuvian area, Herculaneum is served efficiently by the Circumvesuviana railway, which provides fast, frequent, and economical connections; from Naples' Stazione Centrale in Piazza Garibaldi, take the Circumvesuviana train to the Ercolano stop (five per hour, 20 minutes east, €1.80). The ruins are a five-minute walk downhill along Via IV Novembre toward the Bay of Naples. ■TIP→ Archaeology buffs will want to bring a flashlight to better see into the dark corners of the excavated houses and bottled water to pour on in situ mosaics to brighten them up.

Lying more than 60 feet below the town of Ercolano, the **Scavi di Ercolano** (Excavations of Herculaneum) now stand among acres of

The colors remain vivid on many of Herculaneum's frescos.

greenhouses that make this area one of Europe's chief flower-growing areas. It was named, like several other Greek colonies around the Mediterranean, after its legendary founder Heracles (Hercules), but details surrounding the date of its foundation by its Greek settlers have yet to be revealed. Certainly the grid plan of the town's layout suggests affinities with nearby Neapolis (now Naples), so it could have been an offshoot of its neighbor on the Bay of Naples. Like many Greek sites in southern Italy, in about the 4th century BC it fell under Samnite influence. It finally became a *municipium* (municipality) under Roman dominion in 89 BC. At the time of its destruction in AD 79, it had fewer than 5,000 inhabitants (as compared to Pompeii's 10–20,000), many of whom were fishermen, craftsmen, and artists, while a lucky few patricians owned summer villas overlooking the sea. In contrast to Pompeii, most of the damage here was done by volcanic mud. This semiliquid mass seeped into the crevices and niches of every building, covering household objects and enveloping textiles and wood—sealing all in a compact, airtight tomb.

Casual excavation—and haphazard looting—began at the beginning of the 18th century under the prince of Elboeuf, who purchased the land after a farmer had made several chance finds of marble relics while digging for a well. The excavation technique at the time consisted of digging vertical shafts and horizontal galleries, and whenever possible, gunpowder was used to speed up the work—techniques that make those of the much-maligned Heinrich Schliemann, discoverer of Troy, sound positively scrupulous. It was precisely through this network of underground tunnels that 18th-century visitors from northern Europe on their Grand Tour—such as Horace Walpole and Thomas Gray—were to experience the buried city. Open air digs were not initiated until 1828, by which time many of the sugarplums buried within the cake had already been plucked or damaged. Today less than half of Herculaneum has been excavated; with present-day Ercolano and the unlovely Resina quarter (famous among bargain hunters as the area's largest secondhand-clothing market) perched on top of the site, progress is understandably limited.

WORD OF MOUTH

"I love both Herculaneum and Pompeii, but if I had to choose I would say Herculaneum—it seems to be more personal somehow. It is more compact and easier to do justice to it if time is limited."
—travel2live2

Although Herculaneum had only one-fourth to one-half the population of Pompeii and has been only partially excavated, what has been found is generally in a better state of preservation. In some cases you can even see the original wooden beams, staircases, and furniture. Lending a touch of verdant life, some of the peristyle gardens have been replanted. Today much excitement is focused on one excavation adjacent to the main site, the **Villa dei Papiri,** built by Julius Caesar's father-in-law. The building takes its name from the 1,800 carbonized papyrus scrolls dug up here in the 18th century, leading scholars to believe it may have been a study center or library. Now Italian archaeologists and geologists have uncovered part of the villa itself and hope to unearth more of the library—given the right funds and political support. ■ TIP➔ The villa is closed to the public for restoration, but you can see over 100 bronze statues recovered from the villa at the Museo Archeologico Nazionale in Naples.

For all visits to the site, walk through the archway at the very bottom of Via IV Novembre, which houses the ticket office. Here you should also pick up a free booklet and map to the site, and then make your way downhill, pausing to view Herculaneum's grid system of roads from above, with the three *cardines* (avenues running north–south) being intersected by two *decumani* (east–west axes). The blocks, as in Pompeii, are referred to as *insulae,* each containing shops and villas on the ground floor and apartments on upper stories. In general, and unsurprisingly, the best mosaics, wall paintings, and any organic remains such as wooden furniture are found in those parts that were excavated in the 20th century. The 19th-century open-air excavators—though systematic—took few precautions to preserve the upper stories (just note the ruinous state of Insula II, in the southwest corner) and, in addition, the artwork has been exposed to the air for an extra century.

Continue downhill past the large modern structure of the Antiquarium (built in the 1980s, though yet to be opened). At this stage you may want to pick up an audio guide to the site at the kiosk on the right after the Antiquarium (€6.50 for one, €10 for a pair; ID required), which gives helpful house-by-house information. Ignore the pedestrian bridge leading straight into the northern sector (use that for the exit instead) and enter the site via an underground passage behind the audio-guide kiosk, which cuts down through 60 feet of volcanic deposits and emerges by the southern (lower) end of the site. The path then crosses

THE BAY OF NAPLES THROUGH THE AGES

Rich archaeological and literary evidence reveals a continuous human presence in Campania for millennia. Used as an outpost probably by the Minoans and Mycenaeans in the second millennium BC, the area was first colonized by Greeks from Euboea in the 8th century BC; they settled on the island of Pithekoussai (modern-day Ischia) and later on the mainland at Cumae. The Greek geographer Strabo (64 BC–after AD 21), who appears to have traveled extensively in the area, provides further documentation to the area's history. The early Greeks traded widely with the Etruscans and local Italic peoples, eventually extending their sphere of influence to Neapolis and southward and northward along the shores of the Tyrrhenian Sea.

Greek civilization flourished for hundreds of years along this seaboard, but there was nothing in the way of centralized government until centuries later, when the Romans extended their domain southward and began to set up colonies of their own for added protection, especially after incursions led by such flamboyant figures as Pyrrhus and Hannibal in the 3rd century BC.

From the 1st century BC onward, Campania became synonymous with sybaritic living. It was here that wealthy Romans built palatial residences, tapping the natural hot springs for their fabled baths and harnessing the area's rich volcanic soils to produce wines lauded by Latin poets. Here emperors indulged in vices that would have been unseemly in the capital, and there was the usual complement of public baths and spectacle to keep the plebeians happy.

The merrymaking to the east of Naples was stilled in AD 79 by a jolt from Vesuvius, believed by few at the time to harbor any danger for those living at its base. We are fortunate to have Pliny the Younger's memorable description of his uncle being overwhelmed by fumes and dying of asphyxiation in Stabiae, now Castellammare di Stabia. Although written some years after the event, Pliny's letter to Tacitus is a unique and moving account of the disaster. But as so often happens in history, other people's catastrophes are an archaeologist's dream: Pompeii, Herculaneum, and outlying lesser-known sites such as Oplontis were spared the ravages of the centuries and have been remarkably preserved for posterity.

a marshy area, which was the original sea level and the site of a small port. This means that thanks to various eruptions (especially AD 79 and 1631), the topography of the land has changed beyond all recognition. It's now hard to believe that Herculaneum lay "*inter duos fluvios infra Vesuvium*" (between two rivers below Vesuvius).

The most gruesome find to be made in modern times at Herculaneum was in the *fornici* (storehouses) located in the warehouses to the left as you cross small footbridge. Here, about 300 skeletons were excavated, all "frozen" in place as they slept their troubled sleep after the first day of volcanic destruction when a surge cloud swept the town. As they cannot normally be viewed in situ, for sheer poignancy the Garden of the

Fugitives in Pompeii is more effective, as there you get to see the casts of bodies at the bottom of the garden where they were found.

★ Walk up to the town past the **Terme Suburbane** *(Suburban Baths)*, closed for restoration at this writing. In the courtyard outside the building is an altar erected by the town benefactor, Marcus Nonius Balbus, and the base for his marble statue, long since removed to the Museo Archeologico in Naples. Much of the volcanic mud here has been left in situ, so you get a good idea not only of a Roman baths complex, but also of the problems that confronted the archaeologists when excavating it. ⊠ *Il Quartiere Suburbano.*

In antiquity, the **Casa dei Cervi** was one of the first houses that visitors to the town would have passed as they entered the city from the seaward side. As in most top-notch town residences, however, the entranceway is plain and leads into a *vestibulum,* a small vestibule, that opens onto an open courtyard called a *peristylium.* The showpiece in this particular house is the garden area, surrounded by a so-called *cryptoporticus* embellished with fine still life frescoes and terminating in a partially reconstructed gazebo. Of course, prior to the eruption, the house would have had a fine view over the Bay of Naples. ⊠ *Insula IV.*

As you walk around Herculaneum, you'll notice the narrow entrances of the houses and the wider entrances for shops, inns, and other buildings where large numbers of people required access. A case in point is at the corner of Cardo V and the Decumanus Inferior, where you'll see two access points and counters with large amphorae for keeping dishes warm. This was one of the town's **Thermopolia,** the fast-food outlets of the ancient world. Next door, for relaxed, discreet dining where, judging from the warren of private chambers within, more than just food and drink was on offer, there was the **Taberna di Priapo** *(Priapus's Tavern),* complete with its waiting room at the back right. ⊠ *Insula IV.*

Of course, no town would have been complete without its sports facilities, and Herculaneum was no exception. Just opposite the *thermopolium* on Cardo V is the entrance to the large **Palaestra,** where a variety of ball games and wrestling matches were staged. Here, when you look at the peristyle columns and realize that only three of a total of more than 20 have been excavated, you appreciate how much of the ancient town still lies buried under solidified volcanic mud. ⊠ *Insula Orientalis II.*

On Cardo IV parallel to Cardo V, close to the Forum Baths, is the **Casa del Nettuno ed Anfitrite** *(House of Neptune and Amphitrite).* It takes its name from the mosaic that still sports its bright blue coloring and adorns the wall of the small secluded *nymphaeum,* or shrine with fountains, at the back of the house. According to legend, in the time-honored fashion of the Olympians, Neptune (or Poseidon) saw Amphitrite dancing with the Nereids on the island of Naxos, carried her off, and married her. The adjacent wall, in similar mosaic style though less well preserved, has a hunting scene with a stag being pursued by a dog. Annexed to the same house is a remarkably preserved wine shop, where amphorae still rest on carbonized wooden shelves. ⊠ *Insula V.*

Stories of Roman licentiousness are belied by the **Terme del Foro** *(Forum Baths),* where there were separate sections for men and women. Here you see most of the architectural ingredients of *thermae* (baths). But besides the mandatory trio in the men's section (a round *frigidarium*, a cool swimming pool; a *tepidarium*, a semi-heated pool; and a *calidarium*, or heated pool), there's also an *apodyterium*, or changing room, with partitioned shelves for depositing togas and a low podium to use as seating space while in line to use the facilities. For more attractive mosaics—particularly a spectacular rendition of Neptune—go around into the women's baths (with seemingly no frigidarium). The heating system in the tepidarium was also different (no hot air piped through or under, only braziers). Note the steam vents ingeniously built into the bath's benches and the small overhead cubbies in which bathers stored their togas. ⊠ *Insula VI.*

An outstanding example of carbonized remains is in the **Casa del Tramezzo di Legno** *(House of the Wooden Partition)*, as it has been prosaically labeled by archaeologists. Following renovation work in the mid-1st century AD, the house was designed to have a frontage on three sides of Insula III and included a number of storerooms, shops, and second-floor habitations. This suggests that the owner was a wealthy *mercator*, a member of the up-and-coming merchant class that was starting to edge the patricians out of their privileged positions. The airy atrium has a lovely garden. Look closely at the *impluvium* (a channel to collect rainwater), and you'll see the original flooring below, which was later replaced with marble, perhaps after a change of owners. Next to the *impluvium* is an elegant marble table, or *cartibulum*, while behind is the *tablinum* (reception room), partially screened off by a bronze-studded wooden partition (the central part of which is missing) that would also have had hooks for hanging *lucernae* (lamps). ⊠ *Insula III, 11–12, Corso Resina 6, Ercolano* ☎ *081/8575347* ⊕ *www.pompeiisites.org* 💶 *€11 for Herculaneum only; €20 for biglietto cumulativo ticket to 5 sites (Pompeii, Herculaneum, Boscoreale, Oplontis, and Stabiae) valid for 3 days* ⊙ *Nov.–Mar., daily 8:30–5, ticket office closes at 3:30; Apr.–Oct., daily 8:30–7:30, ticket office closes at 6. Closed Jan. 1, May 1, Dec. 25.*

Leave the archaeological site of Herculaneum and head southeast along Corso Resina, keeping Vesuvius on your left and the Bay of Naples on your right; after about a five-minute walk you'll pass the entrance to **Villa Campolieto,** one of the most attractive Vesuvian villas, which, like most historic buildings still standing in the area, has survived centuries of volcanic eruptions, earthquakes, and post-Bourbon neglect. Go in through the well-tended gardens past the ticket kiosk (leaflets are available in English) and turn left into the main building. If you're motorized, ask at the kiosk to use the parking facilities at the far end of the gardens.

The construction of Villa Campolieto was commissioned by Prince Luzio of Sangro and entrusted to no less than four architects during its troubled conception from 1755 to 1775, with the final touches added by the architect Luigi Vanvitelli, better known for his work on the Royal Palace of Caserta, and his son Carlo. After entering through the gardens—this was the original main entrance, as the large doorway on the Via Nazionale delle Calabrie (now Corso Resina) was reserved for carriages—proceed up the Vanvitellian staircase (similar to the one at the palace at Caserta) to the piano nobile, currently used for temporary exhibitions and events. Note the classical scenes in most of the frescoes on this floor, with fine illusionist work by Jacopo Cestaro, including depictions of Minerva and Mercury set in a Vanvitelli-style colonnade. Cestaro was also responsible for the beautifully restored fresco ceilings in both of the front rooms facing Vesuvius. At ground-floor level, the main peculiarity is the elliptical rotunda, which provides a picturesque setting for outdoor concerts and theatrical performances during the Vesuvian Villas Festival in the summer. Note the natural gray shading of the steps and lower facade, characteristic of many buildings erected in the Bourbon era, from the local volcanic *piperno* stone. This villa is the headquarters for the Ente per le Ville Vesuviane association. ⊠ *Corso Resina 283, Ercolano* ☎ *081/7322134* ⊕ *www.villevesuviane.net* ⊡ *€3* ⊗ *Tues.–Sun. 9–1.*

WHERE TO EAT

¢

SOUTHERN
ITALIAN

✕ **La Fornacella.** Doing a brisk trade for both *stranieri* and locals—always a good sign—this ristorante–pizzeria is a 10-minute walk up from the excavations of Herculaneum on the roundabout near the Circumvesuvi-ana station. Dishes and wines vary according to season but always draw on local recipes: pasta *e fagioli* (with beans) is a winter favorite, while richly garnished *schiaffoni* (flat tube pasta) with seafood is a summer stalwart. If sensitive to traffic noise, you're best avoiding the outside tables. ⊠ *Via IV Novembre 90–92, Ercolano* ☎ *081/7774861* ⊟ *AE, DC, MC, V* ⊗ *Closed Mon.*

SHOPPING

Donadio Manifattura Coralli (⊠ *Piazzale L. Sapio, near Ercolano exit of Napoli–Salerno autostrada, Portici* ☎ *081/7752900* ⊕ *www.donadio. it*) is first and foremost a cameo factory; it also sells directly to the public. Local artisans can be observed making the cameos, an age-old tradition in which shells—now virtually all imported—are meticulously carved to produce mythological scenes in relief, exploiting the natural layering and contrasting colors of the raw material.

VESUVIUS

Fodor's Choice
★

16 km (10 mi) east of Naples, 8 km (5 mi) northeast of Herculaneum, 40 km (25 mi) northwest of Salerno.

GETTING HERE

To arrive by car, take the A3 Napoli–Salerno highway exit "Torre del Greco" and follow Via E. De Nicola from the tollbooth. Follow signs for the Parco Nazionale del Vesuvio.

There's regular bus service up Vesuvius operated by **Vesuviana Mobil-itá** (☎ *081/9634420* ⊕ *www.vesuvianamobilita.it*)(€10.60 return from Pompei Piazza Anfiteatro, €9.60 from Ercolano Circumvesuviana sta-tion), although it's far quicker to take the trips up Vesuvius on mini-buses run by **Vesuvio Express** (☎ *081/7393666* ⊕ *www.vesuvioexpress. it*) (€10 return from Ercolano Circumvesuviana station). Both services will take you up to the car park and the starting point of the path up to the cone's top.

CLOSE UP

Hiking around the Bay: Vesuvius and Beyond

For challenging hikes off the beaten track, parts of Vesuvius have been mapped out with trails for public access. What looks like a barren wasteland from down below turns out to be a profusion of well-adapted plant and animal life, which is at its best in spring and early summer. Deserted paths cut across ancient lava fields and pyroclastic material, through lunarlike terrain and then suddenly into Mediterranean scrub and woodland. As an alternative, on torrid summer days, take an eight-minute cable car ride from Castellammare di Stabia up to Monte Faito, which rises impressively to almost 4,000 feet on the southeastern sweep of the Bay of Naples. A short walk takes you into shady beech woods reminiscent of Italy's Apennine backbone, while more ambitious trails marked by the Club Alpino Italiano lead across imposing landscapes to the Amalfi Coast.

If you're suffering from a surfeit of archaeology or feel the need to counteract an overindulgence in the local *cucina,* a visit to one of the extinct volcanic craters near Naples could produce dividends. The Astroni crater, now a preserve maintained by the World Wide Fund for Nature,

offers breathtakingly beautiful walks amid Mediterranean woodland, and it's only 16 km (10 mi) from the very heart of Naples. Picnic sites have been thoughtfully laid out in shady spots within the crater's perimeter. At the base, there's the added interest of small brackish lakes overlooked by an observation hide, so there's a good chance of seeing a variety of bird species (bring binoculars). Like so many places here, the crater is steeped in history: once studded with Roman natural thermal baths, this whole area became the hunting domain of the Aragonese in the 15th century and then of the Bourbon kings in the 18th and 19th centuries.

A smaller crater near the coast to the west of Pozzuoli offering shorter and less shady walks is Monte Nuovo, whose cone formed in just eight days of explosive activity in 1538. Innovatively co-managed by the town council of Pozzuoli and a local school, the cone exhibits residual volcanic activity in the form of fumaroles. This is the place to hone your botanical skills, with many of the main species of the Mediterranean maquis having been planted and clearly labeled close to the site's offices.

A branch of the aptly named Circumvesuviana railway (☎ *800/053939* ⊕ *www.vesuviana.it*) serves the main archaeological sites at the foot of Vesuvius. Trains leave from the Porta Nolana-Corso Garibaldi station in Naples, stop at the main terminal at Piazza Garibaldi 10 blocks away to link up with the Naples *metropolitana,* and then head southeast for Sorrento (about two trains per hour; €1.80 to Ercolano and Torre Annunziata, and €2.40 to Pompei Scavi–Villa Dei Misteri). Confusingly, the station called "Pompei-Santuario," which is the stop for the modern city, lies on a different line, which will leave you not at the main entrance to the archaeological site but just behind the Santuario, closer to the amphitheater.

Vesuvius is a commanding presence in the region.

EXPLORING

Vesuvius may have lost its plume of smoke, but it has lost none of its fascination—especially for those who live in the towns around the cone. They've now nicknamed it the "Sterminator." In centuries gone by, their predecessors would study the volcano for signs of impending destruction. *Napoli fa i peccati e la Torre li paga*, the residents of nearby Torre del Greco used to mutter—"Naples sins and the Torre suffers." When reports of depraved behavior circulated about Neapolitans across the bay, chastisement was only to be expected.

Today, the world continues to watch *'O Vesuvio* with bated breath. Although its destructive powers are undoubtedly diminished, the threat of an eruption is ever present. In bygone ages the task of protecting the local inhabitants fell to the martyred patron saint of Naples, San Gennaro, or St. Januarius, whose statue was often borne aloft through the streets of the city in an effort to placate the volcano's wrath.

Volcanic activity is attentively monitored by the Osservatorio Vesuviano. Founded under Bourbon king Ferdinand II in the mid-19th century, it's the facility where the seismic scale was invented. The original observatory, conspicuous with its Pompeian-red facade, has survived unscathed on the volcano's upper slopes and now serves as a conference center and small museum: the **Museo dell'Osservatorio Vesuviano** houses a mineralogical display, characteristic landscape gouaches, early seismographs, and information panels. Access during the week is restricted to scientific groups, associations, and schools. ⊠ *Via Osservatorio, Ercolano* ☎*081/7777149 081/6108483* ⊕*www.ov.ingv.it* ✉*Free* ☉ *Weekends 10–2.*

Seen from the other side of the Bay of Naples, Vesuvius appears to have two peaks: on the northern side is the steep face of Monte Somma, possibly part of the original crater wall in AD 79; to the south is the present-day cone of Vesuvius, which has actually formed within the ancient crater. The AD 79 cone would have been considerably higher, perhaps peaking at more than 6,000 feet. The upper slopes

3

bear the visible scars left by 19th- and 20th-century eruptions, the most striking being the lava flow from 1944 lying to the left (north side) of the approach road from Ercolano on the way up. Halfway up, the **Park Info Point** (☎081/7710911 ⊕*www.parconazionaledelvesuvio.it*) has information on a series of trails; a favorite one includes footpath up from San Sebastiano, following the course of the old rack railroad wiped out by the 1944 eruption and emerging close to the Osservatorio.

For public transport users, Vesuviana Mobilita' runs a bus service that leaves the Circumvesuviana station for Vesuvius's 1,000-meter point (€9.60 return). A bit more reliable is are the 10-seat minibuses run by **Vesuvio Express** (☎081/7393666 ⊕*www.vesuvioexpress.it*), a quick, painless, and relatively cheap way of getting to the top (€10 return from Ercolano station). Departures are scheduled every 20 minutes, but at peak times you may have to wait (in the office to the left of the station exit). The minibus then threads its way rapidly up on back roads, reaching Quota 1000 (the car park) after about 20 minutes and will wait to take you down. Allow at least 2½ hours for the round-trip, including your walk up to the crater. For those driving up, the road is sometimes confusingly marked, but as a general rule look for the brown PARCO NAZIONALE DEL VESUVIO signs from the Herculaneum (Ercolano) or Torre del Greco autostrada exits and keep heading upward for about 20 minutes. (For taxi rides up Vesuvius from Torre del Greco or Pompeii, there is a flat fare of €90 for a two-hour round-trip.)

When you get to the parking lot at the top, for extra security opt to pay the €2.50 parking charge. The parking lot, minibus terminal, and ticket office at Quota 1000 lie roughly 20 minutes' walk (about a 400-foot climb) from the nearest viewing point down into the crater. You have to pay an entrance fee at the National Park kiosk in the car park of €6.50 (open from 9 AM until two hours before sunset), which covers the cost of a compulsory but somewhat elusive guide service. You will be offered a sturdy walking stick on leaving the parking lot (a small tip is appreciated on your return). The path is kept in good repair, but wear nonskid shoes (not sandals) and come prepared for strong winds. Once you've seen the fumaroles and gazed down as much as 600 feet into the wondrous depths of the crater, take in the broad sweep around the Bay of Naples—though you'll probably find the city of Naples more photogenic from lower down the slopes, near the observatory.

Times have changed considerably since the days of Lord and Lady Hamilton: the tarmac road served around 600,000 visitors in 2007, though facilities at the parking lot and above are still skeletal. Ugly souvenir stands grate with the wilderness, and there may be as many as 30 tour buses offloading their cargoes at any one time. It's even more reason to get here first thing in the morning to appreciate the sharper vistas and raw beauty of the volcano. ■ TIP→Bring binoculars for bird-watching and taking in the sweeping panorama across the bay.

TORRE DEL GRECO

16 km (10 mi) southeast of Naples, 11 km (7 mi) northwest of Pompeii.

GETTING HERE

To get to Torre del Greco by car, take the A3 Naples–Salerno highway, exit at "Torre del Greco" and follow Via Cavallo into the center of town. The FS (state train line) station links Torre del Greco to Naples, Portici, and Salerno), while the Circumvesuviana connects Torre del Greco to Naples, Portici, Herculaneum, Torre Annunziata, Pompeii, and Sorrento. Bus No. 255 arrives from central Naples, via Protici and Herculaneum.

EXPLORING

Being in an area of high volcanic risk, Torre del Greco has borne the brunt of Vesuvian eruptions over the centuries. The demolition of the historic center begun by Vesuvius was almost completed by the time of the postwar building boom; with more than 100,000 inhabitants, Torre del Greco is now close behind its neighbor Portici as one of the most densely populated towns in the world. However, some architectural jewels have survived—including the 18th-century Vesuvian villa Palazzo Vallelonga, at Via Vittorio Emanuele 92—and the **Museo del Corallo** on Piazza Palomba 6. As it turns out, this museum is sited on the first floor of an art school and is only open by appointment (call ☎081/8811360 a few days in advance; the secretary speaks only Italian). No admission is charged and the times more or less coincide with classes (usually from 8:30 to 1), but there are no permanent staff attached to the museum, so it's all on an informal, ad hoc basis. In any event, the exhibits reveal why the Torresi, or Corallini (the townspeople), are still considered the world's best fashioners of coral and cameos. If you're motorized, Torre del Greco is a good base camp for exploring the Vesuvian area, with well-paved, clearly signposted roads north of the Torre del Greco autostrada exit.

WHERE TO EAT AND STAY

$–$$ ⬚ **Hotel Marad.** Dominated by huge spreading umbrella pines and close
★   to the Torre del Greco exit of the Naples–Salerno A3 Autostrada, the Marad bristles with efficiency and is an obvious base for exploring the area around Vesuvius and Herculaneum, especially if you have a car. In the middle of the price scale, the hotel offers good facilities at competitive prices. Though a little unadventurous in its range of main courses and dessert, the ground-floor restaurant produces trusty local pasta dishes, like *Paccheri con cozze e pomodorini* (pasta with mussels

The villa at Oplontis is another of the bay area's archaeological treasures.

and cherry tomatoes). The Marad doubles as a conference center, so book well in advance. **Pros:** half- and full-board available; newly refurbished; pleasant garden, Wi-fi throughout complex. **Cons:** impersonal business travelers hotel; far from restaurants and town; car is a must. ⊠ *Via Benedetto Croce 20* ☎*081/8492168* 🖷*081/8828716* ⊕*www. marad.it* 🗖*74 rooms* ⌂*In-hotel: 2 restaurants, pool, Wi-Fi* ▭*AE, DC, MC, V* ⍟*BP.*

OPLONTIS (TORRE ANNUNZIATA)

Fodor'sChoice
★
20 km (12 mi) southeast of Naples, 5 km (3 mi) west of Pompeii.

GETTING HERE

By car, take the A3 Napoli–Salerno highway to the "Torre Annunziata" exit. Follow Via Veneto west, then turn left onto Via Sepolcri for the excavations.

EXPLORING

Surrounded by the fairly drab urban landscape of Torre Annunziata, thrown up in the 1960s, Oplontis justifies its reputation as one of the more mysterious archaeological sites to be unearthed in the 20th century. The villa complex has been imaginatively ascribed—from a mere inscription on an amphora—to Nero's second wife, Poppaea Sabina, whose family was well known among the landed gentry of neighboring Pompeii. As Roman villas go, Poppaea's Villa, or Villa A, as it's called more prosaically by archaeologists, is way off the top end of the scale. What has so far been excavated covers more than 7,000 square meters (75,000 square feet), and because the site is bound by a road to the west and a canal to the south, we are unlikely to ever gauge its full extent. Complete with porticoes, a large peristyle, *piscina* (pool), baths, and extensive gardens, besides the standard atria, triclinia, and a warren of cubicula, the villa is thought by some to have been a training school for young philosophers and orators. Certainly, for those overwhelmed by the throngs at Pompeii, a modern-day visit to the site of Oplontis offers a chance for contemplation and intellectual stimulation.

Access is easiest from the Circumvesuviana station of Torre Annunziata (about 600 feet away). Outside the station turn left and then right downhill, and the site is just after the crossroads down on the left. If coming by car, take the Torre Annunziata Sud turnoff from the Naples–Salerno autostrada, turn right, and then look for signs on the left for Oplontis at the first major crossroads. Try to negotiate a parking space in the site car park, especially if your car is laden with luggage. At the ticket office you should be given a site map and a helpful information booklet. The main entrance to the site is from the north—you basically go into the villa through the gardens, with the atrium on the southern side lying under about 16 feet of pumice and pyroclastic material from Vesuvius.

Now that many of the frescoed houses in Pompeii are closed for restoration or for limited viewing, you have to come to Oplontis to appreciate the full gamut of Roman wall paintings. Its occupants showed a particular penchant for the illusionist motifs of the so-called Second Pompeian Style. There are some good examples in the west wing of the villa, especially in the triclinium (Room 6) opening onto a small portico, which abuts the west end of the site and the road above. Although the stucco work in the thermae, or baths, is less impressive than in Pompeii and Herculaneum, the calidarium (Room 3) has a delightful miniature landscape scene surmounted by a peacock in a niche at its eastern end, above a more visible fresco of Hercules in the Garden of the Hesperides. In Room 3 and next door in the tepidarium (Room 4) there's an interesting glimpse into the structural design of Roman baths; here the floor is raised by *suspensurae*, small brick supporting pilasters, enabling warm air to pass beneath. Note that Oplontis is sometimes used as a theater venue between June and September, with productions featuring ancient Greek and Latin playwrights (in Italian); tickets can be bought at the Proloco in Torre Annunziata (close to the Oplontis site at Via Sepolcri 16). ⊠ *Via Sepolcri 1, Torre Annunziata* ☎*081/8621755* ⊕*www.pompeiisites.org €5.50 for Oplontis, Stabia, and Boscoreale; €20 for biglietto cumulativo pass to 5 sites (Pompeii, Herculaneum, Boscoreale, Oplontis, and Stabiae) valid for 3 days* ⊙*Nov.–Mar., daily 8:30–5, ticket office closes at 3:30; Apr.–Oct., daily 8:30–7:30, ticket office closes at 6. Closed Jan. 1, May 1, Dec. 25.*

POMPEII: CITY OF VESUVIUS

GETTING HERE

To get to Pompeii by car, take the A3 Napoli–Salerno highway to the "Pompei" exit and follow signs for the nearby "Scavi" excavations. There are numerous guarded car parks near the Porta Marina, Piazza

Essedra, and Anfiteatro entrances where you can leave your vehicle for a fee.

Pompeii has two central Circumvesuviana stations served by two separate train lines. The Naples–Sorrento train stops at "Pompei Scavi-Villa dei Misteri," 100 yards from the Porta Marina ticket office of the archaeological site, while the Naples–Poggiomarino train stops at Pompei Santuario, more convenient for the Santuario della Madonna del Rosario and the hotels and restaurants in the modern town center. A third FS (state) train station south of the town center is only really convenient if arriving from Salerno or Rome.

WORD OF MOUTH

"For Pompeii, you need about four hours—mostly walking on rugged terrain in the shadeless sun. Even if you have stamina, you will need a rest." —traveller1959

VISITOR INFORMATION

The Pompeii offices of **Azienda Autonoma di Cura Soggiorno e Turismo** (✉ *Via Sacra 1, Pompeii* ☎ *081/8507255* ⊕ *www.pompeiturismo.it*) are open 8–3 in winter, 8–7 in summer, closed Sunday. The **Ufficio Informazione** (✉ *Piazza Porta Marina, Pompei* ☎ *081/8575347* ⊕ *www. pompeiisites.org*) outside the archaeological site is open 9–5 daily.

EXPLORING

Mention Pompeii and most travelers will think of ancient Roman villas, prancing bronze fauns, writhing plaster casts of Vesuvius's victims, and the fabled days of the Emperors. Mention Pompeii to many southern Italians, however, and they will immediately think of Pompei (to use the modern-day Italian spelling, not the ancient Latin), home to the Santuario della Madonna del Rosario, the 19th-century basilica in the center of the new town, with the archaeological ruins taking second place. Although millions of culture seekers worldwide head for ancient Pompeii every year, the same number of Italian pilgrims converge on Pompei's basilica as a token of faith—joining processions, making *ex-voto* offerings, or just honoring a vow. Wealthy Neapolitans come to make their donations to help the Church carry out its good deeds. New-car owners come to get their vehicles blessed—and given driving standards in these parts of the world, insurance coverage from on high is probably a sensible move.

Caught between the hammer and anvil of cultural and religious tourism, the modern town of Pompei has shaken off its rather complacent approach and is now endeavoring to polish up its act. In attempts to ease congestion, parts of the town have been made pedestrian-friendly and parking restrictions tightened. Departing from the rather sleazy reputation of previous years, several hotels have filled the sizable niche in the market for quality deals at affordable prices. As for recommendable restaurants, if you deviate from the archaeological site and make for the center of town, you will be spoiled for choice. The modern town may be a circus but the center ring is always Pompeii itself.

CLOSE UP

Pompeii Prep

Pompeii is impressive under any circumstances, but it comes alive if you do some preparation before your visit.

First, read up—there are piles of good books on the subject, including these engaging, jargon-free histories: *Pompeii: The Day a City Died* by Robert Etienne, *Pompeii: Public and Private Life* by Paul Zanker, and *The Lost World of Pompeii* by Colin Amery. For accurate historical information woven into the pages of a thriller, pick up *Pompeii: A Novel* by Robert Harris.

Second, be sure to visit the Museo Archeologico Nazionale in Naples, where most of the finest art from Pompeii now resides. The museum is a remarkable treasure trove—it's a rewarding place to visit even if Pompeii isn't in your plans.

WHERE TO EAT

$$–$$$ ✕**Il Principe.** This is the closest you'll get to experience the tastes of
SOUTHERN ancient Pompeii, though the wines (fortunately) will be quantum leaps
ITALIAN better. At times the food is so artistically presented that it seems boorish
★ to pick up a knife and fork. Try the *pasta vermiculata garo*, otherwise
known as spaghetti with *garum pompeianum*, a fish-based sauce consumed widely in Roman times. Round off the meal with the *cassata di Oplontis* (a sweet made with ricotta cheese and honey), inspired by a famous still-life fresco found in a triclinium at the site of Oplontis. If you're overawed by the grandiose decor inside, opt for more informal outdoor dining. ⊠*Piazza B. Longo 8* ☎*081/8505566* 🖷*081/8633342* ⊕*www.ilprincipe.com* ⊟*AE, DC, V* ⊘*Closed Sun. dinner, Mon. (except lunch in summer), and 3 wks in Aug.*

$ ✕**Ristorante dei Platani.** The simple, seasonal food at this family-run
SOUTHERN establishment a few minutes' walk from the Anfiteatro ticket office will
ITALIAN take your mind off the kitschy faux frescoes inspired by the Villa dei
★ Misteri. Locals and informed tourists alike are drawn to their classic
stand-bys like *gnocchi alla sorrentina* (with tomato and mozzarella) and *frittura di paranza* (fried fish) as well as to their more inventive takes on local tradition—try the *fusilli con crema di ceci e frutti di mare* (with pureed chickpeas and seafood). Those who make it through to the *dolce* (desserts) should sample the delicate *delizia al limone* (lemon profiteroles) brought in daily from Minori on the Amalfi Coast. ⊠*Via Colle S. Bartolomeo 8* ☎*081/8633973* ⊕*www.ristorantedeiplatani. it* ⊟*AE, DC, MC, V* ⊘*Closed Wed.*

$$ ✕**Ristorante President.** The Gramaglia brother-and-sister team is well
SOUTHERN versed in top-level catering and makes sure that customers sigh with
ITALIAN satisfaction after every course. For something different, try the *aragosta*
★ *ubriacata* ("drunken" lobster cooked in white wine) accompanied by
some imaginative side dishes, like *sfoglie di zucca in agrodolce* (sweet-and-sour pumpkin strips). Beautiful presentation, impeccable service, and excellent value all add up to a stellar meal. They also host decadent Roman inspired banquets with musical accompaniment, worth a

Continued on page 169

ANCIENT POMPEII
TOMB OF A CIVILIZATION

The site of Pompeii, petrified memorial to Vesuvius's eruption on the morning of August 24, AD 79, is the largest, most accessible, and probably most famous of excavations anywhere.

A busy commercial center with a population of 10,000–20,000, ancient Pompeii covered about 160 acres on the seaward end of the fertile Sarno Plain. Today Pompeii is choked with both the dust of 25 centuries and more than 2 million visitors every year; only by escaping the hordes and lingering along its silent streets can you truly fall under the site's spell. On a quiet backstreet, all you need is a little imagination to sense the shadows palpably filling the dark corners, to hear the ancient pipe's falsetto and the tinny clash of cymbals, to envision a rain of rose petals gently covering a Roman senator's dinner guests. Come in the late afternoon when the site is nearly deserted and you will understand that the true pleasure of Pompeii is not in the seeing but in the feeling.

A FUNNY THING HAPPENS ON THE WAY TO THE FORUM

as you walk through Pompeii. Covered with dust and decay as it is, the city seems to come alive. Perhaps it's the familiar signs of life observed along the ancient streets: bakeries with large ovens just like those for making pizzas, tracks of cart wheels cut into the road surface, graffiti etched onto the plastered surfaces of street walls. Coming upon a *thermopolium* (snack bar), you imagine natives calling out, "Let's move on to the am-phitheater." But a glance up at Vesuvius, still brooding over the scene like an enormous headstone, reminds you that these folks—whether

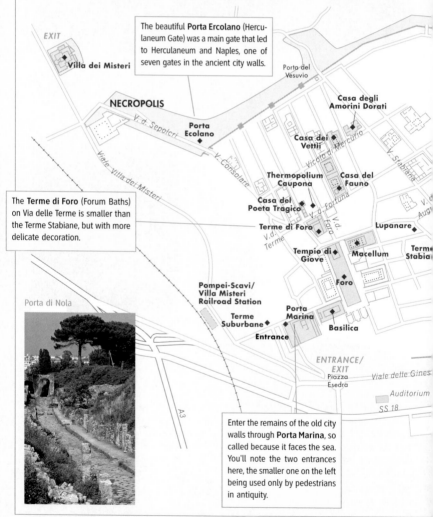

The beautiful **Porta Ercolano** (Herculaneum Gate) was a main gate that led to Herculaneum and Naples, one of seven gates in the ancient city walls.

The **Terme di Foro** (Forum Baths) on Via delle Terme is smaller than the Terme Stabiane, but with more delicate decoration.

Enter the remains of the old city walls through **Porta Marina**, so called because it faces the sea. You'll note the two entrances here, the smaller one on the left being used only by pedestrians in antiquity.

EXIT

Villa dei Misteri

NECROPOLIS

V. d. Sepolcri

Viale Villa dei Misteri

Porta Ecolano

Porta del Vesuvio

Casa degli Amorini Dorati

Casa dei Vettii

Vicolo di Mercurio

V. Consolare

V. di Fortuna

Thermopolium Caupona

Casa del Fauno

Casa del Poeta Tragico

Terme di Foro

V. d. Foro

V. d. Terme

Lupanare

Tempio di Giove

Macellum

Foro

V. Stabiana

V. di Augu...

Terme Stabia...

Porta di Nola

A3

Pompei-Scavi/ Villa Misteri Railroad Station

Terme Suburbane

Entrance

Porta Marina

Basilica

ENTRANCE/ EXIT

Piazza Esedra

Viale delle Gines...

Auditorium

SS 18

Via dell'Abbondanza

imagined in your head or actually wearing a mantle of lava dust—have not taken a breath for centuries. The town was laid out in a grid pattern, with two main intersecting streets. The wealthiest took a whole block for themselves; those less fortunate built a house and rented out the front rooms, facing the street, as shops. There were good numbers of *tabernae* (taverns) and *thermopolia* on almost every corner, and frequent shows at the amphitheater.

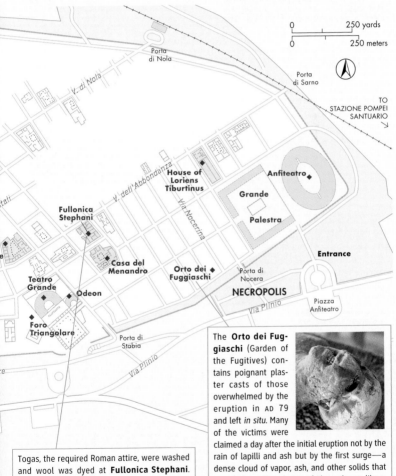

The **Orto dei Fuggiaschi** (Garden of the Fugitives) contains poignant plaster casts of those overwhelmed by the eruption in AD 79 and left *in situ*. Many of the victims were claimed a day after the initial eruption not by the rain of lapilli and ash but by the first surge—a dense cloud of vapor, ash, and other solids that swept down the slopes of the volcano like a boiling avalanche at 40–50 mi per hour.

Togas, the required Roman attire, were washed and wool was dyed at **Fullonica Stephani**. Urine was used to bleach and clean garments.

PUBLIC LIFE IN ANCIENT POMPEII

Forum

THE CITY CENTER

As you enter the ruins at Porta Marina, make your way uphill to the **Foro** (Forum), which served as Pompeii's cultural, political, and religious center. You can still see some of the two stories of colonnades that used to line the square. Like the ancient Greek *agora* in Athens, the Forum was a busy shopping area, complete with public officials to apply proper standards of weights and measures. Fronted by an elegant three-column portico on the eastern side of the forum is the **Macellum**, the covered meat and fish market dating to the 2nd century BC; here vendors sold goods from their reserved spots in the central market. It was also in the Forum that elections were held, politicians let rhetoric fly, speeches and official announcements were made, and worshippers crowded around the **Tempio di Giove** (Temple of Jupiter), at the northern end of the forum.

Basilica

On the southwestern corner is the **Basilica**, the city's law court and the economic center. These rectangular aisled halls were the model for early Christian churches, which had a nave (central aisle) and two side aisles separated by rows of columns. Standing in the Basilica, you can recognize the continuity between Roman and Christian architecture.

THE GAMES

The **Anfiteatro** (Amphitheater) was the ultimate in entertainment for Pompeians and offered a gamut of experiences, but essentially this was for gladiators rather than wild animals. By Roman standards, Pompeii's amphitheater was quite

Amphitheater

small (seating 20,000). Built in about 80 BC, making it the oldest permanent amphitheater in the Roman world, it was oval and divided into four seating areas. There were two main entrances—at the north and south ends—and a narrow passage on the west called the Porta Libitinensis, through which the dead were probably dragged out. A wall painting found in a house near the theater (now in the Naples Museum) depicts the riot in the amphitheater in AD 59 when several citizens from the nearby town of Nocera were killed. After Nocerian appeals to Nero, shows were suspended for three years.

Fresco of Pyramus and Thisbe in the House of Loreius Tiburtinus

BATHS AND BROTHELS

In its day, Pompeii was celebrated as the Côte d'Azur, the seaside Brighton, the Fire Island of the ancient Roman empire. Evidence of a Sybaritic bent is everywhere—in the town's grandest villas, in its baths, and especially in its rowdiest *lupanaria* (brothels), murals still reveal a worship of hedonism. Satyrs, bacchantes, hermaphrodites, and acrobatic couples are pictured indulging in hanky-panky.

The first buildings to the left past the ticket turnstiles are the **Terme Suburbane** (Suburban Baths), built—by all accounts without permission—right up against the city walls. The baths have eyebrow-raising frescoes in the *apodyterium* (changing room) that strongly suggest that more than just bathing and massaging went on here. Reservations are required for entry.

On the walls of **Lupanare** (brothel) are scenes of erotic games in which clients could engage. The **Terme Stabiane** (Stabian Baths) had underground furnaces, the heat from which circulated beneath the floor, rose through flues in the walls, and escaped through chimneys. The water temperature could be set for cold, lukewarm, or hot. Bathers took a lukewarm bath to prepare themselves for the hot room. A tepid bath came next, and then a plunge into cold water to tone up the skin. A vigorous massage with oil was followed by rest, reading, horseplay, and conversation.

GRAFFITI

Thanks to those deep layers of pyroclastic deposits from Vesuvius that protected the site from natural wear and tear over the centuries, graffiti found in Pompeii provide unique insights into the sort of things that the locals found important 2,000 years ago. A good many were personal and lend a human dimension to the disaster that not even the sights can equal.

At the baths: "What is the use of having a Venus if she's made of marble?"

At the entrance to the front lavatory at a private house: "May I always and everywhere be as potent with women as I was here."

On the Viale ai Teatri: "A copper pot went missing from my shop. Anyone who returns it to me will be given 65 bronze coins."

In the Basilica: "A small problem gets larger if you ignore it."

PRIVATE LIFE IN ANCIENT POMPEII

The facades of houses in Pompeii were relatively plain and seldom hinted at the care and attention lavished on the private rooms within. When visitors arrived they passed the shops and entered an open peristyle, from which the occupants received air, sunlight, and rainwater, the latter caught by the *impluvium*, a rectangular-shaped receptacle under the sloped roof. In the back was a receiving room, the *tablinum,* and behind was another open area, the atrium. Life revolved around this uncovered inner courtyard, with rows of columns and perhaps a garden with a fountain. Only good friends ever saw this part of the house, which was surrounded by *cubicula* (bedrooms) and the *triclinium* (dining area). Interior floors and walls usually were covered with colorful marble tiles, mosaics, and frescoes.

Several homes were captured in various states by the eruption of Vesuvius, each representing a different slice of Pompeiian life.

House of Paquius Proculus

The Casa del Fauno (House of the Faun) displayed wonderful mosaics, now at the Museo Archeologico Nazionale in Naples. The Casa del Poeta Tragico (House of the Tragic Poet) is a typical middle-class house. On the floor is a mosaic of a chained dog and the inscription *cave canem* ("Beware of the dog"). The Casa degli Amorini Dorati (House of the Gilded Cupids) is an elegant, well-preserved home with original marble decorations in the garden. Many paintings and mosaics were executed at Casa del Menandro (House of Menander), a patrician's villa named for a fresco of the Greek playwright. Two blocks beyond the Stabian Baths you'll notice on the left the current digs at the Casa dei Casti Amanti (House of the Chaste Lovers). A team of plasterers and painters were at work here when Vesuvius erupted, redecorating one of the rooms and patching up the cracks in the bread oven near the entrance—possibly caused by tremors a matter of days before.

Small Garden

Triclinium

Owner's Quarters

Kitchen

Servant's Quarters

Secondary Atrium

Entrance

Garden

Main Peristyle

Impluvium

Atrium

CASA DEI VETTII

The House of the Vettii is the best example of a house owned by wealthy *mercatores* (merchants). It contains vivid murals—a magnificent *pinacoteca* (picture gallery) within the very heart of Pompeii. The scenes here—except for those in the two wings off the atrium—were all painted after the earthquake of AD 62. Once inside, cast an admiring glance at the delicate frieze around the wall of the *triclinium* (on the right of the peristyle garden as you enter from the atrium), depicting cupids engaged in various activities, such as selling oils and perfumes, working as goldsmiths and metalworkers, acting as wine merchants, or performing in chariot races. Another of the main attractions in the Casa dei Vettii is the small cubicle beyond the kitchen area (to the right of the atrium) with its faded erotic frescoes now protected by Perspex screens.

UNLOCKING THE VILLA DEI MISTERI

Villa dei Misteri

There is no more astounding, magnificently memorable evidence of Pompeii's devotion to the pleasures of the flesh than the frescoes on view at the **Villa dei Misteri** (Villa of the Mysteries), a palatial abode 400 yards outside the city gates, northwest of Porta Ercolano. Unearthed in 1909, this villa had more than 60 rooms painted with frescoes; the finest are in the *triclinium*. Painted in the most glowing Pompeiian reds and oranges, the panels relate the saga of a young bride (Ariadne) and her initiation into the mysteries of the cult of Dionysus, who was a god imported to Italy from Greece and then given the Latin name of Bacchus. The god of wine and debauchery also represented the triumph of the irrational—of all those mysterious forces that no official state religion could fully suppress.

Pompeii's best frescoes, painted in glowing reds and oranges, retain an amazing vibrancy.

The Villa of the Mysteries frescoes were painted circa 50 BC, most art historians believe, and represent the peak of the Second Style of Pompeiian wall painting. The triclinium frescoes are thought to have been painted by a local artist, although the theme may well have been copied from an earlier cycle of paintings from the Hellenistic period. In all there are 10 scenes, depicting children and matrons, musicians and satyrs, phalluses and gods. There are no inscriptions (such as are found on Greek vases), and after 2,000 years historians remain puzzled by many aspects of the triclinium cycle. Scholars endlessly debate the meaning of these frescoes, but anyone can tell they are the most beautiful paintings left to us by antiquity. In several ways, the eruption of Vesuvius was a blessing in disguise, for without it, these masterworks of art would have perished long ago.

PLANNING FOR YOUR DAY IN POMPEII

GETTING THERE

The archaeological site of Pompeii has its own stop (Pompei–Villa dei Misteri) on the Circumvesuviana line to Sorrento, close to the main entrance at the Porta Marina, which is the best place from which to start a tour. If, like many visitors every year, you get the wrong train from Naples (stopping at the other station "Pompei"), all is not lost. There's another entrance to the excavations at the far end of the site, just a seven-minute walk to the Amphitheater.

ADMISSION

Single tickets cost €11 and are valid for one full day. The site is open Apr.–Oct., daily 8:30–7:30 (last admission at 6), and Nov.–Mar., daily 8:30–5 (last admission at 3:30). For more information, call 081/8575347 or visit www. pompeiisites.org.

WHAT TO BRING

The only restaurant inside the site is both overpriced and busy, so it makes sense to bring along water and snacks. If you come so equipped, there are some shady, underused picnic tables outside the Porta di Nola, to the northeast of the site.

MAKING THE MOST OF YOUR TIME

Visiting Pompeii does have its frustrating aspects: many buildings are blocked off by locked gates, and enormous group tours tend to clog up more popular attractions. But the site is so big that it's easy to lose yourself amid the quiet side streets. To really see the site, you'll need four or five hours.

Three buildings within Pompeii—Terme Suburbane, Casa del Menandro, and Casa degli Amorini Dorati—are open for restricted viewing. Reservations must be made on-line at www.arethusa. net, where you can find information on opening times.

TOURS

To get the most out of Pompeii, rent an audio guide (€6.50 for one, €10 for two; you'll need to leave an ID card) and opt for one of the three itineraries (2 hours, 4 hours, or 6 hours). If hiring a guide, make sure the guide is registered for an English tour and standing inside the gate; agree beforehand on the length of the tour and the price, and prepare yourself for soundbites of English mixed with dollops of hearsay. For a higher quality (but more expensive) full-day tour, try Context Travel (⊕ www.contexttravel.com).

MODERN POMPEI

Caught between the hammer and anvil of cultural and religious tourism, the modern town of Pompei (to use the modern-day Italian spelling, not the ancient Latin) is now endeavoring to polish up its act. In attempts to ease congestion and improve air quality at street level, parts of the town have been pedestrianized and parking restrictions tightened. Several hotels have filled the sizable niche in the market for excellent deals at affordable prices. As for recommendable restaurants, if you deviate from the archaeological site and make for the center of town, you will be spoiled for choice.

IF YOU LIKE POMPEII

If you intend to visit other archaeological sites nearby during your trip, you should buy the *biglietto cumulativo* pass, a combination ticket with access to four area sites (Herculaneum, Pompeii, Oplontis, Boscoreale). It costs €20 and is valid for three days. Unlike many archaeological sites in the Mediterranean region, those around Naples are almost all well served by public transport; ask about transportation options at the helpful Porta Marina information kiosk.

try if you are spending the night in town. ⊠ *Piazza Schettini 12* ☏ *081/8507245* 🖷 *081/8638147* ⊕ *www. ristorantepresident.com* ☰ *AE, DC, MC, V* ⊘ *Closed Mon. Nov.–Mar.*

WHERE TO STAY

$ ★ 🛏 **Hotel Amleto.** *Appassionati* and connoisseurs of historical styles of furnishings will find this hotel a real treat. Enjoy the Pompeian-type mosaic in the reception room and the mesmerizing House-of-the-Vettii–type scene in the breakfast room before retiring to your quarters, either 19th-century Neapolitan in style or Venetian in taste. Convenient to say the least, this spot is near the archaeological site and close to Pompei's cathedral. As traffic noise may be a problem, ask for a quieter room on the upper floor. **Pros:** very convenient location near sites and restaurants; excellent, attentive service. **Cons:** books up in high season; rooms facing are street noisy. ⊠ *Via B. Longo 10* ☏ *081/8631004* 🖷 *081/8635585* ⊕ *www.hotelamleto.it* 🛏 *26 rooms* ⚇ *In-hotel: Bar, Internet, parking (no fee)* ☰ *AE, D, MC, V* ⦿ *BP.*

$ 🛏 **Hotel Diana.** At the lower end of the price range, this small family-run hotel is a convenient base for budget travelers who wish to be in striking distance of Pompeii's ruins or the Sanctuary. It's a 3-minute walk from the train, a 10-minute walk from the Amphitheater entrance and close to the action in Pompeii's main square—yet seemingly miles away from the tourist throngs—and ideal for travelers without private transport. Clean and well-appointed rooms and an outgoing young staff make this place an attractive. **Pros:** 10-minute walk to archaeological site; convenient location for strolling in evening; charming garden, quiet setting and very helpful staff; 2 wheelchair accessible rooms. **Cons:** no pool; a bit noisy when fully booked due to tiled halls and echoes; smallish rooms. ⊠ *Vico Sant'Abbondio 12* ☏ *081/8631264* ⊕ *www. pompeihotel.com* 🛏 *13 rooms with private bath* ⚇ *In-room: Internet* ☰ *AE, DC, MC, V* ⦿ *BP.*

WEST OF NAPLES: THE PHLEGREAN FIELDS

Extinct volcanoes, steaming fumaroles, bubbling mud, natural spasms, and immortal names, all steeped in millennia of history, are the basic ingredients of the Campi Flegrei, or Phlegrean Fields (from the ancient Greek word *phlegraios,* or burning). Pompeii and Herculaneum, to the east of Naples, may be the most celebrated archaeological sites in Campania, but back in the days of the Emperors they were simple middle-class towns compared to the patrician settlements to the west of Naples. Here, at Baia, famed figures like Cicero, Julius Caesar, Claudius, Nero, and Hadrian built sumptuous leisure villas (*villae otiorum*) and ports for their gigantic pleasure barges; here St. Paul arrived at Puteoli (to use Pozzuoli's ancient Latin moniker) on board an Alexandrian ship; here the powerful came to consult the oracles of the Cumaean Sibyl; and here Virgil visited Lago d'Averno—the legendary entrance to the Underworld—to immortalize it in his *Aeneid*. Although several villas have now sunk beneath the sea, there are many archaeological sights still extant: the Flavian Amphitheater, which, if not as imposing aboveground as the Colosseum at Rome, is far better preserved in the galleries and cages below the arena in which wild beasts, gladiators, and stage props were kept in readiness; the ancient acropolis area of Puteoli now known as Rione Terra, the ruins of the Sibyl's cave in Cumae; and the ancient baths of Baia. In 2003, the Parco dei Campi Flegrei was established, providing additional funding and protection for the natural and archaeological treasures of the area. A sluggish but steady refurbishment of park grounds is underway.

THE SOLFATARA

Fodor's Choice
★

8 km (5 mi) west of Naples, 2 km (1 mi) east of Pozzuoli.

GETTING HERE

By car take the Tangenziale (bypass) from Naples toward Pozzuoli, getting off at the Agnano, Exit 11, about 4 km (2½ mi) away from the crater. Then follow signs to Pozzuoli and look for the VULCANO SOLFA-TARA sign when beginning the descent into Pozzuoli. The Solfatara lies on the 152 bus route from Naples' Piazza Garibaldi, with a stop just outside the main entrance, and on the M2 metro line from Piazza Garib-aldi Station. It is a 15-minute walk uphill (1 km [½ mi]) from Pozzuoli's Metropolitana station (or take bus P9; no extra fare necessary).

EXPLORING

Here at the sunken volcanic crater Solfatara you can experience firsthand the otherworldly terrain of the Campi Flegrei. The only eruption of this semi-extinct volcano was in 1198, though according to one legend, every crater in the area is one of the mouths of a 100-headed dragon named Typhon, which Zeus hurled into the crater of Epomeo on the island of Ischia. According to another, the sulfurous springs of the Solfatara are poisonous discharges from wounds the Titans received in their war with Zeus. Both legends, of course, are attempts to dramatize man's struggle to overcome the mysterious and dangerous forces of nature. Appropriately, the crater was given the name of *Forum Vulcani* by the ancient Romans, who thought it the residence of the god Vulcan.

Enter the Solfatara through the arch of the turn-of-the-20th-century, long-defunct baths complex (parking facilities and ticket office inside). You approach the volcanically active area down an avenue of holm oak trees, with the attractive Solfatara campsite making full use of all available shade on either side. Complete with year-round bar and **seasonal restaurant** (☎ *081/5262341*), open April–October, providing honest fare to campers and other visitors, this must be one of the best-appointed volcanic craters in the world. After you have cleared the refreshment area, emerge from the vegetation into a light clay expanse that in bright sunlight makes you reach instinctively for your sunglasses. Helpful information panels about the surrounding vegetation and the volcanic action at the core of the crater will steer you past the century-old brick

Solfatara gives you an up-close look at the region's volatile geology.

stufe (ovens) resembling a Roman *sudatorium* (sauna), where you can be parboiled in a matter of seconds. The sulfur fumes were supposed to cure those afflicted with diseases of the respiratory tract, the skin, and the joints. While musing on advances in modern medicine, move on to the fenced-off area of the fumaroles, known as the *Bocca Grande,* where steam whooshes out at about 320°F (160°C). Continuing the circuit, note the *fangaia,* or mud baths, whose mineral-rich mud is highly prized for medicinal purposes. ⊠ *Via Solfatara 161, Pozzuoli* ☎*081/5262341* ⊕*www.solfatara.it* ☐*€5.50* ⊗*Daily 8:30–1 hr before sunset.*

WHERE TO EAT AND STAY

$ ✕ **Taverna Viola.** A three-minute walk down the road from the Solfatara,
PIZZA this rustic-style restaurant–pizzeria has a pleasing view over the Bay
★ of Pozzuoli and the added attraction of serving pizzas at lunchtime. This is the place to deviate from a pizza Margherita and have one *con prosciutto e rughetta* (with ham and arugula) or even branch out into a fish-based dish, drawing on the day's catch from the famous Pozzuoli fish market below the volcano. ⊠ *Via Solfatara 76, Pozzuoli* ☎*081/5269953* ☐*MC, V* ⊗*Daily.*

¢ 🏕 **Camping Vulcano Solfatara.** This campsite, complete with bungalows for hire, is in Mediterranean woodland within the Solfatara Crater. It offers tranquillity, unique ambience, and good facilities at reasonable prices. Tent pitches are €9.60 per person plus €5.60 for a small tent in the high season. **Pros:** pets allowed; budget accommodations; spa treatments. **Cons:** sulfur smell; buggy in summer. ⊠ *Via Solfatara 161* ☎*081/5267413* 🖨*081/5263482* ⊕*www.solfatara.it* ⟳*In-room: No a/c, no TV. In-hotel: Restaurant, pool* ☐*AE, DC, MC, V* ⊗*Closed late Oct.–late Mar.* ✌*EP.*

$ ⓘ**Hotel Solfatara.** This is a clean, newly refurbished and functional hotel located just outside the Solfatara entrance and a 20-minute walk from the center of Pozzuoli. Due to its proximity to the volcano, the smell of sulfur is fairly constant. Front rooms have views over the bay and some have balconies. For extra peace and quiet—but also a stronger smell of sulfur—ask for a room at the back with no view. **Pros:** easy walk to town downhill; half and full board also available; free parking. **Cons:** walk back from town is uphill; front rooms face main road; sulfur smell. ⊠ *Via Solfatara 163* ☎*081/5267017* 📠*081/5263365* ⊕*www. hotelsolfatara.it* ↗*31 rooms* ♨*In-hotel: Restaurant, parking (free)* ⊟*AE, DC, MC, V* ⦿*BP.*

POZZUOLI

FodorśChoice   *8 km (5 mi) west of Naples.*

★   **GETTING HERE**

By car take the Tangenziale (bypass) from Naples toward Pozzuoli and get off at the Pozzuoli-Via Campana exit. At the roundabout, follow the signs for "Porto" to get to the port and the town center. There are subsequent signs for the "Anfiteatro" and Solfatara. The FS (state run) Metropolitana Linea 2 from Naples (Piazza Garibaldi, Cavour, and Montesanto stations) stops at Pozzuoli-Solfatara near the Anfiteatro. Bus No. 152 departs Naples Piazza Garibaldi and ends at the Port in Pozzuoli.

VISITOR INFORMATION

The Pozzuoli office of **Azienda Autonoma di Cura Soggiorno e Turismo** (⊠ *Via Campi Flegrei 3, Pozzuoli* ☎*081/5262419* ⊕*www.infocampiflegrei.it*) is open 8–3 in winter, 8–7 in summer, closed Sunday.

EXPLORING

Legendary spirits populate Pozzuoli. St. Paul stepped ashore at the harbor here in AD 61 en route to Rome: his own ship had been wrecked off Malta, and he was brought here on the *Castor and Pollux,* a grain ship from Alexandria that was carrying corn from Egypt to Italy. Not far from the harbor esplanade, San Gennaro, patron saint of Naples, earned his holy martyrdom by being thrown to the lions at an imperial gala staged in the town's enormous amphitheater, constructed by the Flavian emperors (the wild beasts were said to have torn the rags from Gennaro's body but to have left him unharmed—at which point he was taken to the Solfatara and decapitated). More recently, that latter-day goddess Sophia Loren was raised in a house still standing on a backstreet; later she set off to Naples and celluloid fame. Today Pozzuoli is a well-connected, busy town with about 80,000 inhabitants who are mainly employed by its fisheries, docks, and the tourism industry. Built on geologically unstable land, the area near the port was partially evacuated in the early 1980s due to a phenomenon known as *bradyseism,* or the rise and fall of the land surface. Since then it has been gradually recolonized and partially gentrified: many of the buildings in the Centro Storico have been given a face-lift, the main park (Villa Avellino) has become a mecca for open-air summer festivals, and the town's reputation as a center for gastronomy has been firmly

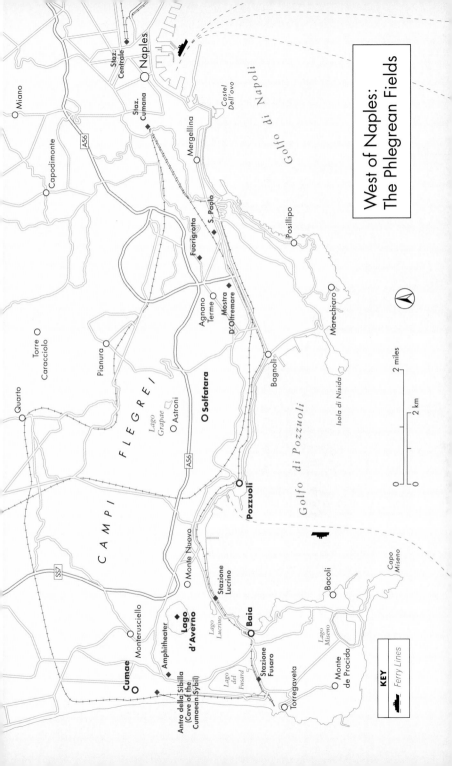

West of Naples: The Phlegrean Fields

Naples
Staz. Centrale
Miano
Capodimonte
A56
Staz. Cumana
Mergellina
Castel Dell'ovo
Golfo di Napoli
Fuorigrotta
S. Paolo
Posillipo
Agnano Terme
Mostra D'Oltremare
Torre Caracciolo
Pianura
C A M P I   F L E G R E I
Lago Grande
Astroni
O Solfatara
A56
Bagnoli
Marechiaro
Isola di Nisida
Quarto
Golfo di Pozzuoli
Pozzuoli
Monte Nuovo
Stazione Lucrino
Lago Lucrino
Monterusciello
Amphitheater
Lago d'Averno
Lago del Fusaro
Baia
SS7
Bacoli
Capo Miseno
Lago Miseno
Antro della Sibilla (Cave of the Cumaean Sybil)
Cumae
Stazione Fusaro
Torregaveta
Monte de Procida

2 miles
2 km

KEY
Ferry Lines

The Amfiteatro Flavio is a marvel of ancient Roman architecture.

established. Pozzuoli has also capitalized on its strategic position close to two of the islands in the Bay of Naples, Procida and Ischia. One of its main selling points is its main arena—Puteoli was the only place in the Empire to boast two amphitheaters—offering glimpses into the life of *panem et circenses* (bread and circuses) in classical times, when Puteoli was one of the busiest ports in the Mediterranean and easily eclipsed Neapolis (today's Naples).

★ The **Anfiteatro Flavio** (seating capacity, 40,000) is a short walk from the Pozzuoli Metropolitana railway station and about 15 minutes' walk down from the Solfatara. Despite the wear and tear of the millennia and the loss of some of the masonry to lime making in the Middle Ages, the site is one of the marvels of Roman architecture in the Campi Flegrei area. The foundation date is open to question. Like many sites in antiquity, the period from conception to completion could stretch over decades. It was probably built under Vespasian (AD 70–AD 79), given various inscriptions reading COLONIA FLAVIA AUGUSTA PUTEOLANA PECUNIA SUA ([built] by the Flavian colony of Puteoli with its own money), although some maintain that work may have started under Nero (AD 54–AD 69) and merely completed later. As you approach the site, note the external part in *opus reticulatum* (volcanic stone masonry arranged in a net-shaped pattern) and *opus latericium* (horizontal bands of brick). When used together, they are called *opus mixtum*, a technique typical of the late 1st and early 2nd centuries, designed to reduce stress and minimize damage during seismic events. Although we now get a fairly good idea of the horizontal ground plan in ancient times, comparison with the Colosseum in Rome shows that much of the superstructure has been lost: the outside part consisted of three stories surmounted by an *atticus* (decorative attic), while the *cavea* (sitting area) would have had a portico above the top row of seats, decorated with a number of statues and supported by columns. At ground level there was an *ambulacrum* (covered walkway) along which spectators would have passed to reach the *vomitoria* (exits).

Near the entrance and ticket office is the passageway leading down into the complex underground network of *carceres* (cells), well worth a visit. Unfortunately, apart from the arena and the outer walkway, much of the amphitheater has been roped off, with access to the cavea only allowed for evening open-air performances between July and September.

In Classical times, entertainment here consisted mainly of *venationes* (animal hunts), often involving exotic animals like lions and tigers brought from far-flung corners of the Roman Empire through the port of Puteoli, public executions, and *munerae* (gladiator fights). The *fossa*, or large ditch in the middle of the arena, may well have contained the permanent stage setting, which could be raised when necessary to provide a scenic backdrop. According to tradition, several early Christians—including the Naples protector St. Januarius, or San Gennaro—were condemned to be savaged by wild beasts in Puteoli under the Fourth Edict, passed in AD 304 by Diocletian, but the sentence was later commuted to a less spectacular *decapitatio* carried out farther up the hill in the Solfatara at a site now commemorated by the Church of St. Januarius.

For information on upcoming events, phone the tourist office in Pozzuoli (☎*081/5262419*), contact the site office at the Anfiteatro, or check the tourist office Web site (⊕*www.infocampiflegrei.it*). ⊠*Anfiteatro Grande, Via Terracciano 75* ☎*081/5266007* ☑*€4, including admission to Cumae and Museo Archeologico dei Campi Flegrei, and site of Baia* ♥*Daily 9– 1 hr before sunset. Closed Tues., Jan. 1, May 1, and Dec. 25.*

WHERE TO EAT

$
SOUTHERN
ITALIAN
★
✕**Bobò.** Just across from the ferry terminal—with the somewhat unromantic parking lot in between—is this stylish but *simpatico* restaurant. There is a *menu degustazione* (€50) for the truly ravenous, and an ample à la carte menu of mainly fish. Exquisite antipasti, delicately garnished pasta, and *pesce* straight off the boats make this a favorite with the locals so book ahead on the weekends and at dinner. A meal here is a fitting way to round out a day in the Campi Flegrei with some of the best the region has to offer. ⊠*Via C. Colombo 20* ☎*081/5262034* ⚑*Reservations essential* ▭*AE, DC, MC, V* ♥*Closed Tues. and 2 wks in Aug. No dinner Sun.*

¢–$
SOUTHERN
ITALIAN
★
✕**Ristorante Don Antonio.** Despite its unflattering location up a *vicolo* (alley) one block from the Pozzuoli waterfront, this restaurant has achieved cult status in Neapolitan circles for its fresh seafood and unbeatable prices. Unlike other eateries, which will happily serve well into the afternoon siesta or late at night, this spot rolls down the shutters as soon as the day's catch has been consumed. ⊠*Vico Magazzini 20, off Piazza San Paolo* ☎*081/5267941* ⚑*Reservations not accepted* ▭*No credit cards* ♥*Closed Mon.*

LAGO D'AVERNO

11 km (7 mi) west of Naples, 3 km (2 mi) north of Baia.

GETTING HERE

To reach Lake Avernus by car, take the Tangenziale from Naples and take the Pozzuoli-Arco Felice exit and follow signs for Lago d'Averno. Alternatively, take the Cumana railway from Stazione Montesanto in Naples to Lucrino, turn left (head west) along Via Miliscola for 250 yards, then turn right on Via Lucrino Averno and walk north until you reach the lake (about ½ mi). SEPSA Bus Linea 1 leaves from Piazza Garibaldi in Naples and stops at the Cumana station in Lucrino before heading on to Baia.

EXPLORING

When the great poet Virgil wrote *"Facilis descensus Averno"*—"The way to hell is easy"—it was because he knew what he was talking about. Regarded by the ancients as the doorway to the Underworld, the fabled Lago d'Averno (Lake Avernus) was well known by the time the great poet settled here to write the *Aeneid*. As with Lago Lucrino (the Lucrine Lake) less than 1 km (½ mi) to the south, a tarmac road skirts much of the lake, opening out at times into litter-strewn lay-bys. However, some of the spell is restored by the backdrop: forested hills rise on three sides and the menacing cone of Monte Nuovo looms on the fourth. (At the time of writing, the Parco dei Campi Flegrei was restoring trails leading up from the lake to the slopes of Monte Nuovo.)Landscaping has restored the path skirting the lake, and bilingual information panels are found at various stages around the perimeter. The water is indeed "black," the smell of sulfur sometimes hangs over the landscape, and blocked-off passages lead into long-abandoned caves into which Virgil might well have ventured. Not far away is the Mare Morto of ancient Romans, who identified it as the Stygian Lake of the Dead, where Charon plied his trade, ferrying souls into the Underworld. Nearby is the spring that was thought to flow directly from the River Styx, and it was there that Aeneas descended into the Underworld with the guidance of the Cumaean Sibyl, as famously recounted in the *Aeneid* of Virgil.

WHERE TO EAT

$ ✕ **La Cucina di Ruggiero.** In antiquity the site of some of the most celebrat-

SOUTHERN ed oyster beds and fish farms, Lake Lucrino is now the setting for this

ITALIAN rustic *trattoria*. Quirky Ruggiero runs the dining room with a whimsical charm—don't be shocked when he addresses you through his megaphone or if he warmly embraces you when you leave—while his wife Maria lovingly prepares local specialties from the land, sea, and lake. Booking is essential in the evening and on the weekends when locals cram into this place for its home cooking and convivial atmosphere. ⊠ *Via Intorno al Lago 3, Pozzuoli, loc. Lucrino* ☎*081/8687473* ▭*AE, DC, MC, V* ⊘ *Closed Sun. dinner and Wed.*

BAIA

12 km (7 mi) west of Naples, 4 km (2½ mi) west of Pozzuoli.

GETTING HERE

To arrive by car take the Tangenziale from Naples and exit at Pozzuoli-Arco Felice and follow the indications for Baia. By train, take the Cumana railway (trains leave every 20 minutes from Montesanto in Naples, travel time 30 minutes, nearest stop Fusaro) followed by a SEPSA bus for the last 3 km (2 mi). On Friday, weekends, and public holidays, take the City Sightseeing Campi Flegrei bus from Piazza della Repubblica in Pozzuoli (or from other sites in the area). Where the bus stops in the square outside the Baia station, cross the disused railway line on a footbridge. Continue upward for about five minutes until you reach the entrance to the site (limited parking is available). The same SEPSA bus also stops at the Museo in the Castle. To arrive from Naples by bus, take the SEPSA Linea 1 from Piazza Garibaldi and ask to get off at either the Parco Archeologico or the Museo.

EXPLORING

Now largely under the sea, ancient Baia was once the most opulent and fashionable resort area of the Roman Empire, the place where Sulla, Pompey, Cicero, Julius Caesar, Tiberius, and Nero built their holiday villas. Petronius's *Satyricon* is a satire on the corruption, intrigue, and wonderful licentiousness of Roman life at Baia. (Petronius was hired to arrange parties and entertainment for Nero, so he was in a position to know.) It was here that Cleopatra was staying when Julius Caesar was murdered on the Ides of March (March 15) in 44 BC; here that Emperor Claudius built a great villa for his third wife, Messalina (who is reputed to have spent her nights indulging herself at local brothels); and near here that Agrippina (Claudius's fourth wife and murderer) is believed to have been killed by henchmen sent by her son Nero in AD 59. Unfortunately, the Romans did not pursue the custom of writing official graffiti—"Here lived Crassus" would help—so it's difficult to assign these historical events to specific locations. Consequently, conjecture is the order of the day: Julius Caesar's villa is now thought to be at the top of the hill behind the archaeological site and not near the foot of the Aragonese castle, though we cannot be absolutely certain. We do know, however, that the Romans found this area staggeringly beautiful. A visit to the site can only confirm what Horace wrote in one of his Epistles: *Nullus in orbe sinus Baiis praelucet amoenis* ("No bay on Earth outshines pleasing Baia").

★ At the ticket office for the **Parco Archeologico e Monumentale di Baia** you should receive a small map to the site while information panels in readable English are posted at strategic intervals. In antiquity this whole area was the Palatium Baianum (the Palace of Baia), dedicated to *otium*—the ancient form of dolce far niente—and the residence of emperors from Augustus to as late as Septimius Severus in the 3rd century AD. The first terrace, the aptly named Villa dell'Ambulatio, is one of the best levels from which to appreciate the topography of the site: the whole hillside down to the level of the modern road near the waterfront has been modeled into flat terraces, each sporting different architectural features.

CLOSE UP

Viewing Underwater Baia by Boat

From the small modern-day port of Baia you can board a boat with glass panels on its lower deck and view part of the *città sommersa*, the underwater city of ancient Baia.

The guided tour—usually in Italian, but given in English if arranged well in advance—lasts about 1¼ hours and is best undertaken in calm conditions, when you can get good glimpses of Roman columns, roads, villa walls, and

mosaics. The fare (€10) also includes a brief talk about significant changes to the coastline over the last two millennia and the main underwater sights.

There are sailings Tuesday–Sunday at 10, noon, and 3; booking ahead essential. For further information and bookings, contact **Baiasommersa** (☎ *349/4974183* ⊕ *www. baiasommersa.it*).

While up on this terrace look for the exquisite stuccoed artistry, with its depictions of dolphins, swans, and cupids in the *balneum* (thermal bathing, Room 13), and admire the elaborate theatrical motifs in the floor mosaic in Room 14. Below the balneum and inviting further exploration is a nymphaeum shrine, which can be reached from the western side. Make sure you get down to the so-called Temple of Mercury, on the lowest level, which has held so much fascination for travelers from the 18th century onward. It has been variously interpreted as a frigidarium and as a *natatio* (swimming pool) and is the oldest example of a large dome (50 BC–27 BC), predating the cupola of the Pantheon in Rome. (Test the impressive echo in the interior.)

In the summers, the archaeological site provides an unusual backdrop to evening opera performances and concerts. For information on similar and other upcoming events, phone the tourist office in Pozzuoli (☎ *081/5262419*), contact the site office at Baia, or check the tourist office Web site (⊕ *www.infocampiflegrei.it*). ⊠ *Parco Archeologico e Monumentale di Baia, Via Sella di Baia 22, Bacoli, loc. Baia* ☎ *081/8687592* ⊠ *€4 including Cumae, site at Museo Archeologico dei Campi Flegrei, and Flavian amphitheater in Pozzuoli* ☉ *Tues.–Sun. 9–1 hr before sunset. Closed Jan. 1, May 1, Dec. 25.*

★ Housed in the Castle of Baia, which commands a fine 360-degree view—eastward across the Bay of Pozzuoli and westward across the open Tyrrhenian—is the exquisite **Museo Archeologico dei Campi Flegrei**. A regular bus service leaves the old Baia station (in the direction of Bacoli; buy a ticket for the return journey, too, at the kiosk outside the old railway station) and stops about a minute's walk away, just opposite the ramp ascending to this impressively located castle. On Friday, weekends, and public holidays, take the Archeobus Flegreo from Piazza della Repubblica, Pozzuoli or from other sites. Though its foundation dates to the late 15th century, when Naples was ruled by the House of Aragon and an invasion by Charles VIII of France looked imminent, the castle was radically transformed under the Spanish viceroy Don Pedro de Toledo after the nearby eruption of Monte Nuovo in 1538. Indeed, its bastions bear a striking resemblance to the imposing Castel Sant'Elmo in Naples, built in the same period. This is an ideal spot for museumphobes: spacious, uncluttered rooms display tastefully contextualized finds; there's a virtual absence of large tour groups; there's access to bastion terraces; and it only takes about an hour to see.

Of the various exhibitions, the first on the suggested itinerary consists of plaster casts from the Roman period found at the Baia archaeological site. This gives valuable insights into the techniques used by the Romans to make copies from Greek originals in bronze from the Classical and Hellenistic periods.

Pride of place in the museum goes to the *sacellum,* or small sanctuary, transported from nearby Misenum and tastefully displayed inside the Aragonese tower, the Torre Tenaglia. Standing about 20 feet high, the sacellum has been reconstructed, with two of its original six columns (the rest in steel) and a marble architrave with its dedicatory inscription to the husband-and-wife team of *Augustales* (imperial cult devotees), who commissioned restoration of the sanctuary in the 2nd century AD, this surmounted by a pediment depicting the beneficent couple. Behind the facade are the naked marble figures of Vespasian (left) and Titus (right) in a flattering heroic pose, at least from the neck downward.

Moving on to the upper floor of the tower, you come to the other *capolavoro,* or showpiece, of the museum, the reconstruction of Emperor Claudius's nymphaeum. Discovered in 1959 but only systematically excavated in the early 1980s, the original nymphaeum now lies together with much of the ancient site of Baia under 20 feet of water in the Bay of Pozzuoli. The sculptural elements salvaged from the seabed include a recognizable scene of a headless Odysseus plying Polyphemus (statue never found) with wine, aided by a companion with a wineskin. The function of the nymphaeum is suggested by the marble supports for *klinai* (couches) set on the floor near the entrance: this must have been a showy triclinium, with its full complement of statues and fountains designed to ease the weight of imperial cares and provide due source for reflection and inspiration. ✉ *Via Castello 39, Bacoli, loc. Baia* ☎ *081/ 5233797* 🖅€*4, including Cumae, site at Baia, and Flavian amphitheater in Pozzuoli* ☉ *Tues.–Sun. 9–1 hr before sunset. Closed Jan. 1, May 1, Dec. 25.*

WHERE TO EAT

¢–$ ✕**Azienda Agrituristica Il Casolare.** Il Casolare offers the rare chance of
SOUTHERN dining and lodging within a 10,000-year-old volcanic crater (thankfully
ITALIAN extinct). This place is particularly known for its restaurant, perched on the inner slopes of the volcano, offering a view of the patchwork of farmed plots on the crater floor. Specializing in *cucina contadina napoletana* (Neapolitan rustic cuisine), the owner Tobia serves whatever is in season. The set price menu is about €30: expect a cornucopia of antipasti and some nouvelle vegetarian dishes like pasta *e cicerchia* (with vetchling). The inn's four *mini-appartmenti* are small but tastefully furnished, a perfect base for exploring the surrounding area. Transfers can be arranged from the nearby railway station of Lucrino.**Pros:** quiet; fresh air; excellent local products produced on-site; small communal

kitchen. **Cons:** car essential; poor public transport connections. ✉ *Via P. Fabbris 12–14, Bacoli, loc. Coste dei Fondi di Baia* ☎ *081/5235193* 🌐 *www.datobia.it* *Booking essential for lodging and dining* *4 rooms* *In-hotel: Restaurant, spa* *No credit cards* *Closed Mon. No dinner Sun.* *EP.*

¢ MEDITERRANEAN **Down Town.** Unlike at other eateries in this area, you won't be pressured to have a *Satyricon*-style banquet at Down Town. Check the whiteboard inside for the day's specials, which often include exotic items (for Naples) like couscous, and always something for nonseafood eaters. Vaulted ceilings and wooden tables inset with tiles give the place a fairly Spartan but distinctive feel. Refreshingly good local wines are served by the glass pair perfectly with their fried appetizers and pizzas. The main entrance is right off the little port of Baia. Reservations essential on weekends. ✉ *Via Lucullo 39* ☎ *081/8687261* 🌐 *www.downtown.it* *DC, MC, V* *Closed Wed. and lunchtime, except Sun.*

CUMAE

Fodor's Choice ★ *16 km (10 mi) west of Naples, 5 km (3 mi) north of Baia.*

GETTING HERE

If driving, take the Cuma exit 13 of the Naples Tangenziale and proceed along Montenuovo Licola Patria, following signs for Cuma. At the first major intersection, take a left onto Via Arco Felice Vecchio, pass under the arch, and make a right at the next intersection and after around 400 yards turn left into the site. There is a free parking lot. There is no train station in Cuma, so to arrive from Naples, take the Cumana railway to Fusaro, then the SEPSA Miseno–Cuma bus to Cuma. SEPSA also runs buses to Cuma from Pozzuoli's station and Baia.

EXPLORING

Being perhaps the oldest Greek colony on mainland Italy, Cumae overshadowed the Phlegrean Fields and Neapolis in the 7th and 6th centuries BC, since it was home to the **Antro della Sibilla,** the fabled Cave of the Cumaean Sibyl—one of the three greatest oracles of antiquity—who is said to have presided over the destinies of men. In about the 6th century BC the Greeks hollowed the cave (closed for restoration at the time of writing) from the rock beneath the ridge leading up to the present ruins of Cumae's acropolis. Today you can walk—just as Virgil's Aeneas did—through a dark, massive 350-foot-long stone tunnel that opens into the vaulted Chamber of the Prophetic Voice, where the Sibyl delivered her oracles. Standing here in one of the most venerated sites of ancient times, the sense of the *numen*—of communication with invisible powers—is overwhelming. "This is the most romantic classical site in Italy," claimed famed travelogue writer H. V. Morton. "I would rather come here than to Pompeii."

Cumae was founded in the third quarter of the 8th century BC by Greek colonists. The name has legendary origins: myth has it that Euboean mariners found a woman who had miscarried a baby on the beach here, and the fetus was washed out to sea by great breakers on the shore. Thinking this an omen from the gods of fertility, the mariners built an altar here and called their new settlement *kuema* (or "fetus" in Greek).

Centuries later Virgil wrote his epic of the *Aeneid,* the story of the Trojan prince Aeneas's wanderings, partly to give Rome the historical legitimacy that Homer had given the Greeks. On his journey, Aeneas had to descend to the underworld to speak to his father, and to find his way in, he needed the guidance of the Cumaean Sibyl. Virgil did not dream up the Sibyl's Cave or the entrance to Hades—he must have actually stood both in her chamber and along the rim of Lake Avernus, as you yourself will stand. When he described the Sibyl's Cave in Book VI of the *Aeneid* as having "*centum ostia*"—a hundred mouths—and depicted the entrance to the underworld on Lake Avernus so vividly, "*spelunca alta . . . tuta lacu nigro nemorum tenebris*"—"a deep cave . . . protected by a lake of black water and the glooming forest"—it was because he was familiar with this awesome landscape. In Book VI of the *Aeneid,* Virgil describes how Aeneas, arriving at Cumae, sought Apollo's throne (remains of the Temple of Apollo can still be seen) and "the deep hidden abode of the dread Sibyl/An enormous cave . . ."

Although Cumae never achieved the status of Delphi, it was the most important oracular center in Magna Graecia, and the Sibyl would have been consulted on a whole range of matters. Governments consulted the Sibyl before mounting campaigns. Wealthy aristocrats came to channel their deceased relatives. Businessmen came to get their dreams interpreted or to seek favorable omens before entering into financial agreements or setting off on journeys. Love potions were a profitable source of revenue; women from Baia lined up for potions to slip into the wine of handsome charioteers who drove up and down the street in their gold-plated four-horsepower chariots. Still, it was the Sibyl's prophecies that ensured the crowds here, prophecies written on palm leaves and later collected into the corpus of the Sibyline books.

Allow at least two hours for this visit to soak up the ambience and study the ruins. Unlike in Greek and Roman times, when access to Cumae was through a network of underground passages, an aboveground bus service leaves the old Baia station at regular intervals. ✉ *Via Acropoli 1 80078* ☎ *081/8543060* 🎟 *€4, including museum and site at Baia and Flavian amphitheater in Pozzuoli* ⏲ *Daily 9–1 hr before sunset. Closed Jan. 1, May 1, Dec. 25.*

WHERE TO STAY

$–$$ ★ **Villa Giulia.** Built with characteristic yellow tuff walls and restored in immaculate taste, this historic farmhouse provides an excellent base for the Cumae area provided you have a car. The decor and atmosphere are those of a top-notch hotel, while the price is refreshingly accessible. As the villa is hard to find, owner-manager Giulia—a fluent English speaker—will prearrange a meeting point closer to Naples and escort you to her home. For an extra €30, try Giulia's inventive cuisine (evenings only) served under her leafy pergola. **Pros:** excellent food and service; charming surrounds and garden; pool, family-friendly. **Cons:** isolated-car is essential; buggy in the summer. ✉ *Via Cuma–Licola 178,* ☎ *081/8540163* 📠 *081/8044356* 🌐 *www.villagiulia.info* *6 rooms* *In-hotel: Pool, parking.* 💳 *AE, DC, MC, V* 🍽 *BP.*

Capri, Ischia, and Procida

WORD OF MOUTH

"We spent three nights on Capri in May, and had a wonderful time. We did a lot of hiking, and I mean a lot. One must really walk to see this beautiful island."

—Tuscanlifeedit

WELCOME TO CAPRI, ISCHIA, AND PROCIDA

Capri

TOP REASONS TO GO

★ **The Living Room of the World:** Pose oh-so-casually with the beautiful people sipping their Camparis on La Piazzetta, the central crossroads of Capri Town: a stage-set square that always seems ready for a gala performance.

★ **Spa-lendid Ischia:** Rebellious daughter of a distant volcanic eruption, Ischia was compensated for her rocky complexion with gorgeous spas famed for their seaweed soaks and fango mud cures.

★ **Marina di Corricella, Procida:** Lilliputian-sized Procida has numerous harbors, but none will have you reaching for your paintbrush as quickly as this rainbow-hue, horizontal version of Positano.

★ **Anacapri's Siren Heights:** Be sure to be nice to the bus driver when you take the precipitously steep road up to Capri's bluff-top village—you're nearly a thousand feet above the Bay of Naples here.

1 Capri. A tiny energy point in the universe with a magnetic pull far exceeding its size, Capri is a balmy and palmy never-never land that has been the darling of tourism for 2,500 years. While its hotels rank among the priciest (and perchiest) around, its incomparable views and natural wonders—I Faraglioni and the Blue Grotto, to name but two—come with no price tags. Capri Town is the place to head for jet-setter glamour, while Anacapri—sitting high up on Monte Solaro—is noted for its understated charm, a fact that accounts for a disproportionate number of easel-toting visitors at the Villa San Michele, with its nonpareil bay view.

Panorama of Capri's harbor

Old house window, Anacapri

GETTING ORIENTED

4

Geological stepping-stones anchored in the Bay of Naples, the islands of Capri, Ischia, and Procida tip the two points of the bay's watery crescent. A mere drop in the blue Mediterranean with a popularity way out of proportion to its size, Capri is a *piccolo paradiso* often swamped by tidal waves of day-trippers. Happily, its more rustic sister islands in the archipelago offer something for escapists of every ilk.

2 **Ischia.** More than twice the size of Capri, lesser-known Ischia may have lost the beauty contest to its sister, but it has something Capri doesn't: paradisial white-sand beaches, thermal hot-spring spas, and many fewer day-trippers. And don't miss the island's delicious Epomeo wine, produced on the slopes of its extinct volcano.

3 **Procida.** Although it's a short trip, 3 km (2 mi) from the mainland, this little volcanic outcropping remains a secret to many. Sun, cliffs, and sea combine to create the distinctive atmosphere so memorably immortalized in the film *Il Postino.*

The Town of Terra Murata is barnacled onto the hillside, ancient baroque abbeys like San Michele glitter amid the rocky terrain, while bird-lovers flock to the Vivara nature preserve.

Map labels

Naples 18
Bay of Naples
Mergellina
Agnano
Solfatara
Pozzuoli
Bagnoli
Posillipo
Marechiaro
Isola di Nisida

Sorrento
Marina di Puolo
Massa Lubrense
Sant'Agata sui Due Golfi
Metrano
Nerano
145
Punta Campanella
Bocca Piccola

Blue Grotto/ Grotta Azzurra
P. dell' Arcera
Anacapri
Marina Grande
Capri Town
Monte Solaro
ISOLA DI CAPRI
Belvedere del Migliara
I Faraglioni

CAPRI, ISCHIA, AND PROCIDA PLANNER

Making the Most of Your Time

Each of the three islands has its own individual charm—the chic resort of Capri, the volcanic spas of Ischia, and the rustic Procida. If you are unable to overnight, it is worth getting to Capri as early in the morning as possible, to see the main sites before the human tsunami hits the island. Take a round-the-island boat trip and gaze at the natural beauty of the Fariglioni and the Blue Grotto, two of the unmissable sights on this fabled isle. If archaeology and history are at the top of your list of priorities, choosing between Ischia and Capri can be difficult. Ischia has the added bonus of its natural thermal baths—if you want the gamut of natural saunas and access to a dreamy beach, head to Poseidon in Forio; for much more stylish surroundings and landscaped Mediterranean gardens, check out Negombo in Lacco Ameno. Moving around Capri to the main sites is generally easier—and can be done in a day if pushed—while Ischia calls for more chilling out at your destination. If time is limited, Procida and its magical waterfront, as immortalized in the Oscar-winning film *Il Postino*, can be tacked on to your stay as a day trip from Ischia or from the mainland.

Getting Around

Ferries and hydrofoils take you from the mainland, with some connections also between the islands. Schedules are listed every day in the local newspaper *Il Mattino*—buy a single ticket rather than a round-trip, which would tie you to the same line on your return journey.

Day-trippers need to remember that the high-season crowds on the last ferries leaving the islands make this crossing riotously reminiscent of packed subways and buses back home; in addition, rough bay waters can also delay (and even cancel) these boat rides.

Once on the islands you can do without a car as the bus service is good—the trip from Capri to Anacapri is breathtaking both for its views and the sheer drops just inches away. Tickets should be bought before boarding, and stamped on the bus. For those with deeper pockets, microtaxis are readily available to whiz you to your destination. Capri's funicular from Marina Grande to Capri town is an attraction in itself, as is its chairlift to Monte Solaro.

Be prepared, especially on Capri and Procida, to do a lot of walking—many of Capri's narrow alleys allow no alternative, and it is the only real way to find the hidden wonders of Procida. Renting a scooter on Ischia gives you the freedom to explore at will, as well as giving you that real Italian experience.

Finding a Place to Stay

On Capri, hotels fill up quickly, so book well in advance to be assured of getting first-pick accommodations. Although island prices are generally higher than those on the mainland, it's worth paying the difference for an overnight stay. Once the day-trippers have left center stage and headed down to the Marina Grande for the ferry home, the streets regain some of their charm and tranquillity.

Although Ischia can be sampled piecemeal on day excursions from Naples, given the size of the island, you'd be well advised to arrange a stopover. Ischia is known for its natural hot-water spas, and many hotels have a wellness or beauty center, meaning you may be tempted not to venture any farther than the lobby for the duration of your stay.

Hotels in Procida tend to be family-run and more down-to-earth. Note that booking is essential for the summer months, when half-board may be required. Most hotels close from November to Easter, when the season is at its lowest.

WHAT IT COSTS (IN EUROS)

	¢	$	$$	$$$	$$$$
Restaurants	under €20	€20–€30	€30–€45	€45–€65	over €65
Hotels	under €75	€75–€125	€125–€200	€200–€300	over €300

Restaurant prices are for a first course (*primo*), second course (*secondo*), and dessert (*dolce*). Hotel prices are for two people in a standard double room in high season, including tax and service.

Taking to the Water

Unsurprisingly the islands are a haven for fans of water sports. Apart from the ample opportunities for swimming in crystal-clear water (but if it's sandy beaches you want, avoid Capri), all three islands have long-established scuba-diving centers (although the prices on Capri are exorbitant). Windsurfers should head to Ischia, while Procida is the ideal place to rent a yacht for short or long trips. Boat and canoe rental is available on all three islands. You might prefer, however, to just avail yourself of the thermal baths for which Ischia is renowned.

Walking and Hiking

With their high peaks, both Capri and Ischia offer spectacular trekking opportunities. Ischia's Monte Epomeo, at 2,582 feet, is somewhat more challenging than the 1,932 feet of Monte Solaro in Capri, especially as on the latter you can choose to use the chairlift for one leg (if not both) of the trip. The path from Capri Town to the Faraglioni is one of the most beautiful seaside walks in the world, although a strong competitor is the four-hour trek past five Napoleonic towers on the island's west coast. Vivara, Procida's protected wildlife islet, is also not to be missed.

CAMPANIA'S SEAFOOD BOUNTY

Fish and other sea creatures are mainstays of the Campanian diet, especially along the region's stunning coastline, and on the islands ringing the Bay of Naples.

The waters along Campania's shore are regarded as some of the cleanest in Italy. Evidence of that claim comes from the ubiquity of anchovies (*alici* or *acciuga*) that are said to only swim in pristine waters. Fishermen in some villages still go out at night in lighted fishing boats to attract and net anchovies, which are cooked fresh or cured with salt.

The Mediterranean Sea's bounty extends far beyond *alici*. Some of the most popular fish varieties are listed on the following page, but there are scores more waiting to be tasted. Gustatory explorers eating their way down the coastline might also encounter these sea creatures: *aguglie* (needle fish); *calamari* (squid); *cicale* (mantis shrimp); *cozze* (mussels); *mazzancolle* (a type of prawn); *orata* (seabream or daurade); *pesce spada* (swordfish); *seppia* (cuttlefish); *scorfano di fondale* (ocean perch); *scorfano rosso* (scorpion fish); and *scampi* (langoustines).

MENU DECODER

Campanian chefs know how to treat fresh fish, using simple preparations that showcase the fresh flavors of the region. These are some of the typical preparations.

-baked (*al forno*)

-baked in a paper pouch (*al cartoccio*)

-cured (*salato*)

-fried (*fritto*)

-grilled (*alla griglia*)

-marinated (*marinato*)

-poached (*affogato*)

-raw (*crudo*)

-roasted (*arrostito*)

-roasted in salt (*al sale*)

-smoked (*affumicato*)

Alici (anchovy)

Highly flavored, small fish that may be served fresh or cured. Grilled or fried anchovies have a milder taste than the cured fish, which can be quite pungent. Fried anchovies are a popular snack along the coast.

Baccalà (salt cod)

Cod that has been dried and cured in salt. Before use, the dried baccalà fillet is soaked repeatedly in water to reduce saltiness and reconstitute the flesh. It is used in myriad dishes for protein and flavor. Common dishes include sautéed baccalà with potatoes, and baccalà baked in spicy tomato sauce.

Bottarga

Salt-cured fish roe, typically from tuna or mullet. A prized flavoring aid, bottarga is often grated or shaved on pasta. The flavor is briny and unctuous, but not fishy. Some people call it the "essence of the sea."

Branzino (European sea bass)

A medium-sized fish with lean, flaky white meat and a slightly sweet, mild flavor. May also be called spigola. It is often grilled and served with potatoes, or baked *al cartoccio*.

Gallinella (gurnard)

A meaty white fish that may also be called mazzole or tub fish. Gallinella *all'acqua pazza* is cooked in "crazy water" flavored with tomatoes and herbs. A related fish is cappone gallinella (red gurnard).

Polpo (octopus)

The firmly textured, gently flavored octopus may be boiled in simple soups, stewed (polpi *in cassuola*), or simply sautéed with garlic and olive oil, among myriad preparations. Polpetto is the term used for little octopi.

Sarde (sardines)

Sardines are considered *pesce azzurro*—small blue fish that swim near the ocean's surface—along with anchovy and cecinelli (smelt). These fish typically appear in seafood fritto misto, a mixture of small fried fish.

Totani (flying squid)

These squid closely resemble calamari, and likewise are popular a popular snack when cut into rings and deep-fried. May be stuffed with diced vegetables, fried as a snack, or boiled and served cold in salads.

Triglia (red mullet)

Small bony fish with moderately fatty flesh and delicate flavor. Often featured in fish stews, and may also be served sautéed, baked, or roasted.

Vongole veraci (striped Venus clams)

These tiny, sweet clams are prized throughout Italy, where they play a star-ring role in spaghetti vongole. They also are served in simple soups and risottos.

Opposite page: A typical Amalfi meal.
top right: Fresh fish in Naples.
bottom left: Octopus, a staple in the Campania diet.

Updated by Fergal Kavanagh

The islands off Naples are so different from each other that you wonder how they can possibly be in the same bay—indeed, some would say they are not true water mates, as they lie just beyond the bay's outer fringes. The contrast goes beyond mere geology and vegetation. They all occupy different niches in the traveler's mind.

Capri panders to the whims of the international great-and-good. Ischia serves the needs of a predominantly German and Italian clientele. Procida—the closest to the mainland—is more dependent on the weekend and summer influx of Neapolitans. Chosen by the Greeks, the supreme connoisseurs and aesthetes of antiquity, as their first base in Italy, the islands of Capri, Ischia, and Procida combine a broad gamut of experiences.

Islandophiles, of course, have always had a special love for Capri (the first syllable is accented— "*Ca*-pri"). Pleasure dome to Roman emperors, and still Italy's most glamorous seaside getaway, this craggy, whale-shaped island has an epic beauty: cliffs that are the very embodiment of time, bougainvillea-shaded pathways overlooking the sea, trees seemingly hewn out of rock by the Greeks. It's little wonder that tales tell of tourists snapping up villas while their unsuspecting wives were, so they thought, doing last-minute souvenir shopping, or of American industrialists who, determined to stay on, sent a wire home with a brisk "sell everything" order. Capri has always been a stage that lesser mortals could share with the Beautiful People, often an eclectic potpourri of duchesses who have left their dukes home, fading French film actresses, pretenders to obscure thrones, waspish couturiers, and sleek supermodels.

Today Capri's siren song continues to seduce thousands of visitors. On summer days the port and *piazzetta* are often crammed, so if you can visit in spring or fall, do so. Yet even the crowds are not enough to destroy Capri's very special charm. The town itself is a Moorish stage set of sparkling white houses, tiny squares, and narrow medieval alleyways hung with flowers, while its hillsides are spectacular settings for luxurious seaside villas. The mood is modish but somehow unspoiled. The upper crust does its sunbaking in private villas, hinting that you, also, should retreat when the day-trippers take over—offering yourself to the sun at your hotel pool or exploring the hidden corners of the island. Even in the height of summer, you can enjoy a degree of privacy on one of the many paved paths that wind around the island hundreds of feet above the sea.

Recent years have seen a diversification of the experiences offered on the three islands. Once entirely dependent on its thermal springs, Ischia is now the archaeological front-runner in the bay, thanks to its noted museum in Lacco Ameno. Procida has opened up to tourism, with some newer, smaller hotels remaining open throughout the year. As always, you need to book a room well in advance to fully discover Procida's fascinating Easter procession, replete with handcrafted wooden sculptures representing religious scenes. On Capri, for those seeking peace and quiet away from its main thoroughfares, walks introducing some of the island's major geological landmarks have been mapped out through species-rich Mediterranean maquis.

EXPLORING CAPRI, ISCHIA, AND PROCIDA

Lying equidistant from Naples (about 25 km [16 mi]), Ischia and Capri stand like guards at the main entrance to the Bay of Naples, with Ischia to the west and Capri to the south, while Procida is like a small stepping-stone halfway between Ischia and Capo Miseno (Cape Misenum), on the mainland. The islands can be reached easily from various points in and near Naples, with the port of Pozzuoli offering the closest access to Procida and Ischia, and the port of Sorrento lying almost opposite Capri.

CAPRI: A SIREN LANDSCAPE

D.H. Lawrence once called Capri "a gossipy, villa-stricken, two-humped chunk of limestone, a microcosm that does heaven much credit, but mankind none at all." He was referring to its once rather farouche reputation as well as its unique natural beauty. Fantastic grottoes, soaring conical peaks, caverns great and small, plus villas of the emperors and thousands of legends combine with Suetonius's ancient Roman tales of "exquisite tortures" to brush the isle with an air of whispered mystery and an intoxicating quality as heady as its rare and delicious wines. Emperor Augustus was the first to tout the island's pleasures by nicknaming it Apragopolis—the city of sweet idleness—and Capri has drawn escapists of every ilk since. Ancient Greek and Roman goddesses were moved aside by the likes of Jacqueline Onassis, Elizabeth Taylor, and Brigitte Bardot, who made the island into a papparazzo's paradise in the 1960s. Today, new generations of glitterati continue to answer the island's call.

Of all the peoples who have left their mark on the island during its millennia of history, the Romans with their sybaritic wealth had the greatest effect in forming the island's psyche. Capri became the center of power in the Roman Empire when Tiberius scattered 12 villas around

Capri is laced with spectacular walking paths.

the island and decided to spend the rest of his life here, refusing to return to Rome even when, 10 years on, he was near death. Far from being a dirty old man only interested in orgies, this misunderstood gentleman used Capri as a base to run the ancient Roman Empire. All Tiberius's hard work and happy play—he indulged in his secret passion for astronomy here—were overlooked by ancient scandalmongers, prime among them Suetonius, who wrote: "In Capri they still show the place at the cliff top where Tiberius used to watch his victims being thrown into the sea after prolonged and exquisite tortures. A party of mariners were stationed below, and when the bodies came hurtling down, they whacked at them with oars and boat-hooks, to make sure they were completely dead." Thankfully, present-day Capri is less fraught with danger for travelers, or even to dignitaries from afar. The main risks now are overexposure to the Mediterranean sun, overindulgence in pleasures of the palate, and a very sore wallet.

VISITOR INFORMATION

Azienda Autonoma di Cura, Soggiorno e Turismo (⊠ *Banchina del Porto, Marina Grande* ☎ *081/8370634* ⊠ *Piazza Umberto I, Capri Town* ☎ *081/8370686* ⊠ *Via G. Orlandi 59, Anacapri* ☎ *081/8371524* ⊕ *www.capritourism.com*) offices in Capri, Capri Town, and Anacapri are open daily 8:30–8:30 in high season, and 9–1 and 3:30–7 (approximately) in winter. Their excellent Web site has an English-language version.

CAPRI: GETTING HERE AND AROUND

GETTING HERE BY BOAT

Capri is well connected with the mainland in all seasons, though there tend to be more sailings between April and October. However, you can't return to Naples after about 10:20 PM in high season (in low season often 8 PM or even earlier). Hydrofoils, Seacats, and similar vessels leave from Molo Beverello (below Piazza Municipio) in Naples, while ferries leave from Calata Porta di Massa, 1,000 yards to the east, and *aliscafi* (hydrofoils) also sail from the small marina of Mergellina, a short distance west of the Villa Comunale in Naples. There's also service to and from Sorrento's Marina Piccola. For locals in Naples there are restrictions on taking cars onto the island; the rules don't apply to non-Neapolitans, but much of Capri is pedestrianized, and a car is almost always more of a hindrance than a help.

Several ferry and hydrofoil companies plying the waters of the Bay of Naples, making frequent trips to Capri. Schedules change from season to season; the most reliable source for departure times is *Il Mattino,* Naples' daily newspaper.

Caremar (☎ *081/5513882 or 081/8370700* ⊕ *www.caremar.it*) has four hydrofoil departures from Molo Beverello (€17, with a travel time of 50 minutes) and three ferry departures per day (€10 high season, with a travel time of 1 hour, 20 minutes). Four ferries leave daily from Sorrento (€9.80, travel time 25 minutes).

Linee Marittime Partenopee (☎ *081/8781430 or 081/8071812* ⊕ *www.consorziolmp.it*) has one to three hydrofoil departures every hour from Sorrento (€14.10, travel

time 20 minutes) and one hydrofoil per day from Ischia (in the morning, €13, one hour).

From Naples, **Navigazione Libera Del Golfo** (☎ *081/5527209 hydrofoils from Naples, 089/5520763 ferry and hydrofoils from Positano* ⊕ *www.navlib.it*) has roughly one hydrofoil departure per hour (€14, travel time 40 minutes). From Easter to October, the company also offers one jetfoil from Positano and Amalfi (approximately €15, travel time 50 minutes), and one ferry from Positano and Amalfi (€11, travel time 1 hour, 20 minutes).

SNAV (☎ *081/7612348 or 081/8377577* ⊕ *www.snav.it*) offers one hydrofoil every hour from Mergellina or Molo Beverello (€17, travel time 40 minutes).

There's little to be gained—sometimes nothing—from buying a round-trip ticket, which will just tie you down to the return schedule of one line. Book in advance in spring and summer for a Sunday return to the mainland.

GETTING AROUND

Most of Capri's sights are reasonably accessible by either boat or bus, except for Villa Jovis and Cetrella, which require some walking (about 40 minutes). The bus service is relatively cheap and frequent, while taxis are likely to cost 10–20 times as much as public transport. Don't buy a *biglietto giornaliero* (day pass) for the bus and funicular unless you're thinking of covering almost every corner of the island—you would need to make six separate trips to make it pay, and locals deem it a bit of a rip-off.

CAPRI TOWN AND ENVIRONS

This fantasy of white-on-white Capriote architecture, flower-filled window boxes, and stylish boutiques rests on a saddle between rugged limestone cliffs to the east and west, where huge herds of *capre* (goats) once roamed, hence the name of the island. Beyond Capri Town lies some of the island's most spectacular sights, including I Faraglioni and the Villa Jovis. As you disembark at the marina quay,

note that unlike the other islands in the Bay of Naples, Capri is not of volcanic origin but was formed by marine deposits laid more than 100 million years ago and then uplifted during plate tectonic activity in the Pleistocene era (as recently as 1–2 million years ago); Monte Tiberio, to the south of the Marina Grande, and Monte Solaro, to the west, powerfully attest to these upheavals.

GETTING HERE

From the main harbor, Marina Grande, you can take a bus or funicular to reach Capri Town, the island's hub.

TOP ATTRACTIONS

Arco Naturale *(Natural Arch).* One of Capri's most famous natural wonders, this geologic arch is all that remains of a large limestone cave that has suffered the erosive effects of wind and rain over the millennia. Once a cave that was likely hollowed out by wave action, it broke apart when lifted up to its present position, hundreds of feet above sea level, in relatively recent geological times (about 1–2 million years ago). Engraved by 19th-century artists, it became a favorite landmark for travelers in the Romantic era. ⊠ *Via Arco Naturale, at the end of Via Matermania.*

Fodor'sChoice **Certosa di San Giacomo** *(Charterhouse of St. James).* Nestled between
★ the Castiglione and Tuoro hills, this grand, palatial complex was for centuries a Carthusian monastery dedicated to St. James. It was founded between 1371 and 1374, when Queen Giovanna I of Naples gave Count Giacomo Arcucci, her secretary, the land and the means to create it. The count himself then became devoutly religious and retired here until his death. After the monastery was sacked by the pirates Dragut and Barbarossa in the 16th century, it was heavily restored and rebuilt—thanks in part to heavy taxes exacted from the populace. The friars within were detested by many Capresi for refusing to open the gates to minister to the people when plague broke out.

The complex was reopened to the public in 2008 after major renovations lasting four years. You enter via a grandly imposing entryway, which leads to the **Biblioteca Comunale Popolare Luigi Bladier** (public library—Capri's only free Internet point) and the spacious church of **San Giacomo** (built in 1690). After admiring the church's Baroque frescoes, follow the signpost down toward the *Parco,* which

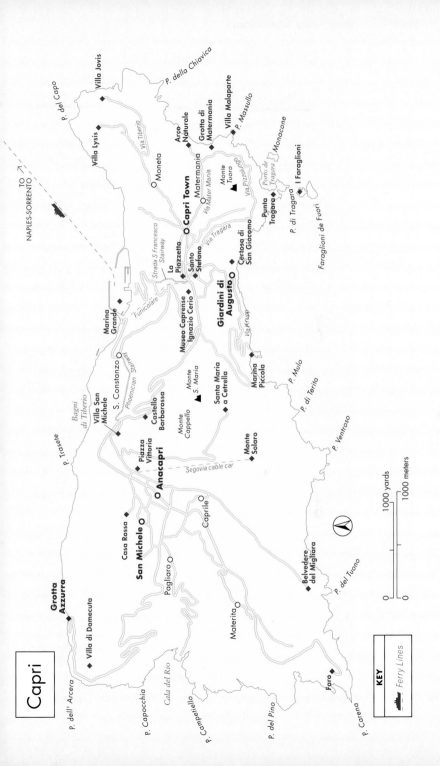

A GOOD WALK: CLASSIC CAPRI

Capri is a walker's paradise, with the added bonus of a detailed history of the main streets displayed on painted tiles at many points, erected by the Lions Club. Once you get off the ferry and have picked up a decent map of Capri (€1 at the information office on the main jetty), take a funicular ride up from the harbor area of **Marina Grande** to Capri Town (only one stop, €1.40 one-way; if for any reason it's not working, there's a bus and taxi service). For energetic foot soldiers, there's a former mule track starting from a small square on the quayside called Largo Fontana that will place you at the top in about 15 minutes, emerging just below the clock tower in Capri Town. The top funicular station brings you out onto Piazza Umberto I, better known locally as **La Piazzetta**.

On peak days in summer this area gets extremely crowded, so don't expect to be allowed to sip your Campari for more than 20 minutes without being encouraged to move on. Admire the majolica decoration of the clock tower dial and inspect the 17th-century church of **Santo Stefano**, just off the upper side of the square in Piazzetta Cerio. On the same tiny square is the **Museo Caprense Ignazio Cerio**, a small four-room exhibition of archaeological and fossil finds, and useful as a backup site on a rainy day. Then forge your way across the main Piazzetta to Via Le Botteghe; if you're thinking about a picnic lunch, you can stock up on provisions here (try Sfizi di Capri, a baker at Via Le Botteghe 15 for a slice of frittata *di spaghetti* or a more orthodox *panino*, or roll, and fixings). Just across the alleyway is a small supermarket to complete the meal or just to stock up on liquid refreshments at reasonable prices.

The farther away you get from La Piazzetta, the quieter this pedestrianized road becomes. Via Le Botteghe becomes Via Fuorlovado and then Via Croce, developing gradually into an avenue fringed by bougainvillea and spreading oleander trees. This is an area where real estate now changes hands for upward of €14,000 a square meter (more than $1,300 per square foot).

After about 10 minutes, at the Bar Lindos, the road to the Arco Naturale branches off to the right. Art and archaeology buffs will instead want to continue straight on, past the Chiesa di San Michele (a powder store in the 19th-century French occupation), and up Monte Tiberio. A turnoff along the way takes you to the **Villa Lysis**, one of Capri's most legendary private homes, built by the poet Baron Fersen and now open to the public (look for the signpost off Via Tiberio). Return to Via Tiberio and continue onward—the full hike may take 45 minutes up the hill—to reach Tiberius's famous mountaintop **Villa Jovis**.

Heading back down Via Tiberio, the café at the crossroads is one of the last watering holes before heading out to the Arco Naturale. Follow the ceramic signs for Arco Naturale along Via Matermania for about 15 minutes until the path forks (Arco Naturale, to the left; Grotta di Matermania, to the right). Peer at the **Arco Naturale**, keeping in mind that the path is a cul-de-sac, so every step you go down has to be retraced.

Then, knee joints permitting, take the hundreds of steps—and we mean hundreds (don't worry, you won't have to backtrack)—down to the **Grotta di Matermania**, an impressive natural cave where ancient Romans worshipped the goddess Cybele every dawn.

Where the path levels out begins one of the most beautiful seaside walks in the world—the Via Pizzo Lungo. This path continues southward through fine Mediterranean maquis vegetation (most of the evergreen trees are holm oak) high above the shoreline, affording fine views of Punta Massullo where **Villa Malaparte**—possibly the most important creation of 20th-century Italian architecture—perches over the sea. Two hundred yards farther on is a panoramic point from which you can gaze at **I Faraglioni**, Capri's famous cluster of offshore rocks.

As you continue westward, look first for the most romantic house on Capri, the Villa Solitaria—once home to novelist Compton MacKenzie, it's set on a bluff high over the sapphire sea and was built in the early 1900s by famed Capriote architect Edwin Cerio—then look for the towering rock pinnacle Pizzo Lungo (High Point), which the ancients thought was the petrified form of Polyphemus, the giant blinded by Odysseus's men.

At the end of the Giro dell'Arco Naturale (Natural Arch Circuit) is another panoramic point, the **Punta Tragara**, which marks your arrival back in Capri Town. From here take Via Tragara, lined with elegant hotels and villas, until it joins with Via Camerelle. Look for a left turn down Via Cerio to the **Certosa di San Giacomo** (Charterhouse of St. James), a former monastery that is Capri's grandest architectural setpiece. About five minutes' walk away up Via Matteotti are the **Giardini di Augusto** (Gardens of Augustus), which give an excellent view over the southern side of the island toward the Faraglioni.

The impressive Via Krupp was reopened in 2008 after 32 years, and it's well worth taking this hairpin-turned walkway to Marina Piccola. Alternatively retrace your steps until you get to Via Serena, a mere five-minute walk from the Piazzetta.

Once back at base, you might splurge on a granita or a cocktail at the Piccolo Bar, the very first bar to grace the square and the only one with an upstairs terrace.

TIMING

Allowing time for a refreshment stop, a little shopping, and a fair amount of photo-snapping, the walk will take between three and five hours, plus an extra half hour if you visit the Certosa museum. Those who aren't up for much hiking should choose either the trek to the Villa Jovis or the Giro dell'Arco Naturale; the latter is a cliff-side path that includes hundreds of steps (going downhill mostly), so be prepared. Most of the sites and shops are open throughout the day, but as there's more than a fair amount of up-and-down, you'd be well advised to avoid the stickiest hours—weather-wise—from noon to 3 in summer.

DID YOU KNOW?

I Faraglioni, Capri's landmark rock formation, rises to a height of 350 feet. Plus, the rock farthest from shore, known as the Faraglione di Scopolo, is home to a blue-tinted lizard found nowhere else.

leads down an avenue flanked by pittosporum and magnolia toward the monastery gardens and some welcome benches. Take heed of the signs reminding you to watch your step, as the ground is uneven in places. Beyond a covered road lies the **Chiostro Grande** (Large Cloister)—originally the site of the monks' cells and now the home of a high school. Nearby is the much prettier 15th-century **Chiostro Piccolo** (Small Cloister), often the venue for summertime open-air concerts. The showstopper here is the **Museo Diefenbach,** comprising a collection of large canvases by the German painter K. W. Diefenbach, who visited Capri in 1900

and stayed until his death in 1913. Although his protracted stay may have cured Diefenbach of his chronic depression, his tormented soul emerges clearly in his powerful paintings, filled with apocalyptic storms and saintly apparitions. For years, Diefenbach rivaled the Blue Grotto for sheer picturesqueness—he was given to greeting visitors replete with flowing white beard, monk's cowl, and primitive sandals. From La Piazzetta take Via Vittorio Emanuele and then Via F. Serena to reach this beautiful monastic complex, one of the highlights of historic Capri. ⊠ *Viale Certosa 40, Capri Town* ☎ *081/8376218* ⊕ *www.capricertosa. com* ⊠ *Free* ⊙ *Tues.–Sun. 9–2, park 9–1 hr before sunset.*

Fodor'sChoice **I Faraglioni.** Few landscapes set more artists dreaming than that of the ★ famous Faraglioni—three enigmatic, pale-ocher limestone colossi that loom out of the sea just off the Punta Tragara on the southern coast of Capri. Soaring almost 350 feet above the water, the Faraglioni have become for most Italians a beloved symbol of Capri and have been poetically compared to Gothic cathedrals or modern skyscrapers. The first rock is called Faraglione di Terra, since it's attached to the land; at its base is the famous restaurant and bathing lido Da Luigi, where a beach mattress may accompany the luncheon menu. The second is called di Mezzo or Stella, and little boats can often be seen going through its picturesque tunnel, which was caused by sea erosion. The rock farthest out to sea is Scopolo and is inhabited by a wall lizard species with a striking blue belly, considered a local variant by biologists although legend has it that they were originally brought as pets from Greece to delight ancient Roman courtiers. ⊠ *End of Via Tragara, Capri Town.*

La Piazzetta. The English writer and Capriophile Norman Douglas called this square, officially known as Piazza Umberto I, "the small theater of the world." The rendezvous point for international crowds, this "*salone*" became famous as the late-night place to spot heavenly bodies—of the Hollywood variety, that is. Frank Sinatra, Rita Hayworth, Julie Christie, Julia Roberts, and Mariah Carey are just a few of the

THE ISLANDS THROUGH THE AGES

In terms of settlements, conquests, and dominion, the history of the islands echoes that of Campania's mainland. For eastern Mediterranean traders in the second and first millennia BC, Capri and Ischia were both close enough to the mainland to provide easy access to trade routes and impervious enough to afford natural protection against invaders.

Ischia, or Pithekoussai, as it used to be called—a word probably derived from the Greek term for a large earthenware jar (*pithos*) rather than the less plausible word, *pithekos*, meaning monkey—is renowned in classical circles as the first colony founded by the Greeks on Italian soil, as early as the 8th century BC.

Capri, probably colonized a century or so later, is amply described in the early years of the Roman Empire by authors such as Suetonius and Tacitus, as this was the island where Tiberius spent the last 10 years of his life.

After the breakup of the Roman Empire, the islands, like many other parts of the Mediterranean, suffered a succession of incursions. Saracens, Normans, and Turks all laid siege to the islands at some stage, between periods of relative stability under the Swabians, the Angevins, the Aragonese, and the Spanish.

After a short interregnum under the French at the beginning of the 19th century, a period of relative peace and prosperity ensued. Over the next century, from the opening of its first hotel in 1826, Capri saw an influx of visitors that reads like a Who's Who of literature and politics, especially in the first decades of the 20th century. Ischia and Procida established themselves as holiday resorts much later, with development taking place from the 1950s onward.

celebs who have made La Piazzetta the place where the rich and famous come to watch other rich and famous folk. These days, if the high flyers bother to make an appearance, they're likely to show up at 8 in the evening for an aperitif and some peppery *tarallucchi* bread sticks, with a possible return visit for a late-night limoncello.

In any event, the square is never less than picturesque and has been a natural crossroads and meeting point since Roman times. The religious complex of Santo Stefano was built around the square in the 17th century, but the clock tower and Municipio, or town hall (once the archbishop's palace) are the only remnants of its cathedral. Capri's version of Big Ben—the charming bell tower, or Torre dell'Orologio—is perched over the ancient gateway. ⊠ *At intersection of vias Botteghe, Longano, and Vittorio Emanuele, Capri Town.*

Fodor'sChoice ★ **Marina Piccola.** A 10-minute ride from the main bus terminus in Capri (Piazzetta d'Ungheria), Marina Piccola is a delightfully picturesque inlet that provides the Capresi and other sun worshippers with their best access to reasonable beaches and safe swimming. The entire cove is romantically lined with *stabilimenti*—elegant bathing lidos where the striped cabanas are often air-conditioned and the bodies can be Modigliani-sleek. The most famous of these lidos (there's a fee to use the facilities), found closest to I Faraglioni, is **La Canzone del Mare,**

Villa Jovis was the home of Emperor Tiberius during the final years of his rule over ancient Rome.

once presided over by the noted British music-hall singer Gracie Fields and for decades favored by the smart set, including Noël Coward and Emilio Pucci (who set up his first boutique here). La Canzone del Mare's seaside restaurant offers a dreamy view of I Faraglioni and a luncheon here, although pricey, can serve as an iconic Capri moment. Jutting out into the bay at the center of the marina is the **Scoglio delle Sirene,** or Sirens' Rock—a small natural promontory—which the ancients believed to be the haunt of the Sirens, the mythical temptresses whose song seduced Odysseus in Homer's *Odyssey*. This rock separates the two small beaches: Pennaulo, to the east, and Marina di Mulo, site of the original Roman harbor, to the west. The small church, **Chiesa di Sant'Andrea,** was built in 1900 to give the local fishermen a place of worship. ⊠ *Via Marina Piccola.*

Punta Tragara. The "three sons of Capri" can be best seen from the famous lookout point at Punta Tragara at the end of gorgeous Via Tragara. At this point, a path—marked by a plaque honoring the poet Pablo Neruda, who loved this particular walk—leads down hundreds of steps to the water and the feet of I Faraglioni, and perhaps to a delightful lunch at one of the two lidos at the rock base: Da Luigi, a household name in the Bay of Naples, or La Fontelina, an exclusive sun-drenched retreat nearby. After lunch, habitués then hire a little boat to ferry them back to nearby Marina Piccola and the bus back to town. Near the start of the Neruda path turn left to find the most gorgeous seaside walk in Capri—the Via Pizzo Lungo. Another place to drink in the view of I Faraglioni, which is most romantic at sunset, is the Punta Del Cannone,

CLOSE UP

Hiking Capri

While Capri may first conjure up chichi cafés and Gucci stores, it's also a wonderland of idyllic pathways running beside cactus-covered cliffs and whitewashed Arabian houses overlooking some of the bluest water on Earth. So when Capri Town swarms with summer crowds and begins to feel like an ant farm, take to the hills—in a few minutes, you can find yourself atop a cliff without a trace of humanity in sight. The island is a novice hiker's paradise, with plenty of moderate hikes that lead to stunning vistas.

One of the simplest routes is to take Anacapri's Via Caposcuro and Via Migliera south to the Belvedere di Migliera, a lookout point above a cliff on the island's south side. For another great hike, from Capri Town follow Via Camerelle–Via Tragara past the ritzy hotels and villas to the terrific south-side vista, within spitting distance of the Faraglioni rocks. From here there's a path leading down to the secluded beaches under the Faraglioni. From the area around the island's famous

Arco Naturale, descend hundreds of steps past the Grotto di Matermania to find the stunning southern hillside path called the Via Pizzo Lungo, passing several famous villas. At Via Arco Naturale, you can climb the hill to see this famous natural rock bridge that overlooks the sea.

To return to town, exit the Via Pizzo Lungo onto enchanting Via Tragara and head back to Capri Town. A short but dizzying hike descends the cliff beneath the Giardini di Augusto. Just beneath the gardens the famous Via Krupp was closed for many years, because of the risk of falling rocks, but was restored to its former beauty in 2008. After the path straightens out, there's a path on your left; the Grotta dell'Arsenale is down here, a large cave in the base of the cliff, on one of Capri's most secluded beaches. Via Krupp continues downhill to Marina Piccola. Capri is considered by many to be one of the most beautiful places on Earth, and the good news is that its trails allow you to discover its every nook and cranny.

a hilltop belvedere reached beyond the Certosa di San Giacomo and the Giardini di Augusto. ⊠ *End of Via Tragara, Capri Town.*

Fodor'sChoice **Villa Jovis.** Named in honor of the ancient Roman god Jupiter, or Jove, ★ the villa of the emperor Tiberius is riveted to the towering Rocca di Capri like an eagle's nest overlooking the strait separating Capri from Punta Campanella, the tip of the Sorrentine peninsula. Lying near the easternmost point of the island, the villa is reached by a well-signposted 50-minute walk that climbs gradually from the Piazzetta in Capri Town and offers several opportunities along the way to slake your thirst and catch your breath (if possible, resist temptation until you get to the welcoming Bar Jovis, on Via Tiberio, about five minutes' walk from the site). Although criticized by locals for the visible conditions of neglect, Villa Jovis is nonetheless a powerful reminder of the importance of the island in Roman times. What makes the site even more compelling are the accounts of the latter years of Tiberius's reign from Capri, between AD 27 and 37, written by authors and near-contemporaries Suetonius and Tacitus. They had it that this villa was famous for its sybaritic

living, thus sounding a leitmotif whose echo can be heard at the luxurious hotels of today.

There are remarkably few discrepancies between the accounts of the two historiographers. Both point to Tiberius's mounting paranoia in Rome, while Tacitus outlines his reason for choosing Capreae (*Annals*, Book IV). "Presumably what attracted him was the isolation of Capreae. Harborless, it has few roadsteads even for small vessels; sentries can control all landings. In winter the climate is mild, since hills on the mainland keep off gales. In summer the island is delightful, since it faces west and has open sea all round. The bay it overlooks was exceptionally lovely, until Vesuvius's eruption transformed the landscape." Capri in Roman times was the site of 12 spacious villas, but Villa Jovis is both the best preserved and must have been the largest, occupying nearly 23,000 square feet.

The entrance to the site lies just beyond the *pharos* (lighthouse) built under Tiberius and used until the 17th century to warn ships away from the narrows between Capri and the mainland. Pick up a site map at the ticket office, which gives a useful breakdown of the various areas of the villa to be visited. Nearby, you can find the **Salto di Tiberio** (Tiberius's Leap), the place where ancient gossips believed Tiberius had enemies, among them his discarded lovers and even unfortunate cooks, hurled over the precipice into the sea some 1,000 feet below. After taking stock of this now-harmless viewing platform and its information panels, take the upper path past the baths complex around the palace residential quarters to view the heavily restored Chapel of Santa Maria del Soccorso and its large bronze statue of the Madonna, a gift to the island from the Caprese painter Guido Odierna in 1979. The walk around the perimeter of the site gives an idea of the overall layout of the palatial residence, which in places rose to five stories in height. From here descend some steps and then a ramp to the *ambulatio* (walkway), which offers additional spectacular views and plenty of shade, as well as a *triclinium* (dining room) halfway along. The center of the site is a complex devoted to cisterns. Unlike in Pompeii, there was no aqueduct up here to provide fresh running water, so the cisterns next to the bath complex were of prime importance. ⊠ *Via A. Maiuri* ☎ *081/8374549* ⚏ *€2* ⊙ *Feb.–Oct., daily 9–1 hr before sunset; Nov.–Jan., daily 9–3:15.*

Fodor's Choice ★ **Villa Lysis.** Opened to the public in 2003, this legendary domain looms large in Capri's consciousness. The island's Xanadu, Manderlay, and San Simeon, it was originally known as the Villa Fersen, after Baron Jacques d'Adelsward-Fersen, the builder. Fleeing to the island from a scandal involving Parisian schoolboys, the French aristocrat had this white-stucco pile designed by Edouard Chimot in 1903 in shimmering belle epoque style, replete with gilded-mosaic columns and floors looted from the island's ancient Roman sites. Past the impressive columned entrance, inscribed in stone with "Amori et Dolori Sacrum" (A Shrine to Love and Sorrow), the baron would retire to write poems and paint pictures in his Liberty Style (art nouveau) salons. Sadly all the furnishings are gone, but you can still gasp at the ballroom open to the sea and the large smoking room in the basement, where, in a titled pool, Fersen committed suicide by ingesting a lethal mix of opium and champagne in

Continued on page 211

CAPRI BY BOAT

To savor Capri to the fullest you must sail its blue waters as well as wander through its squares and gardens. Happily, the famous "giro" cruises around the island allow you to enjoy the perfect sailing safari.

Sooner or later, the beautiful coastline of Capri will lure you to its shores, where you'll be in good company: ancient heroes, emperors, Hollywood divas, and legions of mere mortals have been answering the same siren call from time immemorial. Fact is, you haven't fully experienced Capri until you've explored its rocky shoreline, a veritable Swiss cheese of mysterious grottoes tucked into its myriad inlets and bays. As you'll learn, the Blue Grotto may be world famous, but there's also a Green Grotto, a Yellow Grotto, a Pink, and a White. And unless you possess fins, the only way to penetrate many of these secret recesses is to book yourself on one of the island's giro (tour) cruises—they have been an iconic Caprese experience since the 19th century. Offered by a flotilla of companies ranging from bare-bones to high luxe, these roundabout tours—many last only two hours but you can also sign on for daylong cruises—give you the chance to travel the island's "highway," marvel at sights immortalized in 1,001 travel posters, and, for one magical afternoon, take possession of one of the horseshoe-shape inlets where movie stars are as much at home as dolphins.

above, Capri's iconic Faraglioni rock formation

A "GIRO" TOUR AROUND CAPRI

An aquatic version of the famous Italian *passeggiata* (stroll), the Capri giro cruise is offered on two main types of boat. The classic craft is a *gozzo*—once the traditional fishing boat of the Bay of Naples, it now varies in comfort from luxe (shower, lunch, aperitif) to basic (BYO *panino*). Or opt for a *gommone*, a speedboat: this gives you a chance to create your own itinerary—but watch out for gas prices. Coastal highlights are outlined below, but you can always opt to follow your instincts, take an inviting side lagoon, and Robinson Crusoe the day away in one of the innumerable small inlets.

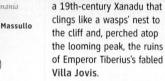

Grotta Bianca

a 19th-century Xanadu that clings like a wasps' nest to the cliff and, perched atop the looming peak, the ruins of Emperor Tiberius's fabled **Villa Jovis**.

STARTING YOUR ROUNDS

Capri's gateway harbor, the **Marina Grande**, is where most giro cruises start. Time, budget, weather, and confidence will determine your choice of tour—long or short, cheap or ritzy, guided

Villa Jovis

or independent—but the more extensive ones should cover the following sites. East of the marina lies the **Grotta del Bove Marino** (Sea Lion's Cave). Listen for the distinctly mammalian howl, amplified naturally by the cave walls: local fishermen may tell you the creature is still in residence, but what you're hearing is the wail of the wind and sea. You soon reach **Punta Capo**, marked by its welcoming statue of the Madonna del Soccorso. Here, atop the **Rocca di Capri**— Capri's own Gibraltar—catch a glimpse of the **Villa Lysis**,

SEA FOR YOURSELF

Rounding Capri's eastern coast you arrive at the **Grotta dei Polpi**, originally named for its abundance of octopus and cuttlefish; recently fished dry, it is now called the Coral Cave. Past a gorge, you'll arrive at **Grotta Meravigliosa**— the "cave of marvels," as its innumerable stalagmites and stalactites prove (look, as most people do, for one that is said to resemble the Madonna). You'll need a sweater and even a scarf in here—it's glacial even in peak summer.

Farther along is the **Grotta Bianca** (White Grotto), whose opal waters—their

Marina Grande

color is due to the mix of seawater and deep-spring water—shimmer against a spectacularly jagged white backdrop; past the entrance a large crevice has produced a natural swimming pool, known as the Piscina di Venere (Pool of Venus). Entering the **Cala di Matermania**, spot the distant square-shaped sea rock known as Il Monacone, once home to a hermit-monk who kept a net hanging off its side (woe betide any fisherman who did not throw in some fish!). Astride the promontory of **Punta Massullo** is that modernist eyeknocker, the red-hued **Villa Malaparte**.

Past the ancient Roman port of **Tragara** lies the famed **Faraglioni**, the earthen powerhouse of three massive rocks rising from the sea that remain the scenic masterpiece of Capri. The "Faraglione di Terra" is linked to land and nestles two famous lido restaurants, Da Luigi and La Fontelina. The next rock monolith out is the "Faraglione di Mezzo"

(Middle)—this one has the tunnel that is so much fun to sail through—while the farthest one out is the Scopolo, or "Faraglione di Fuori" (External). If you have an expert guide ask him to take you into the little blue grotto—a small cave illuminated by an underwater window of aquamarine light—tucked behind the Faraglioni.

Faraglioni

Villa Malaparte

Cala di Matermania

WATER COLORS

Farther on sits the **Grotta Albergo Marinari**. Despite its name, there is no hotel here; the cave was used by sailors as shelter from sudden sea storms. Next lies the **Grotta Oscura**, whose deceptively narrow entrance opens up to reveal the largest cave on the island, its two large oval caverns a showplace of stunning light reflections. Drifting up the southern coast of Capri, the

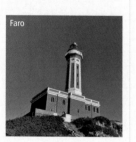
Faro

zigzagging drama of **Via Krupp** threads its way over the hillside to chic **Marina Piccola**. It was here on the Scoglie delle Sirene (Siren's Rock), immortalized in Canto XII of the *Odyssey*, that mermaids tried to lure Odysseus, the world's first tourist, onto its hazardous shoals.

Just after **Punta Ventroso** look for the Cala di San Costanzo, where a "face" in the rock presumably resembles St. Costanzo, the patron saint of Capri. A few hundred meters farther on is the **Grotta Verde** (Green Grotto), whose waters resemble an enormous deep-sea daiquiri, and which in turn is followed by the **Grotta Rossa**, whose red hue is caused by algae buildup. A little way beyond

Marina Piccola

is the **Grotta dei Santi** (Saints' Cave), whose rocky outcrop resembles human figures at prayer. Take some time to enjoy the truly stunning waters of **Cala Marmolata**, which you'll sail through before coming to the lighthouse, or **Faro**. Sail the length of the west coast to the cape landmarked by the Torre Damecuta. From the Gradola shore you will find your spectacular finale, the **Grotta Azzurra** (Blue Grotto).

MAKING THE MOST OF THE GROTTA AZZURA

Grotta Azzurra

siesta, many native Capresi insist that the optimum time to see the unearthly blue is between 10 AM and 1 PM. However, more objective observers advise that the best time is around 4 PM or 5 PM, when the raking light of the sun is most brilliant. At this hour, many—though not all—of the boatmen have departed along with the tour buses, so you may have the Blue Grotto pretty much to yourself.

Today, many travelers visit Capri's fabled Grotta Azzurra (Blue Grotta) using tour boats departing either from Capri's Marina Grande or from the small embarkation point below Anacapri (reached by bus from Anacapri Town). This approach can prove frustrating: you have to board one boat to get to the grotto, then transfer to a smaller one to pass through the 3-foot-high cave opening, and then are allowed—due to the midday traffic jam of boats—disappointingly little time once inside the cave. Instead, in late afternoon—not midday—take the bus from Anacapri's Piazza Vittoria to the Strada della Grotta Azzurra. Interested in protecting the early-afternoon hours for their traditional

- 🖂 € 15 from Marina Grande, €10 by rowboat from Grotta Azzurra
- 🕘 8:30–1 hr before sunset, closed if sea is even minimally rough

Grotta Azzurra

THE BEST CRUISE OUTFITTERS

INDEPENDENCE

If you're keen on exploring the island on your own, you can hire a speedboat (gommone)—with a skipper provided on request—from the following:

LEOMAR (follow the stairs to the passageway; Spiaggia Marina Grande, 081/8377181, www.leomarcapri.it). Based on the beach at Marina Grande next to the bus stop, Leomar offers hourly and full-day rentals starting at €35–€45 per hour, six people maximum.

BANANA SPORT (Spiaggia Pontile Privato, 081/8375188). This popular outfitter offers boats starting at €75 for a minimum two-hour rental.

QUICK OVERVIEW TOURS

If time is short, catch a tour on a larger, quicker, and sometimes more fun-packed boat.

MOTOSCAFISTI CAPRI (Via Provinciale 282, 081/8377714, www.motoscafisticapri.com). With offices right on the dock at Marina Grande, this cooperative of gozzo boat owners offers three set tours that leave on the hour. Admission is depending on choice of tour, €11–€14. Their "Blue" and "Yellow" tours include the Blue Grotto.

LASER CAPRI (Via Don Giobbe Ruocco 45, 081/8375208, www.capri.net/en/c/laser-capri). For those who want to make a tour on a larger, sturdier sightseeing boat, Lazer has a fleet of larger ships which can take up to 100 people. Tickets run €10 to the Blue Grotto, €14 for full-island tour. Their ticket booth is just past the main funicular station landing.

A PERSONAL TOUCH

On some of these guided tours, a lively combination of anecdotes (and folk songs!) accompany you throughout: Proffer a gratuity if you are happy with the trip.

CAPRI RELAX BOATS (Via Cristoforo Colombo 34, 081/8374559, www.caprirelaxboats.com). One of the best and most stylish of the outfitters, Capri Relax has a comprehensive range of tours. The island tour will take you into caves that larger boats can't reach, and their flexibility allows you to decide the itinerary.

GENNARINO ALBERINO (Capri Whales, Via Cristoforo Colombo 17, 081/8377118, www.caprinautica.it). Alberino's tours are virtually living island history, as he was one of the divers who unearthed the ancient marble statues found in the Blue Grotto. Each of his boats is furnished with freshwater showers and iceboxes. Gennarino's knowledge of the island is encyclopedic, and few others can match it.

CAPRI TIME BOATS (Truglio 19, 081/3509173, www.capritimeboats.com). This very suave option not only offers island tours but goes beyond to the Amalfi Coast and islands in the bay.

CAPRI SEA SERVICE (Via Cristoforo Colombo 64, 081/8378781, www.capriseaservice.com). A wide panoply of options are offered, from gozzo tours to specialized diving trips.

CAPRI BOATS (Via Largo Fontana 53, 081/19726872, www.capriboats.com). Those wanting to experience the "Capri moon" over the Faraglioni, nighttime fishing expeditions, and an array of gozzo tours should contact this outfitter.

■ TIP→ Giro passengers often have to purchase separate tickets to use the rowboats that tour the Blue Grotto. Check when signing up for your giro cruise.

Grotta Verde

1923. Outside are magical terraces with views to rival the adjacent Villa Jovis. ⊠ *Via Lo Capo* ☎*081/8386111* *Capri municipal office* 🖃*Free* ⏱ *Apr.–mid-Oct., Mon.–Sat 9:30–12:30 and 2:30–5:30.*

WORTH NOTING

Giardini di Augusto *(Gardens of Augustus)* and **Via Krupp.** You'll see some spectacular views of the southern side of Capri from the southernmost terrace of this well-kept park lying on both sides of Via Matteotti. In one corner of the gardens is a monument to Lenin, who visited Gorky and his Capri-based school for revolutionaries between 1907 and 1913. This school, above the gardens, is now the hotel Villa Krupp, named after the German industrialist Friedrich Alfred Krupp. An amateur marine biologist, Krupp fell in love with Capri after coming to Naples to visit its aquarium. In 1900 he decided to fund a paved walkway to connect the Hotel Quisisana, where he then lived, to the Marina Piccola. The zigzagging Via Krupp is considered a masterpiece, demonstrating that roads can be works of art in themselves. Designed by Emilio Mayer, it features no less than eight whiplash switchbacks, hugging the cliff face and engaging the stroller in an ever-changing panorama that stretches from the Giardini di Augusto and the Punta del Cannone to the waterfront. After a hiatus of 32 years the road was reopened in 2008 by Italian president Giorgio Napolitano, who unveiled a plaque exulting the sinuous curves as an eternal symbol of liberty and homage to the beauty of nature. Although heir to the great munitions fortune, Krupp was the most peaceful of men and bestowed monies on many island charities. Despite his good works, he was hounded by malicious gossip that he held orgies at his villa and in the island grottoes, and he committed suicide in 1902. ⊠ *Via Matteotti and Via Krupp, Capri Town.*

Grotta di Matermania. Set in the bowels of Monte Tuoro, this legend-haunted cave was dedicated to Cybele, the Magna Mater, or Great Mother of the gods—hence the somewhat corrupted name of the cave. A goddess with definite eastern origins, Cybele did not form part of the Greek or Roman pantheon: worship of her was introduced to Italy in 204 BC at the command of the Sibylline oracle, supposedly for the purpose of driving Hannibal out of Italy. At dawn the cave is touched by the rays of the sun, leading scholars to believe it may also have been a shrine where the Mithraic mysteries were celebrated. Hypnotic rituals, ritual sacrifice of bulls, and other orgiastic practices made this cave a place of myth, so it's not surprising that later authors reported (erroneously) that Emperor Tiberius used it for orgies. Nevertheless, the cave was adapted by the Romans into a luxurious nymphaeum (small shrine), but little remains of the original structure, which would have been covered by tesserae, polychrome stucco, and marine shells. If you want to see the few ancient remains, you have to step inside the now-unprepossessing cavern. ⊠ *Giro del'Arco Naturale.*

Marina Grande. Besides being the main harbor gateway to Capri and the main disembarkation point for the mainland, Marina Grande is usually the starting point for round-island tours and trips to the Blue Grotto. The marina has faded in the glare of neon since the days when it was Sophia Loren's home in the 1958 film *It Started in Naples.* Originally a conglomeration of fishermen's houses built on ancient Roman foundations, it's now an extended hodgepodge of various architectural styles, with buildings that almost exclusively service the tourist industry. Warehouses and storerooms in which fishermen once kept their boats and tackle are now shops, restaurants, and bars, most either tacky or overpriced. To the west, however, lie three sights worth exploring: the historic 17th-century church of **San Costanzo,** the ruins of the **Palazzo a Mare** (the former palace of emperor Augustus), and the chic **Baths of Tiberius beach.** ⊠*Marina Grande, Capri Town.*

Museo Caprense Ignazio Cerio. Former mayor of Capri Town, designer of the island's most ravishing turn-of-the-20th-century villas, author of delightfully arcane books, and even paleontologist par excellence, Edwin Cerio was Capri's leading genius and eccentric. His most notorious work was a Capri guidebook that all but urged tourists to stay away. His most beautiful work was the Villa Solitaria—once home to famed novelist Compton Mackenzie and set over the sea on the Via Pizzo Lungo path. He also set up this small but interesting museum, which conserves finds from the island. Room 1 displays Pleistocene fossils of pygmy elephant, rhino, and hippopotamus, which all grazed here 200,000–300,000 years ago, when the climate and terrain were very different. Although most of the important archaeological finds—such as the statues found in the Blue Grotto—have been shipped off to Naples, Room 4 displays the leftovers, a scantily labeled collection of vases, mosaics, and stuccowork from the Greek and Roman periods. ⊠*Piazzetta Cerio 5, Capri Town* ☎*081/8376681* 🖷*081/8370858* ⊕*www.centrocaprense.org* ✉*€2.60, guided tours by appointment €15.50* ⊙*Tues.–Sat. 10–1*

Santo Stefano. Towering over La Piazzetta, with a dome that is more sculpted than constructed and with *cupolettas* that seem molded from frozen zabaglione, Capri's mother church is a prime example of *l'architettura baroccheggiante*—the term historians use to describe Capri's fanciful form of baroque architecture. Often using vaulting and molded buttresses (since there was little wood to be found on such a scrubby island to support the ceilings), Capri's architects became sculptors when they adapted Moorish and Grecian styles into their own "homemade" architecture. Sometimes known unglamorously as the ex-cathedral, the church was built in 1685 by Marziale Desiderio of Amalfi on the site of a Benedictine convent (founded in the 6th century), whose sole relic is the clock tower campanile across the Piazzetta. As in so many churches in southern Italy, there has been a good deal of recycling of ancient building materials: the flooring of the high altar was laid with polychrome marble from Villa Jovis, while the marble in the Cappella del Sacramento was removed from the Roman villa of Tragara. Inside the sacristy are some of the church treasures, including a silver statue of San Costanzo, the patron saint of Capri, whose holy day is celebrated every May 14. Opposite the church on the tiny Piazzetta I. Cerio are the Palazzo Cerio Arcucci, with its Museo Caprense Ignazio Cerio; the Palazzo Farace, which houses the Biblioteca Caprense I. Cerio (I. Cerio Library); and the Palazzo Vanalesti, the executive offices of the Capri tourist board. ⊠*Piazza Umberto I, Capri Town* ☎*081/8370072.*

Villa Malaparte. Nicknamed the *Casa Come Me* (House Like Myself) and perched out on the rocky Punta Massullo, this villa is considered by some historians to be a great monument of 20th-century architecture. Built low to be part of the ageless landscape, the red-hue villa was designed in Rationalist style by the Roman architect Adalberto Libera in the late 1930s for its owner Curzio Malaparte (author of the novel *La Pelle,* which recounts various World War II experiences in Naples). Unfortunately, the aesthetic concerns of the villa are inextricably entailed with political ones: Curzio Malaparte was a full-blown Fascist, and the only reason why this house was allowed to be built along this otherwise unsullied stretch of coast was by special fiat from none other than Mussolini. Malaparte was unhappy with the design and made a number of alterations during the construction phase, including the famous trapezoidal staircase that seems to grow out of the roof. The villa is private, but if you want to see it up close, it was featured as a suitably striking backdrop for Brigitte Bardot in Jean-Luc Godard's underrated film *Contempt* (1963). ⊠ *Giro dell'Arco Naturale.*

FROM ANACAPRI TO THE BLUE GROTTO

One of the most breathtaking bus rides anywhere follows the tortuous road from Capri Town 3 km (2 mi) up a dramatic escarpment to Anacapri. At 902 feet over the bay, Anacapri is the island's only other town and leading settlement on the island's peaks, poetically referred to as the Monte Sirene (Siren Heights). Crowds are thickest around the square, which is the starting point of the chairlift to the top of Monte Solaro and close to Villa San Michele, the main magnet up here for tour groups. Allow plenty of time when traveling to or from Anacapri, as space on the local buses is usually at a premium. Alternatively, the athletically inclined can hike from Capri up to Anacapri by taking the 900 steps of the Scala Fenicia (the Phoenician Stairway, more likely to have been built by the Greeks than the Phoenicians), leading almost down to Marina Grande, to a point on the main road about 15 minutes' walk from Capri Town For access, continue walking past Villa San Michele away from Piazza Vittoria. Long in a state of disrepair, this ancient pathway has been restored and reopened. Needless to say, most people will want to tackle the Scala Fenica going down, not up. As a fitting finale to a visit to Anacapri, take the convenient bus down the hill to the water's edge and the fabled Blue Grotto.

GETTING HERE
There's regular bus service to Anacapri from Marina Grande or Capri Town (Piazzetta d'Ungheria).

TOP ATTRACTIONS
Fodor'sChoice ★ **Casa Rossa** *(Red House).* Capri is famous for its villas built by artists, millionaires, and poets who became willing prisoners of Capri during the Gilded Age. Elihu Vedder, Charles Coleman, Lord Algernon, and the Misses Wolcott-Perry were some of the people who constructed lavish Aesthetic Movement houses. Built by the American colonel J. C. Mac-Kowen, this particular villa, near the center of Anacapri, was erected between 1876 and 1899. With walls hued in distinctive Pompeian

A GOOD WALK: AROUND ANACAPRI

From Anacapri's main square of Piazza Vittoria, take Via Capodimonte opposite the Seggiovia (chairlift) to **Villa San Michele**, about a five-minute walk, past a formidable array of garish boutiques, bars, and liqueur factories, all vying to ensnare passersby. As with many sites on the island, it's best to get to the villa shortly after it opens, or in the early evening when the day-trippers have moved through. After browsing through its rooms and strolling through the gardens and the ecomuseum, retrace your steps to Piazza Vittoria and make for the lower station of the *Seggiovia* to **Monte Solaro**. You'll soon be whisked out of town over whitewashed houses and carpets of spring-flowering broom and rockrose to the viewing platform at the top of Solaro. From here a path leads north downhill toward the sublimely picturesque church of **Santa Maria a Cetrella** through some of the most beautiful wooded countryside on Capri. In spring and autumn watch for migrating birds. A splash of yellow combined with an undulating flight could be the golden oriole; the multicolor bee-eater also migrates via Capri in May and September. On the way back down from Cetrella, follow the signs to Anacapri along Via Monte Solaro (downhill), passing close to the ruins of the **Castello Barbarossa** and then emerging

close to the Villa San Michele. If you have time and energy left over, make for Via Orlandi, a useful street for stocking up on provisions. Pass the impressive **Casa Rossa** (Red House), on your right, and then take the next right turn (Via San Nicola) to Piazza San Nicola and the church of **San Michele**. If possible, climb to the organ loft to savor its magnificent majolica tile floor depicting the Garden of Eden, then head back to the Piazza Vittoria. By mid- to late afternoon, the crowds will have vanished from the **Grotta Azzurra** (Blue Grotto), at the sea below Anacapri. Catch the convenient bus that links the town with the grotto and enjoy this fabled sight around 4 PM or 5 PM, when connoisseurs swear that the light is best. History buffs and vista lovers will want to finish their day with a trek to the nearby **Villa di Damecuta**, thought to have been one of Emperor Tiberius's secret retreats.

TIMING

The walk takes approximately three hours, allowing at least one hour for the visit to Villa San Michele and its gardens, and a further two hours' leisurely amble on the round-trip. If armed with a packed lunch, you're most likely to find a picnic site near Cetrella—in attempts to discourage low-spending day-trippers from the mainland, consumption of picnics is made fairly difficult on Capri.

red, the villa incorporates a noted 15th-century Aragonese tower. A historian and archaeologist, MacKowen wrote a guide to Capri and brought to light marble fragments and statues inside the Blue Grotto, thus revealing and validating its importance as a nymphaeum in Roman times. Local legend says that Anacapri's menfolk locked their women in Casa Rossa when they went to work in Naples, but the villa now houses a permanent exhibition called "The Painted Island," featuring 32 canvases from masters such as Giordano and Brancaccio, depicting images of Capri in the 19th and 20th centuries. ✉ *Via G. Orlandi, Anacapri* 📞*081/8382193* 💶*€2* 🕐*May–Sept., Tues.–Sun. 10:30–1:30 and 6:30–9.*

★ **Grotta Azzurra** *(Blue Grotto).* Contrary to the legend claiming that the Blue Grotto was discovered by two travelers as recently as the 19th century, the truth is it has been an island landmark since time immemorial. Extensive sub-sea-level remains as well as several large statues (some now on view at Capri's Certosa museum, others in Naples) reveal it had been in use as the elegant, mosaic-decorated nymphaeum of the adjoining Roman villa of Gradola. Historians can't quite agree if it was simply a lovely little pavilion where rich patricians would cool themselves in preparation for midday picnics, or if it was a site where sacred rituals were practiced. It is thought that Tiberius may have accessed the grotto through Anacapri's *cloaca maxima* (sewer) from his adjacent Villa Damecuta.

The Blue Grotto famously burst upon the modern consciousness with its rediscovery on August 18, 1826, by the Polish poet August Kopisch and his Swiss friend, the artist Ernest Fries. Two years later, the poet Wilhelm Waiblinger wrote an ode to it as a tribute to the era of Romanticism and man's "return to nature." It subsequently inspired Hans Christian Andersen's 1835 novel, *The Improvisor,* a 19th-century bestseller that triggered an unending flow of Grand Tour visitors to Capri.

Hued in such vivid blue as to demote cerulean to green, the Grotta Azzura remains Capri's greatest natural wonder. Don't be surprised to see visitors dunk glasses into its opaline liquid, half-expecting to see the glasses filled with neon-blue water. In fact, the intense color is caused by sunlight refracting through the entrance's enormous underwater arch. Back when Emperor Tiberius used to haunt this cave, the water level was considerably lower than now, so today's visitors are enjoying a light spectacle the ancient Romans missed out on.

The Grotta Azzurra can be reached from Marina Grande or from the small embarkation point below Anacapri on the northwest side of the island, served by bus from Anacapri. It must be said that while the grotto is spectacular, the experience of viewing it can be frustrating. You board one boat to get to the grotto and transfer to another smaller one in order to get inside (the opening is only just over 3 feet high). If there's a backup of boats waiting to get in, you'll be given precious little time to enjoy the gorgeous color of the water and its silvery reflections. Instead of taking a boat from Marina Grande, from Anacapri you can head to the Piazza Vittoria for the bus that connects the town with the seaside grotto. Either way you go, though, is going to be time-consuming. Be prepared to dicker with the boatmen at the grotto entrance. ✉ *Grotta Azzurra* 💶*€21 from Marina Grande, €10 by rowboat from Grotta Azzurra near Anacapri* 🕐*9–1 hr before sunset, closed if sea is even minimally rough.*

Monte Solaro. An impressive limestone formation and the highest point on Capri (1,932 feet), Monte Solaro affords gasp-inducing views toward the bays of Naples and Salerno. A 12-minute chairlift ride will take you right to the top (refreshments available at bar), which

A chairlift makes ascending Monte Solaro a breeze.

is a starting point for a number of scenic trails on the western side of the island, most particularly down the slope to the lovely area around Santa Maria a Cetrella. Picnickers should note that even in summer it can get windy at this height, and there are few trees to provide shade or refuge. ⊠ *Piazza Vittoria, Anacapri* ☎ *081/8371428* 🎟 *€6 one-way, €8 round-trip* ⊗ *Daily 9:30–1 hr before sunset. Closed in adverse weather conditions.*

Fodor'sChoice ★ **Santa Maria a Cetrella.** Scenically perched on the slopes of Monte Solaro, this small sanctuary in late-Gothic style—with its older parts dating to the late 14th century—offers a truly picturesque frame for a panorama that takes in much of the island. It also marks the top of the second access route (Il Passetiello) used in ancient times, which linked Capri Town with Anacapri. Steep, slippery, and in spots still dangerous, this is the pathway that the Carthusian monks of San Giacomo would have used to reach their properties in the upper part of the island. Congregants were mainly fisherfolk whose boats were moored in the Marina Piccola directly below; they also used this cliff-top aerie as a lookout against Saracen pirates. The church was substantially rebuilt by Franciscan monks in the early 17th century, when a sacristy was added. To reach Santa Maria, you can climb a path leading off Viale Axel Munthe (an hour-long walk); an alternative is to descend a path leading from the Monte Solaro chairlift. The church has erratic opening times; ask at the chairlift for further information. Mass is celebrated at dawn every Sunday in September, but the site remains unforgettable year-round. ⊠ *Monte Solaro.*

FodorśChoice ★ **Villa San Michele.** Henry James called this villa and garden "the most fantastic beauty, poetry, and inutility that one had ever seen clustered together." At the ancient entranceway to Anacapri just at the top of the Scala Fenicia and occupying the site of an ancient Roman villa, Villa San Michele was built (beginning in 1896) in accordance with the instructions of its owner, Axel Munthe (1857–1949). Physician to the Swedish royal family, Munthe practiced both in Paris and in Rome, thereby building up a substantial fortune, much of which he plowed into real estate in Anacapri.

WORD OF MOUTH

"When we arrived in the center of Anacapri we decided the first thing we wanted to do was ride the chairlift up to the top of Mt. Solaro. This was one of the things that was on my 'really want to do this' list, and I'm very happy that we did. It was such a beautiful day…clear blue sky, sun shining, sharing the experience with great friends, I couldn't have asked for a more perfect setting."
—LowCountryIslander

He was a philanthropist with a lifelong dedication to the sick and destitute. Munthe's *The Story of San Michele* is an evocative—if not entirely reliable—autobiography.

The 19th-century artists Alma-Tadema and Lord Leighton—specialists in painting scenes *all'antica* ("of antiquity")—would have set up their easels in a minute at the villa, thanks to its Roman-style courtyards, marble walkways, and atriums. Rooms display the doctor's varied collections, which range from bric-a-brac to classical antiquities (once thought so important J. Pierpont Morgan offered millions for them, but the good doctor knew that most were fakes so refused all offers). Medieval choir stalls, Renaissance lecterns, and gilded statues of saints adorn various rooms, while the doctor's personal memorabilia enables the visiting public to learn more about this enigmatic patron of the arts and humanist.

The villa is connected by a spectacular pergola path overlooking the entire Bay of Naples. This leads to the famous **Sphinx Parapet,** where an ancient Egyptian sphinx looks out over to Sorrento (you cannot see its face—on purpose). It's said that if you touch the sphinx's hindquarters with your left hand while making a wish, it will come true. The parapet is connected to the adorable little Chapel of San Michele. Dr. Munthe was initially drawn to San Michele because of this chapel, abandoned at the time, which was believed to stand on the grounds of one of Tiberius's villas. Rumor has it that its missing bells were said to ring as a sign that the emperor was seeking forgiveness for having sentenced a certain carpenter from Galilee to death. Munthe proceeded to banish all shadows and made his new home Capri's most welcoming showplace.

Oddly enough, the only person Munthe allowed to live at the Villa San Michele (the doctor's real home was the Torre di Materita, up the mountainside) was the Marchesa Casati, the notorious fin de siècle fashion plate who was fond of walking diamond-collared leopards down the Champs-Élyseès.

Besides hosting summer concerts on Friday evenings, the Axel Munthe Foundation has an ecomuseum that fittingly reflects Munthe's fondness

for animals, where you can learn about various bird species—accompanied by their songs—found on Capri. Not only did Munthe aid people, he bought up the hillside as a sanctuary for birds, which prevented the Caprese from capturing quail by terrible means (lured by songbirds that had been blinded to make them sing better). Today, thanks to Dr. Munthe, this little realm is still an Eden. ✉ *Viale Axel Munthe, Anacapri* ☎*081/8371401* ⊕*www.villasanmichele.eu* ✇*€5* ⊙*Nov.–Feb., daily 9–3:30; Mar., daily 9–4:30; Apr. and Oct., daily 9–5; May–Sept., daily 9–6.*

WORTH NOTING

Castello Barbarossa. The foundation of this ruined castle, almost clinging to the side of the cliff above Villa San Michele, dates to the late 10th century, when Capri was ruled by the ancient maritime republic of Amalfi. Named after the admiral of the Turkish fleet, Khair-Eddin, or Barbarossa (Redbeard), who stormed and took the castle in 1535, much of the original layout has been changed over the centuries. The castle is part of the Swedish-run Axel Munthe Foundation, which organizes weekly guided visits on Thursday afternoons from May to October (call the foundation to reserve a place) besides carrying out ornithological research in the surrounding area. ✉*Axel Munthe FoundationAnacapri* ☎*081/8371401* ⊕*www.villasanmichele.eu* ✇*Free.*

San Michele. The octagonal Baroque church of San Michele on Piazza San Nicola, finished in 1719, is best known for its exquisite majolica pavement (1761), designed by Solimena and executed by the Abruzzese *mastro-riggiolaro* (master tiler) Leonardo Chiaiese. A walkway skirts the rich ceramic carpet depicting Adam and a duly contrite Eve being expelled from the Garden of Eden, but you can get a breathtaking overview from the organ loft, reached by a winding staircase near the ticket booth. Outside the church is the Via Finestrale, which leads to Anacapri's noted **Le Boffe quarter.** This section of town, slightly lower on the hillside, is centered around the Piazza Diaz and the church of Santa Sofia and owes its name to the distinctive domestic architecture prevalent here, which uses vaults and sculpted groins instead of cross beams. The word *boffe* comes from the Neapolitan dialect for "swollen." ✉*Piazza S. Nicola, Anacapri* ☎*081/8372396* ✇*€2* ⊙*Apr.–Oct., daily 9–7; Nov.–Mar., daily 10–2.*

Villa di Damecuta. Sited strategically on a ridge with views sweeping across the Bay of Naples toward Procida and Ischia, the main access to this Roman villa would have been from the landing stage right by the Blue Grotto at Gradola. This was probably one of the villas mentioned by Tacitus in his *Annals* as having been built by Tiberius: "Here on Capreae, in twelve spacious, separately named villas, Tiberius settled." Like Villa Jovis to the east, Villa di Damecuta was extensively plundered over the centuries prior to its proper excavation in 1937. Below the medieval tower (Torre Damecuta) there are two rooms (*domus* and *cubiculum*) that are thought to have been Tiberius's secret summer refuge. Affinities with Villa Jovis may be seen in the *ambulatio* (walkway), complete with seats and stunning backdrop. To reach Villa Damecuta, get the bus from Anacapri to Grotto Azzurra and ask the driver to let you off at the right stop. Alternatively, you can walk from the center of Anacapri down the bus route (about 30 minutes, but no sidewalks) or try your luck in the network of virtually traffic-free little alleyways running parallel to the main road. ⊠ *Via A. Maiuri* 🎟*Free.*

WHERE TO EAT

IN AND AROUND CAPRI TOWN

$$ ✕**Al Grottino.** This small and friendly family-run restaurant, which is
SOUTHERN handy to the Piazzetta, in a 14th-century building, has arched ceil-
ITALIAN ings and lots of atmosphere; autographed photos of celebrity custom-
ers cover the walls. House specialties are *scialatielli ai frutti di mare*
(homemade seafood pasta) and linguine *ai gamberetti* (with shrimp and
tomato sauce), but the owner delights in taking his guests through the
menu. ⊠ *Via Longano 27, Capri Town* ☎*081/8370584* ⌁*Reserva-*
tions essential ☰*AE, DC, MC, V* ⊙*Closed Nov.–mid-Mar.*

$$$ ✕**Edode.** When you've had enough of florid, flowery Caprese decor,
SOUTHERN head here to this sleek entry among the island's restaurants. The name
ITALIAN may come from the ancient Greek for food, the seats may have been
imported from Austria, the gray-on-white columns hail from Paris, but
the ambience conjures up New York's hot–cool Meatpacking district.
From the menu, you can't go wrong with the fresh fish, the specialty
being *paccheri con gamberi e crema di zucchini* (large pasta with shrimp
and cream of zucchini). The wine list has more than 700 choices from
all over the world. Enjoy a fine bottle and settle in for some nice people-
watching. ⊠ *Via Camerelle 81/83, Capri Town* ☎*081/8388252* ☰*AE,*
DC, MC, V ⊙*Closed mid-Oct.–Mar.*

$$$ ✕**I Faraglioni.** With natural shade provided by a 150-year-old wisteria
SOUTHERN plant, this is a popular, fairly stylish restaurant, which is both centrally
ITALIAN located and yet almost immersed in Mediterranean greenery. Meals
here usually kick off with *uovo alla Monachina*, an egg-shaped dish
filled with creamy bechamel sauce and breadcrumbs. For a first course,
try the *straccetti con gamberi e pomodorini* (fresh green pasta with
shrimp and small tomatoes). ⊠ *Via Camerelle 75, Capri Town* ☎*081/*
8370320 ⌁*Reservations essential* ☰*AE, DC, MC, V* ⊙*Closed mid-*
Oct.–Mar.

$$$ ✕**La Canzone del Mare.** This is the legendary bathing lido of the Marina
SOUTHERN Piccola, with two seawater pools as well as rocky beach, erstwhile
ITALIAN haunt of Gracie Fields, Emilio Pucci, Noël Coward, and any number
★ of 1950s and '60s glitterati. The VIPs may have departed for more
private beaches, but this setting is as magical as ever: enjoy luncheon
in the covered pavilion looking out over the sea with I Faraglioni in
the distance—this is Capri as picture-perfect as it comes. You need
to pay a fee to actually use this bathing *stabilimento* (club) but why
not make a day of it? There are also a few suites available if a day is
not enough. ⊠ *Via Marina Piccola 93, Capri Town* ☎*081/8370104*
⊕*www.lacanzonedelmare.com* ☰*AE, DC, MC, V* ⊙*Closed mid-Oct.–*
Mar. No dinner.

$$$ ✕**La Capannina.** For decades one of Capri's most celebrity-haunted res-
SOUTHERN taurants, La Capannina is a few steps from the busy social hub of the
ITALIAN Piazzetta. The walls are covered with photos of celebrities enjoying
★ their meal here, and the discreet covered veranda, with its hanging

baskets, is ideal for dining by candlelight in a florid garden setting, all pink, green, and white. Another alternative to avoid the stuffy indoor rooms is to join the regulars in the outdoor courtyard. The specialties, aside from an authentic Capri wine with the house label, are homemade *ravioli capresi* and *linguine con lo scorfano* (flat spaghetti with scorpion fish), the squid stuffed with caciotta cheese and marjoram, and the "Pezzogna," an exquisite sea bream cooked whole in a copper casserole and garnished with a layer of baked potatoes. The small bar across the side alleyway is run by the same owners. ⊠ *Via Le Botteghe 12b, Capri Town* ☎081/8370732 ⊕*www.capannina-capri.com* ⚐*Reservations essential* ⊟*AE, DC, MC, V* ☉*Closed Nov.–mid-Mar. and Wed. in Mar. and Oct.*

$$
SOUTHERN
ITALIAN
★

✕**La Fontelina.** Lying just below Punta Tragara at the base of Capri's impressive offshore rocks (the Faraglioni), this is the place to enjoy a delightfully comatose day on the island. Given its position right on the water's edge, seafood is almost de rigueur. For a slightly different starter, try the *polpette di melanzane* (eggplant fritters), and then dip into the vegetable buffet. Highly recommendable is the house sangria, a blissful mix of white wine and fresh fruit. If you're overwhelmed by large portions of pasta, order a half portion (and pay half). La Fontelina also functions as a lido, with steps and ladders affording access to fathoms-deep blue water. Access is by boat from Marina Piccola or on foot from Punta Tragara (10 minutes). Only lunch is served. Across the way is the archrival lido-restaurant, Da Luigi, with a more evocative setting but now a bit too famous for its own good. ⊠ *I Faraglioni, at end of Via Tragara, Capri Town* ☎081/8370845 ⊟*AE, MC, V* ☉*Closed mid-Oct.–Easter. No dinner.*

$$
SOUTHERN
ITALIAN
★

✕**L'Aurora.** Though often frequented by celebrities—photographs of famous guests adorn the walls inside and out—this restaurant offers courtesy and *simpatia* irrespective of your persona. Although the oldest restaurant on the island, now in its third generation, its decor is sleekly minimalist. If you want to see and be seen, reserve a table outside on one of Capri's most chic thoroughfares; otherwise go for extra privacy and ambience within. The cognoscenti start by sharing a pizza all'Acqua, a thin pizza with mozzarella and a sprinkling of *peperoncino* (chili). If tiring of pasta, try the *sformatino alla Franco* (rice pie in prawn sauce) but leave room for the homemade sweets. The place fills up quickly, so be sure to reserve. ⊠ *Via Fuorlovado 18–20, Capri Town* ☎081/8370181 ⊕*www.auroracapri.com* ⚐*Reservations essential* ⊟*AE, DC, MC, V* ☉*Closed Jan.–mid-Mar.*

$$$
SOUTHERN
ITALIAN
★

✕**Le Grottelle.** Enjoying one of Capri's most distinctive settings, this extremely informal trattoria is built up against the limestone rocks not far from the Arco Naturale—a cave at the back doubles as the kitchen and wine cellar. Whether you stumble over this place, or make it your destination after an island hike, Le Grottelle will prove memorable, thanks to that ambience and sea view taking in the Amalfi Coast's Li Galli islands. The food? Oh, that . . . the menu includes local rabbit, but go for the seafood, with *linguine con gamberetti e rucola* (pasta with shrimp and arugula) one of the more interesting specialties. ⊠ *Via Arco*

Naturale 13 ☎*081/8375719* *Reservations essential* ═*DC, MC, V* ⊘*Closed Nov.–mid-Mar.*

IN AND AROUND ANACAPRI

$$
PIZZA
✗**Barbarossa.** This ristorante–pizzeria is the first you'll see if you arrive in Anacapri by bus. Its panoramic covered terrace takes in views of the Barbarossa castle on the hill as well as the sea. The no-frills ambience belies the quality of the *cucina*: besides *pizze* they specialize in local dishes—be sure to try the *risotto con gamberi a limone* (shrimp with lemon). Barbarossa is open all year. ⊠*Piazza Vittoria 1, Anacapri* ☎*081/8371483* ═*AE, DC, MC, V.*

$$
SOUTHERN ITALIAN
✗**Da Gelsomina.** Set amid its own terraced vineyards with inspiring views to the island of Ischia and beyond, this is much more than just a well-reputed restaurant. The owner's mother was a friend of Axle Munthe and encouraged her to open a kiosk serving hot food, which evolved into Da Gelsomina. It has an immaculately kept swimming pool, which is open to the public for a small fee—a buffet is served as you lounge here. Located close to one of the island's finer walks, it's an excellent base for a whole day or longer. There's also a five-room pensione, with free transfer service by request from Anacapri center. ⊠*Via Migliera 72, Anacapri* ☎*081/8371499* ⊕*www.dagelsomina. com* ═*AE, DC, MC, V* ⊘*Closed Jan.–mid-Feb. and Tues. in winter. No dinner in winter.*

$$
SOUTHERN ITALIAN
✗**Il Cucciolo.** Nestling in thick maquis high above the Blue Grotto and a five-minute walk from the Roman site of Villa Damecuta, this must be one of the most romantic locations on the Capri, perfectly placed to catch the setting sun. The cucina is refreshingly inventive with fish being a specialty: ask for *pasta fresca con zucchini e gamberi* (fresh pasta with zucchini and shrimp). There's a free evening chauffeur service to and from Anacapri. Reservations are essential in the evening. ⊠*Via La Fabbrica 52, Anacapri* ☎*081/8371917* ═*AE, DC, MC, V* ⊘*Closed Nov.–mid-Jan. and Wed. Oct. and Feb.–May.*

$$
SOUTHERN ITALIAN
✗**La Rondinella.** This is an airy ristorante–pizzeria looking onto the main pedestrianized street of Anacapri. In summer make sure you reserve a table out on the popular terrace. If you have difficulty choosing from the extensive menu, ask for advice or opt for one of their best pasta dishes, linguine *macchiavelle* (with capers, olives, and cherry tomatoes). ⊠*Via Orlandi 295, Anacapri* ☎*081/8371223* ═*DC, MC, V* ⊘*Closed Nov.–Feb. and Thurs. Oct.–May.*

WHERE TO STAY

IN AND AROUND CAPRI TOWN

$$$
⌂**Il Gatto Bianco.** Once the spot where Jacqueline Kennedy famously sought refuge when hounded by paparazzi, this is still a favorite destination to channel Capri's Sunset Boulevard-y ghosts. With greater crowds packing Capri, the hotel does suffer a bit from its location—just around the corner from the Piazzetta and right in the thick of crowds, cafés, and discos. That noted, the lovely atmosphere inside the public salons is quintessential Caprese—it was recently refurbished, with a new blue-on-white bar area, majolica-lined stairs, and antique-y accents. It used

to be a bargain option but has grown more pricey over the years. Matisse, the resident *gatto bianco* (white cat), adds an authentic touch to this taste of Capri. **Pros:** central location; wonderful atmosphere. **Cons:** perhaps too close to the action; no sea view. ⊠ *Via Vittorio Emanuele 32, Capri Town* ☎081/8370203 ⊕*www.gattobianco-capri.com* ⟿*40 rooms* ⊟*AE, DC, MC, V* ⊘*Closed Nov.–mid-Mar.* ⭢BP.

$$$$ ⌂**J.K. Place.** Slightly up the hill from the port, this luxury boutique hotel is situated in an imposing mansion with breathtaking views of the Bay of Naples—a bronze sphinx gazes toward the horizon, evoking its stone equivalent in Anacapri's Villa San Michele. The reception area is discreetly tucked away, so you would be forgiven for mistaking the lobby for a multimillionaire's entrance hall. The neoclassical decor is straight out of the Hamptons, but the teak-floored terrace is pure Mediterranean. This is the only hotel in Capri with direct access to a beach, but with the heated pool surrounded by lemon and palm trees you may never venture that far. **Pros:** pure luxury; beach access. **Cons:** a bit distant from Capri's action; only for those with fat wallets. ⊠ *Via Provinciale Marina Grande 225, Marina Grande* ☎081/8384001 ⊕*www. jkcapri.com* ⟿*22 rooms* ⌂*In-hotel: Gym, pool, sauna, Turkish bath* ⊟*AE, DC, MC, V* ⊘*Closed Nov.–Mar.*

$$$$ ⌂**La Palma.** Though the oldest on Capri (1822), this attentively run hotel has not rested on its laurels. When you arrive at its front door you're immediately given a blast of island glamour, with gleaming lobby, and majolica-tile rooms providing a delightful contrast to the hustle at street level outside (this is just down the street from La Piazzetta). Through the lobby, make for the hotel's magical courtyard, lined with coves and columns sculpted in archetypal Caprese "zabaglione" stucco. Beginning life as the Locando Pagano, this hostelry first hosted August Kopisch, who then went on to "discover" the Blue Grotto. What he would think of the highly lush guest rooms, now dripping with "frescoes" and Dolce Vita accents remains to be seen. The outdoor restaurant is on the much frequented Via Vittorio Emanuele—*the* place to see and be seen. **Pros:** the most central of Capri's luxury hotels; real island glamour. **Cons:** perhaps too central; rather far from the sea. ⊠ *Via V. Emanuele 39, Capri Town* ☎081/8370133 ⊕*www.lapalma-capri.com* ⟿*72 rooms* ⌂*In-hotel: Restaurant, bar* ⊟*AE, DC, MC, V* ⊘*Closed Jan.–Easter* ⭢MAP.

$$$$ ⌂**La Scalinatella.** If you're bronzed and beautiful, or just bronzed, or
★ even just beautiful, this is your kind of hotel. A white Moorish mansion out of the Arabian Nights, it conjures up Capri in finest Hollywood fashion. The name means "little stairway," and that's how this charmingly small hotel is built, on terraces following the slope of the hills, with winding paths and bougainvillea arbors. Inside, the decor is *Architectural Digest*–opulent, with Venetian blackamoor statues, Empire-era consoles, and Valentino fabrics. Guest rooms have overstuffed sofas, bright colors, large terraces, and his-and-her bathrooms (most have whirlpool baths). Outside, one of Capri's bluest pools is the fetching setting for delicious luncheons. **Pros:** all rooms have a sea view; his-and-her bathrooms. **Cons:** a bit removed from the center; main pool visible from main road. ⊠ *Via Tragara 10, Capri Town* ☎081/8370633 ⊕*www.*

4

scalinatella.com ✆ *30 rooms* ♿ *In-hotel: Restaurant, bar, tennis court, 2 pools* ☰ *AE, DC, MC, V* ⊗ *Closed Nov.–Mar.* ⦿*BP.*

$$$$
Fodor'sChoice
★

Punta Tragara. Soigné, adorable, and drop-dead gorgeous, clinging to the Punta Tragara lookout point, this has a hold-your-breath perch directly over the famed rocks of I Faraglioni. Originally a villa, it once hosted a secret war-time meeting between Churchill and Eisenhower. Le Corbusier renovated its exterior in traditional Capri style, and it was subsequently opened as a hotel in the 1970s by Count Manfredi. Baronial fireplaces, gilded antiques, and travertine marble set the style in the main salons, while guest rooms—no two are alike—are sumptuously cozy-casual. The dreamy garden area is the showstopper here and it comes studded with two saltwater pools. One is a jet-powered, aquamarine jewel set a foot away from Don Pablo, an idyllic restaurant that just might be the prettiest spot on the island. To top it off, the entire staff seems to have been sent to the finest finishing schools. **Pros:** a taste of the good life; the view of I Faraglioni. **Cons:** a 10-minute walk from the center; some find the decor dated. ⊠ *Via Tragara 57, Capri Town* ☎*081/8370844* ⊕*www.hoteltragara.com* ✆*43 rooms* ♿*In-hotel: Restaurant, bar, 2 pools* ☰*AE, DC, MC, V* ⊗*Closed mid-Oct.–mid-Apr.* ⦿*BP.*

$$$$
★

Quisisana. Some people say there are really three villages on Capri: Capri Town, Anacapri, and this celebrated landmark, which looms large in the island's mythology. Superstar of Capri hotels, the "Quisi" draws "didn't-I-meet-you-in-St-Tropez?" guests who wouldn't *dream* of staying anywhere else. The Quisi's popularity has made it led to its expansion over the years: the lobby is Las Vegas–size, the pool seems ready for an Esther Williams MGM production number, and the theater-cum-convention center is a jewel designed by noted modernist Gio Ponti back in the 1930s. But the hotel can't be beat for its shiny and luxe restaurants, see-and-be-seen bars, QuisiBeauty parlor, professional service, and location (just down the street from the crowded Piazzetta, this may be *too* convenient). These days, the Quisisana legend remains strong: if you want to plug into Capri's network of the rich and famous, one of the best places to start is the hotel's Bar Quisi with its Krug Room. The fact remains that even though this is Capri's biggest hotel, it is also its hardest-to-get reservation in high season. **Pros:** lux atmosphere on a large scale. **Cons:** the food isn't all star quality (steer clear of the pizza); far from cozy. ⊠ *Via Camerelle 2, Capri Town* ☎*081/8370788* ⊕*www.quisisana.com* ✆*148 rooms* ♿*In-hotel: Restaurant, bar, tennis court, 2 pools, gym* ☰*AE, DC, MC, V* ⊗*Closed Nov.–mid-Mar.* ⦿*BP.*

$$

Villa Helios. An art nouveau treasure, the charming Villa Helios is in a 19th-century, lilac-hue, Moorish-inspired villa, surrounded by extensive orchards on a quiet Capri lane—birdsong provides the soundtrack here. Rooms are simple with ceramic floors, and peace reigns—a lovely chapel occupies part of the first floor. For a small fee all guests become members of the Centro Italiano Turismo Sociale, a Christian organization operating Italy-wide. The operation is run by Franciscan nuns, who channel profits into the hospice next door—the residents often take a shortcut through the garden. **Pros:** beautiful quiet villa. **Cons:** slightly run down; a short climb from the center. ⊠ *Via Croce 4, Capri Town*

☏081/8370240 ⊕*www.villahelios.it* ↘*28 rooms, 20 with bath* ⚘*In-room: no TV* ▭*AE, MC, V* ⊘*Closed mid-Oct.–Apr.* ⎮◯⎮*BP.*

$$ 🏨**Villa Krupp.** Occupying a beautiful house overlooking the idyllic Gar-
★ dens of Augustus, this historic hostelry was once the home of Maxim
Gorky, whose guests included Lenin. Rooms are plain but spacious, with
comfy beds, and some have south-facing terraces with awesome views.
Breakfast is served on the glorious terrace and Certosa di San Giaco-
moand I Faraglioni are just a few minutes away. **Pros:** direct access to
the Gardens of Augustus. **Cons:** a lot of steps to be negotiated; rooms are
simple. ✉*Viale Matteotti 12, Capri Town* ☏081/8370362 ↘*12 rooms*
⚘*In-room: No TV, no elevator* ▭*MC, V* ⊘*Closed Nov.–Mar.* ⎮◯⎮*BP.*

$$–$$$ 🏨**Villa Sarah.** Particularly lovely and gently priced (for Capri), this is a
Fodor'sChoice wonderful option. Lovingly run by the De Martino family, this Capri-
★ yellow Mediterranean building has a sweet Caprese style and is sur-
rounded by lush gardens, abloom with flowers, fruit, and peace. Guest
rooms are homey and furnished with bright, simple accents. The Villa
Sarah is close enough to the Piazzetta (a 10-minute walk) to give easy
access to the goings-on there, yet far enough away to ensure restful
nights. Few can resist the swimming pool and Jacuzzi. **Pros:** gorgeous
pool; wonderful gardens. **Cons:** a steep climb back from the Piazzetta;
no elevator. ✉*Via Tiberio 3/a, Capri Town* ☏081/8377817 ⊕*www.
villasarah.it* ↘*19 rooms* ⚘*In-hotel: Bar, pool, no elevator* ▭*AE, DC,
MC, V* ⊘*Closed mid-Oct.–Mar.* ⎮◯⎮*BP.*

IN AND AROUND ANACAPRI

$$ 🏨**Biancamaria.** This tastefully refurbished hotel with its pleasing facade
and whitewashed spreading arches lies in a traffic-free zone close to
the heart of Anacapri. The front rooms have large terraces looking
toward Monte Solaro; those at the back are quieter and more private.
Pros: friendly staff; Anacapri literally at your doorstep. **Cons:** on the
main pedestrian road; no gardens. ✉*Via G. Orlandi 54, Anacapri*
☏081/8371000 ⊕*www.hotelbiancamaria.com* ↘*25 rooms* ▭*MC,
V* ⊘*Closed Nov.–Mar.* ⎮◯⎮*BP.*

$$$$ 🏨**Caesar Augustus.** A continuing favorite of the Hollywood set, this
Fodor'sChoice landmark has long been considered a Caprese paradise thanks to its
★ breathtaking perch atop an Anacapri cliff. Of course, let's not forget the
grandeur of its villa, gardens, terraces, and pool. As for accommodations, think chic, charming, and casual: the chairs are plump, the beds
enormous, the bouquets fragrant, and every room has a Jacuzzi. You
won't give a second's thought to decor, however, once you catch sight
of the fabled stone terrace and its Cinerama view of the Bay of Naples
or the pool—a jaw-dropping extravaganza nearly levitating 1,000 feet
over the sea and easily one of the most glamorous spots on Earth. But
beware: the rooms on the back of this hotel are very close to the main
Anacapri road—be sure to get a bayside room. Blissfully distant from
Capri Town's crowds, the hotel has a private van to shuttle pampered
guests back and forth. The poolside restaurant is open to nonguests, as
are the hotel's lovely summer weekly classical concerts. **Pros:** possibly
the most glamorous place on earth; summer concerts on site. **Cons:** a bit
far from the action for some; noisy road. ✉*Via G. Orlandi 4, Anacapri*
☏081/8373395, 081/8371421 *reservations* ⊕*www.caesar-augustus.*

com ⟲*55 rooms* ⌂*In-room: Wi-Fi. In-hotel: Restaurant, bar, pool, Turkish bath* ⊟*AE, DC, MC, V* ⊙*Closed Nov.–mid-Apr.* †○|*BP.*

$$$$ ⊞**Capri Palace.** This is *the* place to stay in Anacapri. The entrance is hidden behind a long hedge as you leave the town for Villa San Michele, but you can't miss it. With its own designer boutique and an exceptional restaurant, it is no surprise that this is a favorite of the *cognescenti*, famous or otherwise. Some choose one of the seven suites with private pools, while others are content with the luxurious art- and film-themed rooms—ask for the Monroe, Callas, or Warhol. The Capri Beauty Farm operates from here. If you can tear yourself away from the hotel, you can avail of one of their private boats. **Pros:** this is what Capri is about; excellent restaurant. **Cons:** unattractive entrance; a bit too close to the center of Anacapri. ⊠ *Via Capodimonte 2b, Anacapri* ☎*081/9780111* ⊕*www.capripalace.com* ⟲*77 rooms* ⌂*In-hotel: Restaurant, pool, spa, gym* ⊟*AE, DC, MC, V* ⊙*Closed Nov.-mid-Mar.*

$$$–$$$$ ⊞**San Michele.** Surrounded by luxuriant gardens, in a large cream villa, the San Michele offers solid comfort and good value, along with spectacular views from sky-high Anacapri. The showstopper here is the vast pool—the largest on Capri—surrounded with umbrellaed tables for fine dining and lounging. The interiors are modern, with some Neapolitan period pieces adding atmosphere; most rooms have a terrace or balcony overlooking either sea or island. **Pros:** large pool; spectacular views. **Cons:** some rooms are tiny; the staff is not the friendliest. ⊠ *Via G. Orlandi 5, Anacapri* ☎*081/8371427* ⊕*www.sanmichele-capri.com* ⟲*64 rooms* ⌂*In-hotel: Restaurant, pool* ⊟*AE, DC, MC, V* ⊙*Closed Nov.–Mar.* †○|*MAP.*

NIGHTLIFE

As would be expected, Capri offers a fair spread of evening entertainment, especially on weekends and during the busier months of July and August, when many upper-crust Italians from the mainland occupy their holiday homes on the island. For music that's fairly gentle on the ears, try one of the traditional *taverne*, which are peculiar to Capri Town. There are also a number of discos and piano bars from which to choose, but the nightlife is more laid-back than Naples or even Ischia. On summer nights the place to be seen showing off your tan and sipping your extra-dry martini is the Piazzetta. Christmas on Capri is a special time, when most of the island visitors are Italians. On New Year's Eve, the Piazzetta is definitely the place to be seen, with dancing and music culminating in a magnificent fireworks display. On New Year's Day there are marching bands, pageants, and all the revelry you would expect on this exuberant island.

BARS

Panta Rei. Billing itself as a sophisticated bar, this is where to find the cognoscenti sipping their *aperitivi* on the terrace overlooking Marina Grande. In a converted cinema down a short flight of stairs off Via Roma, this doubles as a Beauty Spa by day, with sauna and heated pool, but by night the minimalist lounge bar area comes alive with the coolest sounds from the "guru DJ," live music, or piano bar. ⊠ *Via Lo Palazzo 1, Capri* ☎*081/8378898* ⊕*www.pantareicapri.it* ✉€*20* *including drink at bar* ☉ *Beauty spa daily 10 AM–8 PM, lounge bar daily 7 PM–1:30 AM. Closed mid-Nov.–mid-Dec., Jan.–Mar.*

Bar Tiberio (✉ *Piazza Umberto I 880073* ☎ *081/8370268*) is where the locals go to people-watch in the Piazzetta. Great cakes and a good selection of nibbles with your pricey cocktail make this a classic choice in the square. Under the shadow of the Piazzetta's clock tower is **Pulalli** (✉ *Piazza Umberto I 4* ☎ *081/8374108*), where you can enjoy tapas-style snacks while sipping wine on the open terrace.

DISCOS

For 360-degree music almost any night of the year, **Underground** (✉ *Via Orlandi 259, Anacapri* ☎ *081/8372523*) is the clubbing spot for cognoscenti of various ages. Unlike most other discos in Italy, no admission fee is charged, though you're expected to knock back the odd drink (about €15 each). A new "wine corner" is pulling in the thirtysomethings. This is the only club open all year. On Thursday in July and August, make a point of going down to Antonio Beach near the Faro, where Underground arranges open-air discos by the water's edge beginning at 10:30 PM. **Zeus** (✉ *Via Orlandi 103* ☎ *081/8371169*) pulls in a young crowd that dances the night away at the beach parties held at the Faro di Punto Carena in summer.

TAVERNE

Anema e Core (✉ *Via Sella Orta 39/e, Capri Town* ☎ *081/8376461* ⊕ *www.anemaecore.com*) means "soul and heart" in Caprese dialect. This popular place is tucked down a quiet side street, a two-minute walk from the Piazzetta. Admission (€25) includes an eclectic range of lightish live music (after 11 PM) and a drink from the bar. No food is served, so come well-sated. There's no dancing here officially, though some patrons—including celebrities—occasionally take to the tables. The spot is closed Monday and is usually open 9 PM to 3 AM. Reservations are essential on weekends. Tucked well away from the hub of the Piazzetta is **Guarracino** (✉ *Via Castello 7, Capri Town* ☎ *081/8370514*), the place for traditional Neapolitan guitar music with a hint of Latin-American rhythm.

THE ARTS

Culturally speaking, Capri has a fairly long hibernation, awakening briefly for the New Year celebrations. Recitals and other low-key cultural events are held in October and January in the Centro Caprense Ignazio Cerio, though from June through September the island comes alive with various events, including an outdoor concert season. It's a magical experience to see works performed at Anacapri's Villa San Michele (on Friday evenings) or on the spectacular terrace of the Hotel Caesar Augustus. In general, for information about cultural events and art exhibitions, ask at the local tourist information office or scan the posters in shop windows.

The Certosa di San Giacomo is the cultural heart of the island, hosting events throughout the year. Classical concerts are held in the attractive Chiostro Piccolo from June through September (usually Wednesday and weekends), with a special July program organized by Altera Actione (*www.alterazione.com*). The beginning of September sees the Certosa International Arts Festival, hosting film screenings, recitals, and readings (*www.capricertosa.com*), while the New Year's Eve festivities are eclipsed by the film festival Capri Hollywood (*www.caprihollywood.com*).

Capri also caters for the literati, with Le Conversazioni (*www.leconversazioni.it*) presenting well-known authors reading from their works in Piazzetta di Tragara. Held at the beginning of July, previous editions have featured Martin Amis and Ethan Coen.

SPORTS AND THE OUTDOORS

Although there are several tennis courts on the island, most are restricted access, so the vast majority of people looking to burn excess energy do so at sea level or below. For naturalists, bird-watching is particularly good in spring and autumn as Capri lies on a migration pathway, and botany lovers will be thrilled by the island's various nature trails, especially from April to June. For a simple workout, the **Capri Gym Fitness Center** (*Via Roma 10, Capri* 081/8375430) allows one-off visits.

SWIMMING AND STABILIMENTI

Sorry—Capri is not noted for fine beaches. "Strand-ed" habitués cram onto **Marina Piccola,** generally considered to have the best beach on the island. It's certainly the most historic: Homer believed this to be the legendary spot where the Sirens nearly snared Odysseus. Social go-getters seem to prefer the less picturesque Bagni di Tiberio beach near Marina Grande. At Marina Piccola, expect to pay about €14 per person for the use of showers, lockers, and a sun chair/sun bed. It's definitely worth investing in snorkeling gear, as the sea is rich in marine life, and visibility is often excellent.

Rather than visiting public beaches, many sunworshippers opt to enjoy the fabled *stabilimenti balneari* (private bathing lidos) scattered around the island, some of which offer real relaxation and unbelievable views. One of the most famous is **La Fontelina** (*Località Faraglioni, Capri Town* 081/8370845 *€16 admission includes locker and sun chair; €8 for beach umbrella*), open from April to October. At the foot of the Faraglioni rocks, the lido has a magical setting. There's no beach here, so the lido isn't suitable for children. You can get to La Fontelina by using a rocky path that begins at the end of Via Tragara; others prefer to take a ferry (€3) from the more accessible Marina Piccola during the afternoon. The excellent but pricey restaurant is only open for lunch. The **Lido del Faro** (*Località Punta Carena, Anacapri* 081/8371798 *www.lidofaro.com €10 admission includes locker and sun chair; €16 sun bed, €7 beach umbrella*), on the Anacapri side of the island, is set amid rocks with a natural basin as a seawater swimming pool and is open from April to October during daylight hours. The sun usually beats down on this westerly headland all day while on summer nights the restaurant provides a unique setting for enjoying the freshest fish. The lido is easily accessible by bus from Anacapri. Note that many other stabilimenti are set on the enchanting Marina Piccola, particularly the famous Canzone del Mare *(⇨ see Where to Eat, above)*.

SHOPPING

Although Capri is unlikely to be a bargain hunter's paradise, shopping here is almost an experience in its own right. In the main town near the Piazzetta, the shop windows are usually immaculately dressed, although the shops themselves are generally designed to be low impact and pleasing on the eye. Large neon signs are definitely out. Frustratingly though, goods are often displayed without price tags, which means you have to shop Italian-style: decide whether you like an article first and then inquire about its price, rather than vice versa.

BOOKSTORES

An antiquarian's delight and one of the most elegant bookstores in Italy, **La Conchiglia** (⊠ *Via Camerelle 18, Capri Town* ☎ *081/8378199* ⊕ *www.laconchigliacapri.com* ⊠ *Via Le Botteghe 12, Capri Town* ☎ *081/8376577* ⊠ *Via Orlandi 205, Anacapri* ☎ *081/8372646*) not only offers the largest selection of books on Capri and the Bay of Naples islands but publishes many sumptuous tomes through its own imprint. In addition to their own books, an attractive array of 19th-century prints, gouaches, and vintage editions of English books on Capri and the south of Italy is offered at their art gallery–cum–store on Via Camerelle, although a greater variety of titles is offered at their Via Le Botteghe location. There's also a branch in Anacapri.

JEWELRY

The extra security of being on a virtually crime-free island means that you can actually wear the expensive items you might want to buy. Some tax-free "bargains" might be possible from that Capri institution, **Chantecler** (⊠ *Via Vittorio Emanuele 51, Capri Town* ☎ *081/8370544* ⊕ *www.chantecler.it*), where you can find a miniature replica of the Bell of Good Fortune, from the church of San Michele in Anacapri, presented to President Roosevelt at the end of World War II. Alternatively, try **La Campanina** (⊠ *Via Vittorio Emanuele 18/20, Capri Town* ☎ *081/8370643* ⊕ *www.capridream.com/linacapri*) for a distinctive locally crafted brooch or some cuff links displaying ancient Roman coins.

PERFUME

If you're looking for something that's easily portable to take back from Capri, then eau de toilette, a potpourri, or perfumed soap might be just the thing. **Carthusia** has been making perfumes since 1948, but—as they will proudly tell you—the tradition of perfumery on the island stretches back hundreds of years to the days of Queen Giovanna of Anjou. The factory, close to the Certosa di San Giacomo, is open for visits and a limited range of purchases, although there are no official guided tours of the premises. ⊠ *Factory: Via Matteotti 2d, Capri Town* ☎ *081/8370368 Showroom:* ⊠ *Via Camerelle 10, Capri Town* ☎ *081/8370529 Showroom:* ⊠ *Via Capodimonte 26, Anacapri* ☎ *081/8373668* ⊕ *www.carthusia.com.*

RESORTWEAR

Capri's main shopping streets—the Via Vittorio Emanuele and Via Camerelle, down the road from the island's main square, La Piazzetta—are crammed with world-famous names (Fendi, Gucci, Prada, Dolce & Gabbana, Benetton, Ferragamo, Hermès). But if you're overwhelmed by the choice and are looking for something stylish but Capri-distinctive—in an astonishing range of colors—then check out the bright hand-block prints on clothes, bags, and shoes by Capri-local Livio De Simone at **La Parisienne** (⊠ *Piazza Umberto I 7, Capri Town* ☎*081/8370283* ⊕*www.laparisiennecapri.it*); here, too, you can purchase copies of the original capri pants worn by such gilded folk as Audrey Hepburn. The boutiques of Roberto Russo are favored by fashion folk. **Russo Uomo** (⊠*Piazzetta Quisisana, Capri Town* ☎*081/8388200*) has one of the largest selections. Sandals are a Capri specialty. With a family business stretching back to 1917, **Giuseppe Faiella** (⊠ *Via Le Botteghe 21, Capri Town* ☎*347/6780079*) is justifiably proud of his made-to-measure footwear. Expect to pay €60–€110 for a carefully handcrafted pair.

ISCHIA: THE SEASIDE CURE

While Capri leaves you breathless with its charm and beauty, Ischia (pronounced EES-kee-ah, with the stress on the first syllable) takes time to cast its spell. In fact, an overnight stay is definitely not long enough for the island to get into your blood. Here you have to look harder for the signs of antiquity, the traffic can be reminiscent of Naples—albeit on a good day—and the island displays all the hallmarks of rapid, uncontrolled urbanization. Ischia does have its jewels, though. There are the wine-growing villages beneath the lush volcanic slopes of Monte Epomeo, and unlike Capri, the island enjoys a life of its own that survives when the tourists head home. Ischia has some lovely hotel-resorts high in the mountains, offering therapeutic programs and rooms with dramatic views. If you want to plunk down in the sun for a few days and tune out the world, go down to sea level: against the towering backdrop of Monte Epomeo and with one of the island's inviting beaches—or natural hot baths—close at hand, you might wonder what Emperor Augustus could have been thinking when he surrendered Ischia to the Neapolitans in return for Capri. Still, many find Ischia's physical charms pale in comparison to Capri's splendor.

Unlike Capri, Ischia is volcanic in origin. From its hidden reservoir of seething molten matter come the thermal springs said to cure whatever ails you. Today the island's main industry, tourism, revolves around the 103 thermal baths; most of them are attached to hotels. In the height of summer, the island's population of 60,000 swells more than sixfold, with considerable strain placed on local water resources and public transport facilities and with decibel counts rising notably. However, most of the *confusione* is concentrated within the island's six towns and along its main roads, and it's relatively easy to find quiet spots even close to the beaten path.

Much of the 23 mi (37 km) of coastline are punctuated with a continuum of *stabilimenti balneari* (private bathing establishments) in summer

ISCHIA: GETTING HERE AND AROUND

GETTING HERE

Ischia is well connected with the mainland in all seasons. The last boats leave for Naples and Pozzuoli at about 8 PM (though in the very high season there is a midnight sailing), and you should allow plenty of time for getting to the port and buying a ticket. Ischia has three ports—Ischia Porto, Casamicciola, and Forio (hydrofoils only)—so you should choose your ferry or hydrofoil according to your destination. Many of the sailings go via Procida, giving you an attractive glimpse of its waterfront but extending travel time by 10–15 minutes. Locals are subject to restrictions on taking cars over to the island, but non-Italians can move relatively freely.

Alilauro (081/7611004 www.alilauro.it) has roughly one hydrofoil per hour traveling from Mergellina, Naples, to Ischia Porto (€16.70, travel time 40 minutes). From May through September, five hydrofoils per day depart for Forio (€17.60, travel time 50 minutes).

Caremar (081/5513882 www.caremar.it) has 10 hydrofoil departures from Molo Beverello, Naples, to Ischia Porto (€15, travel time between 45 minutes and 1 hour) and five ferry departures per day (€9.30, travel time 1 hour, 30 minutes). Ferry departures are also available from Pozzuoli (€6.50, travel time 1 hour).

Linee Lauro (081/5522838) sends roughly one hydrofoil every two hours from Molo Beverello, Naples, to Ischia Porto (€15, travel time 40 minutes), and eight ferry departures per day to Ischia Porto (€9.30, travel time 1¼ hours).

SNAV (081/7612348) offers a hydrofoil every hour from Mergellina or Molo Beverello, Naples, to the marina of Casamicciola (€14, travel time 50 minutes).

Traghetti Pozzuoli (081/527736 www.traghettipozzuoli.it) has a ferry departing every hour from Pozzuoli, sometimes docking at Casamicciola (€7, travel time 1 hour).

GETTING AROUND

Ischia's bus network reaches all the major sites and beaches on of one of its 10 lines. Runs continue on some routes until well after 10 PM. The main bus terminus is in Ischia Porto at the start of Via Cosca, where buses run by the company SEPSA radiate out around the island. There are also convenient *fermate* (stops) at the two main beaches—Citara and Maronti—with timetables displayed at the terminus. Tickets cost €1.20; note that conditions can get hot and crowded at peak beach-visiting times.

A number of car and scooter rental facilities are available. Given the much larger size of Ischia compared to Capri and Procida, having your own transport can be handy, but in most towns there are strict parking regulations. Police are also vigilant about seat belt violations.

If you use a bicycle on the island, be prepared for lots of ups and downs, and where possible take to the minor roads. About 100 yards from Ischia Porto's ferry terminal, **Del Franco** (*Via Alfredo De Luca 127, Ischia Porto* 081/991334), opposite Hotel Jolly, has a fair range of sturdy bicycles costing €12 per day.

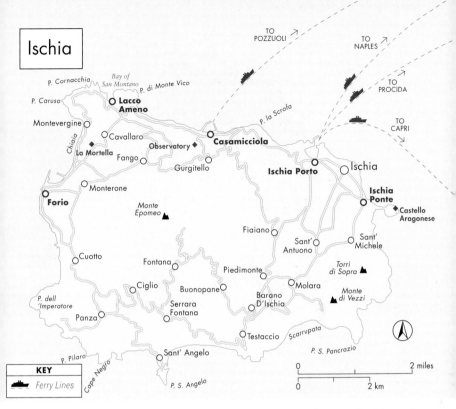

(there are also lots of public beaches), set against the scenic backdrop of Monte Epomeo and its verdant slopes. Most port traffic to the island—mainly ferries and hydrofoils from the mainland—is channeled into Ischia Porto, Casamicciola, and Forio, all burgeoning resorts and busy spa centers. The Castello Aragonese in Ischia Ponte, which is a vast medieval complex rather than just a castle, is one of the island's main historic sights; Lacco Ameno, with its immense archaeological heritage and more upmarket ambience, is a good base for exploring the north of the island; Forio is famous for the grand gardens of La Mortella and the Poseiden thermal baths. Buses between the main towns are frequent and cheap, though somewhat overcrowded.

VISITOR INFORMATION

Azienda Autonoma di Cura, Soggiorno e Turismo (⊠ *Ufficio Informazioni, Banchina Porto Salvo, Ischia Porto* ☎*081/5074231* 🖷*081/5074230* ⊕*www.infoischiaprocida.it*) in Ischia Porto is usually open daily 9 AM–2 PM and 3–8 PM.

Ischia's Castello Arogonese sits on its own island, just off shore from Ischia Ponte.

ISCHIA PORTO

4 km (3 mi) east of Casamicciola.

GETTING HERE

Ferries and hydrofoils bring you here from Naples and Pozzuoli.

EXPLORING

Ischia Porto is the largest town on the island and the usual point of debarkation. It's no workaday port, however, but a pretty resort with plenty of hotels and low, flat-roofed houses on terraced hillsides above the water. Known by the Romans as Villa dei Bagni, its villas and gardens are framed by umbrella pines and locals mingle with German tourists in the narrow streets. The port area was originally a landlocked lake in a volcanic crater: the Bourbon king Ferdinand II had a channel cut to create an opening seaward, and then created a sheltered port (1854). As you walk into the town along the waterfront, note the grandiose facade of the municipal baths (where Ferdinand II used to take the waters), now used for town council offices and occasional art exhibitions. While exploring Ischia Porto, be sure to stop by **Ciccio** (⌧ *Via Jasolino*), near the ferry piers, for the best gelato on Ischia.

WHERE TO EAT AND STAY

$$
SOUTHERN
ITALIAN

✕**Da Gennaro.** The oldest restaurant on the island, this has been a favorite of the stars, including Rod Stewart and Sophia Loren. Family-run, it opened on the seafront overlooking the boats in 1965 and continues to serve excellent fish in a convivial atmosphere. Specialties include *gnocchi alla pescatore* (dumplings with shell fish) and linguine *all'aragosta* (with lobster). In perfect English, friendly owner Gennaro will happily take you through the celebrity-laden wall of photos. ⊠ *Via Porto 59* ☎ *081/992917* ⊟ *AE, DC, MC, V* ⊘ *Closed Nov.–mid-Mar.*

$$–$$$ ⊞ **La Villa Rosa.** A highlight at this gracious family-run hotel, set in a villa, is the thermally heated pool in the garden. Rooms are bright and airy, with varied decor—some rooms have charming antiques, others are more modern. In high season half-board is required—meals are served in the roof garden, overlooking the town of Ischia and the Bay of Naples—and you must reserve well in advance. It's in the heart of Ischia Porto and a short walk from the beach. **Pros:** view from roof garden; wonderful pool. **Cons:** maybe too close to the town; some rooms are more attractive than others. ⊠ *Via Giacinto Gigante 5,* ☎ *081/991316* ⊕ *www.lavillarosa.it* ⟿ *37 rooms* ♨ *In-hotel: Restaurant, pool* ⊟ *AE, DC, MC, V* ⊘ *Closed Nov.–Mar.* ⦿ *MAP.*

NIGHTLIFE AND THE ARTS

In Ischia Porto, nightlife is concentrated around what the locals know as the Rive Droite, the eastern side of the port. In some private gardens, occasional concerts and cultural events are offered during the summer months. Nightlife on Ischia starts late in the evening, and you should be prepared to stay the course until the early hours.

Valentino Club (⊠ *Corso Vittorio Colonna 97, Ischia Porto* ☎ *081/982569* ⊕ *www.valentinoischia.it*), in the center of Ischia Porto, is the focal point for all but the gel-and-scooter set, with clientele in its early twenties and above. Admission varies between €16 and €25, depending on what's on offer.

ISCHIA PONTE 🛈

2 km (1 mi) southeast of Ischia Porto.

GETTING HERE
Take Bus No. 7 from Ischia Porto.

EXPLORING

★ The spectacular **Castello Aragonese,** towering atop an islet just off the main shore, landmarks Ischia Ponte. The town's name (Ischia Bridge) refers to the striking causeway built in the mid-15th century to connect it with the rest of Ischia. The little island was settled as early as the 5th century BC, when the tyrant Hiero of Syracuse came to the aid of Cumae in its power struggle against the Etruscans. This was his reward: an almost unassailable natural islet more than 300 feet high, on which he erected high watchtowers to monitor movements across the Bay of Naples. The island changed hands in the succession of centuries, with Greeks from Neapolis, Romans, Visigoths, Vandals, Ostrogoths, Saracens, Normans, Swabians, and Angevins successively modifying the fortifications and settlements. Ischia Ponte was where the population of Ischia sought refuge in 1301, when Epomeo's last eruption buried the town of Geronda on the other side of the causeway. The new influx of inhabitants led to a flurry of building activity, most notably the **Cattedrale dell'Assunta,** built above a preexisting chapel that then became its crypt. In the following century the Angevin castle was rebuilt by Alfonso of Aragon (1438), who gave it much of its present form.

However, its turbulent history continued well into the 19th century, when it was seriously damaged by the English in their attempts to dislodge the French during the Napoleonic Wars (1809).

Two hours should be enough to give you a feel of the citadel, stroll along its ramparts, and visit its key religious sites. Don't miss the frescoed 14th-century crypt beneath the cathedral (Giotto school), although the ruined cathedral itself, with its noticeable 18th-century additions—

WORD OF MOUTH

"On Ischia, I daytripped to Sant'Angelo and Forio. Sant'Angelo is really lovely with wide expansive beaches, much quieter than Forio. I couldn't say it's inconvenient as there are buses to the port too, it's just more isolated. Forio has a lovely old town center and walks along the coast."

—JudyC

such as the baroque stucco work—is quite atmospheric. Occasional exhibitions are held in the Chiesa dell'Immacolata, and there are two bars. Access to the citadel is via an elevator from the base, and the various walks at the top are clearly signposted. While taking in the whole site, enjoy the stunning views from the various vantage points. ⊠ *Castello Aragonese, Ischia Ponte* ☎ *081/992834* ⊕ *www.castelloaragonese. it* ⚏ *€10* ⊙ *June–Sept., daily 9–7:30; Mar.–May, Oct.–Jan. 8, daily 9–5. Closed Jan. 9–Mar. 1.*

Housed in the Palazzo dell' Orologio, the town's **Museo del Mare Ischia** is dedicated to the daily life of fishermen. Ship models, archaeological finds, nautical instruments, and the stray modern art show make up the small holdings. ⊠ *Via Giovanni Da Procida 3* ☎ *081/981124* ⊕ *www. museodelmareischia.it* ⚏ *€2.60* ⊙ *July and Aug., daily 10:30–12:30 and 6:30–10; Sept and –Oct., Apr.–June, daily 10:30–12:30 and 3–7; Nov.–Jan. and Mar., daily 10:30–12:30; Closed Feb.*

WHERE TO EAT AND STAY

$$
SOUTHERN
ITALIAN
✕ **Ristorante Cocò Gelo.** This inviting restaurant sits on the causeway linking the Aragonese castle to the rest of Ischia and is renowned for its fresh fish, which is highly prized by the Ischitani. Try the linguine *ai calamaretti* (with squid); a good starter in winter months is the vegetable-based *zuppa di fagioli e scarola* (bean and escarole soup). ⊠ *Via Aragonese 1* ☎ *081/981823* ▭ *AE, DC, MC, V* ⊙ *Closed Jan. and Feb. and Wed. Oct.–Mar.*

$–$$
★
🏨 **Albergo Il Monastero.** Within the Castello Aragonese at Ischia Ponte, with rustic rooms that peer down into the Mediterranean hundreds of feet below, this is the ultimate in ambience combined with the peace and quiet of a traffic-free area. Rooms are on the simple side, but the management is friendly and tries to warm things up. You can also choose to dine here (guests only) on the spectacular terrace, if you can't face the climb down to the town. This is a highly popular hotel, so book way in advance. **Pros:** stunning views; how often do you get to stay in a real castle? **Cons:** rather difficult to negotiate the steps before reaching the elevator; just a bit too far away from the action. ⊠ *Castello Aragonese 3* ☎ *081/992435* 🖶 *081/991849* ⊕ *www.albergoilmonastero.it* ⤢ *21 rooms* 🛠 *In-room: No TV. In-hotel: Restaurant, Internet access* ▭ *AE, DC, MC, V* ⊙ *Closed mid-Oct.–late Mar.* ⍥ *BP.*

$ ★ ⓘ **Villa Antonio.** Blessed with a stunning perch over the Bay of Cartaromana, with the Castello Aragonese posing front and center in a panoramic vista, the Antonio offers a quiet haven five minutes from the crowds. Direct access to the sea is a few private steps away from the lovely whitewashed and casual villa, but sun beds abound at several garden levels so most guests tend not to stray too far. Owner Antonio's brother Giovanni is a sculptor—his granite and marble works are scattered around the flower-decked terraces. Rooms are basic, but most have air-conditioning and all have sea views. **Pros:** no better view of the castle; seaside location. **Cons:** many steps to negotiate before elevator; small windows don't do justice to the view. ⊠ *Via S. Giuseppe della Croce* ☎ 📠 *081/982660* ⊕ *www.villantonio.it* ⇆ *18 rooms* ⚷ *In-hotel: Bar* ⊟ *No credit cards* ⊘ *Closed Nov.–mid-Mar.* ⥮ *BP.*

4

NIGHTLIFE AND THE ARTS

There's a rich tradition in Ischian local festivals, with the **Feast of Sant'Anna** (July 26) holding pride of place with its skillful choreography and floating procession in the marina at Ischia Ponte below the Aragonese Castle.

Midway between Ischia Porto and Ischia Ponte, **'O Spasso** has all you need for a good night out in one garden—you can choose between live music, a nightclub, a piano bar, or a more traditional café offering a late-night snack. Calise Caffè runs this place (and has since 1925), as well as four other bars and *pasticcerie* (try their specialty Monte Epomeo on Sunday) around the island. ⊠ *Piazza degli Eroi, Ischia* ☎ *081/991270* ⊕ *www.grancaffecalise.com* ⊘ *Nov.–Easter, Thurs.– Tues. 7:30–3.*

CASAMICCIOLA

2 km (1 mi) east of Lacco Ameno.

GETTING HERE
Take Bus No. 1 from Ischia Porto.

EXPLORING
Known properly as the spa town of Casamicciola Terme, the town revolves around the busy Piazza Marina with its large bust of the Italian king Vittorio Emanuele II and its marble plaque honoring Henrik Ibsen, who was inspired by the beauty of the area to write *Peer Gynt* here. Although much of the town was destroyed in an 1883 earthquake, it has retained some charming examples of 19th-century architecture.

About 2 km (1 mi) from the center is a small **geophysical observatory** from the 19th century, set up to monitor the seismic activity on the island. The *osservatorio* has various antique monitoring devices and a cranky seismic tank designed by the scientist Giulio Grablovitz. ⊠ *Osservatorio Geofisico, Località Sentinella* ☎ *081/996163* ⊘ *By appointment only.*

WHERE TO STAY

$$ ⓘ **Albergo l'Approdo.** Near Casamicciola's port, spas, and town center, this is a small hotel with a fine array of facilities. Guest rooms have private terraces, but tear yourself away to pamper yourself with the beauty

treatments on offer, including ayurveda massage and reflexology. An elevator whisks those who prefer the beach down to sea level, but most stick by the pool. **Pros:** wonderful elevated views; pool perched above bay. **Cons:** the beach is across a busy road; showers are tiny. ⊠ *Via Eddomade 29* ☎*081/994077* 🖷*081/980185* ⊕*www.lapprodohotel. com* ➦*39 rooms* ⚏*In-hotel: Restaurant, bar, pool, spa* ☰*AE, DC, MC, V* ♨*MAP.*

$$$$ 🖬**Terme Manzi.** One of Ischia's newest luxury hotels (yet also the oldest),
★ Terme Manzi originally opened in the mid-19th century and reopened in 2006 after four years of restoration. It was here that so-called "thermal tourism" began, in one of the largest spas in the south of Italy—the bath where Giuseppe Garibaldi bathed is conserved in a corner. Sybaritic is the word to describe the decor: hypercolorful mosaic columns, gilded Stil Empire furniture, and lots of Las Vegas–ian glitz. The staff is ready to pamper you with every kind of beauty treatment imaginable, and you can top it all off in the open-air roof pool, surrounded by Ischia's rich vegetation. The Mosaic restaurant is successfully ambitious. **Pros:** some say five stars is not enough; wonderful indoor pool. **Cons:** located in a nondescript square; very far from beach. ⊠*Piazza Bagni 4* ☎*081/994722* 🖷*081/900311* ⊕*www.manziterme.it* ➦*62 rooms* ⚏*In-hotel: Restaurant, bar, pool, spa* ☰*AE, DC, MC, V* ♨*BP.*

LACCO AMENO

6 km (4 mi) west of Ischia Porto, 3 km (2 mi) north of Forio.

GETTING HERE
Take Bus No. 1 from Ischia Porto

EXPLORING
The smallest of the six *comuni* (municipalities) on the island, Lacco Ameno is a mecca for some of Italy's rich and famous. Magnate Gianni Agnelli used to anchor his yacht every summer close to the Fungo, a most distinctive mushroom-shaped rock in volcanic tufa sculpted by wave action in the small marina, now one of the most notable natural landmarks on Ischia. Luchino Visconti, the noted realist film director and opera designer, had his Villa La Colombaia nearby in Baia San Montano, now used by the local council to promote the film industry on the island. The Bay of San Montano, a brilliant blue-sapphire buckle along the coast, is now the setting for the Giardini Negombo, the most stylish of the thermal complexes on the island. Lacco Ameno was colonized by the Greeks as early as the 8th century BC, and the landscape here has remained epic: it was used as the backdrop for the barge scene in Elizabeth Taylor's *Cleopatra*. The main road along the seafront (Corso Rizzoli) has thankfully been pedestrianized and is now virtually a large promenade flanked by low-key shops, cafés, and restaurants.

★ Lacco Ameno's archaeological importance—it rests below the first Greek settlement on Italian soil on the island, at Monte Vico to the west—is amply reflected by the finds displayed in Ischia's top museum, the **Museo Archeologico di Pithecusae**, and the ancient site beneath the church of Santa Restituta. The museum occupies much of the Villa

The Santuario del Soccorso in Forio is Ischia's most picturesque church.

Arbusto, built by Carlo d'Aquaviva in 1785 on top of a Bronze Age settlement. Inaugurated in 1999, with the directors of both the British Museum and the Louvre in attendence, its eight rooms house a wide range of Greek pottery unearthed at the ancient necropolis site near the Baia di San Montano, much of it dating to the earliest years of the Greek colony (late 8th century BC), including Nestor's Cup, the oldest known kotyle vase in existence. There is also a room dedicated to internationally renowned filmmaker Angelo Rizzoli, who once lived in the villa, as well as a section devoted to dolphins. Villa Arbusto combines musical *serate,* or evening soirées, in summer months with visits to the antiquities museum. ✉ *Villa Arbusto* ☎ *081/996103* 🖷 *081/3330288* ⊕ *www.pithecusae.it* 🎫 *€5* ⊙ *June–Sept., daily 9:30–1 and 4–8; Apr., May, and Oct.–Dec., daily 9:30–1 and 3–7. Closed Jan.–Mar.*

Beside the nearby church of Santa Restituta, almost completely rebuilt following a catastrophic earthquake in 1883, you can gain access to the underground excavations at the **Museo e Scavi Santa Restituta,** which are a memorable lesson in stratigraphy. Discovered in 1950 when the old majolica pavement above was removed, the underground site shows the building activities of several different periods (archaic Greek, Hellenistic, Roman, and early Christian), faithful reconstructions of an ancient loom and a miller's workshop, and the various finds discovered in situ. Although the structures are poorly labeled and it takes an expert eye to discern which buildings belong to which periods, this gives you a good idea of historical continuity on the island. ✉ *Piazza Santa Restituta* ☎ *081/980538* 🎫 *€3* ⊙ *Apr., May, and Oct., Mon.–Sat. 9:30–12:30 and 4–6, Sun. 9:30–12:30; June–Sept., Mon.–Sat. 9:30–12:30 and 5–7, Sun. 9:30–12:30. Closed Nov.–Mar.*

WHERE TO STAY

$$$$ 🏨 **Albergo della Regina Isabella.** Built in the early 1960s and tucked away in an exclusive corner of the beach in Lacco Ameno, Ischia's largest luxury hotel has full resort facilities and also pampers guests (some of whom are here to attend conventions) with spa treatments. Rooms are ample and decorated in warm Mediterranean colors, and most have terraces or balconies, many overlooking the sea, others the hotel gardens. Don't miss the fun of socializing with chic vacationers in the elegant bar or restaurant—a meal here is worth it just for the fabulous views over the harbor. When filming *Cleopatra* on Ischia, Elizabeth Taylor and Richard Burton camped out here. **Pros:** central location; considered by locals the top hotel on the island. **Cons:** not the most elegant of facades; rooms are fairly spartan for a hotel in this the price category. ⊠ *Piazza Santa Restituta* 🕾 *081/994322* ⊕ *www.reginaisabella.it* ➶ *128 rooms, 8 suites* ⚲ *In-hotel: Restaurant, bar, tennis court, pools, spa, beachfront* ▤*AE, DC, MC, V* ⊘ *Closed Nov.–mid-Apr.* ‖⊙‖*BP.*

$$$$ 🏨 **Grande Albergo Mezzatorre.** Far from the madding, sunburned crowds

Fodor's Choice   that swamp Ischia, this luxurious getaway perches in splendid isola-

★   tion on the extreme promontory of Punta Cornacchia. The complex is reached through an imposing gate, and a mile or so along a country lane. Standing on the terraces of this renovated *castello*, set over the blue Bay of San Montano, with yachts parading below you, it's not hard to understand why film director Luchino Visconti chose to live just up the hill. This hotel has nearly everything to tempt its privileged guests to stay put and *relax*: storybook cove, glamorous pool area, a cosseting restaurant, full health and beauty treatments housed in a separate building just down the hill, and hundreds of pine trees for true peace and quiet. The ancient fortress has been sleekly renovated, perhaps too much so from the look of its umber-red exterior. Inside, all is white-on-white glamour with antiques and ancestral portraits as accents. The official address is Forio but this is much closer to Lacco Ameno, where you should get off if you're on the bus; a shuttle bus is available there to pick you up. **Pros:** the ideal getaway location; wonderful views. **Cons:** a bit isolated; health facilities in separate buildings. ⊠ *Via Mezzatorre 13, Località San Montano, Forio d'Ischia* 🕾 *081/986111* ⊕ *www. mezzatorre.it* ➶ *61 rooms* ⚲ *In-hotel: Restaurant, tennis court, pool, spa* ▤*AE, DC, MC, V* ⊘ *Closed Nov.–Apr.* ‖⊙‖*BP.*

THE ARTS

Though it's only been in existence since 2002, the **Ischia Film & Music Global Fest** (⊕ *www.ischiaglobal.com*) has become an important festival, attracting such stars as Burt Bacharach, Dennis Hopper, Val Kilmer, Harry Belafonte, Naomi Watts, and Jean-Claude Van Damme. Hosted in July by the luxurious Regina Isabella Hotel in Lacco Ameno, the event is pleasingly informal.

THE OUTDOORS

If you visit one of Ischia's many *terme*, or spa baths, you will not only be following a well-established tradition stretching back more than 2,000 years but also sampling one of the major contemporary delights of the island. You should allow at least half a day for this experience, but better value is to get there early and indulge until sunset. If you do decide to restrict yourself to half a day, then go in the afternoon, when the hefty entrance fees are lowered. The larger establishments have a plethora of pools offering natural hydromassage at different temperatures and in different settings, with a complement of bars and restaurants to enable customers to stay on the premises right through the day. Most terme are equipped with beauty centers, offering an unbelievably broad range of services, from mud-pack treatments and manicures to tattoo removal and bioenergetic massage.

For the ultimate Ischian spa escape, try the stylishly landscaped park of **Giardini Negombo**. Designed around a beach of the finest sand, by the scenic bay of San Montano, it was created decades ago by Duke Luigi Camerini, a passionate botanist (who named his resort in honor of its resemblance to a bay in Sri Lanka). There are 12 saltwater or thermal pools here, plus facilities for hydromassage, a beauty center with sauna and Turkish bath, sports facilities for diving, windsurfing, volleyball, yoga, a bar, restaurant, and, according to the brochure, "a boutique for irresponsible purchases." All this is set in gardens with 500 species of Mediterranean plants and several panoramic views. Everything here—modern stone waterfalls, elegant poolside tables with thatched-leaf umbrellas, sensitive landscaping—is in the finest taste. At night, the outdoor arena hosts big-name concerts. ✉ *Baia di San Montano, Lacco Ameno* ☎ *081/986152* ⊕ *www.negombo. it* 🎟 *€28 all day, €23 after 12:30 PM, €13 after 4:30 PM; add €3 to prices in Aug.* ☉ *Mid-Apr.–mid-Oct., daily 8:30–7.*

FORIO

9 km (6 mi) west of Ischia Porto.

GETTING HERE

Take Bus No. 1 from Ischia Porto.

EXPLORING

Lying close to the main wine-producing area of the island, Forio is a busy seaside resort with beaches barely a minute's walk from its town center. At first glance, it seems to provide sad evidence of suburban sprawl (there are more houses without planning permits here than with), and its natural setting of flat coastline is not the most alluring.

★ However, the island's most picturesque church is here: the 14th-century whitewashed church of Santa Maria della Neve, down at the harbor, better known as the **Santuario del Soccorso**. This is a good spot for a sunset stroll and for getting an overview of the town from the Torrione, one of 12 towers built under Aragonese rule in the 15th century to protect Forio's inhabitants from the ever-present threat of pirate raids.

Fodor's Choice
★ Two kilometers (1 mi) north of Forio is one of the most famous gardens in Mediterranean Italy, **La Mortella**. The garden was a labor of love designed in 1956 by the landscape architect Russell Page for Sir William Walton and his Argentine-born wife, Susana. The garden was created within a wide, bowl-shaped, rocky valley, originally not much more than a quarry, overlooking the Bay of San Francesco and with spreading views toward Monte Epomeo and Forio. Lady Walton, now a talented gardener in her own right, first planted the trees of her childhood here:

The Giardini La Mortella was built by British composer Sir William Walton and his wife, Lady Susana.

jacaranda and the rare bromeliad. Native wild plants were encouraged in the upper reaches of the gardens, with dainty vetches and orchids as well as myrtle, from which the garden got its name, La Mortella. Considering the volcanic valley out of which the gardens were sculpted, they are appropriately threaded with pathways of rocks hewn from Vesuvius. In homage to the hot springs of the island, the centerpiece is an elliptical pond with three small islands adorned with the immense boulders that once littered the grounds. Below, underground cisterns were excavated to catch natural drinking water.

Besides some soothing strolls among the well-labeled flower beds and landscaped rock gardens, try to spend some time in the museum dedicated to the life and works of the late English composer, William Walton. The gardens have excellent facilities, including a shop selling Sir William's music and Lady Walton's lively biography of her husband, *Behind the Facade*, as well as light, homemade refreshments. A theater was opened in 2006, and hosts a concert series on most weekends. Book well in advance for these tickets. ✉ *Via Francesco Calise 39* ☎ *081/986220* ⊕ *www.lamortella.org* 🎫 *€15, €20 for concert, including visit to garden* 🕐 *Apr.–mid-Oct., Tues., Thurs., and weekends 9–7.*

A crenelatted white fortress, **La Colombaia** was once the summer residence of noted film director Luchino Visconti, and now houses a permanent exhibition of photographs outlining the history of cinema and theater, as well as promoting art and cultural activities on the island. The Visconti Foundation, based here, awards an international prize in the director's name, and plans to host contemporary art exhibitions. The villa itself, unchanged since the director's death in 1976, boasts stunning views over the Baia San Montano. It was closed at the time of this writing, with discussions underway for a reopening but no target date in sight. The official address is the town of Forio but the site is actually closer to Lacco Ameno. ⊠ *Via Francesco Calise 130* ☎ *081/3332945* 💶 *€6* 🕓 *Call to check open status.*

WHERE TO EAT

$

SOUTHERN
ITALIAN

✕ **Bar-Ristorante Bagno Teresa.** This is an unpretentious restaurant on Citara Beach (no dress code) that offers a range of fresh seafood at reasonable prices served with lively local wine. If you want to stay light for the afternoon swim, this is the place to come—there's no need to order a full Mediterranean splurge. ⊠ *Baia di Citara* ☎ *081/908517* ▤ *AE, MC, V* 🕓 *Closed mid-Nov.–Mar.*

$$$

MODERN ITALIAN

✕ **Il Melograno.** One of the island's finest restaurants is tucked away on the road leading to Citara Beach. Try the *crudo italiana* (an Italian take on sushi) to start and then just indulge in food that tastes as good as it looks. New dishes with a twist are regularly introduced—the fried anchovies stuffed with provola cheese and homemade tomato bread was one year's winner. Another specialty is the *beccaccia*, a rabbit dish. Those on a higher budget and with a healthy appetite should treat themselves to the featured special menu, replete with local fish and vegetables given a nouvelle twist. There's an excellent if pricey wine-cellar. Popular as this place is, be sure to reserve for summer dinners. ⊠ *Via G. Mazzella 110* ☎ *081/998450* ⊕ *www.ilmelogranoischia.it* ▤ *AE, DC, MC, V* 🕓 *Closed Jan.–mid-Mar., Mon. and Wed. Nov.–Dec.*

WHERE TO STAY

$$

🏨 **Hotel Semiramis.** A quiet family-run hotel, this is within a minute's walk of Citara Beach and the crowded Giardini Poseidon spa. The rooms are decorated tastefully in thematic styles, with the best and most expensive in the panoramic wing on the upper terrace. Breakfast is served overlooking the beach, and to cap it all, there's a child-friendly, secluded swimming pool tapping water from geothermal aquifers 30 feet down. **Pros:** great views; friendly staff. **Cons:** a lot of steps to negotiate; not much action in the evening. ⊠ *Spiaggia di Citara* ☎ *081/907511* 📠 *081/907511* ⊕ *www.hotelsemiramisischia.it* ⬩ *33 rooms* ⚖ *In-hotel: Bar, pool, no elevator* ▤ *AE, DC, MC, V* 🕓 *Closed Nov.–Mar.* 🍴 *BP.*

$$–$$$

★

🏨 **Il Gattopardo.** Surrounded by verdant Ischian maquis and a vineyard, this modern-style hotel is in the most striking and quiet area of Forio. The two solariums are the ideal place to enjoy the splendid view of the Citara bay and the Epomeo mountain. Thermally heated swimming pools, both indoor and outdoor, are part of the facilities offered in the beauty farm, along with mud therapy, Finnish sauna, and massages. Rooms are airy and comfortable, with either terrace or balcony, and the restaurant boasts a wine cellar where you can sample the fruits of the surrounding vineyard. There is also a chapel with daily services. **Pros:** the outdoor pool under the olive trees; friendly staff. **Cons:** the entrance is more akin to a sports club than hotel; some rooms are too close to the action. ⊠ *Via G. Mazzella 146* ☎ *081/997714* ⊕ *www.ilgattopardo. com* ⬩ *72 rooms* ⚖ *In-room: Wi-Fi. In-hotel: Restaurant, bar, pools, tennis court* ▤ *DC, MC, V* 🕓 *Closed Nov.–Mar.* 🍴 *MAP.*

$$ 🏨 **La Bagattella.** Run by the Lauro family, also responsible for Alilauro ★ hydrofoils, this high-style oasis has a white wedding-cake, Arabesque ambience, with flower-covered balconies, sleek illuminated pool, exotic plants, and palm trees. The lobby is handsomely accented with antique upholstered wood furniture, and guest rooms are as modern and spacious as apartments. Most are warmed up with charming Stile Liberty antiques or Baroque-style mirrors. The restaurant menu has all the usual suspects, with an ambitious array of Mediterranean specialties. A newer wing has less desirable accommodations, but everyone staying here can enjoy the truly orchidaceous atmosphere. **Pros:** wonderful grounds; lovely pool. **Cons:** the newer wing lacks atmosphere; a bit kitschy for some. *⊠ Via Tommaso Cigliano 8* 🕾 *081/986072* ⊕ *www. labagattella.it* 🛏 *54 rooms* ⌂ *In-hotel: Bar, 2 pools* ▤ *AE, DC, MC, V* ⊗ *Closed Nov.–Mar.* 🍴 *MAP.*

SPORTS AND THE OUTDOORS

The largest spa on the island, with the added boon of a natural sauna hollowed out of the rocks, is the **Giardini Poseidon Terme.** Here you can sit like a Roman senator on two stone chairs recessed in the rock and let the hot water cascade over you. With countless thermally regulated pools, promenades, and steam pools, plus lots of toga-clad kitschy statues of the Caesars, Poseidon exerts a special pull on Germans, many of them grandparents shepherding grandchildren. On certain days, the place is overrun with people, so be prepared for crowds and wailing babies. *⊠ Citara Beach, Forio* 🕾 *081/9087111* ⊕ *www.giardiniposeidon.it* 🎟 *€28 all day, €23 after 1 PM; add €2 to prices in Aug., €5 for visitors (no bathing) between 6 PM and 7 PM* ⊗ *Apr.–Oct., daily 9–7.*

Unlike on Capri, aficionados of water sports are unlikely to leave Ischia dissatisfied. On a calm day a canoe will carry you into that secluded bay you've spotted from afar, perhaps with its sea cave that's worth exploring. A good place to start—considered by locals to be one of the best beaches on the island—is Citara, near the Giardini Poseidon, on the edge of the township of Forio. Canoe and boat rental from many beaches on Ischia is run by **Dario Mazzara Marine Service** (*⊠ Via F. Di Lustro 10, Forio* 🕾 *081/998630* ⊕ *www.dmms.it*).

SHOPPING

With all the beauty farms on Ischia, ladies might enjoy visiting the main cosmetics factory on the island, **Ischia Thermae** (*⊠ Via Schioppa 17, Forio* 🕾 *081/997745* ⊕ *www.ischiathermae.com*), which occupies an 18th-century palazzo in the town center of Forio. Besides poring over some of the formidably named articles in their retail outlet (such as Thermal Mud Purifying Mask Exfoliator), you might enjoy guided tours of the factory, offered three days a week (Monday, Wednesday, and Friday at 4:30 and 7:30) with the bonus of a free sample of their products.

SANT'ANGELO

2 km (1 mi) south of Serrara Fontana.

GETTING HERE

Take Bus CD or CS from Ischia Porto and Forio.

EXPLORING

A sleepy fishing village out of season, Sant'Angelo, with its promontory of La Roia, has preserved its character remarkably well. The area has been spared much of the *speculazione edilizia* (speculative building, often without planning permission) that has hit the rest of the island, and the steep, winding paths by the sea are closed to traffic. Well connected by public transport this is a perfect site for an early evening *passeggiata*: you can peek into local pottery shops or tasteful boutiques, and then settle into a café near the quayside for an aperitivo.

PROCIDA: ISLAND OF CONTRASTS

Lying barely 3 km (2 mi) from the mainland and 10 km (6 mi) from the nearest port (Pozzuoli), Procida is an island of enormous contrasts. It's the most densely populated island in Europe—just over 10,000 people crammed into less than 3½ square km (2 square mi)—and yet there are oases like Marina Corricella and Vivara, which seem to have been bypassed by modern civilization. The inhabitants of the island—the Procidani—have an almost symbiotic relationship with the Mediterranean: many join the merchant navy, others either fish or ferry vacationers around local waters. And yet land traffic here is more intense than on any other island in the Bay of Naples.

In scenic terms this is the place to admire what the Italians call "Spontaneous," or folkloric Mediterranean, architecture: look for the tall archways on the ground floor, which signal places where boats could be stowed in winter, the outside staircases providing access to upper floors without cramping interior living space, and the delicate pastel colors of the facades contrasting with the deeper, bolder blues of the sea. Picturesquely scenic, it's no surprise that Procida has strong artistic traditions and is widely considered the painters' island par excellence. If you're here at Easter, make sure you see the striking Good Friday procession through the island's major streets.

VISITOR INFORMATION

Tourist information (⊠ *Via Marina Procida* ☏*081/8101968* ⊕*www. infoischiaprocida.it*) for Procida is run from Ischia, but the office here accepts left luggage and organizes guided tours (be sure to book in advance). It's open daily 9–2 and 3–8.

TERRA MURATA AND ABBAZIA DI SAN MICHELE

GETTING HERE

Ferry or hydrofoil from Naples/Ischia/Pozzuoli to Marina Grande Sancio Cattolico, then bus C2 to Terra Murata.

EXPLORING

Boats pull into the main port, **Marina Grande Sancio Cattolico,** which is fetchingly adorned with pastel-hue houses and the church of Santa Maria della Pietà (1760). Hike up to the Piazza di Martiri on your way up to the **Castello** (a prison until 1986). Magnificent views can be seen from the piazza in front of the castle, including the enchanting fishing village of the Marina della Corricella. For a fascinating glimpse of the traditional

PROCIDA: GETTING HERE AND AROUND

GETTING HERE

Procida's ferry timetable caters to the many daily commuters who live on the island and work in Naples or Pozzuoli. The most frequent—and cheapest—connections are from the Port of Pozzuoli. After stopping at Procida's main port, Marina Grande Sancio Cattolico, many ferries and hydrofoils continue on to Ischia, for which Procida is considered a half-way house.

Caremar (☎081/5513882 ⊕www.caremar.it) has seven hydrofoils departing from Molo Beverello, Naples (€11.30, travel time 35 minutes), and five ferry departures per day from Molo Beverello, Naples (€8.20, travel time 1 hour). There are four departures per day from Pozzuoli (hydrofoil €6, travel time 15 minutes; ferry €5, travel time 40 minutes).

Ferries of **Procida Lines 2000** (☎081/8960328) leave six times a day from Pozzuoli (€5 Sunday, travel time 40 minutes).

SNAV (☎081/7612348) hydrofoils leave every two hours from Mergellina or Molo Beverello, Naples (€10, travel time 35 minutes).

As with the other islands, buy a single ticket rather than a round-trip (there's virtually no saving on a round-trip ticket, which is usually twice the single fare, and it ties you down to one operator on your return).

GETTING AROUND

There are four main bus routes that will take you to practically every corner of the island as well as a fleet of microtaxis operating round island tours and plying the route between the port and the Marina di Chiaiolella, on the southwest of the island. To get to Vivara, a road climbs westward out of Chiaiolella, and motorized access is barred shortly before reaching the causeway linking the two islands.

The bus terminus in Procida is at the disembarkation point in Via Roma. Provided there's no traffic gridlock along the island's narrow streets, the buses run by the company SEPSA will get you to most destinations within about 10 minutes for €1. Chiaiolella is the most frequently served destination (about every 15 minutes) and timetables are displayed—and tickets bought—at a newsstand next to the hydrofoil ticket office. In summer the bus service runs until about 4 in the morning. Tickets can be bought for €1.30 from the bus driver. Keep in mind that on-the-spot checks and hefty fines are frequently imposed on riders without a ticket.

Although Procida has fewer hills than either Ischia or Capri, cycling is really only feasible when the roads are closed to motorized traffic (evenings in summer). Most islanders get around on mopeds and scooters, which means the streets between the port and the center of the island are both noisy and loaded with pollutants, making casual strolling and window-shopping stressful. Beaches can be reached by sea or land, with fishermen improvising as water-taxi drivers.

architecture, once you reach the Piazza turn left and walk about 600 feet until you come to a tiny passageway that leads to the **Vascello,** originally a gated area of tumbling-down fishermen's cottages. Continue along Via San Michele to the highest point on the island, the old town of Terra Murata—a fascinat-

ing cluster of ancient buildings, including churches, palazzi, fortifications, ancient walls, and gateways, mostly in yellow-gray tufa stone. A Benedictine abbey was founded here in the 7th century, safely tucked away from mainland marauders, and the area became the focal point for the inhabitants of the island.

Perched precariously at the top of a cliff facing the small bay of Corricella is the 16th-century **ex-convent of Santa Margherita Nuova,** recently renovated.

The easily distinguishable and now abandoned **Palazzo Reale,** built at the same time—confusingly, sometimes called Il Castello—was used as a prison until 1986. Rumor has it that its inmates were a little miffed at having to abandon the sun-drenched island of Procida.

Within Terra Murata is the **Abbazia di San Michele.** San Michele (St. Michael) is the island's patron saint and a key figure in its history and traditions. Legend has it that in 1535, when the sultan of Algeria's admiral laid siege to the island, San Michele appeared above the pirate force and put them to flight (the 17th-century painting depicting the scene is in the choir of the abbey's 17th-century church; one of the invaders' anchors can also be viewed). On the wall close to the richly coffered ceiling of the church is another depiction of San Michele, this time by the grandmaster Luca Giordano (1699). As you walk around the church, note the holes in marble flagstones on the floor, which were in effect trapdoors through which bodies could be lowered to the underground crypt below. Children will be fascinated by the skulls still lurking in the maze of catacombs leading to a secret chapel. ⊠ *Terra Murata* ☎ *081/8967612* ⊕ *www.abbaziasanmichele. it* ☎ *Free* ☞ *Guided tours, €2 per person to museum and catacombs available on request at bookstore at entrance to abbey* ☉ *Apr.–Oct., Mon.–Sat. 9–1 and 3–6, Sun. 9–1; Nov.–Mar., call for times.*

CORRICELLA

Fodor'sChoice **GETTING HERE**
★ Take Bus C2 from Marina Grande Sancio Cattolico to Terra Murata, then on foot.

EXPLORING
Perched under the citadel of the Terra Murata, the **Marina di Corricella** is Procida's most iconic sight. Singled out for the waterfront scenes in *Il Postino* (*The Postman,* the 1995 Oscar-winner for Best Foreign Film), this fishermen's cove is one of the most eye-popping villages in Campania—a rainbow-hue, horizontal version of Positano, comprising

Procida is famed for its Good Friday procession.

hundreds of traditional Mediterranean-style stone houses threaded by numerous *scalatinelle* (staircase streets). The inhabitants of Corricella have been relatively immune to life in the limelight, and apart from the opening of an occasional restaurant and bar, there have been few changes in this sleepy village. This is the type of place where even those of us with failing grades in art classes feel like reaching for a paintbrush to record the delicate pinks and yellows of the waterfront buildings.

WHERE TO EAT

$
SOUTHERN
ITALIAN

✕ **Graziella.** This atmospheric restaurant sits right on the waterfront down at Corricella. It's family run and as rustic as they come, with food served on plastic tables outside. For starters try the *bruschette* and the seafood specialty, a selection of shellfish, octopus, and anchovies big enough for two. The *impepata di cozze* (mussels in pepper) is a must, and top it all off with a homemade *granita di limone* (lemon crushed ice), made freshly everyday here, and undoubtedly the best on the island. Leave space for the locally made cakes. ⊠ *Via Marina Corricella 14* ☎ *081/8967479* ▬ *No credit cards* ⊗ *Closed Dec.–Feb.*

$$
SOUTHERN
ITALIAN
★

✕ **La Conchiglia.** A dinner at this beachfront spot really lets you appreciate the magic of Procida. Beyond the lapping of the waves, Capri twinkles in the distance. The seafood is divinely fresh, the pasta dishes usually soul-warming. Access here is either by foot down the steps from Via Pizzaco or by boat from the Corricella harborfront—phone owner Gianni if you want the boat to pick you up. ⊠ *Via Pizzaco 10* ☎ *081/8967602* ⊕ *www.laconchigliaristorante.com* ▬ *AE, MC, V* ⊗ *Closed mid-Nov.–Mar.*

$ ✕**La Medusa.** Owner Biagio is in front of the stove in this smallest of the
SOUTHERN   harbor restaurants, just where the ferries dock. The locals bring him
ITALIAN   their catch direct, so don't be surprised if he closes early because he's run
out of fish. On tap are traditional Procida dishes such as spaghetti with
sea urchin and lemon, fish soups, and delicious antipasto, all washed
down with locally produced wine. ⊠ *Via Roma 116* ☎*081/8967481*
▭*AE, DC, MC, V* ⊗*Closed Jan. and Feb. and Tues. Oct.–May.*

WHERE TO STAY

$$ ⊺⊤**La Casa sul Mare.** One of Procida's best boutique hotels, this charmer
overlooks the fishing village of Corricella and the bay. The south-facing
private terraces of the jewel-like, individually designed bedrooms have
stunning views and are the perfect place to lap up winter sunshine.
Antiques and traditional ceramics complete the decor. Breakfast is
served in the garden, and in the summer months a shuttle bus will take
to any beach on the island. **Pros:** stunning views; wonderful atmo-
sphere. **Cons:** tiny bathrooms; guests have complained about the ser-
vice. ⊠*Salita Castello 13* ☎*081/8968799* ⌗*081/8967255* ⊕*www.*
lacasasulmare.it ⇆*10 rooms* ⌂*In-hotel: Bar, no elevator* ▭*AE, DC,*
MC, V ⑩*BP.*

VIVARA

GETTING HERE
Take Bus from L1/L2 from Marina Grande Sancio Cattolico to Marina
di Chiaiolella.

EXPLORING
On the western coast of Procida, beyond the quiet beach of Pozzo Vec-
chio and the busy Lido is the small port of the **Marina di Chiaiolella,**
studded with a few hotels and bars and basically known as a port-of-call
for all sorts of water activities, ranging from boating to scuba diving.
Opposite Chiaiolella is Vivara, a crescent-shaped island and terminal
segment of a volcanic cone, today a living museum of natural history
with unsullied Mediterranean maquis vegetation. Vivara is officially
closed to the public because its access bridge was damaged in a storm
and never repaired. However, visitors are welcome to scramble over to
it across the ruined waterfront mole.

The main path winds up from the causeway to a cluster of abandoned
settlements at the highest point of the island (357 feet above sea level).
On the way, admire the dense maquis on either side, with characteristic
plant species like tree heather, strawberry tree, and rockrose, the latter
of which sports delicate pink flowers in spring.

WHERE TO EAT AND STAY

$ ⊺⊤**Crescenzo Hotel-Ristorante.** A short walk from Vivara, this refurbished
three-story whitewashed hotel overlooks the small yachting marina of
Chiaiolella. Half-board is required here in August, although with the
quality of the food offered you should consider half-board at other
times of the year as well. Even if you're not a hotel guest, enjoy a sea-
food delight or two here. The small hotel has recently been refurbished.
Rooms facing the tiny port are charming but noisy in summer. **Pros:** one

of the cutest corners of the island; great food. **Cons:** rooms are small; some noisy in summer. ✉ *Via Marina Chiaiolella 33* ☎ *081/8967255* 🖷 *081/8101260* ⊕ *www.hotelcrescenzo.it* 🛏 *10 rooms* 🛎 *In-hotel: Restaurant, bar, parking (no fee), no elevator* ═ *AE, DC, MC, V* 🍴 *MAP.*

NIGHTLIFE AND THE ARTS

Procida's nightlife revolves around Via Roma in the port town of Marina Grande Sancio Cattolico, although there are also a number of late-closing bars and restaurants around the Marina di Chiaiolella. The one disco tends to be populated by high school students. The rest of the islanders while away summer evenings strolling the bay-side strip along the Marina Grande and the new tourist harbor.

Il Capriccio (✉ *Via Roma 99, Procida* ☎ *081/8969506*) is the closest bar to the port, open from morning to the small hours, and an ideal place to meet locals, sip a cocktail, enjoy a snack, or use the Internet.

The **Birreria Pub Sotto Sopra** (✉ *Via Roma 11, Procida* ☎ *081/8101013*) serves good draft lager for a young crowd almost around the clock in a congenial quasi-nautical setting. **Bar del Cavaliere** (✉ *Via Roma 42* ☎ *081/8101074*) is where yachting types, wealthy Neapolitans, and thirtysomethings gather to drink cocktails until the wee hours in a relaxing but crowded atmosphere—get here early for the people-watching tables outside.

THE OUTDOORS

With its famous nautical school and centuries-old seafaring traditions, Procida is an ideal base for chartering yachts of various sizes or just exploring the seabed with one of the diving schools on the island.

SAILING One of the market leaders in Italy is **Sail Italia** (✉ *Via Roma 10, Sancio Cattolico Marina Grande* ☎ *081/8969962* ⊕ *www.sailitalia.it*). Except for the even-pricier month of August, chartering a 10-berth 41-foot yacht for a week will set you back about €4,000. Reckoned on a daily per-person basis, this is an interesting alternative to hotel stays. Hire a typical Procida wooden fishing boat for the day to chug around the island and escape the crowds from **Ippocampo** (✉ *West side, Marina Chiaiolella* ☎ *081/8101437* ⊕ *www.ippocampo.biz/procida. asp*). Prices run from €100 per day for up to 10 people excluding fuel; no prior boating experience is said to be required. They also provide a boat-taxi service and island tours from €15 per person, depending on the number of passengers.

Sorrento and the Sorrentine Peninsula

WORD OF MOUTH

"Sorrento is a fine place to spend a few days. Easy to catch ferries to islands. Convenient to Naples, Pompeii, etc."

—Julia 1

WELCOME TO SORRENTO AND THE SORRENTINE PENINSULA

TOP REASONS TO GO

★ **Medieval Times:** The Church of Sant'Antonino was built to the patron saint of navigators 1,000 years ago. See how sorrentini rich and poor have paid tribute to him with their donations large (chapels) and small (votive offerings).

★ **Shopping along Via San Cesareo:** Sorrento's regional trifles are world-famous, and this charming street is just the place to find embroideries, inlaid wooden intarsia, music boxes, and dolls in tarantella costumes.

★ **"Turna a Surriento":** At the heart of Sorrento's historic quarter is the Sedile Dominova, a 16th-century frescoed loggia that is a colorful backdrop for caffès and serenading waiters warbling "Come Back to Sorrento."

★ **Passeggiare:** Join the passeggiata (evening strolling ritual) at Piazza Tasso and follow the locals as they make the rounds of Sorrento's historical center to gossip, strut, and see and be seen.

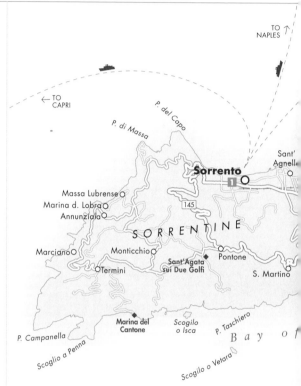

1 **Sorrento.** When literati sang Sorrento's praises in the Grand Tour era, palatial hotels went up to accommodate the titled lords who rushed to visit. The English, especially, left their stamp on the city, which is still notably civil and genteel. Perched on a cliff across the bay from Naples—with Vesuvius front and center—it has no major tourist attractions; the belle epoque city itself, with its enchanting sherbet-hued *palazzi* and bouquets of villas, is the draw. The charming historic quarter is centered around Piazza Tasso. Follow Via San Cesareo through a labyrinth of 19th-century alleys to the Chiesa di San Francesco

Country villa in Sorrento

Marina Grande, Sorrento,

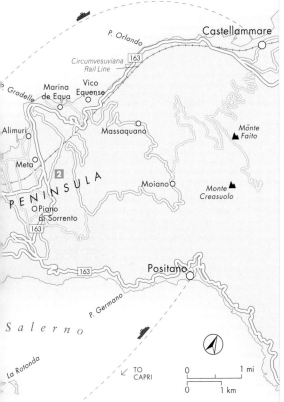

P. Orlando

Castellammare

Circumvesuviana Rail Line 163

P. Gradelle

Marina de Equa

Vico Equense

Alimuri

Massaquano

Monte Faito

Meta

2

P E N I N S U L A

O Piano di Sorrento 163

Moiano

Monte Creasuolo

Positano

P. Germano

Salerno

La Rotonda

TO CAPRI

0   1 mi

0   1 km

GETTING ORIENTED

Connected to Naples via the famous Circumvesuviana train and the Metro del Mare, to Capri and Amalfi via the ferries and hydrofoils that depart its Marina Piccola, and set equidistant from Pompeii and the Amalfi Coast, Sorrento is a convenient home base for visiting the region. Set high atop a bluff on the peninsula created by the Lattari mountains, it has a stunning view of the Bay of Naples. Beyond the town lies a scenery-rich peninsula famous for fabulous restaurants, Edenic parks, and the best beach in Campania at Marina del Cantone.

Limoncello

(with its famous Cloister of Paradise) and the Villa Communale, where you get a Cinerama view of the bay.

2 The Sorrentine Peninsula. When the crowds of Sorrento get too much, you can always get out of town. Northeast of the city, the route leads to Sant'Agnello, an aristocratic beauty spot hallowed by two historic

hotels, the Cocumella and the Parco dei Principi (the latter with a famous botanical park). South of Sorrento, Sant'Agata sui Due Golfi crowns a peak that overlooks both the Bay of Naples and the Bay of Salerno. Travel south down the peninsula to reach the delightfully festive beach at Marina del Cantone.

SORRENTO AND THE SORRENTINE PENINSULA PLANNER

Making the Most of Your Time

Sorrento has plenty of appeal in its own right, but its greatest virtue is its central location—it makes a fine base, putting you within day-trip distance of Pompeii, the Amalfi Coast, and the islands of the bay.

You should spend a day taking in Sorrento itself and the surrounding area, plus another leisurely day exploring the Sorrento Peninsula, enjoying the best beaches and restaurants in the area or taking a rural hike. For day trips, an excursion along the Amalfi Drive is a rise-early, full-day excursion. You can easily get from Sorrento to the Amalfi Coast by bus, or ferry around the peninsula in the summertime. Other day-trip alternatives include an excursion to the archaeological sites around the Bay of Naples—the train from Sorrento will deposit you right in front of Pompeii or a short distance from Herculaneum. Boat, ferry, and hydrofoil services also connect you with Naples and environs, plus the islands of Capri and Ischia, all valid day-trip alternatives.

Keep in mind that if you're driving, and you wind up not heading back to Sorrento until after dark, you should stick to the main roads. It's easy to get lost on backroads at night.

Getting Around by Car

All traffic from Naples to Sorrento is ultimately channeled onto the SS 145, which must be one of the slowest state highways in southern Italy. The road is single lane all the way from the A3 Autostrada turn off at Castellammare di Stabia. Though you'll get some scenic vistas as you inch along the peninsula, it's only when you get beyond Sorrento, on the road to Massa Lubrense or Sant'Agata, that a car becomes more of a benefit than a liability.

Don't expect excellent driving standards in the Sorrento area, and be especially careful of scooters, which tend to take considerable liberties. Avoid traveling from Naples to Sorrento on Saturday evenings and on fine Sunday mornings even in winter. The same applies to the SS 145 late on a Sunday afternoon, when immense numbers of day-trippers and weekenders return home to the Naples area.

Finding a Place to Stay

The ghosts of a vacationing Empress Eugénie and an ailing Caruso haunt Sorrento's hotel corridors. Sorrento has a plethora of upper-range hotels with fin de siècle charm, perched on top of impressive tuff cliffs, with balconies and terraces giving an immediate this-is-it sensation. If traveling on a tighter budget, as a rule the farther you are from Sorrento town center and from the coastline, the better value—and quieter—your accommodation will be. If staying on the peninsula, don't assume you'll be a stone's throw from the shoreline: at times access to the sea is lengthy and arduous, and most of the coastline is rocky.

WHAT IT COSTS (IN EUROS)

	¢	$	$$	$$$	$$$$
Restaurants	under €20	€20–€30	€30–€45	€45–€65	over €65
Hotels	under €75	€75–€125	€125–€200	€200–€300	over €300

Restaurant prices are for a first course (*primo*), second course (*secondo*), and dessert (*dolce*). Hotel prices are for two people in a standard double room in high season, including tax and service.

Getting around by Train

The train stations on the **Circumvesuviana** (☎ 081/7722444 ⊕ www.vesuviana.it) line serving the Sorrento Peninsula are Meta, Piano di Sorrento, Sant'Agnello, and Sorrento, in order of increasing distance from Naples. The main transport hub for cheap, efficient bus services radiating to destinations along the coast and inland is the Circumvesuviana station in Sorrento.

If heading to Sorrento from Naples, use the Stazione Centrale (Piazza Garibaldi), which is the second stop on the Circumvesuviana line as it departs from Naples. At this writing, the station was undergoing substantial renovations, which may be completed in 2010. Follow the *Circumvesuviana* signs, which will take you through the ticket barriers down into what must rank as one of the world's most unwelcoming train stations. Trains to Sorrento run approximately every half hour from Naples; some trains are *direttissimo* (express), only stopping at major stations; they take half the time of local trains. Round-trip fares are €6.60 for Naples to Sorrento (if traveling round-trip the same day, purchase a day pass good for unlimited stops on the line for €6.50) and €3.60 for Pompei Scavi–Sorrento. In Sorrento the train station is opposite Piazza Lauro and a five-minute walk from Piazza Tasso.

Getting around by Bus

At €1.10 for a one-way *extraurbano* bus ticket from Sorrento to other locations on the peninsula—and some lines with departures every 20 minutes—the bus is a good way to get around quickly and cheaply. Municipal **Circumvesuviana** (☎ 081/7722444 ⊕ www.vesuviana.it) buses radiate out from the Circumvesuviana station to most major destinations on the peninsula, while **SITA** (⊕ 089/405145 ⊕ www.sitabus.it) buses go farther afield to Positano, Amalfi, and Naples. Inform the driver of your destination when boarding to avoid missing your stop. If traveling up from the port of Sorrento at Marina Piccola, or the waterfront at Marina Grande, you'll need to get a Circumvesuviana orange bus. The main orange bus stop in Sorrento is on Piazza Tasso.

Tickets must be purchased in advance (though for a surcharge of €0.50 you can buy a ticket on the orange bus). Time-stamp your ticket in the machine at the front of the bus as you board. You can buy tickets at cafés, bars, tobacco shops, and newsstands area-wide.

Getting around by Boat

Headquartered in Naples, the **MetrodelMare**(☎ 199/600700 ⊕ www.metrodelmare.com) is a scenic, seasonal alternative to ground transport around the bay. Commuter ferries service all the main ports throughout the gulf and, while more expensive and slower than ground travel, offer spectacular views of the coastline and Vesuvius. Lines 1, 2, 3, and 6 all connect Sorrento with Naples and numerous other locations. Fares are roughly €7 to €10, depending on the trip. Check the local papers (*Il Mattino* or *La Repubblica*) for timetables or go to ⊕ www.metrodelmare.com for departure times.

In addition, many commercial ferries and hydrofoils run year-round (with more trips in high season). To get to smaller towns or to take private boats, you can make arrangements with private boat companies or independent fishermen. Seek out people who are recommended by the tourist office or your hotel. Ferries and hydrofoils to and from Sorrento, with connections to Naples, Capri, Positano, and Amalfi, are operated by **Alilauro** (☎ 081/8781430 or 081/4972222 ⊕ www.alilauro.it), **SNAV** (☎ 081/4285555 ⊕ www.snav.it), **Caremar** (☎ 892/123 ⊕ www.caremar.it), and **Linee Maritime Partenopee** (☎ 081/8781430 ⊕ www.consorziolmp.it).

5

CAMPANIA'S SUN-SOAKED HARVEST

Campanians have historically been known as *mangiafolie*, or leaf eaters, for the abundance of fruits and vegetables in their diets. And it's no wonder why—the region is internationally celebrated for the quality and flavors of its natural products.

Fertile volcanic soils. Mild, sunny climate. Cleansing sea breezes. These characteristics contribute to a bountiful growing environment throughout the region. In fact, the soils here are thought to be among the best in the entire country, incorporating volcanic ash from Mount Vesuvius with the rich earth of the pre-Apennine hills.

Many natural products from the Campania have DOP or IGP status, meaning they are prized examples of authentic foods from specific geographic areas, recognized for their significance by the EU. Certified products include lemons from Sorrento and the Amalfi Coast, hazelnuts from Giffoni, tomatoes from San Marzano, chestnuts from Montella, and olive oils from Cilento, Salerno, and the Sorrentine Peninsula.

LOCAL LIQUEURS

Liquori (liqueurs) are made from myriad fruits and herbs from the region, from *finocchio* (fennel) to *albicocche* (apricot). These liqueurs are used typically sipped after a meal, as a *digestivo* (digestive drinks). The best-known liqueurs here are *limoncello* and *nocino*. Limoncello is a sweet, lemon-yellow liqueur created from the skins of IGP-protected lemons that are macerated in alcohol and sugar. Nocino, an inky brown, bittersweet, spiced liqueur, is made from IGP-recognized *noci* (walnuts) from the Sorrento hills. In summer, green walnuts and husks infused in alcohol for months with cloves, nutmeg, and cinnamon for wintertime consumption.

Tomatoes

The most significant tomato of Campania is the *pomodoro di San Marzano*, a thin-skinned, sweet plum tomato with low acidity and few seeds. Also abundant are Sorrento's fist-sized pink-green tomatoes and *pomodorini a piénnolo*, which look like cherry tomatoes with pointed tips. They are sold in hanging bunches that resemble grape clusters.

Olives

Olive cultivation has a lengthy tradition in Campania, preceding even ancient Romans. Olive oils from Cilento, Salerno, and the Sorrento peninsula are expecially prized. The oils may be green to straw-yellow, with flavors that range from fruity to peppery and bitter.

Lemons

The large lemons of Capri, Sorrento, and the Amalfi Coast are renowned for their flavor. The *limone di Sorrento* has an elliptical shape with a highly aromatic yellow peel and juicy pulp. Lemons of the Amalfi Coast, called *limone Costa d'Amalfi*, are distinguished by a pale yellow rind, pointed shape, and strong aromatic scent.

Figs

Figs are thought to have been introduced to Cilento by early Greek settlers. In ancient times, dried figs were considered a rare luxury, inspiring many poems and proverbs. Today, dried figs are used in myriad ways. They may be

used in baked goods or sausages, or offered as a stand-alone treat.

Artichokes

Although artichokes have grown here for centuries, large-scale farming didn't begin until the 1920s. Now, artichoke farming is a major industry in the region. The most common type of artichoke here is the *carciofo tondo di Paestum*, or round artichoke of Paestum.

Apples

The *mela annurca* is prized as one of Campania's most delicious fruits. These apples are harvested early, while reddish-green, because they are thought to mature unevenly if left on the tree. Instead, they are set out in the sun on straw mats or wood shavings and rotated periodically until they turn red.

Nuts

Ancient Greeks and Romans brought chestnuts to Campania. The chestnut is grown in the mountains of Avellino, with nuts that are white, dense, and sweet. Hazelnuts from Campania are highly prized by confectioners, especially those of Salerno, which have a firm texture, white flesh, and fragrant aroma. Walnuts from the Sorrento hills also are well-known. The unripe, green walnuts are used in Nocino liqueur. Ripe walnuts appear in baked goods and candies.

Opposite page: Fresh produce and spices for sale in Sorrento.
top right: A round artichoke of Paestum.
bottom left: A basket of lemons found in Sorrento.

Updated by
Katie Parla

Like the familiar song "Come Back to Sorrento," with its long, mournful closing notes (listen to the Pavarotti version and you may shed a few tears), the beautiful, belle epoque resort town of Sorrento is tinged with melancholy.

Its streets seem like 19th-century sepia photographs, vestiges of the Roman Empire's ruins are strewn about, and tiers of votive offerings of hopeful Sorrentines flicker in the crypt of the basilica of Sant'Antonino. Vesuvius, as always, looms in the distance. And with the sun's heart-stopping descent into the Bay of Naples, the isle of Capri fades into the purple twilight, as if to disappear forever. But touched with sadness or not, Sorrento is a temptress above all.

As a hub for a banquet of must-see sites—Pompeii and Naples to the north, Capri to the west, and the Amalfi Coast to the south—Sorrento is unequaled. Because of its convenient location, the city can become over-run with visitors in summer, so it's fortunate that the rest of the Sorrento Peninsula, with plains and limestone outcroppings, watchtowers and Roman ruins, groves and beaches, monasteries and villages, winding paths leading to isolated coves and panoramic views of the bays of both Naples and Salerno, remains relatively undiscovered. Eons ago, when sea levels dropped during the glaciations, the peninsula's tip and Capri were joined by an overland connection, and today it still seems you can almost make it in a single jump. Separating grande dame Sorrento from the relatively arriviste Amalfi Coast, this hilly, forested peninsula provides the famed rivals breathing space, along with inviting restaurants and an uncrowded charm all its own.

EXPLORING SORRENTO AND THE SORRENTINE PENINSULA

From Sorrento on the north coast of the Sorrento Peninsula to Vietri at the eastern edge of the Amalfi Coast, from the Bay of Naples to the Bay of Salerno, this small ledge of land is a poem of compressed beauty, with two main "verses" and a bridge. Sorrento, on the Bay of Naples, is set solidly on a steep cliff, and neighboring towns slope over the gulf, with deep valleys breaking the terraced watershed behind. The rural, sometimes mountainous peninsula is rimmed by the two bays and

Statali (state highways) 145 and 163, the two narrow, winding roads that feed into the Amalfi Drive at the peninsula's southern edge, which faces the Bay of Salerno, near Positano.

SORRENTO

Gently faded, in the manner of a stereopticon image, Sorrento still exudes a robust appeal. For anyone suffering "nostalgia di Napoli"— a longing for tarantellas, strumming mandolines, and *dolce far niente*— this is the ideal place, since it's relatively free of the urban grit found in the real Naples. Sorrento's tourist industry that began centuries ago is still dominant, although the lords and ladies of bygone days have been replaced with (mainly English, German, and Japanese) tour groups.

Sorrento has become a jumping-off point for visitors to Pompeii, Capri, and Amalfi, but you can find countless reasons to love it for itself. The Sorrentine people are fair-minded and hardworking, bubbling with life and warmth. The tufa cliff on which the town rests is like a great golden pedestal spread over the bay, absorbing the sunlight in deepening shades through the mild days, and orange and lemon trees waft a luscious perfume in spring. In the evening, people fill cafés to nibble, sip, and talk nonstop; then, arms linked, they stroll and browse through the maze of shop-lined lanes.

GETTING HERE

From downtown Naples, take a Circumvesuviana train from Stazione Centrale, SITA bus from in front of the station, or ferry from Molo Beverello. If you're coming directly from the airport in Naples, pick up a direct bus to Sorrento. By car, take the A3 Naples–Salerno highway, exiting at Castellammare, and then following signs for Penisola Sorrentina, then for Sorrento.

TOURIST INFORMATION

In Sorrento the office of the **Azienda Autonoma di Soggiorno Sorrento-Sant'Agnello** (⊠ *Via L. De Maio 35, Sorrento* ☎*081/8074033* ⊕*www. sorrentotourism.com*) is open Monday to Saturday 8:45–6:15. Besides dispensing a wealth of information they also have a useful booking service for hotels, B&Bs, and holiday flats throughout the peninsula.

EXPLORING SORRENTO

Winding along a cliff above a small beach and two harbors, the town is split in two by a narrow ravine formed by a former mountain stream. To the east, dozens of hotels line busy Via Correale along the cliff— many have "grand" included in their names, and some indeed still are. To the west, however, is the historic sector, which still enchants—it's a relatively flat area, with winding, stone-paved lanes bordered by balconied buildings, some joined by medieval stone arches. The central piazza is named after the poet Torquato Tasso, born here in 1544. This part of town is a delightful place to walk through, especially in the mild evenings, when people are out and about, and everything is open. Craftspeople are often at work in their stalls and shops and are happy to let you watch; in fact, that's the point.

SORRENTO THROUGH THE AGES

Around the 6th century BC, Samnites (a local tribe) appear to have settled in the area, followed by Greek, Etruscan, and Roman presence. It was the Romans who called the city Surrentum—"city of the Sirens"—taking the name from a temple to the Sirens built nearby. Later rulers included Goths and Byzantines, followed by sacking Lombards, Saracens, and Amalfitans. Next were the Normans, in the early part of the 12th century, and the beneficent Aragonese. Decimated in 1558 by the Turks, the city later rebuilt its walls, and in the early 1700s began a comeback that peaked in the following century when Sorrento became a prescribed stop for "Grand Tour" travelers, who savored its mild winters while sopping up its culture and history. According to a letter from his traveling companion in 1876, the philosopher Nietzsche, not generally known for effervescence, "laughed with joy" at the thought of going to Sorrento, and French novelist Stendhal called it "the most beautiful place on earth."

The Sorrento Peninsula was first put on the map by the ancient Romans. Emperors and senators—who knew a good thing when they saw it—claimed the region for their own, crowning the golden, waterside cliffs of what was then called Surrentum with palatial villas. Modern resorts now stand where emperors once staked out vacation spots. Reminders of the Caesars' reigns—broken columns, capitals, marble busts—lie scattered among the region's orange trees and terraces. Sorrento goes as far back as the Samnites and the Etruscans, the *bons viveurs* of the early ancient world, and for much of Sorrento's existence it has remained focused, in fact, on pleasure.

The Sorrento Peninsula became a major stop on the elites' Grand Tour itineraries beginning in the late 18th century, thanks to glowing reports from Goethe, Lord Byron, Shelley, and Richard Wagner, Keats, Scott, Dickens, and Ibsen. By the mid-19th century, grand hotels and wedding-cake villas had sprung up to welcome the flow of princes, khans, and tycoons.

TOP ATTRACTIONS

❺ Basilica di Sant'Antonino. Gracing Piazza Sant'Antonino and one of the largest churches in Sorrento, the Basilica di Sant'Antonino honors the city's patron saint, St. Anthony the Abbot. The church and the portal on the right side date from the 11th century. Its nave and side aisles are divided by recycled ancient columns, and the interior is Baroque style, with fine paintings, including one on the nave ceiling painted by Giovan Battista Lama in the mid-16th century. Directly opposite across the piazza is the turn-of-the-20th-century *Municipio* (town hall). ⊠ *Piazza Sant'Antonino* ☎ *081/8781437* 🖃 *Free* ⊗ *Daily 7–noon and 5–7.*

❻ Convento di San Francesco. Near the Villa Comunale gardens and sharing
★ its vista over the Bay of Naples, this church is celebrated for its 14th-century cloister. Filled with greenery and flowers, the Arab-inspired cloister has interlaced pointed arches of tufa rock, alternating with octagonal columns topped by elegant capitals, supporting smaller arches, and makes a suitably evocative setting for summer concerts

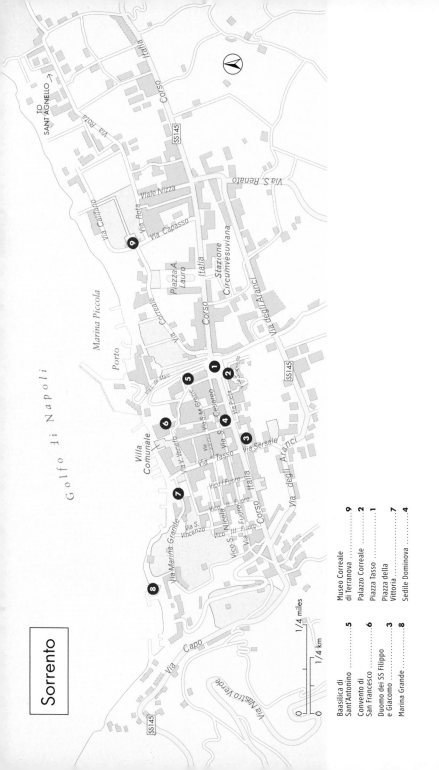

Sorrento

Baasilica di
Sant'Antonino 5

Convento di
San Francesco 6

Duomo dei SS Filippo
e Giacomo 3

Marina Grande 8

Museo Correale
di Terranova 9

Palazzo Correale 2

Piazza Tasso 1

Piazza della
Vittoria 7

Sedile Dominova 4

A GOOD WALK: TAKING IN SORRENTO

Begin at Sorrento's historic center, **Piazza Tasso ❶**, watched over by statues of the namesake poet and the city's patron saint, St. Anthony the Abbot. Avoid busy Corso Italia for the moment and head instead to the southwest corner of the piazza to Via Santa Maria della Pietà to take a look at the noted Palazzo Veniero (No. 14) and the **Palazzo Correale ❷** (No. 24), whose 18th-century majolica courtyard, now a flower shop, overflows with charm.

Follow this street until you reach the Largo Arcivescovado, site of the **Duomo dei SS Filippo e Giacomo ❸**. After viewing this grand cathedral, head for its wedding-cake campanile, then make a right off Corso Italia down Via Giuliani to enter Sorrento's most picturesque quarter. Here, on Via San Cesareo, is the beautifully frescoed **Sedile Dominova ❹**, the ancient, open-air site of civic discourse. At night, the little piazza beside it, called the Largo Dominova, is illuminated and makes a fetching backdrop for diners at the cafés and restaurants on the square.

Return to Piazza Tasso along Via San Cesareo, lighted with 19th-century lanterns and one of Sorrento's most picturesque streets. When you arrive at the edge of Piazza Tasso, go left toward the bay, a block or so along Via De Maio, to pretty Piazza Sant'Antonino, the site of stately palm trees and the 11th-century **Basilica di Sant'Antonino ❺**. Across the piazza is the Municipio (town hall), the former monastery of Santa Maria delle Grazie, with cloister and church. From there, take Via Santa Maria delle Grazie and Via Donnorso to the church

of **San Francesco ❻**, and its legendary 14th-century "Paradise" cloister. Relax in the adjoining Villa Comunale gardens and enjoy the Cinemascope-wide view of the Bay of Naples.

Keep going west along Via Veneto to the **Piazza della Vittoria ❼**. Here the rear facade of the Imperial Hotel Tramontano bears a faded "Casa di Tasso" sign, marking the birthplace of the revered poet. Cross the piazza to the aristocratic Hotel Bellevue Syrene, perhaps to enjoy a drink on the hotel's garden belvedere out front. At the back of the hotel is the Villa Pompeiana, a re-creation of a Pompeian villa built for Lord Astor (whose own magisterial house— still private—is just along the cliff), functioning now as hotel reception rooms. Just beyond is the grand cliffside terrace built in spectacular ancient Roman style by Lord Astor, which today is the impressive setting for private parties and wedding receptions.

Continue past the hotel to exit the walls near the Porta Greca (Greek Gate) and take the stairway down to the fishing port of **Marina Grande ❽**, where seafood restaurants abound. Catch a bus on the Via del Mare (they run frequently) back up to the old town, or just hike back along Via Marina Grande and the Strettoia San Vincenzo. Once back at Piazza Tasso, walk east along the Via Correale, lined by villas-turned-hotels, to the **Museo Correale di Terranova ❾**, where its collection of ancient artifacts is set within a pretty garden.

PARK AND RIDE IN SORRENTO

If you make a stop in Sorrento by car, head for the large parking lot called Ulisse (after the hotel of which it is a part): take a left turn into Via degli Aranci when you meet the "no entry" signs as you enter Sorrento, pass under the railway bridge, and turn right at the round-about. This road skirts the town center (to the right). At the stop sign on Corso Italia take a right turn, and turn right immediately down toward the Marina Grande. **Ulisse Parking** (⊠ *Via Del Mare 22* 🖀 *€2 per hr*) is on your left after the road bridge,

and within easy walking distance of the town center and Marina Grande.

An alternative to driving is the dou-ble-decker tour bus operated by **City Sightseeing Sorrento** (⊠ *Via degli Aranci 172* 🖀 *081/8774707* ⊕ *www. sorrento.city-sightseeing.it*). (For a daily fare of €15, it takes you from its terminus at Piazza Lauro (oppo-site the Circumvesuviana station) out of Sorrento to Massa Lubrense, Termini, and Sant'Agata. You can get off along the way, hike perhaps for a few hours (especially from Termini *Punta Campanella*) and then board once again.

and theatrical presentations—make this a must if you can catch an event. The church portal is particularly impressive, with the original 16th-century door featuring intarsia (inlaid) work. Note the exterior bronze work by Nena. The interior's 17th-century decoration includes an altarpiece depicting St. Francis receiving the Stigmata, by a student of Francesco Solimena. The convent is now an art school, where stu-dents' works are often exhibited. ⊠ *Piazza S. Francesco* 🖀 *081/878126* 🖀 *Free* 🕾 *Daily 8* AM–*10* PM.

❸ Duomo dei SS Filippo e Giacomo. Ancient, but rebuilt from the 15th-centu-ry right up to 1924, the town's cathedral follows a Latin-cross design; its nave and two side aisles are divided by thick piers with round arches. A Renaissance-style door and artworks, including the archbishop's 16th-century marble throne and ceiling paintings attributed to the 18th-century Neapolitan school, are easily viewable. Outstanding 19th- and 20th-century marquetry ornaments a magnificent choir loft, entrance panels, and representations of the stations of the cross. Look for the unusual 10th-century marble slab used as a gravestone, with a lioness on the front and a depiction of the deceased on the back. The delight-fully florid three-story campanile, topped by a clock and a belfry, has an open, arcaded base and recycled Roman columns. ⊠ *Largo Arcivesco-vado, at Corso Italia and Via S. Maria della Pietà 44* 🖀 *081/8782248* 🖀 *Free* ⊕ *www.cattedralesorrento.it* 🕾 *Daily 7:30–noon and 4–7.*

❾ Museo Correale di Terranova. In an 18th-century villa and lovely garden on land given to the patrician Correale family by Queen Joan of Aragon in 1428, this museum has an excellent private collection amassed by the count of Terranova and his brother. The building is fairly charmless, with few period rooms, but the garden offers an allée of palm trees, citrus groves, floral nurseries, and an esplanade with a panoramic view of the Sorrento coast. The collection is one of the finest devoted to Nea-politan paintings, decorative arts, and porcelains, so for connoisseurs of

Marina Grande is Sorrento's main fishing harbor, as well as a popular tourist hangout.

the Seicento (Italian 17th century), this museum is a must. Magnificent 18th-century inlaid tables by Giuseppe Gargiulo, Capodimente porcelains, and Rococo portrait miniatures remind us of the age when pleasure and delight was all. Also on view are regional Greek and Roman archeological finds, medieval marble work, glasswork, old-master paintings, 17th-century majolicas—even Tasso's death mask. ⊠ *Via Correale 50* 🕾 *081/8781846* ⊕ *www.museocorreale.com* 🎫 *€6* ☉ *Wed.–Mon. 9–2; July–Sept., also open Wed.–Mon. 8:15* PM*–10:45* PM.

❹ **Sedile Dominova.** Enchanting showpiece of the Largo Dominova—the
Fodor$Choice little square that is the heart of Sorrento's historic quarter—this is a pic-
★ turesque open loggia with expansive arches, balustrades, and a green-and-yellow-tile cupola, originally constructed in the 15th century. The open-air structure is frescoed with Baroque-era trompe l'oeil columns and the family coats of arms, which once belonged to the *sedile* (seat), the town council where nobles met to discuss civic problems as early as the Angevin period in the 15th century. The sediles resolved regional differences and members were granted privileges by powerful Naples during the days of the Spanish occupation. Today, Sorrentines still like to congregate around the umbrella-topped tables near the tiny square; in the evening, under the still vibrant and now softly illuminated frescoes, men sitting in the forecourt may still be discussing civic problems while playing cards. ⊠ *Largo Dominova, at Via S. Cesareo and Via R. R. Giuliani.*

WORTH NOTING

8 Marina Grande. Close to the historic quarter (but not that close—many locals prefer to use the town bus to shuttle up and down the steep hill), the port, or *borgo*, of the Marina Grande is Sorrento's fishing harbor. In recent years it has become unashamedly touristy, with outdoor restaurants and cafés encroaching on what little remains of the original harbor. Most establishments down here are geared to the English-speaking market—expect a *Good evening* rather than a *Buona sera* as you enter, and menu listings that may make you think you've been teleported into a British fish-and-chip shop. The Marina still remains a magical location for an evening out on the waterfront, but if you're interested in a dip—given the dubious sea water quality here and the cramped conditions—head out instead toward Massa Lubrense and Nerano. Don't confuse this harbor with Marina Piccola, at the base of the cliff, below Piazza Tasso and the Hotel Excelsior Vittoria; that's the area where ferries and hydrofoils dock. ⊠ *Via del Mare.*

> **WORD OF MOUTH**
>
> "This is one of my favorite things—might not be to anyone else—but very early in the morning, head down to the marina (the smaller one, as I remember) to see the fish catches being brought in. It was beautiful and amazing to see giant fish being lifted out of the boats with the aid of winches, and taking three or four hefty men to get each one onto a cart to take it up to the restaurants."
> —Sassafrass

2 Palazzo Correale. Just off the southeast corner of Piazza Tasso, this palazzo was built in the 14th century in Catalan style but transformed into a Rococo-era showstopper, thanks to its exquisite **Esedra Maiolicata** (Majolica Courtyard, 1772). This was one of the many examples of majolica and faienceware created in this region, a highlight of Campanian craftsmen. (Other notable examples are the Chiostro delle Clarisse at Naples' Santa Chiara and the grand terrace of Positano's Hotel San Pietro.) In 1610 the palazzo became the Ritiro di Santa Maria della Pietà and today remains private, but you can view the courtyard beyond the vestryway. Its back wall—a trompe l'oeil architectural fantasia, entirely rendered in majolica tile—is now a suitably romantic setting for the Ruoppo florist shop. Buy a rose here and bear it through the streets of old Sorrento, an emblem of your pleasure in the moment. As you leave the palazzo, note the unusual arched windows on the palace facade, a grace note also seen a few doors away at **Palazzo Veniero** (No. 14), a 13th-century structure with a Byzantine-Arab influence. ⊠ *Via Pietà 24.*

7 Piazza della Vittoria. Tree-shaded Piazza della Vittoria is book-ended by two fabled hotels, the Bellevue Syrene and the Imperial Hotel Tramontano, one wing of which was home to famed 16th-century writer Torquato Tasso. Set by the bay-side balcony, the facade of the **Casa di Tasso** is all the more exquisite for its simplicity and seems little changed since his day. The poet's house originally belonged to the Rossi family, into which Tasso's mother married, and was adorned with beautiful gardens. (Not surprisingly, Tasso's most famous set piece—the meeting of Rinaldo and the Saracen girl Armida—takes place within a sylvan setting.) The piazza itself is supposedly the site where a temple to Venus

EATING WELL IN AND AROUND SORRENTO

With southern Italy's most acclaimed restaurant in Sant'Agata, a cluster of gastronomic destinations in nearby Marina del Cantone, and excellent *pizzerie and trattorie* in Sorrento itself, the Sorrento peninsula has an excellent range of dining options. The region's greater concentration of tourists means there are fewer inexpensive restaurants for locals than Naples, but you are more likely to find waiters who speak some English and *trattorie* that stay open right through August. Venturing away from Sorrento's historic center generally yields higher levels of cuisine and service.

Betraying its rural origins, Sorrento's meal times are earlier than in Naples; you may have trouble finding a place willing to serve after 10 PM in smaller towns. As a rule of thumb, avoid set menus (called *menu turistico* or *menu fisso*) and go for whatever looks freshest. Remember that fish and steak prices on menus are often indicated by a price per 100 grams. Don't be reluctant to negotiate over the weight of your serving.

once stood, and the scattered Roman ruins make it a real possibility. ✉ *Via Veneto and Via Marina Grande.*

➊ **Piazza Tasso.** This was the site of Porta Catello, the summit of the old walls that once surrounded the city. Today it remains a symbolic portal to the old town, overflowing with apricot-awninged cafés, Stile Liberty (Italian art nouveau) buildings, people who are congregate here day and night, and horse-drawn carriages clip-clopping by. In the center of it all is Torquato Tasso himself, standing atop a high base and rendered in marble by sculptor Giovanni Carli in 1870. The great poet was born in Sorrento in 1544 and died in Rome in 1595, just before he was to be crowned poet laureate. Tasso wrote during a period when Italy was still recovering from devastating Ottoman incursions along its coasts—Sorrento itself was sacked and pillaged in 1558. He is best known for his epic poem *Jerusalem Delivered,* which deals with the conquest of Jerusalem during the First Crusade. At the northern edge of the piazza, where it merges into Corso Italia, is the church of Maria del Carmine, with a Rococo wedding-cake facade of gleaming white-and-yellow stucco. Step inside to note its wall of 18th-century tabernacles, all set, like a jeweler's display, in gilded cases, and the fine ceiling painting of the Virgin Mary. ✉ *Western end of Corso Italia and above Marina Piccola, at eastern edge of historic district.*

★ **Villa Comunale.** The largest public park in Sorrento, the Villa Comunale sits on a cliff top overlooking the entire Bay of Naples and offers benches, flowers, palms, and people-watching, plus a seamless vista that stretches from Capri to Vesuvius. From here steps lead down to Sorrento's main harbor, the Marina Grande. ✉ *Adjoining the church of San Francesco.*

NEED A BREAK? The unassuming Bar Villa Comunale (✉ *Villa Comunale* ☎ *081/8074090*), closed mid-November to March, is the perfect spot to sit with Sorrento's cardplayers or just gaze across the Bay of Naples at the perfect scenery.

The Majolica Courtyard is a highlight of the Palazzo Correale.

For an afternoon delight, why not head across the road to **Davide** (✉ *Via Giuliani 39* ☎ *081/8781337*) to indulge in a gelato? For something with a local twist, try *profumi di Sorrento*, the in-house citrus fruit sorbet, or a cream-laden *semifreddo al delizie a limone*. Davide is closed November through March.

WHERE TO EAT

¢–$$

SOUTHERN
ITALIAN

✕**Aurora–'O Canonico 1898.** This century-plus-old institution actually consists of two eateries side by side differing in tone, cost, and cuisine. To make up your mind, just look at the two menus outside: while Aurora serves wood-oven pizzas with a choice of 50 toppings, 'O Canonico specializes in homemade pasta and fresh fish, complete with a 1,500-label wine cellar. Wherever you sit, you can be assured of the local specialty, *Delizia al limone*, a lemon profiterole. Both sets of outdoor tables look discreetly onto Piazza Tasso in the very heart of Sorrento. ✉*Piazza Tasso 7/10* ☎*081/8783277* ⏶*www.ristorantecanonico.com* ▭*AE, DC, MC, V* ☉*Closed Mon. Nov and Dec. and Mar. and Apr. Closed Jan. and Feb.*

$$

SOUTHERN
ITALIAN

✕**Da Emilia.** Near the Marina Grande, and not the most visually prepossessing place in Sorrento, this spot has a happy plus with Signora Emilia herself in the kitchen (and often out front as well). The rickety wooden tables and red-check tablecloths are a refreshing change from the town's (occasionally pretentious) elegance. Go for a plate of honest spaghetti with clams, wash it down with a carafe of the slightly acidic white wine, and watch the fishermen mending their nets. ✉*Via Marina Grande 62* ☎*081/8072720* ▭*No credit cards* ☉*Sept.–June, closed Tues.*

$$ ╳**Il Buco.** In the spirit of "Slow Food," this restaurant just off Piazza
MODERN ITALIAN Sant'Antonino uses only local and seasonal ingredients of the highest
quality in its nouvelle creations. Dine on inventive sea and land dishes
like risotto with shrimp, pumpkin, and arugula pesto or suckling pig with
sweet peppers. Round out the meal with a hazelnut and almond flan and
chilled limoncello. Reservations recommended for dinner. ⊠*Seconda
Rampa di Marina Piccola, 5* ☎*081/8782354* ⊕*www.ilbucoristorante.
it* ▭*AE, DC, MC, V* ⊗*Closed Wed. and Jan. and Feb.*

$ ╳**Il Delfino.** Right on the sea, this restaurant is attached to a *stabilamento*
SOUTHERN (beach club). You can eat in the sunshine or in a glassed-in nautical-motif
ITALIAN dining area. Though you won't see many locals here—they're unlikely
to be impressed by the four-language menus—seafood platters are fresh
and flavorful, and this informal, economical venue also has a snack bar
for light meals. You can even swim off the pier—but please: wait two
hours after eating! ⊠ *Via Marina Grande 216* ☎*081/8782038* ⊕*www.
ristorantebagnidelfino.it* ▭*MC, V* ⊗*Closed Nov.–Mar.*

$–$$ ╳**La Favorita—'O Parrucchiano.** This restaurant is in a sprawling, multi-
SOUTHERN level, high-ceiling greenhouse and orchard, with tables and chairs amid
ITALIAN enough tropical greenery to fill a Victorian conservatory—the effect is
★ enchantingly 19th century. Opened in 1868 by an ex-priest ('o Parrucchiano means "the priest's place" in the local dialect), La Favorita
continues to serve classic Sorrentine cuisine. The shrimp baked in lemon
leaves, white-bean soup, cannelloni, chocolate and hazelnut cake, and
lemon profiteroles are all excellent, but they can't compete with the
unique decor. ⊠*Corso Italia 71* ☎*081/8781321* ⊕*www.parrucchiano.
it* ▭*MC, V* ⊗*Closed Wed. and mid-Nov.–mid-Mar.*

$$ ╳**La Lanterna.** On the site of ancient Roman thermal baths (you can still
ITALIAN see ruins under a glass section in the floor), this is a historic venue as
well as a beloved eatery. Whether dining outdoors under the lanterns, or
indoors under the beamed ceiling and stucco arcades, you'll enjoy *cucina
tipica, locale e nazionale,* traditional local and national dishes, includ-
ing old favorites such as *calamaro ripieno* (stuffed calamari). ⊠*Via S.
Cesareo 25* ☎*081/8781355* ⊕ *www.lalanternarestaurantsorrento.com*
▭*AE, DC, MC, V* ⊗*Nov.–Apr., closed Wed.*

$$$ ╳**Ristorante Museo Caruso.** A classic international and operatic theme is
SOUTHERN carried out from *preludio* appetizers, such as shrimp in a limoncello
ITALIAN dressing, to the *rapsodia delicatesse* desserts, including crêpes suzette.
Sorrentine favorites are tweaked creatively as well, including ravioli
with broccoli sauce and squid with almonds. The staff is warm and
helpful, the singer on the sound system is the long-departed "fourth
tenor" himself, and the operatic memorabilia with posters and old photos of Caruso is viewed in a flattering blush-pink light. This elegant
restaurant deserves its longtime reputation and popularity. It is open
right through the afternoon, from noon to midnight, to cater for hunger
pangs at any time of day. There are five-course tasting menus from €50.
⊠*Via S. Antonino 12* ☎*081/8073156* ⊕*www.ristorantemuseocaruso.
com* ▭*AE, DC, MC, V.*

$$ ╳**Zi'Ntonio.** Not to be confused with Zi'Ntonio Mare (their other
SOUTHERN branch in Marina Grande), this rustic restaurant is the original Uncle
ITALIAN Tony. For six generations the family has been serving huge portions of

5

delectable food. Try specialties including savory San Daniele ham served with mozzarella (from the same distributor since the 1950s), seafood risotto, and *pesce san pietro* (tilapia) with artichokes, or the Zi'Ntonio pizza with the aforementioned ham, mozzarella, and arugula. Local wines are well priced. Up a chestnut-wood staircase, it's fun to eat aloft in the balcony, but all of the three floors and several rooms are evocative and filled with tiles, flags, murals, and plates, along with hearty diners. ⊠ *Via Luigi De Maio 11* ☎ *081/8781623* ⊕ *www.zintonio.it* ⊟ *AE, DC, MC, V* ⊗ *No dinner Sun. Closed Wed. Nov.–Mar.*

WHERE TO STAY

$$$$ 🏨 **Bellevue Syrene.** In the late 19th century, Empress Eugénie of France
★ came here for a week and wound up staying three months. You'll understand why if you stay at this retreat magisterially placed on a bluff high over the Bay of Naples. (Wait until you see the view of Sorrento from the glass-enclosed lobby.) One of Italy's most legendary hotels, this connoisseur's favorite is a gentle fantasia of Venetian chandeliers, Louis-Phillipe rugs, and Belle Epoque murals painted to make the King of Bavaria feel more at home back in the 1860s. Or was, until a recent renovation transformed a block of the guest rooms into visions right out of today's sizzling South Beach. The gilded chandeliers have been replaced by hip and modern ones, avant-garde artworks rub shoulder with trompe l'oeil frescoes, and plate-glass coffee tables now adorn the ducal salons. Don Giovanni, the main restaurant, has plate-glass windows with panoramic vistas over the bay and a truly tempting menu (Li Galli Lobster with Melon Pearls, anyone?). Many, however, will want to head outdoors to enjoy elegant meals under the clifftop wisteria pergola. No less an authority than Heinrich Schliemann, discoverer of Troy, declared the hotel's vistas of distant Vesuvius the grandest in the land. **Pros:** spectacular views; impeccable design elements; elegantly furnished common areas; half board available. **Cons:** very expensive (parking alone costs €25 a day). ⊠ *Piazza della Vittoria 5* ☎ *081/8781024* ⊕ *www.bellevue.it* ⟿ *65 rooms* ⌂ *In-hotel: 3 restaurants, bar, gym, private beach, some pets allowed* ⊟ *AE, DC, MC, V* ⊗ *BP.*

$$ 🏨 **Del Corso.** This centrally located, family run hotel located close to Sorrento's major hub, Piazza Tasso, is homey and comfortable, with pleasant common areas and basic, clean rooms. Fresh flowers, an occasional antique, a solarium, courtyard entrances for some rooms, and a breakfast terrace nudge up the comfort level. Reception is on the second floor (an elevator is provided from the street). For a quieter stay, opt for a room away from the front overlooking the busy Corso Italia. **Pros:** open year-round; pleasant, accommodating staff; centrally located 100 meters from the station. **Cons:** no pool; some rooms are small; no parking. ⊠ *Corso Italia 134* ☎ *081/8071016* ⊕ *www.hoteldelcorso. com* ⟿ *26 rooms* ⌂ *In-hotel: Bar, safe* ⊟ *AE, DC, MC, V* ⊗ *Closed Nov.–Feb.* ⊗ *BP.*

$$$$ 🏨 **Excelsior Vittoria.** Overlooking the Bay of Naples, this Belle Epoque
Fodor's Choice dream offers gilded salons worthy of a Proust heroine; gardens and
★ orange groves; and an impossibly romantic terrace where musicians sometimes lull guests with equal doses of Cole Porter and Puccini. This complex of two mansions and two 19th-century chalets has been run by

The Villa Pompeiana at Bellevue Syrene is a truly unique setting.

the same family for 175 years; they have traded witticisms with Alexandre Dumas and Oscar Wilde, welcomed crowned heads, and comforted Caruso in his final days. The public salons are virtual museums, with potted palms, Victorian love seats, and Stile Liberty ornamentation; like the Bellevue Syrene hotel, this hotel offers the truly magical experience of staying in a veritable "palace" in a casual resort town. Guest rooms are usually spacious and airy, with tile floors, soigné furnishings, and balconies and terraces overlooking bay or gardens. Dine in the open-air seaside restaurant Bosquet or in the magnificently grand dining hall of Vittoria, where waiters in starched white jackets don't look a bit foolish. Outside is a lulling, Edenic park, lined with arbored promenades, shaded by orange trees, studded with statues, and home to a giant pool. Step outside the protected gates and you're right in the heart of Sorrento. **Pros:** unbeatable location in the center of town; gardens buffer city noise. **Cons:** not all rooms have sea views; some rooms are on the small side; some readers mention rude service. ⊠ *Piazza Tasso 34* ☎*081/8071044, 800/980053 in Italy only* ⊕ *www.exvitt.it* ⤶ *105 rooms* ⛱ *In-room: Safe. In-hotel: 2 restaurants, bars, pool, gardens, spa parking (no fee), some pets allowed* ▭ *AE, DC, MC, V* ⑩ *BP.*

$$$ ⍟ **Royal.** Lush, landscaped gardens surround this hotel, which features a pool with sun lounges practically leaning over the bay. An elevator descends to sea level and a private beach. The hotel is an oasis of quiet and cool, with a spacious lobby, lounge, and indoor or alfresco dining. Ask for a room with a balcony and superb view of the pool, gardens, and bay. **Pros:** centrally located; private beach, friendly staff. **Cons:** minimum three-night stay in high season; some first floor rooms have obstructed rooms. ⊠ *Via Correale 42* ☎*081/8073434* ⊕ *www.*

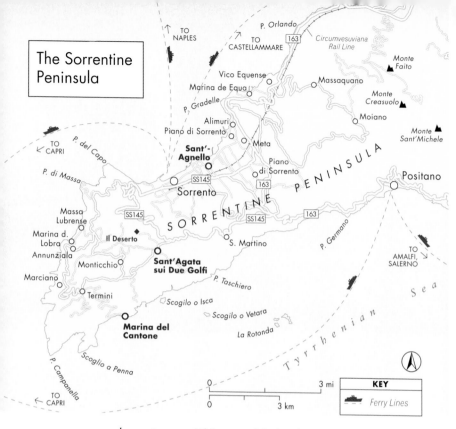

The Sorrentine Peninsula

royalsorrento.com ↗96 *rooms* In-hotel: 2 restaurants, bars, pool, private beach, some pets allowed AE, DC, MC, V Closed mid-Nov.–Easter BP.

$$
Fodor's Choice
★

$$ **Settimo Cielo.** Even if your wallet won't allow a stay at one of Sorrento's grand hotels, you can still find lodgings overlooking the water. This hotel, an excellent choice for budget travelers, is on the road to capo Sorrento. The grounds have pretty gardens and a swimming pool. The rooms, which all face the sea, are simple and modern. **Pros:** plenty of parking; excellent views. **Cons:** no-frills decor, long walk along busy road into Sorrento. ✉ *Via Capo 27* 📞*081/8781012* ⏺*www. hotelsettimocielo.com* ↗*20 rooms* In-room: Safe. In-hotel: Bar, pool AE, DC, MC, V BP.

$$ **Villa di Sorrento.** The best and the worst thing about this self-proclaimed "homely environment," built in 1854, is its central location—an easy walk to most attractions, but right off a noisy street, so request a room overlooking the quiet rear garden. Tile-floor rooms are meticulously clean, with Danish-modern furnishings. The lobby has wood trim, vintage photos, and old-fashioned touches such as embroidered antimacassars on its many, many chairs. Most rooms have either balconies or terraces, with views of the azure sea and red-clay rooftops. **Pros:** central location; child-friendly; double-glazed windows on some rooms. **Cons:** some rooms a bit noisy; few amenities; some readers note staff indifference; no parking. ✉ *Viale E Caruso 6/8* ☎*081/8781068* ⊕*www.villadisorrento.it* ⌁*21 rooms* ⚄*In-hotel: Some pets allowed* ⊟*AE, DC, MC, V* ⦿*BP*.

NIGHTLIFE AND THE ARTS

Music spots and bars cluster in the side streets near Piazza Tasso, among them Fauno Notte Club, Artis Domus, and Chantecler's. Ask at your hotel about clubs that might interest you and to get the latest news. The main watering hole for Sorrento visitors is the **Circolo dei Forestieri** (✉ *Via L De Maio 35* ☎*081/8773012* ⊗*Closed Dec.–Feb.*), traditionally packed with Americans, Brits, and Australians. Crowds begin to descend on this large villa (also home to the Sorrento tourist office) for an aperitif or beer at sunset; others arrive for casual dinner, while merrymakers hold out for the late-night band and karaoke.

The **Tarantella Show** (✉*Fauno Notte Club* ☎*081/8781021* ⊕*www.faunonotte.it*) presents tarantella dances with masks, costumes, and tambourines, as well as classic Neapolitan folklore performances complete with *pulcinelle* (comedic prankster figures in Neapolitan theater) and *pazzarielli* (jesters).

Feste *(religious festivals)* include an atmospheric procession in the thick of Thursday night before Easter, with locals donning eerie white hoods, followed by a less awesome "black" procession on Good Friday evening. Christmas has its usual accompaniment of crèches, while further celebrations are held on February 14—not St. Valentine's Day, but St. Anthony's Day; he's the patron saint of Sorrento.

Incontri Musicali Sorrentini (✉*Cloister of Chiesa di San Francesco* and ✉*Piazzetta Angri and Largo Annunziata in Sant'Agnello*) is the main cultural event of the year, offering a bevy of concerts and theatrical entertainments from the last week of August to the end of September, many held in the famous Moorish-style cloister of the church of San Francesco. There are several outdoor venues in Sant'Agnello nearby. Tickets cost €15–€30; check with your hotel or the Sorrento tourist office (⊕*www.sorrentotourism.com*) for schedules and information. Throughout the year, free municipal concerts—usually jazz or classical music—are held in several other venues.

A five-minute bus ride away in the adjacent township of Sant'Agnello, the **Concerti di Cocumella** hosts chamber music concerts between June and August at the magnificently restored Baroque chapel on grounds of the luxurious **Hotel Cocumella** (✉ *Via Cocumella 7, Sant'Agnello* ☎*081/8782933* ⊕*www.cocumella.com*).

SHOPPING

The main shopping street is Via San Cesareo—along this pedestrian thoroughfare, lined with dozens of shops selling local and Italian crafts, the air is pungent with the perfume of fruit and vegetable stands. Corso Italia has more modern boutique offerings. Wood inlay (*intarsia*) is the most sought-after item, but you'll be surprised by the high quality of embroidery and metalwork. Keep your eye out for stalls selling tiny crèche figures that go beyond the traditional Nativity participants— miniature *Pulcinelle*, hunchback dwarfs, and elaborate market scenes.

Apreda (⊠ *Via Tasso 27* ☎ *081/8782351*) produces delicious *treccia*, braided strands of mozzarella made from cow's milk. **Fattoria Terranova** (⊠ *Piazza Tasso 16/18* ☎ *081/8781263*) sells all kinds of produce— from cheeses to preserves to liqueurs—made on the eponymous family-run farm in nearby Massa.

Bottega d'Arte (⊠ *Via Luigi de Maio 18/20* ☎ *081/8781162*) offers a top selection of old glass, tiles, and jewelry—antique and new.

Rosbenia (⊠ *Piazza Lauro 34* ☎ *081/8772341*) is renowned for traditional hand-embroidered linen and lace.

La Bottega del Gioiello (⊠ *Corso Italia 179/181* ☎ *081/8785419* ⊕ *www. bottegadelgioiello.com*) employs master goldsmiths producing jewelry, including cameos and coral.

Libreria Tasso (⊠ *Via S. Cesareo 96* ☎ *081/8071639* ⊕ *www.libreriatasso. com*) has a browse-worthy stock of English books and maps.

Limonoro (⊠ *Via S. Cesareo 49/53* ☎ *081/8785348* ⊕ *www.limonoro. it*) produces the lovely local lemon liqueur, limoncello. You can observe the production process in the back of this tiny white shop, and watch the owners paint designs on the pretty bottles.

Stinga Tarsia (⊠ *Via L. De Maio 16* ☎ *081/8781165*) has been crafting and selling fine-quality marquetry and inlaid wood, coral, and cameos since 1890.

It's worth making the trek out to the **Wine Corner** (⊠ *Via Capo 12, start of main road leading westward out of town* ☎ *081/8074731*), which has an excellent range of competitively priced local wines and a well-versed shop manager for advice. This is also a focal point for small-scale wine and food tours in the Sorrento peninsula.

SANT'AGNELLO TO MARINA DEL CANTONE

Grand monasteries, the finest beach along the Gulf of Positano, an Edenic botanical park, and southern Italy's finest restaurant are just a few of the discoveries that await the traveler willing to leave Sorrento's belle epoque splendor behind and take to the scenic hills and coasts of the Sorrento Peninsula. As it turns out, many people do just that—the towns here get crowded with weekenders from Naples and Rome, and the two-lane state roads 145 and 163 are often congested. The sights here, however, are worth the bother. For those without a car, blue-color SITA lines and Circumvesuviana orange-color buses run regularly throughout the peninsula, with most routes stopping in Sorrento. Bus stops are frequent along the peninsula roads, but it's always best to be armed with a local timetable to avoid long waits at stops. Buses stop by request and only at official stops, so flag them down when you would like to get picked up and on boarding request the desired stop.

The villas of Sant'Agnello overlook the Bay of Naples and Vesuvius.

SANT'AGNELLO

2 km (1 mi) east of Sorrento.

GETTING HERE

Take the A3 Napoli-Salerno highway to the Castellammare di Stabia exit. Take SS145 south and follow signs for "Penisola Sorrentina" and Sant'Agnello. By train, take the Circumvesuviana to the Sant'Agnello stop. There is regular municipal bus service from downtown Sorrento.

EXPLORING

Back in the 18th and 19th centuries, the tiny hamlet of Sant'Agnello was an address of choice. To escape Sorrento's crowds, Bourbon princes and exiled Russian millionaires vacationed here, some building sumptuous villas, others staying at the Hotel Cocumella, the oldest hotel on the Sorrento Peninsula. On the quieter coastal side of town, Sant'Agnello still possesses a faintly ducal air. The 15th- to 16th-century parish church, Chiesa Parrocchiale di Sant'Agnello, is as lyrical as its name: swirls of lemon-yellow and white, decorated with marble-gloss plasterwork. Nearby is a spectacular belvedere, the Terrazza Punta San Francesco, complete with café, which offers a hold-your-breath view of the Bay of Naples. Sant'Agnello's two most famous estates sit side by side nearby. In the early 19th century, the **Cocumella monastery** was transformed into a hotel, welcoming the rich and famous. Today, only lucky guests can enjoy its gardens, but everyone can attend the chamber music concerts presented by the hotel in its 17th-century church of Santa Maria. Next door is the **Parco dei Principi, a hotel built by Gio Ponti in 1962 surrounded by** a botanical park laid out in 1792 by the

Count of Siracusa, a cousin to the Bourbons. Traversed by a diminutive Bridge of Love, this was a favorite spot for Désireé, Napoleon's first amour, who came here often. Shaded by horticultural rarities, this park leads to the count's Villa di Poggio Siracusa, a Rococo-style iced birthday cake of a house perched over the bay. Green-thumbers and other circumspect visitors can stroll through the romantic park, now part of the Hotel Parco dei Principi.

WHERE TO STAY

$$$$ ⬛ **Cocumella.** Though its luster has faded a bit, many conoscenti adore this hotel, once one of the most aristocratic in Italy. Set in a cliff-top garden overlooking the Bay of Naples, the Cocumella occupies a baroque monastery, complete with frescoed ceilings, antique reliquaries, and a marble cloister. The lobby is Italian-Victorian, and 19th-century grace notes continue in grand suites, which have stone fireplaces, Empire-style bureaus, and marble-clad bathrooms; even smaller rooms have their charm. Added amenities include a vast pool, a beauty-spa and exercise room, a 90-foot-long 19th-century yacht for daily excursions on the bay, and even summer-night chamber-music recitals in the monastery's former church. **Pros:** quiet location; elegant and romantic. **Cons:** far from off-site restaurants; car a necessity; many rooms and areas of hotel need renovation. ⊠ *Via Cocumella 7* 🕾*081/8782933* ⊕*www.cocumella.com* ⟳*53 rooms* ⌂*In-hotel: 2 restaurants, tennis court, pool, gym, private beach, some pets allowed* ⊟*AE, DC, MC, V* ⊗*Closed Nov.–Mar.* ⊺⊙*BP.*

$$$ ⬛ **Hotel Mediterraneo.** With its understated Old World charm, sweep-
★ ing bay views, and impeccable service, Hotel Mediterraneo is the logical choice for a four-star hotel experience in Sant'Agnello. Immersed in well-kept orange and lemon tree gardens and with its own beach access, it seems worlds away from bustling Sorrento, but is actually a 15 minute, 1 km stroll to town. (The hotel also offers a shuttle service.) Some rooms have balconies with their sea views—it pays to request one upon booking. There are panoramic views from the Vesuvio restaurant, and you can tuck into a pizza at the poolside bar. **Pros:** spectacular views; free shuttle into town; bright and spacious rooms. **Cons:** not all rooms have sea views; decor in some rooms could be spruced up. ⊠ *Via Crawford 85* 🕾*081/8781352* ⊕*www.mediterraneosorrento. com* ⟳*70 rooms* ⌂*In-hotel: restaurant, bar, pool, beachfront, Wi-Fi* ⊟*AE, DC, MC, V* ⊗*Closed Nov.–Mar.* ⊺⊙*BP.*

SANT'AGATA SUI DUE GOLFI

7 km (4½ mi) south of Sorrento, 10 km (6 mi) east of Positano.

GETTING HERE

By car, take the A3 Napoli–Salerno highway to the Castellammare di Stabia exit. Take SS145 south and follow signs for "Penisola Sorrentina." Once you reach Piano di Sorrento, take SS163 (direction Positano) and after about 3 km (2 mi), turn back onto SS145, following signs for Sant'Agata sui Due Golfi. By public transport, take the Circumvesuviana to Sorrento, then a SITA bus to Sant'Agata sui Due Golfi.

EXPLORING

Because of its panoramic vistas, Sant'Agata was an end-of-the-line pilgrimage site for beauty-lovers through the centuries, especially before the Amalfi Drive opened up the coast to the southeast. As its name suggests, this village 1,300 feet above sea level looks out over the bays of Naples and Salerno (Sant'Agata refers to a Sicilian saint, honored here with a 16th-century chapel) and it found its first fame during the Roman Empire as the nexus of merchant routes uniting the two gulfs. Now that the town has become slightly built up, you have to head to its outskirts to take in the vistas.

Sant'Agata's most famous vantage point is on the far north side of the hill, where an ancient Greek sanctuary is said—somewhat fancifully—to have been dedicated to the Sirens of legend. That choice location became **Il Convento di San Paolo al Deserto**, a monastery built by the Carmelite fathers in the 17th century and now occupied by an order of nuns. Partly crumbling and partly restored, the monastery's famed belvedere—with panoramic views of the blue waters all around, and of Vesuvius, Capri, and the peninsula—was a top sight for Grand Tour–era travelers. To access the belvedere's tower, ring the bell at the monastery and ask for the key to open the gate. To get to the Deserto from the center of Sant'Agata, take the main road (Corso Sant'Agata) past the church of Santa Maria delle Grazie on your right, and keep walking uphill on Via Deserto for a little more than half a mile. If traveling by car, park in the raised lot opposite the hotel O Sole Mio. ⊠ *Via Deserto* ☎*081/8780199* ✆*Donations welcome* ⊙*Oct.–Mar., daily 8:30–12:30 and 2:30–4:30; Apr.–Sept., daily 8:30–12:30 and 5–8.*

Today's travelers head to Sant'Agata less for the sublime beauties of Il Deserto than for its lodging options and to dine at Don Alfonso 1890, the finest restaurant in Campania. Across the way from Don Alfonso on the town square is the beautiful 16th-century Renaissance church of **Santa Maria delle Grazie.** The shadowy, evocative interior features an exceptional 17th-century altar brought from the Girolamini church in Naples in the 19th century. Attributed to Florentine artists, it's inlaid with lapis, malachite, mother-of-pearl, and polychrome marble.

WHERE TO EAT AND STAY

$

SOUTHERN
ITALIAN

Fodor'sChoice
★

✕**Antico Francischiello da Peppino.** Located halfway between Sant'Agata and Massa Lubrense and overlooking olive groves that seem to run into the sea, this fourth-generation establishment has been welcoming hungry travelers for more than 100 years. Two huge, beamed rooms with sprays of fernery, antique mirrored sideboards, hundreds of mounted plates, brick archways, old chandeliers, fresh flowers, and tangerine-hue tablecloths are quite a sight—a virtual living museum to traditional Sorrentine arts and crafts. *Tagliolini con zafferano, zucchine e gamberi* (pasta with saffron, zucchini, and prawns), ravioli with clams and arugula, and other bountiful country cuisine is *tutto buono.* Reservations are essential for weekend dinners and Sunday lunch. Perched above the restaurant, with sweeping views over to Capri and across the Bay of Naples, are eight well-appointed rooms ($)—much better than those under the same management across the road in the Villa Pina. ⊠ *Via Partenope 27, halfway between Sant'Agata and Massa*

Meals at Don Alfonso 1890 are flights of fancy for the eyes, as well as the taste buds.

Lubrense ☎081/5339780 ⊕*www.francischiello.com* ▭*AE, DC, MC, V* ⊘*Closed Wed. in Nov.–Mar.*

$$$$
MODERN ITALIAN
Fodor's Choice
★

✕**Don Alfonso 1890.** The greatest restaurant in Campania, this is the domain of Alfonso Iaccarino. Haute-hungry pilgrims head here to feast on culinary rarities, often centuries-old recipes given a unique Iaccarinian spin. Lobster, for instance, is breaded with traditional Sorrentine "porri" flour, then drizzled with sweet-and-sour sauce influenced by the Arabian traders who came to Naples. The braciola of lamb with pine nuts and raisins is a recipe that also shows an Arab influence, while the cannoli stuffed with foie gras pays homage to age of Napoleon. Nearly everything is home-grown, with olive oils *di produzione propria* (created on the family farm), vegetables so lovingly grown they have bodyguards, not gardeners (so jokes the staff). Hand-churned butter finds its way into sublime desserts such as the *pizza di cioccolato* (white sugar "mozzarella" on a chocolate "pizza") or the *soufflé di liquore di limone.* The restaurant decor is pastel and staidly traditional—the fireworks are reserved for the food (and the occasional Vesuvio flambéed cocktail). Don Alfonso has one of the finest wine cellars in Europe, set deep in an Oscan cave—don't be surprised if the sommelier tells you his earliest bottle is a Roman amphora dating from 30 BC. If you want to make a night of it, Alfonso and his enchanting wife, Livia, also run an inn ($$$) above the restaurant, with eight suites and an apartment furnished in traditional style. Light sleepers should note that the nearby church bells ring on the half hour throughout the entire night. ⊠*Corso Sant'Agata 13* ☎☎*081/8780026* ⊕*www.donalfonso.com* ▭*AE, DC, MC, V* ⊘*June–Sept., no lunch and closed Mon.; Apr., May, and Oct. closed Mon. and Tues.; closed Nov.–Mar.*

$ ⛉ **Sant'Agata.** If you wish to stay in hilltop Sant'Agata sui Due Golfi, this efficiently run hotel provides airy and pleasant lodging and a good bed to fall into after a meal at Don Alfonso 1890 or a walk to the Deserto belvedere. The second floor on the road-side has a glimpse of a sea-view, but for mere stylish furnishings you should opt for the newer annex. The swimming pool is a welcome addition if you don't want to trek down for a dip at sea level. **Pros:** recently renovated; easily accessible by SITA bus; free Wi-Fi; quiet location. **Cons:** far from the beach. ⌧ *Via dei Campi 8/A* ☎ *081/8080800* 🖷 *081/5330749* ⊕ *www.hotel-santagata.com* 🛏 *48 rooms* ⚙ *In-hotel: Restaurant, bars, pool, parking (no fee)* ▤ *AE, DC, MC, V* ⊗ *Closed Dec.–Feb.* ⦿ *BP.*

MARINA DEL CANTONE

★ *5 km (3 mi) southwest of Sant'Agata sui Due Golfi.*

GETTING HERE

By car, take the A3 Napoli–Salerno highway to the Castellammare di Stabia exit. Take SS145 south and follow signs for "Penisola Sorrentina." Once you reach Piano di Sorrento, take SS163 (direction Positano) and after about 3 km, turn back onto SS145, following signs for Sant'Agata sui Due Golfi, then Metrano, then Nerano-Marina del Cantone. By public transport, take the Circumvesuviana to Sorrento, then a SITA bus to Nerano-Marina del Cantone.

EXPLORING

The largest (pebble) beach on the Sorrento Peninsula attracts weekend sun-worshippers and foodies drawn by the seaside restaurants here. To get to the beach, usually dotted with dozens of festive umbrellas, a slender road winds down to the sea through rolling vineyards and the small town of Nerano, ending at the Gulf of Positano near the Montalto watchtower. This is a good launching pad for whole-day tours to nearby Capri. Alternatively, hire a boat to visit the islets of **Li Galli**—Gallo Lungo, Castelluccia, and La Rotonda—which sit on the horizon to the east of the beach. They're also called Isole Sirenuse (Isles of the Sirens), after the mythical girl-group that lured unwitting sailors onto the rocks. What goes around comes around: legend says the Sirens' feet became flippers, because the Three Graces were envious of how they danced the tarantella; and, as the folkloric tale concludes, the mermaids' dancing days were really *finito* when they petrified into the isles themselves. With all this dancing going on, it's not surprising that the great Russian ballet choreographer Leonide Massine purchased the Li Galli islands as his home in the 1950s; in the 1980s, they were sold to Rudolf Nureyev, who made them his last residence. The beach at Marina del Cantone was reputedly the superstar dancer's favorite coastal hangout.

Nautica 'O Masticiello (⌧ *Waterfront, Marina Del Cantone* ☎ *081/8081443* ⊕ *www.masticiello.com*) runs daily trips to Capri from June to September, and regular tours along the Amalfi Coast including Li Galli, Amalfi, and Positano, weather permitting. They also offer a wide selection of boat rentals, with or without a captain.

WHERE TO EAT AND STAY

$$
SOUTHERN
ITALIAN

✕ **Maria Grazia.** A great story lies behind this area favorite. Signora Maria was running this little waterfront trattoria between the world wars when an aristocrat came round unexpectedly to eat with the marina fishermen; Maria cooked up the best she had on hand—spaghetti with stuffed zucchini blossoms.

WORD OF MOUTH

"Nerano is a charming yet small place right on the water. It would be a very romantic and restful place to overnight. We had lunch, walked on the beach and looked in some shops." —jetsetj

Through the well-satisfied aristocrat, the dish and the restaurant became famous. You can still enjoy it, even without a noble title, in season. ⊠ *Spiaggia di Marina del Cantone* ☎ *081/8081011* ⊟ *AE, DC, MC, V* ⊘ *Closed mid-Nov.–Feb.*

$$$
SOUTHERN
ITALIAN

✕ **Taverna del Capitano.** The fascinating cuisine here is based on old recipes from the various cultures—Norman and Moorish among them—that loom large in the history of the region. The captain's son, Chef Alfonso Caputo, is a wizard at conjuring up not-available-anywhere-else combinations: for example, chicory-and-prawn soup, and tagliatelle with anchovies, sardines, and fennel. You can rely on the knowledgeable maître d' for an absorbing commentary on the various dishes and advice on the right wine from a siege-ready cellar. For dessert, opt for candied eggplant filled with ricotta and topped with chocolate sauce. Above the restaurant area is a select 10-room hotel—called La Locanda del Capitano—run by the same family, with the best rooms overlooking the waterfront. Lodging prices ($$–$$$) include full beach facilities. ⊠ *Piazza delle Sirene 10/11, Massa Lubrense, loc. Marina del Cantone* ☎ *081/8081028* ⊕ *www.tavernadelcapitano.com* ⊟ *AE, DC, MC, V* ⊘ *Closed Jan. and Feb. and Mon. and Tues., except in summer.*

$$–$$$

⊓ **Quattro Passi.** "A hop, skip, and a jump" is how the name of this hotel and Italian-nouvelle restaurant translates colloquially—appropriately so, because it's in Nerano, a five-minute drive from Marina del Cantone, in the groves of the peninsula hillsides. Here, the focus is on relaxation and fine food, but the comfortable environs also make it a pleasure to fall into bed. Guest rooms are simple, and casually elegant, with tile floors, quilts, antiques, and some two-person whirlpool tubs. Some of the young chefs are Japanese, and their delicate touches are evident in the dollop of ham-and-cheese napoleon, or a petit shrimp potpie. Dine indoors in modern white decor, on the big terrace in a lemon grove, or have a homemade limoncello in the brick-arched cantina stocked from fine vineyards north of Salerno. **Pros:** close to the beach; truly exceptional restaurant; cooking lessons on request. **Cons:** grounds can be a bit buggy in the summer; no sea view. ⊠ *Via A. Vespucci 13N, Massa Lubrense, loc. Nerano* ☎ *081/8082800* ⊕ *www.ristorantequattropassi. com* ⤸ *7 rooms* ♿ *In-hotel: Restaurant, bar, parking (no fee), no elevator* ⊟ *AE, DC, MC, V* ⊘ *Closed Wed. and Nov.–mid-Mar.* ⍾⊚ *BP.*

The Amalfi Coast

WORD OF MOUTH

"The Amalfi Coast can be a beguiling place of exceptional natural beauty, fun-loving hedonism, and a hint of Italy's ancient Greek antecedents. It is this part of Italy that breaks everybody's heart, and everybody longs to return to: the mozzarella, the pasta, the lemons, the blue of the sea, the friendly people."

—zeppole

WELCOME TO THE AMALFI COAST

Positano

TOP REASONS TO GO

★ **A World Made of Stairs:** Built like a steep amphitheater, Positano may very well be the best triathlon training ground imaginable. The town's only job is to look enchanting—and it does that very well.

★ **Amalfi, City of the Sea Doges:** Offering a dazzling layer cake of civilizations—Norman, Saracen, and Arab-Sicilian—this medieval city is so picturesque it will practically click your camera for you.

★ **Paradise Missed:** Getaway for the rich and famous, Conca dei Marini is an overlooked treasure with sky-kissing churches, a miniature harbor, and a blue-glass lagoon.

★ **Villa Cimbrone, Ravello:** No one should miss the spellbinding gardens of this villa and its Belvedere of Infinity, set like an eagle's nest 1,500 feet over the sea.

★ **Grecian Glory:** Paestum has three sublime temples sitting side by side—some of the best preserved of ancient architectural monuments anywhere (including Greece).

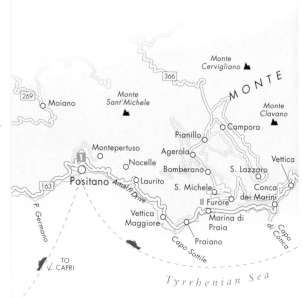

1 Positano to Conca dei Marini. Emerging from Sorrento's peninsula, the Amalfi Drive wriggles its way 5 mi south to Positano, the seaside village that, brilliantly two-faced, moves between luxe-sophisticated and beachcomber-casual. Sheltered by Monte Comune (which keeps the town warm in the winter and cool in the summer), Positano's three districts—the Sponda Lower Town, the central Mulini

area, and the Chiesa Nuovo Upper Town—are all connected by endless staircases offering views well worth the blistered feet. Farther south along the Amalfi Drive is picturesque Praiano; the adorable anchorage-lido of Marina di Praia; a tchotchke hamlet called Il Furore; and Conca dei Marini, noted for its Emerald Grotto and gorgeous Santa Maria della Neve harbor.

Temple of Poseidon, Paestum

Monte
Finestra

18

A3

Salerno

Vietri
sul Mare

163

Bay of Salerno

LATTARI

Ponte
Primario

Vecite

Monte
dell'Avvocata

Cetara

S. Lorenzo

Minori

Marina di
Erchie

Ravello

Scala

Maiori

163

Pogerola

Atrani

THE AMALFI COAST

Amalfi

Capo d'Orso

Lone

6

0   2 mi

0   2 km

2 Amalfi. Nestled between the green Valle dei Mulini and the blue Gulf of Salerno, Amalfi is threaded with Moorish rambling passages that suggest the Oriental caravansary of romance, testimony to the city's Norman and Arab-Sicilian past. A great medieval maritime republic, the city's former glory is best seen in its fantastic cathedral. The transportation hub of the coast, Amalfi's waterfront Piazza Flavio Gioia serves as the terminus for SITA's major bus routes.

3 Ravello to Paestum. Just beyond the Valley of the Dragon lies Ravello, perched "closer to the sky than the sea" atop Monte Cereto and set over the breathtaking Bay of Salerno. Famed for its medieval gardens (one of which inspired Wagner) and its bluer-than-blue vistas, this mountain aerie is often called the most beautiful town in Italy. Return to earth along the Amalfi Drive past modern Maiori to the Marina di Erchie, with its famous Norman tower, and Cetara's quaint fishermen's beach. Leapfrog over chaotic Salerno to the Cilento Coast where Paestum's legendary Greek temples make a rousing finale to any trip.

GETTING ORIENTED

With a thrill every 100 yards and a photo-op at nearly every bend, the Costiera Amalfitana is about the most satisfying 30 mi of coastline to be found in tourist Europe. Winding its way south of Sorrento, its Amalfi Drive—the "road of a 1,001 turns"—threads a string of towns that glisten like pearls in a necklace. Locals dare you to conjure up places that are as lovely as Positano, Amalfi, and Ravello, even in your imagination.

AMALFI COAST PLANNER

Making the Most of Your Time

The Amalfi Coast is laid out in the easiest possible way for touring—it kicks off in Positano and then heads down the coastline for 19 km (12 mi) to Amalfi, with innumerable towns set along the main coastal drive. If a once-over of the coast's most fascinating sights is enough, three days will allow you to see Positano, Amalfi, and Ravello—the absolute musts.

However, a practical minimum for an overview of the splendors to be found here, visiting also Paestum and smaller village treasures along the coast (such as Conca dei Marini or Erchie), is five days.

If staying in one place is a priority, and you will not be going exploring, start by picking a favorite base (obvious boxes for ticking are the three towns mentioned above), but it's best to arrange for at least two of these overnight destinations.

You could opt to pull up camp every night and move on to a different town but since this stretch of the coast is only 24 km (15 mi) long the best option might be to base yourself in only one or two towns and day-trip from them: not only will you feel less travel-weary, you'll begin to actually feel like a "native" of your home base.

Finding a Place to Stay

Most lodgings in this part of Campania have been owned by the same families for generations, and whether the owner is plain mama-and-papa or an heir to a ducal line, personality is evident. Along with local management may come quirks, even in the fanciest establishments.

But the 21st century has finally wrought change, and with it, numerous 19th-century cliff-side villas and palazzi, with their big gardens and grand staircases, huge baths and tile floors, have recently been transformed into hyperluxury hotels. Three of the landmark hotels of Ravello—the Villa Cimbrone, Palazzo Sasso, and the Caruso—have all been newly outfitted with the latest mod-cons. Happily, you don't need to be a millionaire to enjoy comfy lodgings along the Costa Divina: there are many "cheaper" options; the quote marks are used because many of these places cost more than €100 a night, due to their prime real estate overlooking the sea, but there are also plenty of bargains to be had, such as the Albergo S. Andrea, where €35 buys you a single room overlooking the million-euro view of Amalfi's Duomo steps. *Agriturismo* (country living) sets up farmhouse stays in rural and upland areas; check with local tourist boards.

When booking, note that a few hotels *require* half or even full board, usually hand-in-hand with a minimum stay of two or three nights. Some hotels have minimum stays for the peak periods of July and August and around holidays. If you're traveling by car and reserving rooms in advance, ask about parking fees. Many guests staying in Positano and Amalfi suffer a nasty shock when they find they have to shell out up to €20 per day. Porterage is run by cooperatives, not by hotels, in central Positano and Amalfi, and is another extra charge to be factored in.

WHAT IT COSTS (IN EUROS)

	¢	$	$$	$$$	$$$$
Restaurants	under €20	€20–€30	€30–€45	€45–€65	over €65
Hotels	under €75	€75–€125	€125–€200	€200–€300	over €300

Restaurant prices are for a first course (*primo*), second course (*secondo*), and dessert (*dolce*). Hotel prices are for two people in a standard double room in high season, including tax and service.

Getting Around by Boat

The **Metro del Mare** (☎199/600700 ⊕ *www.metro delmare.com*) connects the northern ports of Bacoli and Pozzuoli to Naples and from there goes to Sorrento, Positano, Amalfi, and beyond. Service runs from May through October, with two to three boats a day between Naples and Positano (€14). Check the Naples daily paper, *Il Mattino,* for timetables.

To get to smaller towns make arrangements with private boat companies or independent fishermen recommended by the tourist office or your hotel. Ferries operated by **Travelmar** (☎089872950) and **Linee Marittime Partenopee** (☎089/227979 ⊕ *www.consorziolmp.it*) cover the region. Tickets can be purchased at booths on piers and docks.

Getting Around by Car

Running between the Sorrentine peninsula and Salerno, Statale 163 (or State Highway 163) is known as Amalfi Drive to English-speakers and to Italians the Via Smeraldo (Emerald Road). It can be reached from Naples via the A3 Autostrada to Castellammare di Stabia, then linked to Sorrento via Statale 145.

When driving round-trip, many choose to go only in one direction on the seaside road, going the other way via the inland highway threading the mountains. If you do drive, prepared to pay exorbitant parking fees (and to consider yourself lucky when you find a parking space). There's much to be said for traveling the Amalfi Drive by bus. For more on the subject, see the feature "Buckle Up for the Amalfi Drive" in this chapter.

Getting Around by Train

The towns of the Amalfi Coast aren't directly acessible by train. You can go by train to Sorrento or Salerno and then use bus service from there. The **Circumvesuviana railway** (☎800/181313 ⊕ *www.vesuviana.it*), which runs along the curve of the Bay of Naples from Naples to Sorrento, runs approximately every half hour. The state railway train stops in Salerno on the Milan–Reggio Calabria line. The station here is a good starting point for buses to the Amalfi Coast

Getting Around by Bus

Most travelers tour the Amalfi Drive by bus. **SITA buses** (⊕ *www.sitabus.it*) make the trip 22 times daily between 6 AM and 10 PM (festival, Sunday, and bank holiday schedules vary from weekday schedule).

Major bus stops from Sorrento are: Sant'Agnello, Piano di Sorrento, Meta, Positano (at Chiesa Nuova then at Sponda), Praiano Conca dei Marini, and then Amalfi. SITA bus drivers will stop anywhere on the main route as long as you inform them of your destination when boarding.

Tickets are called Unico Costiera, and cost from €2 for 45 minutes to €6 for 24 hours. They must be purchased in advance and inserted in the time-stamp machine when you enter the bus. Ticket vendors can be found in cafés, bars, and newsstands region-wide. For more about bus travel along the coast, see the feature "Buckle Up for the Amalfi Drive" in this chapter.

Updated
by Fergal
Kavanagh

One of the truly gorgeous places on Earth, this corner of Campania tantalizes, almost beyond bearing, the visitor who can stay but a day or two. Poets and millionaires have long journeyed here to see and sense its legendary sights: perfect, precariously perched Positano (a claim that is more than alliteration); Amalfi, a shimmering medieval city; romantic mountain-high Ravello; and ancient Paestum, with its three legendary Greek temples.

Today, the coast's scenic sorcery makes this a top destination, drawing visitors from all over the world, who agree with UNESCO's 1997 decision to make this a World Heritage Center. This entire area is also a honeymoon Shangri-la—it is arguably the most divinely sensual 48-km (30-mi) stretch of water, land, and habitation on Earth.

Legends abound, but the Greeks were early colonizers at Paestum to the south, and Romans fled their own sacked empire in the 4th century to settle the steep coastal ridge now called the Lattari Mountains (because of the milk, or latte, produced there). Despite frequent incursions by covetous Lombards, Saracens, and other hopefuls, the medieval Maritime Republic of Amalfi maintained its domination of the seas and coast until the Normans began their conquest of southern Italy in the 11th century. By 1300, Naples, the capital of the Angevin Kingdom, had become the dominant ruler of the region and remained so until Italy unified in the mid-19th century.

By the late 19th century tourism had blossomed, giving rise to the creation of the two-lane Amalfi Drive, what has come to be called the "Divina Costiera." A thousand or so gorgeous vistas appear along these almost 40 km (25 mi), stretching from just outside Sorrento to Vietri, coursing over deep ravines and bays of turquoise-to-sapphire water, spreading past tunnels and timeless villages.

The justly famed jewels along this coastal necklace are Positano, Amalfi, and Ravello, but today's traveler will find the satellite baguettes—including Conca dei Marini, Atrani, Scala, and Cetara—just as sparkling. The top towns along the Amalfi Drive may fill up in high season with tour buses, but in the countryside not much seems to have changed since the Middle Ages: mountains are still terraced and farmed for citrus, olives, wine, and dairy; and the sea is dotted with the gentle reds, whites, and blues of fishermen's boats. Vertiginously high villages, dominated by the spires of chiese (churches), are crammed with houses on, into, above, and below hillsides to the bay; crossed by mule paths; and navigated by flights of steps called scalinatelle often leading to outlooks and belvederes that take your breath away—in more ways than one. Songs have been composed about these serpentine stone steps, and they may come to haunt your dreams as well; some costieri (natives of the coast) count them one by one to get to sleep. Semi-tough realities lurk behind the scenic splendor of the Divina Costiera, most notably the extremes of driving (potentially dangerous, although accidents are reassuringly rare), the endless steps, and virtually nonexistent parking. Furthermore, it often rains in spring, parts of the hills burn dry in summer, museums are few, and until you adjust, people seem to talk at maximum decibels. So what? For a precious little time, you are in a land of unmarred beauty.

EXPLORING THE AMALFI COAST

Europe's unsurpassingly beautiful coastline is ". . . the only delectable part of Italy, which the inhabitants there dwelling do call the coast of Malfie, full of towns, gardens, springs and wealthy men." Thus raves Boccaccio in his 14th-century *Decameron*, writing about the Costiera Amalfitana—the Amalfi Coast. Rugged, craggy, and extending around the Bay of Salerno from Positano on the west to Vietri sul Mare on the east, this is where the Amalfi Republic held sway in the Middle Ages, when Amalfi was one of the richest towns in Italy. The coastal sections—steep, winding, and ultrascenic—can only be traversed by boat or by two-lane roads. When driving round-trip, many choose to go only in one direction on the coastal roads, going the other way via the highway or by train from Salerno, or by boat from Amalfi or Positano. The first town on the Amalfi Drive is, to many travelers, the best: Positano. People head for this most popular of Amalfi Coast destinations, which is set in a natural amphitheater, as though to a hit play. The show does not disappoint.

POSITANO TO CONCA DEI MARINI

As you head past the Sorrentine Peninsula and onto the coastal Amalfi Drive, we trust you are not driving your own car. If you are, you will have to make the trip later, with someone else driving, in order to properly enjoy one of the world's most beautiful scenic roads, because it is likewise a tortuous road, writhing its way along a coast that wriggles past caverns, little inlets, cliffs, and gardens, curving sharply every 20 feet. So save your nerves and tempers by leaving your cars behind and get ready to savor this stretch of the Mali Drive, between Position and

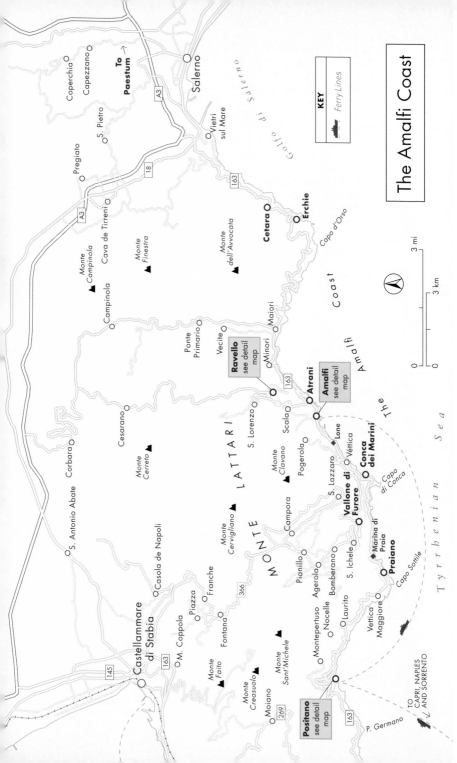

The Amalfi Coast

KEY
Ferry Lines

Coperchia Capezzano

To Paestum →

Salerno

A3

S. Pietro

Pregiato

18

Cava de Tirreni

A3

Monte Campinola ▲

Campinola

Monte Finestra ▲

Vietri sul Mare

163

Cetara

Erchie

Monte dell'Avocata ▲

Golfo di Salerno

Capo d'Orso

Coast

3 mi

3 km

0

Cesarano

Corbara

S. Antonio Abate

Casola de Napoli

Ponte Primario

Vecite

Minori

Maiori

Ravello see detail map

L A T T A R I

Monte Cerreto ▲

S. Lorenzo

Scala

163

Atrani

Amalfi see detail map

Amalfi

Pianillo

Campora

Monte Clavano ▲

Pogerola

S. Lazzaro

Ione ◆

Vética

Conca dei Marini

The

M O N T E

Monte Cervigliano ▲

Agerola

Bomberano

S. Ichele

Vallone di Furore

Marina di Praia ◆

Capo di Conca

Tyrrhenian Sea

Castellammare di Stabia

145

163

M. Coppola

Franche

Piazza

Fontana

366

Montepertuso

Nocelle

Laurito

Praiano

Vettica Maggiore

Capo Sottile

Moiano

269

Monte Faito ▲

Monte Creasuolo ▲

Monte Sant'Michele ▲

Positano see detail map

163

P. Germano

TO CAPRI, NAPLES AND SORRENTO

the city of Mali. Indecently beautiful, the Costiera Amalfitana remains the scenic showstopper of the entire Campania.

POSITANO

56 km (35 mi) southeast of Naples, 16 km (10 mi) east of Sorrento.

GETTING HERE

By car, take the SS163 (Amalfitana) from outside Sorrento or Salerno. By SITA bus from Sorrento/Amalfi, summer ferries from Naples/Amalfi. Purchase tickets prior to boarding at the Tabaccheria. The SITA bus stops here are at Chiesa Nuova and Sponda. SITA buses pass through Positano every 40 minutes or so on the run from Amalfi to Sorrento, 6:30 AM–10 PM from Sorrento to Amalfi, 8:30 AM (earlier on weekdays)–10 PM. In addition to the tobacconist listed below, check around for caffès and additional tobacconists selling SITA tickets.

The ferry and hydrofoil ticket office is beside the Spiaggia Grande; ferries to Amalfi, Sorrento, and Capri are available at a dock under Via Positanesi d'America, near the public beach in the center of town.

Local Flavio Gioia orange buses regularly ply even the smallest roads and make more stops than the SITA buses. Look for the ceramic sign and wait there. Taxis and boats are usually by the harbor, or ask at the tourist office, travel agency, or your hotel. Service on most Flavio Gioia routes begins at 7:30 and ends at midnight; departures are usually every half hour on the main lines.

VISITOR INFORMATION

In Positano, the **Azienda Autonoma Soggiorno e Turismo** (⊠ *Via del Saracino 4, Positano* ☎*089/875067* ⊕*www.aziendaturismopositano.it*) is open weekdays 8:30–2, and June to September, it's also open 3:30–8. You can get information about boats in and out of town at the **Positano ferry and hydrofoil ticket office** (⊠ *Via del Brigantino* ☎*089/811986*).

EXPLORING

When John Steinbeck lived here in 1953, he wrote that it was difficult to consider tourism an industry because "there are not enough [tourists]." Alas, there are more than enough now. What Steinbeck wrote, however, still applies: "Positano bites deep. It is a dream place that isn't quite real when you are there and becomes beckoningly real after you have gone."

The most photographed fishing village in the world, this fabled locale is home to some 4,000 Positanesi, who are joined daily by hordes arriving from Capri, Sorrento, and Amalfi, eager to celebrate the fact that Positano is, impossibly, there. The town clings to the Monti Comune and Sant'Angelo and has been called by artist Paul Klee "the only place in the world conceived on a vertical rather than a horizontal axis." Its arcaded, cubist buildings, set in tiers up the mountainside, reflect the sky in dawn-color walls: rose, peach, purple, some tinted the ivory of sunrise's drifting clouds. In fact, the colors on these Saracen-inspired dwellings may have originally served to help returning fishermen spot their own digs in an instant.

A bronze faun overlooking Positano.

It may have started with bread. Roman Emperor Tiberius, son of poison-happy Livia, sent his three-oar boat to a mill in Positano, understandably afraid that his neighbors on Capri would poison him. The (now modernized) mill still grinds healthful flour, but Positano is now more than just a grocery stop. Its name could be a corruption of the Greek "Poseidon," or derived from a man named Posides, who owned villas here during the time of Claudius; or even from Roman freedmen, called the Posdii. The most popular theory is that the name "Positano" comes from Pestano (or Pesitano), a 9th-century town by a Benedictine abbey near Montepertuso, built by refugees of Paestum to the south, whose homes had been ransacked by the Saracens.

Pisa sacked the area in 1268, but when an elaborate defensive system of watchtowers was in place, Positano once again prospered, briefly rivaling Amalfi. As a fiefdom of Neapolitan families until the end of the 17th century, Positano produced silk and, later, canvas goods, but decline began again in the late 18th century. With the coming of the steamship in the mid-19th century, some three-fourths of the town's 8,000 citizens emigrated to America—mostly to New York—and it eventually regressed into a backwater fishing village. That is, until artists and intellectuals, and then travelers, rediscovered its prodigious charms in the 20th century, especially after World War II; Picasso, Stravinsky, Diaghilev, Olivier, Steinbeck, Klee—even Lenin—were just an inkling of this town's talented fans. Lemons, grapes, olives, fish, resort gear, and, of course, tourism keep it going, but despite its shimmery sophistication and overwrought popularity, Positano's chief export remains its most precious commodity: beauty.

Above It All: Montepertuso and Nocelle

Thousands of travelers head to Positano every summer for some escapist entertainment, but how do *you* escape *them*? The answer lies way up in the Lattari Mountains, where two adorable villages perch on rocky spurs 1,700 feet above Positano's coastline. It's hard to believe two such different settlements share the same air space as their jet-set neighbor while managing, for the most part, to escape the glare of discovery.

Take Positano's village bus 3 km (2 mi) to the village of **Montepertuso** (Pierced Mountain). This sky-high village is where Emperor Frederick II of Sicily bred and trained hawks; some feathery descendants—mainly kestrels and peregrine falcons—still nest on seemingly precarious ledges around the area.

The dramatic hole in the arched rock (*arco naturale*) below Monte Sant'Angelo a Tre Pizzi is one of only three in the world that both the sun's and the moon's rays can penetrate (April–July); the other two are in India. Try to see it in the morning, when the sun shines through.

Legend says the hole was created when the devil challenged the Madonna to a contest: whoever pierced the rock would own the village. In 10 attempts, the devil could

only scratch the limestone, but when the Madonna touched the rock, it crumbled, the sky appeared, and she walked right through, sinking the devil into the hole. On July 2, a holy performance, games, and fireworks commemorate the Virgin's success.

Another popular village festival is the Sagra del Fagiolo, held on the last Saturday in August, which celebrates the humble bean. The town is lined with numerous stalls full of beans and other fare, and waiters dress in traditional folkloric garb.

The Positano bus continues from Montepertuso to just above the "lost" mountainside village of **Nocelle**, but many skip the ride and choose to hike instead.Along a well-paved road, then a curving, tree-shaded pathway, you skirt bottomless crevasses, hike under towering cliffs, and climb stairways that are relatively easy going. Finally, Nocelle appears and, in two minutes, the hamlet fully reveals itself: a stone alley, a scattering of houses and stairways, a pint-size piazza, a church.

Oh, yes, and a panaromantic view—the kind that resets your inner clock. Sheep bleat, children giggle, birds call melodiously, and the rustling wind congratulates you on being far from the madding crowd.

6

Most car travelers leave their wheels either in one of the few free parking spaces on the upper Sorrento–Amalfi main road or in one of the scarce and pricey garages a few minutes' walk from the beach if their hotel doesn't provide parking. The best bet for day-trippers is to get to Positano early enough so that space is still available. Even those arriving in Positano by SITA bus should get a morning start, as traffic on the Via Smeraldo grows combustible by noon. The bus has two main stops in Positano: Transita, or Upper Town—near the large church of Santa Maria delle Grazie, or Chiesa Nuova—and Sponda, closer to the Lower Town, to the east of the main beach. A word of advice: make

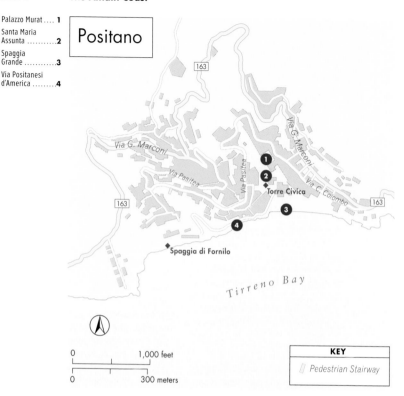

Positano

Torre Civica

Spaggia di Fornilo

Tirreno Bay

	KEY
//	*Pedestrian Stairway*

0 ———— 1,000 feet

0 ———— 300 meters

sure you have some comfortable walking shoes and that your back and legs are strong enough to negotiate those picturesque, but daunting and ladderlike scalinatelle. The municipal bus frequently plies the one-and-only one-way Via Pasitea, hairpinning from Transita to Piazza dei Mulini then up to the mountains and back, making a loop through the town every half hour.

From Piazza dei Mulini you're on your own: make a left turn onto the pedestrianized, boutique-flanked Via dei Mulini to head down to the Palazzo Murat, Santa Maria Assunta, and the beach—one of the most charming walks of the coast.

NEED A BREAK?

If you want to catch your breath after a bus ride to Positano, take a quick time-out for an espresso, a slice of Positanese (a chocolate cake as delectable as its namesake), or a fresh-fruit iced granita, check out **Bar-Pasticceria La Zagara** (⊠ *Via dei Mulini 8* ☎ *089/875964*). Deservedly famous for its lemon profiteroles as much as for its tree-lined terrace, suspended on a wooden platform above the Lower Town, Zagara is ideal for morning coffee, predinner aperitivo, or postdinner digestivo. You can also buy bus tickets here.

1 Past a bevy of resort boutiques,
★ amble down Via dei Mulini to find
the prettiest garden in Positano—
the 18th-century courtyard of the
Palazzo Murat, named for Joachim
Murat, who sensibly chose the
palazzo as his summer residence.
This was where Murat, designated
by his brother-in-law Napoléon as
King of Naples in 1808, came to
forget the demands of power and
led the simple life. Simple may not
be the right word—this "palace"
looks like it was airlifted in from the heart of Naples and seems all the
grander next to the adjacent low-lying houses and harbor beach. Built
in the early 18th century, the palazzo is replete with soaring limestone
walls, shell sconces, and wrought-iron balconies (in summer, adorned
with waterfalls of incredible bougainvillea flowers). Since Murat was
one of Europe's leading style setters, Neapolitan Baroque suited him
perfectly, and he is unlikely to have filed complaints about the views
from the palazzo (now a hotel). ⊠ *Via dei Mulini 23* ☎ *089/875177*
⊕ *www.palazzomurat.it.*

6

2 At the bottom of Via dei Mulini is the Chiesa Madre, or parish church
of **Santa Maria Assunta,** its green-and-yellow majolica dome, topped by
a perky cupola, visible from just about anywhere in town. Built on
the site of the former Benedictine abbey of St. Vito, the 13th-century
Romanesque structure was almost completely rebuilt in the 18th century. The last piece of the ancient mosaic floor can be seen under glass
behind the altar. Note the carved wooden Christ, a masterpiece of devotional religious art, with its bathetic face and bloodied knees, on view
to the left of the choir stalls. At the altar is a Byzantine 13th-century
wooden painting of Madonna with Child, popularly, although erroneously, known as the Black Virgin, carried to the main beach every
August 15 to celebrate the Feast of the Assumption. Legend claims that
the painting was once stolen by Saracen pirates, who, fleeing in a raging storm, heard a voice from on high, *Posa, Posa*— "Put it down, put
it down." When they placed the statue on the beach near the church,
the storm calmed down, as did the Saracens. Positano was saved, and
the town's name was established (yet again). Embedded over the doorway of the church's bell tower, set across the tiny piazza, is a medieval
bas-relief of fishes, a fox, and a Pistrice—the mythical half-fox, half-
fish sea monster, which supposedly characterizes the town's mixture
of mountainous and marine activities. This is one of the few relics of
the medieval abbey of St. Vito. ⊠ *Piazza Flavio Gioia, above Spaggia
Grande beach.*

3 The walkway from the Piazza Flavio Gioia leads down to the **Spaggia Grande,** or main beach, bordered by an esplanade and some of
Positano's best restaurants. Take in the seaside beauty, then be sure
to head over to the stone pier to the far right of the beach as you face
the water.

❹ Here, a tiny road rises to the **Via Positanesi d'America,** the loveliest seaside

Fodor'sChoice walkway on the coast, named for the town's large number of emigrants

★ in the 19th century. Halfway up the path you'll find the Torre Trasìta, the most distinctive of Positano's three coastline defense towers, which define the edges of Positano in various states of repair. The Trasìta—now a residence occasionally available for summer rental—was one of the defense towers used to warn of pirate raids. Beyond the tower is Lo Guarracino, a stunningly idyllic, arbor-covered restaurant. As you continue along the Via Positanesi d'America, you'll pass a tiny inlet and an emerald cove before the large Spaggia di Fornillo beach comes into view. Once you've explored Positano top to bottom (or vice versa), you may want to head heavenward and visit two villages perched directly over Positano high in the crags of the Lattari Mountains. *For this excursion, see the Close Up Box, "Above It All: Montepertuso and Nocelle."*

NEED A BREAK?

Up at the top of the town, **Bar Internazionale** (⊠ *Via G. Marconi 306* ☎ *089/875434*) is more than just a place to wait for the bus (being opposite the main SITA bus stop). As a meeting place for locals and visitors alike, it's a happy spot where you can read newspapers from several countries while mulling over a fine creamy cappuccino.

WHERE TO EAT

$$ ✕**Chez Black.** A local institution, allegedly nicknamed after owner

SOUTHERN Salvatore Russo's eternal tan, this nautically themed place cannot be

ITALIAN beaten for its location (right on the Spiaggia Grande) or as a great spot for people-watching. Regular visitors include Denzel Washington, who was best man at Salvatore's son's wedding. Despite catering to the day-tripping coachloads, the friendly staff will guide you through their specialties, including *zuppa di pesce* (fish soup) and *spaghetti con ricci di mare* (sea urchins), served in a large metal urchin. Start with their *aperativo*, the *grotta dello smeraldo*—gin, lemon, and crème de menthe. ⊠ *Via del Brigantino 19* ☎*089/875036* ⊕*www.chezblack.it* ☐*AE, DC, MC, V* ☉*Closed Nov.–Feb.*

$ ✕**Da Adolfo.** Several coves away from the Spiaggia Grande, on a little

SOUTHERN beach where pirates used to build and launch their boats, this laid-

ITALIAN back trattoria has been a favorite Positano landmark for more than 40 years. The pirates are long gone, but their descendants now ferry you free to the private cove, round-trip from Positano (look for the boat with the red fish on the mast named for the restaurant—it leaves every half hour in the morning; you can also make a steep descent from the main coastal road off the hamlet of Laurito). Sit under a straw canopy on a wooden terrace to enjoy *totani con patate* (squid and potatoes with garlic and oil), then sip white wine with peaches until sundown. Some diners even swim here—so bathing suits are just fine. ⊠*Spiaggia di Laurito* ☎*089/875022* ⊕*www.daadolfo.com* ☐*AE, DC, MC, V* ☉*Closed Oct.–Apr.*

$$$ ✕**Donna Rosa.** Locals in Montepertuso prefer to dine in this family-run

SOUTHERN establishment on the main square, slightly more upmarket than neigh-

ITALIAN boring Il Ritrovo. Watch your meal being prepared in the main room with its open kitchen, snag a seat on the terraces, or join the smokers on the main square. The menu includes fresh homemade pasta, or a

Continued on page 300

BUCKLE UP FOR THE AMALFI DRIVE

The vertical village of Positano

If travelers do nothing else along this coast, they have to experience the Amalfi Drive, a cliff-hugging stretch of road that tests their faith in civil engineering. One of the most beautiful coastal drives in the world, this roller-coastal "route of 1,001 bends" offers views that are drop-dead breathtaking—literally, it sometimes seems.

When visitors to the Amalfi Coast take the spectacular 50-minute bus ride along the sea and begin to note the bus soaring and banking along the cliff-side concrete ribbon, they may well wonder if the driver has a hankering to mature his insurance policy. As the road wiggles in and out of hundreds of feet above the water (while it's still there—landslides, you know), the Mario Andretti at the wheel seems to shift into juggernaut speed. Bottles begin to roll around on the floor and a lady takes out her rosary. With car-chase determination, the driver negotiates a whiplash twist in the road. Terrifying though some switchbacks are, what meets travelers' eyes (when they can bear to open them) is breath-stopping beautiful: bays of turquoise-to-sapphire water, timeless cliff-top villages, vertiginous pinnacles of rock. As the bus finally pulls into Amalfi, passengers congratulate themselves on surviving the ride of their life.

POSITANO TO CONCA DEI MARINI

Positano

POSITANO The most beautiful vertical village in the world suffered from its confined space, so when it grew, it grew up the mountainside.

LATTARI MOUNTAINS

Pianillo

VETTICA MAGGIORE More priceless than any landscape painting in the National Gallery is the panorama you get from Vettica's seaside piazza and its San Gennaro church.

Mount Tre Galli

366

Bomerano

Positano

163

TO SORRENTO & SANT'AGATA SUI DUE GOLFI

FERRY TO CAPRI

TO I GALLI ISLANDS

FERRY TO AMALFI

Punta S. Pietro

163

MARINA DI PRAIA Wedged between two soaring cliffs is this adorable harbor, crammed with dollhouse-issue chapel, restaurant, and beach.

I GALLI ISLANDS Nicknamed "The Birds"—owing to their formation—these three (still private) islets off the Positano coast were famed as Homer's Home of the Sirens and, more recently, as Rudolf Nureyev's last residence.

Vettica Maggiore

Marina di Praia

T. di Grado

Praiano

Capo Sottile

Tyrrhenian

A GUIDE TO THE DRIVE

Statale (Highway) 163—the Amalfi Drive, as we call it—was hewn from the lip of the Lattari Mountains and completed in 1852, varying from 50 feet to 400 feet above the bay. You can thank Ferdinand, the Bourbon king of the Two Sicilies, for commissioning it, and Luigi Giordano for designing this seemingly improbable engineering feat. A thousand or so gorgeous vistas appear along these almost 40 km (25 mi), stretching from just out-side Sorrento to Vietri. John Steinbeck once joked that the Amalfi Drive "is carefully designed to be a little narrower than two cars side by side" so the going can be a little tense: the slender two lanes hovering over the sheer drops sometimes seem impossible to maneuver by auto, let alone by buses and trucks.

Many travelers arrive from Sorrento, just to the north, connecting to the coast through Sant'Agata sui Due Golfi on

Conca dei Marini   San Genarro church, Maggiore   Hotel San Pietro, Positano

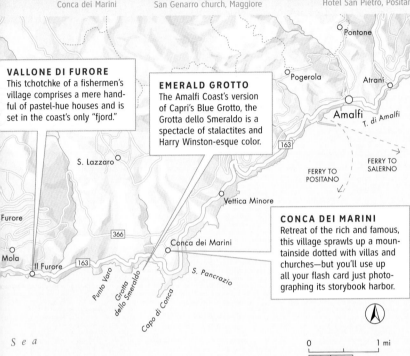

Pontone

VALLONE DI FURORE
This tchotchke of a fishermen's village comprises a mere handful of pastel-hue houses and is set in the coast's only "fjord."

Pogerola

Atrani

EMERALD GROTTO
The Amalfi Coast's version of Capri's Blue Grotto, the Grotta dello Smeraldo is a spectacle of stalactites and Harry Winston-esque color.

Amalfi   T. di Amalfi

S. Lazzaro

163

FERRY TO POSITANO

FERRY TO SALERNO

Vettica Minore

Furore

366

CONCA DEI MARINI
Retreat of the rich and famous, this village sprawls up a mountainside dotted with villas and churches—but you'll use up all your flash card just photographing its storybook harbor.

Mola

Il Furore   163   Conca dei Marini

S. Pancrazio

Punto Varo

Grotta dello Smeraldo

Capo di Conca

S e a

0   1 mi

0   1 km

the Statale 145—the Strada del Nastro Azzurro (Blue Ribbon Road), whose nickname aptly describes its width, and the color at your alternating right and left. The white-knuckle part, or, as some call it, the Via Smeraldo (Emerald Road), begins as the road connects back to Statale 163, threading through coastal ridges at Colli di S. Pietro, and continuing to wend its way around the Vallone di Positano. From ravine to ravine, Positano then begins to beckon out your window, appearing and disappearing like a flirtatious coquette. Just east of Positano, at Punta San

Pietro, Statale 163 again winds sharply around valleys, deep ravines, and precipices, affording more stunning ridge views. Past Praiano, the Furore gorge is crossed by viaduct. From here on to Amalfi, the ridges soften just a bit.

CHICKEN?

If you think a road is just for getting from here to there, the Amalfi Drive is not for you. So if you want to leapfrog over all the thrills, opt for the high mountain pass called the Valico di Chiunzi, easily reached via the A3 Naples–Salerno Autostrada from the exit at Angri.

AMALFI TO CETARA

Villa Rufolo, Ravello

RAVELLO Suspended between sky and sea, this ritzy hilltop village—home to a famous annual music festival—is noted for its spectacular gardens and bluer-than-blue vistas.

Minori

Maiori

Ravello

Scala

Torre Mezza Capo

Torre Paradiso

Torre Normanna

ATRANI Lined with piggy-backed houses and threaded by corkscrew staircases, this stage set of a medieval town revolves around a picture-perfect piazza.

Torre dello Scappariello

Castiglione

Amalfi

Atrani

163

T. di Amalfi

AMALFI The largest town of the Costiera Amalfitana, this is a must-do because of its spectacular Arab-Sicilian cathedral and its impossibly romantic souk-like streets and endless Scalinatelle steps.

FERRY TO SALERNO

FERRY TO POSITANO

DOING THE DRIVE BY CAR

With countless twists and turns, the Amalfi Drive succeeds in making every driver into a Gran Turismo pro. In fact, at times you may feel you've entered the Amalfi Indy: The natives joke that the English complete the "course" in two hours, the Italians in a half hour. The drive is studded with stops built off the roadside for you to pull into safely and experience what your passengers are oohing and ahhing about. The round reflecting mirrors set along major curves in the road intend to

show if others are coming around a bend, but honk before narrow curves to let oncoming traffic know about you, and listen for honks from oncoming curves. Buses and trucks will sometimes require you to back up; if there's a standoff, take it in stride, as it goes on all the time. At various points on the drive, stewards will stop larger vehicles so that cars can pass. Note that the road inevitably is closed some days due to landslides.

Villa Cimbrone, Ravello

Atrani

Cetara

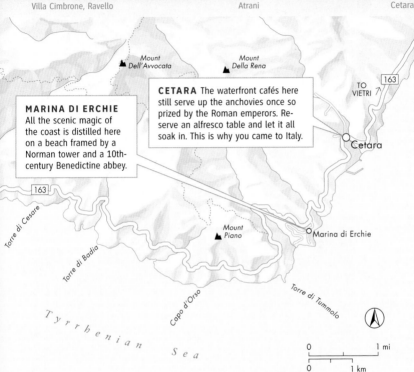

MARINA DI ERCHIE
All the scenic magic of the coast is distilled here on a beach framed by a Norman tower and a 10th-century Benedictine abbey.

CETARA The waterfront cafés here still serve up the anchovies once so prized by the Roman emperors. Reserve an alfresco table and let it all soak in. This is why you came to Italy.

Mount Dell'Avvocata

Mount Della Rena

TO VIETRI ↗

163

Cetara

163

Torre di Cesare

Torre di Badia

Mount Piano

Marina di Erchie

Capo d'Orso

Torre di Tummolo

_T y r r h e n i a n   S e a_

0   1 mi

0   1 km

DOING THE DRIVE BY BUS

There's one main reason why you should forget the car and opt for taking one of the convenient and inexpensive SITA buses that travel the route (usually once an hour: *see* www.sitabus.it): The view is much better, thanks to the mighty elevation of bus seats, which allows you to drink in mountain-meets-sea vistas, often missed in a car because of the highway's low stone barrier. The best views can be yours if you sit on the sea side of the bus (on your right as you board the bus if you're starting in Sorrento, on your left if you begin in Amalfi). The trip between Sorrento and Amalfi generally takes 80 minutes. Buses make regular stops at all the main destinations: happily, the driver will stop anywhere on the main route as long as you inform him of your destination, be it hotel or fork in the road, when boarding. Note that buses fill up in the summer months, and the locals aren't usually orderly when it comes to making a line.

Rules for the Amalfi Drive

As submitted by Az to the Forums at www.fodors.com:

1. Don't look down.

2. Don't look up.

3. Don't look—it's easier that way.

4. Forget about camels not passing through the eye of a needle.

5. Timidity will get you nowhere—literally.

6. The solid center line in the middle of the road is merely a suggestion.

7. Whoever gets to a lane first has the right of way—it doesn't matter whose side the lane is on.

8. Traffic mirrors are put there so that you can see what you are about to hit head on.

9. Tour buses will back up. (This one is true; they don't want a fender bender that will upset the itinerary of all their passengers.)

10. Garbage trucks won't back up.

11. Motorcyclists are fearless.

12. Pedestrians are fearlesser.

13. Five headlights coming toward you equal two cars plus one motorcycle, or one car plus three motorcycles, or five motorcycles, all equally probable.

14. The probability of an accident is very low; at 40 mph around a hairpin curve 1,000 feet above the sea everyone pays attention. (Same is true for the Autostrada: at 130 mph, nobody's attention wanders.)

15. Have plenty of limoncello on hand at the end of a day spent driving the coast.

Rosenatti, another Forums user, added the following coda:

If the large, orderly group of people approaching your car from the opposite direction looks like a marching band, this is because it is a marching band. No, it will not turn around.

---

selection of fresh meat and fish, depending on the day's catch. Digest in style with a glass of their homemade *limoncello*. ⊠ *Via Montepertuso 97/99, Montepertuso* ☎ *089/811806* ⧏ *Reservations essential* ▭ *AE, DC, MC, V* ⊘ *Closed Tues. and mid-Nov.–mid-Mar.*

$$$
SOUTHERN
ITALIAN
✕ **La Cambusa.** The two bronze lions guarding the steps leading up to this "pantry" right off Spiaggia Grande are not actually part of the restaurant, but aptly guide you to this safe haven for tasty local cuisine for 40-plus years. Linguine with mussels and fresh fish with potatoes and tomato sauce are among the favorites. Owners Baldo and Danielle are well known around town for maintaining high standards even during the hectic summer season. The outdoor dining terrace holds pride of place directly above the entrance to the Spiaggia Grande. ⊠ *Piazza Amerigo Vespucci 4* ☎ *089/875432* ▭ *AE, DC, MC, V* ⊘ *Closed Wed. in Nov.–Mar.*

$$$
SOUTHERN
ITALIAN
✕ **La Marinella.** On the Spiaggia Fornillo, it isn't possible to get much closer to the beach than this. Tables and chairs are on a wooden platform above the beach, where you can sample the *zuppa di pesce* (fish soup) or homemade *scialatielli*. Wash it all down with local wine, before availing their deckchair and umbrella rental service to sleep your lunch

The seaside walkway Via Positanesi d'America leads to Lo Guarrancino, a pizzeria with a view.

off. ⊠ *Via Positanesi d'America 22/24* ☎*089/875822* ▬*AE, MC, V* ☽*Mid-Nov.–mid-Mar.*

$$$
SOUTHERN
ITALIAN

✕**La Pergola.** The arbor-covered seating area is about as close to the Spiaggia Grande as you can get, and until the 1970s functioned as a dance floor. Dining here is just as evocative, with seafood unsurprisingly being the main fare—be sure to try the *scialatielli ai frutti di mare* or sea bass in *acqua pazza.* They serve until midnight, so there's plenty of time to digest before trying their *dolci,* desserts and ice cream made in their own *pasticceria,* Il Vicoletto on Via Saricena. ⊠ *Via del Brigantino 35* ☎*089/811461* ⊕*www.bucapositano.it* ▬*AE, DC, MC, V* ☽*Closed Jan. 7–Feb.*

$–$$
SOUTHERN
ITALIAN
Fodor'sChoice
★

✕**Lo Guarracino.** Enjoy a setting to make you fall in love, or rekindle it (be careful who you sit with)—this arbor-covered, perched-on-a-cleft aerie is about the most idyllic place to enjoy your lemon pasta and glass of vino as you watch the yachts come and go. Set a few steps above Positano's prettiest seaside path, the terrace vista takes in the cliffs, the sea, Li Galli islands, Spiaggia Fornillo, and Torre Clavel. Thick, twining vines, little tables covered in cloths that match the tint of the bay, and fine fish specialties are among the big pluses. The super-charming arbor section of the restaurant is home to a pizzeria oven (adorned with an icon of Saint Francesco di Paola, patron saint of bakers, renamed here Saint Pizza). ⊠ *Via Positanesi d'America 12, between Spiaggia Grande and Spiaggia Fornillo* ☎*089/875794* ⊕*www.loguarracino.net* ▬*AE, MC, V* ☽*Closed Jan.–Mar.*

$$ ✕**O' Capurale.** Even though *o' capurale* ("the corporal") himself no
SOUTHERN longer runs the place, his eponymous restaurant is still a great find in
ITALIAN the crowded center of Positano. Positano is about easy-come elegance,
★ and this dining spot sums it all up. Graced with a coved ceiling adorned
with a colorful Fauvist-style fresco, the dining room is filled with happy,
stylish diners, literally unwinding before your eyes, thanks to the deli-
cious, serious food (veal cutlet in white wine, fresh pasta with mussels
and pumpkin, or rockfish *all'acqua pazza* with a few tomatoes and
garlic are favorites) and lovely setting. Walk downstairs to wind up
on a backstreet that has a charmingly framed view of the beach at
tables set for alfresco dining. ⊠ *Via Saracino 7* ☎*089/875374* ⊕*www.
ocapuralepositano.it* ⊟*AE, DC, MC, V* ⊗*Closed Nov.–Feb.*

$ ✕**Pupetto.** A simple place at the end of the Fornillo beach, the Pupetto's
SOUTHERN main feature is its long terrace, stretching almost the length of the
ITALIAN beach and set under heavily perfumed lemon trees. Opt for the excellent
grilled fish, best followed by the homemade limoncello. To get there
from the upper town, take the elevator from the parking lot. The res-
taurant is part of a hotel with spacious guest rooms in pastel shades—
most have lovely views of the sea. ⊠ *Via Fornillo 37* ☎*089/875087*
⊕*www.hotelpupetto.it* ⇆*36 rooms* ⊟*AE, MC, V* ⊗*Closed Nov.–
Mar.* ⊙*FAP.*

$$ ✕**Ristorante il Ritrovo.** Sitting in the tiny town square of Montepertuso,
SOUTHERN 1,500 feet up the mountainside from Positano, the Ritrovo has been
ITALIAN noted for its cucina for over 20 years. The friendly owners will organize
a free shuttle service to and from Positano, making it easy to check out
the terrace's dizzying view while sitting in the wood-paneled dining
room. The menu features a combination of food from the sea and the
hills—try the *scialatielli ai frutti di mare* accompanied by well-grilled
vegetables or the speciality: *zuppa saracena*, a kind of paella brimming
with assorted seafood. Leave space for the *sciuscella*, a homemade chocolate sweet with pine nuts paired with one of their 80 different kinds of
a homemade liqueur (try the carob or even chamomile). Ask for advice
on the excellent wine list from Teresa or Salvatore (if he's not too busy
in the kitchen). Salvatore also runs a cooking school, so you can try to
whip up his creations at home. ⊠ *Via Montepertuso 77, Montepertuso*
☎*089/812005* ⊕*www.ilritrovo.com* ⚲*Reservations essential* ⊟*AE,
DC, MC, V* ⊗*Closed mid-Jan.–mid-Feb.*

$ ✕**Santa Croce.** Perched about 1,400 feet above sea level on the Path
SOUTHERN of the Gods, this is the only restaurant in the dreamy little hamlet of
ITALIAN Nocelle where the dress code is decidedly hiking gear. Try to get a window seat with its view fit for the gods—gazing over Positano, Li Galli
islands, and the Fariglioni of Capri, you can sample their fresh pasta
or grilled meat. On Saturday evenings, the olive wood-fired pizza oven
produces godly delights. ⊠ *Via Nocelle 19, Nocelle* ☎*089/811260*
⚲*Reservations essential* ⊟*AE, MC, V* ⊗*Closed weekdays mid-
Nov.–mid-Mar.*

$$$ ✕**Saraceno D'Oro.** Although open also at lunchtime, this is most defi-
SOUTHERN nitely an evening venue (the outside tables are on the other side of the
ITALIAN busy Via Pasitea). Living up to its name, the restaurant's ambience
inside is distinctly Moorish without being kitschy. This is one of the few

6

restaurants patronized by the *Positanesi*. *Antipasti misti* is a favorite starter, while bass with leeks, veal with provolone, and local wines are all delicious. Pizza is also served. ✉ *Via Pasitea 254* ☎ *089/812050* ⚐ *Reservations essential* ☰ *MC, V* ☉ *Closed Nov.–Dec. 26, Jan. 8–Feb.*

WHERE TO STAY

$$$ 🏨 **Casa Albertina.** Clinging to the cliff, this little house is well loved for its Italianate charm, its homey restaurant, and its owners, the Cinque family, with Mamma Annamaria ruling in the kitchen. Rooms have high ceilings, bright fabrics, tile flooring, and sunny terraces or balconies overlooking the sea and coastline. Car or motorboat excursions to surrounding towns and attractions can be arranged. You can't drive your car to the doorway, but porters will ferry your luggage. Note: it's 300 steps down to the main beach. Half-board available on request. **Pros:** a home away from home; open all year. **Cons:** slightly removed from the action; have we mentioned the 300 steps? ✉ *Via della Tavolozza 3* ☎ *089/875143* ⊕ *www.casalbertina.it* ⌗ *20 rooms* ⚐ *In-hotel: Restaurant, parking (fee)* ☰ *AE, DC, MC, V.*

$$–$$$$ 🏨 **Conca d'Oro.** The name says gold, and the look sure shines at this bright, white-stucco hillside lodging set in a citrus fruit–filled garden. Chintz and hand-painted antique furnishings compete with boldly patterned tile flooring on the terrace. Guest rooms have ceiling fans and balconies, and there's a broad, casual dining veranda and a private stretch of beach. All, of course, overlook the sea and coastline. **Pros:** removed from the bustle of the town; private beach. **Cons:** somewhat distant from the hub of the main town center; rather uninspiring exterior. ✉ *Via Boscariello 16* ☎ *089/811494* ⊕ *www.albergoconcadoro. it* ⌗ *37 rooms* ⚐ *In-hotel: Restaurant* ☰ *MC, V* ☉ *Closed Nov.–Mar.* ⦿ *MAP.*

$$$$ 🏨 **Covo dei Saraceni.** In Positano, sea and town interact, and you see this best from the Covo dei Saraceni, perched on the main beach at the foot of Monte Comune, just steps from the main pier. Modern, charming, and increasingly luxe, this large hotel has a rooftop pool and bar set over the sea. Crisp and cool, the lobby is built around a curved staircase while the Savino restaurant's glass-walled dining area is overhung with bougainvillea vines. Guest rooms are simple but stylized, with wrought-iron balconies; suites are ultradeluxe and spacious, with whirlpools, larger terraces, and fanciful furnishings. The major plus here is the absolutely blissful location—you'd need to stay on a yacht to get any nearer the bay. **Pros:** top location; rooftop pool. **Cons:** a hike to get here, unless arriving by boat; the entrance can be difficult to negotiate as the hordes of travelers arrive by boat. ✉ *Via Regina Giovanna 5* ☎ *089/875400* ⊕ *www.covodeisaraceni.it* ⌗ *61 rooms* ⚐ *In-hotel: 2 restaurants, bar, pool, gym* ☰ *AE, DC, MC, V* ☉ *Closed Nov.–mid-Mar.* ⦿ *FAP.*

$$ **La Fenice.** Paradise found. This tiny and unpretentious hotel on the
Fodor'sChoice outskirts of town beckons with bougainvillea-laden vistas, castaway
★ cottages, and a turquoise sea water pool, all perched over a private
beach (250 steps away), just across a cove from Franco Zeffirelli's
famous villa. Once past the gate, you climb a steep stairway to the
main house—but tread slowly: the paths and stairways here enchant-
ingly frame (sometimes literally with vines) vistas over land and sea.
Thanks to the wonderful family of the owner, Constantino Mandara,
you'll feel right at home in a few minutes—that's because this *is* his
home. Guest rooms, accented with coved ceilings, whitewashed walls,
and native folk art, are simple havens of tranquillity. Several accom-
modations are in a house perched above the road (a bit noisy if trucks
rumble by, but this rarely happens at night), although others are the
adorable little cottages set close to the sea. All are linked by *very* steep
walkways—covered with arbors and zigzagging across the hill, they
tie together these little acres of heaven. **Pros:** paradise; private beach.
Cons: some rooms can be noisy; a 10-minute walk to town. ⊠ *Via G.
Marconi 4* ☎*089/875513* ⤶*14 rooms* ⌂*In-room: No a/c, no TV.
In-hotel: Pool* ⊟*No credit cards* ⍾*BP.*

$$$–$$$$ **L'Ancora.** Set back a little from the main road and a few minutes up
from the main beach, this sunny Mediterranean-style hillside hostelry
commands expansive views of the deep blue, and of local color, too. The
lobby has a sprinkle of antiques, while the guest rooms are bright with
local artwork and boldly patterned mosaic tiling. Guests can use the pool
at the Covo dei Saraceni on the Spiaggia Grande. **Pros:** all rooms have
balconies or terraces and sea views; bright and sunny. **Cons:** a slight climb
from the main drag; no pool in the hotel. ⊠ *Via Cristoforo Colombo 36*
☎*089/875318* ⊕*www.htlancora.it* ⤶*25 rooms* ⌂*In-hotel: Parking
(no fee)* ⊟*AE, DC, MC, V* ⊗*Closed Nov.–Mar.* ⍾*BP.*

$$$$ **Le Sirenuse.** As legendary as its namesake sirens, this exquisite, in-
★ town 18th-century palazzo vies with the Hotel San Pietro for best in
show, but less flamboyantly. This is where John Steinbeck stayed while
writing his famous essay, "Positano," for *Harper's Bazaar* in 1953.
Winner of countless awards, Venetian and Neapolitan museum-qual-
ity antiques and artwork, spacious vine-entwined terraces, a private
yacht for free boating excursions, an iPod for the duration of your stay,
refined service, and the coast's most beautiful pool terrace—*the* place
to have lunch in Positano—are only parts of the whole. A world-class
operation results from the noble Sersale family's constant attentions,
Swiss training, and lots and lots of cash. Rooms, each one special and
many with whirlpool tubs, are accented with great art and artifacts,
such as antique bedsteads or refectory tables. The in-house spa pam-
pers your every need. At night, La Sponda restaurant offers some of
the best (and perhaps the priciest) food in Italy, as you dine by candle-
light. Later, repair to the aristocratic reading room or serpentine bar,
where contented patrons swap experiences and toast their good luck
at being here—and *here.* **Pros:** unrivalled views; pure luxury. **Cons:**
a bit of a climb from the town center; the restaurant is pricey. ⊠ *Via
Cristoforo Colombo 30* ☎*089/875066* ⊕*www.sirenuse.it* ⤶*63 rooms*
⌂*In-room: Safe, Wi-Fi. In-hotel: Restaurant, bars, pool, spa, parking
(fee)* ⊟*AE, DC, MC, V* ⍾*BP.*

6

The majolica-tiled benches of the San Pietro hotel give way to a classic ocean view.

$$$ 🏨 **Miramare.** Prime views and comfortable elegance are pleasing elements of this albergo converted from a 100-year-old mansion. Outdoor and indoor terraces are draped with bougainvillea, and antiques and comfy seating abound. Charming rooms, some with fireplace, are upgraded constantly and offer glazed tiles, balconies or terraces, and windows overlooking the sea. Room 201 is a large suite, and Room 210 has a huge window wall opening to the terrace. **Pros:** this is how the nobility lives; great views. **Cons:** it's 200 steps away from the beach; no pool. ✉ *Via Trara Genoino 27* ☎ *089/875002* ⊕ *www.miramarepositano.it* 🛏 *15 rooms* 🛎 *In-hotel: Bar, parking (fee)* 🖃 *AE, DC, MC, V* ⊗ *Closed Nov.–Mar.* ❋ *BP.*

$$$$ 🏨 **Palazzo Murat.** With a perfect location in the heart of town above
★   the beachside promenade and Santa Maria Assunta, and an even more perfect entrance through a bougainvillea-draped patio and garden, the Murat is one of Positano's winners. The courtyard—part-orchard, part-terrace—is one of the most drop-dead-gorgeous settings in all Campania, the lower section of which offers a sublime area for dining alfresco (the restaurant, Il Palazzo, has a superb and ambitious chef) and the September concert season. The old wing is Positano's very grandest palazzo, with massive limestone walls, carved Rococo delicacies, and wrought-iron balconies swimming in pink flowers; it was built in the early 18th century and used as a summer residence by Joachim Murat, King of Naples. The new wing, also overlooking the garden, is a modern, Mediterranean-style building with arches and terraces—it's cool, lovely, with scattered nautical motifs and tile accents, and very, very pleasant in ambience. **Pros:** one-time home of a king; stunning surroundings. **Cons:** only five rooms with views; a constant stream of

CLOSE UP

Experiencing the Amalfi Coast: Beachgoing

Except for the showpieces at Positano, Atrani, Maiori, and Minori, the area's beaches are generally disappointing, as they usually consist of small patches of coarse gray sand, or just a few rocks below the precipices. In these parts, it's the water that compels: infinite shades of aquamarine, lapis, and amethyst—shimmering in sunshine, glowing silver in moonlight, and becoming transparent in coves.

The longest and widest beaches on the Amalfi Coast are in Maiori and Minori. As space is at a premium, few organized beachside activities are available, the best being at Positano, where you should opt for beautiful Fornillo, the more secluded (but very popular) beach to the west of Spiaggia Grande.

For exercise, folks descend (and later ascend) the scalinatelle to rocky coves, where the adults dip and sunbathe and the children play hide-and-seek. The terrain below sea level is as craggy and steep as the land above—a boon for good swimmers—but as most of the beaches shelve quite steeply, caution needs to be taken, especially with kids.

6

curious day-trippers. ⊠ *Via dei Mulini 23* ☎ *089/875177* ⊕ *www. palazzomurat.it* ➪ *30 rooms* ♿ *In-room: Safe. In-hotel: Restaurant, bar* ⊟ *AE, DC, MC, V* ⊗ *Closed Nov.–Mar.* ❆ *BP.*

$ ⊞ **Pensione Maria Luisa.** With two resident cats and many other felines who are "regular visitors," this place should unfortunately be avoided by anyone suffering from allergies, but is a real find for cat lovers. Very small but very friendly, and wonderfully located in a quiet winding street just above the Fornillo beach, this is as close to staying in a friendly family home as you'll get in Positano. They also organize Italian language courses—even dog lovers could become converts. **Pros:** ideal for cat lovers; the closest to experiencing a real Positano home. **Cons:** not for cat haters; a bit far from the main hub of the town. ⊠ *Via Fornillo 42* ☎☎ *089/875023* ⊕ *www.pensionemarialuisa.com* ➪ *10 rooms* ♿ *In-room: No a/c, no TV* ⊟ *No credit cards* ❆ *BP.*

$$$–$$$$ ⊞ **Poseidon.** More than yet another place with an amazing view and terrace restaurant, the Poseidon now aims at those who wish to holiday and keep themselves trim at the same time. Subscribing to the Five Senses brand, the Beauty Center offers gym, sauna, and hydromassage if you need a break from the stress of lying on the beach. All rooms have a private terrace, most overlooking the bay, and a range of events can be organized, from boat rides to group excursions—they will even help you organize your wedding! **Pros:** a perfect base to organize your holiday; this is a holiday within a holiday. **Cons:** a steep climb from the town center. ⊠ *Viale Pasitea 148* ☎ *089/811111* ⊕ *www.hotelposeidonpositano. it* ➪ *48 rooms* ♿ *In-hotel: Restaurant, pool, gym , parking (fee)* ⊟ *AE, DC, MC, V* ⊗ *Closed Nov.–mid-Apr.* ❆ *MAP.*

$$$$ ⊞ **San Pietro.** Extraordinary is the word for this luxurious oasis, favored ★   by the likes of Julia Roberts, George Clooney, Dustin Hoffman, and Princess Caroline of Monaco, some of whom who prefer this place because it's several leagues out of town (a shuttle bus whisks you back

and forth), far from the crowds and the paparazzi. The place itself is more than camera-ready: set on a cliff high over the sea, with its own chapel for weddings (as well as an English phone box outside the entrance), there are seven levels of gardened terraces. The San Pietro has a frilly, pretty decor that mixes modern (the hotel was built in the early 1970s) with magnificent (great antiques, elegant Vietri tilework). Who can resist idling away hours on the famous majolica benches of the grand terrace? Before you is a god's view of Positano and its bay, magnificently framed by gigantic urns of flowers. Most of the elegantly furnished rooms come with terraces (most look out to the sea, not toward Positano) and plate-glass views; room decors mix chic and charming in best country-style manner. The pool on an upper level is not large, so most guests opt to take an elevator fit for James Bond through hundreds of feet of mountainside to the private beach and beach bar. The proprietors organize boating excursions and parties, while the restaurant's menu is both super-ambitious and stylish. Don't you dare leave without trying the hotel's incredibly delicious signature drink, called Elephant's Milk, a mix of almond milk, mineral water, and lemon juice. They also make a mean Bellini. **Pros:** picture-perfect views from the terrace; mixing with the Modigliani-sleek jet-setters. **Cons:** too far away from Positano to take a stroll; not all rooms served by the elevator. ⊠ *Via Laurito 2* ☎ *089/875455* ⊕ *www.ilsanpietro.it* ⤵ *60 rooms* ⟐ *In-room: Safe. In-hotel: Restaurant, bars, tennis court, pool, gym, beachfront* ⊟ *AE, DC, MC, V* ⊘ *Closed Nov.–Mar.* ⑩ *BP.*

$$
★ ⊡ **Villa Flavio Gioia.** For longer stays this is the ideal option, with a super location overlooking Piazza Flavio Gioia and the town's symbolic parish church, and a hop, skip, and a jump to the Spiaggia Grande. Each mini-apartment has its own terrace or large balcony, and a cooking area. For centuries a private home, it retains its old charm with bright area rooms. Longer stays are preferred, and the minimum stay in high season is one week. The small garden is the ideal place to have breakfast, looking down at the tourists and *Positanesi* trekking down to the beach as you slowly start the day. **Pros:** prime location; ideal for longer stays. **Cons:** short stays are discouraged; no pool. ⊠ *Piazza Flavio Gioia 2* ☎ *089/875222* ⊕ *www.villaflaviogioia.it* ⤵ *13 rooms* ⟐ *In-room: Kitchen* ⊟ *AE, DC, MC, V* ⊘ *Closed Jan.* ⑩ *BP.*

$$$–$$$$ ⊡ **Villa Franca.** Bay blue, lemon yellow, and cool white are the palette here, making for a stress-dissolving retreat, set halfway up the town from the beach. Tile-and-mosaic floors, decorative urns, and graceful archways open to sea air and views, and conversation seating done in bold fabrics marks the public rooms and bar. Similarly furnished, guest rooms, in the main building and the annex, all have terraces over the town, while the smallish pool enjoys a delightful view. **Pros:** the only pool in Positano with a 360-degree view of the gulf; all rooms with terraces **Cons:** a steep climb from the center; small pool. ⊠ *Viale Pasitea 318* ☎ *089/875655* ⊕ *www.villafrancahotel.it* ⤵ *37 rooms* ⟐ *In-hotel: Restaurant, bar, pool, gym* ⊟ *AE, DC, MC, V* ⊘ *Closed Nov.–Mar.* ⑩ *BP.*

NIGHTLIFE AND THE ARTS

Despite its past as a bohemian haven, nowadays Positano is remarkably quiet in the evenings. For entertainment, head down to the waterfront, where the restaurants lined up along the border of the Spiaggia Grande turn into an open-air party on summer nights.

CHAMBER MUSIC
A festival devoted to chamber music, the **Corso Internazionale di Musica da Camera** (⊠ *Via G. Marconi 45* ⊕ *www.icmcfestival.com*) offers two-week master classes, lectures, and concerts open to the public throughout July. The free summer concerts are staged in atmospheric settings throughout Positano.

CULINARY LESSONS
On a centrally located roof garden with sweeping views of the coastline, **Diana Folonari** (of the famous wine family) holds four-day courses on Italian country cooking, offered in English from May through June and September through October, with wine tastings. Bring a notebook, pencils, and your own apron. ⊠ *Viale Pasitea 246* 📠 *089/875784* ⊕ *www.cookingschoolpositano.it.*

DANCE CLUBS
Music on the Rocks (⊠ *Via Grotte dell'Incanto 56* 📠 *089/875874* ⊕ *www.musicontherocks.it* ⊙ *Closed Nov.–Mar.*) is a popular bar with occasional live music, run by the owners of the restaurants Chez Black and Le Terrazze. Set in a seaside cave off the Spaggia Grande beach, it is favored by the likes of Matt Dillon, Lenny Kravitz, Kate Moss, and Denzel Washington. Special events excepted, entrance is free as long as you buy a drink for around €10.

ConWinum (⊠ *Via Rampa Teglia 12* 📠 *089/811687* ⊕ *www.bucapositano.it/winebar.asp* ⊙ *Closed Nov.–Mar.*) is just a few steps up from the Spaiggia Grande and gives you the chance to be a sommelier for an evening. Resident expert Raffaele will talk you through some of the 900 wines available, accompanied by palette-pleasing appetizers and tapas, all in a pastel-color, arched room, with all interiors crafted by local artists. Functioning also as an art gallery and screening all major sporting events, this is a necessary stop for all tastes.

FESTIVALS
Yearlong, the Positano calendar is filled with festivities and religious *feste*. Sole, Mare e Cultura in July hosts national and international authors reading from their books in the shady gardens of Palazzo Murat. The first week in September sees the Premio Leonide Massine dance awards—officially known as the Positano Prize for the Art of Dancing, while the last week brings the Sagra del Pesce (Fish Festival) on Fornillo beach. Fall also brings Quartieri Aperti, with traditional music and regional food from throughout Italy. At Christmas, wreaths are fashioned from bougainvillea, and orchestra and choir concerts pop up all over town; the *Nuovo Anno* (New Year) is greeted with a big town dance and fireworks on the main beach, as well as other folklore and caffè-concerti musical events. In neighboring Montepertuso, a living crèche is enacted. The star event of the year and Positano's main religious *festa* is the **Feast of the Assumption,** held every August 15, with the painting of the Madonna with Child carried from the church to the sea, commemorated by evening fireworks and music on the main beach.

6

SPORTS AND THE OUTDOORS

BEACHES

The Marina is the main boating area, with taupe, semi-sandy Spiaggia Grande the largest and widest beach of the six or so in the area. Fishermen—once the dominant workforce—now function as a cooperative group, supplying local kitchens; they can be seen cleaning their colorful, flipped-over boats and mending their torn nets throughout the day, seemingly oblivious to the surrounding throngs. To the west of town is the less-crowded Spiaggia di Fornillo, which you can get to by walking the impossibly beautiful Via Positanesi d'America (leading from Spiaggia Grande). Fornillo is worth the walk, as it is vast and hemmed in by impressive cliffs. To the east of Positano is a string of small, pretty beaches, separated by coves—La Porta, Arienzo, San Pietro, and Laurito—most of which are accessible only by boat.

BOAT EXCURSIONS

From Spiaggia Grande you can board a scheduled day boat or hire a private one for as long as you'd like, to visit Capri, the Emerald Grotto in Conca dei Marini, or coves and inlets with small beaches. Close by, in the large caves of La Porta (650 feet east of the town center), Mezzogiorno and Erica, tools, utensils, and hunting weapons from the Paleolithic and Mesolithic ages have been discovered, the oldest known remains on the coast. The favorite boating destinations, however, are the rocky Li Galli islets (6 km [4 mi] southwest), seen from any point in Positano (as they are from the beaches of the peninsula), whose name derives from their importance in Greek mythology—resembling pecking birds, the islands were said to be the home of the sirens, part human, part feathered. Originally the site of an ancient Roman anchorage, the islands then became medieval fiefdoms of Emperor Frederick II and King Robert of Anjou. The isles remain tempting enough to lure purchasers in search of an exclusive paradise: Russian choreographer Leonide Massine in 1925, and, in 1988, dancer Rudolf Nureyev, who discovered the islands in 1984 when he came to accept the Positano Prize for the Art of Dancing, given each year in honor of Massine. The islands are still private, now belonging to a Sorrento hotelier, who also purchased the renowned Villa Zeffirelli in 2008—yours for a month for €500,000. **L'Uomo e il Mare** (✉ *Spiaggia Grande pier* ☎*089/811613* ☎☎*089/875475* ⊕*www.gennaroesalvatore.it*) is an outfit run by brothers Gennaro and Salvatore Capraro (Gennaro's wife is English) offering boating excursions to Li Galli and many other coastal destinations, with lunch on board from €80 per person (less if you skip the lunch). Boating excursions can also be organized through **Noleggio Barche Lucibello** (✉*Spiaggia Grande pier* ☎*089/875032* ☎*089/875326* ⊕*www. lucibello.it*), which also rents motorboats and rowboats by the hour.

HIKING

Hikers often pass through Positano on their way to the region's most famed mountainside trail, the **Sentiero degli Dei** (Pathway of the Gods), which can be picked up outside nearby Nocelle. For less professional hikers, Ponte dei Libri (a bridge several miles west) spans a pretty valley with soaring rock pinnacles and is a moderate walk. More serious climbers can hike up to Santa Maria del Castello (just more than

EATING WELL ON THE AMALFI COAST

Locals say they have "one foot in the fishing boat, one in the vineyard"—and a fortunate stance it is, as you can count on eating simple, fresh, seasonal food, and lots of it, with *tutti i sapori della campagna verace* (all the true flavors of the countryside). From the gulfs come *pesce alla griglia* (grilled fish), *calamari* (squid), *aragosta* (lobster), and *gamberone* (shrimp). Wood oven–baked thin-crust pizzas start with the classic *Margherita*—tomato sauce, basil, and cheese—and marinara—"marinated" with tomato, garlic, and oregano—and go from there to infinity.

La Cucina Costiera seems more sensuous amid all this beauty. Sun-dried tomatoes and chili peppers hang in bright red cascades on balconies and shopfronts. (*"Viagra naturale"* boasts a hand-lettered sign in Amalfi.) Ingredients grown in terraced plots include plump olives pressed into oil or eaten whole, tiny spring *carciofi* (artichokes), and sweet figs. *Sponzini,* or *pomodori del pendolo,* the tomatoes carried from Egypt long ago by fishermen, grow in the mountains and muddy fields of Furore and Conca dei Marini. Eggplant, asparagus, and mushrooms thrive in the Tramonte uplands, while tomatoes come from Campora. Soft *fior di latte* (cow's-milk cheeses)—are from the high hill pastures of Agerola, while the world's best buffalo mozzarella comes from Paestum.

Pasta is often served with seafood, but regional dishes include *crespelle al formaggio*—layers of crepes with béchamel sauce—and fettuccine-like *scialatielli,* often a house specialty, served with varied sauces. Clams and pasta baked in a paper bag—

"al cartoccio"—is popular in Amalfi. In Positano, try traditional squid with potatoes, stuffed peppers, and slow-simmering ragù (tomato sauce with meat, garlic, and parsley). Around Cetara, salted anchovies, eggplant, and peppers in oil are the base of the famed sauce called *"garum,"* handed down from the Romans. A lighter version is *colatura di alici,* an anchovy sauce developed by Cistercian monks near Amalfi, served on spaghetti as a traditional Christmas Eve treat. South of Salerno, you can visit working farms, and make friends with the buffalo, before sampling the best mozzarella known to mankind. Artichokes are also a specialty of the Paestum area.

Wine here is light, drinkable, and inexpensive, and often consumed mere months after crushing; don't be surprised if it's the color of beer, and served from a jug (*"sfuso"*–loose wine). Practically all of it comes from Campania, often from the town or village in which it's poured, perhaps even from the restaurant's own centuries-old vines. Little of it transports well. Furore, Gragnano, and Ravello produce good bottled wines, both rosso and bianco, with Furore's Cuomo perhaps the finest white.

Although a few restaurants are world renowned, most are family affairs, with *papà* out front, the kids serving, and mamma, aunts, and even old *nonna* in the kitchen. Smile a bit, compliment the cuisine, and you're apt to meet them all.

6

2,000 feet) from where paths radiate out eastward and westward along the Lattari Mountains. Plant-lovers will find hillside walks particularly rewarding in May, when the mountains turn into a flowering rock garden with fine displays of orchids. As a general rule, allow plenty of time for what look like short distances on paper, take lots of water, and stick to the paths mapped out in red and white stripes by the CAI (Italian Alpine Club). Julian Tippet's hiking guide, *Landscapes of Sorrento and the Amalfi Coast* (available at stores on the coast), is a wonderful book—invest in it. You can also purchase the CAI's official map detailing all paths in the area.

SHOPPING

Although the traditional gaudily colored and lace-trimmed Positano-style clothes have started to look rather too frou frou and dated, some contemporary designers are keeping the fashion alive with a more 21st-century spin. Goods still range from haute to kitsch, often tight tops and casual skirts in vibrant hues, with prices generally higher than in other coast towns. The fabric industry here began long ago with silk, canvas, and hand embroidery, then made headlines in 1959 when Positano introduced Italy to the bikini (following the reasoning that less is more, boutiques now sell even more highly abbreviated ones). The most concentrated shopping area, and the least difficult to maneuver, is the souklike area near the cathedral by the beach, where the crowded pedestrian pathway literally runs through boutiques. Lining steep alleyways covered with bougainvillea, small shops display items such as local foodstuffs, wood, lace, pottery, wines and limoncello, and ceramics; you'll even find artisans who can hand-stitch a pair of stylish sandals while you wait.

Sfizio (⊠ *Via Pasitea 56* ☎*089/875893* ⊠ *Via del Saracino 55* ☎*089/875358*) has a fine selection of bags, shoes, and accessories. It's worth splurging at **Marilù** (⊠ *Via del Saracino 20* ☎*089/875631*) if you want to take something unique home in Positano wear.

Delikatessen Positano (⊠ *Via dei Mulini 5, 13, 15* ☎*089/875489*) is the place to pick up your limoncello or biscuits and also offers candles and soaps made from lemons. At **I sapori di Positano** (⊠ *Via dei Mulini 6* ☎*089/812055*) you can find anything that it's conceivably possible to make from citrus fruits.

PRAIANO

5 km (3 mi) southeast of Positano, 1 km (½ mi) northwest of Marina di Praia.

GETTING HERE

By car, take the SS163 (Amalfitana) from outside Sorrento or Salerno. There is SITA bus service from Sorrento, Positano, and Amalfi.

EXPLORING

From afar, Praiano looks as alluring as a landscape painting. Up close, it turns out to be just your standard-issue village-along-a-road. Praiano has less wealth and sophistication than its neighbors and more olive and lemon trees than tourists. The town's name comes from Plagianum, as the people who first inhabited the site were called. Back in the 13th century, King Charles I of Anjou founded a university here, the doges of Amalfi established a summer residence, and, for a while, Praiano was renowned for its silk industry. But the decline of Amalfi's 12th-century maritime republic hit hard; the charming parish church of San Luca, at the top of the village, is a reminder of those headier times. A medieval lookout tower on the rocks still keeps guard over the coast, and hidden coves are for boating, bathing, and sunning off the rocks. In summer, boats leave the beach here for Capri each morning, and you can clearly see the Faraglioni rocks from here. What really makes it worth stopping here is its vast piazza, in the Vettica Maggiore area of the village, almost levitating over the water. This is a fine place to stretch your legs and view distant Positano, the coast, and the sea. Paved with an intricate, colorful pattern in majolica, the piazza is a fitting setting for the church of San Gennaro, rebuilt in the 16th century, with its notably ornate facade and a gleaming majolica-tile dome. Paintings from the 16th and 17th centuries include *Martyrdom of S. Bartholomew,* by Giovanni Bernardo Lama, decorating the side chapel. You'll find a pretty but hard-to-reach cliff-side beach if you follow the "Spiaggia" signs from the church; it's at the end of an olive grove, hidden at the bottom of the hillside, next to a tiny anchorage.

WHERE TO EAT

$$
SOUTHERN
ITALIAN

✕ **La Brace.** On the second floor of a simple storefront, on the inland side of the drive, the little restaurant you enter looks disappointingly simple. Its fine reputation, however, is validated as soon as you see the fresh, homemade antipasti and when you dig into the hearty Amalfitan cuisine. The friendly owner recommends the seafood (at remarkably accessible prices), and if you sit on the veranda, you can see the jagged coastline and serene sea. ⊠ *Via G. Capriglione 146, Vettica Maggiore, Praiano* ☎089/874226 ▭*AE, DC, MC, V* ☉*Closed Nov. and Wed. Oct.–Mar.*

$$$
PIZZA

✕ **La Taverna del Leone.** A crowd ranging from Ferrari owners to local fishermen is drawn to this rustic, convivial trattoria because of the pizza—reputedly the best around (evenings only). You can choose from a variety of antipasti and creative pizza toppings, or go for a big meal topped off with a cold beer or glass of local wine, in a lusty roadhouse setting where folks mingle happily and noisily. And if you want to stay over rather than face the drive, a few simple rooms with private baths are here as well. ⊠ *Via Laurito 43, Amalfi Dr., between Positano and Vettica Maggiore, Positano* ☎089/875474 ▭*AE, DC, MC, V* ☉*Closed Tues. and Nov.–Mar.*

WHERE TO STAY

$

☂ **Open Gate.** This is a real deal, with much the same view as million-dollar-plus villas nearby. True, you're right on the main road, but the tile-floor guest rooms are white and clean, the private balconies are spacious, and the informal, vine-covered restaurant serves up tasty fare. You can also stay in their villa high in the mountains, with its breathtaking view. **Pros:** coastal views at a fraction of the price of others; simple rooms. **Cons:** on the Amalfi Drive; can be noisy; the owner is often overworked. ⊠ *Via Roma 38* ☎*089/874148* ⊕*www.*

hotelopengate.it ⌘*12 rooms* ⌖*In-hotel: Restaurant, bar* ⊟*AE, DC, MC, V* ⦿*FAP.*

$$$ 🏨**Tramonto d'Oro.** In Praiano's township of Vettica Maggiore and picturesquely sited close to the town's glorious church of San Gennaro, this hotel is a much-loved option on the coast. Modern, clean, and sleek, the guest rooms are casual-traditional in style. The real plus here is the Esposito family—they also run Conca dei Marini's Le Terrazze Hotel—which has presided over the Tramonto d'Oro since 1952 with true warmth and charm. The restaurant has a vast glass wall that frames a picture-perfect view over the church and piazza, while the roof has a pleasant pool. A free shuttle bus will take you to the nearby beaches. **Pros:** the friendly owners; the picture-perfect view. **Cons:** be careful as you step out of the door—the entrance is on the busy Amalfi Drive, not an easy to walk to beach. ⊠ *Via G. Capriglione 119, Vettica Maggiore, Praiano* ☎*089/874955* 🖷*089/874670* ⦿*www.tramontodoro.it* ⌘*40 rooms* ⌖*In-hotel: Restaurant, pool, gym, parking (no fee), some pets allowed* ⊟*AE, DC, MC, V* ⦵*Closed Nov.–Apr.* ⦿*FAP.*

$$$$ 🏨**Tritone.** From afar on the Amalfi Drive, this looks like a shimmering
★   white palace perched on the cliffs. Upon arriving, you'll see no other hotel has such a dizzying roost above the sea. The road level entrance hides the flagstone terraces and gardens set amid soaring rock pinnacles taking full advantage of the location. The seaside bathing area, accessed by an elevator excavated through 1,000 feet of rock, is jaw-dropping and complete with private beach, rocky tunnels, buffet, and bar. Not jaw-dropping, however, are the public and guest rooms, all very standard-issue and staidly traditional in style. Still, they are comfortable and come with grand views of the sea and nearby Praiano. All in all, this is a delightfully low-key and relaxing place. A small rock chapel in a grotto is on the property, if you care to give thanks for the region's natural wonders. **Pros:** feel like an Italian seagull; the amazing private beach. **Cons:** the standard-issue guest rooms; a walk along the busy road to get to Praiano. ⊠ *Via Campo 5* ☎*089/874333* ⦿*www.tritone.it* ⌘*59 rooms* ⌖*In-hotel: Restaurant, bars, pools, beachfront* ⊟*AE, DC, MC, V* ⦵*Closed mid-Oct.–Mar.* ⦿*FAP.*

MARINA DI PRAIA

★   *1 km (½ mi) southeast of Praiano, 2 km (1 mi) west of Vallone di Furore.*

GETTING HERE

By car, take the SS163 (Amalfitana) from outside Sorrento or Salerno. SITA bus from Sorrento/Positano/Amalfi, local bus from Praiano.

EXPLORING

"Whoever wants to live a healthy life spends the morning in Vettica and the evening in Praiano," according to a local adage. The larger township of Praiano may not fulfill that advice, but its scenic satellite, Marina di Praia, indeed does; it's home to a landmark eatery and famous disco. Nestled by the sea at the bottom of a dramatic chasm, this is the only anchorage along this rocky stretch where you can hire a boat and dock it and where ferries depart for points and islands along the coast. The

super-picturesque hamlet, with its year-round nativity scene perched on the cliff above, has a few parking spaces, a small sand beach tucked within cliffs, some excellent seafood restaurants, a hotel, and a tiny church. The L'Africana disco is tucked away on a pretty, winding path along the sea.

WHERE TO EAT AND STAY

$$ ✕**Alfonso a Mare.** Nestled in the Marina di Praia cove, this landmark
SOUTHERN restaurant and hotel is set in a rustic flagstone structure, once a dry
ITALIAN haul for boats, partly open to the sea breezes on one side with an open kitchen on the other. Inside are country-style wooden tables, netting, and ceiling baskets, while outside, colorful boats, peasant dwellings, and the chasm's sheer rock walls catch the eye. The hotel's small rooms have tile floors, windows opening to terraces overlooking the gulf, and a few antique touches. ⊠ *Via Marina di Praia* 🕾 *089/874091* ⊕ *www. alfonsoamare.it* ⤳ *16 rooms* ♿ *In-hotel: Restaurant, bar* ⊟ *AE, DC, MC, V* ⊙ *Closed mid-Nov.–Feb.* ⑩ *MAP.*

$$$ 🖬 **Onda Verde.** Strikingly built on a rock dramatically jutting over the
★ tiny cove of Marina dei Praia, this highly picturesque and popular hotel overlooks a Saracen tower and coastal ridges. Terraces overhang the sea, and common rooms and dining room feature panoramic glass walls and marble flooring. Later, you can climb down a winding path to the beach, where daily boat excursions leave for Positano, Capri, and Ischia. Several minutes away by footpath is the coast's most legendary disco, L'Africana, but you won't hear any music or disturbance from there—if you like to party, you can climb right into bed without having to drive. **Pros:** with these services there's no need to go into town at all; great views. **Cons:** a bit of a walk to get here; not great for mingling as you may never leave the hotel. ⊠ *Via Terra Mare 3* 🕾 *089/874143* ⊕ *www.ondaverde.it* ⤳ *26 rooms* ♿ *In-hotel: Restaurant, bar* ⊟ *MC, V* ⊙ *Closed Nov.–mid-Mar.* ⑩ *MAP.*

NIGHTLIFE

Off a mile-long footpath from the Marina del Praia—or accessed via an elevator from Statale 163—**L'Africana** (Via Torre a Mare 🕾 *089/874042*) is a classic from the 1960s, a golden-oldie on the coast. Jackie O danced one night away on the glass-aquarium floor. With open-to-the-sea atmosphere, an indoor boat that's a buffet of antipasti, animal prints, and wildish shows with partial nudity, you can eat lightly, drink heavily, and dance until the Gulf of Salerno sunrise. If coming from Positano or Amalfi, you can also get here on one of the nightclub's boats.

VALLONE DI FURORE

2 km (1 mi) southeast of Marina di Praia, 2 km (1 mi) west of Conca dei Marini.

GETTING HERE

By car, take the SS163 (Amalfitana) from outside Sorrento or Salerno. There's SITA bus service from Positano and Amalfi.

EXPLORING

Fodor'sChoice The enchanting hamlet of **Marina di Furore**—perhaps 10 houses?—
★   beckons as you pass over it on a towering viaduct. This tchotchke
of a fishermen's village (once a favored hideout of bandits and smug-
glers, including the notorious Fra' Diavolo) seems sculpted out of rock
walls; once mills, these houses (known as *monazzeni,* "places to live in
solitude") and the adjoining paper mill were abandoned when the tiny
harbor here closed. After the hamlet was discovered by vacationers, the
municipality moved in, restoring and gloriously painting it in pastels.
The paper mill is now a *museo della carta,* and the hamlet now calls
itself an "ecomuseum" with short botanical trails laid out (down the
steps, upstream from the viaduct). It's apparently possible to see peregrine falcons here, as well as some rare species of ancient plants found
nowhere else in the region. The Lilliputian settlement is at the base of
a high-wall fissure in the limestone mountains—sometimes hyped as a
fjord. The name is from the "furor" of stormy water that once rushed
down the Torrente Schiato here, now a mere trickle—with a substantial
effluent load from Agerola upstream and uncleared rock slides creating
a less-than-gorgeous gorge, though a recent cleanup operation has made
a significant change. From the beach, the *sentiero della Volpe Pescatrice*
("the fox-fish's path") and the *sentiero dei Pipistrelli Impazziti* ("the
mad bats' path") climb up some 3,000 steps (but who's counting?)
and were built to portage goods from the harbor to the town of Furore
above it. The hard walk up takes a couple of hours, as you climb from
sea to sky. To see any of this by car, you have to pay to park in the layby
some 450 yards away on the Amalfi side of the gorge, just before the
gas station. Unless you're in pretty good shape, it's better to boat to the
beach and just rubberneck.

6

CONCA DEI MARINI

Fodor'sChoice *2 km (1 mi) east of Vallone di Furore, 4 km (2½ mi) southwest of*
★   *Amalfi.*

GETTING HERE
By car, take the SS163 (Amalfitana) from outside Sorrento or Salerno.
There's SITA bus service from Positano and Amalfi.

EXPLORING
In her 2001 book of memories, *Happy Times,* Lee Radziwill declares
that when she thinks of paradise, it is Conca dei Marini that first comes
to mind. If you stay overnight here, we're sure you'll agree. Long a
favorite of the off-duty famous and rich, the town hides many of its
charms, as any sublime forgetaway should. On the most dramatic promontory of the coast, Conca dei Marini (the name means "seafarers'
basin") was originally a province of ancient Rome called Cossa and
later became an important naval base of the Amalfi Republic. Much
later, it became a retreat for high-profile types, including John Steinbeck,
Gianni Agnelli, and Carlo Ponti, who erected a white villa here by the
sea (built for his first wife, not Sophia). You can see why: the green of
terraced gardens competes with (and loses to) the blue sea, while the
town's distinctive houses flanking the ridges have thick, white walls,

Conca dei Marini's 16th-century Watch Tower stands above the Lido Capo di Conca.

with cupolas, balconies, and external staircases, testimony to former Arabic, Moorish, and Greek settlements. Below, on Capo di Conca, a promontory once used as a cemetery, a 16th-century coastal tower dramatically overlooks the sea. On a curve in the road sits the village's most famous attraction, the Emerald Grotto. Coral is still harvested in the waters off the coast here, while boats fish for sardines and squid through the night, their prow lanterns twinkling as if stars had slipped into the sea.

★ The main Conca dei Marini SITA bus stop is directly in front of the Hotel Belvedere. From here head west along the highway to the Sacred Tower and **Lido Capo di Conca** (☎ *089/831512* ⊕ *www.capodiconca. it*) a privately run beach with bar and restaurant within the tower's shadow. Farther along you reach the Emerald Grotto. To the east, you can walk along the highway for views of Conca's harbor and lagoon. But the must-do is a jaunt down the staircase to the left of the Hotel Belvedere. This leads past some gorgeous houses to the dollhouse-size **harbor of Santa Maria della Neve,** one of the most idyllic sights along the entire coast. Closed for many years because of a major landside several years ago, its beach and marina have now reopened, and its darling little Chapel of Santa Maria della Neve should not be missed. From the Amalfi Drive high atop the hill, a view of this harbor is one of the coast's top photo-ops.

For Conca *in excelsis*, however, head up the mountainside to the northern reaches of the town (the road leads upward opposite the Hotel Belvedere, and then you can opt to take the gently climbing roads or the steeper staircase ever upward). Your reward as you climb up the hillside roads and steep scalinatelle is three stunningly sited churches. The first is neo-Byzantine **San Pancrazio**, set in a lovely palm-tree garden. Opposite this church, in the direction of Positano, is a road leading to a sky-high lookout over the coast. Back at San Pancrazio, head up the Scalinatella San Pancrazio to the tiny town piazza.

★ To the east along the cliff-side road is the sky-swimming church and **Convento di Santa Rosa**, which perches, "closer to heaven than to earth," on a bluff 1,000 feet over the sea, looking like some sort of Amalfitan Xanadu. Built as a theological university in the 15th century, and transformed into a Dominican monastery in the 16th century, the convent was abandoned in the 1920s and subsequently renovated into an albergo-inn. Alas, the owners closed up shop, but it is currently being renovated by an American conglomerate, and is expected to open as a luxury hotel in 2009. Its **Chiesa di Santa Rosa**, a 14th-century church, is the site for numerous recitals hosted by the Ravello Concert Society, so attending a performance is the only way you can get past the gates these days. For information, contact the **Ravello Concert Society** (☎089/858149 ⊕www.ravelloarts.org). In the 18th century the nuns of the convent created one of the great local dishes, *sfogliata Santa Rosa* (a sweet cream-cheese-and-ricotta pastry shaped like a nun's hood). The mother superior distributed this delicacy free back then. Today, on Sunday and holy days, the pastries are baked, and savored, by locals and visiting revelers. You can head up to the Santa Rosa bluff by following the road leading up into Conca from the coastline, but if you want to take in the view of the convent from adjacent hills, use the mountaintop highway connecting Amalfi to Sorrento, which (unfortunately) runs right by the convent gates.

★ Heading back to the town piazza from the Convento di Santa Rosa, take Via Due Maggio and Via Roma to **Sant' Antonio di Padova**—an elegant Neoclassical white church spectacularly cantilevered hundreds of feet over the coastline on a stone parapet. The church is only open for Sunday-morning services, but you might ask locals if someone can open the church with a key for a quick visit (*"Dov'è la persona che ci può far visitare la chiesa?"*). For those who want to see churches in coastal villages, this may be the only way to gain entry.

On the outskirts of Conca dei Marini, the **Grotta dello Smeraldo** *(Emerald Grotto)* is a much-touted stop for day-trippers. The rather tacky sign on the road and the squadron of tour buses may put you off, but it's definitely worth a stop. Steps and an elevator bring you almost to sea level, but more delightful is to arrive by boat, which you can hire at just about any port up and down the coast. The karstic cave was originally part of the shore, but the lowest end sank into the sea when the peninsula subsided (the coast remains active, so it may eventually sink even lower—or rise). Intense greenish light filters into the water from an arch below sea level and is reflected off the walls of the cave, quite living up to emerald expectations. You wait to board a large rowboat with about 20 fellow passengers, and then you set off with a guide, gondolier fashion, through the smallish cavern filled with huge stalactites and stalagmites. Don't let the boatman's constant spiel detract from the half-hour experience—this is one of those tours that points out stalactites that look like Lincoln (for Americans), Napoléon (for the French), and Garibaldi (for the Italians) with an underwater nativity scene for the grande finale; just tune out and enjoy the sparkles, shapes, and Harry Winston–esque color. A tourist from Amalfi raved in a hotel log in 1858 that the cave ". . . can compete with Vesuvius," but it was forgotten about for years afterward until the grotto was rediscovered by a local fisherman in the 1930s. The light is best from noon to 3 PM, which is fortunately when hordes of potential visitors will be tucking into their pasta elsewhere. At Christmas there's a special celebration conducted around the underwater crèche. ⊠ *Beyond Punta Acquafetente by boat, or off Amalfi Dr.* ☎ *089/871107 Amalfi tourist board* ⊠ *€5* ☉ *Daily 9–3:30.*

WHERE TO STAY

$$$-$$$$
★
Belvedere. One of the coast's most beloved hotels, the Belvedere is really not a hotel but a "home." This is the sort of place where guests ask for the room their great-grandparents favored. Happily, everyone, not just regulars, is treated like family here, and you'll find it difficult to say good-bye to the remarkably friendly and helpful staff. Set in one of the grande dame villas of Conca dei Marini, featuring salons top-heavy with overstuffed sofas and a ravishing pool area, as well a rocky beach, the Belvedere is handily located for exploring Conca dei Marini, as it's equidistant from the town's lagoon and Saracen tower. A shuttle service will take you to Amalfi. **Pros:** ideal location, with bus stop outside; a home away from home. **Cons:** be careful as you step out of the door—the entrance is on the busy Amalfi Drive; no elevator to the beach. ⊠ *Via Smeraldo 19* ☎ *089/831282* ⊕ *www.belvederehotel.it* ⇆ *36 rooms* ⌂ *In-hotel: restaurant, bar, pool, parking (no fee), some pets allowed* ⊟ *AE, DC, MC, V* ☉ *Closed mid-Oct.–mid-Apr.* ⦿ *FAP.*

$$$-$$$$
★
Il Saraceno. Gothic, Arabic, Oriental—and Las Vegas—influences combine to form this gorgeous extravaganza set on a chunk of cliff 3 km (2 mi) from Amalfi (note that this is its official address, but the hotel is really just a few steps away from Conca dei Marini). Bordering on kitch, the evocatively exotic decor, which refers to Saracen pirates who roamed this coast centuries ago, begins in the lobby adorned with museum-quality 19th-century Orientalist oil paintings and antiques. Below, night-illuminated garden terraces descend the entire hillside to the enormous private beach, which features a saltwater pool. Dining

options include a Romanesque cellar with candelabra and fireplace, and a formal restaurant called Castello, an alfresco terrace under a vine-covered lattice. Mosaic floors, elaborate antique lighting fixtures, a medieval warrior in full armor, and gilded murals are accents, and guest rooms have crown-molded ceilings, rich colors, antiques, and terraces with floor-to-ceiling window panoramas. The hotel also maintains a private Romanesque stone chapel. Whew. **Pros:** ideal for living out your pirate fantasy; gorgeous garden terraces. **Cons:** a little too kitch for some; rather distant from the action. ⊠ *Via Augustariccio 33, Conca dei Marini/Amalfi* ☎*089/831148* ⊕*www.saraceno.it* ⬎*56 rooms* ⚫*In-hotel: 2 restaurants, 2 bars, pool, beachfront, parking (no fee)* ⊟*AE, DC, MC, V* ⊘*Closed Nov.–Mar.* ¶⊚*FAP.*

$$–$$$ ⊞ **Le Terrazze.** As opposed to the yesteryear glow of the Hotel Belvedere, this place, a few feet down the road, is a spankingly modern alternative. The *Wallpaper* crowd might love this place for its sleek, retro-chic '60s style; you half expect to see Monica Vitti and Alain Delon haunting the shadowy corridors, waiting for their cue from director Michelangelo Antonioni. Most rooms have their own balconies, which allow you to look down across the bay at the grand villa built by Carlo Ponti, and—best of all—you are just a few staircases away from Conca's adorable harbor, Jacqueline Kennedy's favorite beach. Guest rooms, delightfully clean and airy, are accented with local Vietri majolica tiles. For those seeking *tranquillità*, this is a fine option. **Pros:** right above the adorable harbor; a view fit for a movie star. **Cons:** so many steps to the harbor; no restaurant. ⊠ *Via Smeraldo 11* ☎*089/831290* ⊕*www.hotelleterrazze. it* ⬎*25 rooms* ⚫*In-hotel: Bar* ⊟*AE, DC, MC, V* ⊘*Closed Nov.– Mar.* ¶⊚*BP.*

AMALFI: FIRST OF THE SEA REPUBLICS

18 km (11 mi) southeast of Positano, 32 km (20 mi) west of Salerno.

At first glance, it's hard to imagine that this resort destination, set in a verdant valley of the Lattari Mountains, with its cream-color and pastel-hue buildings tightly packing a gorge on the Bay of Salerno, was in the 11th and 12th centuries the seat of the Amalfi Maritime Republic, one of the world's great naval powers, and a sturdy rival of Genoa and Pisa for control of the Mediterranean. The harbor, which once launched the greatest fleet in Italy, now bobs with ferries and blue-and-white fishing boats. The main street, lined with leather shops and *pasticcerie,* has replaced a raging mountain torrent, and terraced hills where *banditti* (bandits) once roamed now flaunt the green and gold of lemon groves. Bearing testimony to its great trade with Tunis, Tripoli, and Algiers, Amalfi remains honeycombed with Arab-Sicilian cloisters and covered passages that suggest Asian caravansaries. In a way Amalfi has become great again, showing off its medieval glory days with sea pageants, convents-turned-hotels, ancient paper mills, covered streets, and its mosquelike cathedral.

A plaque under Amalfi's Porta Marina bears this inscription: "THE JUDGMENT DAY, WHEN AMALFITANS GO TO HEAVEN, WILL BE A DAY LIKE ANY OTHER." Visitors to this charming city, set in a verdant valley of the

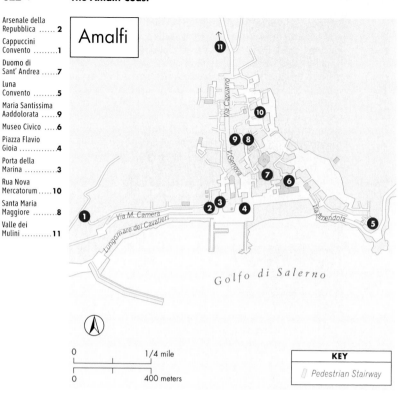

KEY

🕅 *Pedestrian Stairway*

Lattari Mountains, will soon understand what it means. For sheer picturesqueness, it can't be beat. Drinking in the vista of the town against
the sea from the balcony of the Cappuccini Convento is like getting an
advance on paradise. Amalfi's origin is clouded. One legend says that
a general of Constantine's army, named Amalfo, settled here in 320;
another tale has it that Roman noblemen from the village of Melphi (in
Latin, "a Melphi"), fleeing after the fall of the empire, were first in these
parts, shipwrecked in the 4th century on their way to Constantinople.
Myth becomes fact by the 6th century, when Amalfi is inscribed in the
archives as a Byzantine diocese, and the historical pageant really begins.
Its geographic position was good defense, and the distance from Constantinople made its increasing autonomy possible. Continuously ham-
mered by the Lombards and others, in 839 it rose against and finally
sacked nearby Salerno, to which its inhabitants had been deported. In
the 10th century, Amalfi constructed many churches and monasteries
and was ruled by judges, later called doges—self-appointed dukes who
amassed vast wealth and power.

From the 9th century until 1101, Amalfi remained linked to Byzantium
but also was increasingly independent and prosperous, perhaps the
major trading port in southern Italy. Its influence loomed large, thanks
to its creation of the Tavola Amalfitana, a code of maritime laws taken

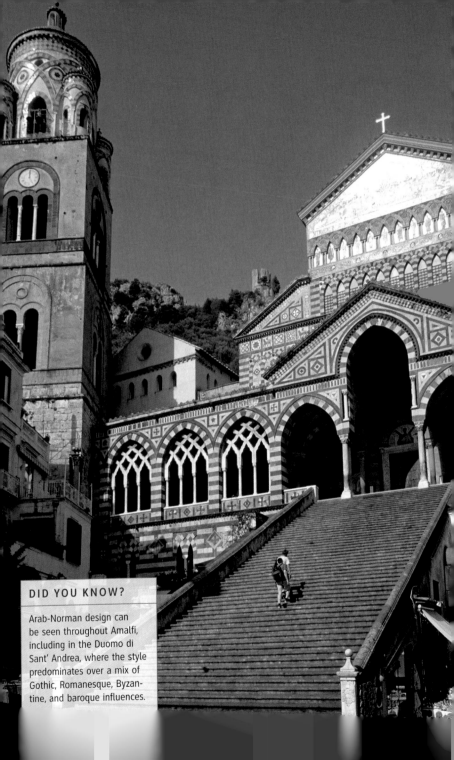

The piazza outside Amalfi's Duomo is a lively gathering place.

up by most medieval-era kingdoms. Amalfi created its own gold and silver coins—or *tari*, engraved with the cross of Amalfi—and ruled a vast territory. With trade extending as far as Alexandria and Constantinople—where a large colony of Amalfitan merchants resided—it became Italy's first maritime republic, ahead of rivals Pisa, Venice, and Genoa; the population swelled to about 100,000, many of them seafarers and traders. As William of Apulia wrote in the 11th century, ". . . No other city is richer in silver, cloth and gold. A great many navigators live in this city . . . famous almost throughout the world as those who travel to where there is something worth buying."

But the days of wine and doges were about to end. In the 11th century Robert Guisgard of Normandy—in the duplicitous spirit of politicos to this day—first aided, then sacked the town, and the Normans from Sicily returned, after a short Amalfitan revolt, in the 12th century. Then, when the Republic of Pisa twice conquered it, Amalfi fell into decline, hastened by a horrific storm in 1343, then by an indirect blow from Christopher Columbus's discoveries, which opened the world beyond to competing trade routes. By the 18th century, the town had sunk into gloom, looking to its lemons and handmade paper for survival. After the state road was built by Ferdinand, the Bourbon king of Naples, in the 19th century, Amalfi evolved into a tourist destination, drawing Grand Tour–era travelers like Richard Wagner, Henry Wadsworth Longfellow, and Henrik Ibsen, all of whom helped spread Amalfi's fame.

GETTING HERE

By car, take the SS163 (Amalfitana) from outside Sorrento or Salerno, or take the Angri exit on the A3 motorway and cross the mountainous Valico di Chiunsi. SITA bus from Sorrento/Salerno, summer ferries from Naples/Sorrento/Salerno. You can purchase tickets prior to boarding at Bar Sita or any port-side bar, travel agency, or tobacco shop displaying a SITA sticker; all SITA buses leave Amalfi from Piazza Flavio Gioia. The special express bus to Naples departs every morning at 8:05 (not Sunday) and 10:15 AM from the port; catching this bus makes for an easy and scenic ride back to the city, allowing you to bypass a transfer from bus to the Circumvesuviana railway in Sorrento.

VISITOR INFORMATION

Azienda Autonoma di Cura, Soggiorno e Turismo ✉ *Corso Reppubliche Marinare 27, Amalfi* ☎ *089/871107* ⊕ *www.amalfitouristoffice.it*) in Amalfi is open weekdays 8:30–1:30 and 3–5 (until 8 mid-June–mid-September); Saturday 9–1.

EXPLORING AMALFI

Amalfi's compact tourist center is split between the bustling *lungomare* (waterfront), with its public and private transportation hubs, and the piazza in front of the Duomo. Parking is a big problem, as the tiny lot on the sea front (€3 per hour) fills up fast. A huge car park is being built into the rock 400 yards east of the town, which may alleviate the situation. Traveling here via ferry and bus or staying in a hotel with a parking garage are good ideas. Once you explore the main sights near the waterfront, take off and explore the souklike center, then escape to the outskirts and the terraced hills of the Valle dei Mulini, site of Amalfi's ancient paper mills. At a little waterfall at the very north of the town, beyond the Museo della Carta, look to the left for a set of scalinatelle and climb the 100-plus steps; follow a footpath to the right, where you're in the middle of a lemon grove. If you buy a fresh lemon along the way—its leaves will be intact and its taste sweeter than you're accustomed to—and down its slices with a pinch of salt, you'll be passing time as the locals have since the age of its republic.

TOP ATTRACTIONS

① **Cappuccini Convento.** Currently closed and undergoing restoration work by new owners (rumor is that it will reopen in 2010), this fabled medieval monastery enjoys a magnificent hilltop perch and was a noted stop for Grand Tour–era travelers. Long famous for its gardens, its ½-km-long (¼-mi-long) terrace over Amalfi's harbor, and its Arab-Sicilian cloister, the monastery was founded by Cistercian monks in the 13th century as the Convento di S. Pietro della Canonica. Then abandoned, the complex was taken over by the Capuchins in 1583, only to be transformed into a hotel in the mid-19th century when the king of Naples suppressed the religious orders. Immortalized in postcards and paintings, the view of Amalfi's waterfront from the hotel terrace became one of the first travel icons of the 19th century. Henry Wadsworth Longfellow composed a poem to celebrate its beauty and Richard Wagner forsook his guest room to camp out under the stars.

FodorsChoice
★

In the recent past, visitors could stroll through the monastery and let the centuries unwind: the 13th-century cloister has the intertwined Arabic columns of the Amalfi cathedral's great Paradise Cloister, the little church is a Rococo confection, and the spirit-warm hallways and salons were barely changed from the 19th century. Let us hope they survive the ongoing renovation to bring them all into the 21st century. ⊠ *Hotel Cappuccini Convento, Via Annunziatella 46* ☏ *089/871877.*

❼ Duomo di Sant' Andrea. Complicated, grand, delicate, and dominating, ★ the 9th-century Amalfi cathedral has been remodeled over the years with Romanesque, Byzantine, Gothic, and Baroque elements, but retains a predominantly Arab-Norman style. Cross and crescent seem to be wed here: the campanile, spliced with Saracen colors and the intricate tile work of High Barbery, looks like a minaret wearing a Scheherazadian turban, the facade conjures up a striped burnoose, and its Paradise Cloister is an Arab-Sicilian spectacular.

The power of Amalfi is evident in the approach to the cathedral, set atop 62 broad steps that lead to a mosaic facade, redone in the 19th century, and framed by bands, arches, and patterned squares. The imposing bronze doors, the first in Italy, were cast in Constantinople before 1066 and signed by Simeon of Syria; they were commissioned by the leader of the large Amalfitan colony there. Silver incrustations on the doors, now difficult to see, are images of Christ, Mary, and saints.

Visitors are now channeled first into the adjoining **Chiostro del Paradiso** (Cloister of Paradise): built around 1266 for Bishop Augustariccio as a burial ground for Amalfi's elite, it's one of the architectural treasures of southern Italy. Its flower-and-palm-filled quadrangle has a series of exceptionally delicate, intertwining arches on slender double columns in a combination of Byzantine and Arabian styles. Note the geometric patterns of colored mosaics in the walls, comprising parts of former pillars and pulpits of the earlier church. Of special note is a 14th-century crucifixion scene by Roberto d'Oderisio, a student of Giotto. The striking 12th-century bell tower in front of the complex has a Romanesque base and an elaborate yellow-and-green-tile top with arches in the local style, a round center surrounded by four smaller cupolas.

The chapel at the back of the cloister leads into the earlier (9th century) basilica. The structure, called the Basilica of the Crucifix, is in Romanesque style, with a nave, two aisles, and a high, deep apse. Note the 14th-century crucifixion scene by a student of Giotto. This section has now been transformed into a museum, housing sarcophagi, sculpture, Neapolitan goldsmiths' artwork, and other treasures from the cathedral complex.

Steps from the basilica lead down into the crypt of St. Andrew. The cathedral above was built in the 13th century to house the saint's bones, which came from Constantinople and supposedly exuded a miraculous liquid believers call the "manna of St. Andrew." Amalfi's cathedral had always lured pious devotees—from Francis of Assisi to Pope Urban IV—but after the 14th-century manna manifestation the pilgrim trade really picked up. The saint's remains (his head was returned from the Vatican in 2008, to coincide with the 800th anniversary of the arrival of the saint's relics in Amalfi) are kept under the 13th-century high altar in this exceptionally beautiful crypt adorned with marble statues sculpted by Pietro Bernini, father of the famed Gianlorenzo Bernini.

Following the one-way traffic up to the cathedral itself, you finally get to admire the elaborate polychrome marbles, and painted, coffered ceilings from its 18th-century restoration; art historians shake their head over this renovation, as the original decoration of the apse must have been one of the wonders of the Middle Ages. However, the original basilica plan has been preserved. The first chapel on the left of the main entrance has a red porphyry baptismal font, supposedly crafted from the ruins of ancient Paestum. Other treasures include a mother-of-pearl cross given by the people of Jerusalem in 1930, in gratitude for Amalfi's help in establishing a 2,000-bed hospital there in 1112, which later became the first military and religious order, the Knights of St. John. ⊠ *Piazza Duomo* ☎*089/871324* ⊠*€2.50* ⊙*Daily: Mar.–June and Oct., 9–6:45; July–Sept., 9–7:30; Nov.–mid-Jan. 10–1 and 2:30–4:30, closed mid-Jan.–Feb. (daily services excepted).*

⑩ Rua Nova Mercatorum. Also known as Via dei Mercanti, evocative Rua Nova was the main thoroughfare of medieval Amalfi, when the main road was a raging torrent, and it remains the most fascinating "street" in town. Claustrophobes, beware: it's completely covered, like a tunnel, but is especially wonderful when the light from alleys and windows plays on its white walls. Stretching almost the length of the main street, it ends at a medieval-era *contrada*, or neighborhood, with a fountain known as *Capo di Ciuccio* (donkey's head), where mules would refesh themselves after the climb down from the hills. ⊠ *Adjacent to Via Pietro Capuano.*

⑪ Valle dei Mulini. The Valley of the Mills, uphill from town, was for centuries Amalfi's center for papermaking, an ancient trade learned from the Arabs (who learned it from the Chinese). Beginning in the 12th century, former macaroni mills were converted to the production of paper made from cotton and linen, among the first in Europe to do so. In 1211 Frederick II of Sicily prohibited this lighter, more readable paper from being used in the preparation of official documents, favoring traditional sheepskin parchment; but by 1811 more than a dozen mills here, with more along the coast, were humming. Natural waterpower ensured that the handmade paper was cost-effective, but catastrophic flooding in 1954 closed most of the mills for good, and many of them have now been converted into private housing. The **Museo della Carta** (Museum of Paper) opened in 1971 in a 15th-century mill; paper samples, tools of the trade, old machinery, and the audiovisual presentation are all enlightening. The admission price gets you a guided tour in English. A 20-minute stroll from the Piazza Duomo will take you to the valley via the main thoroughfare of Via Genoa, turning onto Via Capuano, at the edge of town. ⊠ *Via delle Cartiere 23* ☎*089/8304561* ⊠*€3.50* ⊕*www.museodellacarta.it* ⊙*Mar.–Oct., daily 10–6:30; Nov.–Feb., Tues.–Sun. 10–3 PM.*

CLOSE UP

Experiencing the Amalfi Coast: Boating

People take to boats here with the ease others use around buses and subways. Ferries and hydrofoils run on regular schedules during high season. The waters are calm and beckoning, and boating for pleasure frees you from the tension of coastal driving, giving a different perspective on the coast, so try to arrange to spend at least one day on the water. Bright red-and-blue fishing boats are for hire by the day or for a few hours at the major harbors of Sorrento, Positano, and Amalfi, and by almost any beach wherever you see fishermen.

Boats can take you around the Sorrento area, to the Emerald Grotto, to Capri and offshore islets, to major

towns, and otherwise inaccessible cove beaches. They will drop you off and pick you up, or stay with you, depending on your budget. Look for established sites on major beaches and come a day or so ahead to reserve and bargain, especially if you're with a group.

Pricing could be around €20 an hour, more or less, depending on the market, the season, and your talent at haggling. If in doubt, ask for recommendations about local boatmen at your hotel or at the town tourist board. And don't expect fishermen to speak much English; you'll have to learn to speak with your hands, as many Italians do.

WORTH NOTING

2 **Arsenale della Repubblica.** From the middle of the 11th century, Amalfi's center of shipbuilding, custom houses, and warehouses was the Arsenale, today the only (partially) preserved medieval shipyard in southern Italy. Ships and galleys up to 80 feet long, equipped with up to 120 oars, were built at this largest arsenal of any medieval maritime republic. The boat now used for the historical regatta (held every four years, next in Amalfi in June 2012) and other ship models are kept in the arsenal's two large Gothic halls, which also hosts occasional exhibitions. Completely renovated in 2008, 10 of the original 22 stone piers remain; the others were destroyed by storms and changes in the sea level on this ever-active coast. ⊠ *South of Piazza dei Dogi, at Via Camera, by waterfront* ☎ *089/8736211* ⊗ *Mon.–Sat. 6–10, daily in Aug.*

5 **Luna Convento.** Legendarily founded by none other than St. Francis of Assisi, the Luna Convento was built in the 13th century and retains its famous cloister, with distinctive Arab-Sicilian arcaded columns and a crypt with frescoes. Transformed into the earliest hotel on the Amalfi Coast in the early 19th century, the hotel was where Henrik Ibsen wrote a large chunk of *A Doll's House.* The hotel also owns the famous Torre Saracena (now home to a bar and nightspot) that sits across the highway and stands guard over Amalfi's seaside promontory. ⊠ *Via Pantaleone Comite 19* ☎ *089/871002* ⊕ *www.lunahotel.it.*

9 **Maria Santissima Addolorata.** This church is adjacent to the confraternity founded in 1765 to organize Amalfi's Good Friday celebrations. The entrance gate bears a late-Gothic bas-relief of the Crucifixion, once belonging to nobility from the nearby village of Scala and identified by its coat of arms at the foot of the cross. The interior is neoclassical, with a harmonious scale and coffered ceiling; note the 16th-century marble Madonna and Child in the sacristy. The church is only open on Saturday evening for 7 PM Mass (6:30 November–March). ⊠ *Largo Santa Maria Maggiore.*

6 Museo Civico. The Municipal Museum of Amalfi, sharing space with the municipal offices, contains artifacts from Amalfi's medieval period, including paintings, ancient coins, banners, and jeweled costumes. The highlight is the original 66-chapter draft of the code of the *Tavole Amalfitana,* the sea laws and customs of the ancient republic, used throughout the Italian Mediterranean from the 13th to the 16th century. The Tavole established everything from prices for boat hires to procedures to be followed in case of shipwreck. Long one of the treasures of the Imperial Library of Vienna, the draft was returned to Amalfi after more than 500 years. Note the ceramic panel on the south outside wall of the museum, between Corso delle Repubbliche Marinare and Piazza del Municipio, created by Diodoro Cossa in the 1970s. The scenes provide an overview of local history: Roman refugees establishing themselves in nearby Scala in the 4th century; the founding of Amalfi by these same Romans; Amalfi's commercial and diplomatic role in the Mediterranean; the arrival of St. Andrew's body; the invention of the maritime compass; and other historic events. ⊠ *Piazza Municipio 6* 🕾 *089/8736211* 🎫 *Free* 🕙 *Weekdays 8:30–1:30, Tues. and Thurs. also 3–6 PM.*

4 Piazza Flavio Gioia. A statue, set in an ironically disorienting traffic roundabout in front of the harbor, honors the Amalfitan credited with inventing the maritime compass in 1302. Many say it was the Chinese who invented the compass, passing the idea along to the Arabs, who traded with Amalfi; Gioia may have adapted it for sea use (some even believe there was no such person as Gioia). ⊠ *On waterfront.*

3 Porta della Marina. This gateway "door" to the harbor bears a huge, flaking ceramic panel, created by Renato Rossi in the 1950s, commemorating the trade routes of the republic during the Middle Ages. For one example, ships loaded up with timber from Italy, traded it in North Africa, then used the gold obtained from those sales to buy gems, spices, and silks in Asia to trade in Italy. ⊠ *Across from Piazza Flavio Gioia, next to arsenal.*

8 Santa Maria Maggiore. Next door to Maria Santissima Addolorata, this was constructed by Duke Mansone I in 986, as inscribed on a capital at the entrance, the church has a Byzantine layout, although a 16th-century overhaul inverted the entrance and high altar, and the decoration is now mostly Baroque. The remains of San Felice and an 18th-century crèche scene are worth noting. The campanile dates from the 12th century. ⊠ *Largo Santa Maria Maggiore, near cathedral.*

WHERE TO EAT

$$
SOUTHERN
ITALIAN
✕ **Al Teatro.** Once a children's theater, this informal white-stucco restaurant in the medieval quarter is 50 steps above the main drag and most charming. A house specialty is grilled squid and calamari with mint sauce, reflecting the position of the place—suspended between sea and mountains. Try also the *Scialatielli al Teatro,* with tomatoes and

eggplant. The pizzas, from their wood oven, are terrific. ⊠ *Via E. Marini 19* 🕾*089/872473* ⊟*AE, MC, V* ⊗*Closed Wed. and Jan.–mid-Feb.*

$$$ ✕**Da Gemma.** Cognoscenti have sung the praises of this understated
SOUTHERN landmark since 1872. Tile floors, white tablecloths, and a terrace set
ITALIAN above the main street are soothing elements. The kitchen glistens, the
menu is printed on local handmade paper, and Italian foodies appre-
ciate dishes such as *tubettoni alla masaniello* (tiny pieces of pasta
with capers, mussels, and prawns). For dessert try the local specialty:
eggplant and chocolate. ⊠ *Via Fra Gerardo Sasso 9* 🕾*089/871345*
⊕*www.trattoriadagemma.com* ⌲*Reservations essential* ⊟*AE, DC,
MC, V* ⊗*Closed Wed. and mid-Jan.–Feb.*

$$$$ ✕**Eolo.** One of the most sophisticated restaurants on the Amalfi Coast,
SOUTHERN Eolo is run by the owners of the Marina Riviera hotel. The decor is
ITALIAN suavely tranquil—white-cove ceilings, Romanesque columns, mounted
★ starfish—although the kitchen is anything but . . . it tosses out superb
gastronomic delights. Many dishes are fetchingly adorned with blos-
soms and other visual allures, but nothing compares to the view of
Amalfi's harbor from one of the tables in Eolo's picture-window alcove.
If you don't land one of these, don't fret—the entire room is pretty
enough as it is. ⊠ *Via Pantaleone Comite 3* 🕾*089/871241* ⌲*Reserva-
tions essential* ⊟*AE, MC, V* ⊗*Closed Nov.–Mar. and Tues.*

$ ✕**Il Chiostro.** Just beside the Duomo, up the steps to the left, you can
SOUTHERN dine alfresco in the narrow alley or in the tiny piazza farther up, or sit
ITALIAN inside the cloister, with another room downstairs. The cuisine here is
casareccia, or home cooking. The menu includes the ubiquitous *scial-
atielli ai frutti di mare* (seafood pasta), with fresh fish being a specialty.
You can also try their excellent pizza. The owners will offer you a glass
of their homemade *limoncello* to top off your meal. ⊠ *Via dei Prefetturi
2* 🕾*089/873380* ⊟*AE, DC, MC, V* ⊗*Closed mid-Nov.–mid-Mar.*

$$ ✕**Il Tari.** Locals highly recommend this cozy little ristorante named after
SOUTHERN the ancient coin of the Amalfi Republic and a few minutes' walk north
ITALIAN of the Duomo. In an ex-stable, appealing touches include local art, red
tablecloths, old photos, and tile floors—not to mention wood-oven-
baked thin-crust pizza with fresh sauces, and pasta specialties including *scialatielli alla Saracena,* long spaghetti-style pasta seemingly laden
with everything you can imagine from the sea. ⊠ *Via P. Capuano 9–11*
🕾*089/871832* ⊟*AE, DC, MC, V* ⊗*Closed Nov. and Dec. and Tues.*

$$$ ✕**La Caravella.** Cobalt-blue napery, antiques, tall candles, lace table-
SOUTHERN cloths, floral curtains, marble floors, and Andrea Bocelli's golden voice
ITALIAN on the sound system make this the most romantic restaurant in Amalfi.
This once drew the most gilded guest list in town, including such fans
as Giovanni Agnelli and Federico Fellini. Today, a tasting menu is
available, but don't miss out on the antipasti—especially the slices of
fish grilled in lemon leaves—and the *panzerottini neri* (ravioli stuffed
with ricotta cheese and squid) or the *vellutata di limone* (lemon sauce
with which the fish are dressed). There is also an art gallery displaying
ceramics from Vietri sul Mare. ⊠ *Via Matteo Camera 12, near Arsenale*
🕾*089/871029* ⊕*www.ristorantelacaravella.it* ⌲*Reservations essen-
tial* ⊟*AE, MC, V* ⊗*Closed Nov. and Dec. and Tues.*

Amalfi's Luscious Lemons

Lemons as big as oranges, and oranges as big as grapefruits, and are cultivated on the seemingly endless net-covered pergolas of the Amalfi Coast. From linguine with lemon at trattorias to lemon soufflés at fancy restaurants, the yellow citrus is everywhere, and all parts are used, as can be seen from the delicious habit of baking raisins, figs, or pieces of cheese wrapped in lemon leaves, bound up with thin red thread.

Not only are lemons a main component of meals and drinks, but they are used as a remedy for everything from flu to bunions. But the most renowned end product is that local digestif known as limoncello, which captures in a bottle the color, fragrance, and taste of those tart-sweet lemons. Drink it cold in a tiny, frosty glass or after a shot of hot espresso—a golden memory quenched with each sip.

$$–$$$
SEAFOOD

✕**Lo Smeraldino.** Open since 1949, this airy, popular fish restaurant on Amalfi's almost-emerald waterfront dishes out reasonably priced seafood and *cucina tipica Amalfitana*, such as the tasty penne with tomatoes, cream, eggplant, peppers, basil, and cheese, or excellent simply grilled fish (*grigliata di pesce*). You can see the boats bringing in the day's catch and at night there's pizza on the terrace amid the twinkling lights of hills, sea, and sky. ⊠*Piazzale dei Protontini 1* ☎*089/871070* ▭*AE, DC, MC, V.*

$$
SOUTHERN
ITALIAN

✕**Maccus.** In the heart of medieval Amalfi, with outside seating occupying the small *piazza* outside the churches of Santa Maria Maggiore and the Maria Santissima Addolorata, this gastronomical treat is a testimony to the *maschera* (mask) of Maccus, a lover of good food. Simple seasonal food is prepared by lovers of the craft, using grandma's recipes—try the grilled squid or the buffalo steak. The inside eating area is pianted in vivid yellow and Pompeii red, reflecting the wheat and wine used in this fine restaurant. ⊠ *Largo S. Maria Maggiore 1–3* ☎*089/ 8736385* ⊕*www.maccusamalfi.it* ⌖*Reservations essential* ▭*DC, MC, V* ⊙*Closed Jan. and Feb.*

$$
SOUTHERN
ITALIAN

✕**Stella Maris.** Probably the first restaurant you see on arriving in Amalfi, with its distinctive orange awnings, this boasts a fine location on the beach. Dining outdoors or in front of the glass walls, you can gaze at the fishing boats bob in the bay, or at the sun worshippers on the small beach. The *risotto al pescespada* (rice with swordfish) is a treat, or try a pizza. If you haven't yet worked up an appetite, you can choose an *aperitivo* or cocktail on the terrace. ⊠*Via della Regione 2* ☎*089/872463* ⊕*www.stella-maris.it* ▭*AE, DC, MC, V* ⊙*Closed Nov.–Mar.*

$$
SOUTHERN
ITALIAN

✕**Trattoria da Ciccia-Cielo-Mare-Terra.** Big windows overlook the sky, sea, and land, and there's ample free parking, so this modern seafood restaurant on the Amalfi Drive (approaching from Conca) is a good place to stop if you're driving. Young owner Francesco Cavaliere will give you a warm welcome. After some perfect pasta, finish up with the ricotta-and-pear cake, designed to accompany a tiny glass of well-chilled limoncello.

6

✉ *Via Giovanni Agustariccio 22* ☎*089/831265* ⊟*AE, DC, MC, V* ⊘ *Closed Nov. and Tues.*

WHERE TO STAY

$ **Albergo San Andrea.** With everyone gazing at the magnificent steps
★ leading to Amalfi's cathedral, few turn around to notice that this tiny pensione occupies one of the top spots in town. The cute "Room-with-a-View" lobby is as big as a Victorian closet, while guest rooms range from vast to cozy; most overlook the Duomo, with quieter ones on a side alley. **Pros:** on the main square; best views of Duomo. **Cons:** flight of steps to entrance; rooms very simple. ✉ *Piazza Duomo* ☎*089/871145* ⊕*www.albergosantandrea.it* ↩*9 rooms* ⊟*AE, DC, MC, V* †⊙*EP.*

¢–$$ **Amalfi.** Up a tiny side street not far from the Piazza Duomo, the Amalfi is unassumingly decorated with small, somewhat character-less modern-style rooms (get one with a geranium-filled balcony if you can) without a great view. However, the place's central location, the friendly welcome of the Lucibello family, and the roof terrace where you can breakfast in the warm morning sun, make this a great deal if you want to be in the center of the action while keeping an eye on the budget. **Pros:** great central location; roof terrace. **Cons:** rooms are not very exciting; no access without negotiating steps. ✉ *Via dei Pastai 3* ☎*089/872440* ⊕*www.hamalfi.it* ↩*40 rooms* ⌂*In-hotel: Restaurant, parking (fee), some pets allowed* ⊟ *MC, V* †⊙*FAP.*

$$ **Aurora.** Regarded for its location near the beach of Spiaggia delle Sirene and the fishing harbor, this well-run little hotel is a good deal for sand potatoes who prefer absorbing rays to hiking the highlands. Amid a greenery-filled setting with three levels of arched windows, guest rooms are clean, 16 with water views and private terrace, and although just a flat and easy 10-minute walk from the Duomo, crowds rarely venture to this nook. **Pros:** away from the madding crowds; ideal for a beach-based trip. **Cons:** a bit of a walk to town; the smaller rooms are a bit cramped. ✉ *Piazzale dei Protontini 7, between Scalo d'Oriente and Lungomare dei Cavalieri* ☎*089/871209* ⊕*www.aurora-hotel.it* ↩*29 rooms* ⊟*AE, MC, V* ⊘ *Closed Nov.–Mar.* †⊙*BP.*

$$ **Hotel Floridiana.** Just off the main street, 50 meters from the Duomo, lies the Hotel Floridiana. This was the residence of Pisani in the 12th century, and despite, or rather because of, restoration work in 2004, the surroundings bring you back to those times—look for the frescoed ceiling in the dining room. Rooms are simple, but comfortable, and the owners Agnese and Maria Rosa are extremely helpful and friendly, making you feel right at home in the heart of Amalfi. **Pros:** in the heart of the ancient marine town; friendly owners. **Cons:** the rooms face inward, no sea view. ✉ *Via Brancia 1* ☎*089/8736373* ⊕*www.hotelfloridiana.it* ↩*13 rooms* ⊟*AE, DC, MC, V* †⊙*BP* ⊘ *Closed Nov.–Mar.*

$$$$ **Luna Convento.** Founded as a convent in 1222, allegedly by no less a personage than St. Francis of Assisi, the hotel has been owned by the Barbaro family since 1822 and visited by Otto van Bismarck, Mussolini, Ingrid Bergman, and Tennessee Williams, among other noted figures. One of the restaurants and bar are in the 15th-century Saracen tower, perched on a rock over the sea, providing a view that spans from Capo dei Conca to Capo d'Orso. Coved ceilings, graceful arches, and marble

columns mark the architecture, along with Flemish religious artwork, church and convent artifacts, antique furnishings, and mosaic flooring, all of which mix with modern comforts. The heart of the hotel is the famed southern Romanesque cloisters and the beautiful baroque chapel. Below the tower is a solarium and seawater pool. Ask for a room in the renovated wing, and try to get one with a balcony over Amalfi's bay. The food, alas, does not measure up. **Pros:** staying in a convent: one of *the* Amalfi experiences, a 270-degree view. **Cons:** you need to cross the busy road to get to the pool, the food. ⊠ *Via P. Comite 33* ☎*089/871002* ⊕*www.lunahotel.it* ⤳*43 rooms* ⚲*In-hotel: Restaurant, bar, pool* ⊟*AE, DC, MC, V* ⱺ*BP.*

$$$–$$$$ ⚏ **Miramalfi.** High above the main coastal drive, this white-stucco hotel overlooks deep blue water and coastal ridges. The hotel's elevators, or a steep hike, deposit you at the pool, with a rock ledge for sunbathing carved from the cliff. Lobbies are sleekly decorated, and the dining room serves up wraparound panoramas; guests may also dine on the sea-air terrace. Rooms have vibrant tile flooring, brightly painted furnishings, floral fabrics, wicker, and lots of windows. All have private sea-view balconies, and some have whirlpools. **Pros:** an incredible view; all rooms have balconies. **Cons:** the dining room ceiling is unattractively low; a bit far from town. ⊠ *Via Quasimodo 3* ☎*089/871588* ⊕*www. miramalfi.it* ⤳*49 rooms* ⚲*In-hotel: Restaurant, bar, pool, beachfront, parking (fee), some pets allowed* ⊟*AE, DC, MC, V* ⱺ*BP.*

$$ ⚏ **Piccolo Paradiso.** A location in the Amalfi harbor area across from the Arsenale already makes this upscale B&B a special choice. The atmosphere is more pleasing and elegant than that of a typical pensione. A common area has tile flooring, and rooms are smallish but comfortable, with wicker seating and wrought-iron headboards; some have private terraces. Open only a few years, everything sparkles, and you'll get to know your fellow international guests in this little paradise. **Pros:** great location; friendly atmosphere. **Cons:** a little too close to the center for some; no credit cards. ⊠ *Via M. Camera 5* ☎*089/873001* ⤳*5 rooms* ⊟*No credit cards* ⱺ*BP.*

$$$$ ⚏ **Santa Caterina.** When Elizabeth Taylor and Richard Burton wanted
★ to escape, they headed here and little wonder. Owned by the Gargano family for generations, this quietly elegant, supremely comfortable, and very cherished hotel has long been one of the treasures of the coast. Indeed, many guests have been coming here since great-grandmother's day. Just outside Amalfi proper (giving it a grand vista of the town), the Santa Caterina takes full advantage of its hillside location. There are vast, terraced gardens and orchards overlooking the sea, and down by the water is a luscious seawater-pool area, complete with an idyllic thatched-roof, open-air caffè. The lobby is charmingly coved, while decor is unobtrusively traditional, with Belle Epoque accents. The luckiest guests are allowed to book the hotel's extraordinary, 19th-century hunting-box châlet, set at water's edge at the far end of the hotel's romantic orchards. **Pros:** a treasure on the coast; wonderful view of the town. **Cons:** away from the main town; exhorbitant prices. ⊠*Strada Amalfitana 9* ☎*089/871012* ⊕*www.hotelsantacaterina.it* ⤳*66 rooms* ⚲*In-hotel: Restaurant, bar, pool, gym, parking (no fee)* ⊟*AE, DC, MC, V* ⱺ*FAP.*

The town of Atrani was once a popular residence for the Amalfi aristocracy.

FESTIVALS

Amalfi's festivals best reflect the splendor of its past. The **St. Andrew Race** every June 27 and November 30, dedicated to Amalfi's protector of seamen, is a joyous religious celebration commemorating the defeat of Barbarossa and the Moslem fleet in 1544. A procession of white-robed men carry a silver-gilt replica of the saint to the harbor, and fishermen at the beach run it back to the cathedral and—in one dramatic dash—straight up its 62 steps. Later, the statue gleams silver in the sunshine of the piazza, as fishermen hang tiny wooden and gilt fish amulets from the saint's left wrist as tokens of gratitude. In the evening, guitar music drifts from many boats, and candlelight flickers.

Even more of a pageant is the **Regatta Storica delle Antiche Repubbliche Marinare** (*Historical Regatta* ☎*089/871107*), the mock battles in which four boats, each with eight oarsmen, represent the medieval maritime republics of Amalfi, Pisa, Genoa, and Venice. The prize, held by the winner for a year, is a scale-model gold-and-silver replica of an antique sailing ship. Each of the former republics is represented by 80 participants; Amalfi's musical contingent is adorned in jewel-encrusted costumes on loan from the town museum—doges, dogaressas, merchants, and commoners from the prosperous past come colorfully to life, with the day's festivities culminating in a show of fireworks. Held yearly on the first Sunday in June every four years, with the four cities alternating as the urban stage sets, the pageant is scheduled to be in Amalfi in 2012 (the 2009 edition was brought forward a year to coincide with the 800th anniversary of the arrival of St. Andrew's relics in Amalfi).

Amalfitans love to celebrate holidays. The Good Friday candlelight procession, Easter Sunday, and Christmas pageants with crèche competitions (with cribs mounted in the city fountains) are all excuses for lavish family occasions, with special foods and church ceremonies.

NIGHTLIFE

Amalfi doesn't have many clubs for music or dancing. However, flyers and posters often go up announcing concerts and theatricals during the peak summer months.

SHOPPING

The **Cartiera Amatruda** (⊠ *Via delle Cartiere 100, beyond museum* ☎ *089/871315*), in the Amatruda Mill, is run by descendants of an Amalfi papermaking dynasty dating from at least 1400; it's probably the oldest crafts paper shop in Italy and still produces and sells fine parchment-color handmade paper. **La Scuderia del Ducaartiera Amatruda** (⊠ *Largo Cesareo Console 8, near the Arsenale,* ☎ *089/872976* ⊕ *www.carta-amalfi.it*) is a publisher of fine books and postcards, selling desk accessories, objets d'art, and beautiful art tomes about Amalfi. If you're pining for English-language newspapers, wanting a book on Amalfi's history, or just looking for a suitable poolside novel, try the **Libreria-Edicola Internazionale** (⊠ *Via Repubbliche Marinare 17* ☎ *089/871180*) near the tourist office.

Leather goods are popular items in small shops along the main streets; one good option is **Bazar Florio** (⊠ *Via P. Capuano 5/7* ☎ *089/871980*), with a fair and friendly owner. It features handbags, wallets, and backpacks.

D'Antuono (⊠ *Piazza Duomo 10* ☎ *089/8736374* ⊕ *www.cartadiamalfi. it*) sells art books, old prints, and fine paper goods.

Mostacciulo (⊠ *Piazza Duomo 22* ☎ *089/871552*) has been run by a well-known and respected family of coral craftsmen since 1930.

ATRANI

Fodor's Choice ★ *1 km (½ mi) east of Amalfi, 5 km (3 mi) southwest of Ravello.*

GETTING HERE

On foot from Amalfi; by car, take the SS163 (Amalfitana) from outside Sorrento or Salerno. There's SITA bus service from Sorrento, Positano, and Amalfi.

EXPLORING

Ask hotel owners and longtime residents of the Costiera Amalfitana where their favorite spot is along the coast, and they often respond "Atrani." Most actually whisper, as if it were some secret treasure—and in some respects, it is: set atop a crag between cliffs overlooking the sea, and a 10-minute walk from the western outskirts of Amalfi—take the seaside stairs off the drive, just after the tunnel—this stage set of a medieval town is centered around a small piazza. When closely linked to the republic, the town was the residential choice of Amalfi aristocracy. It gained its independence from Amalfi in 1578, with which it maintains a friendly rivalry; locals say the town holds its processions on its narrow inner streets to discourage Amalfitans from participating.

Now home to less than 1,000 residents, Atrani is largely overlooked by tourists, who drive right by it over the riverbed of the Torrente Dragone. But its special charms are most evident from the sea, as it looks like an amphitheater ready for a royal pageant.

Adorable Piazza Umberto I, entirely enclosed by four-story houses, is the setting for the basics of Italian life: general store, stationery store, coffee shop, bar, fruit stand, restaurant, barber, and, of course, police station (the constable struts about as though in command of the pigeons strutting alongside him). The uncrowded square is filled with simple scenes: children giggle at hide-and-seek, *duenas* gossip, and men debate and take sips from the venerable fountain as if the world had little changed from the days of the doges. An arcade to one side offers a glimpse of beach, fishing boats, a mule or two, and the sea beyond. At Christmas the whole town congregates here at dawn to drink cappuccino and share traditional cakes.

Atrani's closely packed, dollhouse-scaled backstreets are filled with pastel-and-white houses and shops, fragrant gardens, arcaded lanes, and spiraling scalinatelle. But the hamlet's stellar attractions are the baroque-style churches, which dominate the skyline, and around which parish houses cluster in true medieval style.

The bell of the 10th-century church of **San Salvatore de Bireto** tolled to announce the crowning of a new doge. The coronation ceremony was restricted to those wearing a *bireto,* the cloth cap that would be ceremoniously placed on the new doge's head, and someday worn attending his burial in the same church. The church was remodeled in 1810; the dome is beautifully tiled, and the paneled bronze doors cast in the 11th century came from Constantinople, as did the doors in the Amalfi Duomo. Within is a 12th-century marble plaque showing two peacocks, one standing over a human head between two sirens, the other on a hare being attacked by two birds; peacocks were considered immortal, but the symbolism of the two in this setting is open to interpretation.

The church of **Santa Maria Maddalena,** on a piazza, was built in 1274 and given a neo-baroque facade in 1852. The dome is covered in majolica tile, and the bell tower has an octagonal belfry similar to the campanile of the Carmine church in Naples. Among the treasures here are an altar in richly colored marbles and 16th-century paintings attributed to Amalfi Coast artists: *St. Magdalen between St. Sebastian and St. Andrew* by Giovannangelo D'Amato of Maiori, and *The Incredulity of St. Thomas* by Andrea da Salerno.

WHERE TO EAT AND STAY

$$
SOUTHERN
ITALIAN

✕ **A' Paranza.** At the back of the piazza on the main walkway is the best dining option in Atrani. White-cove ceilings reflect immaculate linen tablecloths in a place that is at once homely and quite formal. Entirely seafood-based, each day's menu depends on the catch, though a taster menu (antipasti ranging from marinated tuna to fried rice balls, with a helping of pasta and risotto, followed by a choice of dessert) is recommended. If that sounds like too much, go for the scialatielli ai frutti di mare, but be sure to leave room for the divine cakes. ✉ *Via Dragone*

1/2 ☎*089/871840* ☰*AE, DC, MC, V* ☉*Closed Dec. 8–26 and Tues. Sept.–July.*

$ ✕**Le Arcate.** A cave is not where you'd normally expect to find good
SOUTHERN food, but this one changes the rules. The simple, dark, old restaurant
ITALIAN tucked under the road also has a large terrace overlooking the beach.
Folks dig its *scialatielli Masaniello*—fresh pasta named after the local
boy who became a revolutionary in Naples—as well as its pizza and
grilled fish. It's been here for 50 years, a drop in the gulf around these
parts. Get a table out on the seafront where you can lean over and see
exactly where your meal has come from. ⊠*Via G. Di Benedetto 4,
under arcades of roadway connecting Amalfi and Atrani* ☎*089/871367*
⊕*www.learcate.net* ☰*AE, DC, MC, V* ☉*Closed mid-Jan.–mid-Feb.
and Mon. mid-Sept.–mid-June.*

¢–$ 🏠**A Scalinatella.** Brothers Filippo and Gabriele run just about the only
game in the village, and the cheapest accommodation on the coast,
with hostel beds, private rooms, and apartments (some with kitchens
and washing machines) spread all over the place. These are only modest digs, but if you want to wake up in Atrani, you'll have to deal with
it. Breakfast is served up in the small restaurant on the square (also
owned by the brothers), and you can enjoy inexpensive meals there,
too. **Pros:** in the heart of Atrani; self-sufficient. **Cons:** rather modest
dwellings; not a lot happening in the evening. ⊠*Piazza Umberto I 5*
☎*089/871492* ⊕*www.hostelscalinatella.com* ➘*12 rooms, 10 with
bath* ☰*No credit cards.*

RAVELLO TO PAESTUM

A few minutes west of Amalfi, perched atop a ridge of Monte Cerreto, and "closer to the sky than the sea"—according to French writer
André Gide—the achingly lovely town of Ravello gazes down on the
Bay of Salerno and the humbler villages surrounding it. This cloud-
riding perch is just one reason why some travelers give Ravello the
laurel as the Amalfi Coast's—some say Italy's—most beautiful town
(in fact, the town has long been nicknamed *La Bellissima*). Languor
becomes Ravello's mood, a bit out of sync with the world below, and
it makes this town a lovely place to catch your breath. The slightly
aloof star high above the coast, it remains there for the reaching and
is worth the stretch. Hearty souls trek between Atrani and Ravello by
a path that climbs through the Valle del Dragone, or Dragon's Valley,
a name inspired by the morning mists here (the descent is easier than
the ascent!). Most Ravello-bound travelers, however, take the SITA bus
from Amalfi's Piazza Flavio Gioia, which corkscrews its way up 1,000
feet along a road in the southern Monti Lattari (although the road is
infrequently closed due to landslides). Cars follow the same route and
really come in handy when driving farther south along Statale 163 to
the towns rimming the Bay of Salerno, which have their off-the-beaten-
track appeal. If you're based in Naples and have singled out Ravello for
a day's sampling of the Amalfi Coast, by far the quickest route is via
the mountain pass called the Valico di Chiunzi, easily reached via the
A3 Naples–Salerno Autostrada from the exit at Angri.

Many visitors end their southward journey along the Amalfi Coast in Ravello. They might have a point (what can top that mountain-top paradise?), but other savvy travelers keep heading southward, for ahead lie less crowded seaport villages, the bustling city of Salerno, and fabled Paestum, site of three of the greatest ancient Greek temples in the world.

After dropping down to sea level from Ravello or going eastward from Amalfi, the coast road, Statale 163, descends into Minori, known for its good beach and ancient Roman heritage. The road climbs up the cape by Torre Mezzacapo, then drops back down to sea level near the 15th-century church of San Francesco. Statale 163 then goes though the town of Maiori, with its much broader river valley producing another good beach, and passes Capo di Baia Verde, near the misleadingly named 17th-century Torre Normanna. The coast here becomes dramatic again, giving grand views of the sea as you climb past the promontory topped by Torre di Badia. Capo Tummolo and then Vallone di San Nicola, with the little village of Marina di Erchie, are ahead of you. The drive then descends to the fishing village of Cetara, along a narrow inlet, continues along the coast, passing Torre de Fuenti and Vallone di Albori, and then faces the sea near Torre della Marina di Albori. At the junction of Raito, a lush little village, you cross the bridge over the Vallone Bonea to the town of Vietri, at which point traffic-light reality returns. Follow Statale 163 to the city of Salerno. Autostrada A3 south connects to E45, which leads to Battipaglia and the exit for the ancient temples of Paestum. Alternatively, hug the coast, driving along Salerno's *lungomare*, and continue along the fairly degraded coastline until you reach Paestum, 40 km (25 mi) from Salerno.

RAVELLO

6½ km (4 mi) northeast of Amalfi, 29 km (18 mi) west of Salerno.

GETTING HERE

By car, take the hill road climbing just east of Atrani, or take the Angri exit on the A3 motorway and cross the mountainous Valico di Chiunsi.

SITA buses make the run up and down the mountain between Ravello and Piazza Flavio Gioia in Amalfi, where you can catch the main Amalfi Drive bus to Sorrento. You can purchase tickets prior to boarding at Bar San Domingo, Bar Calce, and Tabaccheria. There are about two buses every hour.

VISITOR INFORMATION

In Ravello, the **Azienda Autonoma Soggiorno e Turismo** (✉ *Via Roma 18b, Ravello* ☎ *089/857096* 🖷 *089/877977* ⊕ *www.ravellotime.it*) is open daily 9–8, and 9–6 November through March.

EXPLORING

Positano may focus on pleasure, and Amalfi on history, but cool, serene Ravello revels in refinement. Thrust over Statale 163 and the Bay of Salerno on a mountain buttress, below forests of chestnut and ash, above terraced lemon groves and vineyards, it early on beckoned the affluent

The Perils of the Ravello Bus

Once known as "*la citta piu tranquilla, solitaria e silenziosa del mondo,*" the mountaintop aerie of Ravello has been discovered by tourists, meaning it's not quite so tranquil as it used to be. Nowhere is that more evident than on the bus ride into town. There's only run one bus an hour (some days feature two) up to Ravello from Amalfi, and it's often crammed to seemingly twice its capacity.

Once the crowds have packed in the fun really begins, as the bus weaves its way up the mountain. There are so many switchbacks you'll think the bus is going to deposit you back in Amalfi. The road is so narrow in places that it can only alternatively accommodate one-way traffic—and who can forget that traffic light with the green neon arrow pointing…directly off the cliff.

Of course, the payoff for this trying bus ride is heavenly Ravello.

with its island-in-the-sky views and secluded defensive positioning. Gardens out of the *Arabian Nights*, pastel palazzos, tucked-away piazzas with medieval fountains, architecture ranging from Romano-Byzantine to Norman-Saracen, and those sweeping blue-water, blue-sky vistas have inspired a panoply of large personalities, including Wagner and Boccaccio, princes and popes, aesthetes and hedonists, and a stream of famous authors from Virginia Woolf to Tennessee Williams. Author and one time resident Gore Vidal, not an easy critic, has called the town's Villa Cimbrone panorama "the most beautiful view in the world."

Though its origins are lost in obscurity, Ravello may have been settled by Romans fleeing the sack of their dying empire. The town itself was founded in the 9th century, under Amalfi's rule, until residents prosperous from cotton tussled with the superpower republic and elected their own doge in the 11th century; Amalfitans dubbed them *rebelli* (rebels). In the 12th century, with the aid of the Norman King Roger, Ravello even succeeded in resisting Pisa's army for a couple of years, though the powerful Pisans returned to wreak destruction along the coast. Even so, Ravello's skilled seafaring trade with merchants and Moors from Sicily and points east led to a burgeoning wealth, which peaked in the 13th century, when there were 13 churches, four cloisters, and dozens of sumptuous villas. Neapolitan princes built palaces; life was privileged.

But as is inevitable with all supernovas, Ravello's bright light diminished, first through Pisa's maritime rise in the 14th century, then through rivalry between its warring families in the 15th century. When the plague cast its shadow in the 17th century, the population plummeted from upward of 30,000 to perhaps a couple of thousand souls, where it remains today. When Ravello was incorporated into the diocese of Amalfi in 1804, a kind of stillness settled in. Despite the decline of its power and populace, Ravello's cultural heritage and special loveliness continued to blossom. Gardens flowered and music flowed in the ruined villas, and artists, sophisticates, and their lovers filled the crumbling palazzos. Grieg, Wagner, D.H. Lawrence, Chanel, Garbo and her

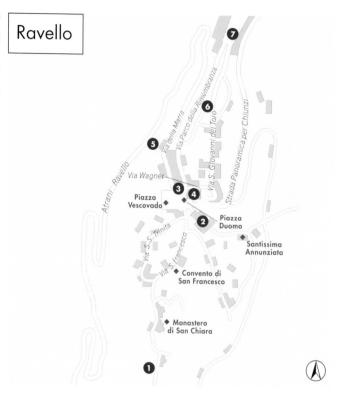

companion, conductor Leopold Stokowski, and then, slowly, tourists, followed in their footsteps. Today, at the Villa Rufolo, the noted Ravello Festival is held in its shaded gardens. Here, special Wagnerian concerts are often held to pay homage to the great composer, who was inspired by these gardens to compose scenes of *Parsifal.*

With the exception of the Villa Rufolo concerts, however, the hush lingers, especially in off-season, when there seem to be more cats than cars. Empty, narrow streets morph into whitewashed staircases rising into a haze of azure, which could be from the sea, the sky, or a union of both. About the only places that don't seem to be in pianissimo slow motion are Piazza Duomo, in front of the cathedral, during the evening passeggiata, or caffès at *pranzo* (luncheon) or *cena* (dinner). Note that the town likes to celebrate religious feste throughout the year—one of the nicest celebrations is the blossom-strewn celebration of Pentecost (usually the first week of June), when Piazza Duomo is ornamented with sidewalk pictures created with flower petals.

Although cars must park in the municipal lot, most arriving buses deposit their passengers near the hillside tunnel that leads to Piazza Duomo, which is lined with hoardings promoting the festival. On the square you'll find the Bric-a-Brac Shop, a great resource for books on Ravello.

CLOSE UP

Experiencing the Amalfi Coast: Hiking

Throughout this entire region, walking *is* hiking, so be prepared. Almalfi, where streets usually take the form of staircases, is a resort where you may leave more fit than you were when you arrived. These towns are picturesque for a reason, and you've probably never seen so many flights of steps—those bothersome *scalinatelle*: thousands of them, leading down to beaches, up to churches, across the hills.

Getting around will take a healthy set of lungs, strong calves, comfortable footwear, time-outs for rest, and a big bottle of Ferrarelle water—slow and steady is the way to go. As for intentional hiking, mule paths and footpaths were the only land-means to get around before the car, and most remain in place for hikers' delight.

Local tourist offices have maps of hikes, and can organize a guide. Check out Julian Tippett's excellent walking book, *Landscapes of Sorrento and the Amalfi Coast* (Sunflower Press), often found at bookstores and newsstands in the area. Even if you're not in shape, you can still participate: take transportation uphill, and let gravity guide you down.

❹ Pride of place on the town piazza is taken by the **Duomo,** the town cathedral, dedicated to patron San Pantaleone and founded in 1086 by Orso Papiro, the first bishop of Ravello. Rebuilt in the 12th and 17th centuries, and completely restored in 1973, the Duomo retains traces of medieval frescoes in the transept, an original mullioned window, a marble portal, and a three-story 13th-century bell tower playfully interwoven with mullioned windows and arches. The 12th-century bronze door features 54 embossed panels depicting Christ's life, and saints, prophets, plants, and animals, all narrating biblical lore. It was crafted by Barisano da Trani, who also fashioned the doors of the cathedrals of Trani and Monreale. (The door is currently under restoration—it was due in 2004, and made a cameo appearance in 2008 only to be whisked away again after it was found to be impossible to hang, due to incorrect measurements. It should return in 2009.) The nave's three aisles are divided by ancient columns, and treasures include sarcophagi from Roman times and paintings by southern Renaissance artist Andrea da Salerno. Most impressive are the two medieval *ambos*, or pulpits: The earlier one, used for reading the Epistles, is inset with a mosaic scene of Jonah and the Whale, symbolizing death and redemption. The more famous one, used for reading the Gospels, was commissioned by Nicola Rufolo in 1272 and created by Niccolò di Bartolomeo da Foggia. It seems almost Tuscan in style, with exquisite Cosmatesque mosaic work and bas-reliefs and six twisting columns sitting on lion pedestals. An eagle grandly tops the colonnette fronting the inlaid marble lectern.

A chapel left of the apse is dedicated to San Pantaleone, a physician, who was beheaded in the 3rd century in Nicomedia. Every July 27 devout believers gather in hope of witnessing a miracle (similar to that of San Gennaro in Naples), in which the saint's blood, collected in a vial and set out on an inlaid marble altar, appears to liquefy and become

The view from Villa Cimbrone's Belvedere of Infinity may be the finest on the coast.

clearer. Use one of the side doors to go behind the altar in the small chapel to get a closer look at the pint of the saint's blood. In the crypt is the **Museo del Duomo,** which displays treasures from around the 13th century, during the reign of Frederick II of Sicily, in an elegant setting. You'll find gold and silver work, sculpture, and a classic Campanian marble bust of a half-smiling woman from the Rufolo dynasty, whose name was Sigilgaita, adorning the cathedral's pulpit. Reliquaries of San Tommaso, Santa Barbara, and San Lorenzo are also displayed here. ⊠ *Museo del Duomo, Piazza del Duomo* ☎ *089/858311* 🖃 *€2* ☉ *Daily 8:30–7, between noon and 5:30, access to church is through museum, to right of steps.*

❸ To the left of the Duomo is the private **Museo del Corallo** *(Coral Museum),* which shows the venerable tradition of Italian workmanship in coral, harvested in bygone centuries from the gulfs of Salerno and Naples and crafted into jewelry, cameos, and figurines. This is a fascinating collection, not confined solely to coral work, with a painting of Sisto IV from the 14th century and what may be an original Caravaggio. Look also in particular for a carved Christ from the 17th century, for which the J. Paul Getty Museum offered $525,000 in 1987 (he was refused) and a tobacco box covered in cameos, one of only two in the world. There is also a statue of the Madonna dating from 1532. Master craftsman in residence Giorgio Filocamo has crafted coral for Pope John Paul II, the Clintons, and Princess Caroline, as well as numerous Hollywood stars. ⊠ *Piazza Duomo 9* ☎ *089/857461* 🖃 *Free* ☉ *Mon.–Sat. 10–noon and 3–5.*

CLOSE UP

The View of Infinity at Villa Cimbrone

A panorama *in excelsis,* the view from the Villa Cimbrone's Belvedere of Infinity is nothing less than an invitation into the Beyond: on many bright-blue days, you can't tell where the sea ends and the sky begins. Little wonder some feel this is the very spot where Satan brought Christ to tempt him with the beauties of the world.

The parapet is adorned with eight *figura di fantasia* depicting Renaissance courtesans and condottieri, fashioned by an 18th-century Neapolitan sculptor. With faces narrowed in contemplation, they stare at you with their backs to That View. You, naturally, instead stare out at infinity—after all, this is the one place the famed poet Gabriele d'Annunzio said "you can be kissed by infinity, as it clasps you with both arms."

❺ Three hundred and fifty yards along Via Roma, to the left of the Duomo, is the three-aisle 13th-century **Santa Maria a Gradillo** with its lovely dome. This was the place where the town noblemen gathered to discuss civic issues; its atrium collapsed in the 18th century. The small Sicilian-Saracenic bell tower has two light mullion windows.

6

❷ Opposite the Duomo is the **Villa Rufolo**, which—if the master story-teller Boccaccio is to be believed—was built in the 13th century by Landolfo Rufolo, whose immense fortune stemmed from trade with the Moors and the Saracens. Now the setting for the Ravello Festival, its Romanesque walls contain a scene that seems from the earliest days of the Crusades. Norman and Arab architecture mingle in a welter of color-filled gardens so lush that composer Richard Wagner used them as inspiration for Klingsor's Garden, the home of the Flower Maidens, in his opera *Parsifal.* Beyond the Arab-Sicilian cloister and the Norman tower are two flower-bedded terraces that offer the prime vista of the Bay of Salerno, set off by the cupolas of the 13th-century church of Santissima Annunziata and a dramatic umbrella pine tree. In 1851 the villa was acquired by Sir Francis Nevile Reid, a Scotsman, who hired Michele Ruggiero, head of the excavations at Pompeii, to restore the villa to its full splendor and replant the gardens with rare cycads, cordylines, and palms. Highlights of the villa are its Moorish cloister—an Arabic-Sicilian delight with interlacing lancet arcs and polychromatic palmette decoration—and the 14th-century Torre Maggiore, the so-called Klingsor's Tower, renamed in honor of Richard Wagner's landmark 1880 visit and today a dramatic spot for chamber music recitals (note that when weather is rainy, concerts are moved into a charmless auditorium). Beyond lie two spectacular terrace gardens, with the lower one, the "Wagner Terrace," often the site for concerts, with the orchestra perched on a precarious-looking platform constructed over the precipice. A musical treat is also in store on nights without concerts—from 9 PM to midnight visitors are given a suggestive night tour accompanied by classical music and poetry readings. Villa Rufolo also houses a library of rare documents and manuscripts. ⊠ *Piazza Duomo,*

Fodor'sChoice
★

☎089/857866 🎫€5, *concerts extra charge* ⊗ *Daily 9–8; closes earlier when concert rehearsals are taking place; winter 9–6.*

The crane blotting the landscape beside the Hotel Graal in 2009 was constructing a 400-seat auditorium, created by modernist Brazilian architect Oscar Nieymeyer (designer of Brasília), as an alternative indoor venue for concerts. At the time of writing it was unclear who would be running the auditorium, but it will almost certainly be open by 2004.

For a closer look at the **Santissima Annunziata** (now a conference center closed to the public), exit the villa and take a sharp right to reach the Via dell'Annunziata stair path, which plummets you down the hillside past the church to the scenic Via della Repubblica.

Head back up the road—which offers a panoramic vista of the blue bay—to the town square and climb the steps of Via Richard Wagner, to the left of the Duomo, to Via San Giovanni a Toro, the address of Ravello's grandest palazzi (now hotels). **Villa Episcopio,** a 12th-century bishop's residence, was formerly called Villa di Sangro. It is currently being renovated, though there's a chance it will be open to the public in 2010. Amid the gardens and ruins, Italy's King Vittorio Emanuele III abdicated in favor of his son, and Jackie Kennedy enjoyed breaks from her public obligations. Wine merchants here have been cultivating grapes since 1860, and varieties of Ravello rosso and bianco, as refined as their namesake, can be purchased in town.

❻ Across the tiny piazza from the Hotel Caruso is the noted 11th-century church of **San Giovanni del Toro.** Its evocative interior has three high apses and a crypt with 14th-century frescoes of Christ and the apostles. A 12th-century ambo (pulpit) by Alfano da Termoli startles the eye with its blue Persian majolica and four columns topped with elaborate capitals. The chapel of the Coppola family in the left aisle has an exceptional 14th-century relief of St. Catherine of Alexandria. The small church's three porticos adorned with lunettes show an Arabian influence, and the tripartite back facade is exquisite. Restoration work on the church commenced in 2003, with no sign of being completed. ⊠ *Piazza San Giovanni del Toro.*

❶ To the west of Ravello's main square, a somewhat hilly 10-minute walk

along Via San Francesco brings you to Ravello's showstopper, the **Villa Cimbrone,** whose dazzling gardens perch 1,500 feet above the sea. The ultimate aerie, this medieval-style fantasy was created in 1905 by England's Lord Grimthorpe and made world-famous when Greta Garbo found sanctuary from the press when she vacationed here with Leopold Stokowski in 1937. The Gothic *castello-palazzo* is in idyllic gardens, which are divided by the grand Allée of Immensity, leading in turn to the literal high point of any trip to the Amalfi Coast—the legendary **Belvedere of Infinity.** This grand stone parapet, adorned with amusing stone busts, overlooks the entire Bay of Salerno and is one of the most magical spots in all Europe. The name Cimbrone derives from the rocky ridge on which the villa stands, first colonized by the ancient Romans and hailed as Cimbronium back then. In the Middle Ages, the noble Accongiogioco clan built a house here. Centuries later, Ernest William Beckett, Lord Grimthorpe (whose main claim to fame is as designer of Big Ben's casement), fell in love with Cimbrone on a Grand Tour of Italy and, with the help of Nicolo Mansi, transformed the gardens into the extravaganza we see today. Since the lord hosted many of England's Bloomsbury set, it is now thought that Vita Sackville-West (just one of the many famous writers and artists who visited here) had some help in the garden design. Be sure to explore all the pathways to find the mock-Gothic crypt (now containing the restaurant Il Flauto di Pan), the Temple of Bacchus *tempietto* (under which Lord Grimthorpe is buried), the tea pavilion done in the style of Florence's Pazzi Chapel, and the Grotto of Venus. Many feel the Cimbrone is the most beautiful garden in Italy; be sure to visit here and decide for yourself. Better yet, overnight at this magical domain, as the villa itself is now a hotel. Begin by logging onto the villa Web site to see its wondrous photos. ⊠ *Via S. Chiara 26* ☎*089/857459* ⊕*www.villacimbrone.it* 🎫*€6* ☉*Daily 9–half hr before sunset.*

Nearly every street in Ravello has a historic church or villa.

Two notable religious sites are the church and convent of **San Francesco,** founded in 1222 by St. Francis of Assisi, with a small Gothic cloister; the church was rebuilt in the 18th century (on Via S. Francesco).

Majolica flooring in the 13th-century **Monastero di Santa Chiara** (on Via S. Chiara), now a closed order, is one special element; another is the *matronaeum,* or women's gallery, the only one left on the Amalfi Coast (not known for segregating the sexes, or anything else). You can visit this church for the early-morning Sunday service, but the wheel used to deliver food (and at one time unwanted children) to the nuns can be seen anytime.

❼ Buy some gelati on the piazza by the Duomo and walk east to the **Piazza Fontana Moresco,** below the Hotel Parsifal and above the gates of the walled perimeter, to check out the two stone lions on the fanciful 1,000-year-old fountain, still spewing water. Unfortunately the lions are imitations; the originals were stolen some 40 years ago.

WHERE TO EAT

$$$
SOUTHERN
ITALIAN
★
✕**Cumpa' Cosimo.** Lustier-looking than most Ravello spots, Cumpa' Cosimo is run devotedly by Netta Bottone, who tours the tables to ensure her clients are content. Her family has owned this *cantina* for 75 of its 300-plus years, and she has been cooking under the arched ceiling for almost 60 of them. You can't miss here with any of the dishes featuring classic Ravellian cuisine. A favorite (share it—it's huge) is a *misto* of fettuccine, fusilli, tortellini, and whatever other homemade pasta inspires her, served with a fresh, fragrant pesto. Meats are generally excellent—after all, they are supplied by the butcher shop next door, also run by Netta. The *funghi porcini* mushroom starter and the house cheesecake are so delicious you'll drop your fork. Local wines ease it all down gently, and homemade gelato is a luscious ending. ⊠ *Via Roma 46* ☎*089/857156* ⌖*Reservations essential* ▭*AE, DC, MC, V* ☉*Sometimes closed Mon. in winter.*

$
SOUTHERN
ITALIAN
✕**Figli di Papà.** The young chef-owners of this restaurant attempt to turn Campania classics into something more—and they usually succeed. Past a fireplace that flickers in season and watercolors by Irish artist Leo

Kennedy, resident in Ravello, you descend into a white, modernized 13th-century setting. The daily menu *turistica* may offer such dishes as *crespolini di pesce* (fish-stuffed crepes), and *lombo di agnello al rosmarino con spinaci all'uvetta* (lamb cutlets with spinach and raisins). Tasting menus—to suit various appetites and wallet sizes—are even more creative, with unexpected combinations. To match the food, the owners provide a wine list featuring the best of the region, which can also be enjoyed on the outside terrace. ✉ *Via della Marra 7* ☏ *089/858302* ⊕ *www.ristorantefiglidipapa.it* ☰ *AE, DC, MC, V* ⊗ *Closed 3 wks in Nov., 6 wks in Jan. and Feb., Tues. in winter.*

$$ \
PIZZA

✕ **Vittoria.** Between the Duomo and the church of San Francesco, this is a good place for a return to reality and an informal bite. Vittoria's thin-crust pizza with loads of fresh toppings is the star attraction, and locals praise it *molto*—it was a favorite of Gore Vidal. But also try the pasta, maybe fusilli with tomatoes, zucchini, and mozzarella. Vittoria is pretty, too, with arches and tile floors. ✉ *Via dei Rufolo 3* ☏ *089/857947* ⊕ *www.ristorantepizzeriavittoria.it* ☰ *AE, DC, MC, V* ⊗ *Closed Nov.–Mar.*

WHERE TO STAY

$$$$ \
Fodor's Choice \
★

Caruso. A beloved Ravello landmark, the Caruso reopened in 2005 after an extensive renovation. Many hail it as a benchmark of 21st-century luxury, while others mourn the loss of its priceless 19th-century patina. Set in a medieval palazzo on the highest point of Ravello (1,150 feet), overlooking an incomparable panorama of the Bay of Salerno, this hotel had always been considered a corner of paradise. In decades past it was a favored home-away-from-home for the likes of Virginia Woolf, Tennessee Williams, Graham Greene, the Khedive of Egypt, Margot Fonteyn, and Peter O'Toole, all of whom came to savor the yesteryear charm, the spectacularly frescoed gran salone, and the pretty terrace restaurant. But as guest rooms had become threadbare, a restoration was ordered by Orient-Express Hotels, with Professor Antonio Forcellino of Rome at the helm (his résumé includes Michelangelo's Moses), aided by Italian designer Federico Forquet. Today, fans rave about the new rooftop dining area and heated infinity pool. The lush hillside garden includes the coast's only herb garden, which provides seasoning for the renowned Caruso restaurant. Guests can also dine alfresco at the Belvedere Restaurant where meals are seasoned by great views over the bay. Too bad that the famous belvedere set with Gothic windows—a postcard icon for centuries of the Amalfi Coast—has been reduced to a beige-on-beige cocktail lobby. Happy guests, however, now enjoy it as a pleasing perch where they can savor a great Bellini and study the Roman ruins unearthed during recent renovations. Rooms are truly sumptuous, most with sea view, some with private garden, and guests are welcomed with strawberries and Champagne. Complimentary boat and shuttle services are offered. Guests are welcome to wrap up the evening, as did Rod Stewart, by joining the pianist for a song in the bar. If the unique ambiance of this hotel has been forever altered, no one can dispute that it is now a ne plus ultra for luxurious accomodation on the Amalfi Coast. **Pros:** experience Ravello like a VIP; pure luxury. **Cons:** out of the price range of most; some consider the restoration work an abhorrence. ⊠ *Piazza San Giovanni del Toro 2* ☎ *089/858801* ⊕ *www. hotelcaruso.com* ⌨ *50 rooms* ♿ *In-hotel: 3 restaurants, bar, pool, gym, spa, some pets allowed, parking (fee)* ▤ *AE, DC, MC, V* ☉ *Closed Jan. and Feb.* ⦿ *FAP.*

$ ▥ **Da Salvatore.** Adjacent to the Hotel Graal and sharing the same glorious view, Da Salvatore has a small garden you enter by walking down into it and then choosing between a large terrace or an indoor area for dining. The family creates classic Campanian cuisine, the service is friendly, and the overlook offers the best view of any inexpensive restaurant in the vicinity. Upstairs guest rooms are surprisingly upscale, with baths, TVs, air-conditioning, and balconies and with a price that makes them a great deal. **Pros:** relatively inexpensive option; glorious view. **Cons:** access is by a long flight of steps; often fully booked. ⊠ *Via della Repubblica 2* ☎☎ *089/857227* ⊕ *www.salvatoreravello.com* ⌨ *6 rooms* ♿ *In-hotel: restaurant* ▤ *AE, DC, MC, V* ☉ *Restaurant closed Mon. in winter; hotel closed Nov.–mid-Mar.* ⦿ *BP.*

$$–$$$$ ▥ **Graal.** The name comes from the Holy Grail, as in Wagner's opera *Parsifal*, but this inn is more an operetta. The walls are adorned with the work of Roman artist Bruno Canova, colorful tiled murals outside, and paintings inside. It's much less grand than Ravello's famous hotels, with a modern decor that's a bit of a downer. Nevertheless, it reaches high-Cs for comfort, cleanliness, and contentment. Hovering over the water on the Via della Repubblica, overlooking the new Nieymeyer auditorium, with a nearly unobstructed view of the breathtaking bay, this hotel possesses one of the friendliest staffs around, a pretty pool area, and whirlpools and fancy baths. In the dining room, meals from a family kitchen are delivered to tables dressed in linen and set near large, arched windows. Most rooms are smallish, some are deluxe (especially No. 342, with a double whirlpool and a bed from which you can see the great view), but all have tiled floors and balconies. **Pros:** friendly staff; great views. **Cons:** rooms on the lower level are disappointing; the modern decor doesn't fit with the surroundings. ⊠ *Via della Repubblica 8* ☎ *089/857222* ⊕ *www.hotelgraal.it* ⌨ *43 rooms* ♿ *In-hotel: 2 restaurants, bar, pool* ▤ *AE, DC, MC, V* ☉ *Restaurant closed Mon. Oct.–Mar.* ⦿ *BP.*

$$$$ ▥ **Palazzo Sasso.** In this 12th-century home of the aristocratic Sasso family, Wagner penned part of his opera *Parsifal* in the 1880s, and in the fashionable 1950s, the palazzo hosted Ingrid Bergman and Roberto Rossellini. Once part of the adjacent Hotel Palumbo, it was opened in its own right by Sir Richard Branson in 1997, after a 19-year hiatus, luring the glitterati—its first guests were Placido Domingo and his entourage. Ordinary mortals, too, can come to sightsee and peek at the gleaming marble lobby (once a chapel), glass elevators, two rooftop hot tubs, and roaring waterfall replete with *Playboy* Mansion statuary. Traditionalists might look askance (if not be totally horrified) at all this glitz in quaint old Ravello, but no one will complain about immaculately furnished guest rooms, with the latest computer-operated lighting and air-cooling systems. Even better, the gilded, Empire-style Rossellini restaurant is now among the finest in Campania and offers the latest in regal, nouvelle fare. **Pros:** one of the finest restaurants in the region; pure luxury.

6

CLOSE UP

Restoring the Swallow's Nest

One of the most spectacular houses in the world, La Rondinaia ("The Swallow's Nest") seems literally pasted to the 2,000-foot-high cliff that looms over the Bay of Salerno. Originally built by Viscountess Frost (as an *oubliette* from the Villa Cimbrone, the estate of her father, Lord Grimthorpe, just up the hill), La Rondinaia was the celebrated residence of author Gore Vidal for three decades until sold in 2006 to Vincenzo Palumbo for a reported €17 million.

Guests at Signore Palumbo's three Ravello hotels can get a sneak peek

at his ongoing restoration. The villa—set with massive, light-filled rooms, Vidal's original furnishings (antiques and California-style touches), and breathtaking parapet terraces over the sea—will become another commercial enterprise, but Palumbo is in no hurry, having not yet (at time of writing) decided to make this a rental villa, a full-fledged hotel or indeed a spa. Whichever way he goes, this will undoubtedly be one of the most talked-about facilities in Europe when it opens.

Cons: out of the price-range of most; beware traditionalists! ⊠ *Via San Giovanni del Toro 28* ☎ *089/818181* ⊕ *www.palazzosasso.com* ⟿ *38 rooms, 5 suites* ⅃ *In-hotel: Restaurant, bar, pool, gym, parking (fee), some pets allowed* ⊟ *AE, DC, MC, V* ☾ *Closed Nov.–Feb.*

$$$$

Fodor's Choice

★

🖼 **Palumbo.** Legendarily old-fashioned, built in the 12th century as a palazzo, this famous hotel has long been a stop for visiting "Someones": Wagner, who composed on the piano in the lobby; Bogart, filming *Beat the Devil*; a young Jack and Jackie. Hollywood's golden couple Brad Pitt and Angelina Jolie filmed a scene from *Mr. & Mrs. Smith* here, so it's unsurprising their relationship also blossomed in real life. This is the real deal—the only great hotel left in Ravello that is still a monument to the Grand Tour sensibility that first put the town on the map. Ancient marble columns, mosaic-tile floors, and museum-quality antiques combine to provide an elegant ambience throughout the hotel, while incredible views of the Bay of Salerno can be enjoyed from your terrace or the lush gardens that sit below the hotel on the hillside. You have the option of being whisked down to a villa at sea level and pampered in the hotel's coastal retreat. The innovative Continental cuisine is served in the exclusive Confalone restaurant, a magnificently gilded ballroom with its original frescoed ceiling and old-master paintings. Or you can enjoy a view as delicious as the food atop the restaurant terrace—finish off your feast with lemon soufflé and Episcopio estate wine (note the restaurant is closed from November to March). Most guest rooms have antiques, vintage fabrics, and modern marble baths, except for those in the annex, where at just over half the cost you still have access to all the facilities of the main palazzo. Lodging prices can include both a sumptuous breakfast and a choice of either a gourmet lunch or dinner. **Pros:** impossibly romantic; wonderful coastal retreat. **Cons:** with all this finery it can be difficult to relax; great restaurant closed in winter. ⊠ *Via S. Giovanni del Toro 16* ☎ *089/857244* ⊕ *www.hotelpalumbo.*

it 🛏18 rooms △In-hotel: Restaurant, bar, parking (fee) ☐AE, DC, MC, V ⦿MAP.

$$ 🏨**Parsifal.** In 1288 this diminutive property was a convent housing an order of Augustinian friars. Today the intact cloister hosts travelers simply intent on enjoying themselves mightily. Ancient, ivy-covered stone arches and a tiled walkway looking out over the coastline lead to a cozy interior that still feels a bit like a retreat. Sun lounges, a garden, a fishpond, a Ping-Pong table, and alfresco dining all overlook the sea. Restoration work is ongoing in the low season, and the swimming pool should be ready for 2010. Rooms are small with coved ceilings (monk's cells, after all), so ask for one with a balcony. The charming young manager dotes on Americans, and gladly accommodates guests all year round. Half-board is often required at peak season. **Pros:** staying in a convent in Ravello; friendly staff. **Cons:** slightly removed from the main town; tiny rooms. ⊠ *Viale Gioacchino d'Anna 5* ☎*089/857144* ⊕*www.hotelparsifal.com* 🛏*19 rooms* △*In-hotel: restaurant, bar, parking (fee), some pets allowed* ☐*AE, DC, MC, V* ⦿*FAP.*

$$$-$$$$ 🏨**Rufolo.** D. H. Lawrence worked on *Lady Chatterley's Lover* during his 1926 visit, so it might be fun to revisit the novel's groundbreaking love scenes while you're here. Some rooms have balconies to liven up the snug quarters with gorgeous sea and sky vistas framed by the palm trees of the Villa Rufolo, just below the hotel. Author Gore Vidal could often be seen strolling along the path beside the hotel—he owned La Rondinaia, the villa at the end of the path, but sold it to a private investor in 2006. **Pros:** as close to La Rondinaia as mere mortals can get; beautiful views over Villa Rufolo. **Cons:** car park clutters the entrance; the staff have been known to be unhelpful. ⊠ *Via San Francesco 1* ☎*089/857133* ⊕*www.hotelrufolo.it* 🛏*34 rooms* △*In-hotel: Restaurant, bar, pool, parking (no fee), some pets allowed* ☐*AE, DC, MC, V* ⦿*Closed mid-Nov.–mid-Mar.* ⦿*FAP.*

$ 🏨**Toro.** Two minutes from the Duomo, this little hotel with a garden and lots of antiques has been in the Schiavo family for three generations. Even this modest inn once boasted visiting VIPs: composer Edvard Grieg wrote in the guest book that he was "*molto contento*" and artist M. C. Escher also stayed here (his celebrated prints of spiraling staircases were inspired by those he discovered in Ravello and Atrani). **Pros:** a small piece of Ravello's artistic history; very central. **Cons:** long flight of steps to climb; space rather cramped. ⊠ *Via Roma 16* ☎*089/857211* ⊕*www.hoteltoro.it* 🛏*10 rooms* △*In-hotel: Some pets allowed* ☐*AE, DC, MC, V* ⦿*Closed Nov.–mid-Apr.* ⦿*BP.*

$ 🏨**Villa Amore.** A 10-minute walk from the Piazza Duomo, this charmingly secluded hotel with a garden is family-run and shares the same exhilarating view of the Bay of Salerno as Ravello's most expensive hotels. Rooms are small, with modest and modern furnishings. Reserve ahead, and specify time of arrival if you need help with luggage from the parking lot or bus stop (you pay about €5 per bag). **Pros:** charmingly secluded; wonderful views. **Cons:** rather far from the main drag; modest rooms. ⊠ *Via del Fusco 5* ☎*089/857135* ⊕*www.villaamore.it* 🛏*12 rooms* △*In-hotel: Restaurant, bar, some pets allowed* ☐*DC, MC, V* ⦿*FAP.*

$$$$
Fodor'sChoice
★
☐ **Villa Cimbrone.** Suspended over the azure sea and set amid rose-laden gardens, this magical place was once the home of Lord Grimthorpe and the holiday hideaway of Greta Garbo. In the mid-1990s it was exquisitely transformed into a hotel by the Vuillemeier family. The hotel is in an intact Gothic-style castle, replete with guest rooms ranging from palatial to cozy. Two rooms are covered with frescoes, and all follow a basic floral theme—we love the small Peony Room because it's the only one with its own terrace overlooking the bay (Garbo's former room only has an enclosed balcony) in the main castello. Happily, a newer wing—antiques and a parchment-hue color scheme make it look as time-burnished as the main house—has a bevy of rooms overlooking the sea bluff and the gorgeous new pool. Tapestried armchairs, framed prints, and vintage art books, which belonged to Viscountess Frost, the lord's daughter, still grace the enchantingly elegant sitting room. Another grand period room, the Music Salon—pomegranate-red and lined with old-master paintings—is just the place to curl up with a Bloomsbury memoir (many members of that Edwardian literary set were houseguests here). The restaurant is near the Cripta, or porticoed crypt, which was built by Lord Grimthorpe to resemble the one at Fountains Abbey, near his birthplace in Malton, England. Best of all, guests have the villa's legendary gardens all to themselves once their gates are closed at sunset. The villa is a bit of a hike along lanes and alleys from the town center, but porters will carry your luggage and the distance helps keep this the most peaceful place on the Amalfi Coast. You can get an advance view of the hotel at its splendid Web site. **Pros:** the gardens are all yours after closing time; stay where Garbo chose to "be alone." **Cons:** a bit of a hike from town; daily invasion of day trippers. ☒ *Via Santa Chiara 26* ☎*089/857459* ⊕*www.villacimbrone.it* ⟿*19 rooms* ⟨ =*AE, DC, MC, V* ☉*Closed mid-Nov.–mid-Mar.* ⚏*BP.*

$$$
★
☐ **Villa Maria.** This pretty-as-a-picture option is fronted by a vast garden terrace and has more sunny warmth than most formal hotels in Ravello. Hued in glowing terra-cotta, adorned with gorgeous flowers, and offering a sweet welcome thanks to entry salons replete with tiled floors, high ceilings, lace, and antiques, the Villa Maria has long been a popular option in Ravello. Other pluses are the delightfully friendly staff, the convenient restaurant, and the hands-on management of Vincenzo Palumbo (who recently bagged Gore Vidal's La Rondinaia villa, with plans to open a spa. All but two rooms are standard, and there's an airy suite that has a large balcony overlooking the coast. Note that views here look out over the Vallone del Dragone, not the bay, but are memorable all the same. Also check out Maria's next-door sibling, the Hotel Giordano, a former 18th-century manor house, which shares facilities with the villa. The rooms are less desirable here, but the pool is closer. **Pros:** friendly staff; convenient restaurant. **Cons:** most views face the valley, rather than the coast; pool is actually in the adjacent hotel. ☒ *Via Santa Chiara 2* ☎*089/858400* ⊕*www.villamaria.it* ⟿*23 rooms* ⟨*In-hotel: Restaurant, bar, pool, parking (no fee)* =*AE, DC, MC, V* ⚏*FAP.*

6

NIGHTLIFE AND THE ARTS

Other than the concerts offered by the Ravello Concert Society and the Ravello Festival, there's little nightlife activity, unless you count moongazing. A few caffès and bars are scattered about, but the general peacefulness extends to evening hours. Hotels and restaurants may offer live music and can advise you about nightclubs, but around these parts the sound is either soft and classical—or silence.

Starting in the 1950s, Ravello became famed as the "City of Music," when concerts began to be performed in the spectacular gardens of the Villa Rufolo. The celebrated **Ravello Festival** (⊠ *Viale Wagner 5* ☎ *089/858360* 🖷 *089/8586278* ⊕ *www.ravellofestival.com*), which evolved from the Festivalè Musicale di Ravello, runs from June to October, with full orchestras performing Wagner, Bach, Mozart, Beethoven, Brahms, Chopin, and slightly less well-known Italian composers such as Scarlatti and Cimarosa. Each year's festival is based on a theme—in 2008 it was Diversity—and this has allowed them to also expand into other genres. The most popular event is the *Concerto all'Alba* (dawn concert), when the entire town wakes up at 4:30 to watch the sunrise over the bay to the accompaniment of music from a full symphony orchestra; this event takes place on August 10 to coincide with the shooting stars on the night of San Lorenzo. The older **Ravello Concert Society** (☎ *089/858149* 🖷 *089/858249* ⊕ *www.ravelloarts.org*) runs a yearlong program, with a few concerts also held in the Chiesa di Santa Rosa in Conca dei Marini and at La Gabella in Praiano. Most evening concerts are held at 9:30, with occasional performances starting at 6:30. Note that the 9:30 concerts begin well after sunset, so come earlier if you want to catch the evening glow. Annual concert schedules—listed on the Ravello Concert Society Web site—are posted outside Villa Rufolo and may also be picked up at tourist information offices on the Amalfi Coast.

CULINARY LESSONS

If you fancy learning how to make some of the things you've been eating, **Mamma Agata** (⊠ *Piazza San Cosma 9* ☎ *089/857019* 🖷 *089/ 858432* ⊕ *www.mammaagata.com*), who has cooked for Elizabeth Taylor, Federico Fellini, Jackie Kennedy, and Marcello Mastroianni, will take you into her kitchen—with the almost obligatory stunning view—and take you through the preparation of the area's pasta dishes and sweets. A four-hour morning session is followed by lunch—that you yourself will have made!

SHOPPING

Bric-a-Brac (⊠ *Piazza Duomo 4* ☎ *089/857153*) has some 19th-century antiques, including historic crèche scenes; in the front of the store is a must for history- and art lovers—a great selection of books and antique prints about Ravello.

Gerardo Sacco (⊠ *Piazza Duomo 8* ☎ *089/858125*) is jeweler to several divas; a brochure in the shop shows Glenn Close, Elizabeth Taylor, Mel Gibson, and Caroline of Monaco (among others) flashing his creations. Theatrical to say the least, his earrings, necklaces, and bracelets are large and showy and not to everyone's taste, but certainly worth a look.

Ceramiche d'Arte (✉ *Via dei Rufolo 16* ☎*089/857303*) ships its good stock of Vietri-made and other hand-painted ceramics all over the world. Bargaining may reward you with a 10% discount, maybe more if you have a talent for it. There are also opportunities for gaining hands-on experience at their showroom and workshop a three-minute walk away in a courtyard at Via Roma 20.

Run by the Hotel Palumbo across the vicolo, **Episcopio Winery** (✉ *Via Giovanni a Toro* ☎*089/857244* ⊕*www.hotelpalumbo.it*), offers selections of fine Ravello vintages.

Gruppo Petit Prince (✉ *Via San Francesco 9* ☎*089/858033*) has a nice selection of stationery, prints, and artworks.

Ravello Gusti & Delizie (✉ *Via Roma 28* ☎*089/857716*) is stocked to the ceiling with *prodotti tipici e naturali della costiera Amalfitana*; this is the place for foodstuffs, as well as delicacies and wines from all over Italy. Sun-dried-tomato pasta, olive oil, and other treats are available, but most intriguing are the lemon products—candles and soaps, and even lemon honey.

ERCHIE

13 km (7 mi) southeast of Minori, 3 km (2 mi) south of Cetara.

GETTING HERE

By car, take the SS163 (Amalfitana) from outside Sorrento or Salerno, or take the Angri exit on the A3 motorway and cross the mountainous Valico di Chiunsi. The SITA bus line runs here from Amalfi and Salerno.

EXPLORING

With a looming Norman tower on the cliff above, the curving beachfront hamlet of Erchie is as romantic as can be, especially when there's no one around but you and the fishermen who haul in their catch in the pink sun of early morning. The little village of Erchie is built around a 10th-century Benedictine abbey destroyed and abandoned in the 12th century; Salerno took over the town in the 15th century. By the 1960s the abbey was restored in neo-Renaissance style, with a portal constructed in dark tufa and stone, and the little village was discovered by city dwellers from Salerno, who now flock here to windsurf along the cove and laze the day away.

CETARA

3 km (2 mi) northeast of Erchie, 4 km (2½ mi) southwest of Vietri.

GETTING HERE

By car, take the SS163 (Amalfitana) from outside Sorrento or Salerno, or take the Angri exit on the A3 motorway and cross the mountainous Valico di Chiunsi. The SITA bus line runs here from Amalfi and Salerno.

EXPLORING

Tourists tend to take a pass on the village of Cetara because of the hairpin turns off the main road. A quaint and quiet fishing village below orange groves on Monte Falerzo, it was held in subjugation to greater powers, like most of these coastal sites, throughout much of its

Paestum is the site of remarkably well-preserved Greek temples, including the Tempio di Cerere.

history. From being a Saracen stronghold in the 9th century, it became the final holding of Amalfi at the eastern edge of the republic, which all through the 11th and 12th centuries tithed part of Cetara's fishing catch, *ius piscariae*—the town's claim to fame. It's rumored that the village's Latin name comes from this big catch—*cetaria* (tuna net), but the town haul is most famous for its anchovies—thousands of years ago, salted and strained, they became a spicy liquid called *garum,* a delicacy to the rich of ancient Rome (it can be purchased at local grocery stores). After the Middle Ages, the village came under the dominion of the Benedictine abbey of neighboring Santa Maria di Erchie and then became the port of the abbey of Cava, above the coast, which traded with Africa and extracted anchorage dues. In 1534 the Turks, led by the tyrant Sinan Pasha—on the invitation, no less, of Prince Ferdinando Sanseverino of Salerno—enslaved 300 Cetaran villagers, spiriting them away in 22 galleys and executing those who would not cooperate. A few survivors fled to Naples, which immediately ordered a watchtower to be raised in Cetara to ward off future raids. This is one of the many landmarks that remind tourists that there were coastal perils previous to the one of driving on Statale 163. Beneath the tower is a rocky little beach, and a small park overlooks the harbor, where fishermen mend their nets and paint their boats. They often are away from home for months, fishing in deep waters. Other than the scenic charm of the waterfront, there are no main sights here, other than the church of San Pietro, near the harbor.

WHERE TO EAT AND STAY

$$–$$$ ✕**Acqua Pazza.** Locals along this part of the coast rave about this tiny
SEAFOOD restaurant. On the main street, it has a modest environment—a spare
interior with a few tables—but its raison d'être is remarkably fresh
seafood, with the spaghetti with *colatura di alici* also a specialty here.
This is a three-minute stroll from the harbor. ✉ *Via Garibaldi 38*
☎ *089/261606* ⊕ *www.acquapazza.it* ▭ *AE, DC, MC, V* ⊗ *Closed
on Mon. mid-Oct.–mid-Mar.*

$ ✕**Al Convento.** Occupying part of a former convent, this restaurant
SOUTHERN receives glowing reviews for its different permutations of the anchovy.
ITALIAN Try the *spaghetti con colatura* (a modern version of the anchovy liquid
known in Roman times as garum) or for the less adventurous, the excel-
lent pizza from their wood oven. The decor is whitewashed with soaring
arches and a ceiling adorned with beautiful old frescoes. ✉ *Piazza San
Francesco 16* ☎☎ *089/261039* ⊕ *www.alconvento.net* ▭ *AE, DC,
MC, V* ⊗ *Closed on Wed. mid-Oct.–mid-Mar.*

$$$–$$$$ ⛱ **Cetus.** Cetara's leading hotel is set in a white-stucco building that
seems to have grown right out of the living rock. The natural theme is
continued within. A summer-light restaurant has floors of marble tile,
a window-wall, and terraces. A steep walk leads to the hotel's private
beach and "American" bar. Shutter doors open onto broad, stone-
flagged spaces, with umbrella tables, casual seating, overflowing flower
boxes, and close-up sea views. **Pros:** amazing view floating above the
sea; no better place in Cetara. **Cons:** 350 yards from town along Amalfi
Dr., not ideal for walking; steep descent to beach. ✉ *Corso Umberto
I 1* ☎☎ *089/261388* ⊕ *www.hotelcetus.com* ⤸ *37 rooms* ♿ *In-hotel:
Restaurant, bar, beach, parking (no fee)* ▭ *AE, DC, MC, V* ⊚*BP.*

PAESTUM

★ *45 km (27 mi) southeast of Cetara, 42 km (25 mi) southeast of Salerno,
99 km (62 mi) southeast of Naples.*

GETTING HERE

By car, take the A3 motorway south from Salerno, take the Battipaglia
exit to SS 18. Exit at Capaccio Scala. By CSTP or SCAT bus hourly
from Salerno, by State railway from Salerno.

EXPLORING

One of Italy's most majestic sights lies on the edge of a flat coastal
plain: the remarkably well-preserved **Greek temples** of Paestum. The S18
from the north has now been rerouted via the train station (Stazione
di Paestum), which is about 800 yards from the ruins. Access can be
gained through the perfectly preserved archway **Porta Sirena**, or—if
motorized—through the northern gate of **Porta Aurea**. The ruins are
part of the ancient city of Poseidonia, founded by Greek colonists in
the 7th century BC. When the Romans took over the colony in 273 BC
and its name was latinized to Paestum, they changed the layout of the
settlement, adding an amphitheater and a forum. Much of the archaeo-
logical material found on the site is displayed in the helpfully labeled
Museo Nazionale. Several rooms are devoted to the unique tomb paint-
ings discovered in the area, rare examples of Greek and pre-Roman

pictorial art. About 600 feet from the museum (in front of the main site offices), framed by banks of roses and oleanders, is the **Tempio di Nettuno** (Temple of Poseidon), a magnificent Doric edifice with 36 fluted columns and an extraordinarily well-preserved entablature (area above the capitals), which rivals the finest temples in Greece. On the left of the temple is the so-called **Basilica,** the earliest of Paestum's standing edifices; it dates from early in the 6th century BC. The name is an 18th-century misnomer, for the structure was in fact a temple sacred to Hera, the wife of Zeus. Behind it an ancient road leads to the **Foro Romano** (Roman Forum) and the single column of the **Tempio della Pace** (Temple of Peace). Beyond—on the north side of the site—is the **Tempio di Cerere** (Temple of Ceres), thought to have originally been dedicated to the goddess Athena. From the thankfully pedestrianized road that runs past the site—actually it cuts the site in half—you can view the temples in the late afternoon or early evening, when the light enhances the deep gold of the limestone. Many people touring the Amalfi Coast take a day trip down to Paestum. ⊠ *Via Magna Grecia* ☎*0828/811023* 🖾*Site €4, museum €4, combination ticket €6.50* ☉*Excavations daily 8:45–1 hr before sunset, 8:45–4 in winter; museum daily 9–7; museum closed Mon.*

WHERE TO STAY

$ 🏨 **Azienda Agricola Seliano.** This working-farm-with-a-difference is about 3 km (2 mi) from the temples and consists of a cluster of 19th-century baronial buildings. The Baronessa Cecilia herself presides over all, with sons Ettore and Massimino handling visitor logistics. Top priority once you have settled in to your refurbished rooms is to make friends with all the farm dogs, who will then be your faithful companions on country walks past apricot orchards and fields of artichokes. Opt for half-board terms as most of the food is home-produced, including the rich buffalo stew, fresher-than-ever mozzarella, and more elaborate dishes brought with relentless regularity from the kitchens; you'll be seated, as is the tradition, with other guests around a banquet table. For those without transport, transfers can be arranged from Paestum main-line station; bicycles may be borrowed on a first-come, first-served basis. **Pros:** a great taste of a working farm; a banquet every evening. **Cons:** confusing to find; not for non-dog fans. ⊠ *Via Seliano, about 1 km (½ mi) down dirt track west off main road from Capaccio Scalo to Paestum, Paestum* ☎*0828/723634* ⊕*www.agriturismoseliano.it* 🛏*14 rooms* ⌂*In-hotel: Restaurant, pool, bicycles, some pets allowed* ⊟*AE, MC, V* ☉*Closed Nov.–Feb., will open for bookings* ¶*FAP.*

ITALIAN VOCABULARY

ENGLISH	ITALIAN	PRONOUNCIATION

BASICS

Yes/no	Sí/No	see/no
Please	Per favore	pear fa-**vo**-ray
Yes, please	Sí grazie	see **grah**-tsee-ay
Thank you	Grazie	**grah**-tsee-ay
You're welcome	Prego	**pray**-go
Excuse me, sorry	Scusi	**skoo**-zee
Sorry!	Mi dispiace!	mee dis-spee-**ah**-chay
Good morning/ afternoon	Buongiorno	bwohn-**jor**-no
Good evening	Buona sera	**bwoh**-na **say**-ra
Good-bye	Arrivederci	a-ree-vah-**dare**-chee
Mr. (Sir)	Signore	see-**nyo**-ray
Mrs. (Ma'am)	Signora	see-**nyo**-ra
Miss	Signorina	see-nyo-**ree**-na
Pleased to meet you	Piacere	pee-ah-**chair**-ray
How are you?	Come sta?	**ko**-may **stah**
Very well, thanks	Bene, grazie	**ben**-ay **grah**-tsee-ay
Hello (phone)	Pronto?	**proan**-to

NUMBERS

one	uno	**oo**-no
two	due	**doo**-ay
three	tre	tray
four	quattro	**kwah**-tro
five	cinque	**cheen**-kway
six	sei	say
seven	sette	**set**-ay
eight	otto	**oh**-to
nine	nove	**no**-vay
ten	dieci	dee-**eh**-chee
eleven	undici	**oon**-dee-chee
twelve	dodici	**doe**-dee-cee

thirteen	tredici	**tray**-dee-chee
fourteen	quattordici	kwa-**tore**-dee-chee
fifteen	quindici	**kwin**-dee-chee
sixteen	sedici	**say**-dee-chee
seventeen	diciassete	dee-cha-**set**-ay
eighteen	diciotto	dee-**cho**-to
nineteen	diciannove	dee-cha-**no**-vay
twenty	venti	**vain**-tee
twenty-one	ventuno	vain-**too**-no
twenty-two	ventidue	vain-tee-**doo**-ay
thirty	trenta	**train**-ta
forty	quaranta	kwa-**rahn**-ta
fifty	cinquanta	cheen-**kwahn**-ta
sixty	sessanta	seh-**sahn**-ta
seventy	settanta	seh-**tahn**-ta
eighty	ottanta	o-**tahn**-ta
ninety	novanta	no-**vahn**-ta
one hundred	cento	**chen**-to
one thousand	mille	**mee**-lay
ten thousand	diecimila	dee-eh-chee-**mee**-la

USEFUL PHRASES

Do you speak English?	Parla inglese?	**par**-la een-**glay**-zay
I don't speak Italian	Non parlo italiano	non **par**-lo ee-tal-**yah**-no
I don't understand	Non capisco	non ka-**peess**-ko
Can you please repeat?	Può ripetere?	pwo ree-**pet**-ay-ray
Slowly!	Lentamente!	**len**-ta-men-tay
I don't know	Non lo so	non lo **so**
I'm American	Sono americano(a)	**so**-no a-may-ree-**kah**-no(a)
I'm British	Sono inglese	so-no een-**glay**-zay
What's your name?	Come si chiama?	**ko**-may see kee-**ah**-ma

My name is . . .	Mi chiamo . . .	mee kee-**ah**-mo
What time is it?	Che ore sono?	kay o-ray **so**-no
How?	Come?	**ko**-may
When?	Quando?	**kwan**-doe
Yesterday/today/ tomorrow	Ieri/oggi/domani	**yer**-ee/**o**-jee/do-**mah**-nee
This morning/	Stamattina/Oggi	sta-ma-**tee**-na/**o**-jee
afternoon	pomeriggio	po-mer-**ee**-jo
Tonight	Stasera	sta-**ser**-a
What?	Che cosa?	kay **ko**-za
What is it?	Chee cos'é?	kay ko-**zay**
Why?	Perché?	pear-**kay**
Who?	Chi?	kee
Where is . . . the bus stop?	Dov'è . . . la fermata dell'autobus?	doe-**veh** la fer-**mah**-ta del ow-toe-**booss**
the train station?	la stazione?	la sta-tsee-**oh**-nay
the subway?	la metropolitana?	la may-tro-po-lee-**tah**-na
the terminal?	il terminale?	eel ter-mee-**nah**-lay
the post office?	l'ufficio postale?	loo-**fee**-cho po-**stah**-lay
the bank?	la banca?	la **bahn**-ka
the . . . hotel?	l'hotel . . .?	lo-**tel**
the store?	il negozio?	eel nay-**go**-tsee-o
the cashier?	la cassa?	la **kah**-sa
the . . . museum?	il museo . . .?	eel moo-**zay**-o
the hospital?	l'ospedale?	lo-spay-**dah**-lay
the first-aid station?	il pronto soccorso?	Eel **pron**-to so-**kor**-so
the elevator?	l'ascensore?	la-shen-**so**-ray
a telephone?	un telefono?	oon tay-**lay**-fo-no
the restrooms?	Dov'è il bagno?	do-**vay** eel **bahn**-yo
Here/there	Qui/là	kwee/la
Left/right	A sinistra/a destra	a see-**neess**-tra/a **des**-tra
Straight ahead	Avanti dritto	a-**vahn**-tee **dree**-to
Is it near/far?	È vicino/lontano?	ay vee-**chee**-no/lon-**tah**-no
I'd like . . . a room the key	Vorrei . . . una camera la chiave	vo-**ray** **oo**-na **kah**-may-ra la kee-**ah**-vay

a newspaper	un giornale	oon jor-**nah**-lay
a stamp	un francobollo	oon frahn-ko-**bo**-lo
I'd like to buy . . .	Vorrei comprare . . .	vo-**ray** kom-**prah**-ray
How much is it?	Quanto costa?	**kwahn**-toe **coast**-a
It's expensive/ cheap	È caro/economico	ay **car**-o/ay-ko-**no**-mee-ko
A little/a lot	Poco/tanto	**po**-ko/**tahn**-to
More/less	Più/meno	pee-**oo**/**may**-no
Enough/too (much)	Abbastanza/troppo	a-bas-**tahn**-sa/**tro**-po
I am sick	Sto male	sto **mah**-lay
Call a doctor	Chiama un dottore	kee-**ah**-mah oon doe-**toe**-ray
Help!	Aiuto!	a-**yoo**-toe
Stop!	Alt!	ahlt
Fire!	Al fuoco!	ahl **fwo**-ko
Caution/Look out!	Attenzione!	a-ten-**syon**-ay

DINING OUT

A bottle of . . .	Una bottiglia di . . .	**oo**-na bo-**tee**-lee-ahdee
A cup of . . .	Una tazza di . . .	**oo**-na **tah**-tsa dee
A glass of . . .	Un bicchiere di . . .	oon bee-key-**air**-ay dee
Bill/check	Il conto	eel **cone**-toe
Bread	Il pane	eel **pah**-nay
Breakfast	La prima colazione	la **pree**-ma ko-la-**tsee**-oh-nay
Cocktail/aperitif	L'aperitivo	la-pay-ree-**tee**-vo
Dinner	La cena	la **chen**-a
Fixed-price menu	Menù a prezzo fisso	may-**noo** a **pret**-so **fee**-so
Fork	La forchetta	la for-**ket**-a
I am diabetic	Ho il diabete	o eel dee-a-**bay**-tay
I am vegetarian	Sono vegetariano/a	**so**-no vay-jay-ta-ree-**ah**-no/a
I'd like . . .	Vorrei . . .	vo-**ray**
I'd like to order	Vorrei ordinare	vo-**ray** or-dee-**nah**-ray

Is service included?	Il servizio è incluso?	eel ser-**vee**-tzee-o ay een-**kloo**-zo
It's good/bad	È buono/cattivo	ay **bwo**-no/ka-**tee**-vo
It's hot/cold	È caldo/freddo	ay **kahl**-doe/**fred**-o
Knife	Il coltello	eel kol-**tel**-o
Lunch	Il pranzo	eel **prahnt**-so
Menu	Il menù	eel may-**noo**
Napkin	Il tovagliolo	eel toe-va-lee-**oh**-lo
Please give me . . .	Mi dia . . .	mee **dee**-a
Salt	Il sale	eel **sah**-lay
Spoon	Il cucchiaio	eel koo-kee-**ah**-yo
Sugar	Lo zucchero	lo **tsoo**-ker-o
Waiter/Waitress	Cameriere/ cameriera	ka-mare-**yer**-ay/ ka-mare-**yer**-a
Wine list	La lista dei vini	la **lee**-sta **day**-ee **vee**-nee

Travel Smart

GETTING HERE AND AROUND

▌ AIR TRAVEL

Air travel to Italy is frequent and virtually problem-free, except for airport- or airline-related union strikes that may cause delays. Alitalia, Italy's national flag carrier, has the most nonstop flights to Rome and Milan, from which you can fly on to Naples.

Flying time to Milan or Rome is approximately 8–8½ hours from New York, 10–11 hours from Chicago, 11½ hours from Dallas (via New York), and 11½ hours from Los Angeles. Flights from Rome to Naples are around 45 minutes and from Milan to Naples, about 1 hour.

Confirm flights within Italy the day before travel. Labor strikes are frequent and can affect not only air travel, but also the local trains that serve the airport. Your airline will have information about strikes directly affecting its flight schedule. If you are taking a train to get to the airport, check with the local tourist agency or rail station about upcoming strikes.

Airline Security Issues Transportation Security Administration (⊕ www.tsa.gov) has answers for almost every question that might come up.

Airline Complaints Office of Aviation Enforcement and Proceedings (Aviation Consumer Protection Division ☎ 202/366–4000 ⊕ airconsumer.ost.dot.gov). **Federal Aviation Administration Consumer Hotline** (☎ 866/835–5322 ⊕ www.faa.gov).

A helpful Web site for information (location, phone numbers, local transportation, etc.) about all of the airports in Italy is ⊕ www.travel-library.com/airports/europe/italy.

AIRPORTS

The major gateways to Italy include Rome's Aeroporto Leonardo da Vinci (FCO), better known as Fiumicino, and Milan's Aeroporto Malpensa (MXP). Most flights to Naples from North America and Australia make connections at Fiumicino and Malpensa or another European airport, though an increasing number of budget airlines offer direct flights to Naples from European destinations. You can also take the FS airport train to Rome's Termini station and catch a train to Naples. It will take about 30 minutes to get from Fiumicino to Rome's main train station.

Located just outside Naples, **Aeroporto Capodichino** (NAP) serves the Campania region. It handles domestic and international flights, including several flights daily between Naples and Rome (flight time 45 minutes). The airport is currently run by the local handler GESAC with some logistical assistance from BAA (British Airports Authority), the majority stakeholder.

Being so close to Naples's city center—a 10-minute drive at nonpeak travel times—Capodichino Airport has little room for expansion. There are skeletal facilities at the airport, so no Internet center, no fitness center, and no airport hotels: on short stopovers—especially if you have to leave early the next morning before road traffic builds up—you're better off staying in the city center. The nearest thing to an airport hotel is the Holiday Inn (shuttle service every hour to the airport): in the *Centro Direzionale* (Business District) close to the industrial eastern suburbs, this is not the sort of place for evening strolls by the Mediterranean.

Airport Information Aeroporto Capodichino (✉ Via Umberto Maddalena, 5 km [3 mi] north of Naples ☎ 081/7896111 ⊕ www.gesac.it). **Aeroporto Leonardo da Vinci-Fiumicino** (Fiumicino ✉ 35 km ([20 mi]) southwest of Rome ☎ 06/65951 ⊕ www.adr.it). **Aeroporto Malpensa** (✉ 45 km ([28 mi]) north of Milan ☎ 02/74852200 ⊕ www.sea-aeroportimilano.it).

FLIGHTS

When flying internationally, you must usually choose between a domestic carrier, the national flag carrier of the country, and a foreign carrier from a third country. You may, for example, choose to fly Alitalia to Italy—as the national flag carrier it has the greatest number of nonstops. However, domestic carriers, such as Air One, AlpiEagles, and Meridiana, may have direct connections between Naples and destinations in other European countries and slightly cheaper flights within Italy.

Until recently, no international carrier made a transatlantic flight to Naples, but EuroFly now connects New York's JFK Airport to Naples' Aeroporto Capodichino three times a week (it also flies to Rome, Bologna, and Palermo). Alitalia offers an extensive schedule of daily flights connecting Naples with the major international hubs of Rome and Milan, as well as Turin and Venice. It continues to offer more nonstop flights to Italy from the United States than any other airline, including a nonstop flight from San Francisco to Milan's Malpensa Airport. Alitalia's North American gateways are Boston, Chicago, Los Angeles, Miami, San Francisco, New York City, Montreal, and Toronto. The main sales offices for the airline in the United States is in New York City, with other offices in Washington, D.C., and San Francisco; the main reservations number and sales office numbers are listed below. For further information about schedules, special fare promotions visit *www.alitalia.com* or *www.alitaliausa.com*.

Domestic connections to Naples are also handled by other carriers, such as Air One (Genoa, Milan Linate, Turin, and Trieste), Alpieagles (Cagliari, Catania, Olbia, Palermo, and Verona), and Meridiana (Cagliari, Milan Linate, and Verona). For connections from abroad, Lufthansa's partner Air One also offer weekend flights from Athens, AlpiEagles offers a daily flight from Barcelona, and Meridiana

compete with Air France on direct flights from Paris. Several other carriers link major European cities with Naples—for instance, British Airways offers a direct route from London-Gatwick, Iberia connects Madrid and Naples, and Lufthansa serves Naples–Munich passengers. Other connections are offered between Naples and Dublin (Aer Lingus), and Malta (Air Malta). Internet bargain hunters appreciate the cut-rate fares from London-Stansted to Naples with the carrier EasyJet, while Ryan Air delivers unbelievable fares to Bari, Brindisi, and Pescara, all on Italy's Adriatic coast, three to five hours away by bus or train. Milan and Rome are also served by Continental Airlines and Delta Air Lines. American Airlines, United Airlines, and Northwest Airlines fly into Milan. US Airways serves Rome. Lower-price charter flights to a range of Italian and other European destinations are available, especially from June through September.

Airline Contacts Air One (☎ 06/48880069, 199/207080 within Italy ⊕ www.flyairone. it). **Alitalia** (☎ 800/223–5730, 800/650055 within Italy ⊕ www.alitalia.com ☎ 212/903–3300 New York, 310/568–5941 Los Angeles, 312/644–0404 Chicago, 617/267–2882 Boston). **British Airways** (☎ 800/247–9297 ⊕ www.britishairways.com). **EasyJet** (☎ 848/887766 ⊕ www.easyjet.com). **EuroFly** (☎ 800/459–4980 www.euroflyusa.com). **TuiFly** (☎ 199/192–692 ⊕ www.tuifly.com).

Domestic Carriers Air One (☎ 06/488800, 199/207080 within Italy ⊕ www.flyairone. it). **Alitalia** (☎ 800/223–5730, 800/650055 within Italy www.alitalia.com). **Meridiana** (☎ 892/928 within Italy ⊕ www.meridiana.it).

▌ BUS TRAVEL

Campania's bus network is extensive and in some areas buses can be more direct (and, therefore, faster) than local trains, so it's a good idea to **compare bus and train schedules.** Bus services outside cities are organized on a regional level, and often by private companies. Campania has three main bus companies, listed below. ANM handles buses within Naples, CTP usually handles medium- and long-distance routes out of Naples, while SITA services the Amalfi Coast. Taking buses from Naples requires both research and patience, since there's no central bus station as such: different bus lines leave from different city squares, with the situation being compounded by recent traffic reorganization in Piazza Garibaldi. Once you've tracked down the schedule and departure point, you'll find the service fairly reliable and uniform. All buses—as indeed all public transport—are non-smoking.

CUTTING COSTS

For bus services within the region of Campania you should buy an **Unicocampania** ticket. For bus trips to Benevento for example, where bus connections are better than train, you should buy a Fascia 6 ticket (€4.20, valid 180 minutes). This will cover combined use of other buses, funiculars, trains, trams, and trolley buses on an outward journey. If you purchase a three-day **Artcard,** this will give you free transport within the region, regardless of the *Fascia*. Children travel free up to six years of age or, curiously, just more than 3 feet tall.

Discount Passes Artecard (☎ *800/600–601 toll-free in Italy* ⊕ *www.campaniartecard.it*). **Unicocampania** (☎ *081/5513109* ⊕ *www. unicocampania.it*).

PAYING

Tickets are not sold on board buses so you must purchase them in advance (cash only) by machine, at newsstands, or at tobacconists. Remember to time-stamp your ticket after you board as conductors often do spot checks. Keep in mind that many ticket sellers close for several hours at midday, so it's always wise to stock up on bus tickets when you have the chance.

Bus Information ANM (⊠ *Piazza Garibaldi, main Servizio CTP bus stop, Napoli* ☎ *081/ 7632177* ⊕ *www.anm.it*). **CTP** (⊠ *Via Sannio 19, Napoli* ☎ *081/7005091*). **SITA** (⊠ *Via*

Pisanelli 3, south of Piazza Municipio, Napoli ☎ *081/5522176 or 081/5934644* ⊕ *www. sitabus.it*).

▌ CAR TRAVEL

Italy has an extensive network of *autostrade* (toll highways), complemented by equally well-maintained but free *superstrade* (expressways). Save the ticket you are issued at an autostrada entrance, as you need it to exit; on some shorter autostrade, you pay the toll when you enter. Viacards, on sale for €25 at many autostrada locations, allow you to pay for tolls in advance. At special lanes you simply slip the card into a designated slot.

An *uscita* is an "exit." A *tangenziale* bypasses a city entirely. *Strade regionale* and *strade provinciale* (regional and provincial highways, denoted by *S, SS, SR,* or *SP* numbers) may be two-lane roads, as are all secondary roads; directions and turnoffs aren't always clearly marked.

Combine the cost of gasoline (as much as €1.40 per liter, or $6 per gallon, at this writing), the languishing dollar, the gridlock traffic in and around Naples, parking fees, and driving standards in southern Italy, and you get five good reasons for not traveling by car in Campania. For recidivist motorists and those who need to reach isolated locations, there's an extensive network of *autostrade* (toll highways), complemented by equally well-maintained but free *superstrade* (expressways). The ticket you're issued upon entering an autostrada must be returned when you exit and pay the toll; on some shorter highways, like the *Tangenziale* around Naples, the flat-rate toll €0.65 is paid upon exiting; the Naples–Salerno toll €1.40 is paid on entry. Viacard cards, on sale at many autostrada locations, make paying tolls easier and faster, although if you're just using the car on local autostrade within Campania you may find yourself with substantial surplus credit on your card at the end of your trip. A *raccordo* or *tangenziale* is a ring road surrounding a city. *Strade statali* (state highways, denoted by *S* or *SS* numbers) may be single-lane roads, as are all secondary roads; directions and turnoffs are not always clearly marked.

Your driver's license may not be recognized outside your home country. An International Driver's Permit is a good idea; it's available from the American or Canadian automobile association, and, in the United Kingdom, from the Automobile Association or Royal Automobile Club. These international permits are universally recognized, and having one in your wallet may save you a problem with the local authorities.

If you want to hire a driver, this service can usually be arranged through hotels or travel agents. Agree on a flat daily rate beforehand, which will include the driver, car, and gasoline. In most cases you would be expected to pay extra for the driver's meals, as well as any parking fees incurred.

AUTO CLUBS

There are two major automobile clubs operative in Italy: ACI (Automobil Club D'Italia), which is in fact less of a club and more of a vehicle ownership registration service, which also provides breakdown assistance coverage; subscription to the TCI (Touring Club Italiano) provides motorists with maps and logistical assistance when planning journeys and holidays, besides taking an active interest in Italian heritage preservation. For a small annual surcharge, the TCI will also provide breakdown assistance.

In Italy Automobil Club D'Italia (☎ *081/ 7253811* ⊕ *www.napoli.aci.it*). **Touring Club Italiano** (☎ *081/4203489 www. touringclubcampania.it*).

In the U.S. American Automobile Association (*AAA* ☎ *315/797–5000* ⊕ *www.aaa.com*); most contact with the organization is through state and regional members.

GASOLINE

Gas stations are located along the main highways. Those on autostrade are open 24 hours. Otherwise, gas stations are generally open Monday through Saturday from 7 AM to 7 PM with a break at lunchtime. Many stations also have self-service pumps, which usually accept bills of €5, €10, or €20. Gas stations on autostrade are open 24 hours, offering motorists the choice of self-service or full-service gasoline (more expensive per liter, no tip required). Credit cards are widely accepted, especially at major stations along main roads. Gas costs about €1.30–€1.40 per liter. Rental cars may take so-called *benzina verde* (unleaded fuel known as "green gasoline") or diesel. Confusingly, the Italian word *gasolio* means diesel fuel. It costs about €1.10 per liter (ask about the fuel type for your rental car before you leave the agency).

PARKING

Parking space is at a premium in Naples and most towns, but especially in the *centri storici* (historic centers), which are filled with narrow streets and restricted circulation zones. It's often a good idea (if not the only option) to park your car in a designated (preferably attended) lot. The *parcometro*, the Italian version of metered parking in which you purchase prepaid tickets (from a newsstand or tobacconist's) that you scratch to indicate time and date of arrival and leave on the dashboard, is common both in Naples and in many of the surrounding towns. You will also find coin-only parking ticket machines at regular intervals. Watch the display panel at the front of the machine, which gives you the expiration time as you insert the coins. If driving to the more popular venues in Naples at night, you may be encouraged to park by a *parcheggiatore abusivo* (unlicensed parking attendant) who will expect a tip (about €1). Bear in mind that this will not stop your car from being clamped or towed away, and such practices are really just fueling the submerged economy.

A red sign with a horizontal white stripe through it means do not enter; a blue circular sign with a red slash or an X means no parking, as do the signs VIETATO SOSTARE, DIVIETO DI SOSTA, and NON PARCHEGGIARE. Wheel-clamping is increasingly common in Naples, making parking offenses potentially costly and time-consuming. ■TIP➔If you have baggage in the car, always park your car in an attended car park or garage.

RENTALS
Most American chains have affiliates in Italy, but the rates are usually lower if you book a car before you leave home. To rent a car in Italy, generally you must be at least 23 years old. Additional drivers must be identified in the contract and must qualify with the age limits. There may be an additional daily fee for more than one driver. Upon rental, all companies require credit cards as a warranty; to rent bigger cars (2,000 cc or more), you must often show two credit cards. There are no special restrictions on senior-citizen drivers. Book car seats, required for children under age 3, in advance (the cost is generally about €36 for the duration of the rental). Most rentals are standard transmissions. You must request an automatic and usually pay a higher rate.

All rental agencies operating in Italy require that you buy a collision-damage waiver and a theft-protection policy, but those costs will already be included in the rates you are quoted. Be aware that coverage may be denied if the named driver on the rental contract is not the driver at the time of the incident. In Sicily there are some roads for which rental agencies deny coverage; ask in advance if you plan to travel in remote regions. Also ask your rental company about other included coverage when you reserve the car and/or pick it up.

Hiring a car with a driver can come in handy, particularly if you plan to do some wine tasting or drive along the Amalfi Coast. Ask at your hotel for recommended drivers, or inquire at the local tourist office.

RENTAL CARS
Renting a car in Italy is helpful when exploring the off-the-beaten-track countryside, but not necessary, as the bus system throughout Campania is excellent and far-flung. Signage on country roads is usually pretty good, but be prepared for fast and impatient fellow drivers. Major car-rental companies have boxy "utility" cars and Fiats in various sizes that are always in good condition.

Your driver's license may not be recognized outside your home country. You may not be able to rent a car without an International Driving Permit (IDP), which can be used only in conjunction with a valid driver's license and which translates your license into 10 languages. Check the AAA Web site for more info as well as for IDPs ($15) themselves.

LOCAL AGENCIES
Major Agencies Alamo (☎877/222–9075 ⊕www.alamo.com). **Avis** (☎800/230–4898 ⊕www.avis.com). **Budget** (☎800/472–3525 ⊕www.budget.com). **Hertz** (☎800/654–3131 ⊕www.hertz.com). **National Car Rental** (☎877/222–9058 ⊕www.nationalcar.com). **Nova** (☎866/668–2227 ⊕www.novacarhire.com).

Car and Driver Due Golfi Car Service (☎339/830–7748 in Italy ⊕www.duegolficarservice.com).

ROAD CONDITIONS
Autostrade are well maintained, as are most interregional highways. The condition of provincial (county) roads varies, but road maintenance at this level is generally decent in Campania. Street and road signs are often challenging—a good map and patience are essential. When stopping to ask locals for directions, it's usually pointless to refer to maps as there is no widespread map-reading culture in southern Italy. Just say the name of your destination and listen carefully or watch for hand gestures. In general, driving standards are poor: some drive fast and are

impatient with those who don't, while others dawdle along oblivious to those behind them. Widespread nonuse of direction indicators means you have to do a lot of guesswork while motoring.

If you have to drive into Naples, Salerno, or into any densely populated urban area in Campania, try to time your journey to coincide with non-peak times. A good time is between noon and 1 PM before kids come out of morning school, and early afternoons between 2:30 PM and 4 PM are usually quiet. Avoid driving to and from the major resorts (Amalfi, Positano, Sorrento, and the Campi Flegrei west of Naples) on Sunday and holidays, especially in spring and summer. Expect considerable traffic entering and within towns on Sunday evenings, a favorite day for a *passeggiata con la macchina* (motorized stroll). Navigating the Amalfi Drive (coastal road) can be an intense experience and should be avoided by inexperienced drivers. Bus and ferry connections link the towns around the coast.

ROADSIDE EMERGENCIES

In the event of a breakdown, if you're on a major highway or autostrada, you should stay in your car and wait for assistance. It can be extremely dangerous to walk by the roadside. If you have to abandon your vehicle, make sure you use the flares and wear the orange jacket that every vehicle in Italy should contain.

In the event of an accident that goes beyond a mild bump or scratch, make sure the emergency services are notified as soon as possible—this is where mobile phones really come in handy. If you have rented the car, there should be an emergency number on the rental contract or on the key ring.

Emergency Services ACI Emergency Service offers 24-hour road service. Dial 116 from any phone to reach the ACI dispatch operator.

RULES OF THE ROAD

Driving is on the right. Regulations are similar to those in the United States, except that a right turn is not permitted

on a red light. Daytime use of headlights is now obligatory on all roads outside urban areas, and seat belts must be worn at all times—despite high noncompliance rates in Campania. In most Italian towns the use of the horn is forbidden; a large sign, ZONA DI SILENZIO, indicates where. Elsewhere, according to the Italian Highway Code, horns can only be used in situations where there is "immediate and real danger." Some drivers interpret this as covering every sharp bend on the Amalfi Coast, although an alternative noise-free technique is to slow down and keep a foot hovering over the brake pedal. In winter you'll often be required to have snow chains, especially when traveling south on the main autostrada from Salerno to Reggio Calabria, and in upland areas within the region. Speed limits are 130 KPH (80 MPH) on autostrade and 90 KPH (55 MPH) on state and provincial roads, unless otherwise marked. If your mobile phone rings while driving, you should either ignore it or pull over and stop when it's safe to do so—stiff sanctions have been introduced to reduce the use of handheld mobile phones while driving. Fines for driving after drinking are heavy, including the suspension of license and the additional possibility of six months' imprisonment.

▌ TRAIN TRAVEL

The fastest trains in Italy are the Alta Velocità (TAV) trains run by Eurostar, operating between Rome and Naples (90 minutes). A close second come the standard Eurostar trains (1hour 53 minutes), which run virtually the length and breadth of Italy, including Naples–Milan via Rome, Florence, and Bologna; seat reservations and supplement are included in the fare. Some of these (the ETR 460 trains) have little aisle and luggage space (although there's a space near the door where you can put large bags). To avoid having to squeeze through narrow aisles, board at your car (look for the number on the reservation ticket). Car numbers are displayed on their exterior. Next-fastest trains are the Intercity (IC) trains, for which you pay a supplement and for which seat reservations may be required and are always advisable. *Interregionale* trains usually make more stops and are a little slower. *Regionale* and *locale* trains are the slowest; many serve commuters.

Note Naples has four main-line stations: Stazione Centrale, Piazza Garibaldi, Napoli Mergellina, and Napoli Campi Flegrei. Stazione Central (ground level) and Piazza Garibaldi (lower level) are in the same building; for Piazza Garibaldi, take the escalator down to the level below Napoli Centrale (follow signs to the *Metropolitana*). Some trains to Rome leave from the classy station of Mergellina, four stops away from Piazza Garibaldi on the Metropolitana. As many as three trains—of varying speed and cost—connect Roma Termini and Napoli Centrale every hour (Alta Velocità: 1 hour 27 minutes, €33.90, second class; Eurostar: 1 hour 45 minutes, €30.40, second class; Intercity: about 2 hour, €19.50, second class); fewer departures on Sunday and after 5 PM.

There is refreshment service on all long-distance trains, with mobile carts and a cafeteria or dining car. Tap water on trains is not drinkable. There's no smoking on any public transport in Italy, though you will find diehards puffing away near the luggage compartments between carriages. As mechanically opening windows are being phased out on all trains, this means you can expect wafts of stale cigarette smoke whenever connecting doors between cars are opened.

When traveling in the Naples area, potential confusion can arise in Pompeii, as the main-line station is a good 20-minute walk from the archaeological site. For the site, you need to take the Circumvesuviana network from Naples to Sorrento and get off at Pompei Scavi (35 minutes).

CLASSES
Most Italian trains have first and second classes. On local trains the higher first-class fare gets you little more than a clean doily on the headrest of your seat, but on long-distance trains you get wider seats, more legroom, and better ventilation and lighting. At peak travel times, first-class train travel is worth the difference. Remember **always try to make seat reservations in advance,** for either class, as you can easily run into long ticket lines at the station just when you're hoping to board a train. One advantage of traveling first class is that the cars are almost always not crowded—or, at the very least, less crowded than the second-class compartments. A first-class ticket, in Italian, is *prima classe*; second is *seconda classe.*

CUTTING COSTS
To save money, **look into rail passes.** But be aware that if you don't plan to cover many miles, you may come out ahead by buying individual tickets.

If Italy is your only destination in Europe, **consider purchasing a Trenitalia pass,** which allows unlimited travel on the entire Italian Rail network for a set number of travel days within two months: $266 for 4 days of travel in first class ($213 second class); 8 days of travel ($385 first class, $310 second class); and 10 days of travel ($444 first class, $359 second class).

Once in Italy, **inquire about the Cartaviaggio Smart (Smart Travel Card) if you're under 26** (€40 for one year), which entitles the holder to a 10% discount on all first- and second-class tickets in Italy, and 25% discounts on international lines. Those under 26 should also inquire about discount travel fares under the Billet International Jeune (BIJ) and Euro Domino Junior schemes. Also in Italy, you can **purchase the Cartaviaggio Relax (Relax Travel Card) if you're over 60** (€30 for one year), which also allows a 15% discount on all first- and second-class rail travel. For further information, check out the Ferrovie dello Stato (FS) Web site (⊕ *www.trenitalia. com*). Toddlers under 4 travel free on trains, though they have no right to a seat, while children under 12 travel for half the fare.

Italy is one of 18 countries in which you can use **Eurailpasses,** which provide unlimited first-class travel in all of the participating countries. If you plan to rack up the miles, get a standard pass. Train travel is available for 3 days (from $248) up to 10 days ($458). You can also receive free or discounted fares on some ferry lines. In addition to standard Eurailpasses, **ask about special rail-pass plans.** Among these are the Eurail Youthpass (for those under age 26), Eurail Saverpass and Eurail Saver Flexipass (which give a discount for two or more people traveling together), Eurail Flexipass (which allows a certain number of travel days within a set period), and the EurailDrive Pass, which combines travel by train and rental car. Whichever pass you choose, remember that you must **purchase your Eurailpass or Eurail Selectpass before you leave** for Europe. You can get further information and order tickets at the Rail Europe Web site (⊕*www. raileurope.com*).

Many travelers assume that rail passes guarantee them seats on the trains they wish to ride. Not so. You need to book seats ahead even if you're using a rail pass. Seat reservations are required on some European trains, particularly high-speed trains, and are a good idea on trains that may be crowded—particularly in summer on popular routes. You'll also need a reservation if you purchase sleeping accommodations. Trains going from the north of Italy via Naples through to Reggio Calabria in the toe of Italy will be particularly tightly packed, especially around weekends and public holidays. If traveling on a Saturday evening or Sunday, it may be worth finding out about important soccer matches and steering well clear of local fans by upgrading to first class or changing your schedule.

If you're on a tight schedule or just want to avoid unpleasant surprises, double-check beforehand whether there's a strike (*sciopero*) planned for the day you're traveling. On average, industrial action is usually planned for 24-hour periods on Friday or Monday, and only limited service may be provided while the strike lasts.

FARES AND SCHEDULES

Trains can be very crowded; it's always a good idea to make a reservation. To avoid long lines at station windows, **buy tickets with seat reservations up to two months in advance** at travel agencies displaying the Trenitalia emblem. Tickets can be purchased at the last minute, but seat reservations can be made at agencies (or the train station) in advance on Eurostar and Alta Velocità trains, your ticket includes a free seat reservation: if you board without a ticket, you will have to pay a surcharge of €25 on application to train staff.

Except on Eurostar and Alta Velocità trains where your ticket is only valid for one train on one day, all **tickets must be date-stamped in the small yellow or red machines near the tracks before you board.** Once stamped, your ticket is valid for six hours if your destination is within 200 km (124 mi), for 24 hours for destinations beyond that. You can get on and off at will at stops in between for the duration of the ticket's validity. If you forget to stamp your ticket in the machine, or you didn't buy a ticket, you are liable to a hefty €50 fine, over and above the fare to your destination. Don't wait for the conductor to find out that you're without a valid ticket (unless the train is overcrowded and walking becomes impossible), as he might charge you a much heavier fine. You can buy train tickets for nearby destinations (within a 200-km [124-mi] range) at tobacconists and at ticket machines in stations.

PAYING

In most cases you can pay for train tickets with any of the major credit cards, though ticket office staff at smaller stations (like Mergellina in Naples) may still raise eyebrows at plastic. Only euros are accepted in cash payment, though at Napoli Centrale station there's a handy exchange bureau right next to the ticket office—and a bank in the same forecourt—where you can change currency.

Information and Passes Eurailpasses are available through travel agents and **Rail Europe** (☎ 800/622–8600 ⊕ www.raileurope. com). **DER Travel Services** (☎ 800/660–5300 ⊕ www.der.com). Italian rail passes can be purchased through DER as well.

Information The main train station in Campania is Naples' **Stazione Centrale** (✉ Piazza Garibaldi ☎ 892/021 ⊕ www.trenitalia.com). The Ferrovia Circumvesuviana leaves for points east from the **Stazione Circumvesuviana** (✉ Corso Garibaldi, 387 ☎ 081/7722111 ⊕ www.vesuviana.it); all trains also stop on the lower level of Stazione Centrale. Destinations include Ercolano (Herculaneum), Pompei Scavi–Villa dei Misteri (Pompeii), and Sorrento. Note that there are two Circumvesuviana stations in the town of Pompeii, served by different lines. For the archaeological site, take the Sorrento line. SEPSA manages two railway lines that leave from the **Stazione Cumana** (✉ Piazzetta Cumana, 100; near Montesanto Metro station ☎ 081/7354111 ⊕ www.sepsa.it). Both end at Torregaveta, at the west end of the Bay of Naples; the Cumana line goes along the coast and stops at Pozzuoli and Lucrino (near Baia), among other places. **Salerno's train station** (✉ Piazza V. Veneto ☎ 892/021 ⊕ www. trenitalia.com) is a stop on the Milan–Reggio Calabria line.

Other Resources *Italy by Train* by Tim Jepson (Fodor's Travel Publications ☎ 800/533–6478 or from bookstores; $16). **Trenitalia** (☎ 892/ 021 in Italy ⊕ www.trenitalia.com).

ESSENTIALS

■ ACCOMMODATIONS

Campania has a varied and abundant number of hotels, bed-and-breakfasts, *agriturismi (farm stays)*, and rental properties. Throughout the cities and the countryside you can find very sophisticated, luxurious palaces and villas as well as rustic farmhouses and small hotels. Six-hundred-year-old palazzi and converted monasteries have been restored as luxurious hotels, while retaining the original atmosphere. At the other end of the spectrum, boutique hotels inhabit historic buildings using chic Italian design for the interiors. Increasingly, the famed Italian wineries are creating rooms and apartments for three-day to weeklong stays.

The lodgings we list are the cream of the crop in each price category. We always list the facilities that are available, but we don't specify whether they cost extra; when pricing accommodations, always ask what's included and what costs extra. Properties are assigned price categories based on the range between their least- and most-expensive standard double room at high season (excluding holidays).

Note that this region of Italy has many resort hotels and in peak-season months (usually June to September), some of them require either half- or full-board arrangements, whereby your (increased) room tab includes lunch or lunch and dinner provided by the hotel restaurant. Board plans, which are usually an option offered in addition to the basic room plan, are generally only available with a minimum two- or three-night stay and are, of course, more expensive than the basic room rate, running from €15 to €50 per meal. Note that the hotel price charts in this book reflect basic room rates only. Inquire about board plans when making your reservations; details and prices are often stated on hotel Web sites.

Useful terms to know when booking a room are *aria condizionata* (air-conditioning), *bagno in stanza* (private bath), *letto matrimoniale* (double bed), *letti singoli* (twin beds), *letti singoli uniti* (twin beds pushed together). Italy does not really have queen- or king-size beds, although some beds, particularly in four- and five-star accommodations, can be larger than standard. Phrases that could come in handy include: *Vi prego di fornire informazioni riguardo il vostro albergo/pensione. Vorrei una camera doppia/camera matrimoniale con bagno in camera.* (Please supply me with information regarding your hotel/pensione. I would like a room with two single beds/a double bed with private bath); *Una camera sul piano alto con vista.* (A room on a high floor with a view.); *Una camera al piano basso.* (A room on a low floor.); *Una camera silenziosa.* (A quiet room.)

Hotels with the designation **BP** (for Breakfast Plan) at the end of their listing include breakfast in their rate; offerings can vary from coffee and a roll to an elaborate buffet. Those designated **EP** (European Plan) have no meals included; **MAP** (Modified American Plan) means you get breakfast and dinner; **FAP** (Full American Plan) includes all meals.

APARTMENT AND HOUSE RENTALS

More and more travelers are turning away from the three-countries-in-two-weeks style of touring and choosing to spend a week in one city or a month in the countryside. Renting an apartment, a farmhouse, or a villa can be economical depending on the number of people in your group and your budget. All are readily available throughout Italy. The rental agent may meet you at the property for the initial check-in or the owner may be present, while the rental agent only handles the online reservation and financial arrangements.

Issues to keep in mind when renting an apartment in a city or town are the neighborhood (street noise and ambience), the availability of an elevator or number of stairs, the furnishings (including pots and pans and linens), and the cost of utilities (ask if they included in the rental rate). Inquires about countryside properties should also include how isolated the property is. (Ask about accessibility to the nearest town.)

Contacts At Home Abroad (☎ *212/421–9165* ⊕ *www.athomeabroadinc.com*). **Barclay International Group** (☎*516/364–0064 or 800/845–6636* ⊕ *www.barclayweb.com*). **Drawbridge to Europe** (☎*541/482–7778 or 888/268–1148* ⊕ *www.drawbridgetoeurope. com*). **Homes Away** (☎*416/920–1873 or 800/374–6637* ⊕ *www.homesaway.com*). **Inter-home** (*800/882–6864* ⊕ *www.interhome.us*). **Suzanne B. Cohen & Associates** (☎*207/622–0743* ⊕ *www.villaeurope.com*). **Villanet** (☎*800/964–1891* ⊕ *www.rentavilla.com*). **Villas & Apartments Abroad** (☎*212/213–6435 or 800/433–3020* ⊕ *www.vaanyc.com*). **Villas International** (☎*415/499–9490 or 800/221–2260* ⊕ *www.villasintl.com*). **Villas of Distinction** (☎*800/289–0900* ⊕*www. villasofdistinction.com*).

Local Agents Cuendet USA (☎*800/726–6702* ⊕ *www.rentvillas.com*). **Vacanze in Italia** (☎*413/528–6610* ⊕ *www.homeabroad.com*).

BED-AND-BREAKFASTS

Increasing numbers of southern Italians, especially Neapolitans, are following the long-tried British formula of bed-and-breakfast. Besides the substantial cost savings, this may be your only chance to peek into an Italian home and experience *vita* (life) as lived by the locals. When booking, try to find out exactly what's on offer: it could be a cramped room in a faceless suburb with overly inquisitive hosts, or you could strike it lucky with a room with an 18th-century frescoed ceiling in a quiet city-center location. For further information, contact the local tourist information office or one of the agencies below.

Reservation Services Bed & Breakfast.com (☎*512/322–2710 or 800/462–2632* ⊕*www. bedandbreakfast.com*) also sends out an online newsletter. **Bed & Breakfast Inns Online** (☎*310/280–4363 or 800/215–7365* ⊕*www. bbonline.com*). **BnB Finder.com** (☎*212/432–7693 or 888/547–8226* ⊕ *www.bnbfinder.com*). **Rent a Bed** (☎*081/417721 www.rentabed.it*).

FARM HOLIDAYS AND AGRITOURISM

Rural accommodations in the *agriturismo* (agritourism) category are increasingly popular with both Italians and visitors to Italy. A little surfing on the Internet can pay dividends: just call up a search engine and key in the words, say, "agriturismo" and "Campania," and see what gives. Although technologically literate, few farms in the Naples area accept credit cards, so remember to load up with cash before your stay.

Information Agriturist (☎*06/6852337* ⊕*www.agriturist.it*). **Italy Farm Holidays** (☎*914/631–7880* ⊕ *www.italyfarmholidays. com*). **Turismo Verde** (☎*06/3240111* ⊕*www. turismoverde.it*).

HOME EXCHANGES

With a direct home exchange you stay in someone else's home while they stay in yours. Some outfits also deal with vacation homes, so you're not actually staying in someone's full-time residence, just their vacant weekend place.

Italians have historically not been as enthusiastic about home exchanges as others have been; however, there are many great villas and apartments in Italy owned by foreigners, such as Americans, who use the home exchange services.

Exchange Clubs Home Exchange.com (☎*310/798–3864 or 800/877–8723* ⊕*www. homeexchange.com*); $99.95 for a 1-year membership. **HomeLink International** (☎*800/ 638–3841* ⊕ *www.homelink.org*); $110 yearly for Web-only membership; $170 includes Web access and two catalogs. **Intervac U.S.** (☎*800/756–4663* ⊕ *www.intervacus.com*); $95 for Web-only membership; $195 includes Web access and consultation.

LOCAL DO'S AND TABOOS

GREETINGS

Upon meeting and leave-taking, both friends and strangers wish each other good day or good evening (*buongiorno, buonasera*); *ciao* isn't used between strangers. Italians who are friends greet each other with a kiss, usually first on the left cheek, then on the right. When you meet a new person, shake hands.

SIGHTSEEING

Italy is full of churches, and many of them contain significant works of art. They are also places of worship, however, so be sure to dress appropriately. Shorts, tank tops, and sleeveless garments are taboo in most churches throughout the country. In summer carry a sweater or other item of clothing to wrap around your bare shoulders before entering a church.

You should never bring food into a church, and do not sip from your water bottle while inside. If you have a cell phone, turn it off before entering. And never enter a church when a service is in progress, especially if it is a private affair such as a wedding or baptism.

OUT ON THE TOWN

Table manners in Italy are formal; rarely do Italians share food from their plates. In a restaurant, be formal and polite with your waiter—don't call across the room for attention.

When you've finished your meal and are ready to go, ask for the check (*il conto*); unless it's well past closing time, no waiter will put a bill on your table until you've requested it.

Wine, beer, and other alcoholic drinks are almost always consumed along with food. Public drunkenness is very much looked down upon.

Smoking has been banned in all public establishments, much like it has in much of the United States.

Flowers, chocolates, or a bottle of wine are appropriate hostess gifts when invited to dinner at the home of an Italian.

DOING BUSINESS

Showing up on time for business appointments is the norm and expected in Italy. There are more business lunches than business dinners, and even business lunches aren't common, as Italians view mealtimes as periods of pleasure and relaxation.

Business cards are used throughout Italy, and business suits are the norm for both men and women. To be on the safe side, it is best not to use first names or a familiar form of address until invited to do so.

Business gifts are not the norm, but if one is given it is usually small and symbolic of your home location or type of business.

LANGUAGE

One of the best ways to make connections with the locals is to learn a little of the language. You need not strive for fluency; even just mastering a few basic words and terms is bound to make chatting with the locals more rewarding.

"Please" is *per favore*, "thank you" is *grazie*, and "you're welcome" is *prego*.

In larger cities such as Venice, Rome, and Florence, language is not a big problem. Most hotels have English speakers at their reception desks, and if not, they can always find someone who speaks at least a little English.

You may have trouble communicating in the countryside, but a phrase book and expressive gestures will go a long way.

A phrase book and language-tape set can help get you started before you go.

Fodor's Italian for Travelers (available at bookstores everywhere) is excellent.

■ COMMUNICATIONS

INTERNET

Getting online in and around Naples isn't difficult: public Internet stations and Internet caffès are becoming more and more common. Prices differ from place to place, so spend some time to find the best deal. Bear in mind that you are required by law to show a photo ID before logging on. Some hotels in Campania have in-room modem lines and have implemented Wi-Fi systems but, as with phones, using the hotel's line is relatively expensive. Always check rates before logging on. You might need an adapter for your computer for the European-style plugs. As always, if you're traveling with a laptop, carry a spare battery and an adapter. Never connect your computer to any socket before asking about surge protection. IBM sells a pea-size modem tester that plugs into a telephone jack to check whether the line is safe to use.

Contact **Cybercafes** (⊕ *www.cybercafes.com*) lists more than 4,000 Internet cafés worldwide.

PHONES

The good news is that you can now make a direct-dial telephone call from virtually any point on Earth. The bad news? You can't always do so cheaply. Calling from a hotel is almost always the most expensive option; hotels usually add huge surcharges to all calls, particularly international ones. In Naples, you can phone from call centers, many of which are found around Stazione Centrale. Calling cards usually keep costs to a minimum, but only if you purchase them locally. And then there are mobile phones; as expensive as mobile phone calls can be, they are still usually a much cheaper option than calling from your hotel.

When calling Italy from the U.S., begin by entering 011 (begin with 00 in other countries), followed by Italy's country code, 39. Note that Italian telephone numbers do not have a standard number of digits (they can range anywhere from four to eight). The area code for Naples is 081.

Essentially, the region from Naples to the islands (Capri, Ischia, Procida) and around the Bay of Naples to Sorrento uses the area code 081; the region along the Amalfi Coast from Positano to Salerno uses the area code 089. For example, a call from New York City to Naples would be dialed as 011 + 39 + 081 + phone number. From the United Kingdom, dial 00 + 39 + 081 + phone number. When dialing an Italian number from abroad, you do not drop the initial 0 from the local area code. The same goes for when you're in Italy. When dialing numbers within Italy, you must always use the area code (e.g., 081 for Naples) even if the number you're calling is just down the road. When dialing from Italy overseas, the country code is 001 for the United States and Canada, 0061 for Australia, 0064 for New Zealand, and 0044 for the United Kingdom.

Mobile phone numbers can be easily recognized; they begin with the digit 3, and run up to about 10 numbers. The first three numbers indicate the service provider (for example, 347 is a Vodafone prefix, 339 is TIM) and are followed by another six or seven digits. Both Vodafone and TIM have good network coverage throughout the Naples area.

CALLING WITHIN ITALY

With the advent of mobile phones, public pay phones are becoming increasingly scarce, although they can be found at train and subway stations, main post offices, and in some bars. In rural areas, town squares usually have a pay phone. Pay phones require a *sceda telefonica* (pre-paid phone card). You buy the card (values vary) at Telecom centers, post offices, and tobacconists. Tear off the corner of the card, and insert it in the slot on the phone. When you dial, the card's value appears in the window. After you hang up, the card is returned so you can use it until its value runs out.

For all calls within Italy, whether local or long-distance, dial the area code followed by the number. Rates for long-distance calls vary according to the time of day;

it's cheaper to call before 9 AM and after 7 or 8 PM. Italy uses the prefix "800" for toll-free or "green" numbers.

CALLING OUTSIDE ITALY

Since hotels tend to charge handsomely for long-distance and international calls, it's best to make calls to the rest of Europe and the United States using a prepaid card. The Europa cards on sale for €5 at major newsstands and tobacconists offer up to 380 minutes' worth of calls. Of course, you need to dial either a local Naples number or a toll-free number first in order to gain access. These numbers are given on the card together with the PIN code.

Alternatively, call from public phones using a *scheda telefonica* (see above). These can be purchased from newsstands and tobacconists. You can **make collect calls from any phone by dialing 170,** which will also get you an English-speaking operator. Calling cards purchased in the United States usually offer terrible rates. Buy a local card when you arrive in Naples. Alternatively, you can call AT&T Direct from Italy using the number below.

The country code for the United States is 1 (dial 00 + 1 + U.S. area code and number).

Access Codes AT&T Direct (☎800/172-444).

MOBILE PHONES

If you have a triband phone (some countries use different frequencies from those used in the United States) and your service provider uses the world-standard GSM network (as do T-Mobile, Cingular, and Verizon), you can probably use your phone abroad. Roaming fees can be steep, however: 99¢ a minute is considered reasonable. And overseas you normally pay the toll charges for incoming calls. It's almost always cheaper to send a text message than to make a call, since text messages have a very low set fee (often less than 5¢).

If you just want to make local calls, consider buying a new SIM card (note that your provider may have to unlock your phone for you to use a different SIM card) and a prepaid service plan in the destination. You'll then have a local number and can make local calls at local rates. If your trip is extensive, you could also simply buy a new cell phone in your destination, as the initial cost will be offset over time.

■TIP→If you travel internationally frequently, save one of your old mobile phones or buy a cheap one on the Internet; ask your cell phone company to unlock it for you, and take it with you as a travel phone, buying a new SIM card with pay-as-you-go service in each destination.

The cost of cell phones is dropping; you can purchase a cell phone with a prepaid calling card (no monthly service plan) in Italy for less than €50. Inexpensive cell phones are dual band and will not allow you to call the United States, but using an international calling card and the cell phone solves that problem in a very inexpensive manner. Most medium to large towns have stores dedicated to selling cell phones. You will need to present your passport to purchase the SIM card that goes with the phone.

Rental cell phones are available from some tour operators in Naples and the Amalfi Coast. Most rental contracts require a refundable deposit that covers the cost of the cell phone (€75–€150) and then set up a monthly service plan that is automatically charged to your credit card. Frequently, rental cell phones will be triple band and allow you to call the United States. Be sure to check the rate schedule before you rent a cell phone and commence calling to prevent a nasty surprise when you receive your credit-card bill two or three months later.

■TIP→Beware of cell phone (and PDA) thieves. Keep your phone or PDA in a secure pocket or purse. Do not lay it on the bar when you stop for an espresso. Do not zip it into the outside pocket of your backpack in the city or public transport. Do not leave it in your hotel room. If you are using a phone with a monthly service plan, notify your provider immediately if it is lost or stolen.

Contacts Cellular Abroad (☎ *800/287–5072* ⊕ *www.cellularabroad.com*) rents and sells GMS phones and sells SIM cards that work in many countries. **Mobal** (☎ *888/888–9162* ⊕ *www.mobal.com*) rents mobiles and sells GSM phones (starting at $49) that will operate in 140 countries. Per-call rates vary throughout the world.

▮ CUSTOMS AND DUTIES

You're always allowed to bring goods of a certain value back home without having to pay any duty or import tax. But there's a limit on the amount of tobacco and liquor you can bring back duty-free, and some countries have separate limits for perfumes; for exact figures, check with your customs department. The values of so-called duty-free goods are included in these amounts. When you shop abroad, save all your receipts, as customs inspectors may ask to see them as well as the items you purchased. If the total value of your goods is more than the duty-free limit, you'll have to pay a tax (most often a flat percentage) on the value of everything beyond that limit.

Travelers from the United States should experience little difficulty clearing customs at any airport in Italy. For returning to the United States, clearing customs is sometimes more difficult. U.S. residents are normally entitled to a duty-free exemption of $800 on items accompanying them. As a general rule, mature cheeses like Parmesan—especially if they're vacuum-packed—are fine, but soft cheeses are not. Condiments such as oil, vinegar, honey, jelly, and jam, are generally admissible. You cannot bring back any of that delicious prosciutto or salami or any other meat product. Fresh mushrooms, truffles, or fresh fruits and vegetables are also forbidden. There are also restrictions on the amount of alcohol allowed in duty-free. Export of antiques and antiquities is best avoided unless you have access to specialist advice; you must have documents such as export permits and receipts when importing such items into the United States. In any case, to avoid unpleasant surprises—and such regulations change with the arrival of every health scare—check with the relevant authorities listed below.

Of goods obtained anywhere outside the EU or goods purchased in a duty-free shop within an EU country, the allowances are: (1) 200 cigarettes or 100 cigarillos or 50 cigars or 250 grams of tobacco; (2) 2 liters of still table wine or 1 liter of spirits over 22% volume or 2 liters of spirits under 22% volume or 2 liters of fortified and sparkling wines; and (3) 50 milliliters of perfume and 250 milliliters of toilet water.

Of goods obtained (duty and tax paid) within another EU country, the guidance levels are: (1) 800 cigarettes or 400 cigarillos or 400 cigars or 1 kilogram of tobacco; (2) 90 liters of still table wine plus (3) 10 liters of spirits over 22% volume plus 20 liters of spirits under 22% volume plus 60 liters of sparkling wines plus 110 liters of beer.

To bring pets into Italy, the animal has to have a certificate of health and origin from a recognized public authority in your country, and may also need a certificate that it's free of infectious diseases. For cats and dogs the health certificate must include a declaration of an anti-rabies vaccination at least 20 days and no more than 11 months after issuing the certificate. Similar rules apply to exporting pets from Italy to the United States.

Information in Italy Italian Customs (*Dipartimento delle Dogane e Imposte Indirette* ⊠ *Via A. de Gasperi 20, Naples* ☎ *081/7803036* 🖷 *081/5528234* ⊕ *www. agenziadogane.it*).

U.S. Information U.S. Customs and Border Protection (⊕ *www.cbp.gov*).

■ EATING OUT

Though pizza, mozzarella, and pasta with seafood are the flagship dishes in the Naples region, regional cuisine in Campania is both varied and distinctive. This is reflected by the choice of eateries, especially in Naples and Sorrento: meals range from on-the-hoof two-euro pizzas at kiosks, to earthy *osterie* serving *cucina povera* (land-based cuisine with a good dose of vegetables), and upscale restaurants where service, location, and *piatti* (dishes) should be worth the higher price tag. Italian restaurateurs have become sensitive to those with special dietary requirements, though vegetarians may still have a rough ride, especially as bacon or kindred pork products may be used to flavor many land dishes but never appear as an item on the menu.

MEALS AND MEALTIMES

Breakfast (*la colazione*) is usually served from 7 to 10:30, lunch (*il pranzo*) from 12:30 to 2:30, dinner (*la cena*) from 7:30 PM until midnight. Although it's not usually necessary to reserve a table, remember that you'll find restaurants deserted before 8 in the evening and packed by 9:30, while lunch can extend until as late as 5 PM on Sunday. Menus often seem to be an optional extra in many restaurants, and even if one exists it often bears little relation to what is actually on offer that day. Tune in carefully as the waiter reels off a list of what's good today—following their advice often pays off. A full-scale meal consists of a selection of antipasti followed by a *primo* (pasta or rice), then a *secondo* (meat or fish), rounded off with *frutta o dolci* (fruit or dessert). And unless you want to shock the locals, *never* order a cappuccino after dinner—but a regular espresso is a perfectly acceptable way to finish a meal. A good compromise—if you like your coffee with a dash of milk—is to ask for a *caffè macchiato*.

In general, Neapolitans are moving away from the classic *abbuffata* (Satyricon-style blowout) toward healthier two-course,

or even one-course, meals. You should not feel guilty about skipping the main course, especially if you've already had a rich antipasto and primo.

Enoteche (wine bars) are open also in the morning and late afternoon for a snack at the counter. An enoteca menu is often limited to a selection of cheese, cured meats, salads, and desserts, but if there's a kitchen you'll also find soups, pastas, and main courses, too. Most pizzerias open at 7:30 PM and close around midnight–1 AM, or later in summer and on weekends. Increasingly, pizzas are being served at lunchtime, too. Most bars and caffès are open nonstop from 7 AM until 8 PM; a few stay open until midnight or so. They can usually fix you up with *un tost* (a toasted sandwich) if every other option is closed.

Not too long ago, *ristoranti* tended to be more elegant and expensive than *trattorie* and *osterie,* which serve traditional, home-style fare in an atmosphere to match. But the distinction has blurred considerably, and an osteria in the center of town might be far fancier (and pricier) than a ristorante across the street. In any sit-down establishment, be it a ristorante, osteria, or trattoria, you are generally expected to order at least a two-course meal, such as: a *primo* (first course) and a *secondo* (main course) or a *contorno* (vegetable side dish); an *antipasto* (starter) followed by either a primo or secondo; or a secondo and a *dolce* (dessert).

The typical pizzeria fare in Naples includes *crostini* (similar to bruschetta, with a variety of toppings) and, especially, *fritti* (deep-fried finger food) such as *crocchè* (fried mashed potatoes) and *arancini* (rice balls stuffed with mozzarella).

The handiest and least expensive places for a quick snack between sights are probably bars, cafés, and *friggitorie* (small stalls selling fritti and small hand-held pizzas) spots.

Bars are primarily places to get a coffee and a bite to eat, rather than drinking establishments. Most bars have a selection of *panini* (sandwiches) warmed up on the griddle (*piastra*) and *tramezzini* (sandwiches made of untoasted white bread triangles). Most bars offer beer and a variety of alcohol as well as wines by the glass (sometimes good but more often mediocre). A café (*caffè* in Italian) is like a bar but usually with more tables. Pizza at a café should be avoided—it's usually heated in a microwave.

If you place your order at the counter, ask if you can sit down: some places charge for table service, others do not. In self-service bars and cafés it's good manners to clean your table before you leave. Note that in some places you have to pay a cashier, then place your order and show your *scontrino* (receipt) at the counter. Menus are posted outside most restaurants (in English in tourist areas); if not, you might step inside and ask to take a look at the menu (but don't ask for a table unless you intend to stay). Italians take their food as it is listed on the menu, seldom if ever making special requests such as "dressing on the side" or "hold the olive oil." If you have special dietary needs, however, make them known; they can usually be accommodated. Although mineral water makes its way to almost every table, you can order a carafe of tap water (*acqua dal rubinetto*).

Wiping your bowl clean with a piece of bread (*fare la scarpetta*) is usually considered a sign of appreciation, not bad manners. Spaghetti should be eaten with a fork, although a little help from a spoon won't horrify locals the way cutting spaghetti into little pieces might. Order your espresso (Neapolitans don't usually drink cappuccino after breakfast time) after dessert, not with it. Don't ask for a doggy bag.

Unless otherwise noted, the restaurants listed in this guide are open daily for lunch and dinner.

PAYING

As indicated on *il conto*—the restaurant check—prices for goods and services in Italy include tax. Most restaurants have a cover charge per person, usually listed at the top of the check as *coperto* or *pane*. It should be a modest charge (around €2 per person), except at the most expensive restaurants. Some restaurants add an additional service charge (*servizio*), a percentage of the total bill, but this must be clearly stated on the menu. If *servizio* is included at the bottom of the check, no tip is necessary. Otherwise, a few extra euros left on the table are appreciated. Remember that there's no line to write a tip on the credit card receipt; you will be presented with a slip that includes only the cost of the meal. Although the vast majority of eateries now accept major credit cards, tips are still left in cash. Visa and MasterCard are more widely accepted than American Express.

The price of fish dishes is often given by weight (before cooking), so the price you see on the menu is for 100 grams or a kilo of fish, not for the whole dish. An average fish portion is about 350 grams. When it comes to smaller *caffès* (cafés) and pizzerias, you sometimes place your order and then show your *scontrino* (receipt) when you move to the counter. Like the rest of Italy, there's a two-tier pricing system in many caffès, one for drinks consumed at the counter, and another if you sit down. If there's waiter service in a caffè, you should sit down and patiently wait for service, and resist the temptation to pay first (counter prices), pick up your drink, and walk to the table.

When you leave a dining establishment, take your meal bill or receipt with you; although not a common experience, the Italian finance (tax) police can approach you within 100 yards of the establishment at which you've eaten and ask for a receipt. If you don't have one, they can fine you and will fine the business owner for not providing the receipt. The measure is intended to prevent tax evasion;

it's not necessary to show receipts when leaving Italy.

RESERVATIONS AND DRESS

Regardless of where you are, it's a good idea to make a reservation if you can. We only mention them specifically when reservations are essential (there's no other way you'll ever get a table) or when they are not accepted. For popular restaurants, book as far ahead as you can (a week or two in advance), and reconfirm as soon as you arrive. (Large parties should always call ahead to check the reservations policy.)

We mention dress only when men are required to wear a jacket or a jacket and tie. But unless they're dining outside or at an oceanfront resort, Italian men never wear shorts or running shoes in a restaurant. The same applies to women: no casual shorts, running shoes, or plastic sandals when going out to dinner. Shorts are acceptable in pizzerias and cafés.

WINES, BEER, AND SPIRITS

Almost all eateries now proudly include a range of local wines from Campania. In terms of grape varieties, Aglianico is the undisputed king of reds, while Fiano, Falanghina, and Greco di Tufo contend for the white crown. Refreshingly, there's a fairly low markup on bottled wines, and a liter of house wine rarely costs more than €8–€10. At the end of your meal you may well be offered some of the house liqueur, probably *limoncello* (a lemon-based liqueur with varying proportions of sugar) or *nocillo* (from green walnuts).

In general, the southern Italians have a relaxed attitude to alcohol consumption. In many homes, a bottle of wine on the dining table is a necessary accompaniment to any meal, like salt and olive oil. All bars and caffès are licensed to serve alcohol, and even takeaway pizzas can be enjoyed with a beer in a city park.

▮ ELECTRICITY

The electrical current in Italy is 220 volts, 50 cycles alternating current (AC); wall outlets take Continental-type plugs, with two or three round prongs.

Consider making a small investment in a universal adapter, which has several types of plugs in one lightweight, compact unit. Most laptops and mobile phone chargers are dual voltage (i.e., they operate equally well on 110 and 220 volts), so require only an adapter. These days the same is true of small appliances such as hair dryers. Always check labels and manufacturer instructions to be sure. Don't use 110-volt outlets marked FOR SHAVERS ONLY for high-wattage appliances such as hair dryers. Adaptors can be found at some *ferramente* (hardware stores) in Naples and the Amalfi Coast. Ask for *"un adattatore per una presa americana."*

Contacts Steve Kropla's Help for World Traveler's (⊕ *www.kropla.com*) has information on electrical and telephone plugs around the world. **Walkabout Travel Gear** (⊕ *www.walkabouttravelgear.com*) has a good coverage of electricity under "adapters" in their product index.

▮ EMERGENCIES

No matter where you are in Italy, **dial 113 for all emergencies,** or find somebody (your concierge, a passerby) who will call for you, as not all 113 operators speak English; the Italian word to use to draw people's attention in an emergency is *"Aiuto!"* (Help!, pronounced "ah-YOU-toh"). *"Pronto soccorso"* means "first aid" and when said to an operator will get you an *ambulanza* (ambulance). If you just need a doctor, you should ask for *un medico*; most hotels will be able to refer you to a local doctor. Don't forget to ask the doctor for *una ricevuta* (an invoice) to show to your insurance company in order to get a reimbursement. Other useful Italian words to use in an emergency are *"Fuoco!"* (Fire!, pronounced " fuh-

WOE-co"), and "Ladro!" (Thief!, pronounced " LAH-droh").

Italy has a national police force (carabinieri) as well as local police (polizia). Both are armed and have the power to arrest and investigate crimes. Always report the loss of your passport to either the carabinieri or the police, as well as to your embassy. When reporting a crime, you'll be asked to fill out una denuncia (official report); keep a copy for your insurance company. Local traffic officers are known as vigili (though their official name is polizia municipale)—they are responsible for, among other things, giving out parking tickets and clamping cars, so before you even consider parking the Italian way, make sure you're at least able to spot their white (in summer) or black uniforms (many are women). Should you find yourself involved in a minor car accident in town, you should contact the vigili.

Pharmacies are generally open weekdays 8:30–1 and 4–8, and Saturday 9–1. Local pharmacies rotate covering the off-hours in shifts: on the door of every pharmacy is a list of which pharmacies in the vicinity will be open late. In the major towns and cities of Campania, you can always find a pharmacy open at any time of day or night.

Foreign Embassies U.S. Consulate Naples (✉ Piazza della Repubblica , at west end of the Villa Comunale Naples ☎ 081/583-8111 naples.usconsulate.gov). U.S. Embassy (✉ Via Veneto 119/A, Rome ☎ 06/46741 ⊕ www.usembassy.it).

General Emergency Contacts Emergencies (☎ 113). Police (☎ 112). Naples' Main Police Station (✉ Via Medina 75 ☎ 081/7941111 ✉ Foreigners' office (Questura): Via Ferraris 131 ☎ 081/6064111) has an ufficio stranieri (foreigners' office) that usually has an English speaker on staff and can help with passport problems.

Ambulance (☎ 081/7520696 or 081/7528282). **Medical emergency** (☎ 081/7613466 or 081/2547215 after 8 PM), ask for an English-speaking nurse. **Car breakdowns and emergencies** (☎ 116).

▌HEALTH

The most common types of illnesses are caused by contaminated food and water. In Italy, tap water is safe to drink and eating out, even in tiny "hole-in-the-wall" places, is perfectly safe. As in every part of the world, avoid vegetables and fruits that you haven't washed or peeled yourself. If you have problems, mild cases of traveler's diarrhea may respond to Imodium (known generically as loperamide) or Pepto-Bismol. Be sure to drink plenty of fluids; if you can't keep fluids down, seek medical help immediately.

SPECIFIC ISSUES IN NAPLES, CAPRI, AND THE AMALFI COAST

The Centers for Disease Control and Prevention (CDC) in Atlanta caution that most of southern Europe is in the "intermediate" range for risk of contacting traveler's diarrhea. Part of this risk may be attributed to an increased consumption of olive oil and wine, which can have a laxative effect on stomachs used to a different diet. The CDC also advises all international travelers to swim only in chlorinated swimming pools, unless they are absolutely certain the local beaches and freshwater lakes are not contaminated.

Contaminated seafood is a risk in Naples as elsewhere, and if you're going to indulge in oysters or other raw seafood, choose your restaurant wisely. Resist the temptation of prying open and eating mussels, clams, or other delicacies on your platter. If the shell doesn't open on cooking, then it's best left alone.

In bars and cafés, especially around areas with heavy human traffic like the Stazione Centrale in Naples or in the depressed areas around Vesuvius, you can ask for your espresso or cappuccino in a bicchiere monouso (nonreusable plastic cup), rather than opting to drink out of the local crockery. However, most mainstream bars and restaurants take hygiene ultra-seriously.

OVER-THE-COUNTER REMEDIES

It's always best to travel with your own medicines. The regulations regarding what medicines require a prescription aren't likely to be the same in Italy as in your home country—all the more reason to bring what you need with you. In general, medications that require prescriptions outside Italy require them in Italy, too. You can buy aspirin (*aspirina*), ibuprofen (Cibalgina, Moment), antihistamines (*antistaminico*), and cough medicines (*sciroppo per la tosse*) at any pharmacy (*farmacia*). *Paracetamolo*, also sold as Tachipirina or Efferalgan, is Italian acetaminophen.

▮ HOURS OF OPERATION

Before you travel, check ahead for public holidays, especially April 25, May 1, and June 2, when public offices and most shops are closed. When holidays fall on a Sunday, one day is effectively lost to merrymaking and Monday is business as usual.

Banks are open weekdays 8:30 to 1:15 and 2:45 to 3:45.

Post offices are open weekdays 8:30 AM to 2 PM and Saturday from 9 AM to 1 PM; central and main district post offices stay open until 6 PM weekdays, 9 to 1 on Saturday.

Gas stations open about 7 AM and close at about 8 PM. In sleepy country areas away from major roads they will close for lunch between 1 and 4 PM, and on Sunday, so make sure you fill up beforehand. Services open around the clock can be found on autostrade and the tangenziale around Naples, and there are about 20 *benzinai notturni* (night-shift gas-stations) operating in various parts of Naples. Details can be found in local newspapers.

The major museums in Naples, such as Museo Archeologico Nazionale, Museo di Capodimonte, Palazzo Reale, and San Martino, are open through to the evening, although you may find some rooms closed due to lack of staff. Many smaller private museums are only open from 9 AM to 1 or 2 PM. The opening times of archaeological sites are subject to seasonal variations, with most sites closing an hour before sunset, and preventing access as much as two hours before. When this book refers to summer hours, it means approximately Easter to October; winter hours run from November to Easter. Most museums are closed one day a week, often Monday or Wednesday. Always check locally.

Most churches are open from early morning until noon or 12:30, when they close for three hours or more; they open again in the afternoon, closing about 7 PM or later. Be as discreet as possible when services are in progress.

Pharmacies are generally open weekdays from 8:30 to 1 and from 4 to 8, and Saturday mornings 9 to 1. Local pharmacies cover the off-hours in shifts: on the door of every pharmacy is a list of pharmacies that will be open in the vicinity on Saturday afternoon, Sunday, or 24 hours.

If the *farmacia* (pharmacy) in Naples's Stazione Centrale is closed, it will post the address of one that's open; the newspaper *Il Mattino* also prints a list of pharmacies that are open nights and weekends.

Most shops are open Monday–Saturday 10–1 and 3:30 or 4–7:30 or 8. Clothing shops are generally closed Monday mornings but open regular afternoon hours, except from July to early September when they close Saturday afternoons and open on Monday mornings. Some bookstores and fashion and tourist-oriented shops are open all day, as well as Sunday. Large chain supermarkets such as Standa and COOP do not close for lunch and are usually open Sunday. *Alimentari* (grocers) and *panifici* (bakeries) open as early as 8 AM every day except Sunday, but are (generally) closed on Thursday afternoons and Sunday—though you can find larger supermarkets and out-of-town malls open at all times except Sunday afternoons. Barbers and hairdressers, with some exceptions, are closed Sunday and Monday. On Sunday the *pasticcerie* (cake shops) do a roaring trade, as most southern Italians like to round off their luncheon ritual with calorie-rich *pasticcini* (little pastries). Most shops in downtown Naples will close for two to four weeks in August. They observe extended hours for the three weeks leading up to Christmas and many close from December 25 to January 6.

HOLIDAYS

If you can avoid it, don't travel through Italy in August, when much of the population is on vacation. Most cities are deserted (except for foreign tourists) and many restaurants and shops are closed. Resort towns burst with Italians on holiday.

National holidays include January 1 (New Year's Day); January 6 (Epiphany); Easter Sunday and Monday; April 25 (Liberation Day); May 1 (Labor Day or May Day); June 2 (Founding of the Italian Republic); August 15 (Assumption of Mary, also known as Ferragosto); November 1 (All Saints' Day); December 8 (Immaculate Conception); and December 25 and 26 (Christmas Day and St. Stephen's Day). During these holidays many shops and restaurants are closed, while decisions about whether to open major museums and archaeological sites like Pompeii and Herculaneum are usually made at the 11th hour.

The feast days of patron saints are observed locally in various towns and villages; some of the more famous *feste* are: San Costanzo, Capri, May 14; San Antonio, Anacapri, June 13; Sant'Andrea, Amalfi, June 25–30; San Pietro, Positano, June 29; Sant'Anna, Ischia, July 26; and San Pantaleone, Ravello, July 27. In Naples, two annual celebrations are held at the Duomo on the first Sunday in May and on September 19 to celebrate the Festa di San Gennaro, or the Liquefaction of the Blood of San Gennaro. For

information on these and other holidays, see also "On the Calendar in the front of this book.

▌MAIL

The Italian mail system has made great progress in speed and reliability, although it can still be slow, so allow up to 10 days for mail to and from the United States and Canada, about a week to and from the United Kingdom.

Standing in line at the *ufficio postale* (post office) in Naples to draw pensions, pay bills, or send registered mail is a major local pastime, and best avoided. You should be able to buy postage stamps at tobacconists without having to line up in post offices. If you still need to go, they are open weekdays 8:30 AM to 2 PM and Saturday 8:30 AM to 1 PM; central and main district post offices are usually open 8:30–6 weekdays, 9–1 on Saturday.

Airmail letters and postcards (lightweight stationery) to the United States and Canada cost €0.85 for the first 20 grams and €1.85 up to 100 grams. Always stick the blue airmail tag on your mail, or write "airmail" in big, clear characters to the side of the address. Postcards and letters in Italy cost €0.60 for the first 20 grams and €1.50 up to 100 grams, while the same categories to other EU countries cost €0.65 and €1.70. Delivery within Italy should take two to three days. To send urgent letters and papers to the United States and elsewhere, consider the *Paccocelere Internazionale* system, which is similar to a courier system, but not necessarily cheaper. This service is offered at several major post offices in Naples and in town post offices throughout the area.

Correspondence can be addressed to you in care of the Italian post office. Letters should be addressed to your name, "c/o Ufficio Postale Centrale," followed by "Fermo Posta" on the next line, and the name of the city (preceded by its postal code) on the next. You can **collect it at the central post office** by showing your passport or photo-bearing ID and paying a small fee. American Express also has a general-delivery service. There's no charge for cardholders, holders of American Express traveler's checks, or anyone who booked a vacation with American Express.

SHIPPING PACKAGES

You can ship parcels via air or surface. Air takes up to two weeks, and surface anywhere up to three months to most countries. If you have purchased antiques, ceramics, or other objects, ask if the vendor will do the shipping for you; in most cases, this is a possibility. If so, ask if the article will be insured against breakage. When shipping a package out of Italy, it is virtually impossible to find an overnight delivery option—the fastest delivery time is 48 to 72 hours.

▮ MONEY

The days when Italy's high-quality attractions came with a comparatively low Mediterranean price tag are long gone. Italy's prices are in line with those in the rest of Europe, with costs in its main cities comparable to those in other major capitals, such as Paris and Madrid. As in most countries, prices vary from region to region and are a bit lower in the countryside than in the cities. Good value for money can still be had in many places in Campania, especially in Naples and on the Amalfi Coast.

Prices throughout this guide are given for adults. Substantially reduced fees are almost always available for children, students, and senior citizens from the EU; be sure to bring EU passports to receive discounts.

▮ TIP➔Banks never have every foreign currency on hand, and it may take as long as a week to order. If you're planning to exchange funds before leaving home, don't wait until the last minute.

ATMS AND BANKS

Your own bank will probably charge a fee for using ATMs abroad; the foreign bank you use may also charge a fee. Nevertheless, you'll usually get a better rate of exchange at an ATM than you will at a currency-exchange office or even when changing money in a bank. And extracting funds as you need them is a safer option than carrying around a large amount of cash. Check with your bank to confirm that you have an international PIN (codice segreto) that will be recognized in Italy, to find out your maximum daily withdrawal allowance, and to learn what the bank fee is for withdrawing money. ▮ TIP➔Be aware that PINs beginning with a 0 (zero) tend to be rejected in Italy.

Fairly common in cities and towns as well as in airports and train stations, ATMs are the easiest way to get euros in Italy. Don't, however, count on finding ATMs in tinier towns and rural areas. Italian ATMs are reliable, and are commonly attached to a bank—you won't find one, for example, in a supermarket. Do check with your bank to confirm you have an international PIN number, to find out your maximum daily withdrawal allowance, and to learn what the bank fee is for withdrawing money. The word for ATM in Italian is bancomat, for PIN, codice segreto.

CREDIT CARDS

Throughout this guide, the following abbreviations are used: **AE**, American Express; **DC**, Diners Club; **MC**, Master-Card; and **V**, Visa.

It's a good idea to **inform your credit-card company before you travel**, especially if you're going abroad and don't travel internationally very often. Otherwise, the credit-card company might put a hold on your card owing to unusual activity—not a good thing halfway through your trip. Record all your credit-card numbers—as well as the phone numbers to call if your cards are lost or stolen—in a safe place, so you're prepared should something go wrong. Both MasterCard and Visa have general numbers you can call (collect if you're abroad) if your card is lost, but you're better off calling the number of your issuing bank, since MasterCard and Visa generally just transfer you to your bank; your bank's number is usually printed on your card.

If you plan to use your credit card for cash advances, you'll need to apply for a PIN at least two weeks before your trip. Although it's usually cheaper (and safer) to use a credit card abroad for large purchases (so you can cancel payments or be reimbursed if there's a problem), note that some credit-card companies *and* the banks that issue them add substantial percentages to all foreign transactions, whether they're in a foreign currency or not. Check on these fees before leaving home, so there won't be any surprises when you get the bill.

■ TIP➔Before you charge something, ask the merchant whether or not he or she plans to do a dynamic currency conversion (DCC). In such a transaction the credit-card processor (shop, restaurant, or hotel, not Visa or MasterCard) converts the currency and charges you in dollars. In most cases you'll pay the merchant a 3% fee for this service in addition to any credit-card company and issuing-bank foreign-transaction surcharges.

Dynamic currency conversion programs are becoming increasingly widespread. Merchants who participate in them are supposed to ask whether you want to be charged in dollars or the local currency, but they don't always do so. And even if they do offer you a choice, they may well avoid mentioning the additional surcharges. The good news is that you *do* have a choice. And if this practice really gets your goat, you can avoid it entirely thanks to American Express; with its cards, DCC simply isn't an option.

MasterCard and Visa are preferred by Italian merchants, so don't expect American Express to be accepted everywhere, even in tourist spots; Travelers Checks are also seldom accepted. Credit cards aren't accepted everywhere; if you want to pay with a credit card in a small shop, hotel, or restaurant, it's a good idea to make your intentions known early on. In general, use cash, not credit cards, for purchases below €20. Southern Italy is still very much a cash-based society, and many shops and smaller *trattorie* have yet to see the benefits of handling plastic.

Reporting Lost Cards American Express (☎ *800/528–4800 in U.S., 336/393–1111 collect from abroad* ⊕ *www.americanexpress. com*). **Diners Club** (☎ *800/234–6377 in U.S., 303/799–1504 collect from abroad* ⊕ *www. dinersclub.com*). **MasterCard** (☎ *800/627– 8372 in U.S., 636/722–7111 collect from abroad* ⊕ *www.mastercard.com*). **Visa** (☎ *800/ 847–2911 in U.S., 800/819–014 collect from abroad* ⊕ *www.visa.com*).

CURRENCY AND EXCHANGE

The unit of currency in Italy is the euro, currently adopted in 16 countries of the European Union (the only EU Member States not to adopt the euro were Britain, Denmark, and Sweden). Italian banks no longer accept the lira—the currency used prior to 2002—but if you have some left over from a previous visit it can be changed at the **Banca D'Italia** (✉ *Via M Cervantes 71* ☎ *081/7975111*), in the center of Naples, until the year 2012. The euro is printed in bills of 500 (practically impossible to change outside of banks), 200, 100, 50, 20, 10, and 5. Coins are €2, €1, 50 cents, 20 cents, 10 cents, 5 cents, 2 cents, and 1 cent. All coins have one side that has the value of the euro on it and the other side with each countries' unique symbol. Notes have principal architectural styles from antiquity onward on one side and the map and the flag of Europe on the other and are the same for all countries. ■ TIP➔When changing money, make sure you ask for small denomination notes, preferably of 50 euros and below, as retailers in Naples and the surrounding area are notoriously bereft of small change.

The euro continues to fluctuate considerably against other currencies. At the time of this writing the exchange rate was about €0.73 to the U.S. dollar.

■TIP➜Even if a currency-exchange booth has a sign promising no commission, rest assured that there's some kind of huge, hidden fee. As for rates, you're almost always better off getting foreign currency at an ATM or exchanging money at a bank.

■ PACKING

The weather is considerably milder in Italy than in the north and central United States or Great Britain. In summer, stick with clothing that is as light as possible, although a sweater may be necessary for cool evenings, especially in the Lattari mountains along the Amalfi Coast (even during the hot months). Sunglasses, a hat, and sunblock are essential. Contrary to myth, the sun does not shine all day, every day on Campania: brief summer thunderstorms are common in Naples, while typhoonlike storms occasionally arrive along the Amalfi Coast, so an umbrella will definitely come in handy. In winter bring a medium-weight coat and a raincoat; winters in Naples can be both humid *and* cold. Even in Naples, central heating may not be up to your standards, and interiors can be chilly and damp; take wools or flannel rather than sheer fabrics. Bring sturdy shoes for winter, and comfortable walking shoes in any season.

For sightseeing, **pack a pair of binoculars;** they will help you get a good look at Naples' wondrous painted ceilings and domes. If you stay in budget hotels, **take your own shampoo and soap;** many such hotels do not provide it, or allot only one tiny bar per room.

■ PASSPORTS AND VISAS

U.S. citizens need only a valid passport to enter Italy for stays of up to 90 days. Ensure that the passport is valid for six months after the date of arrival. Children are required to have their own passport or

be included in the passport of the parent with whom they are traveling.

PASSPORTS

■TIP➜Before your trip, make two copies of your passport's data page (one for someone at home and another for you to carry separately). Or scan the page and e-mail it to someone at home and/or yourself.

VISAS

When staying for 90 days or less, U.S. citizens are not required to obtain a visa prior to traveling to Italy. If you plan to travel or live in Italy or the European Union for longer than 90 days, you must acquire a valid visa from the Italian consulate serving your state *before you leave the United States*. Plan ahead because the process of obtaining a visa will take at least 30 days and the Italian government does not accept visa applications submitted by visa expediters.

U.S. Passport Information U.S. Department of State (☎877/487–2778 ⊕*www.travel.state.gov/passport*).

U.S. Passport Expediters A. Briggs Passport & Visa Expediters (☎800/806–0581 or 202/338–0111 ⊕*www.abriggs.com*). **American Passport Express** (☎800/455–5166 or 603/559–9888 ⊕*www.americanpassport.com*). **Passport Express** (☎800/362–8196 or 401/272–4612 ⊕*www.passportexpress.com*). **Travel Document Systems** (☎800/874–5100 ⊕*www.traveldocs.com*). **Travel the World Visas** (☎866/886–8472 ⊕*www.world-visa.com*).

■ RESTROOMS

Public restrooms are rather rare in Naples; the locals seem to make do with well-timed pit stops and rely on the local bar. Although private businesses can refuse to make their toilets available to the passing public, some bars will allow you to use the restroom if you ask politely. Alternatively, it's not uncommon to pay for a little something—a euro for a mineral water or coffee—to get access to the facilities. Standards of cleanliness and comfort vary greatly. In downtown Naples, restaurants, hotel lobbies, department stores such as Coin, and McDonald's restaurants tend to have the cleanest restrooms. Pubs and bars rank among the worst and, for these, it may help to have your own small supply of tissues. There are bathrooms in most museums and in all airports and train stations. In major train stations you'll also find well-kept pay toilets for €0.50, with the exception of Napoli Centrale where the facilities are best avoided— use the restroom inside McDonald's instead. There are also bathrooms at highway rest stops and gas stations: a small tip to the cleaning person is always appreciated. There are no bathrooms in churches, post offices, public beaches, or subway stations.

The Bathroom Diaries (⊕ www.thebathroom diaries.com) is flush with unsanitized info on restrooms the world over—each one located, reviewed, and rated.

▌SAFETY

Naples, like any modern metropolis, has had certain problems with crime. Although great inroads have been made since the 1990s and the city today is as safe as many other big urban centers in Europe, you should continue to be vigilant, especially around the main rail station of Piazza Garibaldi where petty theft is common. In Italy, in general, violent crimes are rare.

▌TIP➔**Distribute your cash, credit cards, IDs, and other valuables between a deep front pocket, an inside jacket or vest pocket, and a hidden money pouch. Don't reach for the money pouch once you're in public.**

LOCAL SCAMS

The areas round Piazza Garibaldi and near the port in Naples are infamous for a variety of scams. Avoid getting involved in the three-card monte around the station, and never buy any goods from an unlicensed street vendor—you may discover on returning to your hotel or cruise ship that the package with the digital camera you bought at an unbeatable price near the port actually contains little more than wooden chocks. Besides, under current Italian law, any purchase—except at a newsstand or tobacconist's—has to be accompanied by a proper receipt. Without one, both purchaser and vendor are liable to a fine, so you're putting yourself at risk by buying bootleg goods.

Be especially vigilant if traveling on public transport, especially crowded buses, as pickpockets can materialize from seemingly nowhere in large numbers. Dress down rather than up to attract less attention, and never wear gold jewelry.

Both in town and out on the highway, the latest scam is the *cavallo di ritorno*. Car owners lose their cars by some ruse— usually they're told they have a problem at the back or under the chassis; once they get out, and the car is driven off. The owner is then traced and contacted by an intermediary, who will stipulate the ransom for the car (as much as €1,500– €2,500). You do need to stop if you're flagged down by the police; otherwise act with due caution.

The difficulties encountered by women traveling alone in Italy are often overstated. Younger women have to put up with much male attention, but it's rarely dangerous. Ignoring whistling and questions is the best way to get rid of unwanted attention. Fortunately, the vast majority of locals are extremely protective both of foreign visitors and women. As a general rule, in urban areas you're fine walking at street level when the shops are open (until about 8:30 PM). At other times, especially around the seedier parts of Naples, taking a taxi is a sound investment.

▌TAXES

Value-added tax (IVA or V.A.T.) is 20% on clothing and luxury goods. On most consumer goods, it's already included in the amount shown on the price tag, whereas on services it may not be.

At hotels, the service charge and the 10% IVA, or value-added tax, are included in the rate except in five-star deluxe establishments, where the IVA (10%) may be a separate item added to the bill at departure. If your purchases in a single store total more than € 155 you may be entitled to a refund of the V.A.T.

When making a purchase, ask for a V.A.T. refund form and find out whether the merchant gives refunds—not all stores do, nor are they required to. Have the form stamped like any customs form by customs officials when you leave the country or, if you're visiting several European Union countries, when you leave the EU. After you're through passport control, take the form to a refund-service counter for an on-the-spot refund (which is usually the quickest and easiest option), or mail it to the address on the form (or on the envelope with it) after you arrive home. You receive the total refund stated on the form, but the processing time can be long, especially if you request a credit-card adjustment.

Global Refund is a Europe-wide service with 225,000 affiliated stores and more than 700 refund counters at major airports and border crossings. Its refund form, called a Tax Free Check, is the most common across the European continent. The service issues refunds in the form of cash, check, or credit-card adjustment.

V.A.T. Refunds Global Refund (☏ *800/321–11111* ⊕ *www.globalrefund.com*).

▮ TIPPING

In tourist areas like Capri and the Amalfi Coast, a 10% to 15% service charge may appear on your check; this must be clearly written on the menu in order to be applied. If service is added to the bill, it's not necessary to leave an additional tip. If service is not included, leave a cash tip of a couple of euros per person. Usually there will not be a line item on your credit-card slip for a tip—but even if there is, tip in cash. Tip checkroom attendants € 1 per person and restroom attendants € 0.50 (more in expensive hotels and restaurants). Since a

service charge is added at cafés for table service, it is not necessary to leave additionally gratuity. At a hotel bar tip € 1 for a round or two of drinks. At a café, tip € 0.10 per coffee.

Italians rarely tip taxi drivers, and at most round up to the nearest euro. That said, a euro or two is appreciated, particularly if the driver helps with luggage. Service-station attendants are tipped only for special services; give them € 1 for checking your tires. Railway and airport porters charge a fixed rate per bag. Tip an additional € 0.50 per person, more if the porter is helpful. Give a barber € 1 and a hairdresser's assistant € 2–€ 4 for a shampoo or cut, depending on the type of establishment.

On large group sightseeing tours, tip guides about € 5 per person for a half-day group tour, more if they are especially knowledgeable. In monasteries and other sights where admission is free, a contribution (€ 1–€ 2) is expected.

In hotels leave the chambermaid about € 1 per day, or about € 5 a week in a moderately priced hotel; tip a minimum of € 1 for valet or room service. Double these amounts in an expensive hotel. In expensive hotels tip doormen € 0.50 for calling a cab and € 1.50 for carrying bags to the check-in desk and bellhops € 1.50–€ 2.50 for carrying your bags to the room.

▮ TOURS

Guided tours are a good option when you don't want to do it all yourself. You travel along with a group (sometimes large, sometimes small), stay in prebooked hotels, eat with your fellow travelers (the cost of meals sometimes included in the price of your tour, sometimes not), and follow a schedule. But not all guided tours are an if-it's-Tuesday-this-must-be-Belgium experience. A knowledgeable guide can take you places that you might never discover on your own, and you may be pushed to see more than you would have otherwise. Tours aren't for everyone, but they can be just the thing for trips to places where making travel arrangements is difficult or time consuming (particularly when you don't speak the language). Whenever you book a guided tour, find out what's included and what isn't. A "land-only" tour includes all your travel (by bus, in most cases) in the destination, but not necessarily your flights to and from or even within it. Also, in most cases prices in tour brochures don't include fees and taxes. And remember that you'll be expected to tip your guide (in cash) at the end of the tour.

Also keep in mind that the province of Naples has tour guides licensed by the government. Some are eminently qualified in relevant fields such as architecture and art history, but most, especially those that linger outside Pompeii have simply managed to pass the test (or purchase the license!). Few local guides have their own Web sites, though all reputable agencies do. Check online before you leave home. Tourist offices and hotel concierges also can provide the names of knowledgeable local guides and the rates for certain services. Before you hire a local guide, ask about their background and qualifications and make sure you agree on a price, content, and scheduling. Tipping is appreciated, but not obligatory, for local guides.

Recommended Generalists Abercrombie & Kent (☎ 800/554-7016 ⊕ www.abercrombiekent.com). **Andante** (☎ +44 (0) 1722 713800 ⊕ www.andantetravels.co.uk). **Context Travel** (☎ 800/691-6036 or 06/97625204 within Italy ⊕ www.contexttravel.com). **Tauck** (☎ 800/788-7885 ⊕ www.tauck.com). **Travcoa** (☎ 866/591-0070 ⊕ www.travcoa.com).

Biking and Hiking Tour Contacts Backroads (☎ 800/462-2848 ⊕ www.backroads.com). **Butterfield & Robinson** (☎ 866/551-9090 ⊕ www.butterfield.com). **Ciclismo Classico** (☎ 800/866-7314 ⊕ www.ciclismoclassico. com). **Southern Visions** (☎ 713/540-0989 in U.S., 080/416-0030 in Italy ⊕ www. southernvisionstravel.com).

Culinary Tour Contact Epiculinary (☎ 888/380-9010 ⊕ www.epiculinary.com).

Italian Connection (☎ 800/462-7911 ⊕ www.italian-connection.com).

Volunteer Programs Elderhostel (☎ 800/454-5768 ⊕ www.elderhostel.com).

Wine Tour Contacts Cellar Tours (☎ 34/915-213-939 Spanish headquarters ⊕ www. cellartours.com).

▮ TRIP INSURANCE

Comprehensive trip insurance is valuable if you're booking a very expensive or complicated trip (particularly to an isolated region) or if you're booking far in advance. Comprehensive policies typically cover trip-cancellation and interruption, letting you cancel or cut your trip short because of illness, or, in some cases, acts of terrorism in your destination. Such policies might also cover evacuation and medical care. (For trips abroad you should have at least medical-only coverage.) Some also cover you for trip delays because of bad weather or mechanical problems as well as for lost or delayed luggage.

Another type of coverage to consider is financial default—that is, when your trip is disrupted because a tour operator, airline, or cruise line goes out of business. Generally you must buy this when you book your trip or shortly thereafter, and it's available to you only if your operator isn't on a list of excluded companies.

Always read the fine print of your policy to make sure that you're covered for the risks that most concern you. Compare several policies to be sure you're getting the best price and range of coverage available.

Insurance Comparison Info Insure My Trip (☎ 800/487-4722 ⊕ www.insuremytrip. com). **Square Mouth** (☎ 800/240-0369 or 727/564-9203 ⊕ www.squaremouth.com).

Comprehensive Insurers Access America (☎ 800/284-8300 ⊕ www.accessamerica. com). **CSA Travel Protection** (☎ 800/711-1197 ⊕ www.csatravelprotection.com). **HTH**

Worldwide (☎ 888/243–2358 ⊕ www.
hthworldwide.com). **Travelex Insurance**
(☎ 800/228–9792 ⊕ www.travelex-insurance.
com). **Travel Guard** (☎ 800/826–4919
⊕ www.travelguard.com). **Travel Insured
International** (☎ 800/243–3174 ⊕ www.
travelinsured.com).

▮ VISITOR INFORMATION

Italian Government Tourist Board (ENIT
☎ 212/245–5618 in New York ⊕ www.
italiantourism.com ☎ 310/820–1898 in L.A.
☎ 312/644–0996 in Chicago ☎ 416/925–
4882 in Toronto).

Ente Provinciale per il Turismo (EPT)
(☎ 081/268–779 Stazione Centrale ☎ 081/
410–7211 Piazza dei Martiri ☎ 081/761–2102
Stazione Mergellina ⊕ www.enit.it). The official
site of the local region (⊕ www.regione.
campania.it) also provides some coverage.

▮ ONLINE TRAVEL TOOLS

The site for Trenitalia (the national rail),
⊕www.trenitalia.com is a good source
for train information and journey planning, although you can only purchase
tickets online with an EU credit card. On
a local level ⊕www.campaniatrasporti.it
provides an easily downloadable overview
of local transport networks. The Circumvesuviana Web site (⊕www.vesuviana.
it) and Ferrovia Cumana/Circumflegrea
Web site (⊕www.sepsa.it) have public
transport information for getting around
the bay. The SITA site (Italian only) has
schedules for bus travel in Campania,
⊕www.sitabus.it. A handy site for Capri
is ⊕www.capri.net; Ischia has its official
Web site at ⊕www.ischia.com and. Many
hotels now have online reservation facilities and several restaurants have thoughtfully posted menus to whet the appetites of
Internet surfers. Where known, Web sites
have been included at the end of individual
listings.

INDEX

ABOUT OUR WRITERS

Martin Wilmot Bennett's vast background in Italian art and civilization made him a natural to update our Naples Exploring section. A major contributor to *Fodor's Rome* and a graduate of Cambridge University, he teaches at Rome's University of Tor Vergata.

Specializing in the Neapolitan art of *arrangiarsi* (getting by), Fergal Kavanagh has dabbled in teacher training, DJ-ing, writing guidebooks, translating, and organizing cultural exchanges. He currently teaches at the University of Naples and through his Web site (www.tuneintoenglish.com) demonstrates how pop music can help students learn English. For this edition of the guide he updated the chapters covering the Amalfi Coast and the islands of Capri, Ischia, and Procida.

Katie Parla is travel writer and private guide with a degree in art history from Yale and master's in food and wine history from the University of Rome Tor Vergata. She has lived in Rome since 2003 and spends as much time as she can traveling to Puglia, Naples, and Sicily. You can live vicariously through her travel and food experiences at her blog www.ParlaFood.com. Katie updated the "Around the Bay" and "Sorrento and the Sorrentine Peninsula" chapters.

An editor, travel writer, and naturalist, Mark Walters first settled in Naples as a British Council lecturer in the 1980s. He spends several months a year leading tours around the Mediterranean. For our guide he stayed home and ate well, updating the Where to Eat section of the Naples chapter.

Chris Rose arrived in Naples from Manchester, England, planning to stay for three months, but he's now stuck around for over a dozen years. He's worked as the arts manager for the British Council and has contributed to numerous Fodor's guides. He updated the Naples Where to Stay, Sports, Nightlife and Arts, and Shopping sections.

NOTES